MW00895268

Mastering™
Microsoft® Visual Web Developer™
2005 Express Edition

Mastering™
Microsoft® Visual Web Developer™ 2005 Express Edition

John Paul Mueller

Wiley Publishing, Inc.

Acquisitions and Development Editor: Tom Cirtin
Technical Editor: Russ Mullen
Production Editors: Mae Lum, Rachel Gunn
Copy Editor: Cheryl Hauser
Production Manager: Tim Tate
Vice President & Executive Group Publisher: Richard Swadley
Vice President and Executive Publisher: Joseph B. Wikert
Vice President and Publisher: Neil Edde
Book Designers: Maureen Forys, Happenstance Type-O-Rama; Judy Fung
Compositor: Craig Woods, Happenstance Type-O-Rama
Proofreaders: Nancy Riddiough
Indexer: Nancy Guenther
Cover Design: Design Site
Copyright © 2006 by Wiley Publishing, Inc., Indianapolis, IN
Published by Wiley Publishing, Inc., Indianapolis, IN
Published simultaneously in Canada
ISBN-13: 978-0-7821-4423-9
ISBN-10: 0-7821-4423-3

No part of this publication may be reproduced, stored in a retrieval system or transmitted in any form or by any means, electronic, mechanical, photocopying, recording, scanning or otherwise, except as permitted under Sections 107 or 108 of the 1976 United States Copyright Act, without either the prior written permission of the Publisher, or authorization through payment of the appropriate per-copy fee to the Copyright Clearance Center, 222 Rosewood Drive, Danvers, MA 01923, (978) 750-8400, fax (978) 646-8600. Requests to the Publisher for permission should be addressed to the Legal Department, Wiley Publishing, Inc., 10475 Crosspoint Blvd., Indianapolis, IN 46256, (317) 572-3447, fax (317) 572-4355, or online at http://www.wiley.com/go/permissions.

Limit of Liability/Disclaimer of Warranty: The publisher and the author make no representations or warranties with respect to the accuracy or completeness of the contents of this work and specifically disclaim all warranties, including without limitation warranties of fitness for a particular purpose. No warranty may be created or extended by sales or promotional materials. The advice and strategies contained herein may not be suitable for every situation. This work is sold with the understanding that the publisher is not engaged in rendering legal, accounting, or other professional services. If professional assistance is required, the services of a competent professional person should be sought. Neither the publisher nor the author shall be liable for damages arising herefrom. The fact that an organization or Website is referred to in this work as a citation and/or a potential source of further information does not mean that the author or the publisher endorses the information the organization or Website may provide or recommendations it may make. Further, readers should be aware that Internet Websites listed in this work may have changed or disappeared between when this work was written and when it is read.

For general information on our other products and services or to obtain technical support, please contact our Customer Care Department within the U.S. at (800) 762-2974, outside the U.S. at (317) 572-3993 or fax (317) 572-4002.

Wiley also publishes its books in a variety of electronic formats. Some content that appears in print may not be available in electronic books.

TRADEMARKS: Sybex, Wiley, Mastering and related trade dress are trademarks of Wiley Publishing, Inc. or its parent company, in the United States and other countries, and may not be used without written permission. All other trademarks are the property of their respective owners. Wiley Publishing, Inc., is not associated with any product or vendor mentioned in this book.

"Microsoft" is a registered trademark of Microsoft Corporation in the United States and/or other countries and is used by Wiley Publishing, Inc. under license from owner. *Mastering Microsoft Visual Web Developer 2005 Express Edition* is an independent publication not affiliated with Microsoft Corporation.

Screen reproductions produced with FullShot 99. FullShot 99 © 1991–1999 Inbit Incorporated. All rights reserved.

FullShot is a trademark of Inbit Incorporated.

Manufactured in the United States of America

10 9 8 7 6 5 4 3 2 1

This book is dedicated to Eva Beattie: protector of cats, avenger of IT evils, and a friend to me.

Acknowledgments

Thanks to my wife, Rebecca, for working with me to get this book completed. I really don't know what I would have done without her help in researching and compiling some of the information that appears in this book. She also did a fine job of proofreading my rough draft and page proofing the result. Rebecca also helps a great deal with the glossary and keeps the house running while I'm buried in work.

Russ Mullen deserves thanks for his technical edit of this book. He greatly added to the accuracy and depth of the material you see here. Russ is always providing me with great URLs for new products and ideas. However, it's the testing the Russ does that helps most. He's the sanity check for my work and my code.

A number of people read all or part of this book to help me refine the approach, test the coding examples, and generally provide input that every reader wishes they could have. These unpaid volunteers helped in ways too numerous to mention here. I especially appreciate the efforts of Eva Beattie who read the entire book and selflessly devoted herself to this project. Bill Salkin provided me with a great many ideas and URLs, as well as tested some of the examples for me. A number of other readers tested procedures and helped refine the book in other ways.

Finally, I would like to thank Tom Cirtin, Mae Lum, Rachel Gunn, Cheryl Hauser, and the rest of the editorial and production staff at Sybex for their assistance in bringing this book to print. It's always nice to work with such a great group of professionals and I very much appreciate the friendship we have built over the last five books.

About the Author

John Mueller is a freelance author and technical editor. He has writing in his blood, having produced 67 books and over 300 articles to date. The topics range from networking to artificial intelligence and from database management to heads down programming. Some of his current books include a Windows power optimization book, a book on .NET security, and books on Amazon Web Services, Google Web Services, and eBay Web Services. His technical editing skills have helped over 39 authors refine the content of their manuscripts. John has provided technical editing services to both Data Based Advisor and Coast Compute magazines. He's also contributed articles to magazines like DevSource, InformIT, SQL Server Professional, Visual C++ Developer, Hard Core Visual Basic, asp.netPRO, Software Test and Performance, and Visual Basic Developer. He's currently the editor of the .NET electronic newsletter for Pinnacle Publishing (http://www.freeenewsletters.com/).

When John isn't working at the computer, you can find him in his workshop. He's an avid woodworker and candle maker. On any given afternoon, you can find him working at a lathe or putting the finishing touches on a bookcase. He also likes making glycerin soap and candles, which comes in handy for gift baskets. You can reach John on the Internet at JMueller@mwt.net. John is also setting up a Web site at: http://www.mwt.net/~jmueller/, feel free to look and make suggestions on how he can improve it. One of his current projects is creating book FAQ sheets that should help you find the book information you need much faster.

Contents at a Glance

Contents

Introduction

Anyone who's spent any time at all perusing the Internet knows that you can find plenty of Web design tools out there—most of which are free. Therefore, you might ask why you should take time to learn anything about Visual Web Developer Express. It's a Microsoft product and you might end up paying something for it.

You're right, any of these applications can help you design and build a Web site, but you have to ask *how long they require to learn and how much effort you'll have to expend to work with them*. What Visual Web Developer Express is really offering is a friendly environment where you can build Web pages very quickly and with a minimum of fuss. Visual Web Developer Express doesn't require that you reinvent the wheel every time you decide to do something different with your Web site. When you think about it, isn't that what everyone expects from a language product today? It's not sufficient to merely build the application; the language product has to perform the task quickly and effortlessly as well. And even cost isn't a factor because Microsoft is pricing Visual Web Developer Express very inexpensively, and in some cases, it's free of charge.

Seeing the World in a Drop of Rain

I remember watching an ergonomics demonstration once where the product demonstrated illustrated the vendor's inability to grasp the real problem. The product in question looked like a miniaturized version of a large product. It was supposed to help someone with smaller hands perform a task more efficiently by providing a smaller handle. The problem was that the entire tool was smaller and none of those people with smaller hands were able to accomplish the task because the tool was too small. Web design tools for small businesses have a similar feel. They're a downsized, miniaturized version of tools that "real" businesses use. Unfortunately, small businesses quickly realize that these products are toys and end up buying a tool that costs a lot, provides features they'll never use, and is generally unwieldy to use. Visual Web Developer Express isn't like that. It provides you with tools designed for a small business, but with a big business feel. It's like seeing the entire world in a drop of rain. The tool is small—the view is not.

Mastering Visual Web Developer 2005 Express Edition helps you get the most from this great tool. Starting with Chapter 2, you create something new in every chapter. Every time you turn a page, you'll discover something new that you can do today that you couldn't do yesterday—at least not with a tool this size.

The examples in this book start out slow. You'll discover great new ASP.NET features that will save you a lot of time such as master pages and themes. Both of these features let you create new Web pages based on a basic design without working too hard at it. As the book progresses, you'll discover real scripting techniques—the type that professionals use to create all of those interesting effects on the Web sites you visit. You'll also see how to create pop-ups and work with redirection.

Mastering Visual Web Developer 2005 Express Edition doesn't forget about your need to work with data. You'll find three hefty chapters on database management in this book. However, unlike other database books you might have read, these examples make sense for the hobbyist or small- to medium-sized business. You'll put everything you've discovered to work starting with Chapter 13, where you'll create a Web site with pizzazz. In fact, in Chapter 15 you'll create a functional shopping cart application.

Just as Visual Web Developer Express takes care of all of the fit and finish issues for the development environment, *Mastering Visual Web Developer 2005 Express Edition* is a full-fledged programming book, too. The end of the book discusses everything from debugging your application to making it friendly for those with special needs. Two special chapters address any concerns you might have about moving your application around. The first describes how you can update from Visual Studio .NET 2003 to Visual Web Developer Express, while the second tells you how you can move your application to the full Visual Studio 2005 environment should you need to extra power it provides. In short, this is a self-contained environment for all of your Web development needs with Visual Web Developer Express.

Goals for Writing this Book

The little person often gets left out. Everyone seems to focus their attention on large corporations with deep pockets. If you don't belong to such an organization, it's easy to think that no one cares about you unless you're willing to buy the commodity items stocked by big box stores. Visual Web Developer Express immediately struck me as a serious tool for the rest of us—the people who don't have deep pockets. Sure, it does have some limitations, but generally these limitations aren't all that big of a deal for someone writing software for their home office or small organization. Consequently, my first goal for writing this book is to provide you with something that doesn't feel cheap or flimsy. This book provides you with quality applications that really do provide great functionality.

Of course, many large organizations will also want to try Visual Web Developer Express. With ever-shrinking IT budgets, it's hard to find money to go out and buy an application suite. Trying Visual Web Developer Express lets you see what ASP.NET 2.0 and the .NET Framework 2.0 can do without incurring a lot of debt. It's sort of like being a kid in a candy store without the candy store prices. You get to try everything out, get a free sample of the sweets, so to speak, without taking a very big risk. I tried to provide the broadest array of examples possible in this book. The result is a book where you can see what ASP.NET 2.0 buys you when it comes to Web sites.

Finally, this book helps you discover whether Microsoft is telling the truth about the usefulness and effectiveness of this product. Is Visual Web Developer Express really a good tool for creating Web sites? After all, you have a lot of tools from which to choose. I think you'll be surprised at just how easy it is to create Web sites that not only look professional, but don't require a lot of time to build. This book demonstrates that Visual Web Developer Express can help you create Web sites of moderate size without the usual array of widgets and lost time of other products. You can get to work almost immediately and use this book as a guide while you create the masterpiece that is your Web site.

Who Should Read This Book?

This book isn't for everyone. I created a book for someone who wants to see what ASP.NET 2.0 and the .NET Framework 2.0 provide without spending a lot of time and effort doing it. If you're looking for a major enterprise application that takes weeks to explain and requires even longer to comprehend, you won't find it here. This book is all about simplicity—looking for the easy way to accomplish the tasks you need to do to create a great Web site. If you're looking for arcane solutions to very odd problems, this book isn't for you.

I did target this book for two groups. The first group is any small businessperson, hobbyist, or other interested party who doesn't need a very big development system to accomplish everything they need. The projects in this book are designed to help you create a great looking Web site in very little time and with little effort as well. The second group is people who are curious—who want to discover what all the hubbub is about. This book provides the grand tour of all ASP.NET can provide for you.

You do need to have certain knowledge to use this book. I'm assuming that you've worked with your computer long enough to understand how it works—you won't find any button clicking exercises in this book. It's also important that you know a programming language at least a little bit. This book doesn't provide basic instruction on either Visual Basic or C#; the two languages used for the examples. Consequently, if you don't know a loop from an object, you probably need to look through a language book before getting this one, such as *Mastering Visual Basic 2005 Express Edition* by Evangelos Petroutsos and Acey J. Bunch (Sybex, 2006).

Getting the Source Code

This book contains a wealth of programming examples that you'll want to review as part of learning to use Visual Web Developer Express. You're free to type the code in from the book, but you do have an easier means at your disposal for getting the source code. Simply go to the Sybex Web site at `http://www.sybex.com/`, type **Mastering Visual Web Developer 2005 Express** in the search field, and click Go. Click the link for this book and you'll arrive at the book page. Click the Download link and follow the instructions to download the source code for this book. That's all there is to it and you'll save yourself a lot of time typing everything from scratch.

Conventions Used in This Book

TABLE 1.1:   It always helps to know what the special text means in a book. The following table provides a list of standard usage conventions. These conventions make it easier for you to understand what a particular text element means.

CONVENTION	EXPLANATION
`Inline Code`	Some code will appear in the text of the book to help explain application functionality. The code appears in a special font that makes it easy to see. This monospaced font also makes the code easier to read.
`Inline Variable`	As with source code, variable source code information that appears inline will also appear in a special font that makes them stand out from the rest of the text. When you see monospaced text in an italic typeface, you can be sure it's a variable of some type. Replace this variable with a specific value. The text will always provide examples of specific values that you might use.
`User Input`	Sometimes I'll ask you to type something. For example, you might need to type a particular value into the field of a dialog box. This special font helps you see what you need to type.

TABLE 1.1:   It always helps to know what the special text means in a book. The following table provides a list of standard usage conventions. These conventions make it easier for you to understand what a particular text element means. *(CONTINUED)*

CONVENTION	EXPLANATION
Filename	A variable name is a value that you need to replace with something else. For example, you might need to provide the name of your server as part of a command line argument. Because I don't know the name of your server, I'll provide a variable name instead. The variable name you'll see usually provides a clue as to what kind of information you need to supply. In this case, you'll need to provide a filename. Although the book doesn't provide examples of every variable that you might encounter, it does provide enough so that you know how to use them with a particular command.
[*Filename*]	When you see square brackets around a value, switch, or command, it means that this is an optional component. You don't have to include it as part of the command line or dialog field unless you want the additional functionality that the value, switch, or command provides.
File ➢ Open	Menus and the selections on them appear with a special menu arrow symbol. "File ➢ Open" means "Access the File menu and choose Open."
italic	You'll normally see words in italic if they have special meaning or if this is the first use of the term and the text provides a definition for it. Always pay special attention to words in italic because they're unique in some way. When you see a term that you don't understand, make sure you check the glossary for the meaning of the term as well. The glossary also includes definitions for every acronym in the book.
monospace	Some words appear in a monospace font because they're easier to see or require emphasis of some type. For example, all filenames in the book appear in a monospace font to make them easier to read.
URLs	URLs will normally appear in a monospace font so that you can see them with greater ease. The URLs in this book provide sources of additional information designed to make your development experience better. URLs often provide sources of interesting information as well.

Part 1

Discovering Visual Web Developer

In this section you will learn to:

- ◆ **Chapter 1: An Introduction to the Express Products**
- ◆ **Chapter 2: Working with Visual Web Developer**
- ◆ **Chapter 3: Creating a Simple Application**

Chapter 1

An Introduction to the Express Products

The Microsoft Express product line has attracted a lot of attention and for good reason—this series of products can help you create many types of .NET applications without investing a single penny. Unlike Visual Studio .NET, the Express product line includes separate products for desktop and Web development. The topic of this book is Visual Web Developer 2005 Express Edition—the Web component of the Express product line.

It also pays to know something about the other Express products because you can consume (access and use) Web services using these other products from the desktop. Most important, though, is that you'll use one of the Express languages for creating applications in Visual Web Developer and SQL Server 2005 Express Edition as the database server. (The code examples in this book use Visual Basic Express and appear on the CD using Visual C# Express.) Consequently, you'll find at least a little information about the other Express products in this book. I introduce all of the products in this chapter so you know how each product can help you create a complete solution.

TIP   For more information about the Express products, see *Mastering Visual Basic 2005 Express Edition* (Sybex, 2005) by Evangelos Petroutsos and Acey J. Bunch and *Mastering SQL Server 2005 Express Edition* (Sybex, 2005) by Mike Gunderloy and Susan Harkins.

Getting and using the various Express products is easy. All you need to do is download the products you need from the Visual Studio 2005 Express Products Web site. Once you download the product, you'll need to decide how to use it to meet personal, small-to-medium-sized business, or experimental needs. This chapter provides you with a lot of suggestions you can try while working your way through the examples in the book.

One of the most interesting features for Visual Web Developer users is Active Server Pages (ASP) .NET 2.0. ASP.NET 2.0 helps you create more robust Web pages with less effort and greater functionality. You'll find that ASP.NET 2.0 includes new features, such as support for master pages and themes, that make it easier to create dynamic applications with functionality that you might not think possible with the Express products.

An Overview of the Express Product Line

The Visual Studio 2005 Express Edition product line includes six products that you can use to create applications for your system. You don't have to download all of these products to create a complete programming solution. In fact, you can create a complete solution, in many cases, by installing just one of the products.

All of the products share common features. Microsoft has spent a lot of time ensuring the code you develop using an Express product will work in the full version (Visual Studio .NET 2005) so that you can move anything you create. As part of the shared interface, you obtain access to features such as IntelliSense in all Express products. The essential techniques for performing tasks are the same in both the Express products and the full Visual Studio .NET product. For example, the interface for working with a Web page is the same in both environments, so you can easily move from one to the other without losing time relearning the interface.

You'll find many ways in which the Express products mirror the full Visual Studio .NET product, some of which are product specific. The following sections describe the Express product line—you'll discover that Visual Web Developer and other Express products differ from other Microsoft offerings. You'll also discover similarities that will help you understand the products better.

It's not Visual InterDev or Web Matrix

Some developers might remember Visual InterDev (`http://msdn.microsoft.com/vstudio/previous/vinterdev/default.aspx`) or Web Matrix (`http://www.asp.net/webmatrix/default.aspx`). Both of these solutions help you create Web sites. You can still download updates and patches for Visual InterDev. In fact, some of the features found in Visual InterDev are now part of Visual Studio .NET as part of the main language products (it used to be completely separate). Web Matrix is still available as a download and the developers at Microsoft have continued to update this product. Microsoft created both products for the same reason—as starting tools that hopefully lead to someone buying a full copy of Visual Studio. You always had to buy Visual InterDev—Web Matrix is a free download. As the newer product, Web Matrix actually relies on the .NET Framework and the Microsoft developers wrote it using C#.

Both products suffer from the same problem—they don't really work like the rest of Visual Studio. In fact, the IDE (Integrated Development Environment) for both products is very different from the one that Visual Studio .NET uses. Consequently, when you attempt to upgrade to Visual Studio .NET, you're faced with a product learning curve. Not only must you overcome the obstacles of moving your code from one environment to the other, but you must learn a new IDE as well. Figure 1.1 shows a typical Web Matrix IDE view, which is actually closer in some ways to Visual Studio .NET than Visual InterDev was.

FIGURE 1.1
Web Matrix uses the .NET Framework and can create ASP.NET applications, but lacks a compatible IDE.

The IDE problem is one that many developers aren't willing to overcome. When you work with Visual Web Developer, however, you see something surprisingly similar to the Visual Studio .NET IDE, only with a few less features, as shown in Figure 1.2. See the "Understanding the Limitations of Express Products" section of this chapter for details on the differences between Visual Web Developer and Visual Studio .NET. The "Using the IDE" section of Chapter 2 tells you more about working with the Visual Web Developer interface.

Visual Web Developer also streamlines many of the operations that Visual InterDev supports. Many developers find Visual InterDev cumbersome to use. The same can't be said about Visual Web Developer. A combination of simplified interface, improved wizards, and quick methods of performing tasks make this product easier to use and more efficient as well. You spend more time coding and less time trying to figure out how to perform a given task.

The most important consideration is that everything about Visual Web Developer is designed around compatibility. You get a better work environment and improved update options because Microsoft designed the environment to support it. While Web Matrix is an unsupported tool, Visual Web Developer is a fully supported part of the Visual Studio family. The lessons that Microsoft learned from both Visual InterDev and Web Matrix went into the creation of Visual Web Developer. You'll discover techniques for moving your applications from older versions of Visual Studio in Chapter 20 and to the latest version of Visual Studio in Chapter 21.

Understanding Visual Web Developer 2005 Express Edition

Microsoft designed Visual Web Developer to provide basic Web development support. You can create Web applications and Web services using C#, Visual Basic, and Visual J#. This book concentrates on providing examples in C# and Visual Basic. The idea is that Visual Web Developer is a separate environment for creating Web resources. It even includes a special project that generates a fully functional personal Web site that you can use for experimentation. The "Working with the Personal Web Site Starter Kit" section of Chapter 2 discusses many of the elements of this sample application and helps you understand how to use it to your benefit.

FIGURE 1.2
The Visual Web Developer interface looks very much like Visual Studio .NET.

Fortunately, you don't have to rely only on special technologies to use Visual Web Developer. You can create standard Web pages as well using common tags and scripts. Chapter 6 shows how you can perform this type of development. The idea is that sometimes simple is better when it comes to certain page types. For example, you might find yourself using some of these techniques to ensure a page remains accessible as described in Chapter 19.

One of the best features of Visual Web Developer is that you can move any Web application you create from your local drive to the server using the Copy Web tool shown in Figure 1.3. For those familiar with FrontPage 2003 (see Figure 1.4), this feature looks very familiar. The two products use a similar interface for remote connectivity, but not precisely the same. You can learn more about this feature in the "Using the Copy Web Site Tool" section of Chapter 3.

FIGURE 1.3

Use Visual Web Developer to interact with both local and remote sites.

FIGURE 1.4

Visual Web Developer borrows some ideas from FrontPage 2003.

The reason that the FrontPage 2003 connection is so important is that Microsoft did borrow some ideas from FrontPage for Visual Web Developer. These interface elements make Visual Web Developer easier to use and are consistent with Microsoft's goal for this product of creating a great environment for small-to-medium-sized businesses. FrontPage includes functionality that emphasizes simplicity over a heavy-duty programming environment.

Visual Web Express also supports many features that reduce programming complexity. For example, you have full access to the Smart Tags that appear with many Microsoft products today. Smart Tags reduce complexity by limiting the amount of custom code you must create. At the same time, the user gains full access to the functionality that a Smart Tag can provide. For example, when a Web page contains a stock symbol, a special Smart Tag provides information about the stock symbol, such as the number of shares traded. Smart Tags also affect the development environment, as shown in Figure 1.5. This Smart Tag helps you configure a FormView control. You'll discover more about using Smart Tags in the "Working with Control Smart Tags" section of Chapter 3.

Most developers will also appreciate the save/refresh style of working with Web pages that Visual Web Developer Express provides. In the past, you often had to close the browser, make any required changes to your code, and reopen the browser to see the effects. In a worst-case scenario, you might have to restart Internet Information Server (IIS) to see the change. With Visual Web Developer, all you need to do is make the change, save and compile the code in the IDE, and then click Refresh on the browser to see the change. The "Understanding Save/Refresh Style Page Development" section of Chapter 3 describes this technique in detail.

Unlike other simple products that Microsoft created in the past, Visual Web Developer also includes a full and complete debugger. Because debugging Web pages is difficult, in many cases, the inclusion of a complete debugger is important from a productivity perspective. Chapter 16 tells you more about debugging your applications.

Understanding Visual Basic 2005 Express Edition and Visual C# 2005 Express Edition

Visual Basic 2005 Express Edition and Visual C# 2005 Express Edition comprise the desktop application development environments for the Express product line. Obviously, the two languages are different, but for the purposes of this book, they do provide some commonalities that you should consider. These two language products help you use Visual Web Developer in several ways.

Learn the language. It's notoriously difficult to learn a complex language using Web applications because you have fewer resources for dissecting the code to see how it works. Yes, you can do it, but experimenting with simple desktop applications can reduce the learning curve when such functionality is available.

FIGURE 1.5
Using Smart Tags reduces end user interface and other development complexity.

Right-click and select "Save Picture As.." to download the picture.

Common FormView Tasks

Choose Data Source: AccessDataSource1

Configure Data Source...
Refresh Schema

Auto Format...

☐ Enable Paging

Edit Templates

Consume Web pages.   A desktop application can consume Web pages directly. The Web pages can appear as a local source, such as when an application displays help files, or from a remote source, such as when an application provides a user with additional resources. You can use Visual Web Developer to create Web pages of either type and even develop combinations of sources, such as a help system that checks for updates from a remote source every time an application starts. The "Providing User Customized Output" section of Chapter 13 tells you more about consuming Web pages from a desktop application.

Consume Web services.   You can build desktop applications with either Visual Basic Express or Visual C# Express that access the Web services you create using Visual Web Developer. In some cases, you won't want to use a Web application to access the Web service—a desktop application makes more sense. These two products give you the extra flexibility you need. The "Designing Appropriate Middleware" and "Creating the Front End Pages" sections of Chapter 15 tell you more about consuming Web services.

Create server-side applications.   Sometimes you'll want to create utilities that help you manage your Web-based application. Either Visual Basic Express or Visual C# Express can help you create utilities. Of course, neither product provides the functionality that the full product provides, but you can still create classes with them and console applications that are readily accessible from your Web application. Chapter 14 discusses techniques for working with components and controls. The "Managing the Shopping Cart Application" section of Chapter 15 provides additional details on creating server-side applications.

Obviously, you can also use Visual Basic Express and Visual C# Express to create desktop applications. One of the interesting projects that Microsoft supplies with Visual C# Express is a screen saver. Figure 1.6 shows the initial Welcome display that you see when starting the IDE. You can choose one of the task-oriented options in the lists provided or create a new project using the File ➤ New ➤ Project command. Make sure you use the Connecting to the Community options to gain access to additional information about the Express products.

FIGURE 1.6
The IDEs provide helpful, task-oriented links for working with the Express product.

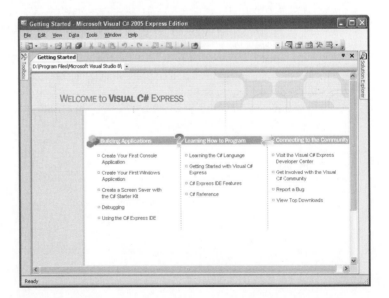

Visual Basic Express also comes with a default project. In this case, you can create a DVD collection manager. The emphasis for Visual Basic Express differs from Visual C# Express. Both products can create console applications, but Visual C# emphasizes it as part of the Welcome display—you can only access this project using the New Project dialog box shown in Figure 1.7 with Visual Basic Express. In addition, while Visual C# Express has a Class Library project, Visual Basic Express supplies a Windows Control Library project. The differences in project types will affect how you use each of these Express products with Visual Web Developer. Visual C# Express is a better choice for components and classes, while Visual Basic Express is a better choice for visual elements. (Discover how to create downloadable applications, pieces of code that you create with Visual C# Express or Visual Basic Express, using Visual Web Developer in Chapter 18.) Interestingly enough, Visual C# includes an Empty Project entry—something you don't get by default with Visual Basic Express.

TIP Visual Basic Express, Visual C# Express, and Visual Web Developer come with an Add New Online Template entry in the New Project dialog box. Click this entry to download additional templates to use with the product. At some point, you'll likely find that community-generated projects more than make up for deficiencies in the Express product projects.

Both of these products do have common features. For example, you gain access to all of the new controls that the .NET Framework provides. In addition, you can consume Web services with either Express language product to create interesting desktop applications.

TIP Microsoft is slowly building a list of interesting projects that you can create using the Express language products. One of the more interesting projects is ExpressPaint—a utility you can use to manipulate images. You can learn more about the ExpressPaint project at http:// msdn.microsoft.com/library/en-us/dnvs05/html/ExprsPaint.asp. View the table of contents on the left side of the display for additional Express product technical articles. General Visual Studio 2005 information and additional Express links appears at http://msdn .microsoft.com/library/en-us/dnanchor/html/vs2005anchor.asp.

FIGURE 1.7

Differences in project type affect how you use each language with Visual Web Developer.

Understanding Visual C++ 2005 Express Edition

Although you won't read much about Visual C++ in this book, you'll find the Visual C++ 2005 Express Edition shares a lot in common with the full-fledged product. You'll find many of the same projects and capabilities in both environments. Unlike Visual Basic Express and Visual C# Express, Visual Web Developer doesn't support Visual C++ Express for creating Web applications. Developers characteristically use Visual C++ to build low-level interfaces such as device drivers, controls, and components. In some cases, Visual C++ also comes in handy when you need to create relatively complex applications—those that interact directly with the Windows 32-bit Application Programming Interface (Win32 API), for example.

In recent years, Microsoft has concentrated hard on creating a compiler that's not only easy to use, but also conforms to all of the standards, especially when it comes to working with templates. Visual C++ Express follows this trend and lets you create C++ code that conforms to the current International Standards Organization (ISO) standards. (ISO also uses the updated name International Organization for Standards.) You can learn more about the American National Standards Institute (ANSI)/ISO C++ draft standard at `http://www.research.att.com/~bs/iso_release.html`, `http://www.open-std.org/jtc1/sc22/wg21/`, and `http://people.msoe.edu/~sebern/resource/ansicpp/`. The bottom line is that Visual C++ Express is a great tool for learning how to create standards compliant C++ code. All standards compliant code that you write using Visual C++ Express is native (unmanaged) and not .NET code.

NOTE　Visual C++ Express won't generate native code immediately after you install it. You have to perform a few extra configuration tasks to obtain this functionality. The instructions for creating native code applications with Visual C++ Express appear at `http://lab.msdn.microsoft.com/express/visualc/usingpsdk/default.aspx`. You can obtain the Windows Platform Software Development Kit (SDK) at `http://www.microsoft.com/msdownload/platformsdk/sdkupdate/`.

Microsoft has become acutely aware of the problems caused by C/C++ code in the past, such as buffer overruns (a major security issue). Consequently, Visual C++ Express contains a new Runtime Checks feature that helps you locate and squash both buffer overruns and other kinds of data-related bugs. The result is that you create better code for whatever environment you want to work in.

Besides writing standards compliant native (unmanaged) applications for Windows (the only .NET Express product that allows you to perform this task), you can also use Visual C++ Express to write managed code using the .NET Framework. This use is where you might create an interface between Visual Web Developer and Visual C++ Express. For example, you can write specialized classes to handle garbage collection needs on active Web sites or perform deterministic finalization of class elements.

Understanding Visual J# 2005 Express Edition

Microsoft envisions Visual J# 2005 Express Edition as a tool for learning Java. The only problem with this vision is that Visual J# Express won't run on any Java Virtual Machine (JVM) and it doesn't necessarily follow the Sun guidelines for Java. The download Web site is very careful about mentioning these problems in the fine print. If you can live with these potential problems and really want to use the Visual Studio .NET IDE for learning Java, downloading Visual J# Express might make sense.

TIP　Although the Express product line is generally well conceived, you'll want to get a real Java development environment if you plan to write Java applications. All you need is a Java editor and the Sun JVM. You can download a free trial version of JCreator Pro (an easy-to-use editor that has many Visual Studio features) at `http://www.jcreator.com` and the free Sun JVM at `http://java.sun.com/j2se/1.4.2/download.html`. Generally speaking, Visual J# Express is an interesting idea and perhaps a good training tool, but don't count on it to create Java applications.

UNDERSTANDING NON-DETERMINISTIC FINALIZATION

Anyone who works with unmanaged code knows that classes always contain a constructor (for creating an instance of the class) and a destructor (for cleaning up after the application no longer needs the object defined by the class). The world of .NET works differently from code you might have used in the past. Classes still contain constructions, but they no longer contain destructors because the Garbage Collector determines when an application no longer needs an object. This loss of ability to determine when an application no longer needs an object is *non-deterministic finalization*.

Behind the fancy term is a simple explanation. The developer loses the ability to determine when an object is going to go away. The object doesn't go away immediately—it may go away after the application terminates. This is a problem if you're using the destructor in an object to perform post-component processing. For example, you may leave a file open the whole time you use a component and close it only when the component no longer needs file access. Using the destructor to close the file is no longer an option in .NET, so you need to use some other method to handle the problem.

You can read more about this particular problem at `http://www.codeproject.com/managedcpp/cppclidtors.asp`. Fortunately, there are workarounds for this problem, most of which following good coding practice addresses. In some cases, however, the Garbage Collector will cost some performance, because you'll need to open and close files more often.

Microsoft did provide access to some Java programming technologies in Visual J#. For example, you can write code that uses the Abstract Windowing Toolkit (AWT), Swing, Applet, and other Java Development Kit (JDK) classes. Unfortunately, Microsoft mixes these Java classes with standard .NET classes, so you can't really be sure that you're writing pure Java code.

NOTE   If you do decide to try Visual J# Express with Visual Web Developer, you must install the package separately. Unlike Visual Basic Express and Visual C# Express, the Visual Web Developer setup program doesn't include Visual J# Express support by default.

Understanding SQL Server 2005 Express Edition

One of the interesting things about the SQL Server 2005 Express Edition entry on the Visual Studio 2005 Express Products Web site (`http://lab.msdn.microsoft.com/express/`) is that you don't really need to download this product when you download any of the others. All of the language products provide a check box for downloading SQL Server Express as part of the installation program. Consequently, the only reason you need to download SQL Server Express is to install this product on another machine.

NOTE   The Express products currently won't work with the full version of SQL Server—you must install SQL Server Express to gain database-processing capabilities with this product. If you didn't install SQL Server Express as part of the Express language product installation, you can install it separately. Microsoft plans to resolve this issue in later versions of the Express products.

There are a number of good reasons to download SQL Server Express. For example, you might find that you need to test a multitiered application strategy, which could mean using multiple machines and placing SQL Server Express on a separate machine. Of course, you could just as easily use the full version of SQL Server for testing, but you have to buy the full version and SQL Server Express is free. You can find a great overview of SQL Server Express at `http://msdn.microsoft.com/library/en-us/dnsse/html/sseoverview.asp`.

Generally, you'll work with SQL Server Express using scripts and the IDEs of the language products. You won't interact with it directly as you would with the full-fledged version of SQL Server (the product lacks the Enterprise Manager and Query Analyzer utilities found in the full product). This omission makes working with SQL Server Express more akin to working with the older Microsoft Database Engine (MSDE) than working with SQL Server. (There are rumors that Microsoft might include graphical tools with SQL Server Express at some point, but these tools aren't available as of the time of writing.) However, the MSDE product lacked a lot of SQL Server functionality that SQL Server Express does include, such as the command line utilities. Microsoft made some compromises in the interest of getting database management into the hands of developers without giving SQL Server away. Chapters 10 (a simple application example) and 11 (detailed SQL Server Express manipulation) are your gateway to understanding SQL Server Express functionality better.

SQL Server Express does include many of the features you'll get with the next version of SQL Server. For example, you can interact with the Common Language Runtime (CLR). It also has full eXtensible Markup Language (XML) support and the capability to use XCopy (a command line utility) to move databases from one location to another. You'll also gain access to support for the Data-GridView, DataNavigator, and DataConnector controls and you can create databases up to 4 GB in size. In short, even though this product does have some of the limitations of MSDE, it also includes a number of features that MSDE didn't—making SQL Server Express a far superior product.

Obtaining the Express Products

Before you can do anything with the Express products described in this book, you need to obtain a copy of the product you want. The best place to get an overview of the products is the Visual Studio 2005 Express Products Web site at `http://lab.msdn.microsoft.com/express/`. The "Installing Visual Web Developer 2005" section of Chapter 2 describes how to install each product so you can use it effectively with Visual Web Developer. Each of the products also has a special Web site. The following list tells you about each product.

Visual Basic 2005 Express Edition (Desktop Applications Only) `http://lab.msdn.microsoft.com/express/vbasic/default.aspx`

Visual C# 2005 Express Edition (Desktop Applications Only) `http://lab.msdn.microsoft.com/express/vcsharp/default.aspx`

Visual C++ 2005 Express Edition (Desktop Applications Only) `http://lab.msdn.microsoft.com/express/visualc/default.aspx`

Visual J# 2005 Express Edition (Desktop Applications Only) `http://lab.msdn.microsoft.com/express/vjsharp/default.aspx`

Visual Web Developer 2005 Express Edition (Web Applications Only) `http://lab.msdn.microsoft.com/express/vwd/default.aspx`

SQL Server 2005 Express Edition (Database Support) `http://lab.msdn.microsoft.com/express/sql/default.aspx`

Unfortunately, the seemingly short download for these products isn't the end of the line—it's only the beginning of a much larger download. Some of these product downloads will exceed 300 MB once you get the entire package. A better option if you have a slow connection is to have Microsoft send you a CD with the Express product that you want. To obtain a CD, start at `http://lab.msdn.microsoft.com/vs2005/get/order/` and fill out the required forms.

NOTE   Remember that the language products will offer to download and install SQL Server Express for you. The only reason you need to download SQL Server Express separately is when you want to place this product on another machine. For example, you might want to see how server access works with your Express language product.

Uses for the Express Product Line

Before you get the idea that the Express product line is just for small time developers with a lack of cash, you need to understand that this is a real tool with real transitioning capabilities. You can use these products to create complete applications or just to test ideas for an application you want to create using Visual Studio .NET. Nothing says that you have to abide by Microsoft's predefined goals for each product—experiment, have fun! The Express product line provides the opportunity to try something new with a minimum of risk. With this idea in mind, here are some ways to use the Express products, most notably, Visual Web Developer Express.

Prototyping   Most developers like to tinker—to take some small bit of code and see what they can do with it. These little experiments can sometimes result in huge time savings later. It's these little experiments that provide the breakthroughs a team needs to accomplish application-programming goals. Unfortunately, trying to place Visual Studio .NET on your laptop so you can play for a while when you fly somewhere might not work well. However, the Express products are smaller, lighter, and very laptop friendly. You can work on your ideas and then move them to the full Visual Studio .NET development environment later.

Experimentation   Let's face it, Visual Studio .NET isn't the least expensive product on the market and you might be hard pressed to get a copy without showing some kind of benefit. Unfortunately, you can't show a benefit to your company without having a copy of Visual Studio .NET to work with. Getting the Express products solves this problem because you can work with .NET long enough to prove that getting the full-fledged product will save time and effort for your programming group.

Application development.   Sometimes you don't need all the bells and whistles that a full-fledged product provides. Visual Studio .NET can actually get in the way of your development efforts because too many goodies attract your attention. Using the Express products lets you develop simple applications with fewer distractions using older equipment that has less memory. What's really interesting is that you get the smaller footprint and still use the latest technology from Microsoft.

Training   Many developers today are self-taught and it's unlikely that this trend will change. Programming is an art that people from many walks of life discover. In addition, companies and educational institutions are constantly looking for ways to reduce their training costs. All of the Express products are currently free. You can download them and learn how to program using something that's free of cost. Later, when your skills improve and the complexity of the applications you develop increases, you can always move to Visual Studio .NET.

Occasional use.   Not everyone uses Visual Studio .NET every day. In fact, some people use more than one language on more than one platform. The Express product line can provide enough functionality for these occasional users to test ideas when they need to write code that works with more than one platform.

TIP Cross-platform solutions are becoming more important to companies as they acquire developers with programming skills that cover more than one discipline. Companies such as Mainsoft (http://www.mainsoft.com/) are trying to solve the problem by creating Visual Studio .NET add-ins that output code in other forms. In this case, Visual MainWin lets a developer write code using C# or Visual Basic .NET and output it as a Java package. You can even use Enterprise Java Beans (EJB) from within Visual Studio .NET as if they were .NET classes. The point is that these add-ins will likely work with the Express products, at some point, too, making it possible for people to interact with multiple environments with great ease.

Quick fixes. Microsoft designed the Express product line to coexist with the released versions of Visual Studio .NET. This is an interesting situation because it actually allows you to perform quick fixes on your Web projects without having to bring up the entire Visual Studio .NET suite. Theoretically, you can view the Express product line as a sort of Wordpad utility compared with using Word. You use Word to write complete and complex documents, but WordPad is best for quick changes to formatted documents that aren't very complex.

Understanding the ASP.NET 2.0 Difference

One of the essential new features for .NET is the introduction of ASP.NET 2.0. The features included with ASP.NET determine what you can do with Web pages and how these pages appear to the end user. The latest version of ASP.NET also promises better performance and security. However, the move from older versions of ASP.NET might not be as seamless as you'd like. As Microsoft begins to overcome security, reliability, and performance issues with Windows and their other products, ASP.NET has to change as well. One of the better places to obtain the insights of developers that have made the move is the ASP.NET 2.0 and Visual Studio 2005 Tips and Tricks forum at http://www.asp.net/Forums/ShowForum.aspx?tabindex=1&ForumID=134.

The first versions of ASP.NET concentrated on functionality—the developer gained important flexibility in creating impressive displays of information. The only problem is that dressing up the display often relied on the talents of the developer, so you still see many plain pages on the Internet. Sure, they work as intended and provide great information in multiple formats, but the pages feel unfinished unless the developer spends time creating additional code. ASP.NET 2.0 fixes the fit and finish problems by incorporating a new concept borrowed from FrontPage 2003—master pages and themes. A master page lets you create a Web page that contains elements that all or a group of Web pages must have and then use that page as a means of starting all of the pages on a Web site. A theme contains graphical and structural elements that define a basic concept for your Web site, such as using red for all title text. Figure 1.8 shows a typical example of a master page (note that it has a MASTER file extension. You'll learn more about working with master pages and themes in Chapter 4.

You'll also find many new developer productivity features in ASP.NET 2.0. For example, Microsoft has made it easier to add security to your Web application. ASP.NET 2.0 includes both credential storage and role management support without adding a lot of additional code. Chapter 17 tells you more about creating secure applications using Visual Web Developer. Personalization services (discussed in Chapter 13) make it easier to store user information so that every user has a custom experience. The use of site navigation to provide better access to Web pages and site counters to measure performance ensure that you can manage a site with greater ease. Both features appear in the "Creating a Custom Site Search" section of Chapter 8.

FIGURE 1.8

Master pages give a Web site a consistent look and greatly reduce development time.

Part of the personalization functionality comes with a new technology called Web Parts. This technology includes a number of controls that let the user change the content, appearance, and behavior of a Web page directly from a browser. You can use this technology to ensure that a Web page meets specific user needs such as accessibility (discussed in Chapter 19) or to allow the user to view content in another way (see the "Using Web Parts to Automate User Customizations" section of Chapter 6).

NOTE   ASP.NET 2.0 supports 64-bit computing. However, it's unclear as of the time of writing, whether you'll be able to create 64-bit applications using the Express products. Generally, working with a 64-bit application in .NET isn't any different than working with a 32-bit application from a coding perspective, so the code you create with an Express product will likely work without modification in the 64-bit environment. You'll need to change the project settings and recompile the application, however.

ASP.NET 2.0 comes with 45 new controls that will make creating applications a lot easier. Many of these controls are encapsulations of features developers requested and many had to be created by hand previously. You'll find examples of these new controls in many places in the book. However, the new controls are so important that you'll find many of them described in the "Working with Forms" section of Chapter 5. These controls also support multiple device types now so you don't have to do anything special to serve up a Web page to someone with a handheld device. The "Working with Multiple Device Types" section of Chapter 12 describes this feature in detail.

Management is a big issue because the Web master or network administrator usually performs the task, rather than the developer who created the application. Microsoft has made management easier by better documenting the WEB.CONFIG and MACHINE.CONFIG files. In addition, you'll find scripts for managing these files as part of the ASP.NET 2.0 installation. You can find out more about these features in the "Employing Server-side Redirection" section of Chapter 9.

There are a number of places online to learn more about ASP.NET 2.0. Of course, you'll discover a lot more about ASP.NET 2.0 functionality as this book progresses. Beginning with Chapter 7, the examples in the book demonstrate various ASP.NET 2.0 features that you get with Visual Web Developer. For example, the "Targeting Feedback Forms to Meet Specific Needs" section of Chapter 7 describes how you can use a master page to develop multiple feedback form types so that ad hoc surveys are much easier to implement. Besides the resources in the book, however, you might also want to obtain *Introducing ASP.NET 2.0* by Dino Esposito (Microsoft Press, 2004), and view these Web sites.

Basic ASP.NET 2.0 overview   `http://www.asp.net/whidbey/whitepapers/`
`AspNetOverview.aspx`

ASP.NET 2.0 and Visual Web Developer 2005 Express Edition forums (Newsgroups)
`http://www.asp.net/Forums/ShowForumGroup.aspx?tabindex=1&ForumGroupID=26`

MSDN ASP.NET 2.0 topics   `http://msdn.microsoft.com/asp.net/whidbey/default.aspx`

ASP.NET security article   `http://www.sitepoint.com/article/asp-net-2-security`

Master Pages in ASP.NET 2.0   `http://www.c-sharpcorner.com/Code/2004/May/`
`MasterPages.asp`

ASP.NET 2.0 internals   `http://www.c-sharpcorner.com/Code/2004/Sept/ASP.NET2`
`.0Internals.asp`

Understanding the Limitations of Express Products

Every .NET product relies on the .NET Framework. All of the capabilities of the platform appear as part of that framework. For example, if you want to program in C#, you might assume that you need Microsoft's Visual C# product, but you don't. All that Microsoft provides with Visual C# .NET is an IDE, which is a graphical way to work with the code. As part of this IDE, you gain access to projects, wizards, utilities, and other features that make development easier, but don't provide actual language functionality. You could also use alternatives, such as the C# editor from Antechinus (`http://www.c-point.com/csharp.htm`), and obtain the same results—only the IDE would differ. The fact that you get the functionality of C# free with the .NET Framework begs the question of why someone would consider buying Visual Studio .NET at all, considering they can get Visual Web Developer free.

The problem is time. Given enough time, you can use a text editor to write all of the code for your Web site and compile it with the features found in the .NET Framework that you download free. You really don't need an IDE at all. Unfortunately, most developers are under such time and productivity constraints that writing code by hand is out of the question. The developer needs an IDE to be productive. Just as the Antechinus editor provides C# developers with a different level of productivity from the Microsoft Visual C# IDE, Visual Web Developer provides a limited level of productivity compared to the Visual Studio .NET IDE.

Microsoft designed Visual Web Developer for small system development—the kind that you use for personal and small-to-medium-sized company needs. It's also the perfect environment for someone to experiment—no matter what the size of the organization. However, Visual Web Developer isn't the right solution for corporate development because it lacks the following productivity features.

No Server Explorer   Server Explorer provides full access to every machine the developer can access on a network. With Server Explorer, the developer has instant access to SQL Server, all of the network services, and even the performance information. To place this information into an application, the developer simply drags and drops it onto a form. Visual Web Developer replaces this important productivity aid with Database Explorer—a simple feature that provides access to databases only after you make a connection to them. Although this might seem like a significant limitation, most developers won't need all of the functionality that Server Explorer provides to create simple applications.

Reduced project availability   Visual Web Developer obviously won't allow any kind of desktop development—something you get free with Visual Studio. However, even with Web projects, Visual Web Developer differs from Visual Studio. It lacks the wizards and other productivity aids that Visual Studio provides and you can't create complex projects. Visual Web Developer does add FrontPage-like simplicity, though. Users work with Webs and can rely on templates to perform some of the work for them. Consequently, the development process is simpler. It's a reasonable trade-off considering the different audiences for each product.

No source control   Because most Visual Web Developer users are individuals, it doesn't make sense to include complex source control. Groups of developers normally require source control to manage complex projects and ensure that none of the developers overwrites another's changes. Again, leaving this feature out of Visual Web Developer is reasonable given the product audience.

Reduced development windows   One of the interesting omissions from Visual Web Developer is the Web Browser emulation window. Microsoft assumes that the developer using Visual Web Developer will check the code with an external browser. Again, it's a productivity and complexity issue. The smaller site probably doesn't need to emulate every browser situation, so Microsoft assumes the developer will create a site that works best with one or two browsers of choice. Visual Web Developer lacks other desktop windows for the obvious reason (it can't create a desktop application).

Fewer development tools   Visual Studio comes with a wealth of development tools such as the ActiveX Control Test Container, Create GUID, Error Lookup, ATL/MFC Trace Tool, OLE/COM Object Viewer, Spy++, and others that make development of complex projects easier. Visual Web Developer doesn't provide access to any of these tools and they aren't accessible externally because they aren't part of the .NET Framework. In general, these tools are for complex programming environments, so leaving them out of Visual Web Developer makes sense.

TIP   One of the easiest ways to get around the lack of development tools in the Express product line is to obtain free versions of these tools online. You'll find a number of sources for these tools in the chapters as the book progresses. In addition, you'll want to review the list of third-party tools in Appendix A. An interesting source of unique developer tools is Chris's Free Developer Tools at http://www.sellsbrothers.com/tools/. This site includes tools that like the Express product line help you experiment with .NET in new ways. For example, the .NET FormatDesigner (http://www.sellsbrothers.com/tools/#FormatDesigner) helps you experiment with formatting strings so you get just the right output from your application.

Slimmer Microsoft Developer Network (MSDN)   MSDN is Microsoft's huge help file for developers. You can access most of it online at http://msdn.microsoft.com/library/, but it's a painful experience. Even Google doesn't work well with this site because it's so complex. Consequently, having MSDN on your hard drive along with Microsoft's custom search engine (it actually does work in this case) is a big productivity enhancer. Visual Studio comes with the complete MSDN so the developer need not get online at all. Visual Web Developer users have to rely on a slimmer version for most, but not all, of their needs. The main reason that Microsoft reduced the size of this feature is to keep the download small—trying to download all of MSDN even with a high-speed connection would keep many developers from even trying Visual Web Developer.

Visual Web Developer is a great development environment, but it won't replace Visual Studio .NET. What Visual Web Developer does is make .NET technology accessible to everyone who can't afford or doesn't need the full Visual Studio environment. Consequently, Visual Web Developer is actually a stepping-stone—something that anyone can use to get started with .NET. When a developer decides that their project warrants the full Visual Studio product, they can move to it without any loss of time or effort.

TIP   Visual Web Developer really is a stepping-stone to other IDEs. When you decide that you want to move up to something with better capabilities, you can still use this book to do it. Chapters 20 and 21 provide that part of the solution as well—the step beyond Visual Web Developer by showing you how to move from one environment to the other.

Defining Your Development Goals

This chapter introduces you to Visual Web Developer and the Express product line in general. It helps you understand how each product fits within the development picture and how you can use each product to create a comprehensive toolbox for small projects or experimentation purposes. The chapter also provides instructions for downloading the express products. Most importantly, you discovered the limitations of each product so you don't have unrealistic expectations of what the product can do for you.

Now it's time for you to act. The first task you need to perform is to decide on how you'll use Visual Web Developer. You might decide to try some simple pages demonstrated in Chapters 4 through 6 first or move right into the complex examples in the latter part of the book. Once you decide what you'd like to do, download the product using the instructions in the "Obtaining the Express Products" section of this chapter. Make sure your setup works and get ready for a delightful experience in the .NET environment.

Chapter 2 moves from a description of Visual Web Developer to a demonstration of how it works. It begins by helping you get Visual Web Developer set up, along with one or two other language products. You'll discover all of the IDE elements and learn how to use them. Once you know a little more about the product, you'll actually create your first Web application. In this case, you'll work with a predefined project that Microsoft provides. This example helps you create a complete personal Web site that you can experiment with and use to discover more about Visual Web Developer and ASP.NET 2.0.

Chapter 2

Working with Visual Web Developer

This chapter begins your journey of using Visual Web Developer. It's important to get a good setup before you begin coding, so the first part of the chapter gets you started. By the time you complete it, you'll have a very usable installation for the rest of the examples in the book and for creating applications of your own.

After you install the product, you'll want to know more about the Integrated Development Environment (IDE). The IDE is the interface you use to create applications using Visual Web Developer and the other Express products. The better you know how to use the IDE features, the faster and more accurately you can create code. In addition, knowing the IDE features can save significant effort because Microsoft designed the IDE to help you perform common tasks efficiently. Unfortunately, there's usually a hard way of performing any task, so this chapter also tells you how to avoid doing more work than you have to.

The final section of this chapter gets you started with your first application. You'll discover how you can use the sample application to create a personal Web site. More importantly, this sample project helps you understand better the features Visual Web Developer provides. You'll discover how things work and how to best use Visual Web Developer's features in a real world–programming environment.

Performing the Visual Web Developer Setup

The Visual Web Developer setup is relatively simple—it's not like installing a complex product such as Office. However, you can create several kinds of setups to meet specific needs. For example, if you plan to create only simple Web sites that never need access to a database or any specialized access, then you might not need anything more than Visual Web Developer. It really is a stand-alone product. The reason that you'll see installation procedures for other products in the sections that follow is that this book helps you explore everything you can do with Visual Web Developer, so you need a larger assortment of products to do the job.

Besides discussing the Visual Web Developer setup, you'll also learn about installing SQL Server Express and a language product (either Visual Basic Express or Visual C# Express). You'll also discover some of the issues you'll encounter when installing Visual Web Developer on a system that already has Visual Studio .NET 2002 or Visual Studio .NET 2003 installed.

Understanding the System Requirements

You need certain system resources to work with Visual Web Developer. Microsoft provides a list of its suggestions at `http://lab.msdn.microsoft.com/express/vwd/readme/default.aspx`. The problem is that these requirements only consider Visual Web Developer—they don't consider a complex setup. In addition, you might be able to get by with a little less when creating only simple applications (not using the full functionality provided by Visual Web Developer). Optimizing your system can also reduce the requirements a little. With these requirements in mind, Table 2.1 provides more realistic system requirements that I based on personal testing (taking Microsoft's suggestions into account).

TABLE 2.1: Express Product Minimum System Requirements

REQUIREMENT	SIMPLE SETUP	AVERAGE SETUP	COMPLEX SETUP
Processor Speed	450 MHz	600 MHz	1 GHz
RAM	128 MB	256 MB	512 MB
Hard Disk	5 GB	10 GB	15 GB
Display	800 × 600 × 16-bit Color	1024 × 768 ×16-bit Color	1024 × 768 × 16-bit Color
CD or DVD Drive for CD Installation	—	—	—

It's important to remember that the requirements in Table 2.1 are the minimum you should consider using. More resources usually result in a better development environment that crashes less often and introduces fewer IDE-related problems during testing. Each product requires a certain amount of hard drive installation space as shown in the following list (full-featured requirement)—this hard drive space requirement is only for installation and doesn't include the extra that you need to write applications.

◆ Visual Web Developer Express: 110 MB

◆ .NET Framework 2.0: 264 MB

◆ Microsoft Developer Network (MSDN) Express: 566 MB

◆ Structured Query Language (SQL) Server Express: 165 MB

◆ Visual Basic Express: 233 MB

◆ Visual C# Express: 188 MB

NOTE The installation programs for all of the Express products check your system for basic requirements before you install the program. If your system doesn't meet the basic requirements, the installation won't start. For example, to install the Express products on Windows XP, you must have Service Pack 1 (SP1) installed as a minimum. Unfortunately, the Express Web site doesn't make you aware of these requirements. The best option is to ensure your system has all of the required patches and updates before you begin the installation.

Installing Visual Web Developer

The Visual Web Developer setup encompasses several phases. Depending on whether you use the Internet download method or the CD installation method, some steps can take a long time. The worst-case scenario is around 3 days using a 128 Kbps Digital Subscriber Line (DSL) connection. You won't want to try using the Internet download method with a dial-up connection. From a procedural perspective, installing the product is the same using either the Internet download method or the CD installation method—only the time required to perform the task differs.

To use the download method, begin at the Visual Web Developer Express site at `http://lab.msdn.microsoft.com/express/vwd/default.aspx`. Click Download Now and follow the prompts. To use the CD installation method, have a credit card ready and go to the CD ordering site at `http://lab.msdn.microsoft.com/vs2005/get/order/`. Select Visual Web Developer from the Select a Product list and your country from the Select a Country list. Click Place Your Order and follow the prompts to order the CD. Once you get the CD, you can begin the installation.

Start installing Visual Web Developer by double-clicking the `VWDSetup.EXE` file (downloaded or on the CD). After the installation program initializes and you accept the licensing agreement, you'll see the configuration dialog box shown in Figure 2.1. All of these optional components provide additional capabilities that you can use as you work with Visual Web Developer. For example, although you don't have to install MSDN, it's a good idea to do so or you won't have any localized help to use. Unless you plan to create and distribute Visual J# Express components with your Web application, you don't need to install the Microsoft Visual J# .NET Redistributable Package. Select the optional components that you want to install and click Next. You'll see a list of features that the installation program will install. Click Install to begin the installation.

FIGURE 2.1

Choose the Visual Web Developer features you want to install.

The following sections discuss specifics about the installation process. For example, you'll discover why you really do need an Internet connection even if you perform an installation using the CD method. These sections also contain hints for making your Visual Web Developer installation work better.

INTERNET CONNECTION REQUIREMENT

No matter which installation method you use, you'll want to have an Internet connection on your development machine. (This connection is mandatory when using the Internet download installation method.) Besides helping you get the product installed, you also need the Internet connection for a number of other reasons including:

◆ Accessing the full version of MSDN as necessary

◆ Obtaining additional templates

- Receiving help from other developers and from Microsoft
- Using the Online Help feature
- Providing input to Microsoft on product performance

MICROSOFT .NET FRAMEWORK 2.0

Installing the Microsoft .NET Framework 2.0 is mandatory. Every aspect of Visual Web Developer relies on the functionality that the .NET Framework provides. For example, you can't even start the IDE without having the .NET Framework installed.

You can install multiple versions of the .NET Framework on a single machine, so if you have older Visual Studio .NET products or applications installed on your system, you don't have to worry about them interfering with each other. The Microsoft .NET Framework 2.0 installs in a separate folder, usually at \WINDOWS\Microsoft.NET\Framework\v2.0.40607. (The minor version number, 40607, will change, but the other parts of the path will remain the same.)

Look into the .NET Framework folder and you'll find a confusing array of files (executable, configuration, support, and initialization to name a few). Many of these utilities appear as the book progresses, so don't worry about discovering what they do now. The important consideration is ensuring that you have access to this folder at the command prompt.

To check for .NET Framework access from the command prompt, select Start ➢ Programs ➢ Accessories ➢ Command Prompt. When you see the command prompt, type **PATH** and press Enter. You'll see a list of the directories that you can access directly from the command prompt.

If you don't see the .NET Framework 2.0 path listed, right-click My Computer and choose Properties from the context menu to display the System Properties dialog box. Select the Advanced tab. Click Environment Variables and you'll see the Environment Variables dialog box. Locate the Path entry in the System Variables list. Click Edit to display the Edit System Variable dialog box, place the cursor at the end of the Variable Value field entry, type a semicolon (if there isn't one), and type the .NET Framework 2.0 path. Click OK three times to close the Edit System Variable, Environment Variables, and System Properties dialog boxes.

VISUAL WEB DEVELOPER EXPRESS

The installation program obviously installs Visual Web Developer by default when you run it. You'll notice that there aren't any configuration settings to change during the installation process except the location of Visual Web Developer on the hard drive (accepting the default location is generally best). However, simply getting the files onto the hard drive isn't the end of the setup process—you also need to modify the Visual Web Developer settings to ensure the IDE works as anticipated. See the "Modifying the Visual Web Developer Options" section later in this chapter for details on changing the Visual Web Developer setup.

MICROSOFT MSDN EXPRESS LIBRARY

If you've worked with previous Visual Studio .NET products, you might be surprised to find that the installation program doesn't ask you which MSDN elements to install. The important point to remember is that this is MSDN Express—a light version of the full-fledged product. Consequently, all you get in the way of support is the Express product support information shown in Figure 2.2. When you need the full functionality provided by MSDN, you need to visit the MSDN site online at http://msdn.microsoft.com/library/. Use the Table of Contents (TOC) on the left side of the display to drill down to the information you need.

FIGURE 2.2
MSDN Express doesn't
provide nearly as much
information as the full
product does.

TIP You can install MSDN Express separately as long as you have an Express language product installed on your system. Simply go to `http://go.microsoft.com/fwlink/?linkid=30100&clcid=0x409` and the download will begin. This link doesn't work if you have only SQL Sever Express installed—you must have a language product installed for the link to work.

SQL SERVER EXPRESS

There are two ways to install SQL Server 2005 Express. The first method is to install this product as part of Visual Web Developer. When you use this method, the installation program won't ask you any questions about the product—it simply installs SQL Server for you. When you use the second method, you'll begin by downloading the `SQLExpr.EXE` file from the SQL Server Express site at `http://lab.msdn.microsoft.com/express/sql/default.aspx`.

WARNING Never install SQL Server Express on a machine that's running an earlier version of SQL Server. The installation program will replace the SQL 8.0 tools with SQL 9.0 versions. As a consequence, you'll lose access to some of the tools that you need to manage the older full version of SQL Server.

The file you download is only the installer. When you run the installer program, you'll begin by accepting the license agreement. After you accept the licensing agreement, the installer creates some setup and configuration files on your system. You'll click Finish when this process is complete, and the installer will display a Welcome dialog box. Click Next and you'll see the System Configuration Check dialog box shown in Figure 2.3.

Notice that this System Configuration Check dialog box has several warnings. (I used it on an older machine.) In some cases, the checks are essential, such as the Operating System Minimum Level Requirement check. However, in other cases, you can get by with fewer requirements for experimentation purposes—some hardware requirements such as processor speed ensure that you get the best possible speed, but you might be able to get by with less. For example, a dual-processor 450 MHz machine won't pass the hardware test, but SQL Server Express runs fine on such a machine (albeit, a little slowly). You can't get by with less memory and, in fact, when you're using a slower processor, more memory is better. To determine precisely how your system failed, select View Report from the Report button drop down. Figure 2.4 shows a typical report.

FIGURE 2.3
Use the System Configuration Check dialog box to determine whether the installation will succeed.

FIGURE 2.4
The View Report dialog box helps you determine whether a particular check is essential.

WARNING Never proceed with a SQL Server Express installation when the System Configuration Check dialog box shows actual errors. Although you can overcome many warnings, errors are an indication that your system won't run the product. Make any required configuration changes before you attempt the installation.

One check is always going to fail when you use Visual Web Developer for local programming tasks (as shown in Figure 2.4). The configuration check doesn't appear to detect the built-in Web server that Visual Web Developer provides, so it will seem as if the Internet Information Server (IIS) check fails. The Web server is still available, SQL Server Express simply doesn't detect it. Normally, you don't have to worry about this issue.

Once you determine that your system will run SQL Server Express, click Continue. Follow the prompts to install the product. Generally, all you need to do is provide your name and company, tell the installation program which features you want installed (Figure 2.5 shows a typical setup), and then let the installation program begin its work. You won't normally need to install Replication support unless your system is running on multiple servers, in which case, you might want to consider a product other than SQL Server Express because Microsoft really didn't design it to work in this environment. The Programming Models feature is an advanced option that you might want to use sometime in the future, but this book won't discuss it.

FIGURE 2.5

Select with care the SQL Server Express features you install.

When you clear the Hide Advanced Configuration Options option on the Registration Information dialog box, you'll also see the Instance Name dialog box shown in Figure 2.6. If the installation program has selected Named Instance and provided a default instance name for you, it means that the system already has a copy of SQL Server or SQL Server Express installed on it. Make sure you check the system setup when you see this configuration unexpectedly (click Cancel to stop the installation process).

Installing a Language Product

You don't have to install a language product such as Visual C# Express or Visual Basic Express to use Visual Web Developer. However, installing one or both of these products will help you use Visual Web Developer in more ways. For example, you can consume Web services that you create with Visual Web Developer using either of these language products. (A Web service is a special kind of application that receives requests from a client through a Web connection, processes the request on the server, and sends the response to the client using a Web connection.) You can also create utilities for building better Web sites using these products. If you add Visual J# Express to the mix, you can also create applets to use on your Web page.

FIGURE 2.6

Make sure you don't install multiple instances unless you really want to.

Installing a second language product is very much like installing Visual Web Developer. In fact, once you start the installation and agree to the licensing terms, you'll see an option selection dialog box very similar to the one shown in Figure 2.1. However, you need to install the optional features only once. When you install Visual Web Developer first with the optional components, all you need to install is the language product. Don't reinstall MSDN or SQL Server. If Microsoft includes other optional features with the language, you should consider installing them. You'll save considerable installation time by requesting only the items you need, especially when you use the download installation method—the installation program still downloads the optional features and then complains when it finds that you installed them earlier.

Once you do install another language product, you should coordinate Visual Web Developer with the other language. For example, when you choose Visual Basic Express as your desktop programming language, you should also use it to write the code behind (the code that makes the Web page functional) for your Web application and Web services. Otherwise, you'll need to use two languages. You'll discover how the combination of the two languages works as the book progresses.

Performing a Side-by-Side Installation with Visual Studio 2002/2003

Developers often complain (and with good reason) that Microsoft finds the most difficult way to implement any given technology. For example, it's not unusual to install an older version of a product to ensure that you can test a newer product with ease. Fortunately, Microsoft has done things right this time—you can create a side-by-side installation of an Express product with Visual Studio .NET 2002 or Visual Studio .NET 2003. In fact, the .NET Framework technology makes this kind of installation possible because each version of the .NET Framework appears in a different folder. The only problem is that Microsoft hid all of the details in the README file that comes with the Express products. (You knew there had to be a hitch, didn't you?)

NOTE   You can safely skip this section unless you have Visual Studio .NET 2002 or Visual Studio .NET 2003 installed on your system. This section doesn't contain any tips or tricks that you can use for other purposes.

WARNING   Some of the early beta Express products don't work well with Visual Studio .NET 2002. Make sure you use a released Express product version with Visual Studio .NET 2002 or uninstall the product before you begin your installation.

As usual, there's no free lunch. Because the Express products use .NET Framework 2.0 and the older Visual Studio .NET versions use either .NET Framework 1.0 or 1.1, you end up with two copies of the .NET Framework on your system. You also have two copies of the programming language IDE and MSDN on your system. In other words, your hard drive must have enough space to support two of everything, including your source code (the Express products convert your source to the newer version so you'll want to save the original and the converted version in different folders).

The resource problem moves from the hard drive to memory and processor resources when you port applications from one environment to the other. The side-by-side installation means that two versions of every support file load into memory—one for the older Visual Studio .NET IDE and another for the Express product IDE. You might notice that your system runs significantly slower when you have only enough resources to run one of the two IDEs. See the "Understanding the System Requirements" section earlier in this chapter for details on the system resource requirements for Visual Web Developer—you'll likely need to double these requirements (at least) to get a workable side-by-side environment.

Another important consideration is to install Visual Studio .NET 2002/2003 before you install the Express product. Otherwise, the Visual Studio .NET installer tends to cause problems with the Express product when you uninstall it. Microsoft's solution to this problem is to reinstall the Express product, which is fine when you use the CD installation method, but not a very pleasant thought when you use the Internet download installation method.

The only downside to installing Visual Studio .NET 2002/2003 first is that you might find some applications that don't work properly because they rely on the .NET Framework 2.0 instead of the older version. You can overcome this issue by creating a CONFIG file for the application (where the configuration filename includes the application name such as MyApp.EXE.CONFIG) like this:

```
<?xml version="1.0" encoding="utf-8" ?>
<configuration>
   <startup>
      <requiredRuntime version="v1.0.3705" safemode="true"/>
   </startup>
</configuration>
```

Notice that the CONFIG file tells the Common Language Runtime (CLR) which version of the .NET Framework to use with the application. This modification might limit the platforms on which the application will run, but it does ensure that the application has the appropriate resources.

Using the IDE

The focus of development language products today is the IDE because the IDE determines how fast and defines how well a developer can write the application. The IDE includes the actual development interface, provides access to components and controls, lets the developer debug the application, and includes the projects and wizards used to create both applications and application elements. You'll find the code used to explore the various view in the \Chapter 02\Views folder of the source code on the Sybex Web site.

NOTE   You could write a .NET Framework application using nothing more than a text editor such as Notepad. The ILASM.EXE file in the \WINDOWS\Microsoft.NET\Framework\v2.0.40607 folder will compile the information you provide into a .NET application. However, working with .NET this way would be one of the most time-consuming and error-prone ways of creating an application imaginable. In short, don't get the idea that the IDE provides the language features—it provides the capability to work with the language in an efficient manner. The .NET Framework provides the language features.

An Overview of the IDE Elements

When you first open Visual Web Developer, you'll see what seems like a confusing array of panes in a main window, as shown in Figure 2.7. However, far from being a confusing array of panes, each one of these client windows is actually a part of the development environment. Figure 2.7 provides a label for each one of the major windows that Visual Web Developer opens. If you don't see one or more of these windows, you can always open it by using the options on the View menu. For example, to open the Solution Explorer window, select View ➢ Solution Explorer.

FIGURE 2.7
The Visual Web Developer IDE provides a number of features for creating applications quickly.

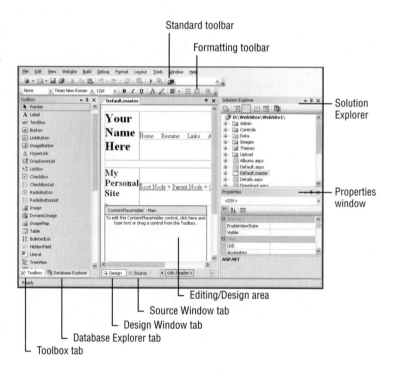

Each of these windows has a special purpose in helping you create applications faster. The following list provides an overview of each of the windows and tells how you'd use the window. You'll obtain additional information about the windows as the book progresses.

Standard toolbar   The Standard toolbar contains common buttons that let you create a new project; add items to a project; save a single or multiple files; cut, copy, or paste items; undo or redo actions; start an application; or find information in the project files. These tasks are common to most file types so Visual Web Developer normally displays the Standard toolbar.

Formatting toolbar   The Formatting toolbar lets you perform a range of text and object configuration tasks. For example, you can choose the style used to display text on screen (a style defines how similar text should look). You can also augment existing text by modifying the font, font size, and attributes. Any object can receive a foreground or background color change. You use the justification options on paragraphs to determine the text alignment. Individual text elements can also include bullets or numbers. Finally, you can convert an URL into a hyperlink that the user clicks to go to a different Web page or download a resource.

Other toolbars   Not shown in Figure 2.7 is the wealth of other toolbars. For example, the Build toolbar contains options that help you compile the application. These other toolbars appear in other sections of this book.

Solution Explorer   Solution Explorer is a kind of outline of your entire project. It shows which files and references your project includes. You can also use Solution Explorer to access the project settings and add new items. Finally, Solution Explorer can help you organize your project to make it easier to work with.

Properties window   The Properties window contains three elements. At the top, you see the selected item. You can select a new item from the drop-down list box. The middle of the Properties window contains the properties for the selected item. Every item contains unique properties based on its object type. The bottom of the Properties window contains an explanation of the selected property when an explanation is available.

Editing/Design area   This is the place where you actually edit or design a Web page. The content changes to reflect the currently selected window tab. For example, when working with a HyperText Markup Language (HTML) document, you'll see tabs for a Source view and a Design view. The Design view lets you modify the graphic elements of the Web page, while the Source view lets you change the code used to create the graphic elements. One or more tabs at the top of the editing/design area let you choose the file you want to work with when multiple files are open. Figure 2.7 shows the Design window (view)—this book examines many other views that Visual Web Developer provides.

Source window tab   Selecting the Source tab displays the Source window where you edit code used to create an application. The Source window lets you edit multiple languages—everything from C# and Visual Basic .NET to HTML and eXtensible Markup Language (XML). The Source window can even appear when there isn't any design to perform. In some cases, you'll create data files using the Source window that provides input to your application. In sum, the Source window is the most common window that you'll see when using Visual Web Developer.

Design window tab   Whenever a file offers a visual element—something the user can interact with—you'll see the Design tab—selecting this tab displays the Design window shown in Figure 2.7. In this case, the display is showing a master file—a new kind of ASP.NET 2.0 feature discussed in Chapter 4.

Database Explorer tab   The Database Explorer tab selects Database Explorer—a feature that Visual Web Developer uses in place of the Server Explorer provided with Visual Studio .NET. Database Explorer helps you create and manage database connections. You can use it to drag and drop tables, fields, views, and other database features to your application. Part IV of this book shows how to work with the database management features of Visual Web Developer.

Toolbox tab   The Toolbox tab selects the Toolbox—a container filled with controls that you use to create the visual elements of an application. Every control has a different purpose and the applications in this book show you how to use many of them. The "Understanding the New ASP.NET 2.0 Controls" section of Chapter 5 also highlights many of the interesting controls in the Toolbox.

TIP   You can click the AutoHide button (the one that looks like a thumbtack) in the upper right corner of any window to hide that window. The window remains accessible—all you need to do is move the cursor over its tab, but the IDE hides the window when you don't need it. To display a window again, simply click the AutoHide button again. The position of the thumbtack on the AutoHide button tells you whether the IDE will hide the window. The IDE always displays the window when the thumbtack points straight down.

Modifying the Visual Web Developer Options

When you first start Visual Web Developer, you'll want to change the IDE options to meet your personal needs. You'll also want to check the settings every time you begin a new project to ensure that the settings meet project needs. To modify the Visual Web Developer settings, start Visual Web Developer using the Start ➤ Programs ➤ Visual Web Developer 2005 Express Edition command. Select the Tools ➤ Options command and you'll see the Options dialog box shown in Figure 2.8. (The figure shows all of the options expanded—these options aren't visible when you initially open the dialog box.)

FIGURE 2.8
The Options dialog box contains the Visual Web Developer settings.

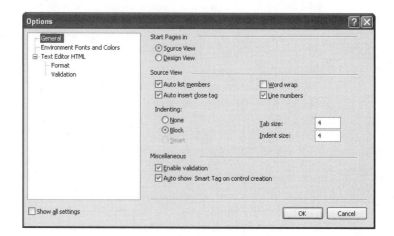

TIP   Most of the dialog boxes in Visual Web Developer include a help button (the one with the question mark in the upper right corner of Figure 2.8). Click the Help button and point to an option or field to obtain additional information about it. The first time you use the help feature, Visual Web Developer displays an Online Help Settings dialog box that determines the source of help. Always choose Use Online Help as Primary Source when you know that you'll always have an Internet connection available and don't mind waiting an additional few seconds to receive the latest help that Microsoft can provide. Choose Use Local Help as Primary Source when you aren't sure that you'll have an Internet connection available or prefer not to wait the additional time for online help unless necessary. Select Do Not Use Online Help when you know you won't have an Internet connection available or don't ever want to wait for the latest help information.

The General options help you control the interface. The Start Pages In group determines whether you view pages starting in Source view (the tags or other code used to create an application) or Design view (the graphical elements that the user sees). Source view includes specialized settings for working with source code. For example, you can display line numbers to make it easier to find errors in the source code (error messages and debugging resources rely on line numbers to tell you the location of an error). Indenting your code is important to improve readability and make it easier to discover how various code elements are related. The Miscellaneous options determine how the IDE reacts to your input and provides other support features. For example, validation checks the code you type to ensure that it's correct. When you make an error, the IDE warns you about it and sometimes provides corrective tips.

The Environment Fonts and Colors options shown in Figure 2.9 help you create a better work environment. The standard settings provide a good environment for someone with average eyesight and a standard-sized display. You might need to modify these settings to meet your specific needs. To change one of the display options, select it in the Show Settings For drop-down list box. Change the environment, font, and color settings as needed to provide a display that's easy to work with. The Sample field in the lower right corner shows the results of any settings changes you make.

FIGURE 2.9
Modify colors and fonts as necessary to create a better work environment.

The Text Editor HTML folder contains two subfolders: Format and Validation. The Format options define how you want the HyperText Markup Language (HTML) tags that Visual Web Developer adds for you and those that you type yourself formatted. The IDE also permits you to differentiate between server-side tags (those that the server interprets) and client-side tags (those that present information to the user), so each tag type can use different formatting. Using different formatting for server and client tags makes it easier to interpret the code you write in many cases. Generally, you won't need to change the Format options unless your company has a specific style guide for formatting HTML. The Visual Web Developer settings tend to follow standard formatting rules.

The Validation options shown in Figure 2.10 are critical, and you should always check them whenever you begin a new project. Figure 2.10 shows the standard settings, which reflect Microsoft's orientation toward Web development. However, you can usually create better applications by changing the value in the Target drop-down list box to match the kind of browser you want to work with. For example, a public Web site that caters to desktop browsers will want to use the Internet Explorer 3.02/Netscape Navigator 3.0 setting to ensure maximum compatibility. As an alternative, you can also rely on the XHTML 1.0 Transitional target, which provides compatibility with Netscape 7, Opera 7, and Internet Explorer 6, but leaves out older browsers that users might own. The targets also include a number of portable devices that you can use.

FIGURE 2.10
Target a specific browser
type and ensure that you
validate code to obtain
better Web pages.

The Options group contains a number of essential features that you should always consider checking (some aren't by default). You should tell Visual Web Developer to show error messages in a number of situations to ensure that your Web pages are standards compliant and will work as anticipated. These error message options should always include:

♦ When tags are not well formed

♦ When attribute values are not quoted

♦ When element or attribute is deprecated (no longer in use or acceptable)

♦ In inline styles

You have good reason for checking these options. The best-case scenario for a tag that isn't well formed is that the browser will ignore it (which means the site won't look like you want it to). A worst-case scenario is that the page won't display at all. Quoting attribute values makes it easier for the browser to interpret your site and ensures that the browser doesn't do anything odd with your content. Although most browsers can interpret old elements that aren't in use, standards committees usually deprecate them for good reason. Generally, different vendors have implemented the element or attribute in different ways, which means that your Web page won't display as it should. In other cases, the ambiguous nature of the element or attribute reduces accessibility or makes it less useful with new devices such as cellular telephones. The problem with inline styles is that they reduce the portability of your Web page. Anyone with a special need (such as being blind) won't be able to use the Web page and you'll find it harder to use with portable devices as well.

Using the Design View

The Design view is where you use graphical elements to create a user display. To create a display, you select items in the Toolbox and drag them to the form. You can also double-click an item in the Toolbox and the IDE will automatically add it to the form for you. Figure 2.11 shows a simple form containing a Label, Textbox, and a Button control. The Label displays text, "Type Something, Anything!" in this case. The user can't edit the content of a Label. A Textbox control accepts input from the user. You can also provide sample text for the user (always a good idea). After the user interacts with the controls on a form, clicking a Button control performs some action—at least it performs an action when you provide supporting code (see the upcoming section "Using the Code View" for details).

FIGURE 2.11
Use Design view to create a user interface for your Web application.

Using Design view isn't simply a matter of placing controls and hoping for the best. You select the controls and organize them in some manner. Normally, you choose an organization that lets the user work without thinking too hard about the organization of the document. For many users, this means placing the controls so they flow from top to bottom and from left to right. You'll see a number of examples of good Web application layouts as the book progresses.

TIP   This book isn't the end-all collection of design ideas. To gain a better appreciation of all of the elements you should consider when designing a great interface, get Mike Gunderloy's *Developer to Designer: GUI Design for the Busy Developer* (Sybex, 2005).

After you place the controls on the form, you'll want to spend a little time configuring them. In all cases, you'll want to provide the control with a meaningful name—one that reflects its use within the application. Every control also has special features that you'll want to configure. For example, when working with a Label control, you'll want to change the Text property so that it includes the text you want to display as shown in Figure 2.11. The Textbox and Button controls also contain the Text property. While you'll want to change the Text property for the Button control, it's an optional change for the Textbox. You'll gain additional insights about controls and their properties as the book progresses.

It's important to consider what's happening as you work on the interface for your Web application. The Visual Web Developer IDE is adding code to the Web page that reflects the changes you make. In many cases, you don't need to worry much about this book—the IDE maintains it for you automatically. However, should you need to see the code so you can fine-tune it, you can click Source at the bottom of the Design view and you'll see the Source view described in the next section.

Using the Source View

Source view shows the code that creates the user interface. Figure 2.12 shows the code used to create the user interface in Figure 2.11. Because Figure 2.11 shows the Label control selected, the IDE highlights that code in Source view. As you work with Visual Web Developer, you can place a control on a form, configure it, and then look at the code that the IDE creates in Source view to gain a better understanding of how the process works.

FIGURE 2.12
Use Source view to
work directly with tags
as needed to create
special effects.

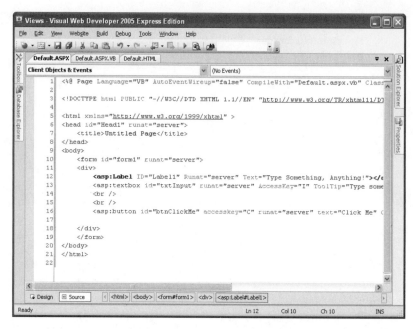

Although Design view is very easy to use, it doesn't provide you with the level of control that Source view does. For example, notice that the IDE created two <br /> tags to create a break on the form. You could replace this code with a <p /> tag if desired to obtain the same result. To test it for yourself, comment out the <br /> tags and replace them with a single <p /> tag as shown here.

```
<!-- <br /> -->
<!-- <br /> -->
<p />
```

Placing the <br /> tags within a comment <!-- --> means that you can still see the tags and restore them if you wish, but the browser ignores them. More importantly, this example shows how Source view provides you with additional options and greater flexibility in creating a Web page. You can't perform this kind of fine-tuning using Design view.

The best way to use Source view is to create your initial design, including all property settings, using Design view, and then fine-tune the page using Source view. When you want to verify that a control is using optimum code, select the control first so you see its code highlighted in Source view. On the other hand, you might simply want to add specialized code to the page, such as the scripting code described in Chapter 6. In this case, you'll place the cursor where the code needs to go and start typing.

Using the Code View

The Code view is where you edit files that don't include a graphical element, such as the code behind files for your Web pages. Figure 2.13 shows a typical example of the Code view. Notice that the window doesn't include a selection for changing to Design view.

FIGURE 2.13
Use Code view to work with code, such as the code behind, for your Web application.

A code behind file contains the code that tells the server what to do when the user performs an action. For example, you might want to calculate an order total when the user clicks Submit to signify that all of the order details are correct. The Code view shown in Figure 2.13 is for the simple Web page shown in Figures 2.11 and 2.12. The act of clicking btnClickMe (the name of the Click Me button in Figures 2.11 and 2.12) is a Click event. The btnClickMe_Click() method is an event handler—it performs a task whenever the Click event for the Click Me button occurs.

You'll also use Code view for other files. For example, whenever you open an XML document, you'll use Code view because XML documents don't have a user interface.

Code view offers two interesting features: IntelliSense (a specialized help system) and Text Editor toolbar support. You can gain limited access to these two features using Source view as well, but they're most useful when working in Code view. The following sections describe these features.

Understanding IntelliSense

IntelliSense is a special automated help feature that Visual Web Developer provides whenever you write code. The .NET Framework objects can contain methods, properties, events, and even other objects. Whenever you type an object name, such as the Response object shown in Figure 2.14, IntelliSense provides a list of items for that object as shown in the Object Member List. As you type more information, IntelliSense refines the Object Member List selection. It also provides a tooltip that describes the selection so that you know when you've found the correct object.

FIGURE 2.14
IntelliSense provides clues that you can use to create code more quickly without accessing help.

TIP   Whenever you type code in Code view (and often when you type it in Source view), you'll see IntelliSense support. In fact, the only time you won't see IntelliSense support is when Visual Web Developer doesn't understand something that you're typing. For example, when you make a typographical error in typing the object name, IntelliSense won't appear on screen. Likewise, when you're missing an object reference or using the wrong object, IntelliSense will clue you in by not displaying any information. Use this IntelliSense cue as an indicator that something's wrong.

USING THE TEXT EDITOR TOOLBAR

The Text Editor toolbar shown in Figure 2.15 provides a number of features that help you create code with greater ease and precision. Each of these buttons helps you perform a code-related task such as displaying an Object Member List like the one described in the previous section, "Understanding IntelliSense." The following list describes the button purposes in detail.

FIGURE 2.15
The Text Editor toolbar helps you work with HTML elements.

Clear All Bookmarks
Move the Caret to the Next Bookmark in the Current Document
Move the Caret to the Previous Bookmark in the Current Document
Move the Caret to the Next Bookmark
Move the Caret to the Previous Bookmark
Toggle a Bookmark on the Current Line
Uncomment the Selected Lines
Comment Out the Selected Lines
Increase Indent
Decrease Indent
Display Word Completion
Display Quick Info
Display Parameter Info
Display an Object Member List

Clear All Bookmarks   Removes all of the bookmarks in a document. A bookmark in Code view works the same as a bookmark in a book—it helps you get back to a specific location quickly. When you complete a book, you normally remove the bookmark and place the book on the shelf. Likewise, when you complete a code editing process, you can click this button to remove all of the bookmarks.

Move the Caret to the Next Bookmark in the Current Document   Moves the caret (cursor) to the next bookmark in the current document. Even if you have bookmarks set in other documents, the IDE will move between bookmarks in the current document only. When you reach the last bookmark in the document, clicking this button again will move you to the first bookmark in the current document.

Move the Caret to the Previous Bookmark in the Current Document   Moves the caret (cursor) to the previous bookmark in the current document. Even if you have bookmarks set in other documents, the IDE will move between bookmarks in the current document only. When you reach the first bookmark in the document, clicking this button again will move you to the last bookmark in the current document.

Move the Caret to the Next Bookmark   Moves the caret (cursor) to the next bookmark. If the next bookmark appears in a different document, the IDE will display that document. When you reach the last bookmark in the current document, clicking this button again will move you to the first bookmark in the next open document that has bookmarks in it. If there aren't any other documents with bookmarks, the IDE will move the caret to the first bookmark of the current document.

Move the Caret to the Previous Bookmark   Moves the caret (cursor) to the previous bookmark. If the previous bookmark appears in a different document, the IDE will display that document. When you reach the first bookmark in the current document, clicking this button again will move you to the last bookmark in the previous open document that has bookmarks in it. If there aren't any other documents with bookmarks, the IDE will move the caret to the last bookmark of the current document.

Toggle a Bookmark on the Current Line   Creates a bookmark on the current line. The bookmark appears as a square box the left side of the editing area.

Uncomment the Selected Lines   Removes the comment character (if any) from in front of the selected lines of code. This process turns the comments back into code that Visual Web Developer will process when you compile the application.

Comment Out the Selected Lines   Adds comment characters in front of the selected lines of code. This process changes the code into a comment that you can still see and modify, but Visual Web Developer will ignore.

Increase Indent   Increases the space between the left side of the display and the start of the code. Indentation makes code easier to read by showing which code is at the same level of execution. Adding indentation can help you reformat code after you add a new type of processing or processing level.

Decrease Indent   Decreases the space between the left side of the display and the start of the code. As the indentation level increases, the code moves to the right side of the screen and eventually out of view. Removing unneeded indentation can help you see the entire line of code, rather than scrolling back and forth to see it.

Display Word Completion   Displays an Object Member List based on the letters typed to the left of the current cursor position. You can use this feature to help type the names of objects. Normally, method, property, and event values appear automatically when you type the period after an object name, but this feature helps you obtain the initial object name and ensure that it appears correctly in the code.

Display Quick Info   Shows a tooltip containing information about the currently selected item. Figure 2.14 shows an example of such a tooltip.

Display Parameter Info   Shows a tooltip containing the parameters for a method or other element that requires input arguments. Figure 2.14 shows a typical example of a tooltip. When a method can accept more than one kind of input argument, the tooltip also includes a method for selecting between the arguments so that you can match the data you want to provide with the arguments the method will accept.

Display an Object Member List   Creates an Object Member List like the one shown in Figure 2.14 for the selected item. You can place the cursor anywhere within the item text and see its entry in the Object Member List. Choosing a new item from the list will replace the selected item in your code.

Working with the Personal Web Site Starter Kit

The Personal Web Starter Kit is a special template that comes with Visual Web Developer. Microsoft included this project to demonstrate the various features that Visual Web Developer provides and help you create a personal Web site very quickly. The project includes a number of features that you'll want for your personal Web site including a Welcome page and the following features:

- Administration pages
- Photo album

The following sections discuss the concept of creating applications using the Personal Web Starter Kit as a starting point. This is actually the first project you'll create with Visual Web Developer. Considering that the project template performs much of the work for you, the project is extremely easy to work with and you'll have a professional looking project to use for reference later. However, the project in Chapter 3 is more realistic in that it shows how you'll start most projects you create. You'll find this example in the \Chapter 02\PersonalWebStarterKit folder of the source code on the Sybex Web site.

Understanding Application Distribution Levels

Not every application that you create will become something that someone else will want to use—sometimes you create applications to meet a personal need. However, don't shortchange yourself. Always create applications as if someone else will use them. That said, developers commonly create several levels of applications based on where they plan to distribute them. Here are some levels to consider.

Experimental   Sometimes you create an application to experiment with a product feature. The application doesn't even have to perform a useful task. The idea is to explore the product feature and learn how it works. You might look at this as playtime—the time you spend with the language product for no purpose other than to see what it can do.

Proof of concept   As you work with Visual Web Developer, you'll discover new features that could work together to create a specific application type. However, you aren't sure that your idea will work. Consequently, you create a proof of concept application that puts all of the required elements together to prove that the idea works. Like the experimental application, this application might not even do any useful work—it's just for testing purposes. It's important to remember, though, that proof of concept applications tend to grow into full-fledged applications, so the design time that you spend today will pay off in a better application tomorrow.

Personal   Developers tend not to work any harder than they have to. Consequently, developers will often create a personal tool that helps them work with the applications they're creating. Something as simple as a new template or a well-designed macro can greatly reduce the time required to create an application. The only problem with personal applications is that people see you use them and then you have to decide whether to let them use it. For example, a network administrator might benefit just as much as you do from a utility that tests application functionality.

Administrative   You'll eventually create some applications that not everyone will use. These applications might include features that help monitor the system or ensure that data remains secure. Administrators and developers alike commonly use Web applications today to monitor server status, application performance, and application error status. Whatever the purpose, you don't want end users to use the tool because it's too powerful.

User   This is the most common type of application that you'll create. Most of the applications that a developer creates end up in the hands of end users. The problem is that many applications that start out at one of the other distribution levels end up in the hands of end users eventually. Even experimental applications end up in the hands of users at times. What usually happens is that someone comes by your desk, sees the interesting new utility you created, and wants a copy for their personal use. It happens all the time, so you have to prepare for it.

Creating the Application

Before you can begin working with any application, you need to create it. The starting point is a project that defines the parameters of the application and stores any special settings that Visual Web Developer requires. You then begin a process of defining the application. This process includes defining a Web site to act as a container for storing the data that you want to display and adding files to the Web site. Each file serves a unique purpose in the overall scheme of creating the Web site that you want to design.

The Personal Web Starter Kit is unique in that you define everything in a single step—the project template performs a lot of the work that you normally need to do. The following steps show how to create the Personal Web Starter Kit application.

1.   Select File ➢ New Web Site. You'll see the New Web Site dialog box shown in Figure 2.16.

FIGURE 2.16
The New Web Site dialog box helps you create a Web site to store the applications that you create.

2.   Choose the language that you want to use from the Project Types list.

3.   Highlight the Personal Web Site Starter Kit project as shown in Figure 2.16.

4.   Type the name and location of the project in the Location field. The name in Figure 2.16 is `PersonalWebStarterKit` and the location is `D:\0197\Chapter 02\`. All projects include these two elements.

TIP   Click Browse to display a Choose Location dialog box. This dialog box lets you find the location you want to use without having to type it. You still need to type a project name after you choose the location.

5. Click OK to create the project or Cancel to close the New Web Site dialog box without creating the project. When you click OK, Visual Web Developer will require several seconds to create the project. Be patient—this process can take a little longer on older machines. Eventually, you'll see the Personal Web Site Starter Kit Design view shown in Figure 2.17.

FIGURE 2.17
The Welcome.HTML file contains information about the Personal Web Site Starter Kit project.

Working with the Application Elements

You have a shiny new Web site filled with pages to work with, but little direction on how to work with them at this point. The Welcome.HTML file supplied as part of the kit tells you how to perform tasks such as creating an administrative user who can upload photographs and perform other tasks on the new site. Make sure you review this file as part of learning about the new Personal Web Site Starter Kit project you created. This section starts where the Microsoft supplied documentation leaves off. For example, you'll discover how to modify the content of the Web site.

Begin exploring the application by opening Solution Explorer. You'll see a list of folders and files for this project. Some folders, such as Themes, contain a number of subfolders—one for each theme that the application supports. To see the contents of a folder, click the plus sign next to it; likewise, click the minus sign to hide the contents of the folder again. Within each folder, you'll normally find one or more files. For example, the Images folder contains a number of placeholder Joint Photographic Experts Group (JPEG) files. These files have either a JPG or a JPEG file extension.

The actual Web pages for the Personal Web Site Starter Kit have an Active Server Pages eXtended (ASPX) file extension. You'll notice a plus sign next to these files—just like the plus signs next to the folders. Click the plus sign and you'll see the code behind file for the Web page. To view the pages in your new Web site, double-click an ASPX entry in Solution Explorer. You'll see the page open in Design view or Source view, depending on how you have your copy of Visual Web Developer configured. Figure 2.18 shows the Links.ASPX page, which is one of the more typical examples.

FIGURE 2.18
Each of the predefined pages has a specific task in making your site usable.

This page has three major sections. You can edit the About the Links and Some Link Trivia sections, but the banner isn't even selectable. The banner material appears as part of the `Default.MASTER` file. To change the banner, you have to edit this file. However, you have to exercise caution in editing the `Default.MASTER` file because it affects every page that relies on this master page—always put common material in `Default.MASTER`, not page-specific material.

The two remaining sections contain three kinds of content. The first kind of content should remain after you perform your edits—it includes headers and other information that you don't need to change. The second kind of content is human readable instructions on how to modify the page. You replace these instructions with content of your own, in most cases, or simply remove the instructions so the Web site users can see them. The third kind of content is unreadable text that takes the place of the content you provide. This is where your main work lies—adding the content that you want to provide to site users.

Modifying the Application Template to Meet Specific Needs

At some point, you might find that the Personal Web Site Starter Kit becomes a major asset. Perhaps you want to set up a personal Web site for every sales member of your small company. You don't really want to invest in a high-end tool to do it, so Visual Web Developer is the best option, but perhaps not the most time-efficient method. You can improve the efficiency of using Visual Web Developer by modifying the application template to meet your specific needs. For example, you might want to add company-specific elements to the template. This section describes how to access the project and modify it to meet your specific needs. It assumes that you're going to create this project more than one time (otherwise, modifying the template doesn't make sense).

WARNING   The procedure in this section is somewhat complicated, and it's going to be a little more than you want to take on if you haven't used .NET in the past. Consider this section food for thought. You might try it now if you've used .NET before, or you might simply decide to come back later after you've gone through more examples in the book. For that matter, you might decide that the projects Microsoft has provided work fine as is and never return to this section.

GETTING STARTED

You'll find the Personal Web Site Starter Kit template in the `\Program Files\Microsoft Visual Studio 8\Common7\IDE\VWDExpress\ProjectTemplatesCache\Web\VisualBasic\1033\PersonalWebSite.ZIP` folder of your hard drive. (Users of other languages will find a folder for that language in the Web folder.) Note that even though the folder has a ZIP extension, it's not a ZIP file. Whatever you do, don't modify this project directly—maintain a clean environment by creating a copy of the folder and renaming it for your personal needs. Call it something such as `ABC_Inc.ZIP`.

TIP   The process outlined in this section works with any project template that Microsoft provides. You might decide to customize the standard ASP.NET Web Site project to include custom content or additional files that you always use with this project. The idea behind customization is to tailor Visual Web Developer to meet your needs, rather than work around any limitations that Visual Web Developer might have (re-creating the same file for every project is a limitation).

The first thing you need to do after you copy the ZIP folder is to open it. Inside you'll find all of the files that make up this project. Modify the existing files to meet your needs. For example, you can modify the master template to include your company name or other features you normally use. Another change is the use of a different template or perhaps a larger font for some design elements. The critical concept is to change only those elements that you change every time you use the project.

ADDING FILES TO A TEMPLATE

Adding new files can become a little trickier, but it's quite doable. Begin by adding the new file to the project folder that you created (`ABC_Inc.ZIP` in the case of the example)—not the original `PersonalWebSite.ZIP` project folder. Once you add the new file, you need to decide where it appears in the project. In fact, you can use the same file multiple times in a project should you decide to.

You might wonder how the project template knows what to do with the file you create. The `PersonalWebSite.VSTEMPLATE` file contains all of the required information. Generally, you want to edit this file with extreme care or the project template changes you perform won't work. In fact, the project template might not work at all. This file is in eXtensible Markup Language (XML) format, so you can use your favorite XML editor to work with it or simply open the file in Notepad. Don't use an editor that will add formatting information to the file, such as Microsoft Word.

After you open the file, skip past the introductory information—you don't want to edit it in any way. Locate the `<ProjectContents>` tag shown in Figure 2.19. This is where you'll add files to the project.

FIGURE 2.19
The *<ProjectContents>* tag shows the beginning of the template file information.

```
<ProjectContents>
    <Folder Name="Admin">
        <ProjectItem>
            <SourceFile>Albums.aspx</SourceFile>
        </ProjectItem>
        <ProjectItem>
            <SourceFile>Albums.aspx.vb</SourceFile>
        </ProjectItem>
        <ProjectItem>
            <SourceFile>Details.aspx</SourceFile>
        </ProjectItem>
        <ProjectItem>
            <SourceFile>Details.aspx.vb</SourceFile>
        </ProjectItem>
        <ProjectItem>
            <SourceFile>Photos.aspx</SourceFile>
        </ProjectItem>
        <ProjectItem>
            <SourceFile>Photos.aspx.vb</SourceFile>
        </ProjectItem>
    </Folder>
    <ProjectItem>
        <SourceFile>Albums.aspx1</SourceFile>
        <TargetFileName>Albums.aspx</TargetFileName>
    </ProjectItem>
    <ProjectItem>
        <SourceFile>Albums.aspx.vb1</SourceFile>
        <TargetFileName>Albums.aspx.vb</TargetFileName>
    </ProjectItem>
    <Folder Name="Controls">
        <ProjectItem>
            <SourceFile>Frame.ascx</SourceFile>
        </ProjectItem>
```

The `<ProjectContents>` element includes a number of interesting child elements. The following list describes each of the elements and helps you understand where they fit into the project definition.

<Folder>   The `<Folder>` element defines the name of a folder. It can also hold one or more `<ProjectItem>` elements. Any `<ProjectItem>` elements that appear in the folder also appear in that folder when you create the project. A `<Folder>` element can also contain other `<Folder>` elements (as subdirectories) or it can be blank to create an empty folder.

<ProjectItem>   The `<ProjectItem>` element defines a single project item—a file that holds some type of project data. As a minimum, the `<ProjectItem>` element contains a single `<SourceFile>` element. However, it can also include optional elements such as `<TargetFileName>` and `<OpenInEditorPropertyGroup>`. In most cases, a `<ProjectItem>` element appears within a *<Folder>* element. When it doesn't, the file appears in the root directory of the project, such as the Albums.ASPX file that appears in Solution Explorer in Figure 2.7. Notice that the declaration for this file appears outside a folder in Figure 2.18.

<SourceFile>   The `<SourceFile>` element defines the name of the file within the project template. It usually defines the name of the file as it appears in the project as well. You can modify this behavior using the optional `<TargetFileName>` element. Visual Web Developer copies this file from the project template and places it in the project you create.

<TargetFileName>   The `<TargetFileName>` element changes the name of a file copied from the project template. Visual Web Developer normally uses the name of the file as it appears in the project template—using this element lets you change the name so a single source file can appear in the project using several different names.

<OpenInEditorPropertyGroup> The `<OpenInEditorPropertyGroup>` element acts as a container for the `<OpenInEditor>` or `<OpenInWebBrowser>` and `<OpenOrder>` elements. As a whole, the group tells Visual Web Developer to open a source file as soon as it's copied into the project folder.

<OpenInEditor> The `<OpenInEditor>` element tells Visual Web Developer to open a source file in an editor so the developer can modify it. Use this element for standard data files that you expect the developer to modify in some way. In many cases, you'll want to open the file automatically to ensure the developer knows that the file requires change.

<OpenInWebBrowser> The `<OpenInWebBrowser>` element tells Visual Web Developer to open a source file in a browser for viewing. You'll normally use this element with informational files (generally in HTML format).

<OpenOrder> The `<OpenOrder>` element tells Visual Web Developer where to place the source file in the open order. For example, if you provide a value of 1, then this is the first file that the developer using your template sees. Make sure that every source file you open has a unique number.

Always remember to place any new entries you create after the opening `<ProjectContents>` element, but before the closing `</ProjectContents>` element. Most of the entries you make are quite simple. For example, to place a file in the root directory, you might include an entry like this.

```
<ProjectItem>
    <SourceFile>SpecialText.TXT</SourceFile>
</ProjectItem>
```

However, let's say you want to rename the file after its copied. To make this change, use the `<TargetFileName>` element like this.

```
<ProjectItem>
    <SourceFile>SpecialText.TXT</SourceFile>
    <TargetFileName>OtherText.TXT</TargetFileName>
</ProjectItem>
```

The file still contains the content of `SpecialText.TXT`, but now it has a filename of `OtherText.TXT`. You can also place the file in an existing folder by looking for the appropriate `<Folder>` element or create a new folder to hold it, as shown here.

```
<Folder Name="Special Folder">
    <ProjectItem>
        <SourceFile>SpecialText.TXT</SourceFile>
    </ProjectItem>
</Folder>
```

In this case, Visual Web Developer creates a new folder named `Special Folder` before it copies `SpecialText.TXT` to it. Let's say that you want to open a file automatically for the developer using your template. First, you need to decide whether this is an informational file or a file that you expect the developer to edit. Use the `<OpenInEditor>` tag for files that you want the developer to edit as shown here.

```
<Folder Name="Another Folder">
    <ProjectItem>
        <SourceFile>SpecialText.TXT</SourceFile>
        <OpenInEditorPropertyGroup>
```

```
            <OpenInEditor>true</OpenInEditor>
            <OpenOrder>11</OpenOrder>
        </OpenInEditorPropertyGroup>
      </ProjectItem>
  </Folder>
```

Notice the combination of tags—you must place the `<OpenInEditor>` element within the `<OpenInEditorPropertyGroup>` element and tell Visual Web Developer when to open the file using the `<OpenOrder>` element. The bottom line is that you can add files to an existing template with relative ease and even change the behavior of the template to an extent by carefully editing the VSTEMPLATE file. The important consideration is that you don't want to change any of the operational information, such as any of the package information that appears at the beginning of the file.

COMPLETING THE TEMPLATE FILE CHANGE

At some point, you'll make all of the changes you want to the project template. You still need to get the template ready for use by Visual Web Developer. The following steps tell you how.

1. Use an application such as WinZip (`http://www.winzip.com`) to create a ZIP file containing the template. (The built-in Windows XP ZIP file support works fine for reading archives, but not as well for creating them.) What you'll end up with is a file named `ABC_Inc.ZIP.ZIP`.

2. Copy the file to the `\Program Files\Microsoft Visual Studio 8\Common7\IDE\VWDExpress\ ProjectTemplates\Web\VisualBasic\1033` folder on your system. (Make sure that you copy the file to the correct language folder—the example is using Visual Basic Express, but you could also use the Visual C# Express or the Visual J# Express folders.)

3. Rename the existing `PersonalWebSite.ZIP` to `OldPersonalWebSite.ZIP`. Saving the file lets you restore it easily later.

4. Rename the ZIP file you created (`ABC_Inc.ZIP.ZIP` in the case of the example) to `PersonalWebSite.ZIP`. This change forces Visual Web Developer to use the new template.

5. Close and reopen Visual Web Developer if necessary. Otherwise, Visual Web Developer might use an older version of the template loaded into memory.

6. Create a new project with the modified template to test it. If you haven't made any errors, the template will use all of the modified settings.

Defining Your Development Goals

This chapter helped you get Visual Web Developer installed and setup for use. In addition, you discovered the various IDE features and how to use them to create code. Finally, you created your first application. Although the Visual Web Developer IDE does most of the work for you, working with this sample application can help you understand how to put pieces together for an application of your own. More importantly, you can easily modify this sample application to meet your specific needs. In this respect, the Personal Web Starter Kit can act as a resource for any predefined Web site need.

It's time to work with Visual Web Developer. You'll want to try out the various IDE features described in this chapter. For example, try creating other projects on your own (we'll explore all of the project types as the book progresses). Try downloading other templates to see what other developers have created. Spend some time understanding how IntelliSense benefits you and work with the various views to see how they affect each other.

Visual Web Developer did most of the work for the sample application in this chapter. Now that you understand the IDE better and know about the various application elements, it's time to create a simple application from scratch. Chapter 3 leads you through the process of creating a simple application using nothing more than the blank project. When you complete Chapter 3, you'll have moved from creating an application based on what Microsoft thinks you need, to creating the application that you know you need. In short, Chapter 3 is the second step to creating that production application you've always wanted to write.

Chapter 3

Creating a Simple Application

The best way to begin using Visual Web Developer is one step at a time. This chapter discusses how to build a simple application—one that's easy to understand and could act as a stepping-stone for something more complex later. More importantly, you'll discover techniques that you can use in any project.

One of the better features of Visual Web Developer is that it provides a built-in Web server. This server isn't accessible to anyone outside your local machine. In fact, the built-in Web server doesn't even run until you tell it to. These features make the built-in Web server very safe to use on just about any machine and very resource friendly, as well, on machines with limitations.

Of course, you'll eventually want to move your application to where someone else can see it. This chapter also discusses how you can use Internet Information Server (IIS) with Visual Web Developer. You'll also discover how to work with other servers such as Apache by using techniques such as File Transfer Protocol (FTP). Eventually, you'll want to publish the site using the Copy Web Publishing Tool.

Because you'll be working with a new project in this chapter, it's also a good time to discuss one of the productivity features that Visual Web Developer provides—control Smart Tags. Using Smart Tags can greatly reduce the time you'll spend trying to configure certain kinds of controls. In some cases, Smart Tags can also provide ideas on how to use the control more efficiently.

Using the Built-in Web Server

Even if you don't have IIS installed on your system, you can test the Web pages you create using Visual Web Developer. The built-in Web server that comes with Visual Web Developer provides everything you need to test a single Web application. You can't use it to build an infrastructure like you can with a full-fledged Web server, but you can use it for local testing. The following sections describe how to work with the built-in Web server so that you can use it to your advantage.

NOTE   It's important to think outside the desktop box when you work with Web applications. An application in this case can include everything from the code behind on the server used to generate the Web page and interact with the user to the script on the client side used to check the user input. An application is a combination of tags, script, and server-side code, plus components and controls. Web application is a flexible term because the Internet is a flexible environment.

Advantages of Using the Built-in Web Server

The built-in Web server might not sound very exciting at first. In fact, it might sound extremely limited. Before you write it off as something that isn't worth your time, you need to consider the advantages it provides. The following list provides some ideas of why you'll want to use the built-in Web server, even if you have another option at your disposal.

Security   No one can access the built-in Web server but you. In fact, you won't access the built-in Web server using the same port twice, making it extremely unlikely that a cracker will gain access. Even if a cracker does gain access, the constantly changing ports means that the cracker will gain access precisely one time before the port changes again. In short, this is an extremely safe way to test your code on the local machine.

Development speed   The built-in Web server is your personal setup. No one else can use it and there aren't any bandwidth concerns. All of your testing happens at the speed of the local machine and there isn't any way to replicate this performance benefit using a remote machine. Even if you use a local copy of IIS, the high degree of connectivity between Visual Web Developer and the built-in Web server means that you don't have to do much to test the application—it all happens at the click of a button.

Testing reliability   Sometimes you can run into errors testing a Web application on an external Web server. For example, a file might not copy or you might forget to set up the project as a Web application. Security can cause problems—you might not have proper access to your own project. Using the built-in Web server eliminates these problems for application testing. Yes, you'll eventually have to face them, but you'll know that the application itself isn't the source of problems when you do. This divide and conquer approach to application testing reduces complexity and improves both testing speed and reliability.

Resource management   You don't have to keep the Web server running—not in the same way that you do with other servers such as IIS. Sure, you can stop the other Web servers too, but it's inconvenient. The built-in Web server creates an icon in the notification area of the Window's Taskbar that you can easily use to stop the server whenever you want. This means that the Web server is only using system resources while you're actually using it.

Creating the Application

Your first application doesn't have to be anything complex. In fact, the example is extremely simple because it's important, at this point, to develop the process you'll use to create complex applications later. The following steps will help you get the application set up—I'm assuming that you've already started Visual Web Developer.

1. Select File ➢ New Web Site to display the New Web Site dialog box shown in Figure 3.1.

FIGURE 3.1
Create a new Web site by selecting the ASP.NET Web Site project.

2. Choose the language that you want to use (the example uses Visual Basic). You can choose from Visual Basic, Visual C#, and Visual J#. However, Visual J# is available only when you install support for this product separately.

3. Highlight the ASP.NET Web Site project. You could also choose the Empty Web Site project when you need complete control over the project, but that level of flexibility isn't required in this case.

4. Type the name and location for the Web site on your location hard drive (the example uses SimpleSite). Click OK. Visual Web Developer creates a new Web site for you with a single ASPX page open.

5. Click Design to show the Design view. You're ready to create your first project.

TIP As you work with Visual Web Developer, you'll find that windows get moved around—sometimes to the point of making the IDE almost useless. You can return the window setup to its pristine state using the Tools ➤ Options command to display the Options dialog box. Check Show All Settings at the bottom of the dialog box. Select the General folder and click Reset Window Layout.

The first project won't do very much, but it will introduce you to several important concepts. Begin by opening the Toolbox (if necessary) using the View ➤ Toolbox command. Drag a Label control from the Toolbox onto the Design area. The controls always contain an icon that shows their purpose and usually include a text description as well, as shown in Figure 3.2.

FIGURE 3.2
The Toolbox provides both an icon and a text description of the controls.

TIP You can work with the Toolbox detached from the side of the Visual Web Developer display. Make sure that the AutoHide feature is deselected, and then drag the Toolbox where you want to work with it using the title bar. You can even drag the Toolbox outside the IDE area if desired, and drag and drop controls from it to the Design area. To dock the Toolbox back on the side of the IDE, simply drag it to the side—the IDE will highlight the location the Toolbox will appear when you release the mouse button.

Drag a Textbox control from the Toolbox to the Design area. Notice that the IDE places the Textbox control next to the Label control. Press Enter to move to the next line of the Design area. Pressing Enter places special spacing tags within the page. Drag a Button control from the Toolbox to the Design area. Notice that the Button control appears one line below the two other controls.

Unlike desktop applications, you must specifically spell out spaces between controls when working with a Web application.

The next step is to add some properties to the application. Begin by selecting the Label control. Display the Properties dialog box (if necessary) using the View ➤ Properties Windows command. Every control you create has a number of properties that define it. Generally, you don't have to change all of the properties. In fact, you'll often change two or three properties out of the many properties that the control provides. Figure 3.3 shows properties associated with a Label control. A Textbox and a Button control will also have some of these properties, but they'll leave some out and add some of their own as well.

FIGURE 3.3
Modify a control's features using the entries in the Properties window.

For this example, type **lblInput** in the (ID) property (near the top of Properties window) and **Type some text.** in the Text property. Notice that the text changes in the Design view as well. The reason you want to change the (ID) property is to make it easier to locate controls using the drop-down list box at the top of the Properties window (Visual Web Developer lists them alphabetically). Using a specific name also makes the control name easier to remember and the control easier to work with when you write code. You also want to give the control a descriptive name to make it easier to remember the task the control performs. The final change for lblInput is to select TextBox1 in the AssociatedControlID property. This property associates the label with the textbox for accessibility purposes—the association makes it easier to group a textbox or other control with its label—the association connects the label so it properly identifies the textbox.

WARNING When you change the name of the text control associated with a label, Visual Web Developer won't update the AssociatedControlID property value automatically. The result is that when you run the application, the Web server will tell you that it can't find the associated control.

Now it's time to change the Textbox control. Type **txtInput** in the (ID) property, **I** in the AccessKey property, **Sample Text** in the Text property, and **Type something interesting.** in the ToolTip property. You make the (ID) property change in the textbox for the same reason that you do with every other control—to make the control easier to locate and work with. The AccessKey property creates a keyboard shortcut for the control so users can access it quickly without removing their hands from the keyboard. The Text property is optional, but you normally want to provide sample text so the user has a better idea of what to type. The ToolTip property tells the application what to display in a tooltip when the user hovers the mouse over the control. Think of tooltips as a form of simplified help.

It's time to work with the Button control. Type **btnClickMe** in the (ID) property, **C** in the AccessKey property, **Click Me** in the Text property, and **See something happen!** in the ToolTip property. You've configured the form well enough to use now.

The only problem is that clicking btnClickMe won't do anything right now because you haven't told btnClickMe to do anything. To create an event handler for the Click event of btnClickMe, you need to double-click the button. Notice that the IDE opens Default.ASPX.VB. This is the code behind file for Default.ASPX, the file that you just configured. The code behind file contains all of the code required to make the ASPX page work. The IDE also automatically adds the event handler declaration—the special code that identifies the Click event for btnClickMe. In fact, the cursor's already in the right place to add some code, so type the following code.

```
txtInput.Text = "You clicked Click Me!"
```

You should already have a good idea of what this code does. The **txtInput** control has a Text property. This code assigns the value You clicked Click Me! to the Text property—changing it on screen. The user sees the new value in place of anything they might have typed. Your code should look like the code in Figure 3.4 at this point. Interestingly enough, you've performed enough work to create your first application. You can run the application by clicking Ctrl+F5.

FIGURE 3.4
Event handlers hold the code required to make a button do something when you click it.

Using the Build Toolbar

Designing and adding code to your application is only the first step of the process. Once you create an application, you need to build it—change the text you typed into Intermediate Language (IL) code so that the Common Language Runtime (CLR) understands what to do with the application. You can build an application using a number of methods, but the easiest method is to use the Build toolbar shown in Figure 3.5. (Right-click the toolbar area and choose Build from the context menu to display the Build toolbar.) The following list describes the purpose of each button.

FIGURE 3.5
The Build toolbar helps
you compile your appli-
cation so you can run it.

Cancel
Build Solution
Build Web Site

Cancel Stops the current build action. You can use this option if you suddenly remember that you forgot to do something with the application in the middle of a long build.

Build Solution Creates an entire solution. A solution usually consists of multiple projects. For example, you might create a solution that includes multiple Web services. Building the solution means creating every project within the solution. Each project will create a separate executable file.

Build Web Site Creates a Web site. Even if the Web site is part of a larger solution, Visual Web Developer builds only the active project—the current Web site.

To perform the next step in the process, click Build Web Site on the Build toolbar. You'll notice that the IDE saves any files with changes first, and then starts building the application. Be patient, the build process can require several seconds to complete, even for a simple project such as this one. When the build process completes, you'll see an Output window at the bottom of the IDE like the one shown in Figure 3.6.

The Output window tells you whether the build succeeded. When the build succeeds, you can begin working with the Web site. Otherwise, you need to correct any problems noted during the build and try building the Web site again. Notice also that the bar on the left side of the IDE across from the code has changed from yellow to green to signify that the code is ready to use.

FIGURE 3.6
The Output window tells
whether the build pro-
cess is successful.

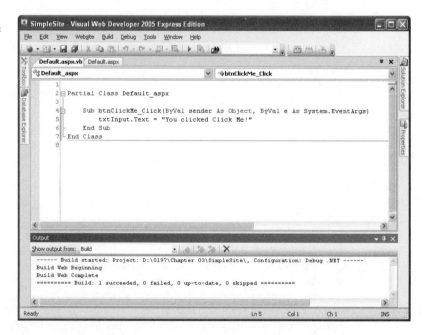

TIP   Visual Web Developer doesn't display all of the available toolbars—in part, because displaying all toolbars at once would create a cluttered display. You display a toolbar by right-clicking the toolbar area and choosing the toolbar that you want to use from the list. To get rid of the toolbar, right-click the toolbar area and choose its entry from the list again.

Using the Standard Toolbar

The Standard toolbar contains a number of buttons that you'll find in any application such as Cut, Copy, and Paste. However, the Visual Web Developer toolbar contains a number of additional options that you need when creating an application. Figure 3.7 shows these special buttons. The following list provides a description of all of the special features on this toolbar.

FIGURE 3.7

The Standard toolbar contains a number of helpful buttons, including one that starts the built-in Web server.

Add Item
New Project

Find
Find in Files
View in Browser
Start
Navigate Forward
Navigate Backward

Add Item   Adds a new item to the project. Whenever you click this button, you'll see the Add New Item dialog box shown in Figure 3.8. Select the item that you want to add from the list, change any required settings for that item, and click Add to add it. Notice that you can also download new items from online sources, so you aren't limited to the selection shown in the figure. Next to the button is a down arrow. Click this arrow and you'll see options for adding a new item (which displays the dialog box in Figure 3.8) or adding an existing item. The Add Existing Item dialog box looks like a standard dialog box that you'd use to open any file. Choose the file you want to open and click Add. Visual Web Developer will create a copy of that item and place it in your project folder.

FIGURE 3.8

Create new items for your project using the supplied list or by obtaining new templates online.

Add New Item - D:\0197\Chapter 03\SimpleSite\

Visual Studio installed templates

Web Form   Master Page   Web User Control
HTML Page   Web Service   Class
Style Sheet   Global Application Class Web Configuration File
XML File   XML Schema   Text File
Assembly Resource File   Data Component   Database
Generic Handler   Image Generator   Site Map

My Templates

Add New Online Template...

A form for Web Applications

Name: Default2.aspx

Language: Visual Basic   ☐ Place code in separate file
                                     ☐ Select master page

Add   Cancel

New Project   Adds a new project to the IDE. When you click this button, the IDE closes the old project by default. It displays the New Web Site dialog box shown in Figure 3.1. Choose the kind of Web site that you want to create and click OK. The down arrow next to this button includes two options. You can create a new Web site or open an existing Web site. When you select Open Web Site, you see the Open Web Site dialog box where you can choose from a Web site on the local hard drive, hosted by a local copy of IIS (not the built-in Web server), hosted on a FTP, or hosted on a remote server using an URL.

Find   Locates text within the current file. Simply type the text that you want to find and press Enter. Press Enter again to find the next location of the word. When you reach the end of the file, the IDE begins again with the first occurrence of the word in the file.

Find in Files   Locates text within all of the files of a project. Type the word that you want to locate in the Find field and click this button. You'll see a Find and Replace dialog box. Select the options that you want to use and click Find. All of the occurrences of the word will appear in the Find Results 1 or Find Results 2 window. See the next section "Finding and Replacing Text" for additional details.

View in Browser   Displays the application in a browser without debugging enabled. You can interact with the application just as the user will and test it for usability, security, reliability, and other requirements. You should also use this mode when checking the localized performance of your application—debugging makes the application slower so you don't get a true indication of application speed.

Start   Displays the application in a browser with debugging enabled. You use this feature for testing your application and locating any bugs it might contain. Use this mode as you write your application code to ensure that you can troubleshoot any errors as they occur.

Navigate Forward   Changes the cursor position and current page to the next entry in the history list. You use this feature to move between application areas as you perform edits. The Visual Web Developer history list works the same as the one for your browser, except it keeps track of the positions within the project, rather than the places that you visit online.

Navigate Backward   Changes the cursor position and current page to the previous entry in the history list.

Now you've built your application, it's time to see how it works. You have two options—you can view the page in your browser without the aid of the debugger or you can start the debugger. For now, click View in Browser so that you can see what the page looks like. After a few seconds, you'll see the page appear in your browser. Click Click Me and you'll see the text in the `txtInput` control change to match the code that you typed earlier. However, the important feature to see is the new Visual Web Developer Web Server icon at the top of the Notification area as shown in Figure 3.9. You can display the menu shown in the figure by right-clicking the icon in the Notification area.

FIGURE 3.9
The built-in Web server appears as an icon in the Notification area.

Open in Web Browser
Stop
Show Details

Right-click this icon and you'll see the context menu with three items as shown in Figure 3.9. Click Stop when you no longer need the built-in Web server. The system releases the resources that the built-in Web server uses. When you want to view the current page in a browser, click Open in Web Browser. Finally, when you click Details, you'll see a Visual Web Developer Web Server dialog box that contains the physical and virtual locations of the current Web site, along with the special port for this application. Click the Stop button on this dialog box to stop the built-in Web server.

Finding and Replacing Text

The Visual Web Developer IDE includes the concept of editing—just as your word processor does. However, you're editing code, in this case, so some of the functionality is a little different from any word processing experience you might have had. Searching and replacing text in a word-processed document requires one set of features; performing the same procedure in code requires different features, even though the result is essentially the same. Visual Web Developer actually provides five kinds of find-and-replace functionality as part of the Edit ➤ Find and Replace menu, as listed here.

Quick Find   Locates the search text in the current file. You search through the file one occurrence at a time.

Quick Replace   Modifies the search text in the current file. You have the option of finding the next occurrence of the search text without replacing the current instance, replacing the current instance and finding the next occurrence of the search text, or replacing all occurrences of the search text.

Find in Files   Locates the search text at several levels including the current file, all open documents, the entire solution, or the current project. The results appear in either the Find Results 1 or Find Results 2 window, so you can scroll the returned values and review only those that you need.

Replace in Files   Modifies the search text at several levels including the current file, all open documents, the entire solution, or the current project. The results appear in either the Find Results 1 or Find Results 2 window, so you can scroll through the returned values and review only those that you need. However, instead of scrolling through the results using the window, you use one of four buttons to locate individual instances and optionally replace the search text. You can choose to find the next instance (meaning you won't replace the current value), replace the current value and look for the next instance, skip the current file completely, and replace all of the values without reviewing them individually.

Find Symbol   Locates the specified object (symbol) within the all of the components, the .NET Framework, the current solution, other areas using the Object Browser, or other areas using criteria specified using the Select Component dialog box. The results appear in the Find Symbol Result window. Instead of seeing text as you do with the other searches, you see the actual object and any other objects it contains. You also see a list of applicable methods, properties, and events for the object.

The quick find and replace are easiest to use and provide the least flexibility in performing a search. The Quick Replace dialog box appears in Figure 3.10. The Quick Find dialog box is similar— the only features it lacks are the Replace With field, the Replace button, and Replace All button.

FIGURE 3.10
Use a quick find or replace to locate and optionally modify information in the current file.

The Find What field contains the search text that you want to find. The Replace With field contains the value that will replace the search text. The Look In field tells Visual Web Developer where to look for the information. It defaults to the current document, but you can also choose all of the currently opened documents and the current project. The Find Options group determines how Visual Web Developer searches for the text you provide. Most of these options are self-explanatory, but several options require special emphasis. For example, as your projects become more complex, Visual Web Developer (and you) will hide some of the text to reduce display clutter. Normally, Visual Web Developer searches only visible text—you must specifically check the Search Hidden Text option to look within the hidden areas.

You can also use either wildcards or regular expressions to perform a search. The wildcards work much like those you use at the command prompt with utilities such as Dir. Wildcards to include a few extensions as follows:

- ◆ * (asterisk) indicates zero or more of any character.

- ◆ ? (question mark) indicates a single character.

- ◆ # (number sign) indicates a single digit.

- ◆ [] (brackets) enclose a series of characters—one of which must be present.

- ◆ [!] (exclamation mark within the brackets) encloses a series of characters—none of which must be present.

Regular expressions offer more options, but require more work. When you initially click Use, Visual Web Developer enables the Regular Expressions options. Clicking the arrow next to either the Find What or Replace With fields displays a list of regular expressions that you can use such as the ones shown in Figure 3.11. Using regular expressions can become a bit of an art when you want to create complex search or replace criteria. The "Using Regular Expressions to Your Advantage" section of Chapter 17 discusses the use of regular expressions in detail. (Even though this section is on using regular expressions for security, the concepts apply to searches as well.)

The options for finding and replacing in files are a little different from those shown in Figure 3.10. Again, the Find in Files dialog box is a less complex version of the Replace in Files dialog box shown in Figure 3.12.

FIGURE 3.11
Regular expressions are complex, but provide extremely flexible search criteria.

FIGURE 3.12
Use the Find or Replace in Files option to locate all instances of a search string within a project.

The options work much the same as those for the quick find or replace, except you have a few more options in the Look In field. Instead of looking for the entries one at a time, you choose an output location in one of the two results windows. You can even perform two searches using two different output windows and compare the output results. The Look at These File Types field becomes active when you select either Entire Solution or Current Project in the Look In field. This field tells Visual Web Developer to limit its search to specific kinds of files—for example, you might only want to search source code files for a particular string.

A symbol search is inherently different from other kinds of searches because it looks for objects and object components such as methods, events, and properties. Figure 3.13 shows the Find Symbol dialog box. As you can see, it includes the Find What and Look In fields, just like all of the other searches. However, notice that this search also lets you look within project references—you can even look in the .NET Framework when desired.

The find and replace options examined in this section produce dramatically different results as shown in Figure 3.14. The top window shows the results of a quick find—you'll see the item highlighted in the code. The middle window shows the results of a find in file search—you obtain a list of strings that match the criteria. Finally, the bottom window shows the results of a symbol search. In this case, you obtain a list of object elements. The icon next to each entry tells you what type of object element the search has found.

FIGURE 3.13

A symbol search looks for objects and object components.

FIGURE 3.14

Make sure you use the correct search to obtain the results you want.

Understanding Save/Refresh Style Page Development

Visual Web Developer includes a new feature that makes it easy to save a change to your application and then simply refresh the browser to see the change. It might seem like an easy concept to include in a development environment, but with older versions of .NET you always needed to close the browser, make your changes, compile the application, reopen the browser, and hope that the server hadn't cached the application (requiring you to reboot IIS). The old way of working with .NET could be frustrating and this new technique is a very welcome change.

Performing Tasks One at a Time

Some developers will create large pieces of code without ever testing them—they keep writing until the code is finished and only then test it out. The result is often a mess because people tend to make the same mistake repeatedly unless corrected. The old way that Visual Studio worked tended to enforce this approach to development. Using the coding save/refresh style means that you can perform one task at a time. The coding cycle works as follows:

1. Divide the code into easily tested pieces called units—a method or property declarations, for example.

2. Write a unit and sight verify that it doesn't contain any errors.

3. Build the code (this step also saves the code to disk) and correct any errors that the compiler finds. Repeat as needed until the code builds.

4. Test the code in the browser. If you already have the browser open, click Refresh to load the newly created version of the Web application. Edit the code to fix any errors and repeat step 3 until the browser tests pass.

5. Repeat steps 2 through 4 until you complete the application.

Visual Web Developer helps you create an environment in which you receive constant feedback. Problematic coding techniques become less pronounced over time because you continuously correct them as you create the application. In addition, errors have less of a chance to get buried because unit testing shows the errors in each unit. Part of the debugging cycle takes place as you write the code, which also reduces the complexity of debugging the application later.

Using the Task List Window

One of the hidden gems for developers is the Task List window. This feature can save you considerable time and help you organize your application development strategy better. Adding the appropriate organizational and task-related information can remind you to fix code, add all of the code you need, and better organize the coding tasks by priority and unit. To view the Task List window, select View ➢ Task List. The Task List window normally appears at the bottom of the display, but you can move it anywhere you like or dock it to another area of the display. Figure 3.15 shows a typical view of the Task List window with a user comment entered.

You can add two kinds of entries to the Task List window—user tasks and comments. Enter the user tasks directly into the window. They work best for tasks that affect the application as a whole, such as when you need to add another unit. Enter comments into the code using a special keyword. Generally, you'll use comments for specific kinds of tasks that affect a particular unit.

FIGURE 3.15
Use the Task List window
to provide reminders to
accomplish specific tasks.

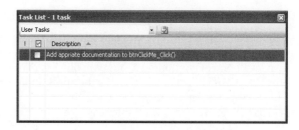

To add a new user task, click Create User Task on the Task List window toolbar. The Task List window will add a new entry and you can type whatever you want to remind you of the task. Because you can sort the Task List window by the Priority, Completed, or Description fields, it pays to use special keywords at the beginning of your comment such as Add Task. The Task List window adds the comment as normal priority. You can change the priority by clicking in the Priority field of the task that you want to change—you'll see a drop-down list box appear with three priority levels: high, normal, and low. When you complete a task, check its entry in the Completed field.

To view the comments task list for the Web application, select Comments in the Categories drop-down list box of the Task List window. Figure 3.16 shows some comments for the example application. In this case, the Task List window sets the priority based on the comments keyword definition, so you can't assign a priority to the task. To show that a task is complete, remove its comment from the code.

FIGURE 3.16
Use comments to create
unit specific tasks within
your Web application.

All of the comments use special keywords. Visual Web Developer supports four keywords, but you can add more as need. Here are the four keywords and their meanings.

TODO   Defines tasks that you still need to perform. The default setting for this keyword is normal priority.

HACK   Defines code that you created to solve an immediate problem, but isn't good production code. For example, you might directly assign a value to a variable that you actually need to compute. The default setting for this keyword is normal priority.

UNDONE   Includes code that you removed to solve a short-term problem. For example, you might comment code out to verify that the application works (up to a point) without it. As another example, you might decide to test two coding techniques to determine which one produces the best result. The default setting for this keyword is normal priority.

UnresolvedMergeConflict   Represents a unit that appears to work find on its own, but doesn't work well with the application as a whole. This comment could also apply to smaller code segments, a partial class, or other coding elements. The idea is that the code should work, but it doesn't when you merge it with something else, so you need to debug the problem. The default setting for this keyword is high priority.

You might have noticed that there's a lack of low-priority keywords and that might not agree with the default settings Microsoft provided. For that matter, you might want to add some keywords of your own because the Microsoft offerings don't do everything you need to do. Fortunately, you can change both kinds of settings using the Options dialog box (select Tools ➤ Options to display it). Begin by checking the Show All Settings option in the lower-left corner. The list of options will grow considerably. Select the `Environment/Task List` folder and you'll see the display shown in Figure 3.17.

FIGURE 3.17
Create new task list keywords or edit existing keywords using this display.

To change an existing entry, highlight it in the Token List field, make the required modifications in the Priority and Name fields, and then click Change. The only keyword you can't rename is TODO. The IDE uses this keyword to alert you to changes that you need to make after creating a new project or using a wizard. You can change the priority of the TODO keyword.

Adding a new keyword is just as easy. Type the new keyword in the Name field, assign it a priority in the Priority field, and click Add. The IDE will add the new keyword to the list.

The `Environment/Task List` folder also contains two options. The first, Confirm Deletion of Tasks, ensures that you don't remove tasks accidentally when checked. This is a good option to check when you first begin using the IDE, but the confirmation messages can become annoying when your skill level increases. The second, Show Only the File Name, Without the File Path, reduces Task List window clutter by removing the path information when checked. This setting works fine for simple projects, but can become a problem when you work with complex projects that span multiple folders. Generally, you'll keep this option checked when using Visual Web Developer.

Using the HTML Source Editing Toolbar

The HTML Source Editing toolbar provides quick access to some of the HTML editing features provided by Visual Web Developer. You access this toolbar by right-clicking the toolbar area and choosing HTML Source Editing from the context menu. Figure 3.18 shows the HTML Source Editing toolbar. The following list describes each of the buttons in detail.

FIGURE 3.18
The HTML Source Editing toolbar makes you more efficient when editing HTML.

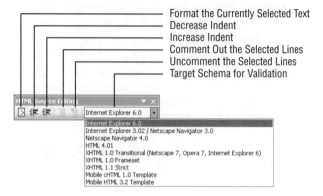

Format the Currently Selected Text   Modifies the text so it fits within the line length you choose and observes any formatting criteria (such as the use of uppercase or lowercase characters) you choose. This feature doesn't check spelling or the usability of the code—it simply formats it.

Decrease Indent   Decreases the space between the left side of the display and the start of the code. As the indentation level increases, the code moves to the right side of the screen and eventually out of view. Removing unneeded indentation can help you see the entire line of code, rather than scrolling back and forth to see it.

Increase Indent   Increases the space between the left side of the display and the start of the code. Indentation makes code easier to read by showing which code is at the same level of execution. Adding indentation can help you reformat code after you add a new type of processing or processing level.

Comment Out the Selected Lines   Adds comment characters in front of the selected lines of code. This process changes the code into a comment that you can still see and modify, but Visual Web Developer will ignore. Visual Web Developer enables this feature only when working with code behind files.

Uncomment the Selected Lines   Removes the comment character (if any) from in front of the selected lines of code. This process turns the comments back into code that Visual Web Developer will process when you compile the application. Visual Web Developer enables this feature only when working with code behind files.

Target Schema for Validation   Selects the kind of browser that the current Web page services. Figure 3.18 shows the options that are accessible from this toolbar. Visual Web Developer enables this feature only when working with Web pages (ASPX or HTML) files.

Working with Control Smart Tags

Microsoft has incorporated Smart Tag technology into many of its products. This technology first appeared in Microsoft Office and now appears in Visual Web Developer as part of the control technology. Not every control has a Smart Tag, but many do. Any time you might benefit from a little extra formatting assistance, Microsoft includes a Smart Tag with the control.

To see this technology for yourself, add two new lines after the `btnClickMe` control shown in Figure 3.3. Double-click the `DropDownList` control in the Toolbox. Visual Web Developer adds the new control to the Web page. Select this control and you'll see an arrow appear in the upper-right corner. Click this arrow and you'll see the Smart Tag shown in Figure 3.19. As you can see, a Smart Tag is essentially a specialized context menu with a list of tasks that you can perform with the control.

FIGURE 3.19
Use Smart Tags to help manage the controls in your application.

Notice that this Smart Tag contains two kinds of configuration. The first is a link such as Choose Data Source. Click a link and you'll see a dialog box containing configuration items. The second is a check box—Enable AutoPostBack in this case. Click this item and the IDE will either enable or disable the feature.

The Smart Tag for a drop-down list box is relatively simple. You'll see more complex Smart Tags as the book progresses. However, it's important to remember that Smart Tags only gather settings that you could change in other areas of the IDE and make them easier to access. None of the settings on a Smart Tag are unique—all of them appear somewhere else, so you can ignore the Smart Tags if you want.

Using Internet Information Server

The built-in Web server is fine for experimenting and beginning projects that you eventually plan to deploy, but at some point, you have to move your application to IIS so that other people can use it. You can accomplish this task using several techniques. The following sections examine several ways to move from the built-in Web server to IIS or another Web server such as Apache.

NOTE   Not all of the techniques in this section will work with every Web server. In fact, Microsoft has every reason to ensure that you don't create Web applications for servers other than IIS. However, you can use the Empty Web Site project to create a project devoid of .NET encumbrances. When you use standard HTML, CSS, XML, and other Web files for your application, you can typically deploy it anywhere—to any server. Of course, taking this approach means that you don't get to use a lot of the great features that ASP.NET 2.0 provides—it's a trade-off and you need to consider how the trade-off affects your application development plans.

Working with Local IIS

You don't have to use the built-in Web server—you can use a local copy of IIS to create applications with Visual Web Developer. The rules are a little different when you use this technique, however, because you already have IIS installed and running. Instead of creating a new Web site, you're opening an existing Web site.

To create a new project using a local copy of IIS, select the File ➢ Open Web Site command. Choose the Local IIS option and you'll see display similar to the one shown in Figure 3.20.

FIGURE 3.20
Open Web applications found on the local copy IIS for testing or modification.

In the upper-right corner of the dialog box, you'll see three buttons: Create New Web Application, Create New Virtual Directory, and Delete. Place the cursor where you want to create a new Web application and click Create New Web Application. Type a name for the Web application and you're ready to go. Click Open and Visual Web developer will open the Web site for you.

NOTE   If you install IIS after you install Visual Web Developer, IIS won't have the proper configuration settings for working with ASP.NET 2.0. Visual Web Developer detects this problem and displays a dialog box telling you about the problem. Click Yes to install ASP.NET 2.0 support so that you can begin working with the new Web application. The configuration can take a few minutes to complete.

Sometimes you don't want to place the Web application in the IIS folder or you might create an application using the built-in Web server and want to test it using IIS. In either case, you can create a virtual directory—a directory that appears to reside in the IIS folder, but really doesn't. To perform this task, choose a location for the folder and click Create New Virtual Directory. Type the name you want to use for the Web site in the Alias Name field and the location of the actual directory on your machine in the Folder field (you can also find the folder by clicking Browse). Click OK and Visual Web Developer will not only create a virtual directory, but will automatically set it up as a Web application for you.

Using the Copy Web Site Tool

The Copy Web Site tool lets you move files to different locations. Visual Web Developer doesn't care where you move the files and it doesn't necessarily care about the kind of server you use. Of course, when you choose something other than IIS, such as Apache, the files you move must work on that server. Microsoft doesn't make it as easy as it could to create applications that don't rely on ASP.NET, but you can do it if you think about the application before you spend much time developing it.

Select Website ➢ Copy Web Site to access the Copy Web Site tool. Figure 3.21 shows a typical view of the Copy Web Site tool after you've created a connection to a remote Web site.

To create a connection to another location (either local or remote), click Connect to a Remote Site. You'll see an Open Web Site dialog box like the one shown in Figure 3.22.

FIGURE 3.21

Once you open a remote Web site, you can move your project to it.

FIGURE 3.22

Use any of four methods to connect to a local or remote file transfer location.

You have four techniques to choose from including: File System, Local IIS, FTP Sites, and Remote Sites. Use the File System, Local IIS, and FTP Sites options for local file copying. The FTP Sites and Remote Sites options work for remote connections. The information you provide depends on the site type. For example, an FTP site requires that you provide the FTP URL, the port, the directory, and any required login information as shown in Figure 3.22. The Remote Sites option requires only that you provide an URL, but the remote server may display a dialog box asking for a username and password (assuming the remote server understands this form of communication). Figure 3.20 shows what you need to enter when working with the Local IIS option. The File System option used a Windows Explorer interface, and you can use it to communicate with both local and networked drives.

Once you choose a connection type and provide the required information, click Open and you'll see the remote Web site appear on the right side of the display as shown in Figure 3.21. You now have several options for copying files. The Move Files drop-down list box includes three options: move the files from the source Web site to the remote site, move the files from the remote Web site to the source Web site, or synchronize the files. After you select any of these options, you click Copy Web Site to move all of the files. The synchronize option is the most interesting because the IDE looks at each file in turn and moves the newest file from each site to the other site. This feature means that some files might move from the source Web site to the remote Web site, while others move from the remote Web site to the source Web site in the same move. When the timestamp on the files on both sites match, then the IDE doesn't move files from either location.

You can also move individual files. Simply highlight the file in the source Web site or remote Web site list and click one of the three movement buttons (only two of which are active). It's possible to move the file or synchronize it. The same synchronization rules apply—the file moves only when it's newer than the one on the other site. Selecting multiple files also works. Choose a starting file, press Shift, and click an ending file to choose files that appear together. Likewise, you can Ctrl+Click to choose individual files without deselecting previous selections.

Defining Your Development Goals

This chapter helped you accomplish a number of important goals, but the most important is taking that first step into creating applications with Visual Web Developer. Even though the project in this chapter is simple, it helps you understand important design and usage principles when you work with Visual Web Developer. This chapter also showed you how to work with several Web servers. Having a local Web server for testing is great—especially when it's a secure setup. However, at some point, you need to upload your Web application to a production Web server so other people can use it. Finally, you discovered the value of control Smart Tags. This feature is so important that you'll see other uses for it as the book progresses.

Now it's time to play. That's right; developers are allowed to play, just like everyone else. Spend some time creating new projects, adding simple controls, and trying the result out locally at least. Try uploading your project to a remote Web server and trying it there as well. (Make sure you don't use a production server for experimentation and have permission to use the server for training purposes.) Check out the Smart Tags for various controls to see what they have to offer.

Chapter 4 shows how to use some new features provided with ASP.NET 2.0. In this case, you'll discover some new visual aids in the form of master pages and themes. The Personal Web Site Startup Kit described in Chapter 2 uses these features, so you've already seen them. However, Chapter 4 provides a hands-on experience where you discover how to implement these features on any Web site you build.

Part 2

Using Built-in Features

In this section you will learn to:

Chapter 4

Working with ASP.NET 2.0 Master Pages and Themes

ASP.NET 2.0 introduces a number of new features—many of which Microsoft added as part of specific developer requests. Two of the most interesting concepts are master pages and themes. These features are so useful as a means of improving developer efficiency and the overall consistency of a Web site that they merit their own chapter.

In some respects, master pages and themes accomplish similar goals—they both create a general look and feel for a Web site. However, a master page and theme differ in their approach to the Web development problem. A master page accomplishes its goal by providing consistent content and, to a certain respect, layout for a Web site. A theme provides consistency through graphical elements, formatting, and layout (among other things).

Master pages and themes aren't necessarily mutually exclusive—Microsoft designed both technologies to mix in a number of ways. You can create a master page that relies on a theme for its formatting and graphical needs. A Web page can have both a master page (for content) and a theme (for formatting and graphics). The idea behind these technologies is to help the developer create pages faster by reducing the need to repeat elements that appear on every page. In addition, both master pages and themes reduce update time because you change a single file that affects the entire Web site, rather than make the change one page at a time.

As worthwhile and useful as master pages and themes are, they don't answer every need and they aren't the right answer in every case. It takes time and coordination to create a master page and theme for your Web site, and then add them to every page. In some cases, you might want to use an alternative such as Cascading Style Sheets (CSS). As you'll discover in this chapter, CSS also provides formatting and, to a lesser degree, some types of layout and graphics. The advantage of CSS is that it's standardized—you can use it on any Web site with any server and expect that any browser with CSS capability will be able to use the page. You might be surprised to learn that you can combine CSS with master pages and themes, so again these options aren't mutually exclusive.

Understanding Master Pages

A master page is a new way of organizing a Web site. It can contain a combination of formatting, graphics, and layout—whatever elements you feel that are common to all Web pages on your site. However, the emphasis is on organization, rather than on content. The idea is to give your Web site a consistent look and reduce the workload on developers. The developer no longer has to create repetitive elements using a number of tried and true methods such as cut and paste. In addition, the developer doesn't have to remember to create the correct elements in the proper order—the master page takes care of everything for the developer.

A master page always has a MASTER file extension. In most respects, it looks and acts just like an ASPX Web page. You add content to a master page just as you would for a standard Web page. Of course, it pays to remember that you won't be using this Web page directly—a master page is always an organization tool for other Web pages, no one actually sees it online.

A master page does have two special features that set it apart from other page types. First, it contains a special tag that identifies it as a master page to the Web server like the one shown here.

```
<%@ master Language="VB"
    CompileWith="Default.MASTER.VB"
    ClassName="Default_master" %>
```

This directive tag (a special tag that the server understands and doesn't send to the client) has four important features.

- The word master differentiates this page from a standard ASPX page, which uses the word page.

- The Language attribute tells you that the page uses Visual Basic for coding needs.

- The CompileWith attribute tells you that this master page uses code behind and that the code is located in the Default.MASTER.VB file.

- The ClassName attribute tells you that the default class for this page is Default_master, not another class that the Default.MASTER.VB file may contain.

Second, a master page contains ContentPlaceHolder controls that tell someone using the master page where to add the unique information for the Web page. Using the ContentPlaceHolder controls means there isn't any chance for confusion—developers working with a master page can only put content in certain places. Figure 4.1 shows the Default.MASTER file from the Personal Web Site Starter Kit example created in Chapter 2.

FIGURE 4.1

Master pages look just like standard Web pages with a few exceptions.

Notice that this page contains everything you might expect to see on every page of a Web site including standard links and a link for the site map. All of the identification information also appears on this page. Consequently, when you want to change the name of your Web site or a company wants to change the logo, all you need to do is change the master page, not all of the pages on the Web site.

As previously mentioned, ASPX pages use a directive similar to the one that the master page uses. One big difference is that the ASPX page uses a page directive, not a master directive. This directive also contains a special keyword that links the ASPX page to the master page. You'll find the `MasterPageFile` attribute shown here.

```
MasterPageFile="~/Default.MASTER"
```

When the server sees the `MasterPageFile` attribute, it reads the information found in the associated MASTER file before it reads the content from the ASPX page. It uses the MASTER file content to build a framework for the ASPX page and then places the unique ASPX page content within the framework. Of course, this begs the question of how the server knows where to place the information. The ASPX page contains special container tags that hold the content that the MASTER file describes such as this one.

```
<asp:content id="Content1" contentplaceholderid="Main" runat="server">
```

The `<asp:content>` tag identifies content information. The `id` attribute provides local identification that you use to interact with the tag. For example, you might decide to write some code behind to work with the content. The `contentplaceholderid` attribute identifies the name of the `ContentPlaceHolder` control in the MASTER file. This value is especially important because it provides the linkage between the ASPX file and the MASTER file—a MASTER file can contain multiple `ContentPlaceHolder` controls. The `runat` attribute tells the server that it should process this tag and not send it to the client for processing.

This process might seem long and arduous, but you don't have to worry about it. Using the procedures found in this chapter, the IDE does most of the work for you and you can perform any additional settings changes using simple properties, rather than write the code. The reason you want to know about these directives is so you understand what's happening and how to fix your pages should they become damaged.

Designing Master Pages

Before you can do anything with a master page, you have to create one. Master pages require a lot more thought than other pages you create because they affect every page on your Web site. It's not simply a matter of creating a great design, but one of determining when content is common to all pages and what type of support the developer using the master page requires. Restricting the master page too much creates an environment where the developer spends a lot of time working around the problems the master page creates. Likewise, developing a generic master page that's completely open to interpretation defeats the purpose of creating the master page in the first place. The following sections discuss these issues and more.

NOTE   Don't be concerned if you receive a script warning message from your antivirus application when adding a master page to a Web site. The error occurs because of the inner workings of Visual Web Developer and not because your machine is suddenly infected with a virus. Of course, you'll still want to react to any warning messages you receive at other times.

Creating the Master Page

Before you can create a master page, you need to create or open a Web site to store it. The "Creating the Application" section of Chapter 3 tells you how to perform this task. The easiest way to add a master page to the Web site is to open Solution Explorer. Right-click the project entry and choose Add New Item from the context menu. You'll see the Add New Item dialog box shown in Figure 4.2. Notice that you can choose to place the code in a separate file—just as you can with a Web Form (ASPX file). In this case, you can't select the Select Master Page option because you can't create a master page based on an existing master page.

FIGURE 4.2
Select the Master Page item from the Add New item dialog box to create a master page.

Select a language for the master page that you want to create. Check the Place Code in Separate File option if you want to store the code behind code in a separate file. Using a separate file is a good idea because doing so helps you create a better development environment—the HTML tags remain separate from the Visual Basic or C# code that you write for the code behind. Click Add to add the master page to the project.

Master pages always have to have one content area as a minimum, so you need to add a `ContentPlaceHolder` control to the master page as shown in Figure 4.3. You should always configure this control before you start adding content to the master page to ensure that you provide it with an easily identifiable name and provide everything the developer using the master page will need.

FIGURE 4.3
Configure the default *ContentPlaceHolder* control before you move on to other tasks.

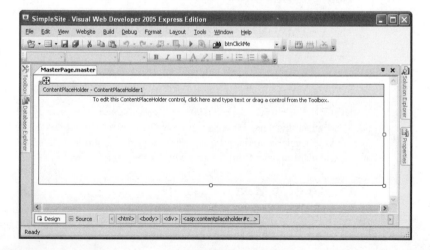

Using Existing Resources

It's quite likely that you'll use the same master page for multiple projects. Once you create the master page, you can make small modifications as needed for other uses. In fact, except for Web Forms, which normally contain unique content, you'll find that many resources you develop are reusable. Consequently, you'll add this existing resource to the project, rather than create a new resource.

To add an existing resource to the current project, open Solution Explorer, right click the project entry, and choose Add Existing Item from the context menu. You'll see the Add Existing Item dialog box shown in Figure 4.4.

FIGURE 4.4
Using existing items for your Web site saves time and effort.

Locate the resource, such as a master page, that you want to use. Don't worry about selecting the code behind page when you select an existing resource because the IDE copies it automatically for you. At this point, you'll see the new file added to Solution Explorer. Look in the project folder and you'll see a copy of the file added there as well. Any changes you make to the resource will affect the local project, but not the project from which you copied the resource.

Defining the Master Page

Now that you have a master page to use, you'll want to define some organizational elements for it. The "Creating a Layout" and "Using the Layout Toolbar" sections of this chapter describe how to add a layout to your master page so that all of the elements you want to add fit nicely.

After you create a layout for your master page, you'll want to add content to it. Generally, you'll want to add basic content to the page, such as a header and footer. This content doesn't have to appear in any special location or rely on complex formatting. Of course, you can always use a theme or CSS to create a specific appearance. The goal is to create a complete page that includes everything that every page on your Web site will need to include. Don't think, however, that these items are limited— consider adding the common elements listed here.

◆ Content

◆ Graphics

◆ Links

◆ Scripts

◆ Controls

◆ Code behind

◆ Anything else common to all pages

That anything else element is substantial. If every Web page will include the same sound or other multimedia file, then you should include it as part of the master page and not repeat it for every Web page on your Web site. Of course, you don't want to drown yourself with detail on the first master page. It pays to spend a little time working with the master page and then create a content page or two to see how it works before you move on to the next task.

Creating a Layout

The Layout toolbar helps you create a well-designed and organized Web page, whether it's a master or a content page. Before you begin using this feature, however, you need to create a layout for your Web page. Layout is actually a fancy term for tables. Just like the tables you create with pen and paper, tables on Web pages let you put anything you want within the rows and columns. With a little effort, tables on Web pages don't have to follow the rigid formatting that you might expect—tables can contain tables, so you can create complex layouts.

To begin the layout process, select the Layout ➤ Insert Table command. You'll see the Insert Table dialog box shown in Figure 4.5. Notice that this dialog box actually contains two methods for creating a table. You can select the Template option to add one of the predefined layouts to your Web page or the Custom option to create a unique layout. Of the two, the Template option is the easiest and you should at least look at the templates to see if any will work for your Web page. In many cases, the template will work, even if you have to make minor modifications. For the purposes of this chapter, choose the Header and Side template.

FIGURE 4.5
Add a table to the master page or content page to organize it.

After you choose a template or create a custom table layout, click OK. Something interesting will occur. You'll see the template added immediately before or after the `ContentPlaceHolder` control. To fix this problem, drag the `ContentPlaceHolder` control into the bottom right square. Your display will look similar to the one shown in Figure 4.6.

FIGURE 4.6
Modify the layout so that the *ContentPlaceHolder* control is in the correct position.

TIP It's important to realize that the IDE is creating an enormous amount of code for this master page in the background. All of these HTML tags do exist and you might eventually need to edit them. That's why it's a good idea to click various elements as you create them, click Source, and view the resulting HTML code. In the case of a table, you'll notice it begins with a `<table>` tag, which contains the entire table. Each row within the table is a `<tr>` tag. Rows contain columns—defined by the `<td>` tags. The bottom of the Design view is also helpful in seeing the relationship between tags. Look at the bottom of Figure 4.6 and you'll see that the tag sequence begins with an `<html>` tag (the entire Web page), followed in turn by the `<body>` (all the content), `<div>` (this section of content), the various table tags, and finally, the actual content, which is the `ContentPlaceHolder` control.

Figure 4.6 shows some other interesting layout features. For example, the sizing handles let you change the size of the layout as needed. When you place the cursor over an inner line, you'll notice that it changes into a sizing cursor. Simply move the line to give one cell of the layout more space (and correspondingly less space to the adjoining cell).

It's also possible to add and remove layout elements using the options on the Layout ➤ Insert menu. The only problem is that the options aren't all that clear unless you spend time working with them. Using Figure 4.6 as a starting point, Figure 4.7 shows the results of six different insertions you can make.

FIGURE 4.7
You can insert new layout features six different ways using the Layout ➢ Insert menu options.

The various additions follow specific rules. To add a column, you must select a row that spans the entire layout. You can still add a column to a row that doesn't span the entire layout, but you must select the entire row or the column addition looks very much like a cell addition. To make it easier to see the changes, the two column additions use the upper row as a starting point, while the remaining additions use the lower right cell as a starting point (the one with the ContentPlaceHolder control). The positioning of your cursor when you insert a new layout item is just as important as the kind of layout item you choose—different cursor positions have completely different effects because the IDE always adds layout elements relative to the current cursor position. In a few cases, you can obtain the same results using two different cursor positions. For example, inserting a column to the left using the upper row as a starting position produces the same results as inserting a cell from the lower right cell in Figure 4.7.

Sometimes, the visual display just doesn't provide enough information or makes it difficult to select just the item you want. When this problem occurs, you can use the options on the Layout ➢ Select menu to choose the entire table, a column, a row, or a single cell. The IDE shows you which items it selected. For example, when you select a row, the IDE highlights the border of the cell that currently contains the cursor and shows all other affected cells highlighted (usually in blue) as shown in Figure 4.8. Once you select an element, you can use the options on the Layout menu to resize or delete the elements. There's also an option to merge all of the cells in a selected row or column to produce a single cell. In short, you don't have to perform all of these tasks using just the features that Design view provides.

FIGURE 4.8
The display uses hints to show the layout selections and make the job of using them easier.

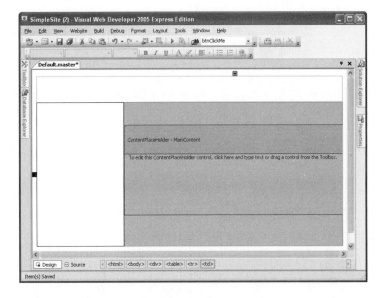

FIGURE 4.9
A good layout and well-defined general content make creating content pages easier.

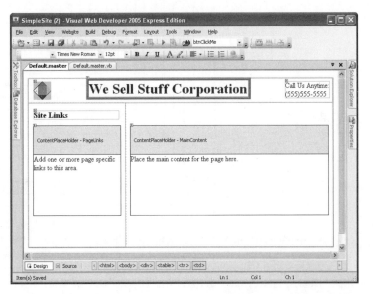

Once you create a layout, you can begin adding items and additional `ContentPlaceHolder` controls to the display. It's important to settle on the layout first because it provides the framework for the remaining controls. Figure 4.9 shows the layout and sample content for the example in this chapter.

Notice that the instructions for using the `ContentPlaceHolder` controls appear within the controls. The developer using the master page you create won't have access to the areas outside the control, so you must put the instructions within the control unless you want the instructions to appear to anyone visiting the page later. The example master page also includes all of the headings, icons, and other resources that appear on every Web page so the content developer performs the minimal amount of work.

Using the Layout Toolbar

At some point, you'll want to add controls to the Web pages you create. Generally, you'll want to create a nice looking layout—one that looks attractive—without doing a lot of work. That's where the Layout toolbar shown in Figure 4.10 comes into play. You use it to adjust the controls you create on a Web page. For example, you can align a series of controls or resize the controls so they all look the same. The following list describes the purpose and use of each control. It's important to realize that Microsoft is attempting to synchronize control and menu sets across products, so some of the buttons are nonfunctional for Visual Web Developer (even though they are functional for the desktop languages).

FIGURE 4.10
Use the Layout toolbar to adjust the default layout settings for a Web page.

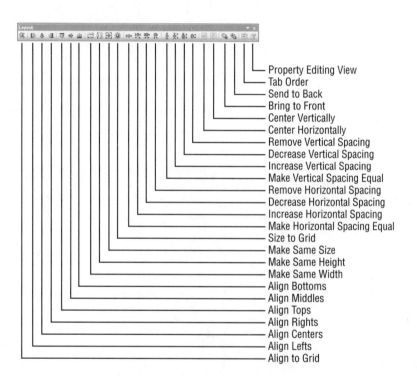

- Property Editing View
- Tab Order
- Send to Back
- Bring to Front
- Center Vertically
- Center Horizontally
- Remove Vertical Spacing
- Decrease Vertical Spacing
- Increase Vertical Spacing
- Make Vertical Spacing Equal
- Remove Horizontal Spacing
- Decrease Horizontal Spacing
- Increase Horizontal Spacing
- Make Horizontal Spacing Equal
- Size to Grid
- Make Same Size
- Make Same Height
- Make Same Width
- Align Bottoms
- Align Middles
- Align Tops
- Align Rights
- Align Centers
- Align Lefts
- Align to Grid

Property Editing View   Changes the Design view to include a Quick Edit Mode bar at the top of the display. A drop-down list box includes common properties such as Name and Text. You change a property by selecting it from the drop-down list box and modifying it directly in Design view, rather than use the Properties window. This feature isn't currently available in Visual Web Developer.

Tab Order   Adds tab order numbers to each of the controls in Design view. Clicking the number lets you edit its tab order. This feature isn't currently available in Visual Web Developer.

Send to Back and Bring to Front   Modifies the stacking order of a series of components. Stacking controls can help you create special effects, but only if the controls appear in the correct order. The last control placed on a form appears in front, while the first control appears behind all other controls. These two buttons let you change the stacking order to achieve specific display results.

Center Vertically and Center Horizontally   Places one or more controls in the center of a form. When you use this feature with all of the controls on a form, you can center the entire display on the form giving it a finished appearance. Unfortunately, browsers don't have a specific form size, so it's no surprise that the Visual Web Developer doesn't support this feature.

Remove Vertical Spacing, Decrease Vertical Spacing, Increase Vertical Spacing, and Make Vertical Spacing Equal   Adjusts the vertical placement between selected controls. Use Remove Vertical Spacing to eliminate all of the spacing between controls—they appear one after the other. Decrease Vertical Spacing removes a little of the spacing between controls, while Increase Vertical Spacing adds a little spacing between controls. Select Make Vertical Spacing Equal when you want to make the spacing between controls equal, without changing the starting and ending positions of the controls as a whole.

Remove Horizontal Spacing, Decrease Horizontal Spacing, Increase Horizontal Spacing, and Make Horizontal Spacing Equal   Adjusts the horizontal placement between selected controls. Use Remove Horizontal Spacing to eliminate all of the spacing between controls—they appear one after the other. Decrease Horizontal Spacing removes a little of the spacing between controls, while Increase Horizontal Spacing adds a little spacing between controls. Select Make Horizontal Spacing Equal when you want to make the spacing between controls equal, without changing the starting and ending positions of the controls as a whole.

Size to Grid   Modifies the size of a control to fit within the grid lines provided in Design view. The IDE normally changes the control size based on the proximity of the grid line to the edge of the control. Using a grid helps you create standardized controls and align them with greater ease.

Make Same Size, Make Same Height, and Make Same Width   Modifies the size of a series of controls to have the same size, height, or width. The last control you select in a group defines the standard for all of the other controls. Making all of the text boxes on a form the same size can give your form a more professional appearance. However, you'll also need to consider the data the user will enter—some controls will be larger because they contain more information that the user must see.

Align Bottoms, Align Middles, Align Tops, Align Rights, Align Centers, Align Lefts, and Align to Grid   Changes the alignment of a series of controls depending on the type of alignment selected. The last control you select in a group defines the anchor point for all of the other controls. Aligning the controls on a form gives the form a more professional appearance and helps the user see the anticipated flow from one control to the next.

When you first display this toolbar (right-click the toolbar area and choose Layout from the context menu), you'll notice that the IDE hasn't enabled any of the buttons. A standard Web page doesn't include the concept of layout and positioning except the positioning you can provide using careful component positioning and aids such as tables and frames. Special control attributes let you add specific positioning information. You add this support using either the Layout ➤ Position ➤ Absolute (for absolute positioning explained later in this section) or Layout ➤ Position ➤ Relative command. Here's an example of a label with positioning information added.

```
<asp:Label ID="Label1"
    Style="z-index: 27; left: 600px; position: absolute; top: 24px"
    Runat="server"
    Text="Call Us Anytime: (555)555-5555"
    TabIndex="3
    Width="104px" Height="19px"></asp:Label>
```

This example uses pixels as a unit of measure. Although the correlation of pixels to inches isn't standardized, most developers use a measure of $\frac{1}{72}$ inch per pixel, which means 72 pixels are equivalent to 1 inch.

The IDE creates all of the code shown, but like most automatically generated code, you need to know something about it so you can repair it later if necessary. The `Style` attribute contains the required positioning information. The `z-index` defines this control's position in the list of controls—this list isn't necessarily zero-based, nor is it necessarily continuous. The `left` value tells you that this control appears 600 pixels from the left side of the display, while the `top` value tells you that the control appears 24 pixels from the top. The `position` value tells you that this is an absolute position, rather than a relative position—the information relates to the upper left corner of the browser display. Relative positioning places the control in relation to some other element, such as a table cell, and requires a little more work to get right, but also provides a more flexible display in that the controls remain positioned well even when the user resizes the browser window.

WARNING Not all browsers can read and understand the styles that Visual Web Developer provides for relative and absolute positioning. Consequently, always assume that some viewers will see that page as if you used relative positioning.

The other attributes for this label help define how it appears on screen and how the user interacts with it. For example, this control runs at the server, so the user sees HTML output based on what the server generates. The `Text` attribute defines the text that the user sees on screen. The `TabIndex` attribute describes the selection order for this control when the user clicks Tab to move from control to control. Finally, the `Width` and `Height` properties tell you the size of the control.

Many of the layout features rely on the grid displayed in Design view. You can control this feature using the Options dialog box that you can access with the Tools ≻ Options command. Select the `Windows Form Designer\General` folder and you'll see the list of grid options shown in Figure 4.11.

The GridSize property defines the number of pixels between grid sections. The LayoutMode determines whether the grid relies on snap lines or actually snaps objects to the grid. (Think of a rubber band—you can place an item outside of the grid lines—the rubber bands, but the grid will snap the item back into place so it lines up with the grid lines.) Set the ShowGrid property to true to see the grid presented on screen. In some cases, developers find this feature helpful because the grid helps the developer place items accurately—other developers find the grid distracting because the form doesn't appear to the developer, as it will to the user. The SnapToGrid property tells the IDE to automatically snap items to the grid when the LayoutMode is SnapToGrid.

FIGURE 4.11
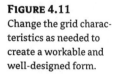
Change the grid characteristics as needed to create a workable and well-designed form.

CONSIDERING THE DOWNSIDE OF USING A LAYOUT

Web sites have used tables for many years as an organizational aid. For the most part, it's a natural decision. The only problem is that tables can cause problems for anyone with special needs or less than the optimal display area. For example, a Web page that uses tables for organization might look great on your desktop machine, but someone using a Pocket PC might see just one square (hopefully, the right square). A page that flows well works best because just about any device can see it, even if the viewing experience is lengthy due to the page size. Given that many people use small devices to view Web pages today, the screen real estate question is a very real concern.

Tables can also cause some compatibility problems because not every browser displays tables the same way or uses the same functionality. A special effect that looks great with Internet Explorer might not display well when using Mozilla or Firefox. The problem is that the standards groups have provided general guidelines for tables, but many of the specifics are vendor specific.

Finally, imagine that you're blind and trying to discover the layout of a Web page by listening to a description of its layout. Listening to a description of a table used for layout, rather than content, is akin to listening to four or five radio stations at the same time and trying to enjoy each of the songs. You can do it, but it's difficult and there are possibly better things to do with your time. The problem is that the table doesn't contain descriptive information when used as a layout, so the screen reader moves from topic to topic without informing the listener of the change or making it clear that the change has occurred.

Tables do have some positive points and you don't always have to avoid using them. For one thing, using tables for layout is better than using frames, which have more severe compatibility problems and are an even bigger nightmare for anyone with special needs. Frames can also pose security risks that many users are unwilling to face today. Another potential problem with frames that you can overcome using tables is that search engines usually display the frame page that contains the content—rather than the container page. In some cases, this means the user doesn't have any way to navigate the size because the navigational aids appear in another frame that isn't displayed. Consequently, when you must organize the data on your Web site and none of the organizational techniques in the "Organizing the Web Page" section of Chapter 19 will work, then using a layout is the best alternative.

Creating a Project with Master Pages

Once you have a master page defined, you can use it to create content pages. A content page has all of the content and organization provided by the master page, plus unique content that the individual page provides. You can use master pages to create content pages in a number of ways. The following sections explore the techniques that you'll commonly use.

Creating a Content Page Using a Master Page

Adding content pages doesn't have to be cumbersome or time consuming. The easiest method for creating a content page based on a master page is to open the master page, right-click anywhere on the form in Design view, and choose Add Content Page from the context menu. The IDE will create a new content page that uses default settings and a generic name based on the master page. Figure 4.12 shows typical results of using this method. Notice the grayed out areas—the developer can't modify this information in the content page. However, the developer can interact with the two content areas and remove the instructions as necessary.

Another way to create a content page using a master page is to right-click the project entry in Solution Explorer. Choose Add New Item from the context menu and you'll see the Add New Item dialog box.

SELECTING USER INTERFACE DESIGN RESOURCES

Getting great user interface design references helps you get started faster and ensures that you won't make as many mistakes during the design process. Typically, you'll find that books are better than Web sites for this kind of information because books have more space to cover contingencies that articles or other online resources can't discuss. However, don't discount Web sites—you might find something that meets a specific need. Newsgroups can help, but you need to state the design issues that you want to overcome very clearly and take any advice with a grain of salt because the developer helping you might not have a clear picture of the issues.

You can find a number of good books online. The trick is to find a book that is either completely generic or meets the need of a specific environment. For example, if you want to design a Web application, then you might consider reading *Designing Web Usability: The Practice of Simplicity* by Dr. Jakob Nielsen (New Riders, 1999). Although Web developers could rely on this book, desktop developers can benefit most from *The Humane Interface: New Directions for Designing Interactive Systems* by Jef Raskin (Addison-Wesley, 2000). Good generic books include *Developer to Designer: GUI Design for the Busy Developer* by Mike Gunderloy (Sybex, 2005) and *Designing Highly Useable Software* by Jeff Cogswell (Sybex, 2004).

It's possible to find good help online. For example, the Microsoft User Interface site at `http://msdn.microsoft.com/library/en-us/dnanchor/html/anch_uidesigndev.asp` provides a wealth of information on topics as diverse as accessibility and Microsoft Agent. Dr. Jakob Nielsen presents a number of usability articles at `http://www.useit.com/alertbox/`. This monthly column can provide continuing help with your application as user needs and expectations change. In some cases, you can even find online books such as *Task-Centered User Interface Design* by Clayton Lewis and John Rieman at `http://www.hcibib.org/tcuid/`. The authors offer this book as shareware, so make sure you support them if you use it.

Locating a newsgroup that offers advice on user interfaces isn't hard—it's hard to find good advice. Generally, you'll need to find a newsgroup that caters to your language and choice of device (such as the .NET Compact Framework for mobile devices at `microsoft.public.dotnet.framework.compactframework`). Some newsgroups, such as `comp.human-factors` provide limited generic help should you need it. After many hours of searching, I couldn't find a suitable newsgroup devoted to the topic of user interfaces. Contact me at `JMueller@mwt.net` if you know of such a newsgroup and I'll post it on my Web site with the updates for this book.

Select the Web Form option, choose a programming language, and type a name for the file. Click the Select Master Page option in this dialog box. Click Add. Normally, you'd see the new page at this point, but you don't in this case—you see the Select a Master Page dialog box shown in Figure 4.13 instead.

As you can see, this is a standard selection dialog box, but it's limited to the current project. You can't choose master pages that reside in other projects because there isn't any guarantee that the other project will even exist on the Web server you use to deploy your project. The limitations of this dialog box are actually a safety feature that ensures your content page has the best possible chance of working. Content pages typically rely on the master page for the <html>, <head>, <body>, and other standard tags, so they might even display without the presence of the master page. Choose a master page from the list and click OK. The IDE will create the required content page for you.

FIGURE 4.12
Content pages are just a few clicks away when you have the master page open.

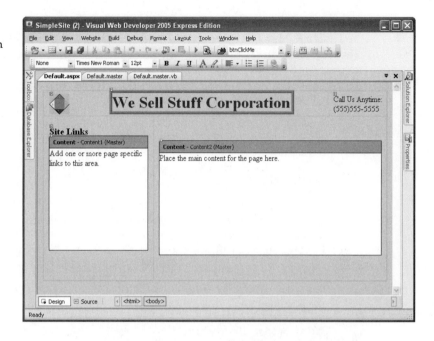

FIGURE 4.13
Choose a master page for your new Web Form using any resource in the current project.

TIP You can change the master page filename if necessary without resorting to hand editing the code. Open the Properties window and select DOCUMENT from the list of objects. You'll see a list of page-related properties including the MasterPageFile property. Change this property to modify the master page that a document uses. Unfortunately, the change in master pages will probably mean hand editing any content areas to match the ID of any ContentPlaceHolder controls in the new master page.

Adding a Master Page to an Existing Web Page

You might create a Web page and only then discover that you forgot to attach the master page to it. Theoretically, with careful editing, you can recover from the error, but it's not easy. Generally, if you can recreate the page using one of the techniques in the previous section, "Creating a Content Page Using a Master Page," you'll save time and effort. If you created the master page as an afterthought, you need to perform the tasks outlined here.

1. Add the appropriate attributes to the page declaration (the `<%@ Page %>` tag) at the top of the file. As a minimum, you need to provide a `MasterPageFile` attribute such as `MasterPageFile="~/Default.master"` and a `Title` attribute such as `title="Untitled Page"`. At this point, you could view the page in Design view and actually see the effect of the master page, but it wouldn't work correctly.

2. Remove the `<!DOCTYPE>`, `<html>`, `<head>`, `<body>`, `<form>`, and `<title>` tags as a minimum. Any common scripts that normally appear as part of the `<head>` tag should appear in the master page, not the content page, so move the code as needed. At this point, the page should work in a browser, but you won't see your old content—it's not part of an `<asp:Content>` tag.

3. Enclose the existing content in an `<asp:Content>` tag. This tag must include `id`, `ContentPlaceHolderID`, and `Runat` attributes. Here's a typical example of an `<asp:Content>` tag for the example master page.

```
<asp:Content ID="Content2"
             ContentPlaceHolderID="MainContent"
             Runat="server">
```

The ID is always unique, but you don't have to provide anything specific. Use a name that you can remember easily in case you have to write code for the content area. The `ContentPlaceHolderID` must match the ID of the `ContentPlaceHolder` control in the master page. This value provides linkage between the content page and the master page. Finally, all pages of this type must run at the server, so you always provide a `Runat="server"` entry.

Sometimes the first conversion attempt fails. In fact, you could experience several failures before you get the page just right. Unfortunately, Visual Web Developer doesn't display a simple message saying that you failed—instead you get the odd-looking page shown in Figure 4.14. This page does contain useful information that Chapter 16 discusses in detail. For now, all you need to know is that this page tells you that the conversion is incomplete and you need to look again at the changes you made.

Using Multiple Master Pages in a Project

A Web site can include more than one master page. For example, you might want one look for pages that have static content, another for survey pages, and still another for pages that contain sales figures or other dynamic content. However, it's best to start by creating a simple Web site that contains just one master page. As the Web site grows, you can add other master pages as needed to serve specific needs.

One thing to remember about master pages is that you can't nest them—a master page can't create another master page. Consequently, when you use multiple master pages, you have to update each master page individually. This is the reason that many developers create a single master page and then augment the master page content using themes or other functionality. Of course, then the master page can become quite generic and not very useful in the construction of a Web site. The decision is ultimately yours—you need to consider the trade-offs of the various options at your disposal.

FIGURE 4.14
Errors can and will occur
when you convert your
existing pages to use a
master page.

There are a number of reasons to use multiple master pages. The best reason is that you have more kinds of content to cover than a single master page can accommodate. Look again at the example master page in Figure 4.9. While this design works fine for a content page, it wouldn't work very well for a feedback page or an order form. You'd need to create other kinds of master pages to serve those needs.

Understanding Themes

Anyone who's used themes in Windows has a basic understanding of themes in Visual Web Developer. As with Windows themes, Visual Web Developer themes appear in a special folder within the project called Themes. You create a special folder to hold each theme that you want to use and place resources within those folders. A theme includes a number of elements such as graphics and formatting information. The idea is to create a concept for your Web page that defines how the page should look. By applying the same theme to every Web page, you can create a consistent look that gives your Web page a professional appearance that users will like.

A theme modifies the appearance of a Web page, but it isn't part of the Web page. Any change that you make to the theme will also appear in the Web page. Consequently, if you decide that a font used to display the company's copyright notice is too small, you can change it in the theme and know that the change will affect all of the documents that use the theme. Like master pages, themes make it possible to produce global changes that ease development and maintenance requirements.

Like master pages, you must create a link between the theme and any Web pages that rely on it. Unlike master pages, themes are relatively unobtrusive from a coding perspective and you can add them at any time. For that matter, as long as your themes are compatible and provide similar resources, you can switch between themes at any point. Even though you'll define the theme connection using the Theme property of the DOCUMENT object, it's important to know what goes on in the background. All that the IDE does is add a `Theme` attribute such as the one that follows to the page directive at the top of the coding area.

```
Theme="MyTheme"
```

Once you add this attribute, all of the features of the theme become available to the Web page. Should you decide later not to use the theme, you can simply remove any resources that the theme provides from the page (such as special buttons or images) and then remove the Theme attribute from the page declaration.

NOTE When you want to use the styles and formatting provided by a theme, but not the content, add the theme name to the `StylesheetTheme` attribute instead of the `Theme` attribute. All of the `SKIN` file information is also available when you use this technique—the only thing missing is any content, such as predefined button names. (A `SKIN` file defines the appearance of the user interface, but not the inner workings of that interface, just as your skin defines your outward appearance.)

The Web page requires a second level of connectivity to make the use of themes complete. You must attach the specific theme entries to the various elements. When working with a `SKIN` file value, you'll make this entry in the `SkinID` property for the control. Likewise, when working with a CSS file entry, you'll make the entry in the `Class` property.

Designing Your Own Themes

Themes can be a little complicated to create, but it's definitely worth the effort. To keep things simple, work on a small portion of the theme at a time. That way you won't get too mired in complexity immediately. You do need to perform four essential steps to create a theme as follow.

1. Create the `Themes` folder.

2. Define a CSS file for the theme.

3. Define the `SKIN` file for the theme.

4. Add any required resources.

You won't necessarily perform these steps one time or even in order. Of course, you have to create a Themes folder before you can do anything, but you might find that you need more than one theme and will add to it later. The following sections describe the process for creating a theme.

Creating a Themes Folder

The Themes folder must appear as part of the root directory for your project and it can't include any resources—only subfolders that will act as theme names. To add the new folder to your project, right-click the project entry in Solution Explorer and choose New Folder from the context menu. You'll see a new folder added to the display. Type **Themes** as the new folder name and press Enter.

Now it's time to create the theme. Right-click the Themes folder and choose New Folder from the context menu. Again, you'll see a new folder added to Solution Explorer, but this one will appear in the \Themes folder. Type the name of the theme that you want to create, such as MyTheme. The \Themes\MyTheme folder will hold all of the resources for the MyTheme theme.

When your theme includes images, you'll want to create an additional subfolder to hold them. Right-click the Theme folder (MyTheme for the example) and choose New Folder from the context menu. Type **Images** as the new folder name and press Enter. Copy any resources that the theme will use into the Images folder for that theme.

Defining a CSS File for a Theme

Most themes include a CSS file that defines the formatting characteristics of any tags that you want to use. You must add this file to the Theme folder. Right-click the Theme folder (\Themes\MyTheme in the example) and choose Add New Item from the context menu. You'll see an Add New Item dialog box. Select Style Sheet from the template list. Type a name for the CSS file. You can use any name desired, but it makes sense to give this file the same name as the theme (MyTheme.CSS in the example). Click Add and you'll see the double-sided CSS display.

Make sure that you provide formatting for both the standard elements and the special classes you want to use. The "Creating and Using a CSS File" section later in this chapter shows you how to define a CSS file. Once you finish applying the changes, save the file.

Defining the *SKIN* File and Adding Theme Resources

The SKIN file contains definitions of the various controls. You can approach this task in two ways—create a single SKIN file for all of the controls or create individual SKIN files for each control. Using the single file is the best approach because it's less confusing and you're less likely to lose one of the files.

Unfortunately, you won't find a SKIN file template, so you'll use the Text File template instead. To add the SKIN file, right-click the template folder and choose Add New Item from the context menu. You'll see the Add New Item dialog box. Select the Text File template and type a filename ending with a SKIN extension (MyTheme.SKIN for the example).

Now it's time to create control definitions for the SKIN file. The definition should never include any identifying or unique information such as the ID property or the caption for a button, unless you plan to use that value for every control and the value won't cause a conflict. Here's the easiest way to create these definitions:

1. Create a scrap page.

2. Select Design view on the scrap page and place the control that you want to create on the scrap page.

3. Configure the control. Make sure that you include all common properties but avoid configuring properties that will change from control to control.

4. Type a value in the SkinID property. This value identifies the control within the SKIN file.

5. Select Source view and highlight the line containing the control that you want to create. Make sure that you copy everything between the beginning and ending tag or the control definition won't work.

6. Click Copy to place the control definition on the clipboard.

7. Select the SKIN file and click Paste. You'll see the control definition displayed in the SKIN file.

8. Repeat steps 2 through 7 for every control you want to add to the SKIN file.

You can add any number and type of controls to the SKIN file. The only requirement is that the control provides some kind of common functionality. For example, if every one of the survey forms that you create includes a Submit Survey button, then you should create this button once and place it in the SKIN file, rather than create the button every time you need it. Here's an example of two controls entered in a SKIN file.

```
<asp:Button AccessKey="C"
            Runat="server"
            Text="Click Me"
            ToolTip="Click this button."
            BorderStyle="Ridge"
            BorderWidth="6px"
            SkinID="ClickMeButton" />

<asp:Image Runat="server"
            BorderStyle="Ridge"
            BorderWidth="6px"
            ImageUrl="Images/TestImage.gif"
            AlternateText="A test image."
            Height="50px"
            Width="50px"
            SkinID="LogoIcon" />
```

Notice that neither of the controls contains specific information except the button control. Because this is a specific kind of button—one that always contains the Click Me caption, it includes the Text property value. The AccessKey property lets keyboard users access the button using Alt+C, rather than using the mouse. The ToolTip property provides explanatory information for people who use accessibility devices and helps other users understand the purpose of the button. The BorderStyle and BorderWidth are actually a decorative element in this case. Finally, the SkinID property contains the name that identifies this particular button—every SkinID is unique.

The <asp:Image> tag includes many similar property values such as the border information and SkinID. Notice that the ImageUrl property points to a theme resource without providing a precise theme name. This technique ensures that you can use the same SKIN file in multiple themes simply by varying the resources that the theme uses and the kind of formatting it provides. The AlternateText property provides an image description for users who require accessibility aids. Finally, because this is a logo and not an image that you might want to resize later, the Height and Width properties contain the logo size.

At this point, you should have a preliminary theme that you'll improve as you test it with your Web site. Figure 4.15 shows a typical simple theme setup. Of course, the theme you create might have multiple SKIN files or it could include other kinds of resource folders (such as Sounds or Multimedia).

FIGURE 4.15
Carefully crafted themes can save the developer time and effort creating consistent pages.

Creating a Simple Project Using Themes

Projects that use themes are similar to those that don't. The only difference is that you have the initial step of creating the theme. This initial step is important because it forces you to think about the project particulars before you begin creating any pages. For example, you must consider how to format the text and how it should appear on screen. A theme helps you consider the functionality of controls and ensures that you've considered all of the resources before you get them on the page. In short, themes aren't just a means of designing pages more efficiently, they're a productivity aid as well. The following sections describe several simple project types that you can create using themes.

Applying a Theme to a Page

Once you have a theme created, you need to test it. After all, you might not have thought about everything the first time. The best way to test a theme is to create a test ASPX file using the Web Form template. All you need to do is create an ASPX file using the standard technique because the Add New Item dialog box doesn't offer any special means of connecting the theme file to the Web page.

After you create the Web page, open the Properties window. Select DOCUMENT in the list of objects and locate the Theme property, as shown in Figure 4.16. If you configured the directory structure correctly, you'll see a listing of any themes you created in the drop-down list box. This is actually the first test of your theme. When you don't see your theme listed, you know that you didn't create the directory structure correctly and need to fix this error.

FIGURE 4.16
Verify that Visual Web Developer can locate the themes that you create.

At this point, you can begin adding controls to your Web page. Whenever you add a control that uses one of the items in the SKIN file, don't make any configuration changes to it. Begin by typing the name of the skin that you want to use in the SkinID property for the control. This example includes only two controls in the SKIN file, so the test page uses those two items: ClickMeButton and LogoIcon.

TIP This is one time when using Source view is actually easier than using Design view. Select the control that you want to modify in Design view, switch to Source view, and add a new SkinID attribute to the end of the control. As soon as you type the = (equals sign), IntelliSense presents you with a list of SkinID values for that control. You won't see any other SkinID values. This technique ensures that you type the SkinID value correctly.

The IDE won't show the changes that the SKIN file makes to your page in Design view, but you can see them when you view the page in a browser. To see the changes made to the controls, right-click anywhere on the form and choose View in Browser from the context menu.

You can customize the controls after you create the required layout and assign the `SkinID` values. It's important to remember that you can't change properties that the SKIN file assigns. For example, when you create an `<asp:Button>` tag with a `Text` property value, every control will have that `Text` property value. The only property values that you can change are those that the SKIN file doesn't specify. Consequently, in the case of the example, you could change the width of the `Button` control, but not its caption.

Adding styles to various elements comes next. You work with styles from a theme precisely the way that you use them when working with a style sheet. The "Working with CSS in the Web Page" section later in this chapter describes this process in greater detail.

Applying a Theme to a Web Site

You don't have to apply themes to Web pages one at a time. When you decide to use the same theme for the entire Web site, you can apply it just once by creating a special Web configuration file. To add the Web configuration file, right-click the project entry in Solution Explorer and choose Add New Item from the context menu. You'll see the Add New Item dialog box. Choose the Web Configuration File template and click Add. (You can change the filename if desired, but it's not necessary because your Web site has only one configuration file.) The IDE creates a new CONFIG file.

The Web configuration file contains a number of entries when you initially create it. You'll find references to these other entries as the book progresses. Locate the `<System.Web>` element. Add a new element to this hierarchy named `<pages>`. This element defines page characteristics for your Web site. In this case, you want to add a `themes` attribute that points to the theme you want to use. Your entry should look similar to the one shown here.

```
<configuration
    xmlns="http://schemas.microsoft.com/.NetConfiguration/v2.0">

    ... Other Entries ...
    <system.web>

        <!-- Tells the System to use MyTheme for all pages. -->
        <pages theme="MyTheme" />

        ... Other Entries ...

    </system.web>
</configuration>
```

Notice that the example includes a comment describing the entry. Always add a comment whenever you make a change to the CONFIG file. Otherwise, you'll look at this file later and wonder what task the entry performs.

Now every Web page that you create will use the global theme unless you specifically override the choice by setting the theme for the individual page. A page level theme declaration always overrides the global theme.

Working with Cascading Style Sheets (CSS)

CSS is perhaps the most useful Web technology that you can learn from an efficiency perspective. Not only will CSS save time and effort formatting the text and controls on your Web site, but it's also a standard technology. You can use CSS on any Web page running from any server and reasonably expect that most people will see the formatting you want to provide—or, at least, a reasonable facsimile. Not every browser renders (interprets and displays) CSS precisely the same, but most do provide an adequate interpretation. The following sections describe how to use CSS.

Using the Style Sheet Toolbar

The Style Sheet toolbar (access it by right-clicking the toolbar area and choosing Style Sheet from the context menu) contains buttons that make performing most CSS editing tasks easier. Figure 4.17 shows what this toolbar looks like. The following list describes each of the button functions.

FIGURE 4.17
Quickly edit a CSS file using the features provided on this toolbar.

Cascading Style Sheet Version for Validation

Add Style Rule

Build Style   View in Browser

Cascading Style Sheet Version for Validation   Determines the rules used to validate the CSS file entries. Older versions are more restrictive, but also less liable to create compatibility problems. The list also includes a special Internet Explorer 6.0 entry that helps you tailor the CSS file to this specific browser.

View in Browser   Creates a special test page that includes a number of standard tags you can use to verify the appearance of your CSS page. The IDE doesn't actually open an external browser—it uses an internal page instead. Although this is a good way to check your entries quickly, you'll also want to test the CSS entries with your Web site to ensure that the entries actually work as intended.

Build Style   Displays the Style Builder dialog box that you use to define an existing style. See the "Creating and Using a CSS File" section later in this chapter for details.

Add Style Rule   Displays the Add Style Rule dialog box you use to add a new style to the CSS file. See the "Creating and Using a CSS File" section later in this chapter for details.

Designing Flexible Interfaces

No matter how well you design your application, someone will complain that some feature doesn't work as expected. During my years of programming, I've personally seen arguments between users about the order of fields on a form. One discussion about a screen degenerated into an intense argument about the order of name elements on the form (one user wanted last name first—the other wanted the first name to appear first). Users will grumble about every aspect of your application given a chance and you'll never satisfy all the users. Some developers solve the problem by giving up and creating the application that they want. However, this solution probably works least often because the user's immediate reaction is that the developer isn't listening and lacks any form of human interaction skills.

Flexible user interfaces resolve the user problem by letting each user design the interface that meets their specific needs. Just how flexible you can make the interface depends on a number of factors including the application environment and the programming language you use. Making Web applications flexible is somewhat harder than most desktop applications because many browsers lack the support required to move visual elements around and perform other manipulations that the user would like. Depending on your programming skill, schedule, programming language, and patience, you can make some desktop applications so flexible that the user has control over every display element and the application will remember its configuration between sessions.

Let's start with something a little more reasonable than complete application configuration. Even the most mundane Web page allows configuration. For example, you can use Cascading Style Sheets (CSS) to format the Web page. Some browsers let the user substitute their CSS file for the default that you provide on your Web site—making it possible for the user to have complete control over the presentation of information even if you don't provide any other form of programming with the Web page. Some sites extend this principle by providing multiple CSS files. A simple cookie entry controls which CSS file the Web site uses when presenting information to the user. Desktop applications are even easier to control in this area. All you need is an Options dialog box containing the display element settings so the user can change them to meet specific needs. Most desktop applications already provide this feature. Make sure you save the user options in a file or other central location (such as the Windows Registry) if you offer this feature.

The next level of application configuration is component selection. For example, not every user will want to sort the output results. It might seem that simply ignoring the sort field would work, but unnecessary fields are annoying to some users. Again, Web pages can use a cookie to store a list of fields or controls that the user doesn't want to see. You'll likely have to provide a configuration page to support this form of configuration—adding a simple link to the page to allow configuration usually works fine. Desktop applications can use an Options dialog box. Most desktop applications don't offer this feature—probably because the developer didn't think to offer the feature or assumed that everyone would want access to every field.

NOTE Don't make every field on a form optional. A user will have to make some entries to perform even basic tasks. For example, a user can't perform an author search without entering an author name, so the author name field isn't optional. However, hiding optional fields can make the application faster and easier to use. You might even find that you want to include some developer-only fields in the list that you control with special entries in the configuration file.

Web applications don't commonly use toolbars or special menus in the same way that desktop applications use them. However, both environments can benefit from some level of customization for both items. Quite a few desktop applications offer this feature. Generally, the user selects a special menu command that allows them to move menu or toolbar elements around, add new menu or toolbar options, or delete options the user feels aren't important. Trying to implement this feature on a Web site would be very hard, but doable if you use some technologies such as ASP.NET. Make sure you offer a feature that returns everything to its default state in case the user makes a few too many changes.

The ultimate level of interface flexibility lets the user move controls around on screen. This feature lets one user place names in last-name order and another user place them in first-name order. Complete interface control is difficult to implement on a desktop application and likely impossible for a Web application. Applications that allow complete interface configuration are extremely rare. However, you'll find that some applications don't suffer from the same level of complexity that other applications do, so this might be a viable solution in some cases. At least you can provide the user with enough flexibility to define precisely how the display appears so that your application works as efficiently as possible for that user.

NOTE   If you plan to provide complete interface flexibility for your application, you should go all the way by allowing the user to change even mundane features such font size and typeface. To an extent, you could even let the user change the button captions and control the color of the tiniest text element. It's even possible to let the user add graphics and perform other odd configuration changes given the right programming language, a platform that supports the changes, and enough time.

Creating and Using a CSS File

CSS files aren't very difficult to create—the biggest problem is deciding how to specify in text the formatting options that you normally see graphically on screen. Every CSS file entry consists of the following three components.

Selector   The value that defines how a browser selects a particular formatting definition contained in a Web page.

Property   The formatting element that you want to define, such as the font face, color, or size, for a particular selector.

Value   The actual formatting information. For example, when working with a color, you might set the value to blue.

Most CSS files use three selector types. The element selector depends on the kind of element. For example, you could define a selector for the <H1> tag. The class selector uses a keyword as a definition. You supply this keyword as part of the element description on a Web page to invoke the selector. The element identifier (ID) relies on the ID value of an element as a selector. This definition will affect one element at most on any Web page because every element has a unique element ID.

When you create a CSS file, the IDE automatically creates a <Body> tag selector for you because most developers create a baseline configuration for the page. The baseline configuration affects all elements contained within the <Body> tag. To configure a tag, place the cursor between the two curly brackets for the body selector in the CSS file. Click Build Style and you'll see the Style Builder dialog box shown in Figure 4.18.

FIGURE 4.18
Use the Style Builder dialog box to add properties and values to a selector.

You don't have to fill out every property contained with the Style Builder dialog box—fill out only those properties that you actually want to change. For example, you might decide to change the font color to Blue (on the Font tab), the background color to PaleTurquoise (on the Background tab), the horizontal alignment to justified (on the Text tab), and the indentation to 6 pixels (px). Click OK once you make the changes. Here's what the resulting body selector looks like.

```
body
{
    color: blue;
    text-indent: 6px;
    background-color: paleturquoise;
    text-align: justify;
}
```

Of course, you can't define everything by using a single selector—you'll want specific formatting for other items as well. Most developers begin by defining the formatting for all of the elements that they intend to use on a page. To create a new selector, place the cursor on the last empty line (press Enter if necessary to create a new blank line) and click Add Style Rule. You'll see the Add Style Rule dialog box shown in Figure 4.19.

FIGURE 4.19
Add new selectors to the CSS file using the Add Style Rule dialog box.

Notice that you can choose from three kinds of selectors: Element, Class Name, and Element ID. When you choose the Element option, you choose the element that you want to define from the drop-down list box. This list box contains an amazing number of elements—at least most of the comment elements and a few of the uncommon elements as well. When working with the other entry types, simply provide the class name or the ID of the object that you want to modify. You don't have to add any special characters to the entries—Visual Web Developer takes care of the special characters for you. After you create the new selector, define its properties just as you did for the <Body> tag earlier.

The CSS file editing display also includes a special view on the left side of the display. This display categorizes the selectors that you create and makes it easy to find the one that you need. All you have to do is click the appropriate entry. Figure 4.20 shows the Visual Web Developer CSS editor display. Notice that the highlighting the IDE provides makes it very easy to see the selector you've chosen in the left pane on the right side of the display.

FIGURE 4.20
The use of color-coding makes it easy to see entries—the hierarchical display makes it easy to find selectors.

Working with CSS in the Web Page

You'll find it very easy to work with CSS on a Web page because most of the entries are automatic. To begin, you must tell the Web page to use the CSS file. When working with a theme, the theme makes the required entry for you automatically. However, when you use a CSS file by itself, you must add the name of the CSS file to the StyleSheet property of the DOCUMENT object (simply select DOCUMENT in the Properties window). Click the ellipsis next to the field entry and you'll see a Select Stylesheet dialog box that you can use to locate the CSS file on your hard drive.

Most of the entries work automatically. When you create an element or element ID selector, the CSS file works automatically. The class selector requires a little more work. You must select the element that you want to work with and then type the name of the style that you want to use in the Class property. This is another case where working in Source view can prove helpful because you can also type the Class attribute by hand and depend on IntelliSense to provide you with useful information. For example, here's <H1> tag with a Class attribute.

```
<H1 Class="SpecialHeader">Header Using CSS</h1>
```

This header will use the properties defined in the .SpecialHeader selector. The interesting thing about CSS is that you define only what you need. If the standard H1 selector provides formatting not found in the .SpecialHeader selector, CSS will continue using the H1 selector formatting. Likewise, all headers will use any properties you define in the Body selector that don't appear in the H1 selector. When working with CSS it's important to remember that a property always has a value once you define it and that you have to override any values you want to change.

Working with Microsoft Using the Web Toolbar

Microsoft provides some help information with Visual Web Developer and you can look at additional resources online. Using the internal help system means that you can find information quickly without leaving the IDE. You can set this option in the Help folder of the Options dialog box you access using the Tools ➤ Options command. Select between the internal and external help format using the Show Help Using field setting. When you do use internal help, you also have access to the Web toolbar for working with help. Figure 4.21 shows this toolbar and the following list describes the various toolbar elements.

FIGURE 4.21
Interact with internal help or directly with Microsoft to learn more about Visual Web Developer.

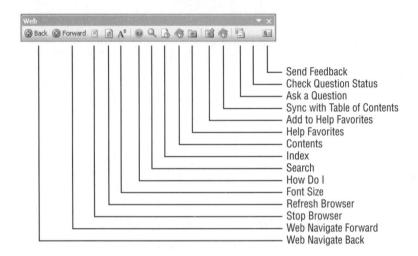

Send Feedback   Sends feedback about the product to Microsoft. When you click this option, the IDE displays a survey type form that you fill out and submit. Someone at Microsoft will review your suggestion and possibly implement it. You generally don't receive feedback when using this option.

Ask a Question and Check Question Status   Accesses the Microsoft newsgroups. When you click Ask a Question, the IDE displays a list of newsgroups where you can ask a question. Click Check Question Status later to determine whether someone has answered your query. This feature relies on a combination of peer and Microsoft help (with a strong emphasis on peer help). When you click Check Question Status, the IDE checks your messages on the newsgroups and provides any feedback you've received.

Sync with Table of Contents   Synchronizes an entry in the Search dialog box or the Index with the table of contents. This feature lets you see where the current topic appears in the hierarchical topic listing. Often, this feature can help you locate related topics that other search techniques might not find. For example, you could use it to locate the next step in a procedure.

Help Favorites and Add to Help Favorites   Displays and adds a topic to the Help Favorites listing in the Help Favorites dialog box. Click Help Favorites to display the Help Favorites dialog box. You can click any of the entries in the Help Topics or Help Searches listings to revisit parts of the helps system that you visited previously. Click Add to Help Favorites when you want to add a new topic to the listing. This feature ensures that you can locate hard-to-find topics when you need them.

Contents, Index, and Search   Displays the Contents, Index, or Search features of the help system. You use these three features to locate topics in the help system. Contents provides a hierarchical display of help topics. Index displays an alphabetical list of common help topics. You can perform a word search using the search feature.

How Do I   Displays a list of how to articles for the product. You can select one of these topics to obtain step-by-step procedures for performing a given task.

Font Size   Modifies the font size of the Help view and associated windows. Larger fonts make the display easier to read and smaller fonts present more information in the same space.

Refresh Browser and Stop Browser   Controls the internal browser actions. The Help view is actually a browser and it displays Web pages. Refreshing the browser displays new content that the Web pages might contain after an update. You can click Stop Browser to end a long download.

Web Navigate Forward and Web Navigate Back   Moves to the next or previous page in the Web page history. The IDE maintains a record of the pages that you visit, so you can move between pages you have already viewed. Click Forward when you want to move to the next page in the list and Back when you want to see the previous page.

Defining Your Development Goals

This is the first chapter to mention the concepts of layout, formatting, graphics, and design, but it won't be the last. The appearance of your Web application follows closely behind its content and usability. Unfortunately, at least a few Web sites seem to consider appearance as the only goal and fail in both content and usability. This chapter also helps you avoid that problem by keeping the issue of appearance where it belongs—as a means to dress up your content.

Now it's time to try these technologies yourself. The only problem with Microsoft's sample application is that it attempts to do everything. Consequently, it's easy to confuse the roles that the various technologies discussed in this chapter play and see their advantages and disadvantages. A better way to work with these technologies at the outset is to create your own Web applications that use just one technology at first. When you're satisfied that you understand a single technology, move on to using two at a time, and finally try all three at once. Only after you've seen how the technologies work alone and together can you gain a full appreciation of what they can do for your Web application.

Most Web sites contain a mix of static and dynamic (changing) pages. A user might view a historical page about a company that doesn't require anything more than serving up the data. Another page might include a survey that asks the user about the Web experience—this page requires support by the server to process the input that the user provides. Still another page could describe the current results of an ongoing event—this is where dynamic content comes into play. You don't know what the page will contain until it's time to serve it up. Chapter 5 helps you discover all of these kinds of interaction and more. It's your next step to creating a truly spectacular Web application.

Chapter 5

Building Intelligent Pages

You can create static pages with Visual Web Developer. Nothing prevents you from creating any kind of page you want. Theoretically, you can even develop pages that rely on other languages, should you wish to do so. However, one of the real reasons to use Visual Web Developer is to create Web pages with intelligence—essentially a Web page that can react to system, user, or environmental events. For example, the Web page might do one thing when the user clicks Submit on a form and quite another when it discovers a virus entered in one of the fields on the submitted form.

Intelligence can occur in one of two places: the server or the client. This chapter helps you understand server-side intelligence, the kind that's used most often with complex Web development technologies such as database applications or those that have to service a broad range of device types. Chapter 6 discusses client-side intelligence, which offloads part of the processing burden from the server and provides better performance in many cases. The kind of intelligence you use for a Web application depends on the effect you're trying to produce and the level of trust the code must have. In some cases, you'll use both kinds of intelligence in one Web application.

Before you can choose which kind of intelligence to use, you need to know what you can do at each end of the communication. This chapter discusses several kinds of server-side communication that you can perform including such tasks as discovering the client browser and how it's configured, as well as simple form processing. You'll also discover how to use eXtensible Markup Language (XML) in place of standard HyperText Markup Language (HTML) to create a simple Web page. The use of XML makes it easier to store content in a database in a form that you can easily modify.

Finally, this chapter discusses an important user issue—one that's becoming increasingly important. Users have an expectation that you'll protect their identity from anyone outside your organization. They also expect you to keep their email address quiet and want to know precisely how you use any information they do provide. This chapter addresses all of these issues.

NOTE   For the purposes of this book, the term *cracker* will refer to an individual who's breaking into a system on an unauthorized basis. It also refers to someone who places software on your system without obtaining your permission first. *Cracking* includes any form of illegal activity on the system such as stealing your identity. On the other hand, the term *hacker* will refer to someone who performs authorized (legal) low-level system activities, including testing system security. Hackers also help find undocumented solutions for many computer needs and create workarounds for both hardware and software problems. In some cases, you need to employ the services of a good hacker to test the security measures you have in place, or suffer the consequences of a break-in.

Understanding Server-side Intelligence

An intelligent Web page includes some type of code—the component that provides the intelligence. Of course, the Web page isn't actually intelligent—it doesn't think or do anything creative, but it does react in a specific way to certain events based on the prerecorded instructions you provide. For example, an intelligent Web page can calculate a total based on the algorithm you provide. The location where the code executes determines certain characteristics of the intelligence. Server-side intelligence means that the server executes the code required to provide Web page intelligence, which provides the following characteristics.

Secure data processing   Using server-side processing reduces security risks for the company or individual providing the data because it provides better control over the data. Nothing leaves the server without getting checked and processed first—at least not if the code is written correctly.

Fewer client requirements   Clients come in all shapes and sizes, so you can't be sure that the client will have the processing power required to perform any work locally. Even when the client has the required processing power, some browsers don't provide all the required support, so you can't tell whether the application will work unless you make a particular browser a requirement. Unfortunately, most browsers include configuration settings that let the user turn off scripting and cookies (with good reason given some of the crackers on the Internet today), so the right browser still doesn't mean that the application will run. In short, clients are unpredictable, so server-side processing is often necessary when you want to make absolutely certain that the application will run.

Consistent results   Using server-side processing exclusively means that the client receives only HTML tags. With a little extra effort, you can ensure that all of the clients you want to support understand the tags the server sends. The Webmonkey chart at `http://webmonkey.wired.com/webmonkey/reference/browser_chart/index.html` (and associated charts with links on this page) can help you determine the kinds of tags that the clients you want to support can understand. For example, if you want to support Internet Explorer 4.0 users, then you can't use eXtensible Markup Language (XML) as an alternative form of data transmission.

Easier debugging   Because the server sends out completed data and all of the processing occurs on the server, you don't have to worry about what the client is doing. The debugging process is easier because you don't have to consider as many variables when you create the application. All you really need to know is what you expect as input from the client, how the server processes that input, and what the client should get as output.

Better stability and reliability   Distributed applications do have many advantages, but they also incur stability and reliability problems. A distributed application—one that relies on a combination of client and server processing—is less stable because both systems must process the data without error and there's less tolerance for even small errors. Reliability also decreases as a factor of the number of failure points—adding client-side processing increases the number of failure points.

Server-side intelligence isn't a one-time process—it's ongoing, just as client-side processing is. The server can process information at several times and in a variety of ways. Here are the most common techniques.

Initial request   A server can read the client's request header (the part of the message that describes the client and its request) during the initial request. It can then offer a response that better meets client needs or information in certain form.

NOTE   Normally, you don't need to worry much about the request or response headers for messages. Request headers are always part of a request message and describe the client making the request. For example, you can learn that the client can accept text output, but not some forms of graphical output. Response headers always describe the server and the processing that it performs to the client. For example, when the server sends one response header, the client knows that an error has occurred, but another response header tells the client that the request succeeded.

After login   The login process, even when you don't see a login screen, requires an initial request, a server response requesting the login information, and a client response with the required login information. At this point, the server knows the identity of the client and can tailor the page content to meet that client's needs. Of course, this assumes there's a login process—many public Web sites don't include one.

Preprocessing   Preprocessing occurs after the server receives the request, but before it does anything with it. In many cases, this is the point in the cycle where the server decides what to do with the request—where to direct it. For example, a request might include invalid data, so the server would send it to an error response, rather than a data processing response. The error response would handle problems such as scripts sent in data fields, rather than the data the server was expecting.

Response   The response is the event that everyone thinks about when it comes to server-side processing. This part of the cycle looks at the input data, decides what to do with it, calculates any results, requests any information from the database, and puts an output page together. The response also considers some special user needs and customizes the output. For example, a potential customer accessing your Web site will require different information from a sales representative on the road.

Post processing   Sometimes a response requires additional tweaking or you might need to verify the response in some way. Post processing provides a means of looking at the entire message, including response headers, to ensure that the client will react in the right way.

Detecting the Client Configuration

The many charts and graphs available on the Internet depicting various browser capabilities and features point to one conclusion—knowing your client can help you provide a better experience for the user. For example, if you find that a client doesn't support I-frames (inline frames that let you embed data from multiple sources as objects in a Web page, instead of using multiple pages accessed from a master page as standard frames use), you can use standard frames or tables for organizational needs instead. A client that doesn't support graphics could use text descriptions instead. The possibilities are endless. The point is that you have to know something about the client to obtain the information.

The problem is that many users now run special applications that block your access to information about the client. You can't determine anything about the client because the user wants to remain completely anonymous. It's not that the user is being contrary or trying to make your life hard. Many Web sites prey on users by detecting them and following them wherever they go. The user ends up with tons of unwanted spam email, pop-ups, pop-unders (windows that appear under the browser in an attempt to be less intrusive), and, in some cases, even identity theft. For many users, your act of customization is a kind thought, but they'd rather not have it at the cost of their identity.

Developers use several techniques to work around this problem. One of the easiest is to ask the user if their browser supports a specific feature. The user selects an option on the Web page and you can customize the input as needed. The only problem is that this solution relies on the user to have the required knowledge—depending on your Web site, many users won't.

Right after you get over the blank expressions on the faces of some users, you can try another alternative. Many browsers now provide a means to let the user trust just your site, without trusting every site on the Internet. For example, when working with Internet Explorer, you can instruct the user to add your site to their Trusted Site zone. To perform this task, select the Tools ➤ Internet Options command. You'll see the Internet Options dialog box. Select the Security tab and highlight the Trusted Site entry to enable the Sites button shown in Figure 5.1.

FIGURE 5.1
Internet Explorer uses the concept of security zones to improve flexibility.

At this point, you can click Sites to display the Trusted Sites dialog box shown in Figure 5.2. Type the URL for the site that you want to trust in the Add This Web Site To The Zone field and click Add. Click OK to make the change permanent. Generally, this change lets you detect the user's client configuration.

FIGURE 5.2
Add the Web site that you want to trust to the list of trusted sites.

You can finally detect the client settings without asking the user many questions that the user might not know how to answer. To perform this task, create a new Web page. Open Solution Explorer, right-click the Default.ASPX.VB entry, and choose Open from the context menu. You'll see the Source view. At the top of Source view, you'll see two fields. Choose form1 in the Class field and Load in the Method Name field. Your display should look like the one shown in Figure 5.3.

FIGURE 5.3
Create a Load event handler that contains the code required to detect the client.

This example uses the Load() event of the form to automatically process the client settings. This event occurs every time you load the form in the browser, so anything you place here happens before you actually see the form on screen. In this case, the form displays the client settings so you can see them, but normally you'll use the code to customize the Web page in some way. Listing 5.1 contains the code you need to perform this task.

LISTING 5.1:   Detecting the Browser Information

```
Private Sub form1_Load(ByVal sender As Object, _
                    ByVal e As System.EventArgs) Handles form1.Load

    Dim Output As New StringBuilder ' Contains the output information.
    Dim Counter As Int32            ' Loop counter variable.
    Dim AgentString As String()     ' A list of user agent values.

    ' Display a heading.
    Output.Append(vbTab + "<h1>Request Header Information</h1>" + _
                vbCrLf)

    ' Get the method used to request the information.
    Output.Append(vbTab + "<h2>Request Type</h2>" + vbCrLf)
    Output.Append(vbTab + vbTab + Request.HttpMethod + vbCrLf)

    ' Get the kind of files the client will accept.
    Output.Append(vbTab + "<h2>Client File Types</h2>" + vbCrLf)

    ' Get the number of file types.
    Output.Append(vbTab + vbTab + "Number of File Types: " + _
                Request.AcceptTypes.Length.ToString() + "</br>" + _
                vbCrLf)
```

```
    ' Get the individual file types.
    For Counter = 0 To Request.AcceptTypes.Length - 1
        Output.Append(vbTab + vbTab)
        Output.Append(Request.AcceptTypes.GetValue(Counter).ToString())
        Output.Append("</br>" + vbCrLf)
    Next

    ' Get the User Agent, which includes the browser type.
    AgentString = Request.UserAgent.Split(Convert.ToChar(";"))
    Output.Append(vbTab + "<h2>User Agent Information</h2>" + vbCrLf)
    For Counter = 0 To AgentString.Length - 1
        Output.Append(vbTab + vbTab)
        Output.Append(AgentString.GetValue(Counter).ToString().Trim())
        Output.Append("</br>" + vbCrLf)
    Next

    ' Get the browser capabilities, a special feature available to
    ' ASP.NET developers.
    Output.Append(vbTab + "<h2>Browser Capabilities</h2>" + vbCrLf)
    Output.Append(vbTab + vbTab + "Supports ActiveX Controls: ")
    Output.Append(IIf(Request.Browser.ActiveXControls, "Yes", "No"))
    Output.Append("</br>" + vbCrLf + vbTab + vbTab + _
                "America Online Browser: ")
    Output.Append(IIf(Request.Browser.AOL, "Yes", "No"))
    Output.Append("</br>" + vbCrLf + vbTab + vbTab + _
                "Plays Background Sounds: ")
    Output.Append(IIf(Request.Browser.BackgroundSounds, "Yes", "No"))

    ' Place the output on the form.
    form1.InnerHtml = Output.ToString()
End Sub
```

This example shows a few techniques that can come in very handy when building a Web page using code. One of the techniques you might wonder about at first is the addition of all of the vbTab and vbCrLf constants in the code. You probably won't insert this code when creating a production application because you won't really care about the appearance of the code in the Web page. However, when you create code for testing purposes, the white space does matter. When you view this Web page, right-click the page and choose View Source from the context menu. You'll see the code that the server actually creates for the browser, including the code that you specifically output as shown in Figure 5.4.

The highlighted code in Figure 5.4 shows the output that the code in Listing 5.1 produces, which begs the question of what all of the other code is. The server produces the other code automatically. For example, the server has to create a package in which to store the Web page, so it automatically adds features such as the <HTML> and <BODY> tags. The hidden __VIEWSTATE control provides status information to the server that you don't have to maintain.

FIGURE 5.4

Adding white space is
important when you
want to view the code
that the server outputs.

FIGURE 5.4

Adding white space is important when you want to view the code that the server outputs.

The next element is the use of the `StringBuilder` control. Relying on the `StringBuilder` control, `Output`, provides a performance boost to the Web application. Standard `String` objects can't grow in Visual Basic, but `StringBuilder` objects can. Whenever you add text to a standard `String` in Visual Basic, CLR actually creates a new `String` object—it doesn't use the old one. Creating the new object takes time that you don't have to expend when using a `StringBuilder`. The downside to using a `StringBuilder` is that it does use more resources than a `String`—essentially, you're trading memory for improved performance in this case.

The example code shows several techniques for gaining access to information that the client provides. All of the techniques rely on accessing the `Request` object—an object that you obtain automatically and don't have to create, it contains the request information from the client. A second object, `Response`, defines the information that the server sends to the client. You use the `Response` object to manipulate the output as a whole, rather than affect just a single page's features.

The first technique shows how to obtain the request method from the client. The request method determines how the client and server communicate. The "Deciding between the GET and POST Data Handling Methods" section later in this chapter describes this issue in more detail. However, look at the code in this case. You can access the `Request.HttpMethod` property directly—no manipulation needed.

The second technique shows that some of the information resides in arrays or collections. In this case, the `AcceptTypes` property is an array where you need to use the `GetValue()` method to obtain a specific element by passing an index (`Counter`). The code obtains the number of elements using the `AcceptTypes.Length` property and used this value to loop through the values.

The third technique shows how to work with encoded data. In this case, `UserAgent` is a string with multiple values separated by a semicolon (;). You could display the string directly, but you wouldn't work with this value as a string in an application. The code shows how to use the `Split()` method to separate the strings so you can examine them using a loop. It's also possible to the `IndexOf()` method to locate a particular value when you know which value you need.

The fourth technique shows a special capability of ASP.NET. In this case, the code accesses the `Browser` object, which contains a number of Boolean property values. The example shows just a few of these values—there are many others and you should spend some time reviewing them. In this case, the code checks whether the browser supports ActiveX controls (`ActiveXControls` property), is a browser provided by America Online (`AOL` property), and supports background sounds using the `<BGSound>` tag (`BackgroundSounds` property). When a browser supports ActiveX controls but the user has this support turned off, the control appears as a box with a red X through it—you have no way of detecting whether the control actually works or not. You can place a message in the `<Object>` tag so the user sees the message, rather than the nondescript box. Simply type the text within the `<Object>` tag like this:

```
<OBJECT CLASSID="CLSID:812AE312-8B8E-11CF-93C8-00AA00C08FDF"
        ID="MyComponent">
    If you see this message without a corresponding pushbutton, then
    your browser doesn't support ActiveX controls.
</OBJECT>
```

The code ends by outputting the information. The `form1` object is the name of the `<FORM>` tag on the Web page—you can access it directly because this is a code behind file. The `InnerHtml` property contains the HTML for this tag, so setting it to `Output.ToString()` fills the property with the information that the example collects. Figure 5.5 shows the output from this example.

The output tells you a lot about the client. For example, this client used the Get method to access the Web site—this is the most common technique for an initial request unless the client already has intimate knowledge of the server (as when using a Web service). The `*/*` output for file types tells you that this client can accept any file type—at least it will try to. However, this value doesn't necessarily mean that the client will understand the file or that the user can work with it—simply that the browser can accept the file.

FIGURE 5.5
The client can provide a lot of configuration information that you can use to tailor a Web page.

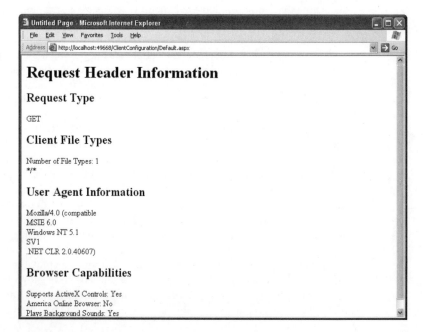

The user agent information is especially interesting. Notice that it tells you that this browser is Mozilla compatible—a requirement for non-IIS Web servers in many cases. The next line tells you that the browser is Microsoft Internet Explorer 6.0 and that it's operating on a Windows NT 5.1 (Windows XP) system. The SV1 tells you that the system has Service Pack 2 installed. You can learn more about what this means to the Web application at `http://msdn.microsoft.com/security/default.aspx?pull=/library/en-us/dnwxp/html/xpsp2web.asp`. Finally, the last line tells you that the client is running the .NET Framework 2.0.

ASP.NET does provide you with many advantages in quickly determining the browser status. As previously mentioned, the last section of the output shows various status indicators. In this case, the browser can work with ActiveX components, it isn't an AOL browser, and it can work with background sounds.

Working with Forms

Forms are an essential part of Web page development because they help you exchange information with a user. The `<Form>` tag in a Web page has the same connotation as a form you use at your desk. Generally, forms let you send a request for information to a user and provide feedback about the information the user provides. In most cases, forms contain a description of the kind of data needed, the reason you need the data, specific descriptions of each data element, and fields the user fills out.

Don't get the idea that computer forms are something you get only with ASP.NET. You can also create forms using standard HTML. The number of controls you can access are a lot more limited, but developers have used standard HTML for years with good success. Consequently, you need to consider both HTML and ASP.NET solutions when working with forms—some simple forms might work better and improve performance when you use straight HTML.

Exchanging data between a client and server isn't quite as easy as giving a form to a supervisor. Forms have specific criteria for exchanging data—a protocol (set of rules) determines how the exchange takes place. For example, you won't place your form in the supervisor's in basket if the supervisor isn't in the office. Likewise, computer forms have rules that the following sections examine and explain.

Of course, there's the little matter of getting the data you want. Fortunately, you don't have to rely on the controls that HTML provides—you also have access to a number of useful and interesting ASP.NET 2.0 controls as well. The last section examines these controls and provides pointers on using them to create extremely flexible forms.

Deciding between the GET and POST Data Handling Methods

Whenever you create a form, you need to decide how the form should interact with the server. For example, you must decide whether the client will use the GET or the POST method to send information to the server. The method appears as part of the `<form>` tag, as shown here. (Note that the use of the term method isn't related to objects it in this case—it refers to the technique used to transfer the data.)

```
<body>
    <form name="MySurvey"
          id="MySurvey"
          action="HTMLPage.htm"
          method="get">
    </form>
</body>
```

As you can see, the `<form>` tag normally appears within the `<body>` tag and includes four attributes as a minimum. The `name` attribute defines the form name and is how you reference the form when you receive the data. The `id` attribute identifies the form and lets you interact with it in both code behind (when using ASP.NET) and script (available for both ASP.NET and HTML developers). The `action` attribute defines where the client sends the data. Finally, the `method` attribute defines how the client and server exchange data.

In many cases, it doesn't matter whether you use the GET or POST method for a form. Both techniques send data to the server. However, any server-side coding must know what to expect from the form, so the techniques aren't interchangeable, but the results are the same. The receiving page must use the correct data transmission method. Fortunately, you can use the `Request.HttpMethod` property to determine whether the client used the GET or POST method. In fact, you could provide code that accepts data using either method to ensure that the page always works.

The POST method sends the information from the client to the server using the request header. Many developers prefer the POST method because the browser's Address field remains clean and it's less likely that the user will modify the contents of the data sent to the server. Unfortunately, the POST technique really doesn't keep the data that much safer—a determined cracker can still access it. Use the POST technique on sites where you want to maintain some level of data hiding. For example, many sites use it for Web services or confidential information sent using an encryption technique such as Secure Sockets Layer (SSL).

The GET method sends the data as part of the address. For example, you might fill out a form that includes your name and a submission button. The address line could look like this after you submit the data.

```
http://localhost:25860/Forms/HTMLPage.htm?txtName=John&btnSubmit=Send+Data
```

The question mark (?) defines the end of the URL and the beginning of the data. Each entry consists of a control name, such as `txtName`, an equal sign (=) and the data value, such as `John`. Each control is separated by an ampersand (&). Some Web sites actually encourage use of the GET method because they want users to maintain the list of values they sent to the server. For example, search pages often rely on the values stored as part of a URL to return the user to the same place without having them fill out the search form again. In fact, some users rely on this behavior to modify the arguments that appear as part of the URL to obtain better results or even create a list of URLs on a custom Web page. For example, you can store these values as shortcuts in Internet Explorer.

Understanding the Four Levels of Data Processing

You have choices to make when it comes to working with data passed by the client. ASP.NET 2.0 actually supports four levels of data processing—the GET method, the POST method, the control method, and a combination of all three. All of these methods rely on the `Request` object. The property you use determines the data you receive from ASP.NET 2.0. Here are the four processing techniques (including three properties) that you need to consider.

QueryString   Contains the values passed using the GET method. ASP.NET automatically separates the data into name-value pairs so that you can use the variable name to access its value.

Form   Contains the values passed using the POST method. ASP.NET automatically separates the data into name-value pairs so you can easily access the posted data by name.

Params   Contains all of the values in the `QueryString`, `Form`, `ServerVariables`, and `Cookies` properties. Because this property combines values from several sources, you can use it to look for data no matter what the source might be. The downside is that you have to sift through a lot of information that you don't need.

Direct variable access   Allows direct manipulation of data values. Unlike HTML tags, you can also access ASP.NET controls (`<asp:control>` tags) directly by name. This means that you can control property values directly as well.

Processing Input Using the GET Method

One of the best ways to begin learning how to process information is to use the GET method. All of the information appears as part of the address—the communication technique doesn't hide anything. In addition, you can use simple HTML tags for the data, which simplifies the actual Web page. This example relies on the simple form shown in Figure 5.6.

FIGURE 5.6
This form contains three simple controls: a label, a textbox, and a submit button.

The example relies on simple HTML tags so you know that the example isn't using any odd ASP.NET technology. You could create this page using a simple HTML document, but the use of ASPX allows code behind. When working with an HTML page, you'd use a script for processing—something that you'll discover in Chapter 6.

The code behind for this example relies on the Load event. Whenever the page loads, the example looks for a specific set of criteria and processes the Web page. Listing 5.2 shows the code for this example.

LISTING 5.2:   Processing GET Method Input Data Using Code Behind

```
Private Sub Page_Load(ByVal sender As Object, _
                      ByVal e As System.EventArgs) Handles Me.Load
    Dim DataOut As StringBuilder    ' Output string.
    Dim ProcOut As StringBuilder    ' Individual query string values.
    Dim Variable As String          ' Single query string variable.

    'Perform processing only after the user sees the initial form.
    If Page.IsPostBack Then

        ' Create the output tags.
        DataOut = New StringBuilder
        DataOut.Append("<h1>Data Output</h1>" + vbCrLf)
        DataOut.Append("<label id='lblOutput' for='txtOutput'>" + _
```

```
                                    "Values: </label>" + vbCrLf)
            DataOut.Append("<textarea id='txtOutput' name='txtOutput' " + _
                           "readonly rows='5' cols='80'>")

            ' Get the input variables, if any, and display them.
            ProcOut = New StringBuilder
            If Request.QueryString.Count > 0 Then

                ' Every variable is a unique entry.
                For Each Variable In Request.QueryString
                    ProcOut.Append(Variable)
                    ProcOut.Append(" equals ")

                    ' Access the variable value by using the variable name.
                    ProcOut.Append( _
                        Request.QueryString.GetValues(Variable).GetValue(0))
                    ProcOut.Append(vbCrLf)
                Next
                DataOut.Append(ProcOut.ToString())
            Else
                DataOut.Append("No Variables")
            End If

            ' End the <textarea> tag.
            DataOut.Append("</textarea>")

            ' Output the response.
            frmGetForm.InnerHtml = DataOut.ToString()
        End If

    End Sub
```

The code begins by declaring variables it needs to process the data. It then checks the Page.IsPostBack property. This Boolean property tells you whether the user has just loaded the page or has clicked Send to transmit the data. (A postback occurs when a control posts information back to the server—it's a communication from the client to the server.) When this value is true, the user has clicked Send and the code can begin processing the data.

The first few lines of code create some HTML tags to display on screen using a StringBuilder, DataOut. Theoretically, you can get by without ever generating any HTML tags manually when using pure ASP.NET code, but reality is often different—it's good to know that you at least have the option of generating the tags when needed. The last part of the tag code creates an open <textarea> tag that contains the output data for the example.

You need a second StringBuilder, ProcOut, to hold the processed output. The processing code begins by checking the number of query strings values available using the Request.QueryString.Count property. When there's at least one value to process, the code uses a For Each loop to process the values. Remember that the QueryString property contains data sent using the GET method only, so it won't contain any other values (even if you send them using some other method).

The For Each loop places each member of the Request.QueryString collection into Variable in turn. The code places the variable name into ProcOut, followed by the word equals and the variable value. The Request.QueryString.GetValues(Variable).GetValue(0) property contains the value. It's possible to simply use the Get() method to obtain a value as well (see the next section "Processing Input Using the POST Method" for details). This method is convenient when the input has variables with multiple values.

The code ends by assigning the ProcOut value to DataOut, closing the <textarea> tag, and placing the result in the frmGetForm.InnerHtml property. Figure 5.7 shows typical output for this application. The technique shown in this example provides you with complete output, including all of the hidden variables that ASP.NET generates. Interestingly enough, this particular technique is helpful for trouble-shooting your Web pages. You can use it to detect problems with inputs as you build and debug the application. It's also possible to view odd problems, such as when you fail to escape a control character such as a space (usually replaced with a plus sign).

FIGURE 5.7

This example processes all of the GET variables, even those that ASP.NET generates automatically.

Processing Input Using the POST Method

The POST method places values in the request header, but you can't gain access to the data using the Request.Headers property. ASP.NET 2.0 separates this information and places it in the Request.Form property instead. However, it's important to know where the data really resides should you ever need to perform low-level troubleshooting. This example uses the same front-end page shown in Figure 5.6, but processes the information differently, as shown in Listing 5.3.

LISTING 5.3:   Processing POST Method Input Data Using Code Behind

```
Private Sub Page_Load(ByVal sender As Object,
                      ByVal e As System.EventArgs) Handles Me.Load

    Dim DataOut As StringBuilder    ' Output string.

    'Perform processing only after the user sees the initial form.
    If Page.IsPostBack Then
```

```
' Create the output tags.
DataOut = New StringBuilder
DataOut.Append("<br/>" + vbCrLf + _
               "<label id='lblOutput' for='txtOutput' " + _
               ">Input Value: </label>" + vbCrLf)
DataOut.Append("<input type='text' id='txtDataEntry' " + _
               "name='txtDataEntry' readonly value=")

' Get the input variables, if any, and display them.
If Request.Form.Count > 0 Then

    ' Get the input value directly.
    If Request.Form.Get("txtDataEntry").Length > 0 Then
        DataOut.Append("'")
        DataOut.Append(Request.Form.Get("txtDataEntry"))
        DataOut.Append("'")
    Else
        DataOut.Append("'Input Value is Blank'")
    End If

Else
    DataOut.Append("No Variables")
End If

    ' End the <textbox> tag.
DataOut.Append("/ >" + vbCrLf)

    ' Output the response.
    frmPostForm.InnerHtml = _
        frmPostForm.InnerHtml + DataOut.ToString()
End If

End Sub
```

The code still begins by creating a few variables and checking whether the user has clicked Send using the Page.IsPostBack property value. In this case, the code produces tags to add to the existing page, rather than overwrite the existing page with new data. Consequently, the tags include a spacing tag, <br /> to provide some additional white space for the output.

This application uses a standard textbox for output. The code still checks Request.Form.Count to verify that there are variables to process. The Request.Form.Get("txtDataEntry").Length check verifies that the txtDataEntry variable contains data. If the variable does contain data, the code uses Request.Form.Get("txtDataEntry") to obtain the value directly. This code assumes that you're working with a single string, not a complex value of some sort.

In this case, the code ends by closing the <textbox> tag. The code then appends the additional data to the end of frmPostForm, so you'll see the original form, plus the new data. Figure 5.8 shows typical results from this example.

FIGURE 5.8
Adding to an existing
Web page is relatively
easy in most cases.

Understanding the New ASP.NET 2.0 Controls

Although you can use standard HTML tags to control input on your Web page, it's a lot easier to use
ASP.NET controls. Previous versions of ASP.NET provide a modest assortment of controls that meet
most common needs, but developers always find something new to try and Microsoft added new controls to ASP.NET 2.0 to address many of these needs. Figure 5.9 shows the standard preselected controls
available to ASP.NET developers.

FIGURE 5.9
ASP.NET 2.0 provides
myriad controls to
address a multitude
of needs.

TIP The Toolbox defaults to a list view of the controls. The list view includes the icon followed by a
descriptive name. This view works best when you dock the Toolbox to the side of the IDE and need to
locate controls quickly. To see the view shown in Figure 5.9, undock the Toolbox. Right-click anywhere
within an area and clear the List View option from the context menu. The descriptive text will disappear and all you'll see is the icon. Hover the mouse over an icon to see the descriptive text.

Some of the controls did appear in previous versions of ASP.NET. For example, if you used previous versions of ASP.NET, you already know about items such as the Textbox control. The controls on the Navigation tab owe their start to FrontPage. Even though these controls aren't a direct copy of the FrontPage equivalents, you'll notice definite similarities if you used FrontPage in the past. The controls on the Login and WebParts tabs are new for ASP.NET 2.0 and you'll use them in several examples in the book. The controls on the HTML tab are the ones that several of the examples in this chapter use.

As you can see from the Toolbox, each group of controls performs a specific task in a particular manner. If you decide that you don't want to use HTML controls, you can simply close the HTML tab or remove the tab from view. To remove a tab from the list, right-click the tab entry and choose Delete Tab from the context menu. Likewise, when you want to add a new tab, right-click within the tab area and choose Add Tab from the context menu. If you end up making a mess of the whole thing, simply right-click the Toolbox and choose Reset Toolbox from the context menu. Of course, using this option resets all of the options and any changes you made are gone for good.

At some point, you might find that you want to use other controls. You can download controls from the Internet, use existing Component Object Model (COM) controls installed on your machine, or create new controls of your own. To add the controls to the Toolbox, right-click the tab where you want the control to appear and select Choose Items from the context menu. You'll see the Choose Toolbox Items dialog box shown in Figure 5.10.

FIGURE 5.10
Add either .NET or COM controls to your Toolbox as needed.

The first thing you'll notice is that even the .NET Framework Components tab contains a number of controls that don't appear in the Toolbox. To add a new item to the Toolbox tab you selected, check the box next to the component name and click OK. The new controls will appear in the Toolbox. Likewise, to remove a control that you no longer want, clear the check box next to the item name. The COM Components tab contains a list of COM components installed on your system. You can select any of the controls that appear in the list.

WARNING   Don't assume that every COM control is going to work with .NET. In fact, some won't because .NET won't be able to build an appropriate compatibility layer. Make sure you run appropriate tests whenever you try to use a COM control in an application. When a control fails in some way, it's usually best to find a .NET alternative if possible.

Using the ASP.NET 2.0 Controls

Using controls to create and manage your Web page has definite advantages over using HTML tags. For one thing, you now have two methods of working with the input data. You can still use the techniques for working with the GET or POST method (depending on how you set up the form) or you can work with the controls directly. Listing 5.4 shows how to use both techniques.

LISTING 5.4:   Managing Input Data Using Controls

```
Sub btnSubmit_Click(ByVal sender As Object,
                    ByVal e As System.EventArgs)
    Dim DataOut As StringBuilder    ' Output string.
    Dim Variable As String          ' Single query string variable.

    ' Create the output variable.
    DataOut = New StringBuilder

    ' Get the input variables, if any, and display them.
    If Request.QueryString.Count > 0 Then

        ' Every variable is a unique entry.
        For Each Variable In Request.QueryString
            DataOut.Append(Variable)
            DataOut.Append(" equals ")

            ' Access the variable value by using the variable name.
            DataOut.Append( _
                Request.QueryString.GetValues(Variable).GetValue(0))
            DataOut.Append(vbCrLf)
        Next
    Else
        DataOut.Append("No Variables")
    End If

    ' Output the GET response.
    lblOutputGet.Visible = True
    txtOutputGet.Visible = True
    txtOutputGet.Text = DataOut.ToString()

    ' Process the variables directly.
    DataOut = New StringBuilder
    DataOut.Append("txtDataEntry equals " + txtDataEntry.Text + vbCrLf)
    DataOut.Append("btnSubmit equals " + btnSubmit.Text)

    ' Output the variable response
    lblOutputVar.Visible = True
    txtOutputVar.Visible = True
    txtOutputVar.Text = DataOut.ToString()
End Sub
```

Notice that this example monitors the `Click` event of `btnSubmit`, rather than the `Load` event. This change means that you don't have to monitor post back status of the Web page to know when to process the data—the code only processes the data when the user clicks Submit. However, the code still monitors `Request.QueryString.Count` because there isn't any way to determine how many input variables the code will process.

The actual processing works much like the processor for HTML code shown in Listing 5.3. However, notice that the output technique is different. Rather than create a series of HTML tags and output them to the page, you now assign the data directly to a textbox, reducing the potential for error. In this case, the textbox remains hidden until it actually has data to display, so the initial display still looks like the one in Figure 5.6.

The real change for this example is working directly with the controls on the form. Notice that you don't have to use the `get` variables to access `txtDataEntry`, simply use the `Text` property. In fact, IntelliSense shows you all of the features that you can access with this control. Using these controls means making a trade-off. You gain all of the flexibility of working with real controls, but you also lose compatibility. Figure 5.11 shows typical output from this example.

FIGURE 5.11
Use any technique that works well for processing ASP.NET control input.

Using controls in this manner means that your page will never run on any server other than IIS and you lose control over how the system creates the output page. To see the actual output code, right-click the Web page and choose View Source from the context menu. You'll immediately see that the output is very different from the hand-coded HTML provided as output from the other examples.

Using XML Instead of HTML for Web Pages

Many companies have moved to XML for storing data because it's easy to transport and manipulate as needed for various presentations. Even if you haven't personally moved to using XML for data storage, it's quite likely that you'll encounter some form of XML while you work with Web pages. For example, some online media use XML to store the data you read, even though it looks like a standard Web page. In addition, all Web services rely on XML and some databases rely on it too. For example, you can output SQL Server data as XML and process it as a Web page. All of the latest Microsoft Office products read and output XML data too. Consequently, you need to know how to work with XML as a kind of Web page. Although the following sections don't provide a complete tutorial, they do give you a better understanding of the power of XML. (XML does appear in other sections of the book, so this won't be the only time you see it.)

Creating the XML Content

XML is a kind of data storage technology that relies on pure text to store the information. In many respects, XML looks like HTML, but the rules are a lot stricter. For example, an XML tag must always include a closing tag. The example in Listing 5.5 shows two address book records. The listing includes the most common XML information, so it's a good way to work with XML if you haven't done so in the past.

LISTING 5.5:   Typical XML Data Example

```
<?xml version="1.0" encoding="utf-8" ?>
<!-- This is a list of my personal names and addresses -->
<AddressBook Version="1.0">
    <!-- Each person record contains the person's name and
         address, as well as one or more telephone numbers. A
         person record can also include special notes and other
         personal data. -->
    <Person>
        <Name>George Smith</Name>
        <Address>
            <AddressLine>1234 West Street</AddressLine>
            <AddressLine>Suite 20</AddressLine>
        </Address>
        <City>Somewhere</City>
        <State>WI</State>
        <ZIP_Code>54001</ZIP_Code>
        <Telephone>
            <Number Location="Home">(555)555-1212</Number>
        </Telephone>
        <PersonalData>
            <Note Type="TimeToCall" Hour="PM">
                8:30
            </Note>
            <Note Type="SpouseName">
                Nancy
            </Note>
        </PersonalData>
    </Person>
```

```
<Person>
   <Name>Amy Wright</Name>
   <Address>
      <AddressLine>99 Lear Street</AddressLine>
   </Address>
   <City>Edge</City>
   <State>CA</State>
   <ZIP_Code>99122</ZIP_Code>
   <Telephone>
      <Number Location="Office">(555)555-1234</Number>
      <Number Location="Home">(555)555-9876</Number>
   </Telephone>
   <PersonalData />
</Person>
</AddressBook>
```

The first line of code is an XML processing instruction. Every XML document must contain the `<?xml ?>` processing instruction. However, you'll encounter other processing instructions in XML documents. An XML processing instruction always includes two angle brackets, with enclosing question marks and the processing instruction name. The `<?xml ?>` processing instruction normally includes the `version` and `encoding` attributes. Attributes always appear as name and value pairs separated by an equals sign as shown in the listing. The values must appear in single or double quotes as shown—the name always appears without quotes.

The second line of code shows a typical comment. Comments always appear within an angle bracket pair that includes an exclamation mark (`<!-- -->`). The XML parser ignores any text within a comment and a comment can appear on multiple lines.

Every XML document includes a root element that contains all of the other elements in the document. In this case, `<AddressBook>` is the root element. The `<AddressBook>` element contains a single attribute, `Version`, which identifies the version of this document. The version number is optional, but it's a good idea to give your documents version numbers so that you know how to process them as your XML coding technology evolves. You'll find that XML documents do change because the data configuration that looks great today might not work very well tomorrow.

The `<AddressBook>` table consists of `<Person>` element records. This example includes two records, but an XML document can contain any number of records you want. The `<Person>` element is a child of the `<AddressBook>` element, while the `<AddressBook>` element is the parent of all of the `<Person>` elements. XML relies on a hierarchical structure—many developers talk of the child and parent relationships between the various elements as a means of understanding the structure. Although XML doesn't require the use of white space, using line spacing and indentation as shown in Listing 5.5 is very helpful in understanding the various relationships.

Elements that appear at the end of the hierarchy are leaves. For example, `<AddressLine>1234 West Street</AddressLine>` is a leaf element because it appears at the end of the hierarchy. This leaf element includes an address, which is the element data. Elements can also contain other elements as shown in the listing. A leaf element that doesn't include data can include the closing tag at the end of the element like this:

```
<PersonalData />
```

The slash at the end of the tag closes the tag. You don't always need an opening and closing tag pair. Of course, it's legal to use an empty pair like this:

```
<PersonalData></PersonalData>
```

Because XML is hierarchical, it doesn't need to include blank elements unless your application expects a particular element. For example, notice that both records include a `<PersonalData>` element because the application is expecting to see it, but that the second record doesn't include any data for this element. Consequently, the second record doesn't include any `<Note>` elements, even though the first record includes two of them.

As you begin working with XML, you'll find that viewing the XML files in a text editor isn't always easy. You can view them in Visual Web Developer, but the IDE doesn't always provide a quick method of viewing the file and assumes that you have the IDE installed on every machine. Likewise, you can get a high-end XML tool such as XMLSpy (`http://www.xmlspy.com`), but again, this tool might not always be available. It turns out you can always rely on one tool no matter what machine you decide to use—the browser. Figure 5.12 shows an example of how an XML document appears in Internet Explorer.

FIGURE 5.12
Even a standard browser works for viewing XML files in many cases.

Internet Explorer even color codes the XML document for you, making it easy to determine whether a line of text is a comment or an element. If the document lacks white space, Internet Explorer adds it for you. The little dashes next to some of the entries in Figure 5.12 let you collapse a parent element so that the child elements remain hidden. This feature lets you view just the parts of the XML document that you actually want to see.

Interpreting the XML Using XSLT

As interesting as XML documents might appear, they really aren't very useful without some kind of interpretation. It turns out that you can create a special kind of XML document that tells a browser or other application how to interpret the XML file you create. The eXtensible Style Language Transformation (XSLT) file is a special kind of XML file that describes how to interpret the XML document. Listing 5.6 shows an example of an XSLT file that interprets the XML document shown in Listing 5.5.

LISTING 5.6:   Interpreting XML Data Using XSLT

```
<?xml version="1.0" encoding="utf-8"?>
<xsl:stylesheet version='1.0'
 xmlns:xsl='http://www.w3.org/1999/XSL/Transform'>
<xsl:output method="html" indent="yes" />
<xsl:template match="/AddressBook">

<HTML>
<HEAD>
    <TITLE>Personal Address List</TITLE>
</HEAD>

<BODY>
<H1>Personal Address List</H1>

<!-- Process all of the people in a loop. -->
<xsl:for-each select="Person">

    <!-- Display each record in a separate paragraph. -->
    <p>

    <!-- Get the person's name -->
    <xsl:value-of select="Name" />
    <br />

    <!-- Display the address information. -->
    <xsl:text>Address: </xsl:text>
    <xsl:value-of select="Address" /><br />
    <xsl:value-of select="City" />
    <xsl:text>, </xsl:text>
    <xsl:value-of select="State" />
    <xsl:text>     </xsl:text>
    <xsl:value-of select="ZIP_Code" /><br />


    <!-- Test to see whether the person has an office telephone. -->
    <xsl:if test="string(Telephone/Number/@Location) != 'Office'">
        <xsl:text>No Office Phone</xsl:text><br />
    </xsl:if>
```

```
    <!-- Process all of the telephone numbers. -->
    <xsl:for-each select="Telephone/Number">

        <!-- Display a telephone number and its length. -->
        <xsl:value-of select="@Location" />
        <xsl:text> Telephone Number: </xsl:text>
        <xsl:value-of select="." /><br />
        <xsl:text>The telephone number is </xsl:text>
        <xsl:value-of select="string-length(.)" />
        <xsl:text> digits long.</xsl:text><br />
    </xsl:for-each>

    <!-- Test for certain types of personal data and act on it. -->
    <xsl:for-each select="PersonalData/Note">
        <xsl:choose>
            <xsl:when test="string(@Type) = 'TimeToCall'">
                <xsl:text>Best Calling Time: </xsl:text>
                <xsl:value-of select="." />
                <xsl:value-of select="@Hour" /><br />
            </xsl:when>
            <xsl:when test="string(@Type) = 'SpouseName'">
                <xsl:text>Spouse Name: </xsl:text>
                <xsl:value-of select="." /><br />
            </xsl:when>
            <xsl:otherwise>
                <xsl:text>Note Type Not Recognized</xsl:text>
            </xsl:otherwise>
        </xsl:choose>
    </xsl:for-each>
    </p>

<!-- End of person processing. -->
</xsl:for-each>

</BODY>
</HTML>

</xsl:template>

</xsl:stylesheet>
```

The XSLT file starts with the same XML processing instruction as an XML document because it really is an XML document. The next line contains the root element for the document, `<xsl:stylesheet>`. The little "xsl" in front of the word stylesheet is a namespace reference. It tells the XML parser that this special kind of element requires instructions from a nonstandard location to understand. The `xmlns:xsl` attribute contains an XML namespace declaration for the `xsl` reference that includes the URL for the instructions.

XSLT files can create a broad range of output types. In fact, you can use them to create any kind of output that you want. Although most XSLT files create some type of text output, it's theoretically possible to create binary output as well. This particular XSLT file creates HTML as output. The `<xsl:output>` element identifies the kind of output, the `method` attribute tells the specific output type, and the `indent` attribute tells the parser to add white space to make the output easier to read. In short, this XSLT file is producing a Web page.

You need to tell the XSLT file where to start processing the input XML file. The `<xsl:template>` element tells the XSLT parser to match the `<AddressBook>` element—the root element of the sample XML file. It's possible to start processing an XML file at any point—you don't have to process the entire document.

At this point, you'll notice that the XSLT file contains standard HTML output. An XSLT file isn't pure XML—it contains a combination of data types. The XSLT parser outputs the HTML directly to the output (no matter what the output might be).

XSLT includes a number of programming instructions. This example shows a few of the common instructions, but there are many others. See the next section, "Learning More about XSLT," for resources that tell you about these other programming instructions. The example begins with a loop instruction, the `<xsl:for-each>` element. The `select` attribute tells the parser what kind of element to use as a looping variable. This loop processes every `<Person>` element in the XML file.

The next line of code is another piece of HTML—it's the open paragraph, `<p>`, tag. Within this tag, the XSLT places the extracted values of the `<Name>`, `<Address>`, `<City>`, `<State>`, and `<ZIP_Code>` elements using the `<xsl:value-of>` programming instruction. Notice how the `select` attribute tells the parser which element to work with.

XSLT understands HTML tags and XML elements, but it doesn't understand freestanding text. The `<xsl:text>` programming instruction tells the parser that the included information is text and not something that XSLT has to process. Notice how the example uses these elements to add identifying information to the various XML data entries.

At some point, you'll need to test values in the XML file to determine what course of action to pursue. The `<xsl:if>` programming instruction performs this task by using the value of the `test` attribute. When the test passes, the XSLT file performs any steps contained within the `<xsl:if>` element. Notice that the code uses a special test function to determine whether the `Location` attribute of the `<Number>` element has a value of `Office`. The `<xsl:if>` programming instruction doesn't include the concept of an `else` clause, so you have to perform every test directly.

Some of the XSLT programming instructions become a little complex. For example, many programming languages include a `Select Case` programming structure and XSLT is no exception. The case statements always appear within an `<xsl:choose>` element. Each of the selection criteria appear within a `<xsl:when>` element. Like the `<xsl:if>` programming instruction, you need to provide a test attribute that succeeds or fails. When the test succeeds, the XSLT parser interprets all of the statements within the `<xsl:when>` element. When all of the tests fail, the XSLT parser looks for an optional `<xsl:otherwise>` element that contains alternative instructions.

Now that you have a better idea of how XSLT works, you need to create a connection between the XML file and the XSLT file. Your browser won't know that it's supposed to use this XSLT file unless you provide a processing instruction to that effect in the XML file. The following processing instruction assumes that the XML and XSLT files are in the same folder.

```
<?xml-stylesheet type="text/xsl" href="First.XSLT"?>
```

As with all processing instructions, the `<?xml-stylesheet?>` processing instruction includes the enclosing question marks. The `type` attribute tells the XML parser what kind of information to expect in the stylesheet file. The `href` attribute tells the parser where to find the XSLT file. When you open the XML file in a browser now, the parser sees the processing instruction and interprets the XML file according to the rules in the XSLT file. Figure 5.13 shows the output from this example. As you can see, it's very hard to tell that this is an XML file.

FIGURE 5.13
Using XSLT transforms unreadable XML into something that looks like a regular Web page.

Learning More about XML

Whether you know it or not, you'll run into XML many times during your computer use. The reason is simple—XML makes a great way to exchange data between disparate systems. Fortunately, XML is relatively easy to learn. Visit the W3C Schools site at `http://www.w3schools.com/xml/` to find a complete XML tutorial. You might also want to review the namespace tutorial at `http://www.zvon.org/index.php?nav_id=172&ns=34`.

Unlike many topics discussed in this book, there are multiple versions of XML so you can't rely on just one reference. The most important reference appears at `http://www.zvon.org/xxl/xmlSchema2001Reference/Output/index.html`. However, make sure you also look at the references at `http://www.zvon.org/xxl/xmlSchemaReference/Output/index.html` for complete information. The annotated XML reference at `http://www.xml.com/axml/axml.html` is also handy for seeing the specification and expert commentary side by side.

You can also find a number of good general-purpose XML sites online. For example, the Microsoft XML Developer Center (`http://msdn.microsoft.com/nhp/default.asp?contentid=28000438`) is a great place to visit if you use Microsoft products.

Learning More about XSLT

This chapter skims only the surface of what you can do with XSLT. You can perform an incredible number of tasks using this technology. One of the better places to learn about XSLT is `http://www.w3schools.com/xsl/`. You should also view the examples in the XSLT reference at `http://www.zvon.org/xxl/XSLTreference/Output/index.html`. The XSL reference at `http://www.zvon.org/xxl/xslfoReference/Output/index.html` can also come in handy when you begin creating complex XSLT pages. You can also find a good tutorial on the Webmonkey site at `http://hotwired.lycos.com/webmonkey/98/43/index2a.html?tw=authoring`.

Make sure you check out some of the better third party XSLT reference sites. For example, the XSLT.com site at `http://xslt.com/` provides links and resources for XSLT from various vendors (not just Microsoft).

It also helps to have some great books on the topic. Make sure you read books such as *Mastering XSLT* by Chuck White (Sybex, 2002). It also helps to know something about XML schemas, so check out *XML Schemas* by Chelsea Valentine, Lucinda Dykes, and Ed Tittel (Sybex, 2002). (Even though these books have 2002 publication dates, they still contain valuable information.)

Developing a Privacy Policy

Privacy has become a major concern for most people because the news contains numerous stories of personal information misuse. One of the major misuses of personal information is identity theft, but that's by no means the largest misuse. Many users also feel that gathering personal information for marketing purposes without permission and full disclosure of how the requestor will use the information is also a major misuse of personal information. People don't want to suffer through a barrage of unwanted sales calls as witnessed by the proliferation of "No Call" lists both locally and nationally. In fact, many people are taking positive steps to take back their personal information or at least block further attempts to acquire new information.

Personal information covers a range of topics today. Most developers recognize that name, address, telephone number, and other personally identifying information is private. However, users don't want developers to know a lot of other information that some developers see as belonging to the public domain. For example, some developers will try to get the `Referrer` (the previous Web page), `User-Agent` (the browser type, version, and host operating system), and `From` (the user's email address) headers of the user's browser. Brisk sales of products such as Norton Internet Security demonstrate that users don't want developers to collect this information. An interesting side effect of this battle between user and developer is that even though the user is using a new version of products such as Internet Explorer and Mozilla, the Web site often reports the user has an outdated version of the product.

Generally, if your Web site doesn't include a shopping cart application or some other form of transaction that the user wants to participate in, you shouldn't collect any personal information at all. You can also avoid collecting browser information through careful design and by following standards. The Webmonkey chart at `http://hotwired.lycos.com/webmonkey/reference/browser_chart/index.html` helps you understand which design features to avoid based on browser compatibility.

Even with the best design, however, you'll eventually encounter a situation where you want to use cookies (assuming that the user has their browser set to accept cookies). Many users realize that cookies aren't inherently evil, but they also realize that a Web site could use cookies for nefarious purposes. All the pop-up ads that you see floating around on your favorite Web site are one reason that people are suspicious. Some of these vendors follow people around to the various sites they visit and keep track of their movements. However, you can overcome the fears of most users by maintaining a privacy policy and including special tags for that policy on your Web site. The most common way to publish and use a privacy policy is Platform for Privacy Preferences (P3P). The World Wide Web Consortium (W3C) sponsors this technique, and you can read about the six easy steps for implementing P3P on your Web site at `http://www.w3.org/P3P/details.html`. The P3P standard (`http://www.w3.org/TR/P3P/`) also contains a wealth of information you should review.

NOTE The example in this section uses the IBM P3P generator (`http://www.alphaworks.ibm.com/tech/p3peditor`). The W3C site lists several other generators—I chose this particular generator because it comes with a 90-day free trial. Your code might turn out different from mine if you use another generator for your code. For some reason, the IBM P3P generator doesn't work with the current version of the Java Runtime Environment (JRE)—version 1.4.2. IBM recommends using the 1.3.1 version of the JRE that you can download at `http://java.sun.com/j2se/1.3/`.

Your privacy statement will consist of several files, including at least one P3P file that you create using the P3P generator and an XML reference file. A good generator will also help you create a generic privacy summary that you can use for queries from the user and a compact policy statement you can use in the response headers of pages that contain cookies. If you own the server that you use for the Web page, you can place the privacy information in the \w3c folder of the Web site. It's also possible to create linkage between the privacy information and your Web page using a `<link>` tag similar to the one shown here.

```
<link rel="P3Pv1" href="http://www.mwt.net/~jmueller/p3p.xml">
```

The problem comes in when you don't own the server that hosts your Web page—the situation for many people, including small business owners. Internet Explorer 6 has several levels of cookie protection built in. The highest level will likely reject your privacy information because Internet Explorer relies exclusively on the compact policy statement supplied as part of the response headers. Adding the compact policy statement is relatively easy if you own the server. Listing 5.7 shows an alternative that you can try when you don't own the server, plus some test code you can use to verify the results.

LISTING 5.7:   Adding a Compact Policy to a Web Page

```
<html>
<head>
<meta http-equiv='P3P'
     content='policyref="http://www.mwt.net/~jmueller/p3p.xml",
     CP="NOI DSP COR NID CURa OUR NOR NAV INT TST"'>
<title>Privacy Demonstration</title>
<script>
function SetCookie()
{
    var  UserCookie; // Stores the user name.

    // Create the username cookie.
    UserCookie = "UserName=" + escape(InputVal.value);
```

```
        // Add the cookie to the document.
        document.cookie = UserCookie;

        // Tell the user the cookie was saved.
        alert("The cookies were saved.");
    }

    function ReadCookie()
    {
        var  ACookie; // Holds the document cookie.
        var  Parsed;  // Holds the split cookies.
        var  Name;    // The user name.

        // Get the cookie.
        ACookie = unescape(document.cookie);

        // Split the cookie elements.
        Parsed = ACookie.split("=");

        // Get the user name.
        Name = Parsed[1];

        // Display the name.
        alert("Your name is: " + Name);
    }
```

The <meta> tag at the beginning of the code is the essential addition to your application. The http-equiv attribute tells the server what kind of response header to add. Some servers don't honor this attribute, so this solution might not work completely in all cases. The content attribute tells the client where to locate the privacy policy for your Web site—it works much the same as the <link> tag discussed earlier in this section. Finally, the CP attribute defines the compact policy for your server. Most tools, such as the IBM P3P Policy Editor shown in Figure 5.14, tell you what these codes mean and generate a text file containing them for you.

The test code consists of two functions attached to buttons on the example form. The first creates a cookie and attaches it to the document. The second retrieves the cookie stored in the document and displays the results on screen. Neither function is that exciting, but this is enough code to create an error with Internet Explorer 6 if the compact policy isn't accepted. You must have a compact policy in place and Internet Explorer 6 must accept it if you want users to use the high privacy setting. However, even if Internet Explorer 6 decides that it won't accept the compact policy, having a privacy policy in place and set up using the information provided in this section lets the user rely on the medium high privacy setting. Although, the medium high setting isn't quite as comfortable as the high setting, it's much better than the low setting your Web site would require if it didn't have a privacy policy.

FIGURE 5.14
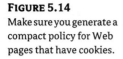
Make sure you generate a compact policy for Web pages that have cookies.

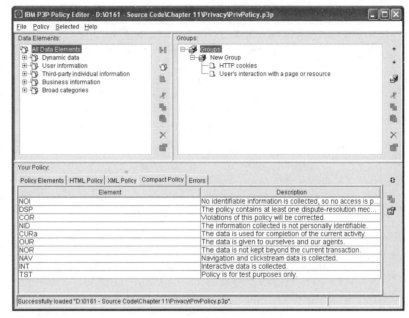

Creating a Safe Environment for User Data

Some kinds of user activity on a Web site will require that you know something about the user. For example, when the user requests that you send your newsletter, you'll need an email address. Even if the user provides you with a false name, the email address has to be real or the user won't receive the newsletter. Consequently, the user has to trust you to keep the email address secure and use it only as your privacy statement specifies. Break this trust and you'll find that your Web site is less effective and will have fewer visitors. The first rule of working with user data is to obtain only the user information that you absolutely have to have in order to provide a service.

Sometimes interacting with the user goes far beyond a simple exchange. For example, you might sell products on your Web site. As a minimum, you'll need to know the person's name and address because you need to know where to send items that you sell. However, it's quite likely that you'll know more information than that—a telephone number is likely and you might even need to work with a credit card number or other sensitive information. Because privacy is such an important issue, the user will want to place significant restrictions on what you can do with personal information. Most users won't want you to sell their name or identifying information because they don't want to receive calls from other vendors. More importantly, with identity theft running rampant, you need to safeguard any sensitive information because you might become responsible for its loss. For example, the identity theft experienced by the University of California, Berkeley, caused major waves. (See the InfoWorld article at `http://www.infoworld.com/article/04/10/20/HNidtheft_1.html` for details.)

Safeguarding user information begins with the lines of communication that you establish. It might seem odd, but some of the worst cracker break-ins begin with an intercepted message. When this information gathering leads to some type of valuable deduction, you have a security leak on your hands. For example, someone can perform a social engineering attack after gathering just enough information about a site visitor to communicate effectively with them directly. Consequently, it's important to keep eavesdropping to a minimum. Encrypt the information before the user sends it to you using a secure setup such as Secure Sockets Layer (SSL)—generally enabled using HyperText Transfer Protocol Secure (HTTPS).

Make sure you protect yourself when you do receive sensitive information from someone else. It's generally a good idea to have an actual agreement page as part of the user sign-up to ensure there's no doubt that the user agreed to provide you with personal information as part of a transaction. In short, make sure you have a strong agreement with the user and stand by that agreement.

TIP Most third-party organizations you interact with, such as eBay, require that you use HTTPS and SSL to protect user data you exchange with them. A good application designer will also use HTTPS and SSL for all local user interaction as well. It's important to secure the data stream to reduce the chance of someone peeking at the data. You can learn more about the HTTPS protocol at `http://www.w3.org/Protocols/` and `http://www.faqs.org/rfcs/rfc2818.html`. Learn about the SSL specification at `http://wp.netscape.com/eng/ssl3/`.

You can add a few commonsense principles to ensure your own privacy policy will reduce your liability for user information. For example, many businesses store user information in a database. When crackers breach that database, the information becomes public knowledge and you have a public relations nightmare on your hands. Even if you use stringent methods and encrypt every piece of information in your database, someone with enough time and a good enough reason will likely break through your protections. The best policy is not to store the information at all.

Unfortunately, it's not always possible to get rid of the user data as soon as a transaction is complete. When you need to store user data for a while, make sure you encrypt the database and that you store the information on a server that lacks access to the Internet. Employ automatic aging if possible, to ensure that the system automatically removes the data from the database after a certain time. Keep only the data that you actually need. For example, although you might need to retain the user's name and address, you probably don't have to keep their credit card number on file. Even though it's more convenient to store the credit card information, removing it from your system is safer. Most users won't object to entering their credit card information for every sale if you explain the policy.

WARNING Always assume that someone's going to feed your application bad data. For example, you'll want to verify that you check data for accuracy before processing it. This means ensuring that the data is the proper length and data type, and that it doesn't contain any character data that could cause problems (such as a hidden script). Whenever possible, check the data against a list of acceptable entries and verify that the user has provided complete entries. You can often use regular expressions, a type of check that validates the form of the data, to ensure that the data meets a particular requirement, such as a telephone number. In addition, always assume there are going to be security breaches. Maintain a log of access events for your application for 60 days so you can locate, isolate, identify, repair, and hopefully prosecute security breaches. The event log needs to include some type of user identifier, the time of access (including both log on and log off), and the activity the user performed.

You need to consider security for your site when it works with sensitive data from any source. One of the better white papers on how the standards groups are meeting security needs appears on the Microsoft site at `http://msdn.microsoft.com/library/en-us/dnwssecur/html/securitywhitepaper.asp`. Even though this white paper is about Web services, the principles apply to any kind of Web communication. This discussion also provides a road map of security services.

As a final security precaution, you should consider some form of physical security for your system. This could be something as simple as ensuring that you lock the system in a room where no one but you can get to it. You could also keep the data held by your system safe by placing the information on a removable disk, removing the disk after each session, and locking it away. There are a number of ways that you can ensure the physical security of your system. For example, companies such as Interface (`http://www.crocodile.de`) provide physical security add-ons for your computer.

TIP One requirement that would be easy to miss is to ensure that you secure all storage media. This means that you shouldn't expose a system with sensitive data to the Internet if possible and that you must take precautions to safeguard the system when you do. However, the requirement goes further than actual application requirements. Have your system disk securely wiped when you get rid of your current machine. Usually, this means destroying the disk or at least exposing it to a strong enough magnetic force to ensure complete data erasure.

Defining Your Development Goals

This chapter has explored the intelligent Web page from the server perspective. The server has the best control over the flow of data because all of that data resides on its own hard drive. In addition, the server is at a better advantage to implement security and to ensure that data receives the proper treatment. Of course, this all comes at a price including additional server loading and loss of user trust in some cases. Generally, server-side intelligence works best for data-gathering projects such as detecting user settings so you can provide a better experience or collecting survey forms. Shopping cart and other financial applications also work best using server-side intelligence.

Now it's time for you to try out server-side processing. Try creating simple applications such as a survey form or an application that collects user data and uses it in a positive manner. While you're working with that user data, you might want to create your own privacy policy. Far too few Web sites provide a privacy policy and lose both user interest and sales as a result. Make plans now for keeping user data safe (when your Web site stores it) or helping the user understand the need to store the data on their machine. Consider using encryption for all storage needs to protect the data from prying eyes (even if the data resides on the user's system).

Chapter 6 considers client-side intelligence. Clients use scripting technology to perform specific tasks, so this chapter also shows how to create and use scripts using one of the most popular languages, JavaScript. You'll find that client-side scripting has many advantages for the developer, but it also comes with problems that you'll need to work around as you create your Web application.

Chapter 6

Working with Scripts

Intelligent pages require code and that code has to execute somewhere. You have two choices: the client or the server. When you want the code to execute on the server, you create code behind, as shown in Chapter 5 to perform the task. However, when you want the client to perform the work, you need to use scripting. The client's browser sees the script and relies on the local script engine to perform the required tasks. The browser doesn't have a script engine, in most cases—it uses the one supplied by the operating system. For Windows users, this means that you have access to JavaScript or VBScript as scripting languages. The Windows script engine is extensible, so you might have access to other options. However, the important consideration is that other operating systems generally support only JavaScript, so if you want your client-side application to run on the most machines possible, you need to use JavaScript as your scripting language. This chapter will fill you in on all the details for working with the scripting engine so you can make a decision about which language to use.

Once you have access to the script engine, you need to make other choices. A language like JavaScript can perform a number of standard tasks. For example, you can access any of the controls on the form—HTML as well as ASP.NET controls, so this is a situation where client-side scripting is actually more flexible than working with the server because code behind can't access HTML directly (it's designed to work with ASP.NET controls).

This chapter shows you how to perform a number of other essential tasks using scripts. For example, many scripts perform calculations or perform other behind-the-scenes tasks. These nonvisual tasks are essential to your application. You'll also want to know how to save cookies on the user's machine. The safest place to store user data is on the user's machine where the cookie will eventually expire. You can also combine client and server processing to produce robust applications that serve a variety of complex needs.

The last part of this chapter discusses a new ASP.NET technology called Web Parts. The interesting point about Web Parts is that this technology lets a user customize a Web application—similar to the customizations that a desktop application can provide. This chapter provides a basic overview and some usage examples. The "Working with Web Parts" section of Chapter 13 provides more details and you'll see an interesting use for this technology in the "Creating Accessible Pages Using Web Parts" section of Chapter 19.

Understanding Client-side Intelligence

Client-side intelligence means that the client executes the code required to provide most Web page intelligence. All client-side processing also involves some level of server processing. For example, even though the client can provide a calculated result, the client must still request new data from the server. Consequently, client-side intelligence is actually a hybrid form of processing that provides the following characteristics.

Reduced network bandwidth needs   When working with a client-side script, the client doesn't have to send requests for updates to the server constantly. The scripts can handle many requirements, especially calculated results. Overall, this feature reduces network bandwidth requirements and can mean a boost in performance.

Better server performance   Anything you can do to remove a little of the processing load from the server pays dividends in better performance. Client-side processing removes a lot of the server-side processing requirements, which means the server can handle more clients, faster, and with fewer delays.

Faster response times   Because the client bundles all of the processed data and sends it to the server without intermediate trips, client-side processing tends to produce better response times. Some responses are almost immediate because the client processes them locally. However, even when the client has to request data from the server, the response is likely faster because the server doesn't have to process the raw data first—the client has already performed this task.

Customizable results   Client-side processing lets the browser perform some analysis of the input and present it to the user in a specific way—independently of the server. The server doesn't have to consider the output as much when using client-side processing—it can provide the same data to everyone. The client can use scripts to manipulate the data and present it the way the user wants.

Increased privacy and personal security   Generally, client-side processing reduces privacy problems and increases user security because the server receives less raw data. In fact, a carefully written set of scripts and cookies can keep all personally identifiable information on the client machine so the server doesn't receive anything that a third party could use. For example, instead of receiving a user name, the server would receive a user identifier. The user doesn't even need to send address, telephone, or credit card information for each transaction because the personal identifier locates the user record in the secure storage on the server.

Client-side intelligence isn't a one-time process—it's ongoing, just as server-side processing is. The client can process information at several times during the request/response cycle and in a variety of ways. Here are the most common techniques.

Form loading   Use form loading techniques to initialize the client-side environment, create a custom page based on a previous result, or ensure that the user environment has specific minimum resources. Form loading is an excellent time to perform any nonvisual tasks you might need to perform to create a good user experience.

Initial request   Use the initial request to perform processing of basic user input, validation of initial form data, to ensure client meets server-side constraints, or ensure server communication can take place. Performing these tasks at the client means that the data doesn't have to take a round trip across the network. Not only does the server receive less bad data, but the user also gets instant feedback on any problems with the initial request. Of course, you can't perform every task during the initial request. For example, you usually can't perform user validation during the initial request—the server must request the security information during the second request/response cycle.

Automatic processing   Use automatic processing to ensure that the user environment meets user expectations or to ensure that your application meets either client or server processing needs. For example, your Web site might allow a lot of customization, but the initial page won't show the user's preferences unless you use automation to obtain the user's preferences and reconfigure the page as needed. Other forms of automation include client-side setups. For example, a client might need to download a special control or application to ensure that your Web application will work as anticipated.

User action response   Whenever possible, perform user action response processing on the client to reduce the time between a user click and the result's appearance on screen. For example, you can always perform calculations locally unless the client is using a resource poor platform such as a Personal Digital Assistant (PDA) or a cellular telephone. (As these devices gain more intelligence, you'll find that client-side scripts become effective even in these limited environments.)

Timed response   Rely on timed responses to overcome a variety of error conditions. For example, you might know that the client should receive a response from the server within a specific time frame and that something has gone wrong if this time expires. A timed response can alert the user to the problem and provide a recommended course of action to fix the error. Likewise, some users won't know that you need a particular response from them. A timed response can provide the user with a friendly reminder that they need to provide input. In some cases, you might be able to overcome the problem by performing a default action when the time elapses. Always provide a means for turning off the timer when you take the default action approach because some users with special needs will require additional time.

The most important consideration for client-side scripting is that it can't replace the server. Yes, you can perform many tasks using client-side scripting—some of which you can't perform at the server. However, some developers use extreme programming techniques to try to shoehorn a client-side script to meet a sever-side need. Always review the task that you want to perform, attempt to perform it at the location you think works best, and then be willing to change course when it becomes apparent that either the client or the server can't perform the task with ease. Complex scripts that use odd programming techniques usually cause more problems than they solve because many browsers simply won't run them.

NOTE   As users become more aware of the problems that scripts can cause, you might find that the client can't run your script at all. Be prepared for this eventuality. Whenever possible, try to provide a non-script or server-side alternative for your application or at least tell the user what they need to do to get the Web page to work right. Some users refuse to enable scripts (and who can blame them given the current Internet environment). The bottom line is that client-side scripting can solve problems, but it also causes problems due to the less than stellar behavior of others on the Internet.

Using Basic Scripting Principles

Scripts have some basic properties that you need to consider before using them. For example, it doesn't matter what operating system or browser you use, a script is always interpreted—the script engine runs after the browser hands the script off to it. Because computers interpret scripts, rather than compile them, all scripts incur a performance penalty. Given that most scripts are short, the performance penalty isn't noticeable, but you definitely don't want to write your next game program using a script without considering the possible performance loss.

Most operating systems provide a generic scripting engine for several needs, and many operating systems provide a special script debugger. Because Visual Web Developer runs only on Windows, this chapter considers only Windows solutions to the problems of working with the script engine. However, the Web application you create using Visual Web Developer could end up running on just about any operating system and the user might select any of a number of browsers. It's important to at least consider some method of working through problems on other systems (using the feedback form in Chapter 7 is a good start). The following sections discuss basic scripting issues such as performance, scripting engine support, and debugging.

Creating Efficient and Effective Scripts

Scripts provide a wonderful alternative to forcing the server to perform every task needed for intelligent Web pages. Of course, you'll want to create the best scripts possible to reduce support requests for your Web site and enhance the user experience. An efficient script is different from an effective script. Efficient scripts perform fast, reduce network traffic, and use the fewest possible resources. Effective scripts perform the task you want while enhancing the user experience. The best situation is where you create scripts that are both effective and efficient.

Unfortunately, some developers attempt to use scripts to offload most of the processing tasks from the server. This approach doesn't work well because the client simply doesn't have the resources required to perform the required tasks in many cases. In addition, when a client has scripts disabled, the Web page either doesn't work at all or must rely on workarounds to get any work done. Consequently, whenever possible, it's best to avoid overwhelming the client to save the server.

Likewise, some developers don't trust the client at all and do everything possible not to use scripts at all. This approach does have the advantage of leaving everything in the developer's hands and in the developer's environment, so there's little chance of unexpected failure. When a client has scripts disabled, you must take this approach, but it's neither effective nor efficient. Using a server-side approach wastes resources, increases network bandwidth requirements, increases processing time, and definitely affects the user experience.

The problem is to create an environment where scripting works with the server to provide specific results. Normally, the best approach is to divide whatever task you want to perform into individual steps and then decide where that step will perform best given the available resources. For example, you can't perform a step on the server when the server lacks the required client information. In some cases, you'll have to add another step to move data from one location to the other to garner a boost in performance. Once you create this task list, you can fine-tune it to provide both efficient and effective application performance. Here are some tips you can use to make the task easier.

Use scripts for personal information processing.   Whenever possible, keep the user's personal data on the local machine. Even moving the data from the client to the server for processing is a bad idea. The only exception is when you must have the personal data to complete a server-side task such as fulfilling an order.

Rely on the server for business processing.   Don't expose your business processes to anyone who could use the information to gain entry to your system. Something as simple as a misplaced database name or a special equation used to calculate a price can cause problems for you or your company. Scripting should always focus on the user, never on you or your system.

Make sure that tasks are small enough.   Any time you find that you have a hard time deciding where to perform a task, it's probably a signal that you haven't made the task small enough. Break the overall task into small enough pieces that your application can perform each subtask in a specific location. It's important to create a task scheme that reflects a reliable order of accomplishing a goal and that means knowing where you can perform the task safely.

Ensure that tasks are specific.   It's easy to write down a generic description of a task and assume that you know precisely what that task entails. The problem is that a general task description often hides complexity that you won't know about until you actually begin creating the application. You'll save time by creating very specific task descriptions as you think about the application, rather than fixing problems caused by a generalized description later. For example, a task description such as "download the client data" is very generic. Make sure you include details such as the exact client data elements you need. You might find that some of these elements aren't stored on the server and that you'll have to request them from the user.

Track the precise location of the data. You should always know where the data is located. Some developers write code that places some data here and other data there. Eventually, the processing becomes a mess, the data becomes corrupted, or errors occur in the result because it isn't possible to ensure the integrity of the data or even know which data is the newest.

Using CScript and WScript

Most Web page developers don't realize that they have more than a few resources at their disposal for working with scripts in Windows without loading even one additional product. One of the most important features is the ability to access the scripting engine without using a Web page. That's right—you can create a standalone script, test it, and then put it into a Web page after testing. Using this technique can save considerable time and effort. For example, consider the following short script. You'll find this example in the \Chapter 06\JS_Script folder of the source code on the Sybex Web site.

```
// Test the script.
WScript.Echo("The sum of 2 + 3 is: " + AddIt(2, 3));

// This is the function that will appear in the Web page.
function AddIt(Value1, Value2)
{
   // Calculate the result.
   return Value1 + Value2;
}
```

The example (named DoAdd.JS) doesn't do much, but it does demonstrate how you can test a function using the desktop interface. The code outputs a simple message telling you the result of the calculation. Windows actually provides two script engine interfaces: CScript (a command line interface) and WScript (a graphical user interface). Because these two applications use precisely the same script engine that your browser uses, any function tests that you perform using either interface also tests the function for your browser. In this case, typing **CScript DoAdd.JS** and pressing Enter at the command prompt displays the output at the command prompt. On the other hand, typing **WScript DoAdd.JS** and pressing enter displays the result in a dialog box. Here are the command-line versions of both interfaces.

```
CScript <Script Name> [<WSH Command Line Switches>] [<Script Arguments>]
WScript <Script Name> [<WSH Command Line Switches>] [<Script Arguments>]
```

CScript and WScript use the same command line. You must provide a script name as the first command-line argument. Most scripts have a VBE or JS file extension, but any extension is acceptable. For example, you can still use VBS files with WSH, but the icon won't look right, in some cases, and you can't double-click it to start the execution with any version of Windows XP. The VBS extension is the right choice for older versions of Windows. The icon is yellow for VBE files and blue for JS files.

WSH provides a wealth of command line switches that you can use to modify its behavior. The following list describes the command-line switches that WSH provides.

//? Displays the currently documented command-line switches. The newest versions of WSH tend to reject older switches, even those of the undocumented variety.

//B Use this mode when you don't want the user to interact with the script. Batch mode suppresses all non-command-line console user interface requests from the script. It also suppresses error message display (a change from previous versions).

//D   Activates debugging mode so you can fix errors in a script.

//H:CScript   Makes `CSCRIPT.EXE` the default application for running scripts. (WScript is the default engine.)

//H:WScript   Makes `WSCRIPT.EXE` the default application for running scripts.

//I   Allows full interaction with the user. Any pop-up dialog boxes will wait for user input before the script continues.

//Job:Job Name   Executes a WSH job. A WSH job has a Windows Script File (WSF) extension. This file enables you to perform tasks using multiple scripting engines and multiple files. Essentially, this allows you to perform a "super batch" process. Creating WSF files is an advanced technique not discussed in this book because it isn't very useful in most cases. You can learn more about this topic at `http://msdn.microsoft.com/library/en-us/script56/html/wsAdvantagesOfWs.asp`.

//Logo and *//NoLogo*   WHS normally prints out a logo message. You'd use the `//NoLogo` switch to prevent WSH from displaying this message.

//S   This command line switch allows you to save current command line options for a user. WSH will save the following options: `//B`, `//I`, `//Logo`, `//Nologo`, and `//T:n`.

//T:Time Limit   Limits the maximum time the script can run to the number of seconds specified. Normally, there isn't any timeout value. You'd use this switch in situations where a script might end up in a continuous loop or unable to get the requested information for other reasons. For example, you might use this switch when requesting information on a network drive.

//X   Starts the script in the debugger. This allows you to trace the execution of the script from beginning to end.

//U   Outputs any console information using Unicode instead of pure ASCII. You use this switch on systems where you need to support languages other than English. This is a CScript-only option.

Notice that all of these command-line switches start with two slashes like this: `//` to differentiate them from switches you may need for your script. WSH passes script arguments to your script for processing. Script arguments can be anything including command-line switches of your own or values needed to calculate a result.

NOTE   Users of older versions of CScript and WScript may remember the `//C` and the `//W` switches used to switch the default scripting engines. Newer versions of CScript and WScript replace these switches with the `//H` switch. You'll also find the `//R` (reregister) and `//Entrypoint` switches missing from WSH because script developers no longer need the functionality. Always use the correct command-line switches for the version of Windows and WSH installed on your machine.

You can work with WSH in either interactive or batch mode. Use batch mode when you need to perform tasks that don't require user input. For example, you might want to run Scan Disk every evening, but use different command-line switches for it based on the day. You could use Task Scheduler to accomplish this task, but using it in conjunction with a WSH script improves the flexibility you get when running the task.

Another kind of batch processing might be to send log files to your supervisor or perhaps set up a specific set of environment variables for a character-mode application based on the current user. On the other hand, interactive mode requires user interaction. You'd use it for tasks such as cleaning the hard drive because you don't always know whether the user needs a particular file. Such a script could ask the user a set of general questions, and then clean excess files from the hard drive based on the user input. The cleaning process would follow company guidelines and save the user time.

TIP   Because batch processing doesn't require any form of user input, it's usually a good idea to include the //T switch with the //B switch. This combination stops the script automatically if it runs too long. In most cases, using this switch setup stops an errant script before it corrupts the Windows environment or freezes the machine. However, you can't time some tasks with ease. For example, any Web-based task is difficult to time because you can't account for problems with a slow connection. In this case, you'll need to refrain from using the //T switch or provide a worst-case scenario time interval.

The next set of command line switches to consider is //Logo and //NoLogo. There isn't any right or wrong time to use these switches, but you usually use the //Logo switch when testing a script and the //NoLogo switch afterward. The reason is simple. During the testing process, you want to know about every potential source of problems in your script environment, including an old script engine that might cause problems. On the other hand, you don't want to clutter the screen with useless text after you debug the script. Using the //NoLogo switch keeps screen clutter to a minimum.

TIP   You can find a number of good resources online for working with WScript and CScript. The two most important resources are the Microsoft WScript site at http://msdn.microsoft.com/library/en-us/script56/html/wsObjWScript.asp and a description of how to run commands from the command prompt at http://msdn.microsoft.com/library/en-us/script56/html/wsruncscript.asp.

Debugging Your Script

At some point, you'll have a Web page that contains a script and you won't be able to test it using either CScript or WScript anymore. You need a debugger that works with the browser so that you can see how the script works in the environment that the user will rely on. To perform debugging, you need to modify a few settings on your machine. First, open Internet Explorer and choose the Tools ➤ Internet Options command. You'll see the Internet Options dialog box. Select the Advanced tab and locate the Disable Script Debugging options shown in Figure 6.1. You'll find the example used for debugging in the \Chapter 06\BrokenScript folder of the source code on the Sybex Web site. Make sure that both options are cleared—checking them will prevent you from debugging the script. Note that not all versions of Internet Explorer have multiple options—you might see a single option for disabling script debugging.

FIGURE 6.1
Make sure that you have debugging enabled in Internet Explorer.

After you check your browser, open the Services console found in the Administrative Tools folder of the Control Panel. Locate the Machine Debug Manager service shown in Figure 6.2. Windows should start the service for you automatically. However, if Windows hasn't started the service, right-click the entry and choose Start from the context menu. The service should start within a few seconds.

FIGURE 6.2
Start the Machine Debug Manager service when required to ensure that the debugger will start.

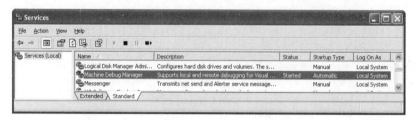

Now that you have everything set up, you can start a project that contains a script. After you load the page, three events will trigger the script debugger. The following list describes each option.

An error occurs. Whenever the scripting engine experiences an error executing the code, it presents an Error dialog box like the one shown in Figure 6.3 that asks whether you want to start the debugger. The dialog box tells you about the error that the scripting engine encountered so you can determine whether you can fix the error. The error message also includes a line number. The line number isn't always correct, but it will get you close to the line with the problem code. Click Yes to start the debugger.

FIGURE 6.3
An error dialog box tells you about the scripting error and describes where to find it.

Open the debugger manually. You can load the page and immediately open the script debugger by selecting the View ➤ Script Debugger ➤ Open command.

Open at the next statement. Sometimes you don't want to start the debugger until you do something. In this case, select View ➤ Script Debugger ➤ Break at Next Statement command. The browser won't appear to do anything. You can type any data you need to test the page. The debugger starts when you perform an action that executes code, such as clicking the Submit button.

TIP If you still can't get the script debugger to start, try downloading and installing the Microsoft Script Debugger located at http://www.microsoft.com/downloads/details .aspx?FamilyID=2f465be0-94fd-4569-b3c4-dffdf19ccd99&displaylang=en. The debugger should start after you install the Microsoft Script Debugger and restart your system. However, the Visual Web Developer installation should allow you to debug script applications—refusal to start normally indicates there's a problem with your setup.

Whenever the debugger starts, you see the Just-In-Time Debugging dialog box. As a minimum, this dialog box will contain the Microsoft Script Debugger as a debugging option. However, when you have other programming products installed, you should also see them listed. For example, when you have Visual Studio .NET installed, it always appears as one of the debugging options. Visual Web Developer should also appear as one of the debugging options, but may not on certain versions of Windows with specific service packs installed.

WARNING   Windows XP Service Pack 2 (SP2) can cause significant problems for any of the language product debuggers, including Visual Web Developer. You can learn more about this issue at `http://blogs.msdn.com/andypennell/archive/2004/08/20/217933.aspx`. The best option is not to install SP2.

Select the debugger that you want to use and click Yes. The debugger will start and load the code from the Web page. The fact that the code comes from the Web page and not from the source is an important issue because the Web page might not be the same as your Visual Web Developer code when you create the page using ASP.NET. Because the script has to run in the environment that the user sees, debugging the output, rather than the ASP.NET code, is the best option for scripts. Figure 6.4 shows the Microsoft Script Debugger with the example code loaded.

FIGURE 6.4

Use the Microsoft Script Debugger to locate and fix scripting errors in your code.

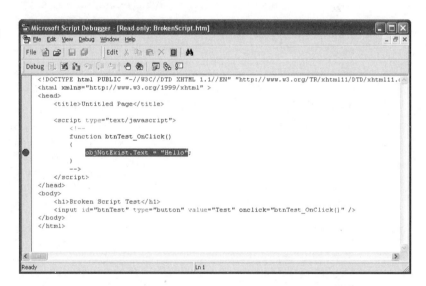

TIP   Another method that you can use to start the script debugger is to load the document you want to debug into your browser. Locate the `MSScrDbg.EXE` file in the `\Program Files\Microsoft Script Debugger` folder. After you start the application, select View ➢ Running Documents. You'll see the Running Documents window. Double-click the running document that you want to debug. The Microsoft Script Debugger will load the document and let you debug it.

The Microsoft Script Debugger isn't fancy, but you can use it to perform basic debugging tasks. The debugger includes a command window where you can test various scripting code while the application runs. You can also view the call stack and set break points. Chapter 16 discusses debugging in detail.

Learning More about JavaScript

Sometimes it's amazing to discover just what you can do with JavaScript because most people don't see JavaScript as a real programming language. However, JavaScript is a very robust language and you can do a lot with it. Not everyone has an eternity, though, to learn a new programming language. One of the best tutorials is the Webmonkey JavaScript Crash Course at `http://webmonkey.wired.com/webmonkey/programming/javascript/tutorials/jstutorial_index.html`. This course covers all of the basics including issues such as creating loops and understanding how JavaScript works with variables. Another great tutorial is the one put out by the W3Schools at `http://www.w3schools.com/js/`. The W3Schools site also has many excellent coding examples.

Once you get past the basics, you'll want to start looking through a manual that contains all of the JavaScript functions. The best source of information is the ECMAScript site at `http://www.ecma-international.org/publications/standards/Ecma-262.htm`. (ECMAScript is a name for standardized JavaScript created by the European Computer Manufacturer's Association.) If you want a strict JavaScript guide, then the JavaScript guide at `http://wp.netscape.com/eng/mozilla/3.0/handbook/javascript/` is a good option.

Many people learn best by seeing coding examples. A good source of JavaScript coding examples is Koders as `http://www.koders.com/default.aspx`. Another good place to look for coding examples is JavaScript Source at `http://javascript.internet.com/`. ScriptSearch.com (`http://www.scriptsearch.com/`) has many script examples to look at. Finally, you might also want to check out the Microsoft Scripting site at `http://msdn.microsoft.com/scripting/`.

Working with Controls

This section uses the term *control* very loosely because that's how JavaScript treats them. A control can be anything from an `<Input>` tag to an actual ASP.NET control. You can also create controls on standard HTML pages using the `<Object>` tag. The only problem with this approach is that the client must support ActiveX controls, must allow you to run them on the client system, and must have the control installed (or you can provide a means of downloading the control when required). The following sections describe three kinds of controls that you can work with using scripts.

Working with HTML Tags

You can treat HTML tags as you would controls when working with scripts. For example, Listing 6.1 includes a simple script that works with a control—an `<Input>` tag in this case. You'll find this example in the `\Chapter 06\Controls` folder of the source code on the Sybex Web site. When the user clicks Test, the script displays a dialog box that shows what the `txtMessage` control, the `<Input>` tag, contains.

LISTING 6.1:   Using a Simple Control

```
<!DOCTYPE html PUBLIC "-//W3C//DTD XHTML 1.1//EN"
                     "http://www.w3.org/TR/xhtml11/DTD/xhtml11.dtd">
<html xmlns="http://www.w3.org/1999/xhtml" >
<head>
    <title>Untitled Page</title>
    <script type="text/javascript">
```

```
    <!--
        function TestMe()
        {
            // Display a message for the user.
            alert(MyForm.txtMessage.value);
        }
    -->
    </script>
</head>
<body>
    <form id="MyForm" name="MyForm">
        <h1>Control Test Form</h1>
        <div>
            <label id="lblMessage" for="txtMessage">
                Type a Message
            </label>
            <input type="text"
                   id="txtMessage"
                   name="txtMessage"
                   value="Hello" />
        </div>
        <div>
            <input type="button"
                   id="btnTest"
                   name="btnTest"
                   value="Test"
                   onclick="TestMe()" />
        </div>
    </form>
</body>
</html>
```

There's nothing special about this page except that it does use a client-side script to perform work with btnTest. The onclick attribute connects btnTest to the TestMe() script. When you begin typing onclick in the IDE, you'll notice that IntelliSense even displays it as an event using the event icon.

The browser supplies the alert() method for you. All that this function accepts is a simple message, but you'll find it quite useful for diagnosing problems with your applications. The message need not be a string—JavaScript doesn't rely on strict typecasting, so you can supply a string, a number, or an object should you wish to do so. However, the output you receive depends on precisely what you provide as input—an object would display an [Object] moniker, rather than a value.

Notice that the actual script appears within a comment (<!-- -->). The reason for this convention is that not all browsers understand scripts. Using the comment keeps browsers that don't understand scripts from choking on the code. Browsers that do understand scripts ignore the comment. Most modern browsers are script friendly, so they'll work with the script without problem. Even so, you should include the comment to ensure that users of older browsers don't experience problems with your Web site.

IntelliSense also plays a role in the use of controls. When you type the name of a control—no matter what kind of control it might be—IntelliSense displays the events, methods, and properties associated with that control. In fact, you can't determine the control type from the IntelliSense display because all controls receive equal treatment. For example, when you type `txtMessage`, Intelli-Sense displays a list like the one shown in Figure 6.5 that includes all of the essentials for this control created from a tag.

FIGURE 6.5

IntelliSense helps you access the events, methods, and properties that controls support.

Using the *<Object>* Tag

Microsoft originally introduced the `<Object>` tag to bring Component Object Model (COM) controls to the Internet. The `<Object>` tag appears on many Web pages and you'll even find it discussed on the World Wide Web Consortium (W3C) school Web site at `http://www.w3schools.com/tags/tag_object.asp`. The `<Object>` tag works with either standard HTML pages or ASPX pages, so this solution is great for situations where you might have to work in more than one environment. The point is that this is a standard way of adding controls to your Web page. Unfortunately, Visual Web Developer doesn't provide very good support for this essential means of working with controls, so you end up doing extra work to use it. You'll find the examples in this section in the `\Chapter 06\Controls` folder of the source code on the Sybex Web site.

GETTING THE *<OBJECT>* TAG DATA

Unless you're creating a special control, you'll want to use a control that everyone has on their machine or that they can easily download from the Internet. Otherwise, you need to consider adding the required support to your Web site and have the user download the control. For example, both Adobe Reader and Shockwave Flash are easy to download from the Internet and all Windows users will have some version of the Windows Media Player already installed. With this problem in mind, the example in this section describes how to use the Windows Media Player—a very common and useful control.

The problem is that you don't know anything about this control, other than it exists somewhere on most machines. The Object Browser can prove invaluable in this case. Select View ➢ Object Browser to display the Object Browser. Click Add Other Components and you'll see the Select Component dialog box shown in Figure 6.6. Locate the component that you want to use and click Add. Notice that this display tells you the name and location of the component DLL. Click OK to add the component to the Object Browser.

FIGURE 6.6

Use the Object Browser to your advantage when working with the *<Object>* tag.

The Object Browser display is very useful because it tells you about the control—how to access its features. The property listing comes in especially helpful later. You need to perform one additional task before you can use the control—you need to learn its class identifier—a special number that uniquely identifies the control. You have two choices for locating this number. The first is to use the OLE/COM Object Viewer utility. This utility doesn't come with the Express products, but you can download it at `http://www.microsoft.com/windows2000/techinfo/reskit/tools/existing/oleview-o.asp`. Normally, you'll find the control that you need in the Control folder shown in Figure 6.7.

FIGURE 6.7

The OLE/COM Object Viewer makes locating controls easy.

You can also use the Registry Editor to locate the class identifier. Open a command prompt, type **RegEdit.EXE**, and press Enter to start the Registry Editor. After you open the Registry Editor, choose Edit ➤ Find. Type the path and name of the component DLL and click Find Next. Components can have a lot of property pages and other entries in the registry. Figure 6.8 shows a typical component entry. Notice that it contains the full component name and entries such as the version number. The property page and other entries won't contain this level of detail, so you can easily identify the component entry. The class identifier appears as the key. Right-click the entry and choose Copy Key Name from the context menu.

> **WARNING** Avoid editing the registry unless you understand precisely what the change will do. Always create a backup of the registry before you make any changes to it. You can find an excellent set of utilities for saving and restoring the registry at `http://home.t-online.de/home/lars.hederer/erunt`.

FIGURE 6.8
Using the Registry Editor lets you copy the class identifier directly.

The `<Object>` tag is somewhat self-contained. You can interact with it using a script, but it's best to configure the object as much as possible when you create the `<Object>` tag. Fortunately, the `<Object>` tag is relatively easy to understand. Here's the `<Object>` tag, default parameters, and default values for the Windows Media Player.

```
<OBJECT id=objMediaPlayer
        classid=CLSID:6BF52A52-394A-11d3-B153-00C04F79FAA6>
    <PARAM NAME="URL" VALUE="">
    <PARAM NAME="rate" VALUE="1">
    <PARAM NAME="balance" VALUE="0">
    <PARAM NAME="currentPosition" VALUE="0">
    <PARAM NAME="defaultFrame" VALUE="">
    <PARAM NAME="playCount" VALUE="1">
    <PARAM NAME="autoStart" VALUE="-1">
    <PARAM NAME="currentMarker" VALUE="0">
    <PARAM NAME="invokeURLs" VALUE="-1">
    <PARAM NAME="baseURL" VALUE="">
    <PARAM NAME="volume" VALUE="50">
    <PARAM NAME="mute" VALUE="0">
    <PARAM NAME="uiMode" VALUE="full">
    <PARAM NAME="stretchToFit" VALUE="0">
    <PARAM NAME="windowlessVideo" VALUE="0">
```

```
            <PARAM NAME="enabled" VALUE="-1">
            <PARAM NAME="enableContextMenu" VALUE="-1">
            <PARAM NAME="fullScreen" VALUE="0">
            <PARAM NAME="SAMIStyle" VALUE="">
            <PARAM NAME="SAMILang" VALUE="">
            <PARAM NAME="SAMIFilename" VALUE="">
            <PARAM NAME="captioningID" VALUE="">
            <PARAM NAME="enableErrorDialogs" VALUE="0">
            <PARAM NAME="_cx" VALUE="6350">
            <PARAM NAME="_cy" VALUE="6482">
        </OBJECT>
```

Just in case you're wondering, unlike some programming languages, the browser doesn't care whether you write your tags in lowercase `<object>`, or initial caps `<Object>`, or uppercase `<OBJECT>`. The reason the code appears as it does, in this case, is this is how the `<Object>` tag stores the data internally using the `outerHTML` property. Listing 6.2 shows a simple page that you can use to test various objects and see which `<Param>` tags they support. Notice that I haven't included any `<Param>` tags in order to see the default values the control uses—the control won't actually work this way.

LISTING 6.2:   Testing *<Object>* Tag Parameter Values

```
<!DOCTYPE html PUBLIC "-//W3C//DTD XHTML 1.1//EN" "http://www.w3.org/TR/xhtml11/DTD/
xhtml11.dtd">
<html xmlns="http://www.w3.org/1999/xhtml" >
<head>
    <title>Show the Object Params</title>
    <script type="text/javascript">
    <!--
        function ViewParams()
        {
            txtOutput.value=objMediaPlayer.outerHTML;
        }
    -->
    </script>
</head>
<body>
    <h1>Show the Object Params</h1>
    <object id="objMediaPlayer"
            classid="CLSID:6BF52A52-394A-11d3-B153-00C04F79FAA6" >
    </object><br />
    <input type="button" id="btnTest" value="Test" onclick="ViewParams()" /><br />
    <textarea id="txtOutput" cols="50" rows="10" />
</body>
</html>
```

DEVELOPING WITH THE *<OBJECT>* TAG

Once you know enough about the control you want to use, it's time to begin creating a Web page with it. Depending on the control, the object could be a single part of a much larger design, or it might be the basis of the entire page. For example, an on-screen drawing application would likely have a number of constituent parts. On the other hand, you could create an entire Web page out of the Windows Media Player. The example that appears in Listing 6.3 shows how you can interact with the Windows Media Player as an application.

LISTING 6.3:   Using the Windows Media Player on a Web Page

```
<!DOCTYPE html PUBLIC "-//W3C//DTD XHTML 1.1//EN"
                    "http://www.w3.org/TR/xhtml11/DTD/xhtml11.dtd">
<html xmlns="http://www.w3.org/1999/xhtml" >
<head>
    <title>Play the Windows Media Player</title>
    <script type="text/javascript">
    <!--
        function ChangeTune()
        {
            // Select the desired tune.
            switch (optSelect.selectedIndex)
            {
                case 0:
                    objMediaPlayer.URL = "Bells.WAV";
                    break;
                case 1:
                    objMediaPlayer.URL = "Cuckoo2.WAV";
                    break;
                case 2:
                    objMediaPlayer.URL = "Shred2.WAV";
                    break;
            }

            // Display the effect of the change.
            txtOutput.value = objMediaPlayer.childNodes(0).name +
                            " is set to " +
                            objMediaPlayer.childNodes(0).value;

            // Play the tune.
            objMediaPlayer.controls.play();
        }
    -->
    </script>
</head>
<body>
    <h1>Play the Windows Media Player</h1>
```

```
<p>Click Play to start the sound.</p>

<!-- The configured Media Player object. -->
<object id="objMediaPlayer"
        classid="CLSID:6BF52A52-394A-11d3-B153-00C04F79FAA6" >
        <param name="URL" value="Cuckoo2.WAV" />
        <param name="autoStart" value="0" />
</object><br />

<!-- Sound selections from the current project and the
     change button. -->
<select id="optSelect">
    <option value="Bells.WAV">Bells</option>
    <option value="Cuckoo2.WAV">Cuckoo</option>
    <option value="Shred2.WAV">Shredder</option>
</select>
<input type="button"
       id="btnChoose"
       value="Choose"
       onclick="ChangeTune()" /><br />

<!-- An output area to monitor the status of the Media Player
     object. -->
<textarea id="txtOutput" cols="50" rows="2" />
</body>
</html>
```

The Web page contains the Windows Media Player control, a sound effect selection, and a button for changing the sound within the Windows Media Player. The example also includes a status window so you can see the effects of the change on the internal Windows Media Player data. The project folder contains three sound files that you can use, or you can create sound files of your own.

When the user clicks Choose, btnChoose calls ChangeTune(). The ChangeTune() function begins by setting the objMediaPlayer.URL property to the name of the new sound file. The next step verifies the setting by outputting the objMediaPlayer.childNodes(0).name and objMediaPlayer.childNodes(0).value properties. The childNodes array contains a list of the parameters described in the "Getting the <Object> Tag Data" section earlier in this chapter in the order described. Every object you create has the same feature, so you can easily track the status of various elements, even those not accessible through properties.

TIP The Internet provides a number of resources for using the Windows Media Player. One of the best sources is the series of articles that Microsoft provides at http://msdn.microsoft.com/library/en-us/wmplay10/mmp_sdk/displayingwebpagesinwindowsmediaplayer.asp. You'll find a streaming media jukebox player application described at http://www.webreference.com/js/column51/install.html. The article at http://cita.rehab.uiuc.edu/media-player/sami-web.html tells you how to add media with captions to your Web site. In fact, this is one of the few examples that also shows you how to request a download of the Windows Media Player when the client machine doesn't have it installed.

The final step tells the Windows Media Player to play the selected file using the `objMediaPlayer`
`.controls.play()` method. Unfortunately, you won't find either the URL property or the `play()`
method listed in IntelliSense—you must know which properties and methods the object supports.
That's why it's handy to have a copy of Object Browser open so you can work with the various properties and controls. Figure 6.9 shows typical output from this application. Notice that even though
you can't see the object in Visual Web Developer, it displays correctly on the Web page and you even
have full access to the various object features.

FIGURE 6.9

The Windows Media
Player and other objects
work great on Web pages.

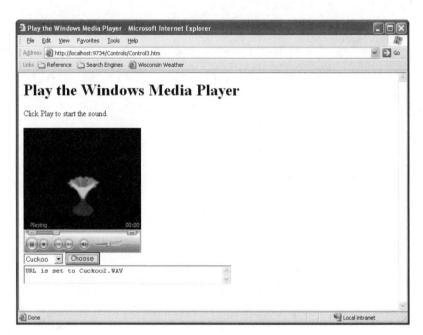

Relying on ASP.NET Controls

Of all the controls you can use with Visual Web Developer, ASP.NET controls prove the least cumbersome and difficult to use. However, there are some odd rules you have to follow when working with
ASP.NET controls, one of which is that you can't always use an ASP.NET control to perform a task. The
control that actually interacts with the script must be an HTML control. For example, you can create an
entire form using ASP.NET controls as long as the button used to submit the form using a script is an
HTML control. ASP.NET controls only support code behind techniques, which means that they always
require server support. Listing 6.4 shows a simple example of working with ASP.NET controls. You'll
find this example in the \Chapter 06\Controls folder of the source code on the Sybex Web site.

LISTING 6.4:   Using Scripts with ASP.NET Controls

```
<%@ Page Language="VB"
        AutoEventWireup="false"
        CompileWith="Control4.aspx.vb"
```

```
        ClassName="Control4_aspx" %>

<!DOCTYPE html PUBLIC "-//W3C//DTD XHTML 1.1//EN"
                    "http://www.w3.org/TR/xhtml11/DTD/xhtml11.dtd">

<html xmlns="http://www.w3.org/1999/xhtml" >
<head runat="server">
    <title>Untitled Page</title>
    <script type="text/javascript">
    <!--
        function btnChange_OnClick()
        {
            var InputString;

            // Get the current string value.
            InputString = form1.txtInput.value;

            // Encode it.
            form1.txtOutput.value = escape(InputString);
        }
    -->
    </script>
</head>
<body>
    <form id="form1" runat="server">
    <div>
        <asp:Label ID="lblGreeting"
                   Runat="server"
                   Text="ASPX Control
                   Demonstration" Font-Bold="True"
                   Font-Size="X-Large"></asp:Label>
        <br />
        <asp:Label ID="lblInput"
                   Runat="server"
                   Text="Type any string: "
                   AssociatedControlID="txtInput"></asp:Label>
        <asp:TextBox ID="txtInput"
                     AccessKey="T"
                     Runat="Server">
            A Sample String
        </asp:TextBox><br />
        <asp:Label ID="lblOutput"
                   Runat="server"
                   Text="Output string: "
                   AssociatedControlID="txtOutput"></asp:Label>
        <asp:TextBox ID="txtOutput" Runat="server"></asp:TextBox>
        <br />
        <input id="btnChange"
```

```
                        accesskey="C"
                        type="button"
                        value="Change the Text"
                        onclick="btnChange_OnClick()" />

        </div>
        </form>
    </body>
    </html>
```

Begin by looking at the HTML for this example. All of the controls are ASP.NET controls, not standard HTML controls, except for btnChange. You need to use a standard HTML control here because the standard ASP.NET button doesn't support scripting through the onclick attribute. The HTML in this example demonstrates a perfect mix of ASP.NET and HTML—at least if you want to use client-side processing to reduce the workload on the server.

WARNING   The features described in this section apply only to ASP.NET 2.0. Older versions of ASP.NET are extremely painful to work with when using scripts because the server mangles the control names. To learn more about this particular problem, see the WWW Coder article at http://www.wwwcoder.com/main/parentid/261/site/3590/68/default.aspx.

Notice that this code does include the usual <%@ Page> directive. You can create a page where some buttons or other controls with events use client-side processing and other controls rely on the server for processing. The point is that you have the freedom to use whatever kind of processing works best for the particular situation.

When a user clicks Change the Text in this application, btnChange calls the btnChange_OnClick() method. This function begins by obtaining the form1.txtInput.value property. IntelliSense won't tell you that this control is available, nor will it tell you about the full list of properties and objects that form1 possesses. Sometimes you have to work with the script for a while in the debugger to understand fully the properties, methods, and events the various controls support in code. Notice, however, that txtInput is an ASP.NET control and you can access it without error in the script.

Once the code obtains the value of txtInput, it uses the escape() function to modify any characters that could cause problems in HTML so that you can transmit them without error. The code places the result in form1.txtOutput.value (another ASP.NET control) and the user sees the value on screen—without a trip to the server. Figure 6.10 shows typical output from this application.

FIGURE 6.10
ASP.NET Web pages can use scripts just as easily as standard HTML.

Notice that the escape() function converts problem characters to other forms. For example, it converts spaces to %20 and the backslash (\) to %5C. This is a standard conversion that all Web servers understand and use. You can find a complete list of these conversions on the User Interface Programming site at http://home.online.no/~pethesse/charcodes.html.

Working with Nonvisual Data and Components

You have access to a vast array of nonvisual data and components on any given user system. For example, you can use special components to modify the registry, create files, and perform other tasks. The power of nonvisual components is the reason that many users are terrified of what your script will do to their system and the reason you must gain their trust through ethical behavior to create an environment where your script can run. Using nonvisual data and components has many positive purposes as well. For example, you can use nonvisual components to make a query on the user's behalf, interpret the results, and provide a nicely formatted display of the information retrieved. Amazon Web Services provides such an opportunity and it's the example used in this section. You'll find this example in the \Chapter 06\AmazonWebService folder of the source code on the Sybex Web site.

TIP You can perform an amazing number of tasks with Amazon Web Services, including managing your own offerings or becoming an Amazon associate. In short, even though the example in this section shows how to create a nice search service for your users, you can actually do a lot more with Amazon Web Services. I based much of the material in this section on my book, *Mining Amazon Web Services* (Sybex, 2004). This book shows you the full extent of the functionality that Amazon Web Services can provide for your Web site.

WHAT IS A WEB SERVICE?

You can look at a Web service from a number of perspectives. The easiest way to view a Web service is as a means of obtaining access to information. Essentially, you ask the server for information and the server returns that information in some form. The request and the returned information normally appear in eXtensible Markup Language (XML) form. Using XML preserves the meaning behind the information so that you receive not only the information, but understand the context in which the information is used as well.

From an Amazon Web Services perspective, you request information on one or more products, vendors, or other search criteria. The request defines the kind of information you want to know and how detailed that information will be. The Amazon Web Service returns the information you request (when available) in a standardized format specified by their database schema. A schema defines the organization of information in a database.

A Web service also performs some type of useful work. The useful work might be something as simple as interpreting your request, calculating the answer, and sending the result back. In the case of Amazon Web Services, the Web service accepts your request (normally, some search criteria), interacts with the database through a search engine to obtain the information you requested, and sends the information back to you. You can also perform other tasks using Amazon Web Services, such as make a purchase or sell goods to others.

The final consideration for a Web service (at least from the Web service user perspective) is that it executes on the remote machine, not on your machine. In short, this means you're using resources on that other machine with the permission of the machine's owner. The remote machine can set requirements for using the Web service, as well as require you to perform specific setup and security checks as part of your request. In the case of Amazon Web Services, you need to obtain this permission by requesting it as part of the Amazon Web Services Kit download process. The next section, "Registering to Become a Developer," tells you how to obtain the required permission and what this permission means to you.

Registering to Become a Developer

Before you begin working with Amazon Web Services, you need to gain access to the online documents and obtain a developer token. Once you have the required resources, you can begin creation applications that use Amazon Web Services.

You'll find the main Web services page at http://www.amazon.com/gp/browse.html?node=3435361. Figure 6.11 shows that this page contains some information, along with three important links. Make sure you perform step 1 before proceeding with this chapter. (To get the most from the Web service, make sure you perform steps 2 and 3 as well, rather than charging ahead.) This chapter assumes that you want to download the Amazon Web Services Kit first.

FIGURE 6.11

The Amazon Web Services site helps you obtain the kit and a developer token.

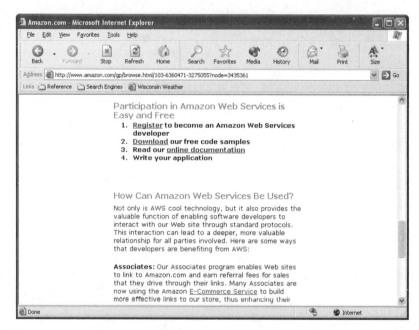

Click the Register to Become an Amazon Web Services Developer link and you'll see a page that describes the kit. Follow the prompts to register to obtain the kit. You'll see a Web page that requests an email address and password. You'll see a complete copy of the licensing agreement below these fields. Make sure you read the licensing agreement because it contains important usage information in addition to the actual terms of use.

Don't worry about getting your developer token from the Web site. You'll see a message stating that Amazon will send your developer token to your email. The email actually contains a link that takes you to a Web page containing your developer token. I received mine in about an hour—you might need to wait more or less time depending on how busy Amazon is at the time. Make sure you save the email message containing the developer token because you'll need it for every transaction later.

You'll receive a second email that contains detailed information about the Amazon Web Services program. This second email contains links to Amazon Web Services features such as the online reference that tells you about the Web service and how to use it.

Make sure that you eventually go back to the main page and click the Download Our Free Code Samples link. This link takes you to the downloadable portion of Amazon Web Services, including all of the example code. However, this page contains a lot more. For example, it includes links for downloading the Web Services Description Language (WSDL) file. All of these individual files used to appear in the Amazon Web Services Kit, but now appear as separate downloads. Even if you download everything, the kit will consume less that 4 MB on your hard drive.

It's also important to look at the various tools that Amazon makes available. You can see them listed on the left side of the Web services page shown in Figure 6.11. The tools include an XML scratch pad (for creating queries), seller pricing tool, and an XPath/XSLT development tool.

Creating the Request

No one says that working with a Web service has to be hard or mysterious. Amazon Web Services relies on a very simple technique for receiving requests—all you need to do is type an URL in your browser. You can literally type the following URL in your browser's Address field, press Enter, and get back results. Make sure that you replace the string, `Your-Developer-Token` with your actual developer token. Note also that the URL is very long and wouldn't fit on a single line in the book. Simply type the entire URL without pressing Enter until you get to the end. Be sure you don't add any unnecessary spaces.

```
http://xml.amazon.com/onca/xml3?t=webservices-20&dev-t=Your-Developer-Token&
    AuthorSearch=John%20Mueller&mode=books&type=lite&page=1&f=xml
```

This URL may look complicated, but it's relatively easy once you know what the individual entries mean. The `http://xml.amazon.com/onca/xml3` entry is the actual Web service URL for XML queries—SOAP queries use a different URL. All of the arguments—the description of the query—appear after the URL. You separate each argument with an ampersand (&). Here's a short description of each entry.

t=webservices-20   This entry contains the associate identifier. When you establish an associate relationship with Amazon, any sales that you direct their way will net a commission. If you don't have an associated identifier, use the generic identifier shown.

dev-t=Your-Developer-Token   This entry contains the developer token of the requestor. Every request must include a developer token or the Web service won't honor it.

AuthorSearch=John%20Mueller   This entry contains the kind of search, an author, and the author's name. Notice that the query replaces the space in my name with %20. You can't use spaces in queries, so you use this special character combination instead.

mode=books   This entry tells the Web service to look for books. You can also look for other product types.

type=lite   This entry tells the Web service to provide only an overview of the information. You can also tell it to provide the details by specifying a heavy search.

page=1   This entry tells the Web service to return the first page. If you want the second page, then you type **page=2** instead.

f=xml   This entry defines the query format. In this case, we're using XML. The Amazon Web Services can also work with SOAP requests.

Using a Script to Call an XSLT Page

Amazon doesn't know how you want to present the data they provide, so the XML you receive doesn't include any form of XSLT declaration. This declaration normally appears as `<?xml-stylesheet type="text/xsl" href="amazon-seller-search-popup.xsl"?>` in the XML file. The `href` attribute tells where to find the XSLT file. Without this information, the browser will never display anything but XML on screen. It would seem that the situation is hopeless. However, you have other options, such as writing a script that performs the transformation process using another technique.

The example in Listing 6.5 shows how you can download a response from Amazon, store the information locally, and translate it using XSLT. The result is the same as modifying the XML file to include the required linkage information, but far more automatic.

LISTING 6.5:   Performing a Transformation in JavaScript

```
function GetData(XslFile)
{
   // Convert the author name to use %20 instead of spaces.
   var AuthName = SubmissionForm.AuthorSearch.value;
   AuthName = escape(AuthName);

   // Build a string that will hold the complete URL.
   var XmlFile = "http://xml.amazon.com/onca/xml3?" +
                 "t=" + SubmissionForm.t.value + "&" +
                 "dev-t=" + SubmissionForm.devt.value + "&" +
                 "AuthorSearch=" + AuthName + "&" +
                 "mode=" + SubmissionForm.mode.value + "&" +
                 "type=" + SubmissionForm.type.value + "&" +
                 "page=" + SubmissionForm.page.value + "&" +
                 "f=" + SubmissionForm.f.value;

   // Create an XML document object and load the data from the
   // Amazon Web Service into it.
   var XMLData = new ActiveXObject("Msxml2.DOMDocument.5.0");
   XMLData.async=false;
   XMLData.load(XmlFile);

   // Create an XSLT document and load the transform into it.
   var XSLTData = new ActiveXObject("Msxml2.DOMDocument.5.0");
   XSLTData.async = false;
   XSLTData.load(XslFile);

   // Display the output on screen.
   document.write(XMLData.transformNode(XSLTData));
}
```

The script relies on named text boxes on the Web page for input. The first task the code performs is to URL encode the `AuthName` value using the `escape()` function. The code then combines the various values and the XML site URL into a request URL.

The next step is a little tricky and definitely Windows specific. The code creates an instance of the Microsoft XML component. This component lacks any kind of interface, yet it can have a profound (positive) impact on the user. The `ActiveXObject()` function performs this task. The `Msxml2.DOMDocument.5.0` string identifies the component. You might have to use `Msxml2.DOMDocument.4.0` on older machines—the last part of the string identifies the component version number. Setting the `async` property to false is important because you don't want the call to load the XML to return until the browser actually receives this file. Finally, the `XMLData.load()` function loads the response from Amazon Web Services.

The code now has a local copy of the data from Amazon. This local copy will disappear as soon as the function ends, so you don't have to worry about update requirements, but it's important to understand that the copy resides in memory on your machine somewhere.

At this point, the code has data to work with, but no XSLT file. The next step loads the XSLT file defined by the `XslFile` variable. The coupling between the XML response and the XSLT occurs in the `XMLData.transformNode()` function call. This call produces output that the `document.write()` function then sends to the current page. The result is that you see the transformed XML on screen, as shown in Figure 6.12. Notice that the URL doesn't change, even though the content differs, because you're still theoretically on the same Web page.

FIGURE 6.12
The results of using a script to transform XML data received from Amazon.

Writing a Simple XSLT Page

This section describes the XSLT page used with the transformation described in the previous section, "Using a Script to Call an XSLT Page" (see Listing 6.5). Listing 6.6 shows how to create an XSLT page that outputs HTML code. You could use the same technique to create a report or any other form of output based on the XML input received from Amazon.

LISTING 6.6:   Designing an XSLT Page

```
<?xml version="1.0" encoding="UTF-8"?>
<xsl:stylesheet version="1.0"
 xmlns:xsl="http://www.w3.org/1999/XSL/Transform"
 xmlns:fo="http://www.w3.org/1999/XSL/Format">
<xsl:template match="/">
<html>
<head>
   <title>XSLT Transformation Example</title>
</head>
<body>
   <!-- Display a heading. -->
   <h1 align="center">Translated Amazon Web Server Results</h1>

   <!-- Displays the arguments used_u102 ?or the call. -->
   <table align="center" border="1" width="60%">
      <caption>Search Result Arugments</caption>
      <tbody>
         <tr>
            <th>Name</th>
            <th>Value</th>
         </tr>
         <xsl:for-each select="ProductInfo/Request/Args/Arg">
            <tr>
               <td><xsl:value-of select="@name"/></td>
               <td><xsl:value-of select="@value"/></td>
            </tr>
         </xsl:for-each>
      </tbody>
   </table>

   <!-- Display the search result values. -->
   <table align="center" border="1" width="100%">
      <caption>Books Returned from Query</caption>
      <tbody>
         <tr>
            <th>Book Title</th>
            <th>ISBN</th>
            <th>Release Date</th>
            <th>Publisher</th>
         </tr>
```

```
        <xsl:for-each select="ProductInfo/Details">
            <tr>
                <td><xsl:value-of select="ProductName"/></td>
                <td><xsl:value-of select="Asin"/></td>
                <td><xsl:value-of select="ReleaseDate"/></td>
                <td><xsl:value-of select="Manufacturer"/></td>
            </tr>
        </xsl:for-each>
        </tbody>
    </table>

</body>
</html>
</xsl:template>
</xsl:stylesheet>
```

The code begins with the usual declarations. It then outputs the heading. Notice that this is pure HTML and that the code isn't doing anything but output this text. The code moves on to the body where it outputs a heading.

The XSLT-specific code begins when the code starts creating a table. Notice the head of the table is standard HTML, but that the next selection is an `<xsl:for-each>` element. This statement tells the parser to look at all of the children of the `ProductInfo/Request/Args/` node. The system will process each `<Arg>` element in turn. The next step is to use the `<xsl:value-of>` element to retrieve the name and value attributes of each `<Arg>` element. Notice how the code uses the attribute axis to ensure that the parser retrieves the attribute values and not the element values.

Once the code processes all of the arguments, it moves on to the `<Details>` element. The code uses the `<xsl:for-each>` element again to select each of the books in turn. It uses the `<xsl:value-of>` element to select each element value in turn. Notice that the code codes rely on an axis, in this case, because it uses the selected element directly. The code ends by completing the HTML page, and then completing both the template and the style sheet.

Storing and Deleting Cookies

No matter how you try to avoid using them, some applications require the use of cookies. The problem is simple. Web communications are one way. A client makes a request and the server responds. When the client makes a second request, the server views it as a new connection, making Web communications stateless. The only way to add state information (maintain a view of the transactions taking place) is to use cookies in many cases. Cookies store the information needed for the system to keep track of the conversation between the client and the server. The following sections describe the two cookie types: temporary and permanent.

Creating and Reading Temporary Cookies

Always use temporary cookies when you can. A temporary cookie lasts only for the current session, which means that you don't have as many privacy and security concerns when using them. In addition, most users are more willing to allow cookies when they know that the cookie will last only a short time. You'll find this example (Listing 6.7) in the `\Chapter 06\TemporaryCookie` folder of the source code on the Sybex Web site.

LISTING 6.7:   Using Temporary Cookies

```
<!DOCTYPE html PUBLIC "-//W3C//DTD XHTML 1.1//EN"
                    "http://www.w3.org/TR/xhtml11/DTD/xhtml11.dtd">
<html xmlns="http://www.w3.org/1999/xhtml" >
<head>
    <title>Temporary Cookie Demonstration</title>

<script language="javascript">
<!--
    function GetCookie()
    {
        if (clientInformation.cookieEnabled)
        {
            // When there aren't any cookie values, ask
            // for new entries.
            if (document.cookie.length == 0)
            {
                // Get the user name.
                txtUserName.value = prompt("Please type your user name");

                // Get a background color.
                document.bgColor = prompt("Type a background color name");
            }
            else
            {

                // Get the cookie values.
                var aCookies = document.cookie.split("; ");

                // Process each of the cookie values.
                for (Counter = 0; Counter < aCookies.length; Counter++)
                {
                    // Divide the cookie into a name and value pair.
                    var aCrumb = aCookies[Counter].split("=");

                    // Determine the cookie type.
                    switch (aCrumb[0])
                    {
                        case "UserName":
                            txtUserName.value = unescape(aCrumb[1]);
                            break;
                        case "bgColor":
                            document.bgColor = unescape(aCrumb[1]);
                            break;
                    }
                }
            }
        }
```

```
          // Display a personalized greeting.
          txtGreeting.innerText =
              "Hello " + txtUserName.value + ", glad to see you!";
       }
       else
       {
          // Provide a greeting for users who don't have
          // cookies enabled.
          txtGreeting.innerText="Hello stranger, glad to see you!";
       }
    }
    function SaveCookie()
    {
       // Determine whether the user has cookies enabled.
       if (clientInformation.cookieEnabled)
       {
          // Normally you don't display a message, but it's
          // good for testing.
          alert("Saving Cookie");

          // Save the user's name.
          document.cookie =
              "UserName=" + escape(txtUserName.value) + ";";

          // Save the user's background color preference.
          document.cookie = "bgColor=" + escape(document.bgColor);
       }
    }
//-->
</script>

</head>

    <!-- Use one function for loading the cookies and another to save
         them -->
    <body onload="GetCookie()" onunload="SaveCookie()">

    <!-- This input is only used for temporary data storage so it has
         no size. -->
    <input type="hidden" id="txtUserName" visible="false" />

    <!-- Display the customized greeting. -->
    <p id="txtGreeting"></p>

</body>

</html>
```

When the form loads, it calls the GetCookie() function. This code considers three situations.

♦ The user has cookie support, but hasn't visited the site before, so there aren't any cookies to read.

♦ The user has visited the site before and there are cookies to read.

♦ The user's browser doesn't have cookie support.

The first if statement checks the clientInformation.cookieEnabled property to determine whether the user has cookie support enabled. When the user doesn't have cookie support enabled, the code executes the else clause of this if statement to display a generic greeting. The code doesn't change the background color because there isn't any way to determine the user's preference. You could easily add the generic greeting to the form and avoid using scripts at all when the client doesn't support cookies.

NOTE   Checking for client cookie support illustrates an important concept—always provide an alternative for the user who doesn't want to use cookies even if that alternative is inconvenient for you. Most Web sites work with cookies or they don't work at all, which is a very poor way of treating the user. Sometimes you can't provide the requested functionality with cookies, but there's usually an alternative even when using shopping carts. Simply display a message asking the user to call your customer support line to make the order over the telephone. Using this technique means that you won't lose out on a sale.

The next step is to determine whether the user has any cookies for your site. When the document .cookie.length property is 0 there aren't any cookies to process and you can assume this is a first-time user. The code prompts for values to store in the cookies, but you can obtain the cookie data using any other technique you want. Notice that the code doesn't store the data in variables—it uses form entries to store the information. This is a common practice because the form entries are global to the entire Web page.

The else clause executes when the user has cookie support enabled and there are cookies to process. The code uses the special split() method to divide the cookie entries. The split() method creates an array that JavaScript stores in aCookies. The array contains one entry for each cookie.

TIP   You might have noticed the use of the escape() and unescape() functions in the example. Always escape (also known as URL encoding) the values you save to a cookie to ensure that the script converts any control characters into a form that the text file can accept. Likewise, un-escape the values when you retrieve them from the cookies to ensure that the control character data is restored.

Now that the cookies are split, the code uses the aCookies.length property to determine how many cookies there are and processes each cookie in turn using a for loop. To process a cookie, you must break it into crumbs (a name and value pair). The code uses the split() method again to perform this task and places the name and value pair in the aCrumb array.

NOTE   A cookie consists of two crumbs: a name and a value. The name is the identifier you use for the cookie. Listing 6.7 shows two cookies named: UserName and bgColor. Always choose a name that identifies the purpose of the cookie so you can retrieve and understand its purpose later. The value is the information you want to save. You can retrieve any variable or object property that you want to save as a value.

The name crumb always appears in array element 0, so the code can use a switch statement to process it. A switch is an extended version of the if statement. Every case entry acts as an if statement.

Therefore, the code asks whether the name equals `UserName` first and `bgColor` second. When the name doesn't match either value, nothing happens.

When the name does match one of the target values, JavaScript follows the code between the case entry and the break entry. For example, when working with the `UserName` crumb, the code places the value, which always appears in `aCrumb` element 1, into the `txtUserName.value` property.

When the form unloads, it calls the `SaveCookie()` function. Notice that this form contains event handlers for two `<body>` tag events—you can assign as many scripts as needed to various tag events to create a complete solution. This function begins by determining whether the client has cookies enabled. If the client doesn't have cookies enabled, the function exits without doing anything. Otherwise, the code displays a message box using the `alert()` function. It then saves the cookie using the `document.cookie` property.

Unlike many properties, the `document.cookie` property is a collection. Every time you supply a new name and value pair, JavaScript creates a new entry for it in the collection. Consequently, when the code assigns the `UserName` value and then the `bgColor` value to the `document.cookie` property, JavaScript actually creates two entries—one for each value.

Creating and Reading Permanent Cookies

Permanent cookies let you save data between sessions. Some less-than-honorable Web sites use them to do things such as track user movements. Fortunately, you have many useful and positive ways to incorporate permanent cookies into your applications too. A common need is saving user configuration information so that you can restore the user experience for each visit. For example, you could use a cookie to store the user's preferred CSS file as suggested in the "Designing Flexible Interfaces" section of Chapter 4. Always make sure that you provide a privacy policy when using cookies as outlined in the "Developing a Privacy Policy" section of Chapter 5. You'll find this example (Listing 6.8) in the \Chapter 06\PermanentCookie folder of the source code on the Sybex Web site.

LISTING 6.8:   Using Permanent Cookies

```
<!DOCTYPE html PUBLIC "-//W3C//DTD XHTML 1.1//EN" "http://www.w3.org/TR/xhtml11/DTD/
xhtml11.dtd">
<html xmlns="http://www.w3.org/1999/xhtml" >
<head>
    <title>Permanent Cookie Demonstration</title>

    <script language="javascript">
    <!--
    function btnSave_Click()
    {
        var UserCookie;          // Stores the user name.
        var TheDate = new Date(); // Date object.
        var Expire;              // Expiration date.

        // Build an expiration date. Begin by getting the day.
        // of the week.
        switch (TheDate.getUTCDay() + 2)
        {
        case 1:
```

```
        Expire = "Sun, ";
        break;

... Other Cases ...

case 7:
    Expire = "Sat, ";
    break;

}

// Add the date.
Expire = Expire + (TheDate.getUTCDate() + 1);

// Add the month.
switch (TheDate.getUTCMonth() + 1)
{
case 1:
    Expire = Expire + " Jan ";
    break;

... Other Cases ...

case 12:
    Expire = Expire + " Dec ";
    break;
}

// Add the year.
Expire = Expire + TheDate.getUTCFullYear() + " ";

// Add the time.
Expire = Expire + TheDate.getUTCHours() + ":" +
        TheDate.getUTCMinutes() + ":" +
        TheDate.getUTCSeconds() + " UTC";

// Create the username cookie.
UserCookie = "UserName=" +
            escape(prompt("Type your name")) +
            "; expires=" + Expire + ";";

// Add the cookie to the document.
document.cookie = UserCookie;

// Tell the user the cookie was saved.
alert("The cookies were saved and will expire on: " +
    Expire + ".");
}
```

```
    function btnGet_Click()
    {
        var  ACookie; // Holds the document cookie.
        var  Parsed;  // Holds the split cookies.
        var  Name;    // The user name.

        // Get the cookie.
        ACookie = unescape(document.cookie);

        // Split the cookie elements.
        Parsed = ACookie.split("=");

        // Get the user name.
        Name = Parsed[1];

        // Display the name.
        alert("Your name is: " + Name);
    }

    //-->
    </script>
</head>
<body>

    <h1>Permanent Cookie Demonstration</h1>
    <p>
        <button id="btnSave" onclick="btnSave_Click()">
            Save Cookie
        </button>
        <button id="btnGet" onclick="btnGet_Click()">
            Get Cookie
        </button>
    </p>

</body>

</html>
```

The actual cookie creation process is the same as Listing 6.7. In this case, you have access to two buttons on the form—one saves the cookie, while the other gets the cookie. Defining the date takes a little more work. You must create a Universal Time Code (UTC) date for your cookie. The date must appear in a very specific format. The code in Listing 6.8 shows how to create such a date. The final date appears like this:

```
Sat, 5 Jun 2004 18:44:53 UTC
```

To begin the process, the code creates a Date object, `TheDate`. This object provides access to a number of date and time functions, including the UTC functions shown in the code. For example, the `getUTCDay()` function retrieves the day of the week as a number between 0 and 6. Because the date must contain the day as a name, the code uses a switch to convert it to text form.

One of the problems with working with the time functions is that you can't retrieve the time directly. You must use the method shown. The `getTime()` method returns the number of milliseconds since midnight January 1, 1970, which isn't particularly helpful in this case.

Notice that adding an expiration date is simply adding another cookie to the document. The expiration date relies on the keyword `expires`, which you can't use for any other purpose. When JavaScript sees this keyword, it reads the date supplied and acts according to specific rules. When the date is in the past, JavaScript erases the cookies immediately. On the other hand, when the date is in the future, JavaScript creates a file on disk that holds the information. The precise location varies, but when you use Windows 2000 or Windows XP, the cookie appears in the `\Documents and Settings\<Your Login Name>\Cookies` folder. The cookie has your name and the folder in which the associated Web page appears, along with a TXT extension. You can easily open the file and see what it contains using Notepad

Using Web Parts to Automate User Customizations

Web Parts help you create pages that users can customize as desired. One of the interesting features of Web Parts is that they rely on a combination of server-side and client-side code. When you create a Web page that includes Web Parts, you'll find that it contains scripts that the server automatically generates based on the content of the page you design. The server side of the code manages the page, and it stores the changes that the user makes in the local Access database. You'll find that this technique eliminates the need for cookies, but it also creates a requirement for a strong privacy policy that users will accept. Note that this chapter outlines only the basic scripting and database considerations for working with Web Parts. The "Working with Web Parts" section of Chapter 13 provides additional details. You'll find this example in the `\Chapter 06\WebParts` folder of the source code on the Sybex Web site.

TIP   Web Parts is an exciting new technology and some early adopters have already begun working with them. You can find an interesting tutorial from one of these early adopters at `http://www.carlosag.net/Articles/WebParts/connectionsTutorial.aspx`.

Adding the *WebPartManager*

The `WebPartManager` control is the component that coordinates the efforts of all of the other controls that you add to the Web page. This control doesn't actually create any content and you don't have to do anything to configure it. However, you must have one (and only one) of these controls on the page before you add any other WebPart controls to the page. You can drag and drop this control from the Toolbox or add it to the page in Source view, as shown here:

```
<asp:WebPartManager ID="WebPartManager1" Runat="server">
</asp:WebPartManager>
```

Changing Selections using a Custom Control

Before the user can work with Web Parts, you must provide a means for them to change selections. Theoretically, Microsoft could provide a control to perform this task, but for whatever reason, they decided not to do so. Consequently, you need to create a custom control to perform the task. You begin this task using the Add New Item dialog box to add a Web User Control to your project. This file type has an ASCX file extension.

Custom controls have two parts. The first part is the display you provide to the end user. The control interface for this product includes a drop-down list box for selecting the editing mode, a reset link, and two radio buttons that determine the scope of the changes you make. The scope is important. When you choose the user scope, the changes affect only the local user. Choosing the shared scope means that everyone is affected.

After you create the basic appearance for the control, you need to add code to make it function. The code in Listing 6.9 shows the initialization portion of a very basic control based on the Microsoft example. You can use this code directly or modify it to meet your needs. However, unless you have a pressing reason to change something, you should stick with this basic example.

LISTING 6.9:   Defining Editor Handling Features for Web Parts

```
' Use a field to reference the current WebPartManager control.
Dim WPM As WebPartManager

Sub Page_Init(ByVal sender As Object, ByVal e As EventArgs)
    ' Tell the Web page to use this handler for Web Parts.
    AddHandler Page.InitComplete, AddressOf InitComplete
End Sub

Sub InitComplete(ByVal sender As Object, ByVal e As System.EventArgs)
    Dim DisplayMode As WebPartDisplayMode   ' A list of zones.
    Dim ModeName As String                  ' A mode title.
    Dim ddlModeItem As ListItem             ' One mode entry.

    ' Get the current Web Part Manager for the page. The Web Part
    ' Manager will know about all of the editor zones for the
    ' current page.
    WPM = WebPartManager.GetCurrentWebPartManager(Page)

    ' Fill the drop-down list with the names of display modes
    ' that the page supports.
    For Each DisplayMode In WPM.SupportedDisplayModes

        ' Get the current display mode.
        ModeName = DisplayMode.Name

        ' Make sure a mode is enabled before adding it.
        If DisplayMode.IsEnabled(WPM) Then

            ' Define a new mode list item and add it.
            ddlModeItem = New ListItem(ModeName, ModeName)
            ddlMode.Items.Add(ddlModeItem)
        End If
```

```
        Next DisplayMode

        ' Determine whether this user can work with shared scope
        ' items. Only administrators normally have this privilege.
        If WPM.Personalization.CanEnterSharedScope Then

            ' Make the personalization scope panel visible.
            pnlPersonalizeMode.Visible = True

            ' Select the correct scope for the current setup.
            If WPM.Personalization.Scope = PersonalizationScope.User Then
                rbUserScope.Checked = True
            Else
                rbSharedScope.Checked = True
            End If
        End If
    End Sub
```

The central focus of most activities in this custom control is the `WebPartManager` control that you added to the Web page. The `WebPartManager` control, `WPM`, tracks all of the page activity, knows which zones the page contains, and can interact with the various zones you provide. Consequently, the code defines `WPM` as a global variable to make the process of working with the page easier.

The Web page only calls the custom control during the page initialization process. To make the control active, you must provide one or more event handler additions during the `Page_Init()` method call performed by the Web page as part of initializing your control. In this case, the only handler that the `Page_Init()` method adds is one that calls `InitComplete()` once the page initialization finishes. The reason for using this approach is that `WPM` won't know about the various zone controls on the page until after the initialization completes, so the code can't create a menu before that time.

The `InitComplete()` method begins by obtaining a copy of the `WebPartManager` for the current page. It then uses `WPM` to obtain the name or title of the mode that the Web page currently supports. The modes appear in the `WPM.SupportedDisplayModes` collection. The code gets the name for a mode, verifies that the page has the required control for that mode, and then adds the mode name to the list. The WebPartManager supports several modes including:

◆ BrowseDisplayMode

◆ CatalogDisplayMode

◆ ConnectDisplayMode

◆ DesignDisplayMode

◆ EditDisplayMode

The initialization ends by verifying the user's capabilities. Administrators can change both their personal settings and the settings for everyone who uses the Web page. The ability to change individual or all settings is called scope and the `WebPartManager` currently supports two scopes: user and shared. The code detects people who can use shared mode (the default is use) and makes the Personalization Scope panel available to those who have the proper credentials.

Once the initialization is complete, you need to add code to handle the individual controls. The only control that you must implement is the drop-down list box that lets the user choose an editing mode. Everything else is optional. Here is the code for the drop-down list box.

```
Sub ddlMode_SelectedIndexChanged(ByVal sender As Object, _
                                 ByVal e As EventArgs)
    Dim SelMode As String                  ' The User Selected Mode.
    Dim DisplayMode As WebPartDisplayMode  ' Web Parts Properties.

    ' Get the editor mode that the user selected from the drop down
    ' list box.
    SelMode = ddlMode.SelectedValue

    ' Get the information for that mode from the list of supported
    ' modes.
    DisplayMode = WPM.SupportedDisplayModes(SelMode)

    ' Change the page to the selected display mode.
    If Not (DisplayMode Is Nothing) Then
        WPM.DisplayMode = DisplayMode
    End If
End Sub
```

The code begins by obtaining the mode that the user selected from the drop-down list box, `ddlMode`. It uses this information to obtain properties for that particular mode from the list of modes that the `WebPartManager` supports using the `SupportedDisplayModes()` method. Finally, the code sets the current `WPM` mode to match the mode the user selected by changing the `WPM.DisplayMode` property.

Users will make mistakes, so it's nice to provide a means for resetting the display. The Reset User State hyperlink performs this function. When the user clicks this link, the following code changes the `WPM` state.

```
Protected Sub lbtnReset_Click(ByVal sender As Object, _
                              ByVal e As EventArgs)

    ' Reset all of a user's personalization data for the page.
    WPM.Personalization.ResetPersonalizationState()

End Sub
```

Fortunately, the `WebPartManager` provides everything needed to perform this task, so you don't have to perform any messy state tracking. The `ResetPersonalizationState()` method call takes care of everything.

The final task is to let an administrator switch from user to shared mode. You only need to implement this feature when the Web site uses shared settings and allows someone to change them. Here is the code you use to perform this task.

```
Protected Sub rbUserScope_CheckedChanged(ByVal sender As Object, _
                                         ByVal e As EventArgs)
```

```
        ' Verify the current scope setting.
        If WPM.Personalization.Scope = PersonalizationScope.Shared Then

            ' Change to user scope if necessary.
            WPM.Personalization.ToggleScope()
        End If
    End Sub


    Protected Sub rbSharedScope_CheckedChanged(ByVal sender As Object, _
                                    ByVal e As EventArgs)
        ' Verify the current scope setting. Make sure the user is allowed
        ' to enter the shared scope.
        If WPM.Personalization.CanEnterSharedScope AndAlso _
            WPM.Personalization.Scope = PersonalizationScope.User Then

            ' Change to the shared scope.
            WPM.Personalization.ToggleScope()
        End If
    End Sub
```

The only call of concern in both cases is ToggleScope(). Of course, this means that you must verify the current scope before you call the ToggleScope() method. Otherwise, the toggling sequence will get out of order. Notice also that you must verify a user's credentials before switching into the shared scope mode. Otherwise, anyone could change the shared settings.

Once you complete the custom control, drag it from Solution Explorer onto your application form. The control will only display the mode selection and reset options when you add it to the Web page since the personalization scope features are only available at runtime after verification of the user credentials.

Creating Content with the *WebPartZone*

A Web Part Web page contains two kinds of content. The first kind is content that the user can't modify. For example, you wouldn't want to let the user remove the company logo from a Web page or modify important content such as warnings. The second kind is content that helps the user in some way that you want to allow the user to change as needed. For example, if your Web page includes the local weather and you feel that information is ancillary, you can let the user remove it or at least move it out of the way. The second kind of content appears in a WebPartZone control.

Normally, you'll include several WebPartZone controls on a page so the user can move items around. A page might contain a sidebar for less important information, a main area for important materials, and a lower section for items that the user wants, but doesn't use very often. The point of this example is to show the Web Part technology, rather than interesting content, so the two WebPartZone controls shown here contain simple labels and hyperlinks.

```
<asp:WebPartZone ID="wpzTest"
                Runat="server"
                HeaderText="Content Selections"
                EditVerb-Text="Edit">
    <ZoneTemplate>
```

```
                <asp:Label Runat="server"
                           Text="Hello the First Time"
                           ID="lblGreeting1" />
                <asp:HyperLink ID="hlNowhere"
                               Runat="server"
                               NavigateUrl="Default.aspx">
                    Goes Nowhere
                </asp:HyperLink>
        </ZoneTemplate>
    </asp:WebPartZone>
    <asp:WebPartZone ID="wpzTest2"
                     Runat="server"
                     HeaderText="Alternate Content Selections"
                     EditVerb-Text="Edit">
        <ZoneTemplate>
            <asp:Label Runat="server"
                       Text="Hello the Second Time"
                       ID="lblGreeting2" />
        </ZoneTemplate>
    </asp:WebPartZone>
```

Notice that the controls appear within a `<ZoneTemplate>` tag. You must include this tag as a container for the content. The content itself is relatively simple. The point is that you can include any content you want within the `<ZoneTemplate>` tag.

Modifying the Content with an *EditorZone*

Depending on what you want the user to do with the page, you can provide the design, edit, or both verbs on the `WebPartPageMenu` control. The design verb only lets the user move things around, while the edit verb allows a lot more. When you include the edit verb, you also need to add an `EditorZone` control. The Web page automatically displays the content of this control when the user selects the edit verb. Here's an example of an `EditorZone` control with two kinds of editors.

```
    <asp:EditorZone ID="EditorZone1" Runat="server">
        <ZoneTemplate>
            <asp:AppearanceEditorPart Runat="server"
                                      ID="AppearanceEditorPart1" />
            <asp:LayoutEditorPart Runat="server" ID="LayoutEditorPart1" />
        </ZoneTemplate>
    </asp:EditorZone>
```

As with most zone controls, you must place the `EditorZone` control content within a `<ZoneTemplate>` tag. In this case, the application uses an `AppearanceEditorPart` (changes the appearance of the control) and a `LayoutEditorPart` (lets the user move the data elements around) control. As you can see from the code, you don't have to perform a lot of work to make these controls functional. Figure 6.13 shows both controls in action.

FIGURE 6.13
Make changes to
the appearance
(AppearanceEditor-
Part) and layout
(LayoutEditorPart)
of the Web page.

To make this display appear, the user first chooses Edit from the Change the Layout menu. This selection displays the various controls, as shown in Figure 6.13, and makes the Edit selection for each control accessible. Choosing the Edit option for a particular control displays both the AppearanceEditorPart and LayoutEditorPart controls. Notice that the AppearanceEditorPart control lets the user change the title for the display element, as well as its width and height. The user can also choose to display the element with a title and border, or without either item. The user can even hide unwanted items from view. The LayoutEditorPart control makes it possible to move Web page elements around and change their state from normal (viewable) to minimized (just the title showing). The Zone Index field changes the control's position within a particular zone.

It's important to note that you can add other controls to the list. The BehaviorEditorPart control lets the user change how the control interacts with the Web page. The PropertyGridEditorPart control lets the user change individual properties for the controls. Both of these controls require special programming, so they appear in the "Working with Web Parts" section of Chapter 13.

Adding New Items with the *CatalogZone*

Think of a catalog as something you don't have now, but would like to have on the Web page. For example, when a user closes an element on a Web page and wants it back later, they open the catalog and select the missing item. Visual Web Developer supports three kinds of catalogs through the CatalogZone control. The PageCatalogPart control is the easiest to use and the one that you'll add most often. It lets a user add closed items back onto the page. The `DeclarativeCatalogPart` and `ImportCatalogPart` controls provide access to external elements and require special handling, so you'll find them discussed in the "Working with Web Parts" section of Chapter 13. Here's a sample of the `PageCatalogPart` control.

```
<asp:CatalogZone ID="CatalogZone1" Runat="server">
    <ZoneTemplate>
        <asp:PageCatalogPart ID="PageCatalogPart1" Runat="server" />
    </ZoneTemplate>
</asp:CatalogZone>
```

This control becomes active when the user selects the catalog verb from the `WebPartPageMenu` control. Figure 6.14 shows a typical example of the `PageCatalogPart` control in action. Notice that it contains the closed element on this Web page. To display the element, the user checks the element option (`Untitled [1]`), chooses a location from the Add To field, and clicks Add.

FIGURE 6.14

Add elements back onto the Web page using a PageCatalogPart control.

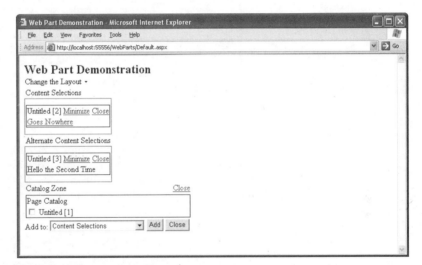

Viewing the Script behind the Controls

It's interesting to note that even though you don't write any script to use Web Parts, the IDE adds these scripts for you automatically. Right-click the example Web page and choose View Source from the context menu. You'll see the source code for the example Web page as the browser sees it. The first thing you'll notice is that the page contains many scripts sprinkled throughout the page, as shown in Figure 6.15.

Viewing the source for this Web page points out an important reason for learning the scripting language that you choose for Visual Web Developer. Even if you decide not to use scripting for your page, there's a good chance that anything you ask the IDE to perform automatically will produce some client-side code. Knowing how this code works can help you diagnose problems with the Web page. No, you can't modify the code directly, but the code that the IDE produces does help you understand what's going on in the background. In some cases, a change to the settings can make a big difference in the script that you see in the output.

FIGURE 6.15
Web Parts really do rely
on a combination of
client-side and server-
side scripting.

```
<script type="text/javascript">
<!--
var theForm = document.forms['form1'];
function __doPostBack(eventTarget, eventArgument) {
    if (theForm.onsubmit == null || theForm.onsubmit()) {
        theForm.__EVENTTARGET.value = eventTarget;
        theForm.__EVENTARGUMENT.value = eventArgument;
        theForm.submit();
    }
}
// -->
</script>


<script src="WebResource.axd?a=s&amp;r=webParts.js&amp;t=632352954239375000"
type="text/javascript"></script>
    <div>
        <span id="lblPageGreeting" style="font-size:X-Large;font-weight:bold;">Web Part
Demonstration</span>
        <br />

        <span id="WebPartPageMenu1"
style="cursor:hand;display:inline-block;padding:1px;text-decoration:none;">Change the
Layout <span id="WebPartPageMenu1Popup"
style="font-family:Marlett;font-size:8pt;">u</span></span><div id="WebPartPageMenu1Menu"
style="display:none;">
        <table cellspacing="0" cellpadding="1"
style="border-width:1px;border-style:solid;border-collapse:collapse;width:100%;">
            <tr>
                <td style="white-space:nowrap;"><div>
                    <a title="Browse this page in normal read-only mode."
href="javascript:void(0)" onclick="document.body.__wpm.SubmitPage('WebPartPageMenu1',
'Browse');" class="menuItem"><img
src="WebResource.axd?a=s&amp;r=Spacer.gif&amp;t=632352954239375000" alt="Browse" width="16"
height="16" style="border-style:none;vertical-align:middle;" /> Browse </a>
                </div><div style="height:5px;font-size:1pt;">
                    <img
src="WebResource.axd?a=s&amp;r=Spacer.gif&amp;t=632352954239375000" alt="" width="16" height="1"
style="vertical-align:middle;border-style:none;" /><img
```

Keeping Data Safe with Encoding

After you work with the example page for a while, you'll notice that any changes you make appear
the next time you start the application—even if you clear all of the cookies from your system. Web
Parts don't rely on cookies to store settings—the settings appear on the server in the \App Data folder
in the ASPNetDB.MDF database. Look in the aspnet_PagePersonalizationPerUser table and you'll
see at least one entry like the one shown in Figure 6.16.

FIGURE 6.16
The WebPart technology
automatically makes
user selection informa-
tion safe.

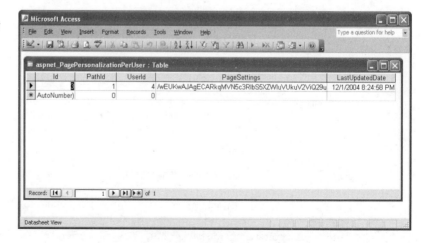

The ID field contains the number of the entry. When you find that a page contains errors, it's usually a good idea to delete the personalization settings to avoid creating problems when you test any changes you make. The `PathId` field contains the number of the Web page affected by the settings. You can find this information in the `aspnet_Paths` table. The `UserId` field contains the number of the user that requested the personalization. This value appears in the `aspnet_Users` table. Now, notice the `PageSettings` field. This information is completely encoded. No one can determine what personalization settings the user had made—not even the developer. Only the page user knows which settings are in force, which is the way things should be.

Defining Your Development Goals

This chapter has demonstrated some interesting uses for scripts in your client-side applications. In addition, you've discovered some interesting testing techniques and even learned more about how scripting works on operating systems such as Windows. Of course, it's important to remember that client-side scripting can't solve every problem, not even if you use some of the convoluted and messy scripts that some developers use to work around client-side scripting issues. You also encountered a new user-friendly technology that helps a user develop a better rapport with your applications—Web Parts.

Scripts can become a favorite tool or a nightmarish experience—it all depends on how much time you spend working with them. The examples in this chapter provide a good starting point for your scripting experience, but serious developers spend time fine-tuning their scripting knowledge by browsing Web sites that specialize in this particular technology. You'll want to work with as many kinds of scripts as possible so you can truly understand the possibilities. Once you feel you have enough information, try creating some scripting scenarios of your own. Begin by determining whether the task would work better on the client or the server and then test your theory by building the required scripts.

Chapter 7 discusses an essential topic—feedback forms. Many developers (and other people for that matter) view feedback forms as a nuisance. Someone writes in about a problem and makes you look bad. However, properly designed feedback forms are actually resources that make your life easier. A feedback form can provide new ideas for your Web site—ideas that you don't have to think about too hard because someone else has already done the heavy lifting for you. Good feedback forms can also provide a foot in the door. Go ahead, contact the sender, and put them on the hot seat with you. Complaining is easy—figuring out a solution is hard. Perhaps the person who sent you the complaint also has a really interesting and useful way to fix the problem. The point is that feedback forms are great—they let you interact with someone using your Web site and use them as a resource.

Part 3

Creating Simple but Effective Pages

In this section you will learn to:

Chapter 7

Creating Feedback Forms

Feedback is one of the most miserable forms of Web site interaction for many developers. In fact, entire companies seem averse to the very notion of feedback because the assumption is that no one fills out feedback forms unless they have an axe to grind. Unfortunately, my own analysis shows that most people fill out feedback for the sole purpose of complaining about something—very little goes on in the feedback department in the way of thanks or congratulations. Consequently, it's easy to wonder why anyone in their right mind would create not one, but several, kinds of feedback forms. The answer is simple: You must view feedback forms from a different perspective and manage the information they provide to obtain something of value from them. That's one of the main points of this chapter—discovering why feedback forms are essential to the success of your Web site.

Once you determine that feedback forms are essential, it's time to consider the kinds of forms you should supply. Every Web site should consider three kinds of feedback form as a minimum. The most negative, and yet most essential, feedback form requests user satisfaction information. A second, less negative, form lets the user request help for using your Web site. Finally, a positive feedback form that few Web sites appear to employ is the beneficial suggestion. Generally, providing these three feedback forms will help you create a great Web site that meets most users' needs. Of course, adding other specific feedback forms is always helpful and demonstrates that you really do have the user's needs in mind.

Developing great feedback forms doesn't mean you'll actually receive great feedback. In fact, designing a feedback form incorrectly simply opens your Web server to attack by crackers. Consequently, the final portion of this chapter discusses principles you should use when designing forms of any kind. Although the information does center on the feedback form, most of the information provided will help you avoid major problems with form security and lackluster input from the user.

Understanding the Need for Feedback Forms

The first consideration for feedback forms is how to make them into a resource, rather than a major nuisance. A feedback form is someone else's interpretation of your Web site. The interpretation isn't always correct or even warranted—it simply reflects their opinion at that moment in time. In fact, you'll find that the opinions change over time, so the feedback you get today won't be the feedback you receive tomorrow. I've actually had people provide negative feedback one day and retract it the next simply because they were having a bad day and I happened to be an easy target. The important thing to remember is that you can make feedback a resource rather than take it as a personal assault on you or your Web site.

Feedback forms also provide an invaluable method of letting people let you know about Web site issues. The alternatives are that the user will leave your Web site for another one or that your Web site will garner a bad reputation—making it less likely that people will visit in the first place. When people know that you care enough to discuss issues and act on them, it's easier to overlook any problems until you have time to fix them. Generally, the positive attitude that well-designed feedback forms provide creates a better Web site environment. Obviously, you'll run into the person who's having a bad day, but even so, you can normally work around a problem when you know about it—not including feedback forms means you won't ever know about it.

It's not always necessary to focus feedback forms on problems. Sometimes it's better to include a number of positive feedback forms as well. For example, instead of asking the user what's wrong about your Web site, ask them what they like about it instead. In addition, you can seek out the user's opinion—give them a chance to help you design a better Web site by creating a beneficial suggestion form. These positive feedback forms not only give the user a chance to voice an opinion, but also provide positive feedback to you as well. More importantly, placing the user on the hot seat with you makes it easier for the user to see things from your perspective.

Feedback forms provide an essential service that you must consider in order to have a successful Web site. You need feedback forms to discover more about the user's needs, wants, and desires. In fact, you might even want to classify the feedback you receive on that basis.

Needs   A need is something the user must have to use the Web site at all. For example, if users complain that the color combinations you use make it hard to read the Web site, you should classify that as a need and fix it as soon as possible.

Wants   A want is something that the user requires to enjoy the Web site, but might not need to use it. For example, a personal page about you is something that helps the user enjoy the site and builds a rapport between you and the user, but the user doesn't have to have a personal page in order to obtain good information from the Web site.

Desires   A desire is something that the user doesn't need to either use or enjoy the Web site, but requests anyway. For example, a user might request that you use animated GIFs to dress up the Web site. Although the animation makes the Web site look nicer, it doesn't really affect the user's enjoyment to any degree—it's a bit of extra fluff that you've added.

Targeting Feedback Forms to Meet Specific Needs

In some respects, feedback forms are a kind of marketing. You're marketing the service aspect of your Web site. A feedback form tells the user that you value their opinion and plan to do something about it. More importantly, the feedback form itself provides you with the ideas required to do something about the information you receive. Unfortunately, just providing the user with a feedback form that asks, "Yeah, what do you want?" isn't going to do the job. You must target the feedback form to achieve certain goals and may find that you have to tweak the feedback form as you get responses in order to fine-tune the result. The following sections describe some of the methods you can use to target a feedback form.

TIP   Don't get the idea that feedback forms always provide two-way communication. In many cases, the user will simply tell you what's wrong and won't want to hear back from you. Of course, this kind of communication is limited in that you can't even ask for additional information. That's why you want to encourage the user to provide some form of two-way communication when you can. Feedback forms can encourage such communication by providing the user with a good reason to continue the conversation. You can offer everything from a pleasant environment to rewards for continuing the conversation so you can obtain all of the information you need. The bottom line is that when you use feedback forms as a resource, you must spend some time cultivating the user response.

Considering What You Expect from the Form

Targeting a specific need means creating forms that have fields that answer the questions for a particular requirement. For example, you might create a number of user feedback forms, but each form will answer specific questions. A product feedback form will have part numbers, color, and other product information, while a Web page feedback form will include the URL and the configuration options that the user selected. You might create special user feedback forms for your information page and others for the site search. The idea is to create specific forms for each need so that the user isn't faced with questions that don't make sense such as asking for the requested URL as part of a product feedback form.

Sometimes you can help yourself by adding hidden fields to the Web page. For example, you don't have to create a special feedback form for every product. However, you also can't assume that the user will know the model number of the product they want to ask about, especially if they don't currently own the product. Consequently, you can add hidden fields to the requesting form that include the information you know you'll need, yet can't provide as part of the generic form. Figure 7.1 shows a typical example of hidden fields. In this case, the first hidden field contains the product name, while the second contains the model number. To use a hidden field, all you need to provide is a unique name as part of the (ID) property and the information as part of the Value property.

FIGURE 7.1

Hidden fields make it easier to pass specifics that you can't count on the user providing.

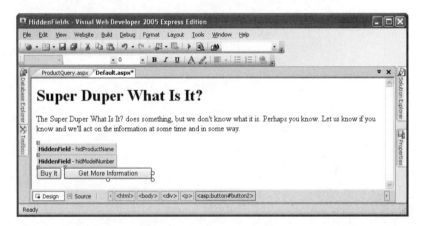

The user won't see the hidden fields when viewing the form using a browser, but the data's there. Notice that this form has a special button for getting more information. The user clicks this button and the Web server passes them along to the generic product request form that you create. However, it won't appear generic—the page actually looks specific because of the hidden fields you provide and even your database will include specific information. Figure 7.2 shows a typical example.

The secret is to modify the form so that the information from the hidden fields configures it as needed. You add this information using the Load event handler shown here.

```
Private Sub form1_Load(ByVal sender As Object, _
                       ByVal e As System.EventArgs) Handles form1.Load


    ' Get the information from the hidden fields.
    txtProductName.Text = Request.Form.GetValues("hidProductName")(0)
    txtModelNumber.Text = Request.Form.GetValues("hidModelNumber")(0)
```

```
        ' Make sure the user can't change it.
        txtProductName.ReadOnly = True
        txtModelNumber.ReadOnly = True
    End Sub
```

Because the form uses the GET method, you can rely on the `Request.Form.GetValues()` method to retrieve the hidden field information. The code assigns these values to the `txtProductName` and `txtModelNumber` text boxes to create the display in Figure 7.2. The code then makes these fields readonly so the user can't change them.

It's interesting to note that the header for the Web page in Figure 7.2 uses two different controls. The "Get More Information About" text appears within a label, so clicking Submit won't send this information to the server. However, the "Super Duper What Is It?" text appears in a textbox, so the form does send this information to the server. As far as the user's concerned, both elements are the same—they look and act the same—only you know the difference.

FIGURE 7.2
Collect and display information from the hidden fields on your generic form.

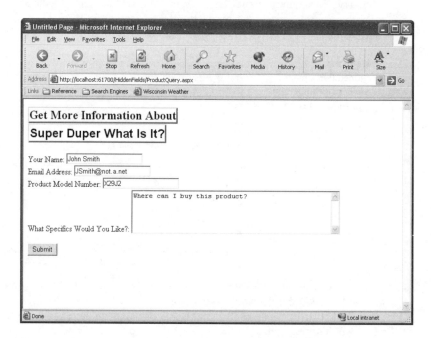

Defining the Basic User Requirements

Users have specific needs when working with forms. For example, you need to explain how to fill out the form without making the user feel silly or stupid. One of the most effective ways to accomplish this goal is to create questions using sentences that include a description of the information you need. For example, a field that says, "Model Number" doesn't really tell the user much, but a field that says, "Provide the model number located on the white tag in back of the product." tells the user precisely what you need and where to find it.

Sometimes a good question isn't enough. That's why you should also provide sample information as part of the input. Make sure this information isn't real, but is a good example. Scan the form after the user submits it to ensure that the form contains a real model number instead of the example you provided.

Another useful addition to a Web page is to provide entries for every `Title` property. The `Title` property displays a tooltip like the one shown in Figure 7.3. When the user hovers the mouse over this control, the browser displays a tooltip that explains what the user will see after clicking Get More Information. Notice that the questions on this form help the user understand what you need, while the tooltips tell what the user gets for filling out the form.

FIGURE 7.3

Collect and display information from the hidden fields on your generic form.

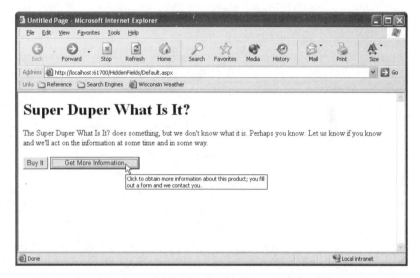

The concept of telling the user what they receive for providing helpful information is central to designing forms that actually work. In fact, the act of telling the user why they're filling out the form is the only way to ensure that your form will work as anticipated. The user has a need to know why you want the data and how you'll use it. This need goes back to the requirement to provide a privacy policy as explained in the "Developing a Privacy Policy" section of Chapter 5.

Using a Master Page to Create Multiple Feedback Form Types

At some point, you'll have a list of feedback forms that you want to implement. Depending on how complex your Web site is, you might have several kinds of user feedback forms, a number of product suggestion forms, even several kinds of help forms. The list of forms might seem daunting at first. However, you can dramatically decrease the complexity of the situations by using master pages.

The goal is to find the common areas of each form and then create a master page to address that particular form. For example, you might create a master page for feedback forms. All of the feedback forms would have common elements such as the user name and email address, so the master page would include these elements. However, a Web page feedback form might include an URL field while a product feedback form includes a model number field. This special information appears on the individual forms in an area that you designate.

It's unfortunate that you can't create master pages based on other master pages. If this feature were available, you could create a master page with all of the company information. Every feedback form master page could inherit from this beginning page so you would ultimately have just one page with each kind of information. Even so, you can cut and paste the common elements between master pages. Figure 7.4 shows an example of a master page you might create. Notice that this master page includes the header, a greeting, some common controls, and an area for adding specific questions.

FIGURE 7.4
Select a master page for the user feedback form that you want to create.

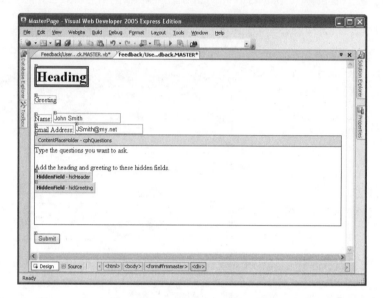

To make this project work better, you'll want to start with the Empty Web Site project. Right-click the project entry in Solution Explorer and choose Add New Item from the context menu. Create a new Master Page. Once you create the master page, start creating the forms you need. Make sure you check Select Master Page on the Add New Item dialog box. Click Add and you'll see the Select a Master Page dialog box shown in Figure 7.5. Notice that the master page appears in a special Feedback folder. Organizing the feedback pages in a special folder can make it easier to create robust Web sites and reduce programming errors. Choose the master page that you want to use and click OK.

FIGURE 7.5
Select a master page for the user feedback form that you want to create.

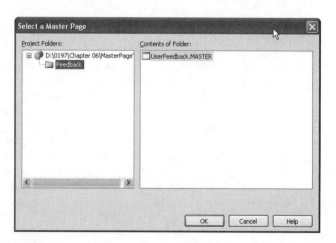

This is a situation where you'll want to add code in a number of places. First, think about the master page itself. This page contains all of the general elements for the Web page such as the heading. Unfortunately, you don't know the heading name, at this point, and you know that more than one page will use the master page, so you couldn't assign a specific name even if you had one in mind. This is another situation where using hidden controls can be quite helpful. The master page would include a Load event handler like this one to ensure that the general elements are set.

```
Private Sub frmMaster_Load(ByVal sender As Object, _
                           ByVal e As System.EventArgs) _
                           Handles frmMaster.Load

    ' Replace the standard heading and greeting.
    If Not (Request.Form.GetValues("hidHeader") Is Nothing) Then
        lblHeader.Text = Request.Form.GetValues("hidHeader")(0)
    End If
    If Not (Request.Form.GetValues("hidGreeting") Is Nothing) Then
        lblGreeting.Text = Request.Form.GetValues("hidGreeting")(0)
    End If
End Sub
```

Using the hidden fields lets the developer implement the form based on the master page to change the heading and greeting text without providing access to any other element. Notice that you need to verify that the caller (not the form based on the master page, but the actual caller) passed the required hidden controls. The `Request.Form.GetValues("hidHeader")` member is nothing when the hidden control is missing. Of course, the form is interested in the presence of the values, so the code uses **Not** to negate the Boolean value so you can determine when the values are present. When the caller does supply these hidden controls, the code applies the values to the header and greeting.

You still have one thing to consider when working with the form based on the master page. It's impossible to edit the two hidden controls supplied as part of the master page in the example. However, the two hidden controls provide default values. The page that calls the form you create will have to include the two hidden controls to change the default text. Fortunately, even if the calling page doesn't supply the required values, the two hidden controls supplied with the example will provide headings. Figure 7.6 shows a test page that includes the two hidden fields—these values override the defaults provided on the master page.

FIGURE 7.6
Developers will need to call the form with the required hidden fields, but make sure that you provide defaults as well.

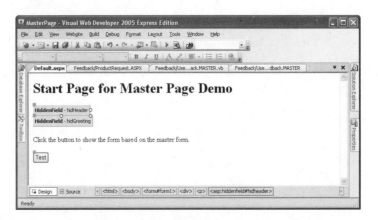

Creating a User Satisfaction Form

Most people have an opinion. The opinion doesn't have a right or wrong value—it's simply how they feel about a particular topic. Getting an honest opinion from people can be difficult, but you can do it. When the topic concerns your application or Web site, the need to get an honest opinion is essential. Otherwise, changes that you make to an application or Web site as the result of user feedback is going to be off target—you want to target the users of your site to ensure that they have a great experience.

> **TIP** Don't assume that every positive feedback message you receive means that you're doing every-thing right with your application. Some people will tell you positive things to obtain benefits they might not normally receive or simply because they don't want to hurt your feelings. Likewise, not every negative message is an indictment against your programming practices. Sometimes a user will have a bad day and decide to take it out on you because you're the nearest target that can't attack back. Deciphering feedback often means reading the message several times and deciding just how it affects your application (or whether it affects your application at all).

The following sections discuss user feedback. This information reflects issues that you need to con-sider when working with your Web site. For example, it discusses some of the problems of sorting information into the right area for consideration.

Designing User Feedback

One of the problems in getting good user feedback is designing the form so that it elicits a response, especially from users who don't normally express themselves well. A nebulous question such as "How do you feel about this input form?" won't net you a very good response. You need to direct the user to the kind of input you want, without contaminating the user's response. For example, "Does the item search form help you find the information you need to make a purchase, or do you find your-self using alternative search techniques?" offers the user a choice and makes them think about alter-natives. The question is still specific enough that even a shy user can provide an answer. Offering yes, no, and other (with a comment field) lets the shy user off the hook, but also lets vocal users state their answers in precise terms.

The simplest method for obtaining user feedback on a Web page is to create a form and send it to your email (or other location). You might have the impression from previous sections of this chapter that Visual Web Developer is effective only when used to create ASP.NET solutions, but it works just fine for creating this plain HTML feedback form as well. The solution in this section is a great option if you're using Visual Web Developer on a hosted site where you don't have access to the Web server. In addition, this solution works with any browser that supports forms, which is essentially every browser in use today.

Although using the email method does require a little interpretation, it has the advantage of allowing you to get feedback almost free. If you use a programmable email reader such as Microsoft Outlook, you can write a macro to interpret and save the results for you. Otherwise, the careful use of form values will let you read the report with a little effort. Listing 7.1 contains an example of a simple form that works with almost all browsers even if the user has turned off scripting support and cookies.

LISTING 7.1:   A Simple, Low-cost Feedback Form

```
<!DOCTYPE html
    PUBLIC "-//W3C//DTD XHTML 1.1//EN"
           "http://www.w3.org/TR/xhtml11/DTD/xhtml11.dtd">
<html xmlns="http://www.w3.org/1999/xhtml" >
<head>
    <title>Simple Response Form</title>
</head>

<body>

    <!-- Display a heading. -->
    <h1 align=center>Simple Response Form</h1>

    <!-- Display some explanatory text. -->
    <p>
        This page asks how the search engine worked for you. It doesn't
        collect any personal information and no one will contact you
        for additional information. The only purpose for collecting
        this information is to improve the Web site search engine.
    </p>

    <!-- Define the form and anticipated action. -->
    <form action="mailto:JMueller@mwt.net?subject=Test Message"
        method=post
        name=SimpleRespForm
        enctype="text/plain">

    <!-- Ask about search engine performance. -->
    <label>Did the search engine work as you expected?</label>
    <input type=hidden
        name="Q1"
        value="Search Engine"/><br/>
    <label>Yes</label>
    <input type=radio name="1A" value="Y"/><br/>
    <label>No</label>
    <input type=radio name="1A" value="N"/><br/>
    <label>Other</label>
    <input type=radio name="1A" value="O"/><br/>
    <label>Additional comment (40 characters max):</label><br/>
    <input type=text name="1E" maxlength=40/><p/>

    <!-- Ask about link descriptions. -->
    <label>Were the link descriptions easy to understand?</label>
    <input type=hidden
        name="Q2"
```

```
                value="Link Description"/><br/>
    <label>Yes</label>
    <input type=radio name="2A" value="Y"/><br/>
    <label>No</label>
    <input type=radio name="2A" value="N"/><br/>
    <label>Other</label>
    <input type=radio name="2A" value="O"/><br/>
    <label>Additional comment (40 characters max):</label><br/>
    <input type=text name="2E" maxlength=40/><p/>

    <!-- Submit the form to email. -->
    <input type=submit value="Send" accesskey="S"/>
    </form>

</body>
</html>
```

For anyone who's spent considerable time working with Web pages, this might look like old technology crying for a makeover. However, this technique works quite well. I didn't include the accessibility information in this example for the sake of clarity. You could also dress it up a bit using Cascading Style Sheets (CSS). The underlying example, however, is easy to understand. Figure 7.7 shows an extremely simple form that anyone could fill out in seconds. The limitations on the length of the input keeps the user focused on a particular requirement. Notice that this form doesn't collect any personal information—the user is completely anonymous, which means more users are likely to fill out the form.

FIGURE 7.7
Sometimes simple forms
are the best.

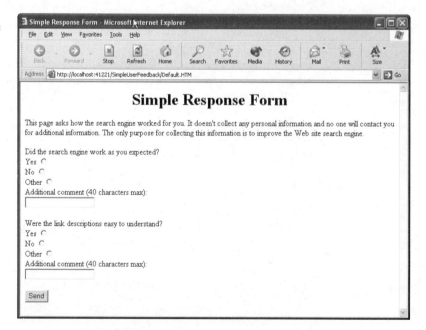

The focus of this example is the `<form>` tag. Notice that the `action="mailto:JMueller@mwt.net?subject=Test Message"` attribute defines my email address as the destination for the data in the form. In addition, the email subject is Test Message. By giving each survey a different name, you know precisely where the user took the survey and what to expect as input. Most developers would stop here and complain about the results received in their email (a rather unattractive attachment). By adding the `enctype="text/plain"` attribute, you can change the output to something that's easy to parse using any script and not all that hard to read using the email application's preview pane, as shown in Figure 7.8.

FIGURE 7.8

Encoding your survey form correctly lets you read it directly in email.

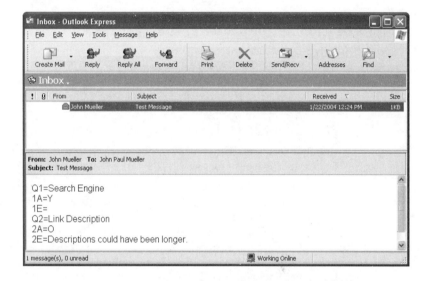

TIP Many developers don't understand the `mailto:` URL very well. The problem is that the protocol doesn't appear very often on Web pages and most Web pages don't use the full potential of the `mailto:` URL. You can use most of the same fields with a `mailto:` that you use with an email program including such features as cc and bcc. You can find several good resources about the `mailto:` URL on the Internet. One of the better places to look is the Web Design Guides site at `http://www.ssi-developer.net/design/mailto.shtml`. Another good place to look for tips of this sort is the Ezine-Tips.com site at `http://ezine-tips.com/articles/format/20001020.shtml`.

Each of the entries in the email has a corresponding tag in the form that has the name attribute shown. Notice how the example separates the questions using a hidden `<input>` tag like this:

```
<input type=hidden
       name="Q1"
       value="Search Engine"/><br/>
```

The value you provide should include a reminder about the question content. In this case, I provided a reminder that the question asks whether the user found every product needed.

WARNING   Some browsers have a content size limit when you use this technique; although none of the newer browsers have this limit, you do need to be aware of it should someone with an older browser visit your site. In some cases, forms can have a 255-character limit on the amount of data that they can send. (Make sure you also check for potential limits with the Web server that you use.) This means you have to provide limits on the size of comment fields using the `maxlength` attribute, as shown in Listing 7.1. You also need to design your form carefully and make answers terse whenever possible if maximum compatibility is the main objective. However, when targeting newer clients, you can easily exceed the 255-character limit without problem and should make your comments verbose enough that the intent of any feedback you receive is clear.

Developing Automated Feedback

Automated feedback systems accept the forms that users provide, process them, and create reports based on the results. All you have to do once you create the initial form is to wait for the system to receive enough results for a report. This book doesn't delve into automated feedback systems because there are a number of resources that you can use for this type of programming. Here are a couple of resources you should consider.

User Feedback HTML Form   `http://www.bytesworth.com/learn/html00009.asp`

Creating Feedback Forms for WAP Sites   `http://www.aspfree.com/c/a/Code%20Examples/ Creating-feedback-forms-for-WAP-sites--By-Michael-Wright`

However, given that many developers want to provide an application that does everything the user could possibly need to do, making the feedback page friendly is critical. In general, the more you automate the feedback to make things easier for your company, the fewer users will be able to use the feedback system. This issue is especially true of form-based Web feedback because many users now turn off scripting, cookies, applets, and plug-ins for fear that their systems will download viruses or experience other problems. Automation usually requires some level of client and server scripting, along with cookies and even plug-ins.

TIP   Some ISPs consider user feedback forms so important that they make it part of the documentation for their service. For example, check out the AT&T site at `http://www.att.com/style/wc_ feedback.html`. This site tells how to create a user feedback for using the special features of the AT&T servers. Your ISP might provide similar services that you can use to make development of automated pages easier.

The problem even occurs with desktop applications. Some vendors make feedback available as part of a Help menu option. In most cases, the feedback form works and sends the information to the vendor (usually over the Internet). However, problems arise when the vendor assumes the user has a permanent connection to the Internet—many users use dial-up connections. Fortunately, every Web site developer can assume that the user has some kind of Internet connection (even if it's through a proxy server); otherwise, the user wouldn't be able to visit the Web site at all.

Creating a Help Request Form

Help request forms are one of the most important forms that you can add to your Web site because they let you interact with the user directly. Of course, simply receiving the request isn't enough to satisfy the user—you have to have someone to answer the query. This application isn't finished to the point where you could use it without some modifications, but it gives you an idea of how you could produce such an application without expending a lot of time or energy.

Designing the Request Page

The example is quite simple, but also quite functional. The request page contains just four fields, yet this information is all you need to answer a help request in many cases (complex forms on most Web sites notwithstanding). The form in Figure 7.9 shows a typical example.

FIGURE 7.9

Keep your request form simple and easy to understand so users will fill it out.

What you can't see in the figure are all of the tooltips provided with the input page. You use the ToolTip property for ASP.NET controls to add a tooltip to the page. The server automatically converts the ToolTip property to the Title attribute for the HTML it outputs. The idea is to provide the user with enough extra information to fill out the form. Theoretically, you should also provide default values in the form fields, but in some cases, this technique actually backfires because the user can't see which fields require additional information.

Notice that this form is almost too simple looking. Part of the reason is that this is an example and I didn't want to clutter it with extra doodads. However, it's always a good rule of thumb to keep things simple when it comes to forms. Use the least possible number of fields. Make sure the fields are always easy to understand. Provide extra help in the form of tooltips so everyone can participate.

Generally, you want the input form to flow from the initial input screen shown in Figure 7.9 to some type of response screen. In most cases, you'll want to give the user a feeling of success as shown in Figure 7.10. Notice that this page also includes a LinkButton control that takes the user back to the main page. Always ensure that your forms flow from one place on your Web site to another so the user doesn't have to click the Back button on their browser constantly. Chapter 8 provides a number of other ideas for making movement on your Web site easy.

Always provide some form of error trapping for your forms. The example is very simple in that it only checks for fields that the user hasn't filled out. You should also explicitly check for fields with the wrong input data and fields that contain viruses, scripts, or simply odd information that you don't want in your database. Some users appear to have so much time on their hands that they'll test for every kind of odd input they can think of when trying out your Web site. In this case, the example displays a simple message as shown in Figure 7.11.

FIGURE 7.10
The user should be able to move from one location on your site to another without much effort.

FIGURE 7.11
Always provide some form of error trapping and messaging with your application.

Enabling Debugging

Because this is the first complex Web project in the book, you'll want to enable debugging so that you can view precisely how the project executes. Adding these features lets you use the Debug ➢ Start command to start the Web page in the debugger. You can also set break points—essentially places where you want to stop code execution—by right-clicking a line of code and choosing Breakpoint ➢ Insert Breakpoint from the context menu. You'll find detailed debugging information in Chapter 16. For now, you can add debugging to this application in case it fails in some way—the application will display detailed information about the error for you. Begin by modifying the page tag in `Default.ASPX` so it contains a `Debug` attribute like the one shown here.

```
<%@ Page Language="VB"
        AutoEventWireup="false"
        CompileWith="Default.aspx.vb"
        ClassName="Default_aspx"
        Debug="true" %>
```

The IDE provides the other attributes for you. An application suffers a significant performance penalty whenever you add debugging to it, so you'll want to remove the `Debug` attribute when you finish working with the application.

After you change `Default.ASPX`, you'll need to add a Web configuration file to the project. Right-click the project entry in Solution Explorer and choose Add New Item. You'll find the Web Configuration File entry in the Add New Item dialog box. Within this file you'll find a special `<compilation>` element that includes a `debug` attribute like the one shown here.

```
<compilation debug="true" />
```

Set the `debug` attribute to true to enable debugging. As with the `Debug` attribute for the page directive, you'll want to set this value to `false` when you finish working with the application. Make sure you rebuild the application afterward by choosing Build ➢ Build Web Site in the IDE. Otherwise, the application will still contain debugging information.

TIP   As your projects get larger and have more Web pages, you'll want to ensure that you set a starting page for the project or Visual Web Developer will simply open the current Web page when you start the project. To set the starting page, right-click the page that you want to use in Solution Explorer and choose Set as Start Page from the context menu. Interestingly enough, the page icon won't change in appearance at all in Solution Explorer, so you don't know whether the change has taken effect until you start the application.

Developing the XML Storage

You have many options at your disposal for processing the forms you receive from users. This example uses a very simple methodology that works quite well. The example relies on an XML file to store the data and XSLT to translate the information into a Web page. The "Transforming the Results with XSLT" section later in this chapter tells you more about the XSLT part of the equation. This section concentrates on the XML storage.

To keep things simple, the example stores each input form in a separate file. As the technician answers a request, the application either archives or deletes the file from the drive. A special algorithm ensures that every form has a unique name, even when one user submits multiple forms. The XML file requires the usual `<?xml?>` processing instruction, a root node, and child nodes for holding the data. Figure 7.12 shows the essential data structure for this example.

As you can see, this XML is very simple. It stores the data items shown in the form in Figure 7.9 in a direct correspondence. Anyone looking at the XML could see how the user provided all of the required information. However, viewing XML directly isn't pleasant, no matter how simple you make it. Consequently, this example also includes the `<?xml-stylesheet>` processing instruction shown here. Whenever someone opens the XML file, they'll see a Web page created by the XSLT file.

```
<?xml-stylesheet type='text/xsl' href='DisplayReport.XSLT'?>
```

FIGURE 7.12
Use a simple data structure to store the information so you can process it easily.

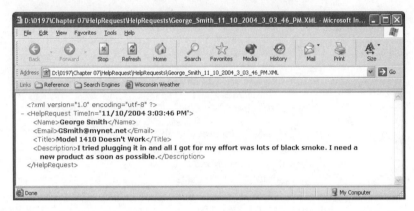

Now that you have a better idea of what tasks the code will perform, it's time to review the code. Listing 7.2 shows how to create and save an XML file based on the contents of a form. You could use this technique for any form, but the code provides specific formatting for the example form in Figure 7.9.

LISTING 7.2: Creating an XML Storage File

```
Sub btnSubmit_Click(ByVal sender As Object, ByVal e As System.EventArgs)
    Dim Output As XmlDocument                  ' Contains all the input.
    Dim PInst As XmlProcessingInstruction      ' A processing instruction.
    Dim Attr As XmlAttribute                    ' A node attribute.
    Dim RootNode As XmlElement                  ' The root node.
    Dim DataNode As XmlElement                  ' Individual data element.
    Dim ThisPath As String                      ' Mapped application path.
    Dim Filename As String                      ' Full path of data store.

    ' Verify that the data fields have all of the required information.
    If txtName.Text.Length = 0 Or _
       txtEmail.Text.Length = 0 Or _
       txtTitle.Text.Length = 0 Or _
       txtDescription.Text.Length = 0 Then

        lblErrorMessage.Visible = True
        Return
    End If

    ' Create the XML document.
    Output = New XmlDocument()

    ' Define the XML processing directive.
    PInst = Output.CreateProcessingInstruction( _
        "xml", "version='1.0' encoding='utf-8'")

    ' Add the XML processing directive to the document.
```

```
Output.AppendChild(PInst)

' Define the XSLT processing directive.
PInst = Output.CreateProcessingInstruction( _
    "xml-stylesheet", "type='text/xsl' href='DisplayReport.XSLT'")

' Add the XSLT processing directive to the document.
Output.AppendChild(PInst)

' Create the root node that holds all of the other data.
RootNode = Output.CreateElement("HelpRequest")
Attr = Output.CreateAttribute("TimeIn")
Attr.Value = DateTime.Now.ToString()
RootNode.Attributes.SetNamedItem(Attr)

' Create the name node and add it to the root node.
DataNode = Output.CreateElement("Name")
DataNode.InnerXml = txtName.Text
RootNode.AppendChild(DataNode)

' Create the email node and add it to the root node.
DataNode = Output.CreateElement("Email")
DataNode.InnerXml = txtEmail.Text
RootNode.AppendChild(DataNode)

' Create the request title node and add it to the root node.
DataNode = Output.CreateElement("Title")
DataNode.InnerXml = txtTitle.Text
RootNode.AppendChild(DataNode)

' Create the description node and add it to the root node.
DataNode = Output.CreateElement("Description")
DataNode.InnerXml = txtDescription.Text
RootNode.AppendChild(DataNode)

' Add the root node to the document.
Output.AppendChild(RootNode)

' Determine the path for this application.
ThisPath = Page.MapPath(Page.AppRelativeVirtualPath)
ThisPath = ThisPath.Replace("\Default.aspx", "\")

' Create the filename. Build a unique name first and then remove
' any elements that might cause problems. Finally, include the
' destination folder.
Filename = txtName.Text + "_" + DateTime.Now.ToString() + ".XML"
Filename = Filename.Replace(" ", "_")
Filename = Filename.Replace(":", "_")
```

```
        Filename = Filename.Replace("/", "_")
        Filename = ThisPath + "HelpRequests\" + Filename

        ' Save the document to disk.
        Output.Save(Filename)

        ' Send the user to the success page.
        Response.Redirect("Success.ASPX")
    End Sub
```

The code begins by verifying the input data. In this case, the code ensures that the user has entered information in all of the fields. You can provide any level of error checking—the important thing is to provide some level of error checking and ensure that it meets your data processing needs. When the user doesn't enter the proper information, the example displays a label on screen, as shown in Figure 7.11. The label is always there, but the server outputs it only when the user makes a mistake.

The center of the XML processing universe is the XmlDocument component, which is Output in this case. The XmlDocument component holds the data, lets you save it, and helps you create new elements as you need them. This example uses only a few of the common elements—the .NET Framework provides a host of useful components for creating the XML document you need.

Once you create a document, you begin filling it from top to bottom. Yes, you can fill it in any order you want, but using the top to bottom order greatly reduces the amount of code you must write and the debugging time as well. Consequently, the code begins by creating an XmlProcessingInstruction component that contains the <?xml?> processing instruction. Notice that you don't create this element (or any other element) directly—you must rely on Output to do it for you using the CreateProcessingInstruction() method.

The CreateProcessingInstruction() method is a little odd. Most elements require that you add attributes separately, as you'll see with the <HelpRequest> element later in this section. When working with a processing instruction, you always include the attributes as data. In fact, if you look at this object in the debugger, you'll see that the Attributes property is Nothing (null)—you couldn't add anything to it even if you wanted to. After the code creates the <?xml?> processing instruction, it uses the Output.AppendChild() method to add the processing instruction to the document. As far as Output is concerned, the processing instruction doesn't exist until the code performs this step. The code performs the same sequence of events for the <?xml-stylesheet?> processing instruction used to link the XML page to the XSLT file.

The next step creates the root node using the Output.CreateElement() method. Remember that the root node in XML acts as a container for all of the data. This root node also includes an attribute called TimeIn that lets the support person know when the user sent the help request. Notice how the code creates the root node, <HelpRequest>, and then adds the TimeIn attribute to it. Even though you use Output to create the various pieces of the element, the element is a stand-alone portion of the document.

Now it's time to add the data elements. Again, the code uses Output to create the elements. In this case, the code creates leaf nodes, so they have a Value property entry. However, to make adding this information easier, the code actually uses the InnerXml property to add the data (using the Value property directly will display an error message). The code then uses the RootNode.AppendChild() method to add the data node to the root node—you don't add this data directly to the document because the document can't see it—only the root node can see it.

This code brings up an important issue. XML uses the concept of data levels. Every time you want to create a new level, you must work directly with the level to ensure that the data is added correctly. Creating a complex XML data storage structure tends to complicate the code and increase the potential for errors. Always create a simple data structure when you can.

At this point, the `RootNode` is complete, so the code uses the `Output.AppendChild()` method to add the `RootNode` to the document. You can output the document, at this point, and it will look like the presentation shown in Figure 7.12 (with the XSLT processing instruction added).

Depending on how you set up your application, you'll want to create some way to store the data so that multiple requests don't interfere with each other. Although the example could use a single XML document to store the data—using a single document would limit the application to processing one request at a time. Therefore, the example uses a separate file for each request. However, now you have to create a unique name for the file to ensure that one request doesn't overwrite another. The next series of coding steps performs this task beginning with locating the application folder so the support personnel know where to find the data. Interestingly enough, if you don't perform this first step, the application attempts to write the data in the `\Program Files\Microsoft Visual Studio 8\Common7\IDE` folder of your hard drive.

The code begins by getting the current path for the Web page using the `Page.MapPath()` method. The page supplies this information as part of the `Page.AppRelativeVirtualPath` property. Unfortunately, the path contains the name of the file. You can use a number of techniques to separate the filename from the path, but the example uses a simple string replacement through the `ThisPath.Replace()` method to create the path.

Knowing where to place the file is only part of the answer. The code now creates a unique filename using the user's name and the current time. This technique ensures that even if the same user submits more than one form, each form will reside in a unique file. Of course, the string form of the time includes colons (:) and the date includes slashes (/). In addition, the space in the name might make it more difficult to locate the file. The code uses the `Replace()` method to replace the potential problem character with underscores. It then adds the path and filename together. The final XML processing step uses the `Output.Save()` method to send the data to disk.

If the code exited now, the user's data would appear on the hard drive, but the user wouldn't know whether the server saved it. The code uses the `Response.Redirect()` method to redirect the user to the success Web page shown in Figure 7.10.

Transforming the Results with XSLT

At this point, the example application has addressed the needs of the user, but hasn't provided a means to process the data. It's tempting to create a special ASP.NET page, load the XML data, and process it using code similar to that shown in Listing 7.2 to gain a little flexibility. However, if you want to save time, then processing the file using XSLT works just fine and you really won't notice much loss in the way of flexibility. Listing 7.3 shows the XSLT used to process the example code.

LISTING 7.3:   Parsing the Output Data

```
<?xml version="1.0" encoding="utf-8" ?>
<xsl:stylesheet version='1.0'
 xmlns:xsl='http://www.w3.org/1999/XSL/Transform'>
<xsl:output method="html" indent="yes" />
    <xsl:template match="/HelpRequest">
```

```
<HTML>
<HEAD>
    <TITLE>Help Request</TITLE>
</HEAD>

<BODY>
    <h1>Help Request</h1>

    <!-- Display the title of the request. -->
    <h2><xsl:value-of select="Title" /></h2>

    <!-- Display the name. -->
    <p>Name:
    <xsl:value-of select="Name" /></p>

    <!-- Display the time the request was received. -->
    <p>Time Received: <xsl:value-of select="@TimeIn" /></p>

    <!-- Display the description of the help need. -->
    <p>Description: <xsl:value-of select="Description" /></p>

    <!-- Display the email address. -->
    <xsl:text disable-output-escaping="yes">
        &lt;a href="mailto:
    </xsl:text>
    <xsl:value-of select="Email" />
    <xsl:text>?subject=</xsl:text>
    <xsl:value-of select="Title" />
    <xsl:text disable-output-escaping="yes">
        "&gt;Contact User&lt;/a&gt;
    </xsl:text>
    <br />
</BODY>
</HTML>

</xsl:template>

</xsl:stylesheet>
```

The code begins with the usual declarations required for an XSLT file. It then selects the root node of the XML document, which is always the same because of the way the application creates the XML document. All processing revolves around the <HelpRequest> node.

The example displays the data in a different order from the XML form. You don't have to display the data in any specific order and can, in fact, use the same data more than one time. For instance, you'll find the `<Title>` node used twice in this example. Figure 7.13 shows how the output looks so you can compare it to the appearance of elements within the XSLT file.

The first processing step displays the `<Title>` element as a heading on the Web page using the `<xsl:value-of>` element. The user's name appears next using the same technique, but within a paragraph this time. Notice how the code retrieves the `TimeIn` attribute and displays it on screen. Always precede attribute names with the at (@) symbol. Processing the `<Description>` element is the same as the `<Name>` element.

The email address presents a bit of a problem. You don't want to force the support person to type the email address into a response by hand. In addition, adding the title to the response automatically saves time for the support person. Consequently, what you need is a link that includes the `mailto` `href` and a subject variable like this:

```
<a href="mailto:JMueller@mwt.net?subject=My Title">
```

Because you have to include variable information as part of the tag, you can't just construct it as you would a header or paragraph tag. The code uses the `<xsl:text>` element to include the less than (<) and greater than (>) symbols in the tag. However, notice that the `<xsl:text>` element also includes an `disable-output-escaping="yes"` attribute that tells the XML parser to output this data as a tag, not as an actual less than or greater than symbol. The code uses the `<xsl:value-of>` element and a plain `<xsl:text>` element to construct the rest of the tag. As this example shows, you can create complex Web page elements using XSLT as long as you think them through. When the support person clicks the link shown in Figure 7.13, they'll see an email response similar to the one shown in Figure 7.14. Notice that the email response already has the correct email address and subject filled out.

FIGURE 7.13

The output from the XSLT file is easy to read, understand, and use.

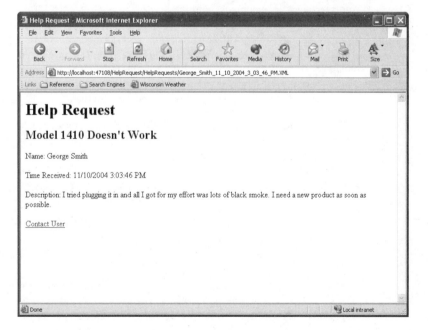

FIGURE 7.14
Using the right tags can
greatly reduce support
time and effort.

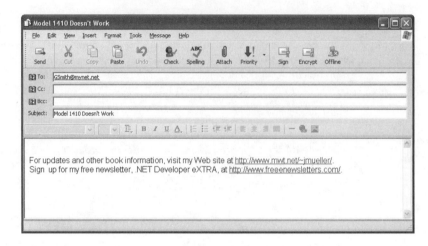

Developing a Beneficial Suggestion Form

Any Web site can benefit from a beneficial suggestion form. You could model it after the help request form described in the "Creating a Help Request Form" section of the chapter. The user would need to provide a name for the idea and an appropriate description as a minimum. However, because there isn't any way to go back and ask who generated an idea later when working on the Internet, you'll probably want to include the user's name and email as well—hoping that the user will provide valid entries so you can contact them later.

The problem with just sticking a beneficial suggestion form on your Web site is that very few people are going to fill it out. Consequently, you need some type of reward for filling out the form, but make it contingent on providing a good idea—one that you can really use to improve the Web site. Otherwise, you'll end up with a ton of useless ideas and people with their hands out expecting the promised reward. The reward also makes it more likely that you'll get a valid user name and email address so that you can contact them later, discuss the idea, and get enough details to implement it.

TIP   Rewards don't have to have monetary value or cost very much to make an impact. Giving the user a public forum—some type of public recognition for the input—is often enough to garner at least some beneficial suggestions. However, even low-cost ideas work. One developer offered gift certificates at Amazon in lieu of cash or products. Another developer offers free consulting time and others offer free products created by their company. You don't have to make the reward expensive—it simply has to have sufficient value in the eyes of the user to make it worthwhile to come up with ideas and submit them.

This kind of form benefits from directed questions. Sometimes a user has a great idea that they don't know how to express. A smart developer knows how to draw the information out of the user. It's easier to discover great communication techniques, rather than reinvent every idea that comes your way. For example, many developers include a list of categories for the beneficial suggestions. The very act of categorizing the idea helps the user articulate it with greater accuracy. A few developers will ask the user to quantify the idea. For example, determining how much of the Web site the idea impacts will give the user a better idea of its usefulness.

Deciding between Required and Optional Data

Most users aren't going to supply every piece of information you request—no matter how aggressively you request it. Some Web sites get around this problem by making their forms obnoxious and persistent. The form keeps returning with all of the cheer of an unloved relative pointing out the fault in every move. Red stars or text describing the stupidity of the form submitter show the glaring hole in the information coverage—the information the user won't provide under any circumstance. Users commonly take care of the problem by either refusing the fill the form out at all or providing false information. In either case, you lose. Either you lose the user's feedback or you lose the integrity of your database.

A positive way to avoid this problem is to make an honest determination of the information you really need. Yes, it's nice to know who you're dealing with, but let's face it, the Internet is all about getting what you need using an anonymous face and most users aren't going to give up that privilege unless you give them a very good reason to do so. For example, a user feedback form is equally valid whether you know the user's name or not. It's true that getting the user's email address will let you ask the user additional questions and ask opinions about the resolution of a problem, but getting the initial feedback is valuable enough that you don't want to create an environment where the user doesn't provide the information at all. Consequently, all you really need is a title for the feedback along with the feedback itself. You should also request amplifying information as needed, but make sure you really need the amplifying information.

TIP   Some kinds of feedback form information are ambiguous. For example, a general comment about your Web site need not include a part number, but a comment about a specific piece of equipment that you sell probably should have the part number. Consequently, you might need to create multiple feedback forms with a number of amplifying fields that include required information. Tailoring a form to meet specific needs makes it more likely that the user will fill out the form completely.

Some forms do require interaction. For example, a help request form requires some level of interactivity to be effective. In this case, you can explain to the user that you must have an email address in order to respond to their question. Failure to provide the information, in this case, means that you can't complete the request for help. The lack of an email address or other means of communication, in this case, really does mean that the form is useless. However, don't limit the user to one kind of input. The required field can include a number of alternatives. Perhaps you can provide places for an email address, written response, or telephone number. Yes, it requires an extra effort on your part, but that's how people develop reputations for providing superior service. You'll have to decide just how much service you can afford to provide, but this is one case where users will understand the need for additional information.

It's possible to coax additional information out of users, in many cases, even when a user could argue that the information isn't essential. For example, a beneficial suggestion form works just fine whether the user provides a name and email address or not. Of course, a beneficial suggestion that isn't complete or doesn't provide some kind of interactivity might not be very useful—perhaps it simply isn't complete and you need more information. Rather than waste a perfectly good idea, try to convince the user to supply the information you need. For example, you could provide some form of gratuity in exchange for the user input. A small token of your appreciation not only makes it more likely that someone will come up with an idea, but that they'll also provide the extra information you need such as a name and email address.

Some Web sites provide registration or other forms full of dubious requirements for information. At least a few users will provide all of the requested information because they just don't know how to say no, but many will provide purposely misleading or false information just to get past the form. According to a number of trade press articles, interviews with users, newsgroup entries, and other sources of information, here are a few of the most common requests for information that go unheeded.

Email address　The only time you should request an email address is when you have to send the user some kind of response to a question. Sometimes you'll want to request an email address as an optional input—such as when the user provides input that could require additional discussion. In many cases, you can avoid the problem by not requesting the user's email address at all.

Address　The only time you should request an address is when you need to send the user a product. Given the nearly constant appearance in the news of stalkers and other nefarious individuals misusing address information, many users are wary about giving out this information. Generally, the address you receive is going to be fake unless the user has a very good reason to give it to you.

Telephone number　Never request a telephone number as a required input—you should always make this information optional. It's unlikely that you'll spend the money to call the user if they supply an email address anyway. Even when a user orders a product from you, you have the option of verifying that their form of payment is valid before you ship the product.

Personal information　Never request personal information such as age, sex, nationality, or religion. With identity theft running rampant, most users are unlikely to provide you with valid information. Invalid personal information could color a survey you make by providing useless demographics. Likewise, many users are going to provide false information because they fear prejudice. The anonymity of the Internet makes it impossible to verify anything other than the answers that the user wants you to have.

Preferences　The only time you should ask about preferences is when you're conducting a survey or trying to fulfill a user need such as selling them a product or providing help. Make sure the preferences that you request are important. For example, you can't sell the user a product without knowing the color in some cases—users understand this requirement and will provide you with good information. However, users are less likely to answer a request for information that has nothing to do with the current topic, such as whether they like men with green or orange hair better.

The main reason that most of these information requests go unheeded is that users value their privacy. They don't want to provide an address because they fear you'll sell their name and address to a marketing firm that will promptly bombard them with home loan advertisements. The user doesn't really care that you think they need a particular service and have an aching desire to buy a new product, so many of them will provide you with what you want least—bad information. The bottom line is that users are more likely provide you with everything you really need when you consider optional versus required information carefully.

Devising Methods of Reducing Repeat Input

Some feedback forms ask the same question in more than one way, supposedly to force the user to provide more information or at least validate the user's assertions. The result of this kind of feedback is repetition. The repeated data consumes more space in your database, requires additional processing time without providing any significant gain in information, and frustrates the user. The user frustration part is especially important because a frustrated user provides less useful information.

VALIDATING REQUIRED INPUT

Once you decide that the user must provide some input to satisfy the basic requirements of a form, you need to validate that input. Chapter 17 provides details on creating secure forms, but you need to perform validation on the form as well. For example, many Web pages fail to verify that the user has entered any information at all until the form goes all the way back to the server. A local script can ensure that the user has provided input in the required spaces. You can also verify that the input meets length requirements and that it doesn't include any special characters that might indicate a virus, rather than useful information.

Validation also means adding some intelligence to the checks. For example, you could parse the input to ensure that it contains a part number as part of the explanation of a hardware failure. You can also verify that the input includes special terms. Input about an application might require some mention of settings, so you can check the input for this term to ensure that the user has included the settings. Of course, you don't want to go too far—language provides myriad ways to express the same idea so you'll want to ensure that you look for reasonable input rather than every specific word you think should appear in the text.

Make sure you also look for potential errors in the input. For example, if some percentage of the input you receive contains two words that users often confuse, you might want to verify that the user actually meant to use the term in the feedback. Some terms are confusing enough that there's an entire Web site devoted to the topic—Confusing Words at `http://www.confusingwords.com/index.php`. In short, always provide the user with helpful assistance.

The problem for many developers is that it's easy to become engulfed in details rather than look at the overall picture. For example, you could begin the user help form by asking for a general description of the problem. The next question might ask for a list of steps required to reproduce the problem. Even though they appear as two different questions, many users will answer them the same way. In fact, some users will go so far as to cut and paste the two answers, so you get precisely the same answer for both. A great way to avoid this problem is to have several people from varied backgrounds test the form. Make sure they haven't seen the form before. When you receive the results, you'll start to notice similarities in the answers and that information will help you prevent some of the repetition.

In some cases, a user will provide a standard "non-answer" in place of real information because they're simply too lazy to provide the information you want. Their goal is to answer the questions as quickly as possible and still receive what they want back from you. Answering the questions quickly, rather than correctly, is a problem that you have to address. You could process the form using some type of string comparison. For example, you could look for duplicate strings, flag them on the form, and ask the user whether they really intended to provide the duplicate answers. Often, this little check is all that you need to get rid of the non-answers. Of course, you have to ask why the user didn't provide the information that you need in the first place. Redirecting the questions so the user can see the need to answer them often helps, but won't solve the problem in every case.

Another potential problem is that your form isn't accessible. Perhaps the questions are worded in such a way that the user can't understand them and provided replicated input as a show of frustration. Avoid using jargon and abbreviations whenever possible—have a nontechnical person review the form for potential problems before you make it available on the Web site. Accessibility problems come in a number of forms and you can discover more of them in Chapter 19.

Defining Your Development Goals

This chapter helps answer some general questions about forms, such as discussing some simple techniques for securing them. However, it also discusses a specific kind of form—the feedback form that you should consider standard fare on your Web site. When a user sees that you care enough to request their input constantly, it's hard for them to go somewhere else and tell other people that you're just missing the point. Most people will take you up on your offer to let them complain and a few will end up providing something much more—good input on how you can create a better Web site. The best part about this kind of input is that it's from the very people who are using your Web site, so it's always pertinent—always right on the mark. Best of all, you don't have to pay anyone to provide the input to you.

At this point, you can build the feedback forms for your Web site. Make sure you create specific feedback forms and change the content as needed to reflect the changing Web site scenery. As you make changes, ask people specific questions about those changes. Not only will asking specific questions help the people who didn't see the changes recognize them, but you'll discover whether the input you received from a boisterous user last week really does reflect the opinion of most of the Web site users. In addition to the three forms described in this chapter, make sure you create some special forms for your Web site as well. For example, if your Web site specializes in greeting cards, ask users what kinds of greetings they'd like to see in the future.

Chapter 8 discusses another important feature that every Web site should include—a site search. Helping people locate essential information on your Web site is just as important as the feedback forms described in this chapter. Unfortunately, creating a great site search is not only time consuming and error prone, but open to interpretation by the people using your Web site. A site search that works great for you and even the majority of the people using your site might not work well for those who need the site search the most. This chapter helps clear some of the ambiguities you have to consider and provides more than one technique for solving everyone's search needs.

Chapter 8

Developing a Site Search

Unless your Web site is extremely small, users will occasionally experience problems finding something. They might know that you have pictures on your Web site, but might not know where to find them. A link from someone else's Web site might provide a tantalizing clue as to what your Web site contains, but the user might not get a good idea until they search your site. In short, most Web sites require at least one and perhaps several ways to search for information.

This chapter begins by examining the kinds of searches you can create and then demonstrating how to create those searches using the custom techniques that Visual Web Developer provides. You'll find that these searches work very well when you have access to the Web site. Although the custom search isn't perfect, you gain flexibility in how the search is weighted and what the user sees.

Not everyone is going to have access to the Web server that hosts their site. Another alternative is to use Google for searching. Google provides several methods that let you incorporate their search engine into your Web site. In fact, some of these techniques rely on simple HTML that you add to your Web page. Other techniques require a little more work but offer greater flexibility.

You might not want to restrict searches to your own Web site. Sometimes you want to provide the capability of searching other Web sites or having those Web sites provide search results for your site. This chapter also examines techniques you can use to make these cross-site searches more efficient.

Finally, this chapter discusses the topic of site maps. A site map is a kind of picture of the layout of your Web site. Users like site maps because site maps help them find information by topic, rather than using a specific search. You should combine site maps with searches on larger Web site. Site maps also work with smaller Web sites, but have a reduced effect on usability because the Web site is easier to navigate.

TIP   It isn't always necessary to write a search routine for your Web site from scratch. Third party vendors such as Wrensoft produce search engines to make the job easier. The Zoom Search Engine (http://www.wrensoft.com/zoom/index.html) is one such offering. You don't need to do much to make these products work. Of course, the speed you gain is offset by the flexibility you lose—a third party vendor will provide you with a generic solution—not the specific solution you can create using hand coding techniques.

Understanding the Site Search Types

Before you can create any kind of search for your Web site, you need to consider what kind of search you need. In some cases, you'll need multiple search engines to address every need, but it pays to start with the one that you need most. Not every Web site relies on precisely the same search. The following list provides the basic kinds of search engines that you'll find on the Internet, but you'll want to note any special search engines you run across because these special engines provide you with great ideas for upgrades of your own. One of the more interesting places to see side-by-side comparisons of search engine output is Dogpile at `http://www.dogpile.com`.

Specific page   The specific page search is the most common. The search engine returns one or more pages that contain keywords or fit within other criteria for the search term that the user provides. Indexing technique (whole page, `<meta>` tags, or some other method), indexing criteria (which words the search engine indexes), and weighting (how much value each word has in determining the search score) all play an important part in determining the results you obtain from a specific page search engine.

Informational   An informational search can retrieve whole Web pages, snippets, or specific page elements, depending on how the developer constructs the search engine. In many cases, the search engine provides options for fine-tuning the search based on the content of a single return. The search engine may or may not provide a link for the Web page itself since the user relies on this kind of search to quickly research specific bits of information.

Downloads   Instead of locating Web pages, this kind of search locates files. Most search engines specify a file type, such as graphics or audio. You could use this kind of search engine to locate a missing DLL on your machine or to find the latest CD from a musical group. Download searches always provide a direct link to the file—clicking the link normally starts the download process.

Creating a Custom Site Search

Visual Web Developer provides the means for creating a custom site search. A custom site search depends on your ability to describe your Web site and define the criteria that you think users will need. The following sections describe the tools that Visual Web Developer provides for creating a custom site search.

Developing a Simple Site Search

Searching a Web site comes down to figuring out how to index the pages and then determining how to use that index to locate content. Although the example in this section only lets you search for one word at a time, it does provide you with the basic principles for creating a custom search. The following sections address both the indexing and the index searching requirements.

INDEXING THE KEYWORDS

You need to carefully consider how to index a Web page. Making the index too small or confined means that users won't be able to search your site completely, reducing the usefulness of the search engine you create. On the other hand, making the index too comprehensive increases search times to the point that no one will want to wait for the search to complete. Consequently, you need to choose a middle ground for the index.

The technique that works best, in many cases, requires that you perform some additional work for each Web page. It relies on the use of special `<meta>` (or informational) tags. A `<meta>` tag always contains a name and content attribute pair. This example uses three common `<meta>` tags, but you can learn about others at `http://www.theemiratesnetwork.com/computers/webmaster/metatag1.htm`. Here are the three `<meta>` tags that appear in the `<head>` tag area of each Web page.

```
<meta name="title" content="Custom Site Search Example">
<meta name="description"
      content="Discover how to create a site search.">
<meta name="keywords" content="Custom Site Search Find Keyword">
```

The title `<meta>` tag provides the title that you want to appear on the search page. Many search engines use the `<meta>` tag version of the title, rather than the actual `<title>` tag information. Supplying both the `<meta>` tag and the `<title>` tag ensures that your Web page is always listed using the title you want. The description `<meta>` tag contains a description of the services that a Web page provides. Shorter descriptions normally work best, but be sure you describe that particular page fully (in other words, don't use the same description for every page on your Web site). The keyword `<meta>` tag is the most important because it contains the list of words that most search engines use to locate content on your site.

You need to create and then store the index in some way. Most commercial Web sites use a special database application to perform the task. However, many smaller Web sites don't need anything that complex. You can easily store the information in an XML file and use a standard Web page to create the information. Figure 8.1 shows a single record from the XML file used for this example.

FIGURE 8.1

Storing the index for a Web site as XML works fine in many cases.

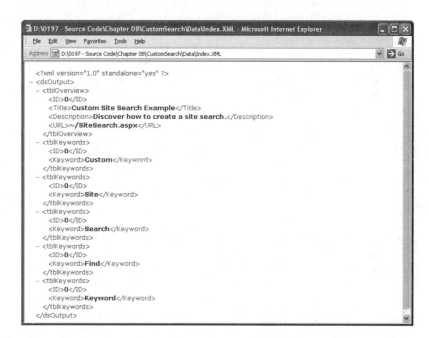

The XML file contains two tables. The first, `tblOverview`, contains the title, description, and URL for the Web page, while the second, `tblKeywords`, contains a list of keywords for the Web page. A single Web page can have only one `tblOverview` entry, but will normally have multiple `tblKeywords` entries. A special ID field in each table provides a link so you can search the keywords and retrieve the information you want to display on screen. Listing 8.1 shows the code required to create this index. (You'll find this example in the `\Chapter 08\CustomSearch` folder of the source code on the Sybex Web site.)

LISTING 8.1:   Indexing the Web Page Data

```
Sub btnStart_Click(ByVal sender As Object, ByVal e As System.EventArgs)
    ... Variable Declarations ...

    ' Determine the path for this application.
```

```
ThisPath = Page.MapPath(Page.AppRelativeVirtualPath)
ThisPath = ThisPath.Replace("\IndexPages.aspx", "\")

' Obtain a list of all of the files to index.
TheFiles = Directory.GetFiles(ThisPath, "*.ASPX")

' Create the DataSet
Output = New DataSet("dsOutput")

' Add the single entry, parent table.
Output.Tables.Add("tblOverview")
Output.Tables("tblOverview").Columns.Add( _
    "ID", GetType(Int32))
Output.Tables("tblOverview").Columns.Add( _
    "Title", GetType(String))
Output.Tables("tblOverview").Columns.Add( _
    "Description", GetType(String))
Output.Tables("tblOverview").Columns.Add( _
    "URL", GetType(String))

' Add the keywords table.
Output.Tables.Add("tblKeywords")
Output.Tables("tblKeywords").Columns.Add( _
    "ID", GetType(Int32))
Output.Tables("tblKeywords").Columns.Add( _
    "Keyword", GetType(String))

' Set a relationship between the tables.
Output.Relations.Add("PageKeywords", _
    Output.Tables("tblOverview").Columns("ID"), _
    Output.Tables("tblKeywords").Columns("ID"))

' Set the record ID
RecordID = 0

' Clear the data entries.
Title = ""
Description = ""
Keyword = ""
ReDim Keywords(0)

' Process one file at a time.
For Each ThisFile In TheFiles
    ' Read the file into memory.
    DataRead = File.OpenRead(ThisFile)
    ReDim ByteData(Convert.ToInt16(DataRead.Length))
    DataRead.Read(ByteData, 0, Convert.ToInt16(DataRead.Length))
```

```
' Convert the byte data to a string.
ReDim CharData(Convert.ToInt16(DataRead.Length))
For Count = 0 To ByteData.Length - 1
    CharData(Count) = Convert.ToChar(ByteData(Count))
Next
TheData = New String(CharData)

' Skip processing if there aren't any <meta> tags.
If TheData.IndexOf("<meta") > 0 Then

    ' Keep processing the <meta>
    Do Until TheData.IndexOf("<meta") = -1

        ' Locate the initial <meta> tag.
        TheData = TheData.Substring(TheData.IndexOf("<meta"))

        ' Look for the title <meta> tag.
        If TheData.Substring(12, 5) = "title" Then
            TheData = _
                TheData.Substring(TheData.IndexOf("content"))
            TheData = _
                TheData.Substring(TheData.IndexOf( _
                    Convert.ToChar(&H22)) + 1)
            Title = _
                TheData.Substring(0, TheData.IndexOf( _
                    Convert.ToChar(&H22)))
        End If

        ... Same Code for the Description <meta> tag ...

        ' Look for the keywords <meta> tag.
        If TheData.Substring(12, 8) = "keywords" Then
            TheData = _
                TheData.Substring(TheData.IndexOf("content"))
            TheData = _
                TheData.Substring(TheData.IndexOf( _
                    Convert.ToChar(&H22)) + 1)
            Keyword = _
                TheData.Substring(0, TheData.IndexOf( _
                    Convert.ToChar(&H22)))

            ' Split the keywords into an array.
            Keywords = Keyword.Split(Convert.ToChar(" "))
        End If

        ' See if we have a complete record.
        If (Title.Length > 0) And _
           (Description.Length > 0) And _
```

```
                        (Keyword.Length > 0) Then

                            ' Add the overview data to the DataSet.
                            DR = Output.Tables("tblOverview").NewRow()
                            DR("ID") = RecordID
                            DR("Title") = Title
                            DR("Description") = Description
                            DR("URL") = Page.ResolveUrl("/CustomSearch/" + _
                                ThisFile.Substring(ThisFile.LastIndexOf("\") + 1))
                            Output.Tables("tblOverview").Rows.Add(DR)

                            ' Add the keywords.
                            For Each Keyword In Keywords
                                DR = Output.Tables("tblKeywords").NewRow()
                                DR("ID") = RecordID
                                DR("Keyword") = Keyword
                                Output.Tables("tblKeywords").Rows.Add(DR)
                            Next

                            ' Clear the data values.
                            Title = ""
                            Description = ""
                            Keyword = ""
                            ReDim Keywords(0)

                            ' Increment the record identifier.
                            RecordID = RecordID + 1
                        End If
                    Loop

                    ' Assign the DataSet to the GridView
                    dgResults.DataSource = Output
                    dgResults.DataBind()
                End If
            Next

        ' Write the results to a database.
        Output.WriteXml(ThisPath + "Data\Index.XML")
        Output.WriteXmlSchema(ThisPath + "Data\Index.XSD")
    End Sub
```

The code begins by retrieving the physical path for the current Web page. It requires this information to retrieve a list of files for processing and eventually to save data to the Web site. The first use of the path is with the `Directory.GetFiles()` method, which returns a list of files for the Web site. The code processes each of the files in turn, looking for the `<meta>` tags required to create the index.

The next step is to create the `DataSet`, `Output`, used to store the data, which includes two tables, `tblOverview` and `tblKeywords`. The `Columns.Add()` method adds the columns to each of the tables. Notice that you must provide a data type for each column using the `GetType()` method. `Output` also defines a relationship between the two tables using the `Output.Relations.Add()` method. Although you don't necessarily have to define this relationship, it helps reduce the chance of data errors in the index. This first section of code finishes by initializing some of the variables used for processing the data.

The file processing loop begins by reading a file into memory. The process requires multiple steps, beginning with the creation of a `FileStream`, `DataRead`. Think of `DataRead` as a conduit that places the information in a `Byte` array, `ByteData`. Unfortunately, you can't process a `Byte` array, so you must convert it to a `String`, `TheData`, through a `Char` array, `CharData`. This entire process is messy because you have to process `ByteData` one byte at a time. (The actual processing is a lot faster than you might think.)

Once the Web page appears as string, the code can begin processing it. The first task is to locate the first `<meta>` tag using `TheData.IndexOf("<meta>")`. Not every Web page will have `<meta>` tags, so this code prevents the loop from failing. A Web page that does include `<meta>` tags won't have them in any particular order, so the loop must process them one at a time and provide logic that processes just the required `<meta>` tags and knows when the Web page has provided all of the required `<meta>` tags. The example performs these tasks by filling three separate variables with the `<meta>` tag information. Notice the amount of string manipulation you must perform to obtain the `<meta>` tags. The code shown should work reliably with any functional `<meta>` tag combination. Note that `&H22` converts to a double quote ("). The keywords require special processing because you need to split them into separate words. The code accomplishes this task by obtaining all of the keywords and then using the `Keyword.Split()` method to place the keywords in a string array.

The code recognizes a complete record by the appearance of text in all three of the `<meta>` tag strings, `Title`, `Description`, and `Keyword`. The code adds the required new rows to the target table using the `NewRow()` method. It fills the resulting `DataRow`, `DR`, with the information obtained from the `<meta>` tags. The data doesn't actually appear in the table, though, until the code calls the `Rows.Add()` method. Notice that the keywords create multiple entries in the associated `tblKeywords` table because there's one entry for each keyword. The table code ends by resetting the various `<meta>` tag variables so the loop can recognize when the next record is ready.

The next task is to display the resulting data on screen. The loop performs this task by assigning `Output` to the `dgResults.DataSource` property. Calling `dgResults.DataBind()` makes the data visible. Figure 8.2 shows typical results of an indexing session.

FIGURE 8.2
The Web page output tells you about the index file entries.

Having a great looking display doesn't do much for the application. The final two lines of code write the data and the associated schema (a description of the database structure) to the application's \Data folder. Figure 8.1 shows typical XML file output. You can view the resulting XML Schema Definition (XSD) file in Visual Web Developer. Figure 8.3 shows the database structure for this application. Notice that the fields are as you expect and that the XSD file shows the relationship between the two tables.

FIGURE 8.3
Use XSD files to describe complex XML table relationships.

SEARCHING THE INDEX

At this point, you have an index based on the keywords <meta> file to use for the custom search. It's important to note that many search engines today index the entire Web page, so the indexing code in Listing 8.1 is the minimum you can use to obtain a relatively simple search. (Many modern search engines rely on spiders, special applications that constantly look for Web page changes, to ensure that any Web page changes appear in an updated index.) The search in this section only accepts a single keyword. The main reason for this limitation is that adding Boolean searches makes the quote quite complex and tends to hide the basic principle—looking for something in the index. Listing 8.2 shows the code used to search the index. (You'll find this example in the \Chapter 08\CustomSearch folder of the source code on the Sybex Web site.)

LISTING 8.2:   Getting Data from the Index

```
Sub btnSearch_Click(ByVal sender As Object,
                    ByVal e As System.EventArgs)

    ... Variable Declarations ...

    ' Determine the path for this application.
    ThisPath = Page.MapPath(Page.AppRelativeVirtualPath)
    ThisPath = ThisPath.Replace("\SiteSearch.aspx", "\")

    ' Read the raw DataSet from disk.
    dsInput.ReadXmlSchema(ThisPath + "Data\Index.XSD")
    dsInput.ReadXml(ThisPath + "Data\Index.XML", _
                    XmlReadMode.ReadSchema)

    ' Sort and search the data.
    ThisView = dsInput.Tables("tblKeywords").DefaultView
    ThisView.Sort = "Keyword"
    Hits = ThisView.AddNew().DataView.FindRows(txtSearchTerm.Text)

    ' Define the filtered information DataSet.
    dsFiltered.Tables.Add("tblOutput")
    dsFiltered.Tables("tblOutput").Columns.Add( _
        "Title", GetType(String))
    dsFiltered.Tables("tblOutput").Columns.Add( _
        "Description", GetType(String))
    dsFiltered.Tables("tblOutput").Columns.Add( _
        "URL", GetType(String))

    ' Process the individual records.
    For Counter = 0 To Hits.Length - 1
        SDR = Hits(Counter).Row
        ODR = dsInput.Tables("tblOverview").Rows( _
            Convert.ToInt32(SDR("ID")))
        DR = dsFiltered.Tables("tblOutput").NewRow()
```

```
            DR("Title") = ODR("Title")
            DR("Description") = ODR("Description")
            DR("URL") = ODR("URL")
            dsFiltered.Tables("tblOutput").Rows.Add(DR)
        Next

        ' Display the result.
        gvOutput.DataSource = dsFiltered
        gvOutput.DataBind()
    End Sub
```

The code begins by determining the physical path of the data files and using the physical path to read both the schema and index into a DataSet, dsInput. Notice that the code reads the schema first and then the data to ensure dsInput interprets the information correctly. To ensure that the application interprets the schema correctly, use the XmlReadMode.ReadSchema constant when reading the data.

Now that dsInput has data to work with, the code creates a view of the data. A view doesn't change the data in any way, simply the way that application sees the data. In this case, the code sorts the data by the keyword. Sorting is important to ensure dsInput can locate the information you want to find. It then creates the view using ThisView.AddNew(). The DataView.FindRows() method determines the kind of view—a list of rows that match the search term. The code combines both operations into one statement.

The code has now examined the keywords and obtained a list of rows that contain the search term. These values appear in Hits. The row from tblKeywords consists of the keyword and the ID field, which has the same number as the ID field in tblOverview. It's important to build another DataSet, dsFiltered, to hold the values from tblOverview that match the values in Hits. Even though you could build a view using the current dataset, creating the new dataset has two important advantages. First, you don't need the ID field from tblOverview—it won't help the user in any way. Second, dsFiltered won't require any fancy manipulation to create the required output.

The processing loop comes next. The example relies on three DataRow objects to perform the required manipulation: SDR (the source data row from Hits), ODR (the output data row from tblOverview), and DR (the display data row that contains the manipulated data). The code creates a new DR for each iteration of the loop using the dsFiltered.Tables("tblOutput").NewRow() method. It then fills DR with the data from ODR and finally adds it back into dsFiltered using the Rows.Add(DR) method.

Now that dsFiltered contains the final search output, the code displays it on screen using the GridView, gvOutput. Notice that the code sets the DataSource property first and then displays the information by calling DataBind(). Figure 8.4 shows the output from the example.

You'll notice that Figure 8.4 shows the URL as a hyperlink. The user can click the hyperlink to move from page to page. The secret of this display is to create custom columns for gvOutput. To begin, display the GridView Smart Tag and choose Edit Columns from the menu. You'll see the Fields dialog box shown in Figure 8.5 (the screenshot shows the fields configured). Clear the Auto-Generate Fields option and then begin adding the fields you need. The example uses two Bound Field and one HyperLink Field controls. As a minimum, you must provide values for the HeaderText and DataField properties for each Bound Field controls. The DataField property values must match field names within dsFiltered. The HyperLink Field control requires three entries. The HeaderText property contains the text that appears at the top of the column, the DataTextField property contains the text the user sees on screen, and the DataNavigateUrlFields property contains the actual navigation URL.

FIGURE 8.4

The simple search looks for only one keyword, but demonstrates the complexity of a custom search.

FIGURE 8.5

Configure the *GridView* control with custom column entries to ensure that the user sees the correct display.

Defining Preferred Links Based on Site Counters

ASP.NET 2.0 contains a wonderful new class called SiteCounters. This class lets you create a database that tracks how users work with your site. For example, you could track all of the links that the user clicks. The Microsoft documentation focuses on using the SiteCounters class with the AdRotator control. Combining the two does make sense because you can easily track the number of clicks a particular advertisement receives (see the "Using the AdRotator Control" section of Chapter 13 for additional details on the AdRotator control), but you can use the SiteCounters class for so many other purposes. For example, you could use the counters for statistical purposes—to determine which products are most popular. This section concentrates on using the SiteCounters class to improve the search results for your Web site. By tracking what users click on most often, you can weight the search results you provide to make it easy for users to locate the most popular choices quickly.

One way to track user access to a Web page is to create a custom site counter for each page. Whenever someone loads the page, the site counter records the information. Later, you can create a report on your findings and manually weight the pages or you can simply include the count in your custom search calculations. To begin, here's the simple code you use to create a custom counter for each page.

```
Sub Page_Load(ByVal sender As Object, _
              ByVal e As System.EventArgs) Handles Me.Load
   ' Provide an application name for the site counters.
   SiteCounters.ApplicationName = "Custom Search"

   ' Add a new entry to the database and store it immediately.
   SiteCounters.Write("Page Changes", _
                      "Custom Search Page", _
                      "PageLoad", _
                      "~/SiteSearch.ASPX")
   SiteCounters.Flush()
End Sub
```

The code begins by assigning an application name to the site using the SiteCounters object. You don't have to perform this step, but it helps to add an ApplicationName property value when you work with multiple Web sites. This extra field can help you sort through the data based on the particular site, yet create a comprehensive whole view of all the sites.

The SiteCounters.Write() method lets you create a custom entry and place it in the database. You can include a number of arguments, including the group name, the name of this particular page, the event that triggered the entry, and URL used to navigate to the page. Theoretically, the application should write this data to the database, but testing shows that it's easy to corrupt the database when you move from page to page. Calling SiteCounters.Flush() ensures that the data actually gets to the database.

Once you have the basic code added to the Web pages you want to track, you might want to display some statistics for them on a special administrative page. Listing 8.3 shows typical code for displaying either complete or individual statistics for your custom counters. You'll find this example in the \Chapter 08\CustomSearch folder of the source code on the Sybex Web site.

LISTING 8.3:   Tracking Complete or Individual Page Statistics

```
Sub Page_Load(ByVal sender As Object, _
              ByVal e As System.EventArgs) Handles Me.Load

   Dim ClickStats As DataSet    ' Holds the statistics

   ' Add a new entry to the database and store it immediately.
   SiteCounters.Write("Page Changes", _
```

```
                    "Site Counter Page", _
                    "PageLoad", _
                    "~/SiteCounter.ASPX")
    SiteCounters.Flush()

    ' Display the current statistics.
    ClickStats = SiteCounters.GetGroupRows(DateTime.MinValue, _
                                    DateTime.MaxValue, _
                                    "Page Changes")
    dgStatsView.DataSource = ClickStats
    dgStatsView.DataBind()

    ' Display individual values.
    txtCustomSearch.Text = _
        SiteCounters.GetTotalCount(DateTime.MinValue, _
                                DateTime.MaxValue, _
                                "Page Changes", _
                                "Custom Search Page").ToString()
    txtSiteCounter.Text = _
        SiteCounters.GetTotalCount(DateTime.MinValue, _
                                DateTime.MaxValue, _
                                "Page Changes", _
                                "Site Counter Page").ToString()
    txtSiteControl1.Text = _
        SiteCounters.GetTotalCount(DateTime.MinValue, _
                                DateTime.MaxValue, _
                                "Page Changes", _
                                "Site Counter Page 1").ToString()
    txtSiteControl2.Text = _
        SiteCounters.GetTotalCount(DateTime.MinValue, _
                                DateTime.MaxValue, _
                                "Page Changes", _
                                "Site Counter Page 2").ToString()
End Sub
```

The code begins by writing this page's custom counter to the database. It then begins displaying the statistics. You can choose a number of display scenarios. For example, you could display all of the events for just one page. This example displays the statistics for the entire group because the page statistics use a unique group name. Using a unique name for the group makes sense because you're creating statistics for a search, not for any other purpose. In fact, you can create as many entries in as many groups as you wish in order to keep the data completely separate.

Notice that the code includes a starting and ending time as part of the SiteCounters.GetGroupRows() method. You can use this feature to retrieve a subset of the data—the technique shown retrieves all of the data. Once the code retrieves all of the group data and places it within a DataSet, it sets the DataSource property of a DataGrid control, dgStatsView, and then uses the DataBind() property to cause dgStatsView to display the data on screen.

Obtaining single statistics is a little harder. In this case, the code retrieves a single numeric count using the `GetTotalCount()` method. Again, you can specify a beginning and ending time for the count. In this case, you must specify both the group name and the individual counter name. Figure 8.6 shows the output of this example.

FIGURE 8.6
You can retrieve the site counter data individually or work with it as a data set as needed.

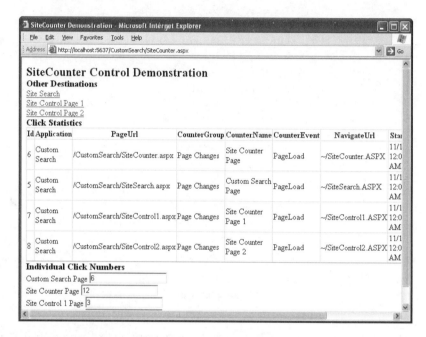

The best solution for working with the `SiteCounters` class would be a way to track unique visits to the page itself, but you can't easily track pages using the `SiteCounters` class, and the results can become skewed when users click the Back and Forward buttons on the browser. Consequently, you can track control activity instead—a user has to click something to move from one page to another and have it count toward the total. This technique still has pitfalls, but it could introduce fewer weighting problems for some Web sites. The biggest drawback to this approach is that it can't track the user's initial entry into the Web site, because that entry relies on loading the page directly or a click from another site.

When using the `SiteCounters` class to track Web site usage for creating weighted search results, you don't want to track every control—just those that transfer control from one page to another. For this reason, you'll normally track the `Button`, `LinkButton`, and `Hyperlink` controls. Depending on the circumstances, you might track other controls as well, but these three buttons normally provide all of the page movement functionality you require.

To start tracking the clicks made by users, you must decide how to organize the database and make three simple changes to each control you want to track. You don't actually have to create the database—Visual Web Developer creates it for you, but you do have to set the appropriate properties shown in Figure 8.7. Begin by setting the `CounterGroup` property to a common value for all page change information, such as Page Changes. The next step is to set the `CounterName` property to the name of the page that the user will go to after clicking the control—make sure each page has a unique name. Once you complete these two steps, set `CountClicks` to True.

FIGURE 8.7

Setting the *CountClicks* property to True is enough to start counting clicks.

Don't get the idea that the `SiteCounters` class uses a mysterious database located in a hidden location that you'll never find. Like many other Visual Web Developer features, this information appears in the `ASPNetDB.MDB` file found in the `\Data` folder for the individual project. When you want to remove old counters or modify existing counters, open the `ASPNetDB.MDB` file and locate the `aspnet_SiteCounters` table. When you open this table, you'll see a list of entries similar to the ones shown in Figure 8.8. You can easily modify or delete entries as needed. Creating a new entry is a little harder, and you should probably rely on code to perform this task.

FIGURE 8.8

Deleting or modifying counters is relatively easy once you know where to look.

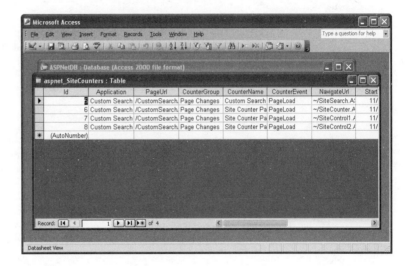

Using Google to Create a Site Search

Creating a custom site search isn't a minor undertaking—you'll spend a lot of time creating the search engine, deciding how to weight the various search factors, and adding new kinds of searches to satisfy user needs. In fact, if your Web site is large enough, you could conceivably end up hiring multiple developers just to maintain the search engine. In many cases, developers don't feel the effort is worth the results. Fortunately, Google provides a ready-made alternative.

The advantage of using Google as your search engine extends well beyond development time, however. Using Google also makes it possible to shift the processing burden from the server to the client. By using scripting techniques, you can provide a great search engine without incurring much development time and still reduce the costs of running your Web site. The following sections discuss the various techniques you can use to add a Google search to your Web site.

USING THE NON-CODED APPROACH

Before you begin writing code, it's important to understand that Google does provide several free search services that don't require much (if any) coding. All you have to do to use these free services is paste a little HTML on your Web page. You can learn more about these free offerings at `http://www.google.com/searchcode.html`. The bottom line is that you can gain site-specific access to what many people consider the most powerful search engine in the world with about 10 seconds of work. However, the non-coded approach does come with a few problems and you need to consider whether another approach will work better.

The main problem with the free search that Google provides is that you lose control of the visitor to your site. The search executes on the Google Web site. Consequently, the person that originally came to your Web site for help could literally end up anywhere on the Internet after the search. In addition, a user who has your site set up as a trusted site will suddenly see messages that they're entering an untrusted zone if Google isn't also part of their trusted list. In short, the transfer from your site to the Google site disrupts the smooth Web surfing experience that users expect—not the impression of your site that you want to promote.

Output is also a problem because you can see the information in only one form: the one that Google chooses for you. If Google's idea of what the display should include matches your own, fine, but this is seldom the case. Most Web site owners want a customized display that meets specific requirements. Consequently, even though the easy solution of using Google works well, the inflexibility of this solution runs counter to what most people want.

Using the Web Service

Before you begin working with Google Web Services, you need to obtain the kit and a developer license. Once you have the kit, you need to install it and become familiar with its content. The following sections describe the kit-related tasks that you need to perform.

TIP Google lets you perform many different tasks with its Web service, and Google has recently added a few additional search features. I based much of the material in this section of the chapter on my book, *Mining Google Web Services: Building Applications with the Google API* (Sybex, 2004). This book shows you the full extent of the functionality that Google Web Services can provide for your Web site.

PERFORMING THE DOWNLOAD

Downloading the kit is easy. You'll find the main Web services page at `http://www.google.com/apis/`. Figure 8.9 shows that this page contains some information, along with two important links. Although the steps shown in the figure are numbered, you can perform the first two steps in any order. This chapter assumes that you want to download the Google Web Services Kit first.

Click the Download link and you'll see a page that describes the kit. This page also includes the licensing agreement for the Google Web Services Kit. Make sure you read the licensing agreement and understand what it means before you proceed. Don't worry about copying the licensing agreement to disk—the kit includes a copy of the licensing agreement that you can use for reference purposes later. Check the "I have read and agree with the Google Web APIs license terms" option and then click Download Now. You'll see a File Download dialog box. Click Save and you'll see a Save As dialog box. The default name of the file is `GoogleAPI.ZIP`, but you can save it using another name if desired. Click Save and you'll receive the file—a mere 666 KB in size.

FIGURE 8.9
You can obtain both the kit and the developer license on this site.

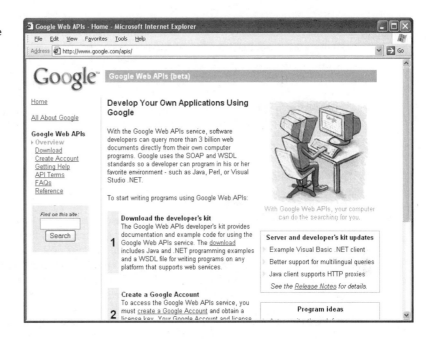

GETTING A LICENSE

Once you complete the download process, click the Create a Google Account link that is available on the same page as the Google Web Services Kit download. You'll see a Web page that requests an email address and password. This page also contains links to Google's terms of service and privacy statements. Make sure that you read both before you proceed. The Google Web Services Kit doesn't include copies of either document, so you might want to copy the information and save it on disk for use later. When you finish reading both documents, check the "I have read and accepted the Google Terms of Service above and Privacy Policy" option and click Create My Google Account.

At this point, you'll see a message stating that Google will send a verification message to your email. Click the link provided by the verification message to activate your account. After you verify your account, Google sends your developer license to your email. The license normally arrives in about an hour—you might need to wait more or less time depending on how busy Google is at the time. Make sure you save the email message containing the developer token because you'll need it for every transaction later.

TIP   You can always change the password and other information associated with your account. Simply go to the Google Accounts site at `https://www.google.com/accounts/Login`. Type your name and password to enter the site. Select the My Account link to change the account information.

INSTALLING THE KIT

The kit is actually a Zip file containing examples and documentation. If you're running Windows XP, the operating system provides a program to unpack the file for you. Otherwise, you'll need a special program that reads the compressed file and unpacks it for you, such as WinZip (`http://www.winzip.com`).

You won't find any actual developer tools in the Zip file. The file does include complete path information, so you can unpack it in the root folder of your hard drive if you like. I used the D drive on my system, so the Google Web Services Kit appears in the D:\GoogleAPI folder.

At this point, the kit is ready for use. However, before you go any further, you need to know about two files in the \GoogleAPI folder. The LICENSE.TXT file contains a copy of the license agreement that you saw online. Make sure you retain this file so that you can refer back to the usage terms as needed.

The README.TXT file contains useful information about the Google Web Services Kit and tells you where you can obtain additional information. This file is very helpful because it contains URLs where you can obtain additional examples. It also has URLs for help sites and additional information. Finally, you'll want to read this file if you want to run the examples because it contains instructions for using them.

Performing a Simple SOAP Call

Google Web Services relies on the use of the Simple Object Access Protocol (SOAP) to make calls. SOAP is yet another form of XML. However, this form of XML provides a means of communication, rather than a means of data storage. As you work with XML, you'll find that it's incredibly flexible and developers use it for many purposes. You get full SOAP support with Visual Studio .NET, and many Windows updates also install it. You can also find the SOAP Toolkit 3.0 at http://www.microsoft.com/downloads/details.aspx?FamilyId=C943C0DD-CEEC-4088-9753-86F052EC8450&displaylang=en.

TIP This section of the chapter doesn't provide a complete SOAP tutorial, but it does provide sufficient information for you to use the example code. However, you can find a great SOAP tutorial at http://www.w3schools.com/soap. It's also helpful to study the official SOAP specification (http://www.w3.org/TR/2001/WD-soap12-20010709), primer (http://www.w3.org/TR/soap12-part0), messaging framework (http://www.w3.org/TR/soap12-part1), and adjuncts (http://www.w3.org/TR/soap12-part2).

SOAP is actually incredibly easy to use to access Google once you understand the basic principles. It's time to try the first SOAP call using a technique that many developers will employ for learning Google Web Services—a simple Web page. Listing 8.4 shows how to make a simple SOAP call using JavaScript. You'll find this example in the \Chapter 08\GoogleSearch folder of the source code on the Sybex Web site.

LISTING 8.4:   Simple JavaScript SOAP Call

```
function CallGoogle()
{
   // Create the SOAP client.
   var SoapClient = new ActiveXObject("MSSOAP.SoapClient30");

   // Initialize the SOAP client so it can access Google
   // Web Services.
   SoapClient.MSSoapInit("http://api.google.com/GoogleSearch.wsdl",
                         "GoogleSearchService",
                         "GoogleSearchPort");
```

```
    // Make a search request.
    var ThisResult =
        SoapClient.doGoogleSearch("Your-License-Key",
                                    SubmissionForm.SearchStr.value,
                                    1,
                                    10,
                                    false,
                                    "",
                                    false,
                                    "",
                                    "",
                                    "");

    // Return the results.
    return ThisResult;
}
```

The code begins by creating a SOAP client. The client communicates with the server—it ensures that the message traffic flows as anticipated and that the request is formed correctly. The `SoapClient.MSSoapInit()` function creates a connection to the server. This step isn't the same as sending data to the server—all it does is create the connection.

At this point, the code can make a request of Google Web Services. Requests take the form of specially formatted function calls. You must know the name of the function call as well as the variables it requires—all of which appear in the Google Web Services Kit that you install. The code makes the request by sending all of the required arguments as part of the `SoapClient.doGoogleSearch()` function call. The following list defines each of the search request arguments. Your application must provide these arguments in order as part of the search request. Otherwise, Google won't honor the request.

key   Every request you make requires the license key you obtained from Google. When you make a request without the license key or using the key found in the Google examples, you'll receive an invalid authorization key message. Google uses a string of zeros (00000000000000000000000000000000) as the sample key—this key looks nothing like the actual key. The examples in this book use "Your-License-Key" as the sample key. In both cases, you must replace the sample key with a real key.

q   This string argument contains the search request. Tests indicate that you can make search requests of any length and Google will honor them. This means you can be quite specific in requesting what you want or you can make a general query and filter the data locally. The one caveat you do need to observe is that complex search specifications tend to reduce the number of results to the point that you don't get any results at all. Smart search techniques make the request specific, without attempting to locate the one result that perfectly matches a need. See Chapter 2 for a complete discussion of search request elements.

start   This numeric argument contains the 0-based starting point for the search. You must couple this starting point with the number of results you request, with 10 results being the maximum. Consequently, if you want to view the third set of results and you request 10 results for each set, you'd set this argument to 30. An odd problem can occur when working with Google Web Services, however. Although the results you receive are sequential, they aren't necessarily complete. The actual results might start at 1 or skip a similar result. This means you can't use a strict starting point; you must base the starting point on the returned values.

maxResults   Google lets you request a maximum of 10 results. However, you can specify less than that amount when you only need a few results. In addition, you may receive fewer results if the search criteria are strict enough. The benefit of requesting fewer results is that you get the response faster, so your application performs better. However, if you plan to request additional results anyway, it's probably better to request the maximum number of results and cache the additional results locally.

filter   The documentation doesn't make this particular argument very clear. You provide true or false as the input values—not the values described in the Automatic Filtering section of the Google Web API Reference. Turning on filtering means that Google looks for results that have the same title and snippet. The Web service only returns the first result and eliminates the others. In addition, Google returns only the first two results from a particular Web host. Filtering means that you have to select the start argument value carefully because Google will leave out some of the results.

restrict   This argument restricts the results you receive to a particular country of origin. Don't confuse this argument with a language restriction. For example, when you select the United States as the country of origin, you could still receive pages written in Spanish or German. However, you won't receive results from either Spain or Germany. The Restricts section of the Google Web API Reference contains a chart of country codes you must use for this argument. As with most restrictions, this argument will create holes in the result set and affect the start argument value.

safeSearch   Generally, you can use this argument to ensure you don't receive any results with pornographic content. However, the filter doesn't work all the time and some search terms will almost certainly retrieve adult content despite the use of this filter. Set the argument to true when you want to avoid adult content. Contact Google at `safesearch@google.com` when you encounter pornographic material that you don't want. Telling Google about the problem will help refine the filter so that others don't encounter the same results.

lr   Sometimes you need a result in a specific language. This argument doesn't restrict the country that you get a result from, but it does restrict the language of the result. For example, you could tell Google that you only want results written in Japanese. The Restricts section of the Google Web API Reference contains a chart of country codes you must use for this argument. As with most restrictions, this argument will create holes in the result set and affect the start argument value.

ie   This argument is ignored. You still need to provide it as part of the SOAP message, but leave the content blank (an empty string).

oe   This argument is ignored. You still need to provide it as part of the SOAP message, but leave the content blank (an empty string).

On return from the call, `ThisResult` contains the return data from Google in the form of a SOAP message. This object isn't an XML document. You must retrieve the XML document using the technique shown in Listing 8.6. However, at this point, you have a pointer to the information you need.

Using a Script to Call an XSLT Page

Google doesn't know how you want to present the data it provides, so the XML you receive doesn't include any form of XSLT declaration. This declaration appears as `<?xml-stylesheet type="text/xsl" href="SearchDisplay.xsl"?>` in the XML file. The `href` attribute tells where to find the XSLT file. Without this information, the browser will never display anything but XML on screen. It would seem that the situation is hopeless. However, you have other options, such as writing a script that performs the transformation process using another technique.

The example in Listing 8.5 shows how you can download a response from Google, store the information locally, and translate it using XSLT. The result is the same as modifying the XML file to include the required linkage information, but far more automatic. You'll find this example in the \Chapter 08\GoogleSearch folder of the source code on the Sybex Web site.

LISTING 8.5:   Performing a Transformation in JavaScript

```
function GetData(XslFile)
{
   // Get the search data.
   var TheResult = CallGoogle();

   // Place the resulting information in an XML document.
   var ProcDoc = new ActiveXObject("Msxml2.DOMDocument.4.0");
   ProcDoc.async = false;
   ProcDoc.loadXML(TheResult.context.xml);

   // Create an XSLT document and load the transform into it.
   var XSLTData = new ActiveXObject("Msxml2.DOMDocument.4.0");
   XSLTData.async = false;
   XSLTData.load(XslFile);

   // Display the output on screen.
   document.write(ProcDoc.transformNode(XSLTData));
}
```

Before the script can do anything, it must obtain the search results from Google. When using Google Web Services, you must rely on SOAP to perform this task. SOAP is extremely flexible, so you can use a number of techniques to make a request with it. The "Performing a Simple SOAP Call" section earlier in this chapter shows one such technique. All you need to know, for the moment, is that the script obtains search results from Google using the CallGoogle() function.

The next step is a little tricky and definitely Windows specific. The code creates an instance of the Microsoft XML component. The ActiveXObject() function performs this task. The Msxml2 .DOMDocument.4.0 string identifies the component. You might have to use Msxml2.DOMDocument.5.0 on newer machines with Microsoft Office 2003 or another new product loaded—the last part of the string identifies the component version number. Setting the async property to false is important because you don't want the call to load the XML to return until the browser actually receives this file. Finally, the ProcDoc.loadXML() function loads the response from Google Web Services. Notice that the code uses the loadXML() function to load text formatted as XML, rather than XML from a file.

NOTE   Most versions of MSXML work fine for this example. However, you'll probably want to get MSXML Version 4.0 Service Pack 2 (SP2) from http://www.microsoft.com/downloads/ details.aspx?FamilyID=3144b72b-b4f2-46da-b4b6-c5d7485f2b42&DisplayLang=en. (MSXML Version 5.0 isn't available for download as of this writing.)This latest version includes a number of features that make working with XML documents a lot easier. In addition, you'll find that the latest versions are slightly faster and contain a number of bug fixes that make your application more reliable.

The code now has a local copy of the data from Google. This local copy will disappear as soon as the function ends, so you don't have to worry about update requirements, but it's important to understand that the copy resides in memory on your machine somewhere.

At this point, the code has data to work with, but no XSLT file. The next step loads the XSLT file defined by the XslFile variable. Notice that the code uses the XSLTData.load() function because the XML appears in a file that the application must load into memory. The coupling between the XML response and the XSLT occurs in the XMLData.transformNode() function call. This call produces output that the document.write() function then sends to the current page. The result is that you see the transformed XML on screen, as shown in Figure 8.10. Notice that the URL doesn't change, even though the content differs, because you're still theoretically on the same Web page.

FIGURE 8.10
The results of using a script to transform XML data received from Google.

Translating the Result with XSLT

This section describes the XSLT page used with the transformation described in the "Using a Script to Call an XSLT Page" section (see Listing 8.5). Listing 8.6 shows how to create an XSLT page that outputs HTML code. You could use the same technique to create a report or any other form of output based on the XML input received from Google. (You'll find this example in the \Chapter 08\GoogleSearch folder of the source code on the Sybex Web site.)

LISTING 8.6:   Designing an XSLT Page

```
<?xml version="1.0" encoding="UTF-8"?>
<xsl:stylesheet version="1.0"
    xmlns:xsl="http://www.w3.org/1999/XSL/Transform"
```

```
      xmlns:fo="http://www.w3.org/1999/XSL/Format">
<xsl:output method="xml" indent="yes"/>
<xsl:template match="/return">
<html>
<head>
    <title>XSLT Transformation Example</title>
</head>
<body>
    <!-- Display a heading. -->
    <h1 align="center">Translated Google Web Services Results</h1>

    <!-- Display some common information. -->
    <h2>Common Results</h2>
    <label>
        Search request:
        <xsl:value-of select="searchQuery"/>
    </label><br/>
    ... Other Common Results ...

    <!-- Display the search result values. -->
    <table align="center" border="1" width="100%">
        <caption><h2>Results Returned from Query</h2></caption>
        <tbody>
            <tr>
                <th>Site Title</th>
                <th>Snippet</th>
                <th>URL</th>
                <th>Cached Size</th>
            </tr>
            <xsl:for-each select="resultElements/item">
                <tr>
                    <td>
                        <xsl:value-of select="title"
                            disable-output-escaping="yes"/>
                    </td>
                    <td>
                        <xsl:value-of select="snippet"
                            disable-output-escaping="yes"/>
                    </td>
                    <td>
                        <xsl:text disable-output-escaping="yes">
                            &lt;a href='
                        </xsl:text>
                        <xsl:value-of select="URL"/>
                        <xsl:text disable-output-escaping="yes">
                            '&gt;
                        </xsl:text>
                        <xsl:value-of select="URL"/>
```

```
                        <xsl:text disable-output-escaping="yes">
                            &lt;/a&gt;
                        </xsl:text>
                    </td>
                    <td><xsl:value-of select="cachedSize"/></td>
                </tr>
            </xsl:for-each>
        </tbody>
    </table>

</body>
</html>
</xsl:template>
</xsl:stylesheet>
```

The code begins with the usual declarations. The `<xsl:output method="xml" indent="yes"/>` tag is important because it determines the kind of output the parser creates. You can also choose text as the output method or tell the parser that you don't want the output indented. Notice that the code also matches the `return` element using the `<xsl:template match="/return">` tag. All of the data appears within this element, so there isn't a good reason to match the root node of the XML document.

The code then outputs the heading. Notice that this is pure HTML and that the code isn't doing anything but outputting this text. The code moves on to the body where it outputs a heading.

The XSLT-specific code begins when the code outputs some of the common information returned by Google. None of this information requires special handling, so the code uses a simple `<xsl:value-of select="searchQuery"/>` tag to retrieve and display the information. The information is surrounded by descriptive text and enclosed within a `<label>` to make it easier to see.

Each return value requires special handling, so the code relies on a table. Notice the head of the table is standard HTML, but that the next selection is an `<xsl:for-each>` element. This statement tells the parser to look at all of the children of the `resultElements/item` node. The system will process each `<item>` element in turn. The next step is to use the `<xsl:value-of>` element to retrieve the name and value attributes of each `<item>` element. Because some of these entries contain the text version of the HTML tags such as `&gt;` for the greater than (>) symbol, you must include `disable-output-escaping="yes"` attribute with the `<xsl:value-of>` element. Otherwise, the code will display the > symbol and not create a tag. The code ends by completing the HTML page, and then completing both the template and the stylesheet.

Getting Your Site on Other Web Sites

Everyone wants a popular Web site. Although this section doesn't provide a comprehensive guide to everything you can do, it does provide some great ideas on how you can improve the visibility of your Web site and attract the kind of traffic that you want.

One of the most important additions to your Web pages is a list of keywords that describe the content fully. As previously noted, you add this list using the `<meta name="keywords">` tag. All you need to add is a `content` attribute that contains the keywords for that page. The more descriptive you become, the more keywords that most search engines will add for that page, which makes it easier for people to find your Web site. This strategy works to a point. Some Web sites add so many keywords that search engines such as Google downgrade them to prevent the Web site from gaining an unfair or unwarranted advantage. In addition, even though most Web sites use automated techniques to locate keywords, spot checks will reveal any use of misleading or incorrect keywords. This act can also downgrade your site. Consequently, you'll want to create keywords that accurately describe your Web page without going beyond the bounds of what the site actually contains.

It doesn't matter how many keywords you use if you don't also provide useful information about your Web page to the search engine. Many search engines provide both a short description that they obtain from the `<meta name="title">` tag and a longer description that they obtain from the `<meta name="description">` tag. Try to create a short, but descriptive title. Search engines generally place a short limit on the amount of information they'll accept for a title and you don't want your title truncated. A description can be quite a bit longer, but it usually has a limit as well. Make sure you check with the individual search engines to discover what these limits are (they change continually).

Now that you have the automated techniques addressed, you'll want to try to garner additional attention. One method of accomplishing this goal is to exchange information with similar or complementary Web sites. In some cases, Web sites form "rings" of sites with content that users might want to see. You place links on your site that let the user move to either the previous or next Web site in the ring. However, sometimes you can just place a link to the other Web site on your Web site in exchange for the same favor on their site. This idea of exchanging links creates a community atmosphere that many Web masters see as a good way of expanding the popularity of their own site while helping the Internet as a whole.

You can also rely on self-marketing techniques. For example, the simple act of placing the URL for your Web site on the bottom of every one of your email messages is a form of advertising. People are bound to see the URL and visit it when they become interested. Make sure you include a short description of what they'll find on your Web site as part of the signature at the bottom of your email.

The Internet provides a wealth of other techniques for gaining additional attention for your Web site. For example, commercial Web sites (even those of small stores) can buy advertising space on other Web sites or as part of newsletters. Of course, you'll pay a price for this particular attention-getter, so you need to weigh the cost against the benefits you'll receive. Generally, you'll find that the more you invest in your Web site, the better results you'll achieve in ensuring that someone will find it.

Discovering Site Maps

Many Web sites now include a site map. In some cases, the Web site relies on a site map in place of a site search, but in most cases, the site map augments any search capability the site search provides. A site map is always some type of text or graphic representation of the site based on the site content. For example, you could create a topical tree that helps the user define the information they need. The following sections discuss site maps and help you create one using the tools that Visual Web Developer provides.

Understanding the Differences Between a Site Map and a Site Search

It's important to understand the differences between a site search and a site map—they accomplish similar goals, but use completely different techniques. A site search relies on the user to provide input in the form of keywords. The user must already have some idea of what they are searching for to use this technique. The results the user receives from a site search vary greatly depending on the flexibility and functionality of the search engine.

A site map provides a representation of the Web site as a whole. The user need not know anything about the Web site to use a site map because the site map presents all of the information at one time.

The user looks through the list of entries to locate the required information. Clicking a link takes the user to the specified Web page.

Even though a site map may appear superior to a site search at first glance, the site map also suffers from limitations. Using a good search engine, a site search can turn up possible pages that the user might not have originally considered. A site search is also more precise—more targeted—because it presents only the hits that relate to the user's search terms. The targeting is important because the user can choose from known good selections, rather than scan an entire Web page looking for potentially good information.

Another point to consider is the number of results that a site search can provide. Even though the user must supply good search terms to begin a site search, a site search ultimately returns more results than a site map can. When creating a site map, the developer must limit the possible search criteria to a topic or other form of descriptive data, rather than a raw collection of words on the page.

Ultimately, it's not a matter of discovering which technique is better. Both a site map and a site search fulfill specific needs for particular users. The choice you make depends partially on who you expect to visit your Web site. A Web site with many first-time novice users generally benefits most from a site map, while a Web site that has a loyal following of advanced users normally does better with a site search. In some cases, providing both search methods is the best choice because a Web site receives a random mix of users.

Using the Site Navigation Features

The site map functionality provided by Visual Web Developer includes a special kind of Web page (described in the "Creating a Site Map" section later in this chapter) and two special controls. These controls appear on the Navigation tab of the Toolbox. The following sections describe the two controls and tell how you can use them to add navigation features to your Web site.

USING THE *SITEMAPPATH* CONTROL

The SiteMapPath control works with the SITEMAP file described in the "Creating a Site Map" section later in this chapter. Any site map entries that you place in the SITEMAP file also appear on this control depending on the Web page's position in the site map hierarchy. You use this control when you want a simple path displayed on screen from the current location to the main page on your Web site (also called the root node).

You can control many of the formatting features of this control. For example, you can change the colors or even the appearance of the various links. You can change the order in which the links appear and features such as the display of tooltips when the user hovers the mouse over the control. It's also possible to choose from one of the predefined templates using the Edit Templates option on the SiteMapPath Smart Tag.

USING THE *MENU* CONTROL

The Menu control can also rely on the content of a SITEMAP file for a list of links. However, this control is a lot more flexible than the SiteMapPath control because you can also use a database as a source of links or you can enter the links manually. In short, you use the Menu control when you need additional flexibility and the use of a drop-down list works as well as the map path provided by the SiteMapPath control.

Besides the flexibility of data source, you can also choose a static or dynamic view that you select using the Views field on the Menu Smart Tag. The static view reads the data source or manual entry when the page loads and only updates the display when the user reloads it. The advantage of this approach is that you conserve network bandwidth and improve application performance. The dynamic view updates the information as needed from the data source while the page is loaded. The advantage of this approach is that you can make new options available as the user needs them.

To change the menu items manually, click Edit Menu Items on the `Menu` Smart Tag. You'll see the Menu Item Editor shown in Figure 8.11. The figure shows one item added. To add an item, click either Add a Root Item or Add a Child Item (the first two buttons above the Items list). You must define the `NavigateUrl`, `Text`, and `Value` properties as a minimum. It's extremely helpful to include a `ToolTip` property value as well so users can obtain additional information about choices they make.

FIGURE 8.11
Create menu items manually using the Menu Item Editor.

To add a data source, select an existing entry in the Choose Data Source field of the `Menu` Smart Tag or choose `<New Data Source...>` to create a new data source. You'll see a Data Source Configuration dialog box. This dialog box lets you choose between a site map and an XML database as a source of entries for your menu. When you select a site map as a data source, you don't have to perform any additional work because the control automatically uses the `SITEMAP` file you define for other purposes. When working with an XML database, you must create the specially formatted XML (see Listing 8.7 for an example). This is a viable option if you store your site map in a database, but isn't especially convenient and you should avoid using it when possible.

Creating a Site Map

A site map requires a little special programming. Visual Web Developer encapsulates this programming as part of the Site Map template located on the Add New Item dialog box. When you select this template, you'll create a new `Web.SITEMAP` file. The special `SITEMAP` extension defines a site map for your Web page. The `SITEMAP` file is yet another example of XML at work. You define the structure of your Web site using a series of XML entries. Subpages appear as child nodes of the parent used to call them. For example, the "Creating a Custom Site Search" section of the chapter used a number of Web pages to perform its work. The first page you access is `SiteSearch.ASPX`, so that page acts as the parent for all other nodes, as shown in Listing 8.7. You'll find this example in the `\Chapter 08\CustomSearch` folder of the source code on the Sybex Web site.

LISTING 8.7:   Defining a Site Map Structure for a Web Site

```xml
<?xml version="1.0" encoding="utf-8" ?>
<siteMap>
    <!-- Node the user accesses first. -->
    <siteMapNode url="SiteSearch.ASPX"
                 title="Custom Site Search Example"
                 description="Discover how to create a site search."
                 roles="">

        <!-- Two nodes accessed from SiteSearch.ASPX. -->
        <siteMapNode url="IndexPages.ASPX"
                     title="Index the Custom Search Pages"
                     description="Create a search results index."
                     roles="" />
        <siteMapNode url="SiteCounter.ASPX"
                     title="SiteCounter Demonstration"
                     description="Shows how to use custom counters."
                     roles="">

            <!-- Two nodes accessed from SiteCounter.ASPX. -->
            <siteMapNode url="SiteControl1.ASPX"
                         title="Control Site 1"
                         description="An extra page."
                         roles="" />
            <siteMapNode url="SiteControl2.ASPX"
                         title="Control Site 2"
                         description="An extra page."
                         roles="" />
        </siteMapNode>
    </siteMapNode>
</siteMap>
```

The site map appears as a series of `<siteMapNode>` elements that you can nest as needed to create the hierarchy for your Web site. Each `<siteMapNode>` element contains four attributes.

url   Contains the relative or absolute URL of the target page. Make sure you include the path from the root node when working with relative URLs.

title   Contains the page title. You should use the same title that appears in the `<title>` tag or the title `<meta>` tag when defining this option.

description   Defines the purpose of the Web page. You can use the content of the description `<meta>` tag for this entry. However, if the standard description is too long to create an effective tooltip, you can always shorten the text so it fits on screen.

roles   Creates a security setting for this site map entry. Only users who exist in the appropriate security role can access the entry. Visual Web Developer uses the concept of roles to enforce security—users exist in roles that have specific security access. The user's role can change depending on circumstances—a user with a local connection acting as a manager might have more rights than with a remote connection as a user. See Chapter 17 for a complete description of security issues in Visual Web Developer.

Once you create a `SITEMAP` file, you can add either a `SiteMapPath` or `Menu` control to the pages on your Web site to display its content. Figure 8.12 shows examples of both kinds of output. The `SiteMapPath` appears at the top of the page immediately below the page title, while the `Menu` appears at the bottom of the page. Notice how hovering the mouse displays a tooltip describing the page.

FIGURE 8.12

Use the appropriate control to display your site map.

Defining Your Development Goals

This chapter has helped you understand the purpose and effectiveness of site searches using various techniques and under a number of conditions. In some cases, you also need to create a site map to ensure that all users can find everything they need. The choices you make determine how easy your site is to search, which ultimately determines its popularity. Users can't tell other people about great information they can't find.

It's time to determine the search setup for your Web site. You can begin by defining the search elements the user is likely to need. After you decide what kind of search to create, you'll need to determine how to create it. Using a custom search does have significant benefits, but also requires a lot of effort on your part. Many developers rely on Google searches to meet their needs. After you create one or more searches for your Web site, think about creating a site map as well. In fact, you might want to use some of the tips from Chapter 7 to design a form to get user feedback on the kind of site they need as well.

Chapter 9 helps you understand both pop-ups and redirection—two resources that you can use with either forms or searches. Some Web sites use these features to good effect in making the user experience better. Of course, it's always easy to misuse a technology. Pop-ups have become a problem for many people because Web site developers have misused them in the past. Chapter 9 not only shows you great uses for both pop-ups and redirection, but also helps you avoid misusing these technologies.

Chapter 9

Using Pop-ups and Redirection

On the Internet, getting to where you really wanted to go is half the adventure. Web sites change their domain names, Webmasters move pages around, sometimes a Web site will choose to provide more than one path to the same information, and there are even times where you'll get the wrong URL the first time. No matter how you get to where you're going, pop-ups and redirection both have a role to play in getting you there. This chapter explores legitimate uses of both techniques and exposes some uses that you'll want to avoid to keep Web site visitors happy.

Many people criticize the use of pop-up forms for good reason—most Web sites use them in unappealing ways to try to sell you something or get you to do something that you don't want to do. However, pop-up forms can have many legitimate uses as well. For example, you can provide a pop-up form that reminds a user to perform a specific task or asks the user's opinion about Web site functionality.

NOTE   This chapter doesn't explore a variation of the pop-up, the pop-under. Proponents of the pop-under say that it's less intrusive than the pop-up, but there are few legitimate uses for the technology. A pop-under appears under the main Web page, which means that the user can't even see it immediately. Some Web sites, such as ASAP! A Stand Against Pop-under ads! (`http://jenett.org/asap`), speak out against pop-under advertisements. A number of articles, such as the Fox News Channel article at `http://www.foxnews.com/story/0,2933,28826,00.html`, also discuss how pop-under advertisements are irritating Web surfers. You can get additional information about pop-under windows in the article, "Pop-Under Windows—The Latest Pop-Window Trend" at `http://www.web-source.net/popunder.htm`.

Like pop-up windows, redirection has a number of legitimate uses. In fact, of the two technologies, redirection probably has the most legitimate use—getting people to the location of a new page on your Web site. Unfortunately, like pop-ups, redirection has a lot of potential for misuse, so users are leery of redirection, in many cases for good reason. You have access to three kinds of redirection when using Visual Web Developer and this chapter explores all three. The kind of redirection you choose depends on the need that your Web site is trying to serve and the security requirements for the redirection. Although using the meta refresh tag is still extremely popular and you can rely on scripted redirection when the client trusts your Web site enough to run scripts, server-side redirection is becoming extremely popular because it's the most secure and reliable method of performing this task.

Understanding User Concerns over Pop-ups and Redirection

Most users understand that Web sites need to earn money to stay in business and most are very happy to accept the banner advertisements that these Web site sport. The problem for the Web site is that most banner advertisements don't garner enough click-through (when the user clicks the advertisement) activity to keep the Web site alive. As a result, developers created the pop-up advertisement. A pop-up advertisement is a window that appears over the top of the browser window. It's annoying because the user has to dismiss the window before viewing the Web site content.

Unfortunately, the problem gets worse. Some developers noticed that the user was dismissing the window without providing a click-through, so they created a setup where the window keeps reappearing until the user clicks the advertisement. The user can even move to a different Web site and the advertisement will keep reappearing. In fact, because some of this code is broken, the advertisement keeps popping up even after the user clicks it. The only way to get rid of the advertisement, in some cases, is to reboot the machine. After having a few of these experiences, most users become quite adamant about not wanting to see any more pop-up windows—ever.

The problem with pop-up advertisements has become so severe that even Microsoft has recognized the need for a pop-up blocker (special software that keeps pop-up windows from appearing on screen). You can now get a built-in pop-up blocker as part of Windows XP Service Pack 2 (SP2), which you control using the Privacy tab of the Internet Options dialog box. Click Settings and you'll see the Pop-up Blocker Settings dialog box shown in Figure 9.1. This dialog box has the highest settings enabled (see `http://www.microsoft.com/windowsxp/using/web/sp2_popupblocker.mspx` for additional details).

FIGURE 9.1

Internet Explorer users now have a built-in pop-up blocker in Windows XP SP2.

Quite a few third-party vendors also supply pop-up blockers for other versions of Windows, many of which are special toolbars for Internet Explorer. The three most common toolbar options are the MSN toolbar (`http://toolbar.msn.com`), Google toolbar (`http://toolbar.google.com`), and the Alexa toolbar (`http://download.alexa.com/index.cgi`). The point is you must provide the user with a good reason to allow your pop-up window other than the fact that you want to sell products.

NOTE   It's interesting to note that pop-up blockers can cause problems of their own. A friend recently related that several employees decided to add pop-up blockers to their system without permission. It wasn't long before the users complained of problems with their systems. A specific combination of applications would cause one of the applications to crash—sometimes the cure is worse than the disease.

Redirection hasn't come under the common definition of a plague that pop-up advertisements have, but it can actually be a bigger problem. It's possible for a cracker with the proper tools to redirect a browser from a legitimate Web site to a look-alike that contains viruses, Trojan horses, or other content of dubious quality. Some of this redirection takes place in situations where the user has no idea that the redirection has occurred, such as the cross-site scripting issue described in the US-CERT article at `http://www.us-cert.gov/cas/techalerts/TA04-163A.html`. You can find a concise description of some of the security problems with redirection on the LWN site at `http://lwn.net/2000/features/Redirect.php3`.

Some users respond to the security issues created by redirection by disabling some browser features such as scripting. In fact, Internet Explorer can also disable the meta refresh tag using the settings on the Security Settings dialog box shown in Figure 9.2. (You can access this dialog box by opening the Internet Options dialog, selecting a security zone on the Security tag, and clicking Custom Level.) Consequently, the only sure way to provide redirection on your Web site is to use server-side redirection. Not surprisingly, this is also the safest method of providing redirection and the one that the user is most likely to accept.

FIGURE 9.2

Disabling both scripted and meta refresh redirection is easy in Internet Explorer.

Although you know that you have no evil intent in using either pop-ups or redirection, convincing the user is going to be difficult given the problems that both technologies can cause. That's why you need to create a written set of policies for your Web site. A privacy policy assures the user that any information you collect as part of pop-ups and the use of redirection will remain private and describes precisely how you'll use the information. You also need a policy that defines why your site is using these technologies and encourages the user to contact you about the legitimacy of this need. It's also a good idea to be proactive about providing the user with facts about both technologies so the user understands the risks on other Web sites. The goal is to provide the user with the education required to understand your use of these technologies and provide a good reason for the user to allow your use of them.

Creating a Pop-up Form

The basic pop-up form is easy to create. The technique relies on a little JavaScript to perform the task, and any kind of Web page can support the form. You'll find this example in the \Chapter 09\ BasicPopup folder of the source code on the Sybex Web site. To begin creating a pop-up, you'll need a method of displaying the window. The Web page shown in Listing 9.1 shows a simple demonstration form you can use.

LISTING 9.1:   Displaying a Pop-up Using JavaScript

```
<!DOCTYPE html PUBLIC "-//W3C//DTD XHTML 1.1//EN"
                      "http://www.w3.org/TR/xhtml11/DTD/xhtml11.dtd">
<html xmlns="http://www.w3.org/1999/xhtml" >
<head>
    <title>Pop-up Window Demonstration Main Page</title>
    <script type="text/javascript">
<!--
    function btnPopup_OnClick()
    {
        var Features;

        // Create a description of the features.
        Features = "height=" + txtHeight.value;
        Features = Features + ",width=" + txtWidth.value;
        if (cbScrollbar.checked)
            Features = Features + ",scrollbars=yes";
        else
            Features = Features + ",scrollbars=no";

        // Display the pop-up
        window.open('PopupPage.HTM', 'TestWindow', Features);
    }
-->
    </script>
</head>
<body>
    <h1>Pop-up Window Demonstration</h1>
    <label>Window Height: </label>
    <input id="txtHeight" type="text" value="200" /><br />
    <label>Window Width: </label>
    <input id="txtWidth" type="text" value="400" /><br />
    <label>Scrollbars: </label>
    <input id="cbScrollbar" type="checkbox" value="Scollbars" /><br />
    <input id="btnPopup"
            title="Displays the popup on screen."
            accesskey="S"
            type="button"
            value="Show Popup"
            onclick="btnPopup_OnClick()"/>

</body>
</html>
```

The demonstration form lets you try various simple pop-up settings to see how they affect the appearance of the page. Figure 9.3 shows the form along with the associated pop-up. As you can see, you can change the size of the form quite easily, as well as the presence of scrollbars in the resulting form. The resulting form doesn't include any of the normal browser toolbars because it's a pop-up.

FIGURE 9.3

The demonstration page lets you test various pop-up form features.

The essential part of this page is the `window.open()` method call in the `btnPopup_OnClick()` function. The page calls this method when the user clicks Show Popup. The code builds up a list of comma-separated features based on the form content before it calls the `window.open()` method. The `window.open()` method accepts up to four arguments including the pop-up form URL, form name, form feature list, and a Boolean value that replaces the current pop-up window when set to true.

NOTE   The features list is optional. If you don't provide a features list, the pop-up form uses the settings the user prefers for the browser. In other words, it looks like another browser window, rather than a pop-up form.

At some point, you'll want to close the window. Most users will figure out that they need to click the close box in the upper-right corner of the form. However, your pop-up will have a nicer appearance when you include a button for dismissing the pop-up from the screen. All you need is a simple function to perform the task like the one shown here.

```
<script type="text/javascript">
<!--
    function btnDismiss_OnClick()
    {
        // Close this window.
        window.close();
    }
-->
</script>
```

The features list for a pop-up can include a number of arguments—all of which affect the appearance of the window in some way. Here's a list of the common pop-up window feature arguments. Note that you must include some arguments, such as `width` and `height`, together, as shown in the list.

width **and** *height*   Determines the size of the form in pixels (the default is the same size as the parent window).

left **and** *top*   Defines the upper left corner of the form on the screen in pixels (the default centers the window on screen).

toolbar   Displays a toolbar (standard buttons toolbar) on the form when set to yes (the default when you provide a list of features is no).

location   Displays a location field (address toolbar) on the form when set to yes (the default when you provide a list of features is no).

directories   Displays a list of popular locations (links toolbar) on the form when set to yes (the default when you provide a list of features is no).

status   Displays a status bar across the bottom of the pop-up form when set to yes (the default when you provide a list of features is no).

menubar   Displays a list of menu items across the top of the form when set to yes (the default when you provide a list of features is no).

scrollbars   Displays a vertical scrollbar as a minimum and an optional horizontal scrollbar when needed when you set this option to yes (the default when you provide a list of features is no).

TIP   Because you can't be sure about the user's display and predetermine how the other settings you choose will affect the display, you should either provide scrollbars in the form or allow the user to resize the form as needed to display the content. For example, the user could rely on a large font to display content—you can't predetermine when the change in font size will occur, so letting the user resize the form to accommodate the larger font is a good idea. (Many users require large fonts to address special visual needs such as low or poor vision.) Using scrollbars would also allow the user to move content around as needed to view the entire form.

resizable   Allows the user to resize the form when set to yes (the default is no, which means the user can't resize the form).

dependent   Sets the form to automatically close when the parent window closes when set to yes (the default when you provide a list of features is no).

fullscreen   Displays the form full screen, rather than as a smaller dialog box, when set to yes (the default when you provide a list of features is no).

channelmode   Sets the form to use channelmode—a feature that is only available to Internet Explorer users when set to yes. The form displays a specialized menu in full screen mode. In some cases, you'll also see an Explorer Bar on the left side of the display.

Using Pop-up Forms

Pop-up forms or windows have a number of legitimate uses. For example, when you visit the Windows Update site at `http://windowsupdate.microsoft.com`, you'll notice that Microsoft uses pop-up windows to display status information as the Web site looks for updates on the host machine. Although this isn't the most common use of a pop-up window, it's a legitimate one and a use that you could consider for a custom Web application. The point is that this window doesn't advertise anything—it's there to help the user. The following sections describe other legitimate uses for pop-up forms.

Additional Information

Sometimes a Web site has instructions that it must present to new users. For example, you might require that the user install a kit prior to installing software updates or perform other tasks as part of a setup. The user will visit your Web site many times, but need the instructions only once or twice. When you use a static page to display the required information, the user has to wade through all of the novice-level material before getting to the needed material during each visit. Using a pop-up window for this information means that the Web site can display just the essentials on the main window. A new user will see the pop-up window on the first visit and read through the required material, but an advanced user can simply dismiss the window and get right down to business.

In fact, you can easily extend this idea by creating a check box on the pop-up form that says something like, "Don't display this information in the future." A cookie on the user's machine alerts you to the fact that the user doesn't want to see the information anymore, so your Web page won't even display the pop-up window. Of course, if you take this approach, you'll also want to include an option to display the pop-up window again when the user needs to display the information. Making changes two-way is an important concept.

The example in this section explores a few new concepts. The first is the use of a shared script file. Sharing a script lets you create the code once, yet use it as many times as needed. Script sharing is a common practice on Web sites because it's such a big productivity enhancer. The second is sharing a cookie between Web pages. Once you create a permanent cookie, you can share it with any page on a particular Web site. By adding some special information (the path and domain elements), you can also share the cookie with pages in a particular path or even within the same domain. (You can learn more about the path and domain elements of a permanent cookie at `http://wp.netscape.com/newsref/std/cookie_spec.html`.) The third is creating a null link—one that doesn't actually lead anywhere. This technique lets you execute a script without actually taking the user anywhere.

CREATING THE SHARED JAVASCRIPT FILE

You can store scripts externally and then reference them from more than one page. Unfortunately, Visual Web Developer doesn't provide a template to perform this task, so you'll need to select the Text File template and type a script filename such as SharedScript.JS. Listing 9.2 shows the shared script file used for this example. You'll find this example in the `\Chapter 09\AddedInformation` folder of the source code on the Sybex Web site.

LISTING 9.2:   Placing Cookie Scripts in a Shared File

```
function GetExpireDate(Days, Months, Years)
{
    var TheDate = new Date(); // Date object.
    var Expire;               // Expiration date.

    // Add the required time intervals.
    TheDate.setHours((Days * 24) + TheDate.getHours());
    TheDate.setMonth(TheDate.getMonth() + Months);
```

```
TheDate.setFullYear(Years + TheDate.getFullYear());

// Build an expiration date. Begin by getting the day.
// of the week.
switch (TheDate.getUTCDay() + 1)
{
case 1:
    Expire = "Sun, ";
    break;

... Other Cases ...

case 7:
    Expire = "Sat, ";
    break;

}

// Add the date.
Expire = Expire + (TheDate.getUTCDate());

// Add the month.
switch (TheDate.getUTCMonth() + 1)
{
case 1:
    Expire = Expire + " Jan ";
    break;

... Other Cases ...

case 12:
    Expire = Expire + " Dec ";
    break;
}

// Add the year.
Years = TheDate.getUTCFullYear();
Expire = Expire + Years + " ";

// Add the time.
Expire = Expire + TheDate.getUTCHours() + ":" +
        TheDate.getUTCMinutes() + ":" +
        TheDate.getUTCSeconds() + " UTC";

// Return the result.
return Expire
}
```

With careful programming, you can move many of your JavaScript applications to a separate file. In this case, the application accepts the number of days, months, and years that you want to add to the current date. The return value is an expiration date that you can use to create a permanent cookie.

The first task is to add the required time intervals to the current date. When working with days, you must actually add the required hours, rather than the number of days, so the code multiplies Days by 24 to obtain the number hours from the current time, which it obtains using the TheDate.getHours() method. The code then uses the TheDate.setHours() method to change the date. If the number of days changes the month or year, the TheDate.setHours() method automatically accounts for the differences. Adding the Months and Years values is easier because you can add them directly to the date, rather than perform a conversion.

The code creates the expiration date by creating a new string value, Expire. It begins by determining the day of the week using a switch statement. The code then adds the day, the month as a text value (using another switch statement), the year, and finally the time. The function passes this information back to the caller.

Now that you have a file with a number of useful scripts, you need to add it to the Web page that relies on them. All you need to do to perform this task is create a blank script in the Web page like this:

```
<script src="SharedScript.JS" type="text/javascript"></script>
```

When the browser sees a <script> tag like this one, it automatically loads the file along with the Web page. The scripts contained within the source file (defined by the src attribute) become available to any part of the Web page.

DESIGNING THE POP-UP FORM

The pop-up form has several tasks to perform in this example. The form stores a cookie that tracks whether the user wants to see the additional information presented by this form, so the form has to work with the cookie. This means that the code must display the current cookie status and let the user change the cookie as needed. In addition, the form must contain some means of dismissal. Listing 9.3 shows the code for this part of the example.

LISTING 9.3:   Displaying and Configuring the Pop-up Form

```
<!DOCTYPE html PUBLIC "-//W3C//DTD XHTML 1.1//EN"
                      "http://www.w3.org/TR/xhtml11/DTD/xhtml11.dtd">
<html xmlns="http://www.w3.org/1999/xhtml" >
<head>
    <title>Added Information Page</title>

    <script src="SharedScript.JS" type="text/javascript"></script>

    <script type="text/javascript">
    <!--
        function PageLoad()
        {
            var ACookie; // Holds the document cookie.
            var Parsed;  // Holds the split cookies.
```

```
            // Get the cookie.
            ACookie = unescape(document.cookie);

            // Split the cookie elements.
            Parsed = ACookie.split("=");

            // Determined the checked value.
            if (Parsed[1] == "true")
                cbDontShow.checked = true;
            else
                cbDontShow.checked = false;
        }

        function btnDismiss_OnClick()
        {
            // Close the window.
            window.close();
        }

        function cbDontShow_OnClick()
        {
            var UserCookie; // Stores the user name.
            var Expire;     // Expiration date.

            // Get an expiration date. Set it to expire one year
            // from the current date.
            Expire = GetExpireDate(0, 0, 1);

            // Create the username cookie.
            UserCookie = "AddedInfo=" + escape(cbDontShow.checked) +
                         "; expires=" + Expire;

            // Add the cookie to the document.
            document.cookie = UserCookie;
        }
    -->
    </script>
</head>
<body onload="PageLoad()">
    <h1>
        Added Information Page</h1>
    <p>
        This section normally contains the instructions that you want
        the user to see the first few times they open the page.
    </p>
    <p>
        <label>Don't Show This Window Again</label>
        <input id="cbDontShow"
```

```
                type="checkbox"
                accesskey="S"
                title="Disables additional information display."
                onclick="cbDontShow_OnClick()" />
    </p>
    <p>
        <input id="btnDismiss"
                type="button"
                value="Dismiss"
                accesskey="D"
                title="Closes the added information window."
                onclick="btnDismiss_OnClick()" />
    </p>
</body>
</html>
```

The form actually contains two controls, as shown in Figure 9.4. Look at the HTML for this example and you'll see that both controls include onclick attributes. That's right, you can attach a script to a check box just as easily as you can a button, so you can use whatever control makes sense for a particular task. The btnDismiss code simply closes the pop-up form, as you'd expect.

FIGURE 9.4
The example uses controls to ensure that the applications meet user needs.

The cbDontShow_OnClick() method uses the GetExpireDate() function to create an expiration date. It then obtains the value of the cbDontShow.checked property and creates a cookie. Because this is a permanent cookie, it appears in the user's \Cookies folder. The example sets the cookie to expire in a year. Consequently, the user will see the additional information pop-up form once a year if the cookie never changes. You could add code to refresh the cookie as needed, but having it pop up occasionally reminds the user that the information is available.

The final task occurs when the page loads. The <body> tag calls the PageLoad() function. This function retrieves the cookie, parses it, and uses the value to determine whether or not the check box is checked. Some developers wouldn't include this feature, but the status information is essential. Strange things can happen when the user sees something unexpected, so this little piece of code can save support calls.

CREATING THE MAIN PAGE

The added information page won't display until the main page, the one that the user initially opens, creates it. This fact means that the code for setting the cookie is inaccessible to the user once the user decides to set the form not to display. Since you don't want to display the form unless the user requests it, the main page requires both an automatic and a manual means of displaying the pop-up form. The user relies on the manual method when needed to display the additional information or change the automatic display setting. Listing 9.4 shows the code required for this part of the example.

LISTING 9.4:   Managing the Pop-up Form

```
<!DOCTYPE html PUBLIC "-//W3C//DTD XHTML 1.1//EN"
                    "http://www.w3.org/TR/xhtml11/DTD/xhtml11.dtd">
<html xmlns="http://www.w3.org/1999/xhtml" >
<head>
    <title>Informational Page Demonstration</title>
    <script type="text/javascript">
    <!--
        function PageLoad()
        {
            var  ACookie; // Holds the document cookie.
            var  Parsed;  // Holds the split cookies.
            var SetIt;

            // Get the cookie.
            ACookie = unescape(document.cookie);

            // Split the cookie elements.
            Parsed = ACookie.split("=");

            // Determine whether the user wants the additional
            // information displayed on screen.
            if (Parsed[1] == "false")
                window.open("AddedInfo.HTM",
                        "AddedInfo",
                        "height=300, width=400, resizable=true, " +
                        "dependent=true");
        }

        function ForceLoad()
        {
            // Force the added information page open.
            window.open("AddedInfo.HTM",
                    "AddedInfo",
                    "height=300, width=400, resizable=true, " +
```

```
                              "dependent=true");
            }
        -->
        </script>
    </head>
    <body onload="PageLoad()">
        <h1>Informational Page Demonstration</h1>
        <p>This page contains the main Web site content.</p>
        <a href="" onclick="ForceLoad()">
            Open the added information page.
        </a>
    </body>
</html>
```

The <body> tag always calls the PageLoad() function when the page loads. The PageLoad() function begins by loading the cookie created by the added information pop-up form. This cookie is available because it's permanent and the main page is in the same path as the Web page that created the cookie. After the code loads the cookie, it determines whether the user wants the additional information pop-up form loaded. If the user wants to see the additional information, the code uses the window.open() method to open the pop-up window. Notice that this pop-up form is dependent on the main page, which means it closes automatically when the user closes the main page.

As you can see, the automation works fine, so long as the user wants to see the information, but won't work at all once the user decides not to see the pop-up form. Notice the special link near the bottom of the page. As you can see from Figure 9.5, it looks like any other link you might have seen in the past. However, the href attribute is a blank string. You always have to include the href attribute or the link won't appear as a link—it'll appear as text, but this href attribute won't take the user anywhere. Notice that the <a> tag does include an onclick attribute, which calls the ForceLoad() function when the user clicks the link. The ForceLoad() function simply displays the pop-up form without any intermediate checks. A null link provides the interface that the user expects, but performs the task that you need.

FIGURE 9.5
Use null links as needed to create the proper presentation without compromising functionality.

Help Pages

Most users like to have help pages side by side with their main page so they can use the two together. Consequently, a help page is an excellent use of a pop-up form. The user can click Help on any given page and get the help required to work with it. This feature gives your Web application a decidedly desktop feel. Besides making the user happy, creating pop-up help pages also reduces support costs for your Web site. You can even add a level of context sensitivity to the help pages by using a different URL for each page or relying on anchors to access a particular portion of a single help page.

Mechanically, help pages are very much like the informational pages described in the "Additional Information" section of the chapter. Of course, you don't need a check box to let the user indicate that they don't want to see the help page because the user will decide when the help page appears. You might want to include the menu bar using the `menubar` feature so the user can add special help pages to their favorites list.

A help page also relies on the fourth `window.open()` method argument. Set the `replace` argument to true to ensure that the user doesn't end up with many copies of the same page. Replacing each old request with a new request means the user sees a single main page and just one help page—avoiding confusion that will certainly keep support costs down.

Users naturally want to move between topics, so your help page will include plenty of content links. However, you might also want to include a list of popular links along with the side of the page or even use a `Menu` control (see the "Using the Menu Control" section of Chapter 8 for details) to display a user's favorite links. You could store the links using cookies and then populate the `Menu` control using code during page loading.

Unlike an information page, where scrollbars work fine, you'll want to make help pages resizable so the user can modify the size as needed. In fact, you might want to store these settings as part of a cookie so that you can restore the window to its original size later. In short, even though help pages work very much like informational pages, they have a few bells and whistles that you need to add to ensure smooth operation and good user support.

NOTE You might have noticed that this chapter relies heavily on cookies. As your Web pages increase in complexity, you need some means of storing both temporary and permanent data. When a user doesn't allow cookies, you'll have to convince them to make an exception, use server-side storage if possible, or use a non-scripting solution for the problem. In general, using cookies on a private Web site is never a problem. Using them on a public Web site can be a problem depending on how much trust the user has in your Web site. Given the current Internet environment, it's not too surprising to find users reluctant to allow cookie support so you need to spell out precisely how you plan to use them in order to garner support.

User Survey

User surveys represent another way to use pop-up forms to benefit the user. In this case, however, using pure HTML could be troublesome. Yes, you can definitely do it, but Visual Web developer offers so many interesting ways to work with data that you won't want to use pure HTML. In fact, this is a perfect time to begin using the `View` and `MultiView` controls to create a great presentation that all of your users can work with. The interesting part of the `View` and `MultiView` controls is that you can present multiple pages of data to the user without leaving the current page.

However, a pure ASP.NET solution doesn't work particularly well either. For example, the very act of presenting the pop-up form is a nightmare when working with ASP.NET. All you need is a few lines of script of accomplish the task. Consequently, this example does use HTML as well. In fact, it demonstrates that you can combine ASP.NET and HTML in one application in a way that the user will never notice or care about. You'll find this example in the \Chapter 09\Survey folder of the source code on the Sybex Web site.

USING THE *VIEW* AND *MULTIVIEW* CONTROLS

The View and MultiView controls work together to create what appears to be multiple Web pages from a single Web page. The idea is to create an environment where you get to work with all of the data in one page, but the user sees multiple, less complex, pages that fit on most screens. Each View control can contain a whole page worth of information. You can select each page independently. Therefore, the user seems to move from page to page, but actually stays in place. Figure 9.6 shows a typical example of multiple View controls contained within a MultiView control.

FIGURE 9.6

Each *MultiView* control contains multiple *View* controls.

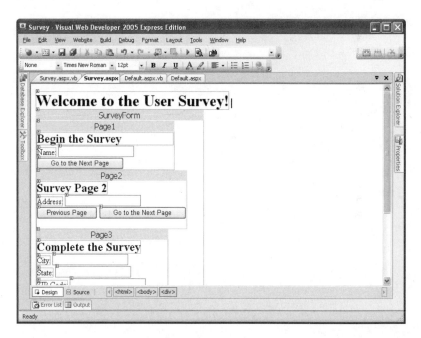

The page shown in Figure 9.6 works as any other ASP.NET page you create. For example, the banner at the top appears on every page because it resides outside of the MultiView control. Nothing stops you from creating common content, and including more than one MultiView control is necessary to display unique content on each page. You could even use the technique to create pages that contain statistics in one MultiView control and one of several graphical representations in another. All the user sees is one of the pages, however, as shown in Figure 9.7.

FIGURE 9.7

The user sees only the part of the display that you want them to see.

You use the `MultiView` control (`SurveyForm` in the example) to switch between `View` control outputs (`Page1` through `Page4` in the example). In fact, the process is incredibly easy, as shown here.

```
Sub Page_Load(ByVal sender As Object, _
             ByVal e As System.EventArgs) Handles Me.Load
    ' Load the first page of the survey.
    SurveyForm.SetActiveView(Page1)
End Sub
```

When the form opens, the code loads the first `View` control, `Page1`, using the `SurveyForm` `.SetActiveView()` method. You don't need to refresh anything or worry that the user won't gain access to all of the form functionality. The server takes care of everything for you. Consequently, you create only one line of code to display a `View` control—the IDE creates all other code for you in the background as you lay out the various page elements. The simplicity of this approach is the reason that you want to avoid using HTML whenever possible to create this kind of pop-up form.

CREATING THE POP-UP SURVEY FORM

All of the survey coding takes place on the server. However, the actual mechanics of displaying the form should take place on the client. Generally, you won't see developers mix ASP.NET and HTML controls on one form. Fortunately, the technique works extremely well and makes a lot of sense when you can employ it successfully. Figure 9.8 shows the combination of ASP.NET and HTML controls used for this example. Notice that the HTML control (highlighted in the figure) has a very familiar look from the example in the "Additional Information" section earlier in this chapter, even though this is essentially an ASP.NET application.

FIGURE 9.8
Mixing ASP.NET and HTML controls really isn't taboo and you should use the technique whenever possible.

The reason that this combination makes sense, in this case, is that you must tell the client to load and unload the pop-up form. Theoretically, you can do this from the server using pure ASP.NET code, but you'll write a lot of code to do it and the resulting application won't perform well. This example uses the same code as the added information example to load and unload the pop-up form.

PROCESSING THE SURVEY

Once you collect all of the survey data, you'll want to process it. Depending on your particular requirements, XML files or a database will work equally well for a smaller organization. Large organizations that expect thousands of survey results will want to use a database. The example relies on an XML file, in this case, that creates a unique entry based on the user name and the time, as shown in Listing 9.5.

LISTING 9.5: Processing the User Input as XML

```
Sub btnSubmit_Click(ByVal sender As Object, ByVal e As System.EventArgs)
    Dim ThisPath As String                   ' Application path.
    Dim Filename As String                   ' Full path to data store.
    Dim Output As XmlDocument                ' Contains all input.
    Dim PInst As XmlProcessingInstruction    ' A processing instruction.
    Dim RootNode As XmlElement               ' The root node.
    Dim DataNode As XmlElement               ' Individual data element.

    ' Determine the path for this application.
    ThisPath = Page.MapPath(Page.AppRelativeVirtualPath)
```

```
        ThisPath = ThisPath.Replace("\IndexPages.aspx", "\")

        ' Create the filename. Build a unique name first and then remove
        ' any elements that might cause problems. Finally, include the
        ' destination folder.
        Filename = txtName.Text + "_" + DateTime.Now.ToString() + ".XML"
        Filename = Filename.Replace(" ", "_")
        Filename = Filename.Replace(":", "_")
        Filename = Filename.Replace("/", "_")

        ' Set the output information.
        txtMoreInfo.Text = Filename

        ' Complete the filename.
        Filename = ThisPath + Filename

        ' Create the XML document.
        Output = New XmlDocument()

        ' Define the XML processing directive.
        PInst = Output.CreateProcessingInstruction( _
            "xml", "version='1.0' encoding='utf-8'")

        ' Add the XML processing directive to the document.
        Output.AppendChild(PInst)

        ' Create the root node that holds all of the other data.
        RootNode = Output.CreateElement("Survey")

        ' Create the Name node and add it to the root node.
        DataNode = Output.CreateElement("Name")
        DataNode.InnerXml = txtName.Text
        RootNode.AppendChild(DataNode)

        ... Other Data Nodes ...

        ' Add the root node to the document.
        Output.AppendChild(RootNode)

        ' Save the document to disk.
        Output.Save(Filename)

        ' Load the final page.
        SurveyForm.SetActiveView(Page4)
    End Sub
```

The code begins by obtaining the application path. It then creates a unique filename based on the user name and the current time. The code outputs the filename to `txtMoreInfo.Text` as part of the final page display shown in Figure 9.9. Providing the user with a filename not only makes it possible for that user to track the survey, but also gives a feeling of completion that many survey applications lack. Notice that the code doesn't provide the user with a path to the file—this action would represent a security risk. After the code outputs the filename, it creates a complete filename by combining the path with the unique filename.

FIGURE 9.9

Providing the user with a survey filename makes it possible to track the survey later.

At this point, the code begins creating an XML document. As normal, the code begins by creating an XML document and placing an XML processing directive within it. The code then begins creating the root node and filling it with the data nodes from the survey form. Finally, the code adds the root node to the XML document, `Output`, and the document is complete. The `Output.Save()` method places the XML file on disk where you can retrieve it later.

The code uses the `SurveyForm.SetActiveView()` method to display the form on screen. However, in this case, the form contains unique data for the user to view. You can perform any code manipulation of the `View` controls necessary during runtime to complete a display. The design time configuration provides only the basic requirements in many cases.

Using Meta Refresh for Redirection

The meta refresh tag is one of the most popular ways of redirecting a Web site user from one page to another. The tag is easy to use and most browsers support it, which means the developer doesn't have to perform any fancy coding or worry about compatibility issues. However, the World Wide Web Consortium (W3C), a standards group that provides information about standardized tag use, does recommend against using this technique in the W3C Recommendation at `http://www.w3.org/TR/html4/struct/global.html#adef-http-equiv`. The fact remains that this is a very easy way to send users to another page and you need to know about it for that reason. Here's an example of a meta refresh tag.

```
<meta http-equiv="refresh" content="3;url=http://www.mysite.com">
```

This tag tells the browser to wait 3 seconds and then redirect the user to `http://www.mysite.com`. The `http-equiv` portion of the tag translates to HyperText Transport Protocol Equivalent. In short, the `<meta>` tag tells the browser that this tag takes the place of an HTTP header that the browser might ordinarily expect to receive from the server. The content contains the number of seconds to wait along with the URL that the browser should load. Notice that you must separate these two arguments by a semicolon (;).

NOTE Don't confuse the meta refresh tag with the completely standard and recommended meta expires tag: `<META http-equiv="Expires" content="Friday, 31 Dec 2004 14:30:00 GMT">`. In this case, the page will expire on Friday, 31 December 2004, at 2:30 in the afternoon. The meta expires tag ensures that the browser always has a fresh copy of the content on your Web site. You set the tag to refresh the page at a reasonable interval to ensure that the user doesn't see the cached version of a page that resides on their hard drive. Caching makes Web pages load faster because the browser uses a local copy, rather than download the content from the Internet. However, this performance boost can cause problems by letting the user see old content.

Unfortunate as it might seem, the meta refresh tag doesn't provide any clues to a user who has the tag disabled. Typically, the user sees a blank page. The only way that a well-informed user knows what to do with this page is to right-click the blank page and choose View Source from the context menu. This action displays the source code for the Web page, where the user can highlight the redirection text and go to the new Web page. A few smart developers have come up with a solution—add a manual tag to the page as well as shown in this code. You'll find this example in the `\Chapter 09\ MetaRefresh` folder of the source code on the Sybex Web site.

```
<!DOCTYPE html PUBLIC "-//W3C//DTD XHTML 1.1//EN" "http://www.w3.org/TR/xhtml11/
DTD/xhtml11.dtd">
<html xmlns="http://www.w3.org/1999/xhtml" >
<head>
    <title>Untitled Page</title>
    <meta http-equiv="refresh" content="3;url=Redirect.HTM">
</head>
<body>
    <h1><a href=Redirect.htm>Click this Link to Go to the Page</a></h1>
    <a href="Policies/UsingRedirection.htm">
        Discover why we use redirection.
    </a>
</body>
</html>
```

Now users who don't have the meta refresh tag enabled or don't have a browser that supports the tag can click the supplied link. Because this fix is relatively simple, you could even implement it as a master page solution. All the developer would need to do is supply the required links. Using this option also means the user doesn't have to guess about your intentions for the redirection—you simply moved the page and the user needs to click the link to find the new location.

TIP If you have a written redirection policy, you can also include the link on the redirected page. The user can click this link to learn more about the reason for the redirection before committing to clicking the link. The reason for adding a written policy is to ensure that the reader understands why you move material or use redirection for other purposes.

Using Scripting for Redirection

The meta refresh tag offers a lot for such a small amount of code—it's easily understood and executes automatically. It's very tough to make anything go wrong with it. However, the meta refresh tag is also somewhat inflexible. You get a selection of precisely one location and one display interval. In many cases, this selection isn't flexible enough to meet a need, so using scripts makes sense. For example, you might detect the client accessing a Web page and provide a special redirection for that client. In other cases, such as in the example program, you might decide to provide redirection based on a user requirement, such as a fancy (one with lots of graphics, color, and sound) versus a plain page (practical for someone with special needs). You'll find this example in the \Chapter 09\ScriptRedirect folder of the source code on the Sybex Web site.

This example needs to perform two tasks. First, it must provide the user with enough time to make a selection. Second, when the user decides not to select an option within a reasonable time frame, the example redirects the user automatically. Listing 9.6 contains the code for this example.

LISTING 9.6:   Redirecting a User Through a Script

```
<!DOCTYPE html PUBLIC "-//W3C//DTD XHTML 1.1//EN"
                      "http://www.w3.org/TR/xhtml11/DTD/xhtml11.dtd">
<html xmlns="http://www.w3.org/1999/xhtml" >
<head>
    <title>Script Redirection Example</title>
    <script type="text/javascript">
    <!--
        function GoSomewhere(Destination)
        {
            // Change the current location.
            window.location = Destination;
        }

        function AutoSelect()
        {
            // Set a timer on the selection.
            self.setTimeout("GoSomewhere('FancyPage.HTM')", 5000);
        }
    -->
    </script>
</head>
<body onload="AutoSelect()">
    <h1>Welcome to Our Web Site</h1>
    <p>
        Please choose a page option.<br />
        If you don't select an option in 5 seconds, the page will
        automatically select the Fancy Page option.
    </p>
    <p>
        <input id="btnPlain"
```

```
                              title="Displays a content-only page."
                              accesskey="P"
                              type="button"
                              value="Plain Page"
                              onclick="GoSomewhere('PlainPage.HTM')" />
                       <input id="btnFancy"
                              title="Page includes graphics, color, and sound."
                              accesskey="F"
                              type="button"
                              value="Fancy Page"
                              onclick="GoSomewhere('FancyPage.HTM')" />
              </p>

    </body>
    </html>
```

The code begins with the `<body>` tag, which calls the `AutoSelect()` function when the page loads. The `AutoSelect()` function makes a single call to `self.setTimeout()`, which sets the page to perform a redirection in 5 seconds. The first argument to the `self.setTimeout()` defines what the call will do. In this case, it calls the `GoSomewhere()` function with the name of the page to select. Notice the formatting used to provide the `GoSomewhere()` function—it must appear as a string. The second argument contains the number of milliseconds (ms)—1,000 ms equals a second, so the example uses 5,000.

At some point, the code calls `GoSomewhere()`. This function accepts a single argument—a string containing the new location. Using this technique means that you can use the same function for multiple buttons or multiple ways of redirecting the page. Both buttons, `btnPlain` and `btnFancy`, call `GoSomewhere()`. The `GoSomewhere()` function relies on the `window.location` property to redirect the user. The browser automatically detects changes to this property and makes the required request.

TIP   You can find many resources for using scripted redirection on the Internet. For example, you'll find an example that shows how to respond to client differences on the JavaScript Redirection site at `http://www.pageresource.com/jscript/jredir.htm`. The irt.org site at `http://developer.irt.org/script/redirect.htm` includes a number of redirection solutions to answer specific needs, such as redirecting a Web page based on an entry in a text box (see FAQ 284 for details). ScriptSearch.com (`http://www.scriptsearch.com/JavaScript/Scripts/Redirection`) includes scripts that a peer group reviews for accuracy and usefulness. The script at `http://grizzlyweb.com/webmaster/javascripts/redirection.asp#Timed-Redirect` shows how to combine JavaScript and a meta refresh tag to provide scripted and non-scripted solutions to the same problem. In short, the topic of redirection is extremely popular and you can find ready-made resources to perform almost any task.

Employing Server-side Redirection

Server-side redirection is the safest and most flexible means of redirecting a client in many cases. The server receives the request, translates it, and then sends the appropriate page to the user. The whole process takes less than a second, in most cases, yet the server performs a lot of work during that time. Because the entire event occurs at the server, you can maintain an extremely secure environment—no outside force can interfere unless you server is compromised. Of course, nothing comes free—you do pay an additional cost in server performance. Because the server performs additional processing, you'll find that you can't handle quite as many users as before. You'll find this example in the \Chapter 09\ ServerRedirect folder of the source code on the Sybex Web site.

Understanding How Server-side Redirection Works

When a server receives a request, it doesn't just fulfill that request immediately. The server first determines where the request is supposed to go and then applies any number of filters to that request. For example, Internet Information Server (IIS) supports a number of filtering features (as do most servers).

An Internet Server Application Programming Interface (ISAPI) filter is a special DLL that you load into the server. The ISAPI filter views the request and performs any required processing on it before passing it to the next ISAPI filter in line or passing it back to the server. You configure the ISAPI filter as part of the Web site or application properties using the Internet Services Manager console located in the Administrative Tools folder of the Control Panel as shown in Figure 9.10. This particular filter looks for FrontPage Server Extension calls and redirects them as needed—it affects every request for this particular Web site. These filters also apply to your Visual Web Developer projects, even though you can't create an ISAPI filter with any of the Express products. The built-in server you use for testing your code doesn't support this kind of filtering.

FIGURE 9.10
ISAPI filters can redirect requests as needed to a specific server application.

Filtering affects requests at many levels. For example, filtering can affect some file types or extensions and not others as shown in Figure 9.11. Click Configuration on the Home Directory tab of a Web site Properties dialog box and you'll see the Application Configuration dialog box shown in Figure 9.11. The Application Configuration dialog box shows the DLL used to handle a particular request based on its file extension. Some DLLs handle entire classes of file types. Notice that IIS handles the ASP file extension directly, but relies on the .NET Framework to handle the ASPX file extension.

FIGURE 9.11

FIGURE 9.11

Filtering also affects requests for specific file types and extensions.

The filters appear in a hierarchy, which the Web request visiting the server filters first, then the Web site, then the application, and finally the individual page filters. The filters don't all appear in the Internet Services Manager console either. Some of them appear as part of the Machine.CONFIG and Web.CONFIG files—others appear as code within the individual page. These individual filters appear lower in the hierarchy and have a smaller effect on the Web site as a whole.

Whatever the level a filter appears at, most filters have the option of performing a redirection of some type. For example, a filter can raise an error and cause the server to display an error message. The filter can directly change the Web page as well. In some cases, a filter can intercept an event caused by another filter and react to it. For example, when the server filter that checks for the presence of the requested file on the machine raises an error because the file isn't present, another filter can intercept the event and react to it. Eventually, the request passes through all of the filters and the server sends a final response to the client.

Using the Coded Method

Any ASPX Web page that you create can perform redirection. You can make the redirection part of a button client or in response to an automatic event such as loading the page. No matter how the event occurs, the code for transferring control from one page to another is relatively easy to create, as shown here.

```
Sub btnCodedTest_Click(ByVal sender As Object, _
                       ByVal e As System.EventArgs)

    ' Transfer control to a different page.
    Server.Transfer("NewPage.ASPX", True)
End Sub
```

This feature relies on the Server object—a special object that you don't have to create that provides an interface with the server. The Transfer() method accepts two arguments. The first contains the URL that you want to use for redirection. The second argument defines whether you want the various arguments, such as the query string, to pass to the redirected page. Setting this value to True does incur a small performance penalty, so pass the information only when you actually need it on the redirected page.

You can use this technique for any kind of redirection. However, it only works for one Web page— the one with the code attached. Other techniques described in this book can garner a better response for multiple pages. For example, you can create an HTTP handler using the techniques in the "Working with HTTP Handlers" section of Chapter 18. The next section "Modifying the `<customErrors>` Element of the `Web.CONFIG` File" also discusses techniques for working with multiple pages.

Modifying the *<customErrors>* Element of the *Web.CONFIG* File

The `Web.CONFIG` file contains a wealth of settings that help the developer create a robust Web site. The `<customErrors>` element of this file contains settings that control how the Web site reacts to errors. The server reports errors in the status member of the header of any response that it creates. The status numbers are standard for every Web server, so you don't have to worry about any odd surprises. A successful response always has a status code of 200. Error messages usually have a 400 series error code. You can find a list of these status codes and their meanings at `http://www.w3.org/Protocols/rfc2616/rfc2616-sec10.html`.

Theoretically, you can handle any status code that you want. However, the error codes are of greatest interest because they affect the client most. Every error that you want to handle requires an `<error>` element in the `<customErrors>` node as shown here.

```
<customErrors mode="RemoteOnly" defaultRedirect="GenericErrorPage.htm">
<!--
    <error statusCode="403" redirect="NoAccess.htm"/>
-->
    <error statusCode="404" redirect="NewPage.ASPX"/>
</customErrors>
```

The default Visual Web Developer `Web.CONFIG` page includes two error handle entries, both of which are commented out using the `<!--` and `-->` pair. This example enables the Not Found status code of 404 that represents a request for a nonexistent resource on the server. The `statusCode` attribute of the `<error>` element tells which status code to detect. The `redirect` attribute defines which Web page to open when this error occurs.

The only problem with this code is that you can't see the result when working with Visual Web Developer. Even with the error handler enabled, you'll see an error message display like the one shown in Figure 9.12. The `mode` attribute of the `<customErrors>` element tells the server how to apply the custom error handler. The default value of `RemoteOnly` is useless for Visual Web Developer users because there isn't any remote access to the server. Always set this value to `On` to see the custom error handler and `Off` to see the standard error message.

Whenever the server intercepts an error, it attaches special information for the error handler as part of the query string. You can detect and use this information in the handle page as shown here.

```
Sub Page_Load(ByVal sender As Object, _
                ByVal e As System.EventArgs) Handles Me.Load

    ' Display the error information, when included.
    txtErrorInfo.Text = Request.QueryString.Get("aspxerrorpath")
End Sub
```

The `aspxerrorpath` query string variable contains the location of the page that failed. You can use this information to create a log or simply display it on screen. Figure 9.13 shows typical results for this example.

FIGURE 9.12
You can't see the full effect of the redirection until you change the mode attribute setting.

FIGURE 9.13
The server passes the failed page information to the page handling the error.

Defining Your Development Goals

This chapter has demonstrated techniques that you can use to create pop-up windows and use redirection to help the user find new or existing materials on your Web site. Whether you use these techniques depends on the goals that you want to accomplish. Given the potential for misuse of these technologies, you'll want to exercise care in relying on them and provide the user with good reasons to accommodate these needs. The bottom line is that you have a number of new useful techniques you can use, but you need to use them wisely.

It's time to decide whether your Web site can benefit from either pop-ups or redirection. One of the essentials, especially when working with pop-ups, is to write a policy that explains the use of the technology. Writing the policy is actually a good test of the actual need for these technologies. The act of writing the policy places you in the position of having to explain the use of the technology in terms that the user will accept. A failure to write a good policy, one that you know the user will accept, usually indicates that you don't need to use the technology.

Chapter 10 explores a new area of Visual Web Developer, database applications. Previous chapters have demonstrated a number of uses of XML files as a means of storing critical data for your Web site. However, XML files can't fulfill every need. In many cases, you need to create a formal storage area, which means using a database to accomplish the task. Fortunately, Visual Web Developer makes this task easy with the use of Database Explorer.

Part 4

Working with Dynamic Data

In this section you will learn to:

Chapter 10

Developing Simple Database Applications

Although generalizing is always dangerous, one generalization you can probably make safely is that all businesses use Database Management Systems (DBMSs) of some sort. In fact, it wouldn't be too much of a stretch to say that most individuals use a DBMS as well. For example, the messages you see in applications such as Outlook Express reside in a database and Outlook Express is the DBMS. A database is the storage container for the data, while the DBMS manages the storage container. The DBMS for Visual Web Developer is SQL Server Express. Yes, you can also use standard SQL Server or Microsoft Access to create applications with Visual Web Developer. In fact, you can create a connection for any database that supports Open Database Connectivity (ODBC), Object Linking and Embedding-Database (OLE-DB), along with SQL Server and Oracle. Visual Web Developer is quite flexible.

NOTE This chapter assumes that you have SQL Server Express installed on your machine. The "SQL Server 2005 Express" section of Chapter 2 tells you how to install SQL Server Express if you haven't done so already. You'll also find examples that show how to work with Microsoft Access and the full version of SQL Server. Even if you don't have these products installed, you can follow along with the examples to see some of the techniques you can use with Visual Web Developer.

Microsoft considers SQL Server Express the replacement for the Microsoft Database Engine (MSDE) found in previous products such as Web Matrix and Visual Studio .NET. This chapter considers the differences between the two DBMSs so that you can make the transition with greater ease if you're already familiar with MSDE. You'll really enjoy some of the new features that SQL Server Express provides including a utility to manage the service. Of course, SQL Server Express still isn't a full-fledged copy of SQL Server, so you still need to consider its limitations.

Visual Web Developer includes a number of features that make working with SQL Server Express (or any DBMS for that matter) easier. For example, the Database Explorer lets you view the content of a database with relative ease so that you can simply drag and drop items onto the form. You'll also find that the concept of code-free data binding saves you considerable time. The IDE also provides a number of toolbars that reduce the time required to perform tasks. In short, Visual Web Developer makes it easier to work with databases than ever before.

This chapter does provide you with a number of simple examples that demonstrate how you can add database management to Visual Web Developer applications. One of the most important examples shows how you can access the `ASPNetDB.MDB` database, which stores the settings for your application. You'll also discover how to access existing databases, such as those that rely on ODBC connections. All of these short examples help you understand the concepts of working with databases in Visual Web Developer.

Considering Differences with Microsoft Database Engine

Microsoft originally created MSDE to provide a quick method for developers to work with SQL Server databases, without actually installing SQL Server. Unfortunately, this cut-down version of the product wasn't very popular for a number of reasons, most significantly, the lack of tools to work with it. In fact, the problem was so bad that some developers created their own tools to work with MSDE. For example, MSDE Query (http://www.msde.biz) provides the graphical interface shown in Figure 10.1. You can still use these tools as required with SQL Server Express, but you'll find that they aren't as necessary because SQL Server Express provides far more in the way of management tools.

FIGURE 10.1

Tools such as MSDE Query made MSDE workable for developers.

The management tools are incredibly important. However, SQL Server Express provides features that make it better suited for modern application development. For example, you'll gain access to full eXtensible Markup Language (XML) support, which means you can import and export data from the databases in a form that works well with Web applications. This particular feature is very important for Visual Web Developer users when you consider how many of the sample applications in this book rely on XML, rather than using full database support. You can experiment with various XML files until you find something that works, and then import it into SQL Server Express for complete testing in a full database environment.

SQL Server Express does sport a management utility, SQL Computer Manager. The "Working with SQL Server 2005 Express" section later in this chapter describes this utility in detail. Essentially, this tool helps you learn more about the state of SQL Server Express so you can make management decisions about it. The utility provides the input you need to determine when an error is a problem with your code or an issue with SQL Server Express. When working with MSDE, you often had to guess about this status information, and some developers found that rebooting the system was the only way to overcome some problems.

Another great feature for Visual Web Developer users is the fact that you can simply copy the database from one machine to other. This means you can develop an application locally, move the database to a network machine, and then begin your multiuser testing without having to reconstruct anything first. It also means that you can move items from a development machine to the production server for smaller projects—everything is ready to go.

MSDE often left developers out in the cold even when it come to command-line tools. With SQL Server Express, you obtain a relatively complete list of command-line utilities. When it comes to graphical tools, SQL Server Express doesn't currently support as many as you might like. The Management Studio, Profiler, and Database Tuning Wizard are all missing in the current version, but Microsoft intends to add this support later.

One of the features that Microsoft discusses most often is Common Language Runtime (CLR) integration with SQL Server Express. This feature is important because it means that you can write stored procedures and functions in the language you like best. However, you still need to use SQL to perform many kinds of database interaction, so while this feature is extremely nice, it's not a major break with the functionality that Microsoft provided in the past.

You'll find performance differences between MSDE and SQL Server Express. For example, you can create a 4 GB database with SQL Server Express—MSDE only supports 2 GB databases. On the other hand, MSDE supports 2 GB of RAM, while SQL Server Express provides support for only 1 GB of RAM. Part of the RAM capacity limitation is offset by the lack of a Workload Governor in SQL Server Express, which caused endless performance problems in MSDE.

Depending on how you use MSDE and SQL Server Express, you might miss SQL Agent in SQL Server Express. Generally, this loss won't affect most forms of development. Hopefully, Microsoft will change its mind later about this particular issue.

Understanding SQL Server 2005 Express Limitations

SQL Server Express isn't a full version of SQL Server—Microsoft designed it for use in experimentation and for your development projects. In fact, the default installation doesn't even enable network access to the database. The "Enabling and Disabling Network Support" section later in this chapter describes how to enable network access, but the fact that SQL Server Express lacks this support at the outset tells a lot about its intended purpose. Fortunately, enabling network support lets you use SQL Server for a small business, a development team, or perhaps a workgroup in a larger organization.

The lack of some features should also tell you about the functionality that SQL Server Express provides. This isn't a multiuser environment. You can probably support several users with it, but it's not something that you would use as a basis for your enterprise network. In fact, you'll find that it's very difficult setting up multiple users when compared to the full version of SQL Server. You can do it, but you won't enjoy getting there.

This product also lacks many of the graphical tools that the full version provides. For example, you won't find a copy of either Query Analyzer or Enterprise Manager with this product. Microsoft has plans to introduce these tools for SQL Server Express, at some point, but you can't obtain them today. Fortunately, you can perform most tasks using the graphical environment provided by Database Explorer (see the "Using Database Explorer" section later in this chapter for details). The SQLCmd command-line utility (see the "Using the SQLCmd Utility" section for details) also reduces the impact of the lack of graphical tools, but the fact that you must rely on these external resources means that your database development is less efficient.

Working with SQL Server 2005 Express

SQL Server Express does provide a few interesting tools that you'll need to create database applications. The most important tool, in many cases, is SQL Computer Manager because it provides the status information you need. However, you'll also want to spend time working with the various command-line tools that SQL Server Express provides because they help you perform the actual management tasks. The following sections describe both kinds of tools.

Working with SQL Computer Manager

The SQL Computer Manager appears as part of SQL Server Express. You'll find this utility in the Start ≻ Programs ≻ Microsoft SQL Server 2005 menu. This utility is the same as the one that the full version of SQL Server 2005 uses, so you can use it to monitor the full version of the product. The following sections describe essential tasks you can perform using this utility.

GETTING SQL SERVER STATUS INFORMATION

One of the more important tasks you can perform with this utility is to obtain status information. The `Services` folder shown in Figure 10.2 contains a list of the SQL Server services—not all of these services appear on your machine when you install SQL Server Express. For example, even though the utility contains an entry for SQL Agent, you won't see an entry in this folder when using SQL Server Express because this version of the product doesn't support SQL Agent.

FIGURE 10.2
SQL Computer Manager provides access to a number of SQL Server Express features.

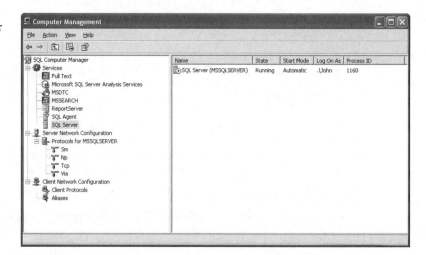

The SQL Computer Manager also provides other forms of status information. For example, look at the `Server Network Configuration` folder and you'll see an entry for each instance of SQL Server (including SQL Server Express) on the machine. Within these instance-specific folders, you'll find the protocols that SQL Server supports including shared memory (Sm), named pipes (Np), Transmission Control Protocol/Internet Protocol or TCP/IP (Tcp), and Virtual Interface Architecture or VIA (Via). A status indicator next to each entry shows whether you have this protocol enabled.

The `Client Network Configuration` folder contains options that the client can use to connect to the server. The `Client Protocols` folder defines which protocols the client can use to connect to the server. This folder has the same four options that the server provides. The `Aliases` folder contains a list of alternate identities that the client can use to connect to the server. This feature is helpful because you can use it to hide connectivity from the client and redirect the client as needed when the server setup changes. In most cases, you won't need to use an alias when working with SQL Server Express.

ENABLING AND DISABLING NETWORK SUPPORT

At some point, you'll want to share the data you've created across a network. For example, you might set up a test site for the other developers on your team. SQL Server Express doesn't enable network support by default, so you need to perform some additional work.

The first task is to start the SQL Browser service so that client computers can locate the instance of SQL Server Express on your system. When you want this feature enabled every time you start the system, you'll want to set the SQL Browser service to start automatically. The downside of starting this service is that viruses and other unappealing intruders can also find your setup. Consequently, you don't want to enable other network connections unless you actually need them. Open the Services console found the in the `Administrative Tools` folder of the Control Panel to start the SQL Browser service. When you want to start the service for a short connection, right-click the SQL Browser service entry and choose Start from the context menu. Otherwise, double-click the entry to open the SQL Browser Properties dialog box. Set the Startup Type field to Automatic and click Start. Click OK to close the SQL Browser Properties dialog box. The Services console will appear, as shown in Figure 10.3, when you finish.

FIGURE 10.3

Start the SQL Browser service to ensure that clients can locate your system.

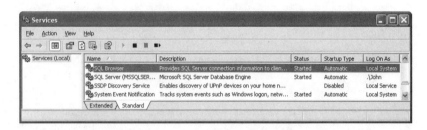

Now you need to enable the desired protocols on the client and server. Begin with the server. Open the `Protocols` folder for the SQL Server Express instance that you want to work with. Locate the protocol that you want to use. Right-click the entry and choose Enable from the context menu. This step is all you need to do for the Sm, Np, and Via protocols. The Tcp protocol entry has several subentries, as shown in Figure 10.4, for the Internet Protocol (Ip) part of the protocol.

FIGURE 10.4

When working with TCP/IP, make sure you enable at least one Ip entry.

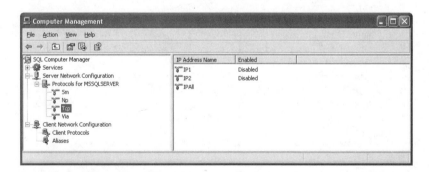

The number of Ip entries that you see depends on the configuration of your machine. Each default Ip entry works with one address on your machine, including the loopback (local) address. The only way to determine which Ip entry to use is to double-click the entry. You'll see the Ip Properties dialog box shown in Figure 10.5. The address you want to look at is in the IpAddress field. Figure 10.5 shows the Ip address for the loopback or local connection. Enable this Ip entry when you want to work with TCP/IP locally but don't want to let outside clients see your machine. To enable TCP/IP connectivity, you must select Yes in the Enabled field. A TCP/IP connection requires that you enable the Tcp entry and at least one Ip entry.

FIGURE 10.5
The IpAddress field tells
you which connection
the Ip entry affects.

NOTE Make sure you disable the server protocols when you no longer need them. Simply right-click the desired protocol and choose Disable from the context menu.

The final step is to enable the required client protocols. Select the `Client Network Configuration\ Client Protocols` folder to view the list of client protocols, as shown in Figure 10.6. Right-click a protocol and choose Enable from the context menu to enable the protocol. The Order column determines the order in which the client calls the various protocols looking for a connection to the server—the client stops when it locates an active protocol, so the order you choose is important.

FIGURE 10.6
Both client and server
must have the same pro-
tocol enabled to create a
connection.

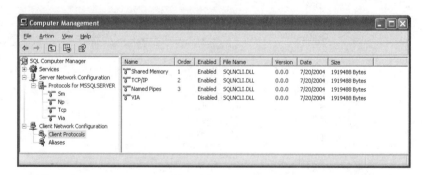

It's easy to change the order of the protocols. Right-click the `Client Protocols` folder and choose Properties from the context menu. You'll see the Client Protocols Properties dialog box shown in Figure 10.7. To change the order, highlight one of the protocols and click either Move Up or Move Down as needed. Notice that this dialog box also lets you selectively enable or disable the client protocols.

FIGURE 10.7
Use the Client Protocols
Properties dialog box to
change protocol order.

CREATING AN ALIAS

An alias provides an alternative means of creating a connection between a client and a server. Normally, when a client makes a request, it uses the default SQL Server instance. The client tries one protocol after another until it locates the server. You can use other instances, but it's time consuming. Using an alias short-circuits the process by specifying a specific SQL Server instance, a particular protocol, and a particular connection methodology.

To create an alias, right-click the Aliases folder and choose New Alias from the context menu. You'll see the Alias – New dialog box shown in Figure 10.8. This dialog box contains everything needed to create a custom connection to SQL Server Express.

FIGURE 10.8
An alias represents a
custom connection to
the SQL Server instance
you want to use.

Begin by typing a name in the Alias Name field. The name you choose is important because this is the value you enter in the Select or Enter a Server Name field of the Connection Properties dialog box in Visual Web Developer. (See the "Creating a Connection to SQL Server and SQL Server Express" section later in this chapter for additional information.) The example uses a value of `SpecialConnect`, but you can use any value you want.

After you enter the alias name, type the name of the SQL Server instance in the Server field. If you want to use the default instance, type a `.` (period) in place of the name. Otherwise, provide the name of the SQL Server instance that you want to use, not the name of the machine. When working with TCP/IP as the protocol, you can also type the IP address in place of the server name. Figure 10.5 shows the IpAddress field for the Ip1 protocol—the loopback or local connection in this case.

Select the protocol that you want to use. An alias can use named pipes, TCP/IP, or VIA as the protocol. The shared memory protocol applies only to direct connections.

Depending on the protocol you choose, you can enter a value in the Connection String field. When working with named pipes, you must enter the named pipe of the server that you want to use. You obtain this value by right-clicking the protocol entry in the `Server Network Configuration\Protocols for Instance` folder and choosing Properties. The named pipe value appears in the PipeName field of the Np Properties dialog box. When working with TCP/IP, you provide the `TcpPort` value (see Figure 10.5) for the Ip protocol that you want to use. When working with VIA, you provide the server port number located in the ListenInfo field of the Via Properties dialog box.

Figure 10.9 shows a completed TCP/IP alias. The connection relies on the default SQL Server Express instance, so the Server field contains a period. The Protocol field shows that this is a TCP/IP connection. The Connection String field shows the TCP/IP port number—the same number that appears in Figure 10.5. With all of the information shown, the machine could now access the server using this alias—all you need to do is type it as the server name when making the connection.

FIGURE 10.9
The SpecialConnect alias provides a TCP/IP connection to the default SQL Server Express instance.

Using the SQLCmd Utility

The SQLCmd (Structured Query Language Command) utility is one of the most useful features of SQL Server and SQL Server Express. You can perform a number of tasks from the command line using this utility. In fact, the utility easily lends itself to use with both scripts and batch files, so you can create a setup once and then execute it whenever needed. The following sections describe how to use to use this utility both interactively and at the command prompt. (You'll see additional usage examples as the book progresses.)

USING SQLCMD INTERACTIVELY

One of the best ways to learn how to use SQLCmd is to create an interactive connection. All you need to do is type **SQLCmd** and press Enter at the command prompt to start an interactive session. It's also possible to specify any required command-line switches that don't cause the program to exit. For example, all the −S, −P, and −U command-line switches work fine. Once you start the interactive session, you'll see a new prompt that lets you enter commands. Figure 10.10 shows an interactive session consisting of several commands using the Northwind database.

FIGURE 10.10

Use SQLCmd interactively to discover how it works and see the best ways to create scripted sequences.

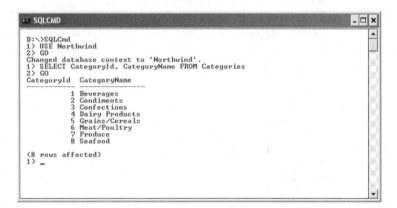

The commands in Figure 10.10 mix standard SQL statements with special commands that the SQLCmd understands. Anyone who uses Query Analyzer regularly will recognize the GO command. The following list describes the commands that the SQLCmd understands.

!! *Command*   Executes any operating-system command. For example, when you want to clear the clutter on your display, you can type ! ! **CLS** and press Enter to clear the screen.

:Connect *ServerName* [*InstanceName*] [*Timeout*] [*Username* [*Password*]]   Creates a connection to a different server and SQL Server or SQL Server Express instance. You can specify the amount of time to wait for the connection to complete and include both a user name and password as needed.

:Error *Filename* | STDERR | STDOUT   Redirects the error output to the specified filename, the standard error device (STDERR), or the standard output device (STDOUT). SQLCmd defaults to sending the error information to the STDERR device, which is the display.

:Help   Displays a list of all the commands that SQLCmd understands along with very brief descriptions.

:List   Prints the content of the statement cache. SQLCmd clears the statement cache after each successful transaction, so this command might not display anything, even after you work with SQL-Cmd for a while.

:ListVar   Displays the script variables you set, along with selected environmental variables, including SQLCMDCOLSEP, SQLCMDCOLWIDTH, SQLCMDDBNAME, SQLCMDEDITOR, SQLCMDERRORLEVEL, SQLCMDHEADERS, SQLCMDINI, SQLCMDLOGINTIMEOUT, SQL-CMDMAXFIXEDTYPEWIDTH, SQLCMDMAXVARTYPEWIDTH, SQLCMDPACKETSIZE, SQLCMDSERVER, SQLCMDSTATTIMEOUT, SQLCMDUSER, and SQLCMDWORKSTATION.

NOTE   Some environment variables are read-only, which means you can view them, but not change them directly. These environment variables include SQLCMDDBNAME (set with the −d switch), SQLCMDPACKETSIZE (set with the −a switch), SQLCMDSERVER (set with the −S switch), SQLCM-DUSER (set with the −U switch), and SQLCMDWORKSTATION (set with the −H switch).

:On Error [EXIT | IGNORE]   Determines the action that SQLCmd performs when an error occurs. When you choose the EXIT option, SQLCmd stops execution and exits when it encounters an error. Otherwise, SQLCmd displays the error information and attempts to execute the next statement.

:Out *Filename* **| STDERR | STDOUT**   Redirects the standard output to the specified filename, the standard error device (STDERR), or the standard output device (STDOUT). SQLCmd defaults to sending the output to the STDOUT device, which is the display.

:Perftrace *Filename* **| STDERR | STDOUT**   Redirects performance information to the specified filename, the standard error device (STDERR), or the standard output device (STDOUT). SQLCmd defaults to sending performance information to the STDOUT device, which is the display.

:ServerList   Displays a list of the available servers. Note that this output isn't always correct. A server might not have the SQL Browser service running, so it won't appear on the list. The server must broadcast and the client must receive the server information for the `:ServerList` command to display it within SQLCmd. In addition, just because you see a server doesn't mean that you can connect to it. You must have the proper rights to access the server.

:SetVar [*VariableName* **[***Value***]]**   Defines the value of a script or environmental variable. For example, to set the SQLCMDCOLSEP environmental variable to use an asterisk, you would type `:SetVar SQLCMDCOLSEP "*"` and press Enter.

:XML ON | OFF   Determines whether SQLCmd outputs data as standard text or XML.

ED   Starts the selected text editor and places the contents of the statement cache in it for editing. When you exit the text editor, SQLCmd places the edited content on screen. The default editor is the DOS Edit.COM. You can change the editor by modifying the SQLCMDEDITOR environment variable using the `:SetVar` command.

EXIT [(*ExitValue***)]**   Ends the interactive session. You can optionally provide an output value to any script that initiated the interactive session. The output can include a numeric value, query, or other statement. When the parentheses are empty (there's no return value), the batch file processing continues without the return value. Using EXIT by itself is equivalent to issuing a QUIT command.

GO [*Count***]**   Executes the content of the statement cache as a batch job. The optional `Count` value defines the number of time to execute the batch.

QUIT   Ends the interactive session without any return value, batch, or scripting support provided.

R *Filename*   Loads a file containing Transact SQL statements for execution as a batch. The file can contain any legitimate commands or SQL statements, including the GO command.

RESET   Empties the statement cache. You can use this command to remove any unneeded commands from the statement cache.

USING SQLCMD AT THE COMMAND LINE

Scripts, batch files, and even you will want to rely on the SQLCmd command-line interface to perform many tasks. For example, you can execute a query at the command line without ever using the interactive interface. In addition, the command-line interface has certain advantages—you can use redirection to obtain specific effects that you might not ordinarily have access to, such as saving the output in a processed file. SQLCmd supports the following command-line switches—all of which are optional (make sure you replace variable information with actual data).

WARNING   Case does count when working with these command-line switches. For example, an uppercase *U* defines your user name, while a lowercase *u* defines Unicode output. The list groups uppercase and lowercase switches when they produce similar results—they never produce the same results. The SQLCmd utility also lets you use the dash (−) or slash (/) for command-line switches—even though the dash appears in the list.

−A   Creates a dedicated administrative connection (DAC) to the database. This feature works with SQL Server 2005—not earlier versions of the product. Normally, you won't need this kind of connection. However, you might want to view hidden tables, such as `sys.sysallocunits`, where SQL Server Express requires you to have a DAC connection. You can't bind to hidden tables unless you have a DAC connection. This connection also works when SQL Server is in an abnormal state and not responding to a SQL Server connection. The "Using a Dedicated Administrator Connection" help file topic provides additional information about this command-line switch.

−a *PacketSize*   Determines the size of the individual transfers between the client and the server. In general, you don't need to worry about the packet size for smaller databases because you won't notice a performance advantage. However, as the database size increases, it pays to optimize the packet size to improve overall performance. Valid packet sizes range from 512 through 65,535.

−b   Configures SQLCmd to exit when an error occurs, rather than ignore the error and simply list it to the default error output.

−c *CommandTerminator*   Defines a command terminator for Transact SQL statements. The default setting uses the word GO, but you can use any terminator desired. Avoid using words or symbols that have special meaning. The terminator you select must still appear on the separate line—just as GO normally does.

−d *DatabaseName*   Loads a specific database when SQLCmd starts.

−e echo input   Adds any input statements to the beginning of any output. This feature is helpful when you use a file or other output other than the display because it repeats the input commands for later analysis.

−E trusted connection   Creates a connection between the client and server using a trusted connection, rather than requesting a user name and password.

−f *Codepage* | i:*Codepage* [,o:*Codepage*]   Determines the language support provided by SQLCmd. The −f switch defines the codepage for both input and output. As an alternative, you can specify the input codepage using the i argument and the output using the o argument. This feature doesn't provide any translation functionality—it simply changes the language support, such as date and monetary format that SQLCmd provides.

TIP The codepage values supported by your system will vary by the languages you have installed. You can find a list of standard Windows codepage values at http://www.microsoft.com/globaldev/reference/cphome.mspx.

–h –1 | 1 Determines whether SQLCmd displays headers as part of the query output. The default setting of 0 outputs headers at the beginning of the query output. Use a value of –1 to inhibit header display. A value of 1 displays the headers for every output row.

NOTE Whenever a command-line switch accepts a negative value, such as –1, you must place the value immediately after the switch. For example, if you want to inhibit header display, you must supply the switch as –h–1. Otherwise, SQLCmd interprets the space as the start of a new switch and displays an error message.

–H *Hostname* Defines the host used to execute commands. This command affects the workstation name that it returned by the sp_who stored procedure by modifying the content of sysprocesses.hostname. The default setting uses the current computer as the host.

–I Sets the QUOTED_IDENTIFIER connection option on.

–i *Filename* Loads the requested filename containing Transact SQL commands into the statement cache for execution within a batch. The file can contain any legitimate commands or SQL statements, including the GO command.

–k [1 | 2] Removes (1) or replaces (2) control characters encountered during processing.

–l *Timeout* Determines the login timeout value—the time that SQLCmd waits for login information from the user. The default value is 8 seconds.

–L[c] Displays a list of servers accessible from the current machine. Note that this output isn't always correct. A server might not have the SQL Browser service running, so it won't appear on the list. The server must broadcast and the client must receive the server information for it to appear in the list.

–m *ErrorLevel* Sets the error level at which SQLCmd displays error information. SQLCmd won't display any errors less than the requested level. Use a value of –1 to display all errors, including informational messages.

–o *Filename* Redirects SQLCmd output to the requested file.

–P *Password* Accepts the user password for access to the requested database.

–p[1] Prints performance statistics. Adding a 1 after the command-line switch tells SQLCmd to use the colon format for output.

–q "*Query*" and -Q "*Query*" Queries the database for data based on the query string. The query string must appear within double quotes. The uppercase version of the switch makes the query and immediately exits from SQLCmd. The lowercase version shows the results of the query and then an interactive prompt.

–R Sets SQLCmd to use the locale settings specified for the client machine.

–r [0 | 1] Redirects the message output to the STDERR device (normally the screen) when you don't specify an argument or use a value of 1. Only error messages with a severity level of 11 or greater are redirected when 0 appears as the argument.

–s *Separator*   Defines the character used as a column separator. SQLCmd normally uses a space between columns. You must enclose special characters (| ; & < >) in double quotes.

–S *Server*   Defines the name of the target server. The target server determines the location of the SQL Server database.

–t *Timeout*   Defines the time that SQLCmd waits for a query before it exits. Commands don't time out if you don't specify this value.

–U *Username*   Accepts the username for purposes of identification.

–u   Outputs the data in Unicode format, even when the input file is in another format.

–V *SeverityLevel*   Defines the level of error severity required before SQLCmd outputs the error information. Any errors less severe than the requested severity level are ignored and not reported.

–v *VariableName* = *"Value"* ...   Defines one or more variables for use in processing commands. SQLCmd accesses the value using the variable name supplied. You must enclose the value within double quotes. A single command-line switch can define multiple variables.

–W   Removes leading and trailing spaces from the output data. Most developers combine this switch with the –s switch to prepare data for use with another application.

–w screen width   Defines a screen width between 8 and 65,535 characters. The default setting of 80 characters matches most screens. Larger values let you prepare data for output to a file as a contiguous string, rather than multiple strings. Whenever the data length exceeds the screen width, SQLCmd wraps the data to the next line.

–X[1]   Disables the ! ! and ED commands to reduce security risks. When you supply a *1*, SQLCmd adds an error message stating "Error: The ED and !!<command> commands are disabled." whenever the user attempts to use the disabled commands.

–y *Width* **and –Y** *Width*   Limits the number of characters displayed on screen. The –y (lowercase) switch controls large variable types including varchar(max), nvarchar(max), varbinary(max), xml, UDT (User-defined Data Types), text, ntext, and image. The –Y (uppercase) switch controls standard variable types including char, nchar, varchar(n), nvarchar(n), and sql_variant. When working with varchar(n), n is between 1 and 8,000. When working with nvarchar(n), n is between 1 and 4,000.

–z *Password* **and –Z** *Password*   Modifies the password of the trusted user. The uppercase version of the switch changes the password and immediately exits from SQLCmd. The lowercase version changes the password and then displays an interactive prompt.

You can use the command-line interface for a variety of tasks such as adding automation to your applications. Of course, you'll want to start by trying the commands manually. For example, Figure 10.11 shows the results of a query made at the command line.

Notice that this query uses the uppercase –Q switch, so SQLCmd simply displays the results on screen. Using redirection, you could place this command in a batch file and execute it whenever necessary. Adding XML functionality by loading a command file would let you extract data from a database and place it in a folder on your Web site. The Web application you create would immediately begin using the new data. Adding this feature to the Task Scheduler would automate the task still further. Your Web application would receive constant updates and you would never have to do anything manually except change the data in the database.

FIGURE 10.11
The command-line interface lets you automate tasks by using batch files or scripts.

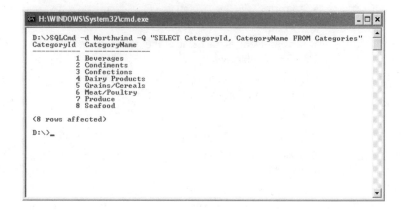

Using Database Explorer

Database Explorer is a unique feature for the Express product line. It replaces the Server Explorer found in the full version of the product. The essential purpose behind this tool is to help you create and manage database connections, and it performs that task very well. The following sections explore several connection scenarios. You'll discover more about the management issues that Database Explorer addresses in other areas of the book, including the "Designing a Database" section later in this chapter.

Creating a Connection to SQL Server and SQL Server Express

Creating a connection to SQL Server or SQL Server Express is relatively easy. All you need to know is the name of the server and the name of the database that you want to use. You can also use an alias as the server name (see the "Creating an Alias" section earlier in this chapter for details). Figure 10.12 shows a typical database connection with the various entries that you might see for a SQL Server Express database.

FIGURE 10.12
Database Explorer provides great access to all of the database elements that you need to manage.

Begin the connection process by right-clicking the Data Connections entry in Database Explorer and choosing Add Connection from the context menu. You'll see the Connection Properties dialog box shown in Figure 10.13. Select the server that you want to access in the Select or Enter Server Name field. Choose a user identification technique. Finally, select the database you want to use. Click Test Connection to verify that the connection actually works and click OK.

FIGURE 10.13
Create a database connection by defining server and database names.

TIP   You'll find three buttons at the top of the Database Explorer window shown in Figure 10.12. The Refresh button creates a new database query and updates the information shown in Database Explorer. The Stop Refresh button helps you end long queries. Finally, click Connect to Database when you want to create a new connection.

Creating a Connection to Other DBMSs

The initial Visual Web Developer setup assumes that you want to use SQL Server or SQL Server Express. Many developers have other kinds of connections to create and Visual Web Developer is up to the task of accommodating them. All you need to do is choose a different setup than the default. Open the Connection Properties dialog box by clicking Connect to Database in Database Explorer and you'll notice that it automatically selects the Connection tab. Choose the Provider tab instead and you'll see a list of provider options, as shown in Figure 10.14.

The default provider is .NET Framework Data Provider for SQL Server. This special provider includes code that enhances the performance of a SQL Server or SQL Server Express connection, but doesn't do much for other databases. Oracle users also have access to a specialized provider, so you should select this option when working with Oracle databases.

The option with the best performance for connections to other databases is the OLE-DB connector. Choose this provider and you'll notice that the Connection tab changes, as shown in Figure 10.15. Notice that you have access to a number of OLE-DB providers—not just one or two. Select the provider that you think matches your database best. For example, when working with Access, you'll want to select the Microsoft Jet 4.0 OLE-DB Provider. The Connection tab changes to meet the needs of the specific provider whenever you choose a different OLE-DB provider.

FIGURE 10.14

Select a provider that matches a connectivity option for your database.

FIGURE 10.15

Choose an OLE-DB provider, whenever possible, for best performance.

Most databases provide ODBC support. Even open source databases such as MySQL provide ODBC support through third party add-ons. Consequently, there's little chance that you can't create a connection to your database, even if you have to use a slower ODBC setup. The next section, "Creating a Connection to Microsoft Access Using ODBC," shows how to use this old and reliable connectivity method.

Creating a Connection to Microsoft Access Using ODBC

ODBC has been around for many years. You can easily find it in products that predate Windows 95. In fact, this technology has been around for so long that many developers view it as a kind of one-size-fits-all solution to database connectivity. It's hard to find a database that can't use ODBC to create a connection. Because Visual Web Developer provides full ODBC support, you should be able to create a connection to any database you want—at least within reason. This section describes how to use ODBC to create a connection to Microsoft Access. The amazing thing is that this process works relatively well for other databases too—most of them simply change the form required to make the connection meet specific driver needs.

NOTE The example in this section relies on a sample Access database that you'll find in the \Chapter 10 folder of the sample code on the Sybex Web site. You can use this database to experiment with connections as needed to see how Access works with Visual Web Developer.

CREATING THE ODBC CONNECTION

Before you can tell Visual Web Developer which ODBC connection to use, you have to create the connection. You define the connection using the ODBC Data Source Administrator that you access using the Data Sources (ODBC) applet in the Administrative Tools folder of the Control Panel. Figure 10.16 shows what this dialog box looks like with the sample database connection entered.

NOTE One of the problems with using ODBC is that you have to define the connection or Data Source Name (DSN) on every machine that requires it. The need to define a DSN on every machine isn't such big deal for a small organization, but imagine doing it for thousands of machines and you'll know why most network administrators want another solution.

FIGURE 10.16
Use the ODBC Data Source Administrator to create an ODBC connection.

To create the connection, click Add. You'll see the Create New Data Source dialog box where you select a connection type. Every ODBC source on your computer has a special driver—the driver has a name such as Microsoft Access Driver (*.MDB). Select the Access driver and click Finish. This act starts the driver and you'll see a driver-specific dialog box such as the ODBC Microsoft Access Setup dialog box shown in Figure 10.17. Note that this dialog box shows the entries required to access the database.

FIGURE 10.17
Fill in the information
required to let the driver
access the database.

The information that you provide to create an ODBC connection varies by driver. In most cases, you'll need to provide a database name and security information as a minimum, but many drivers require additional input. When working with an Access database, you need to provide the location of the database by clicking Select and choosing the database file using the Select Database dialog box. After you add the database connection, type a name for the connection in the Data Source Name field. Even though the Description field is optional, you'll likely want to provide information in it as well, so you can identify the connection easier.

At this point, you need to decide whether to provide a default login for the connection. Most connections are more secure when you request the login information from individual users. When you decide to create a default login, click Advanced. You'll see a Set Advanced Options dialog box. Type the default authorization information in the Login Name and Password fields. Click OK to close the Set Advanced Options dialog box, and click OK a second time to close the ODBC Microsoft Access Setup dialog box.

ADDING THE CONNECTION TO VISUAL WEB DEVELOPER

Once you create an ODBC connection, you can use it within Visual Web Developer. Begin by clicking Connection to Database in Database Explorer. Always remember that Microsoft assumes that you're going to use SQL Server, so the first thing you need to do is click Provider and select the .NET Framework Data Provider for ODBC option. Click Connection and you'll notice that the Connection Properties dialog box changes, as shown in Figure 10.18. Notice that the figure shows the DSN defined in the "Creating the ODBC Connection" section selected under the Use Data Source Name radio button in the dialog box.

Depending on how you plan to use the database, you'll need to provide a user name and password. When the password is blank, you can leave the user name blank as well in some cases. Make sure you check Blank Password. You'll also need to decide whether the user can save the password so they don't need to enter it again.

FIGURE 10.18
ODBC connections
require that you supply a
DSN for the connection.

Something that you might find troubling is that the Enter the Initial Catalog to Use field is blank in many cases. Clicking the drop-down list box doesn't yield any entries to use. You can leave this field blank when working with Access and some other databases. Click Test Connection to ensure that the connection works, especially when you don't know which catalog to use initially. Figure 10.19 shows how the sample database appears when you use an ODBC connection (bottom) contrasted to an OLE-DB connection (top).

FIGURE 10.19
OLE-DB and ODBC con-
nections provide access
to the same data, but with
different performance.

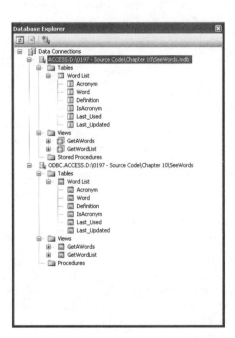

The results are the same—you gain access to the same data no matter which connection you use. The difference is performance. The OLE-DB connection will outperform the ODBC connection. In addition, the OLE-DB connection doesn't require configuration on a machine-by-machine basis. Of course, ODBC is a viable solution when OLE-DB connections aren't possible.

Designing a Database

When you work with data, you need to design a database to store the information for later use. In some cases, this means creating a simple XML storage container, as shown in previous chapters of the book. XML is increasingly becoming a storage medium of choice, especially for simple projects, because it doesn't require any special DBMS to use—it has the advantage of being inexpensive and simple. However, complex data storage usually requires something better. Many small businesses rely on Microsoft Access, while others use third-party solutions such as MySQL. Unfortunately, you can't create an Access or MySQL database within Visual Web Developer. You can define elements of the database, but you must create the initial database using the resources of that DBMS.

Visual Web Developer does provide a means for creating SQL Server databases within the IDE. In addition, when working with SQL Server, you can create databases using scripts. The following sections show how to create a new database using a simple dialog box and how to add the Northwind and Pubs databases to your existing SQL Server Express setup. This part is especially important because many of the remaining database examples in the book rely on the Northwind database.

Developing a SQL Server Database Using the Wizard

Creating a new SQL Server database using Visual Web Developer is relatively easy. To begin, right-click the Data Connections entry in Database Explorer and choose Create New SQL Server Database from the context menu. You'll see the Create New SQL Server Database dialog box shown in Figure 10.20. This figure shows the required entries in place.

FIGURE 10.20
Use the Visual Web Developer IDE to create any new SQL Server database that you need.

Select the server that you want to use for the database from the Select or Enter a Server Name field. Type a name for the database in the Enter a New Database Name field. You can optionally change the database security, but most developers now use the default Windows integrated security option, as shown in Figure 10.20. Click OK and Visual Web Developer will add the new database to the Database Explorer. You can now add tables and other resources as needed to the database. Chapter 11 examines this topic in detail.

NOTE The `\Chapter 10` folder on the companion CD contains the scripts required to create the MovieGuide database and import data for it. To use these scripts, you must edit the location to match a location on your hard drive. The location you choose must contain an uncompressed folder, or the scripts will fail. The failure message tells you that the script attempted to create a compressed read/write database. The `CreateMovieGuide.SQL` script creates the files used to store the data. The `MovieGuide.SQL` script creates the tables within the database. Finally, the `ImportRecords.SQL` script imports the data from the `MovieGuideData.DAT` file into the tables. The `ImportRecords.SQL` script is currently set to use the same folder as the database for the `MovieGuideData.DAT` file, but you can easily change this if necessary.

Obtaining the Northwind and Pubs Sample Databases

Many developers are used to working with the Northwind and Pubs database with other Microsoft products. These two databases have become so standard that many authors, including me, rely on the presence of these databases to ensure that everyone can see example code without a lot of extra effort. Unfortunately, you won't find either database installed as part of the default SQL Server Express installation—you won't find an option for installing them either. However, you can find scripts for creating these databases in SQL Server Express online at `http://www.microsoft.com/downloads/details.aspx?familyid=06616212-0356-46a0-8da2-eebc53a68034&displaylang=en`. The name of the file you'll receive is `SQL2000SampleDb.MSI`. Even though Microsoft originally created this file for SQL Server 2000, it works just fine with SQL Server Express.

TIP Microsoft doesn't make the Books Online feature (the documentation) available during the initial installation. You can obtain Books Online at `http://www.microsoft.com/downloads/details.aspx?FamilyId=2ADBC1A8-AE5C-497D-B584-EAB6719300CD&displaylang=en`. This page also includes links for the Adventure Works database that you can use for experimentation purposes.

After you download the script files, you'll need to run them. Right-click the file and choose Install from the context menu. You'll see a Welcome dialog box that tells you that this file contains the sample databases for SQL Server 2000. Click Next, read the licensing agreement, and agree to it. Keep following the prompts until you install the sample database scripts in the appropriate directory.

At this point, you have two scripts for creating the sample databases. If you used the default installation settings, these files appear in the `\Program Files\Microsoft SQL Server 2000 Sample Database Scripts` folder of your machine. The `InstNwnd.SQL` file will create the Northwind database and the `InstPubs.SQL` file will create the Pubs database.

To install the databases, open a command prompt. Type **OSQL -E -i InstNwnd.SQL** and press Enter. The OSQL utility will create the Northwind database for you (this process can take quite some time). When the utility completes, you'll see the command line along with what appears as nonsensical output, as shown in Figure 10.21. Once the Northwind database is complete, type **OSQL -E -i InstPubs.SQL** and press Enter. The process will repeat itself.

NOTE If you try to run the OSQL utility and find that you receive an error message at the command prompt, it means that the SQL Server Express installation didn't modify the path information for your system as it should have. In some cases, this makes your installation suspect and you should reinstall the product if you experience other problems. To use the installation scripts, copy them from the installation folder to the `\Program Files\Microsoft SQL Server\90\Tools\binn` folder. You can run the OSQL utility at the command prompt from this folder to create the two sample databases.

FIGURE 10.21
The OSQL utility runs for quite a while and displays output like this as it completes.

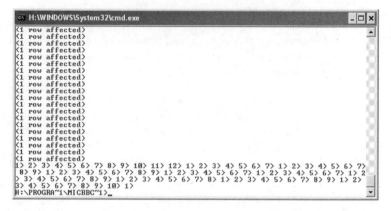

You'll want to test the installation to make sure that it worked. Open a copy of Visual Web Developer and use the View ➤ Database Explorer command to display the Database Explorer. Right-click Data Connections and choose Add Connection from the context menu. Database Explorer will display the Connection Properties dialog box shown in Figure 10.22 (this one already has all of the information filled out).

FIGURE 10.22
Use the Connection Properties dialog box to check for the two databases.

Type the name of your machine in the Select or Enter a Server Name field. Click the down arrow under the Select or Enter a Database Name radio button. You should see both the Northwind and Pubs databases, as shown in Figure 10.22. If you don't see these entries, it means that an error occurred. Try running the scripts a second time. A second failure usually means that there's a problem with your SQL Server Express setup and you might need to reinstall the product.

You need to make sure that you can actually access the database. Choose the Northwind database. Click Test Connection. When the scripts install the databases properly and you can access them, you'll see the success message shown in Figure 10.23. Click OK to clear the success message and Cancel to clear the Database Connection dialog box. You can close Visual Web Developer if desired.

FIGURE 10.23
Verify that you can actually connect to the test databases.

> **NOTE**   Because you're the only one using SQL Server Express, you don't need to worry about assigning login permissions for the test database. If you want to test any applications created in this book with the full version of SQL Server, you probably will need to assign login permissions to the test database to ensure that they work as anticipated.

Relying on Code-Free Data Binding

Once you create a connection to a database, the first concern is using it. The interesting thing about newer Microsoft products is that you don't have to do all of the work. In fact, when you have simple display needs, you don't have to do any of the work. One of the fastest and easiest ways to display data elements on screen is to simply drag and drop what you need onto the form—not code it. Yes, the IDE is creating code for you in the background, but the idea is that you aren't spending the time required to create the code.

In fact, you can get many of the features that developers want today without creating any code at all. Try this experiment. Drag and drop the Categories table from Database Explorer onto a new Web form. You'll find that Visual Web Developer automatically adds a GridView and a SqlDataSource control to the page for you. The Common Grid View Smart Tag does the rest. Simply check the options you want and you'll see them added, automatically, without coding, as shown in Figure 10.24. You'll find this example in the \Chapter 10\CodeFree folder of the source code on the Sybex Web site.

Start up the application. You'll find that all of the functionality works just as advertised and you haven't created a single line of code—at least, not personally. One of the biggest issues that developers need to consider is how much work to allow the IDE to do for them. As you can see, the IDE can do a lot of work, but it's also easy for a developer to feel that the automatic method isn't necessarily best. It isn't the best way to code complete complex applications, but simple pages really do work best when you let the IDE do the coding for you.

Defining Your Development Goals

This chapter shows you some basics of working with databases with Visual Web Developer. You discover the many ways to design databases, create connections for them, access them from Visual Web Developer, and finally create an application using them. This chapter also describes several new Visual Web Developer features, including Database Explorer and a number of toolbars. All of these features make it easier for you to work with database applications.

FIGURE 10.24
The best way to create simple displays is not to code them.

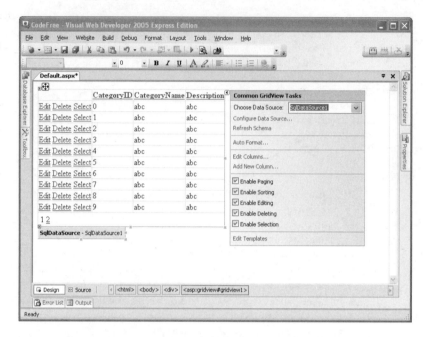

Now it's time to work with the database features in more detail. You might have an existing database that you want to access from Visual Web Developer or simply create a new database for experimental purposes. Don't forget that Microsoft provides you with a number of sample databases you can use for experimentation, so if you want to work on coding technique, you can simply rely on one of the existing databases. The goal is to build proficiency working with Visual Web Developer to create database applications using the vast number of resources that this product provides.

Chapter 11 takes you farther on the road to working with databases efficiently in Visual Web Developer. You'll discover that you have access to a number of database management options that make it easier to manage your database. For example, you can create views to see the data in another way or stored procedures to perform some tasks using the DBMS, rather than writing local code. In many cases, the features described in this chapter can not only reduce the work you have to do, but also make it easier to locate mistakes and even test the database as needed.

Chapter 11

Using SQL Server 2005 Express Efficiently

SQL Server Express doesn't provide all of the functionality that you find in the full version of the product, yet it's fully capable of creating databases that you can move to the full version. Most of the work you do with SQL Server Express actually occurs within the Visual Web Developer IDE. Yes, you can use command line utilities, such as SQLCmd, to perform some tasks, but the daily work that you need to do occurs within the IDE. In fact, the IDE provides a number of resources, including Database Explorer and several toolbars, that help you perform the required work.

Once you create one or more tables that you can use within Visual Web Developer, you'll need to create all of the add-ons that come with database programming, such as views and stored procedures. All of these resources help you define the database application and create something that works efficiently. For example, sometimes it's faster to create a view of the data, rather than construct it from scratch every time someone uses the application. Stored procedures sometimes work faster than local code because they keep all of the data on the server—the client simply receives the finished product. You need to consider where data manipulation occurs to ensure that the application performs well.

A new feature in this version of SQL Server is the existence of a connection to the Common Language Runtime (CLR). Fortunately, you can work with this new feature as part of your application code in SQL Server Express. Although you probably won't see the full effect of CLR within SQL Server Express, you obtain enough information to understand how using CLR can definitely reduce the workload for the developer. Of course, all of that new functionality comes with a stiff price tag.

SQL Server Express, like the full version, also provides full support for XML. Some developers view this feature as nice to have, but not very exciting. XML is an essential feature for Visual Web Developer because you can do so many things with XML within your Visual Web Developer applications. The samples in previous chapters have shown you everything from data storage to survey results to configuration settings. All of these kinds of data manipulation work well with Visual Web Developer and XML. Adding this capability to SQL Server Express only completes the circle because your desktop applications still gain access to the full benefits of a full-fledged database. XML becomes an end location for some types of data storage—not a permanent piece of the application puzzle.

TIP   This book provides a good overview of using SQL Server Express from a Visual Web Developer Express perspective. If you're planning to write a number of database applications, you'll want to learn more about the making SQL queries using a book such as *SQL Queries for Mere Mortals* by John L. Viescas and Michael J. Hernandez (Addison Wesley, 2000). To get the most out of SQL Server Express, you'll also want to get a copy of *Mastering SQL Server 2005 Express Edition* by Mike Gunderloy and Susan Harkins (Sybex, 2005).

Accessing the Database from Visual Web Developer

Creating a database means that you have a container to store data and objects—everything from data tables to triggers used to signal an event. However, SQL Server Express lacks the visual interface supported by the full version of the product. The method you use to manage your database is the Visual Web Developer IDE. The following sections introduce many of the concepts you'll use to create database applications in Visual Web Developer.

RECONFIGURING A DATASOURCE

You will eventually run into trouble where you move a project from one machine to another or install a SQL Server update and your application suddenly forgets everything it ever knew about the data source. Reconfiguring the DataSource control can help in these situations. Simply follow these steps to get back your data source without having to reconfigure the entire page.

1. Select the DataSource control in Design view.

2. Choose the Configure Data Source option from the DataSource control SmartTag. You'll see the Configure Data Source wizard. The important part now is not to change anything.

3. Click Next at each wizard step. Ensure that the settings you previously used are still valid for this setup. If not, change just the settings that you must change to make the DataSource control functional.

4. Click Test Query on the final page to ensure that the data source is working again. If not, click Previous to make any required changes.

5. Click Finish to complete the update. Visual Web Developer will display a message box asking whether you want to refresh the fields and keys for the view controls.

6. Click No each time Visual Web Developer asks to refresh the controls. If you click Yes, you must reconfigure the affected view control.

7. Test your application to ensure the changes work as anticipated.

Using the Database Explorer

Database Explorer is the main interface between Visual Web Developer and SQL Server Express. The "Using Database Explorer" section of Chapter 10 describes how you can create a connection to SQL Server Express using Database Explorer, but Database Explorer can do a lot more than create simple connections. You can use it to create every object type that the database supports, including new tables.

NOTE   Throughout the book, I'll use the technically correct term *fields* to refer to the smallest element that you can access within a database. Most developers know and understand this term, which is the reason I use it in this book. Microsoft has chosen to use *columns* as a replacement term for *fields*, so you'll see this term when working with Microsoft products, but not with products from other vendors. I'll also use the term *records* to refer to a collection of fields that defines a single entry in a table. Microsoft uses the term *rows* to refer to *records*.

DISPLAYING THE DATA

In addition to creating, deleting, and modifying objects, you can use Database Explorer to view the various objects. For example, open the Categories table in the Northwind database. Right-click the Categories entry and choose Show Table Data from the context menu. You'll see the table data, as shown in Figure 11.1. This view lets you edit the data, just as you can when working with an application. More importantly, this view lets you see the effects of tasks that your application performs on the data.

To create a new object, right-click the folder that holds the object (such as Tables) and choose the Add New option on the context menu. You'll normally see the new item created outright or a wizard will take you through the process. Other sections of this chapter discuss the details of creating specific objects such as views.

FIGURE 11.1
Use Database Explorer to perform tasks such as querying the database.

MODIFYING THE TABLE AND ASSOCIATED FIELDS

You might decide at some point that you need to add a new field to the table or change part of the table schema. To view this data, right-click the table and choose Open Table Definition from the context menu. Figure 11.2 shows what you'll see for the Categories table.

The upper half of the display contains a list of fields for this table, defines the field data type, and shows whether the field allows nulls. The display also shows the primary key. To set the primary key, select the fields you want to use to define the key (use Ctrl+Click to select multiple fields), right-click one of the highlighted fields, and choose Set Primary Key from the context menu.

The lower half of the display contains a description of the highlighted field. You use the lower field to add information, such as a field description or select the data type. This is also where you add a default value for the field or define computed fields. The data includes some nonchangeable values as well, such as whether you can use the field in an index. In short, you get all of the same functionality that you'd expect from SQL Server; it's just in a different place.

FIGURE 11.2
Define the table schema using an interface that looks similar to the one in SQL Server.

WORKING WITH INDEXES

The same interface shown in Figure 11.2 lets you create indexes as well. All you need to do is right-click the upper pane and choose one of the indexing options. However, you need to decide which kind of index to create. Visual Web Developer helps you create the following three index types.

Standard A standard index provides indexing for internal SQL Server Express use. You order the data by specifying an index. This option also lets you create keys for use with the table—both primary and foreign. Most developers already know how to use this kind of index.

Full text Some types of data stores require a full text index. For example, you might create a database to hold all of the Web pages on your Web site. To help users locate the information they need quickly, you'd provide a full text index. This kind of index requires that you create a full text catalog as part of the database. Unfortunately, SQL Server Express doesn't support the full text index option. To use this feature, you must rely on the full version of SQL Server. Even when working with SQL Server, the full text index support is a separate installation option and it works only with specific field types. Given the special nature of this index, I don't discuss it in detail in this book. You can find a full discussion of this topic at `http://msdn.microsoft.com/archive/en-us/dnarexnt00/html/ewn0092.asp`.

XML An XML index lets you order data so it works well as XML output. The column contains XML data that SQL Server Express orders for you. This is an especially important feature for Visual Web Developer because it's likely that you'll output data as XML at some point. To use this index, you must add a special field to the table of the XML data type. The "Creating an XML Index" section later in this chapter demonstrates how to create an XML index using Visual Web Developer.

TIP Visual Web Developer users do have options other than using a full text index in SQL Server to perform full text searches of their Web site. Third-party products such as the Zoom Search Engine (http://www.wrensoft.com/zoom/index.html) from Wrensoft Web Software make creating full text searches easier.

Standard indexes work with a subset of the data types that SQL Server Express supports. For example, you can't create a standard index for the `ntext` data type, but you can create it for fields with a specific size such an `int` or `timestamp`. To create a standard index, right-click any of the columns and choose Indexes/Keys from the context menu. You'll see the Indexes/Keys dialog box shown in Figure 11.3. In fact, this dialog box already has one index, `CategoryName`, and one key, `PK_Categories`, defined.

Click Add to add a new index to the list. You must define the index by clicking the ellipsis (…) in the Columns field. This entry displays the Index Columns dialog box where you can choose one or more fields to use for the index. The Index Columns dialog box displays only fields that you can index. As you add fields to the list, you'll see fewer options—you can add a field only one time to an index. Most developers also provide a new, descriptive, entry in the (`Name`) field and a `Description` field entry so that it's easier to remember the purpose for the index later.

FIGURE 11.3

Create new indexes as needed to order the data in your table.

DEFINING RELATIONSHIPS

Relationships define how two or more tables interact. Many database applications provide a visual layout of these relationships with pointers showing the interactions. In fact, the full version of SQL Server does provide this feature, but SQL Server Express doesn't. You can still work with relationships using the Foreign Key Relationships dialog box shown in Figure 11.4.

A relationship between two tables exists when one table defines its content based on the content of another table. For example, the Products table contains a list of products, each of which belongs to a particular product category. Consequently, even a category in the Categories table can have many products listed under it. A customer may request a beverage (the category), but you can't fulfill the request until you know the specific beverage (the product).

FIGURE 11.4
Define relationships be-
tween tables as needed.

To define a new relationship, you begin in the table that needs the data from the other table. The Products table requires a list of Categories, so you'd begin in the Products table. Open the Foreign Key Relationships dialog box by right-clicking anywhere within the table definition and choosing Relationships from the context menu. Click Add. The IDE automatically creates a new entry for you that has FK (for foreign key) and the name *Products* twice, FK_Products_Products. The first name always reflects the table that needs information, while the second reflects the table that has information, so normally, you'd change the name of the new relationship to FK_Products_Categories, but this entry already exists. Leave the name as is for now.

Define the relationship by clicking the ellipsis (...) in the Tables and Columns Specification field. You'll see the Tables and Columns dialog box shown in Figure 11.5. This dialog box already has the relationship defined. Notice that the Categories table appears in the left pane and that it has the CategoryID field selected. Likewise, the Products table appears in the right pane with the CategoryID field selected. Generally, developers create tables with matching field names where relationships exist to avoid confusion and to make the relationships clearer. Notice that the IDE automatically renamed the relationship to reflect the naming convention—it added 1 to the end of the name because this is the second occurrence of that relationship. Click OK to close the Tables and Columns dialog box.

FIGURE 11.5
Always begin defining a
relationship in the table
that needs information.

Deleting a relationship is easy, but the effects can be devastating when your database relies on the relationship. Consequently, you don't want to delete the relationship without thinking about it for a long time first. To remove the relationship you just created, highlight the FK_Products_Categories1 entry in the Foreign Key Relationships dialog box and click Delete. Click Close to close the Foreign Key Relationships dialog box.

MAKING QUERIES

Queries are the basis for obtaining information from the database, so it's important to know how to work with them. Fortunately, you can experiment as much as you want with Visual Web Developer by creating queries with Database Explorer. To try a simple query, right-click the Categories table and choose New Query from the context menu. You'll see an Add Table dialog box, as shown in Figure 11.6. The title of this dialog box is a little misleading because you can also choose views and functions as a source of data. For now, simply select the Categories entry on the Table tab and click Add. Because this is the only table that the example needs, click Close to close the Add Table dialog box.

FIGURE 11.6
Add tables, views, and functions to your queries as data sources.

Once you add the data source, you'll see a display like the one shown in Figure 11.7. This view will also display any relations between multiple tables. The point is that this is where you choose the data you want to see and how you want to see it. (The figure shows the query selections and output in this case—your initial view will contain less information.)

To create a query, select the data fields you want to view, create any required relations between tables (drag and drop a relation between related fields of two tables), and choose any ordering. Figure 11.7 shows that the CategoryID, CategoryName, and Description fields appear in the output, but not the Picture field. In addition, the query sorts the data by the CategoryName field. The grid in the middle of Figure 11.7 shows that it's easy to select just the items you want. The area immediately below shows the SQL statement that the query generates.

The problem is that you don't know whether the query will do what you want. To check the query for accuracy, right-click the upper pane and choose Execute SQL from the context menu. The lower grid in Figure 11.7 shows the results. In this case, the display shows the content of the Categories table sorted by the CategoryName field. The query doesn't contain the Picture field—just as specified. You can save the query for later use in your application, but it's very helpful to try out various queries until you gain a full understanding of how this mechanism works. For example, try opening the Products table next by right-clicking the upper pane and choosing Add Table from the content menu. Create a relationship between it and the Categories table, and then generate a new query. Figure 11.8 shows one way to perform this task. You can find this query in the SampleQuery.DTQ file located in the \Chapter 11 folder of the source code on the Sybex Web site.

FIGURE 11.7

The IDE shows the tables, views, and functions that you've selected, along with any relations between them.

FIGURE 11.8

Work with queries for a while to determine how various additions affect the output.

Using the Table Designer Toolbar

The Table Designer toolbar automatically appears whenever you open a table definition. This toolbar contains features that help you work with tables with greater ease. Figure 11.9 shows how this toolbar looks. The following list describes the toolbar buttons.

FIGURE 11.9
Use the Table Designer toolbar to create and manage tables for your application.

Manage Check Constraints   Displays the Check Constraints dialog box where you can add a constraint for the current database. A constraint ensures that the DBMS enforces whatever database integrity rules you choose in addition to those that SQL Server normally enforces. For example, you might decide that a contact database ensures that a user have at least one, but no more than five, telephone numbers. You can also check for range errors and other kinds of integrity rules.

Manage XML Indexes   Displays the XML Indexes dialog box, which contains a list of the XML indexes for the selected table. See the "Creating an XML Index" section later in this chapter for additional information about XML indexes.

Manage Full Text Index   Displays the Full Text Index dialog box, which contains a list of the full text indexes for the database. You must create a full text catalog to use a full text index.

Manage Indexes and Keys   Displays the Indexes/Keys dialog box, which contains a list of the standard indexes for the database, along with any primary key definitions. See the "Working with Indexes" section earlier in this chapter for details on working with standard indexes. You create a primary key using the Set Primary Key button on this toolbar.

Relationships   Displays the Foreign Key Relationships dialog box, which describes the relationship between this table and other tables in the database. The "Defining Relationships" section earlier in this chapter tells you how to work with foreign keys.

Set Primary Key   Sets the primary key for the table. A primary key consists of the fields required to create a unique table entry.

Generate Change Script   Displays the Save Change Script dialog box shown in Figure 11.10. This dialog box contains all of the changes you propose making to the table. You can use a change script to move a change from one system to another. For example, you can move a change from your development machine to a production server. Change scripts are also a good way to document changes that you make to the table schema.

FIGURE 11.10
Use change scripts to document changes that you make to the database and move them to other systems.

Using the Data Design Toolbar

This toolbar appears when you work with data sources or when you create a Data Component. Figure 11.11 shows how this toolbar appears. The following list describes the features it provides.

FIGURE 11.11
The Data Design toolbar provides quick access to indexes, keys, and change scripts.

Preview Data Displays the Data Preview Dialog box. This is the only control available for both data sources and Data Components. Figure 11.12 shows a typical preview. The Select an Object to Preview field contains the data object that you want to view. You'll see a hierarchical list of available objects, in most cases, with the leave node as the selectable object. Click Preview and you'll see the data provided by a data object such as a query. The purpose of this option is to let you see the results of configuration changes you make before you begin using the object within your code.

Add New Data Source Displays the Data Source Configuration Wizard. You use this wizard to create a connection to a data source on your system.

Generate Dataset Creates a dataset based on a data source. Generally, the IDE automatically creates a `DataSet` control for you, so you won't need to use this option.

Show Data Sources Displays the Data Sources window. This window contains a list of every data source you create. You can use it to add data to your application—either individual fields or entire tables. The window includes a special feature that lets you choose the kind of control it creates. For example, an individual date field could rely on any of these controls: `DateTimePicker`, `TextBox`, `Label`, `ComboBox`, `LinkLabel`, or `ListBox`. Figure 11.13 shows a typical view of a Data Sources window with the control selection list shown. Notice that you can choose the None option when you don't want the field to appear in the output, even when you select the table.

FIGURE 11.12
Preview the data objects you create to ensure that they work as anticipated.

FIGURE 11.13
The Data Sources window helps you choose data items for your application.

Using the Query Designer Toolbar

The Query Designer toolbar becomes active whenever you create a database query. However, the IDE doesn't always display this toolbar automatically, so you may need to activate it by right-clicking the toolbar and choosing Query Designer from the context menu. The Query Designer toolbar always appears, in some cases, such as when you work with the Query Designer window shown earlier in Figure 11.7. Figure 11.14 shows the Query Designer toolbar. The following list describes the features it provides.

FIGURE 11.14

Open and close panes, choose a query type, and perform other query tasks with the Query Designer toolbar.

Add New Derived Table Creates a table that it derived from the other resources in the query. You use derived tables to speed queries by reducing the time required to gather information from multiple sources.

Add Table Displays the Add Table dialog box shown earlier in Figure 11.6. Once you select a table for the query, click Add and the IDE will add it to the Diagram pane where you can choose the fields you want to use.

Add Group By Defines grouping criteria for a result set. Essentially, this means that the system will interpret the tables, rather than present the information directly on-screen. The "Creating a Group" section later in this chapter provides additional information about this particular feature.

Verify SQL Syntax Analyzes the SQL statement created by the various Diagram pane and Criteria pane selections. When the SQL statement is correct, you see a success message stating that the input will work as written. Likewise, when there's an error, the dialog box contains error information. It's a good idea to verify the SQL syntax before you try to execute it so you can receive the results faster (completely incorrect syntax won't execute anyway and partially incorrect syntax may yield erroneous results).

Execute SQL Executes the SQL statement and places the output in the Results pane. The Results pane contains a table that relies on a grid view.

Change Query Type Modifies the query type, which changes the output received from the query. For example, the output could appear as an addition to an existing table, rather than part of the Results pane. See the next section, "Modifying the Query Output Type," for additional information on this feature.

Show Results Pane Displays the Results pane on-screen when selected. The Results pane receives the output from a query in most cases. Keeping the Results pane hidden until you finish designing the query can save screen real estate for query design needs.

Show SQL Pane Displays the SQL pane on-screen when selected. The SQL pane displays the results of selections you make in the Diagram and Criteria panes. You can also manually add SQL information (although this act isn't recommended because the IDE tends to remove any changes you make by hand).

Show Criteria Pane Displays the Criteria pane on-screen when selected. The Criteria pane helps you modify the way in which the IDE reacts to database fields you choose from the list of available fields. For example, you can create field groupings, modify the sort order, and create field evalu-ations rather than use the actual field data. The order of the fields in the Criteria pane also affects the order of the fields in the Results pane (or other output you choose).

Show Diagram Pane   Displays the Diagram pane on-screen when selected. The Diagram pane contains a graphic representation of the tables you choose and the relationships between them. Use this pane to choose the fields you want to appear in the output.

Two of the Query Designer toolbar buttons perform special tasks. The following sections describe these two tasks.

MODIFYING THE QUERY OUTPUT TYPE

The Visual Web Developer IDE always assumes that you can create a selection query—one that selects values from one or more tables and displays the result in the Result pane. Ultimately, you can place the results anywhere, but the Result pane is the output when working in the Query Designer window. However, you have quite a few other query options, as shown in Figure 11.15. All you need to do is choose the new output type. The following list describes each of the query types.

FIGURE 11.15

You have access to a number of query types using the Query Designer toolbar.

Select   Creates a standard output set using the Results pane. This is the default query options.

Insert Results   Places the results in an existing table. When you choose this option, the IDE displays the Choose Target Table for Insert Results dialog box, which contains a complete list of tables for the current database. The table you choose receives the results of the query when you click Execute SQL. Because the changes this option creates are permanent and could damage entries in an existing table, you'll want to use this option with care.

Insert Values   Places the values you supply into an existing table. When you choose this option, the IDE displays the Choose Target Table for Insert Values dialog box, which contains a list of the open tables. You can't save the results into other tables that the database might contain. After you select this option, the IDE automatically closes every other open table. Type the values you want to insert in the SQL pane as part of the VALUES argument or within the New Value column of the Criteria pane. Click Execute SQL to add the new values to the selected table.

Update   Defines an update query where the SET argument contains a list of values to insert into a table. Unlike an insert values query, an update query can affect the content of existing records when you provide filter criterion. Or you could provide a filter that tells the IDE to change a value for every record that contains a CategoryID value of 1.

Delete   Defines a delete query where the IDE removes records from the selected table as defined by the WHERE argument. Because this query permanently removes data from a table, you should use it with care.

Make Table   Creates a new table in the database to hold the results of a query. The IDE displays the Make Table dialog box where you enter the name of the new table. The table appears within the database after you click Execute SQL. It has all of the same features as any other table, so you can modify it as needed to meet specific needs.

CREATING A GROUP

Groups help you derive new information from the existing data by grouping data together and by analyzing it. For example, you can group data by one field and then count how many times that field occurs in another table. The kinds of analysis you can perform depends on the data types of the data fields you choose. You don't have to limit yourself to numeric fields—you can perform analysis on text fields too. For example, it's possible to create statistical information, such as the average length of a customer remark on a survey, based on the survey entries in the database.

To see how this feature works, create a new query that includes the Products and Categories tables. Select the CategoryID and CategoryName fields of the Categories table and the CategoryID field of the Products table. Click Add Group By. You'll see a new Group By column added to the Criteria pane. Change the CategoryID entry for the Products table from Group By to Count. Notice that the Diagram pane now shows a summation symbol for the CategoryID field and that the field is no longer checked. Change the Alias column entry for the CategoryID field to NumberOfProducts and click Execute SQL. Your display should look like the one shown in Figure 11.16.

The point of this exercise is that you've created new information from the existing data. You now know how many products appear in each category. For example, the Beverages category has 12 items in it. You could output this data to another table and use it as an input to an application that tells the user how many of each kind of item to expect. Normally, this kind of data would require analysis every time you needed to do it, but now how you have a special table set aside for the purpose and a query to re-create the totals as needed, rather than every time you want to display them.

FIGURE 11.16
Grouping information can help you learn more about the information the database provides.

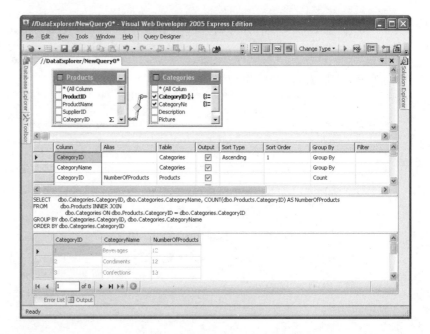

Creating a Blank Database

You can create a blank SQL Server database as an object within Visual Web Developer. This template appears on the Add New Item dialog box you access by right-clicking the project entry and choosing Add New Item from the context menu. Select the Database item and give it a name such as `MySampleData.MDF`. Click Add. The IDE displays a message requesting to create a `\App_Data` folder when your project doesn't include one. Click Yes and the IDE will create the new database for you. (You'll find this example in the `\Chapter 11\SimpleData` folder of the source code on the Sybex Web site.)

The only problem is that after the IDE creates the database you still can't use it because your system lacks a connection to it. Unfortunately, if your drive is compressed, you can't create a connection because SQL Server Express won't connect to compressed database files. To remove the compression from this file, open a copy of Windows Explorer and locate the file. Right-click the file and choose Properties from the context menu. Click Advanced in the Properties dialog box and you'll see the Advanced Attributes dialog box shown in Figure 11.17. Clear the Compress Contents to Save Disk Space option and click OK twice. Perform this process a second time with the folder that holds the database (you need not decompress any other files already in the folder). You're ready to make a connection to this local database.

Creating a connection to a local SQL Server database is a little different from creating a connection to a database that already appears as part of the server. The DBMS doesn't know anything about this database, so you can't simply select it from the Select or Enter a Database Name drop-down list in the Connection Properties dialog box (see the "Creating a Connection to SQL Server and SQL Server Express" section of Chapter 10 for additional information). Select the Attach a Database File as a File Name option instead. Type the name you want to use for the database and use the Browse button to locate the actual database file.

Verify all of the information you entered for the new database. Click OK. The IDE performs several tasks at this point. First, it creates a connection for the database. Second, it introduces the DBMS to the database so the DBMS knows that it's supposed to manage the database. The new database is completely blank—it doesn't contain anything at all, not even a table. Other sections of the chapter discuss how you can create new tables, modify table definitions, create relations, and perform other tasks required to fill a new database with data.

WARNING   Don't delete the database from your hard drive simply because SQL Server Express and Visual Web Developer will continue to look for it. Delete the database connection from Visual Web Developer first, use SQLCmd utility to drop the table from the master table in SQL Server Express (see the "Using the SQLCmd Utility" section of Chapter 10 for details), and finally, remove the database from your project using Solution Explorer.

FIGURE 11.17
SQL Server Express won't work with compressed database files.

Using the Microsoft SQL Server 2005 Express Manager

If you had thoughts that Microsoft would provide a graphical utility for managing SQL Server Express, you're going to be disappointed. The SQL Server Express package doesn't include any graphical tools for managing the database (a flaw in MSDE as well). However, you can download Microsoft SQL Server 2005 Express Manager at http://www.microsoft.com/downloads/ details.aspx?familyid=3212a9a2-b658-4710-b04e-8a28355f836d&displaylang=en. This utility is a marginal replacement for the graphical utilities provided with the full version of SQL Server 2005, but it's much better than having nothing at all.

Once you install the utility, you can start it using the Start ➢ Programs ➢ Microsoft SQL Server 2005 ➢ SQL Server Express Manager command. You'll initially see a Connect to Server dialog box. Type the name of your machine in the Server Instance field when you want to manage a local copy of SQL Server Express. You can also manage other SQL Server instances using this tool by typing the name of the machine where SQL Server is running. SQL Sever Express Manager will make the connection to the database and display a window containing resources for that instance of SQL Server. Figure 11.18 shows a typical view of SQL Server Express Manager with a database loaded and a query in place. The left pane is the Object Explorer, while the right pane is the Workspace window. The following list describes each of the controls.

FIGURE 11.18

Use SQL Server Express Manager to graphically manage your databases.

New Query   Creates a new query file. If you already have a query open, you'll see a second tab added to the top of the Workspace window.

Open Query   Opens an existing query (SQL file) and places it in the Workspace window.

Execute   Executes the selected query. When you have more than one query open, SQL Server Express Manager executes the query that you can see. When you choose the Results to Grid or Results to Text buttons, along with the Show Results button, you'll see the results of the query in the lower half of the Workspace window.

Parse   Tests the selected query and displays any errors in the lower half of the Workspace window.

Save   Saves the current query to a SQL file on disk.

Increase Text Size   Increases the text size. When the text size reaches the largest that SQL Server Express Manager supports, the text size changes to the smallest size on the next click.

Show Results   Displays the results of a query in the lower half of the Workspace window.

Results to File   Places the results of a query into a file, rather than displaying them on screen. You can save the data as a Report (RPT) or Text (TXT) file.

Results to Grid   Places the results of a query in the lower half of the Workspace window in a data grid as shown in Figure 11.18.

Results to Text   Places the results of a query in the lower half of the Workspace window in a report format. The report shows the text separated into columns as you would see them in a TXT file.

Table Selection   Lets you choose a table from the current database to use for queries.

You can use the SQL Server Express Manager to perform any task with a database. However, the utility doesn't provide any automation for performing tasks except to create a new database. To create a new database, right-click the Databases entry in Object Explorer and choose New Database from the context menu. You'll see a New Database tab added to the Workspace window as shown in Figure 11.19. Type the name and location of the new database. Click OK to create the new database.

FIGURE 11.19
The only automation SQL Server Express Manager provides is database creation.

After you create the database, you must use SQL statements to perform every other task. For example, you must create all tables using this technique. Consequently, this utility is of limited use when you create a database for your personal use—the Visual Web Developer Express IDE provides a lot more automation. However, this utility does come in handy for testing the queries you want to make, exporting the database for someone else to use, or even to create scripts by hand. SQL Server Express Manager is a good addition to, not a replacement for, the features that Visual Web Developer Express provides.

NOTE You must refresh the view every time you complete a SQL statement using SQL Server Express Manager. Right-click the database in question and choose Refresh from the context menu. The database will close and you'll need to reopen it to see the results of any changes.

Accessing Stored Procedures

Stored procedures provide an application-like functionality to SQL Server Express. You write these functions as separate entities and then call on them as needed to perform tasks at the database. The advantage of using stored procedures is that you don't have to move the data across a network—it stays right at the server, which means you gain a performance advantage in processing large amounts of data. However, the performance gain for the client comes at the cost of server processing cycles. The server performs the analysis and sends just the result to the client. Consequently, you have to consider where to spend processing cycles. In many cases, stored procedures are the best option when you work with large data sets because the network performance penalty is enormous.

TIP Many developers use stored procedures to help keep data secret. A stored procedure processes the data on the server, away from prying eyes. The client sees only the information that you want seen, so the changes of security breach are less. Breaches can still occur, but using the stored procedure provides one less avenue that a cracker can use for gaining access.

Working with Stored Procedures

Both the Northwind and Pubs sample databases come with a number of stored procedures you can try—they're all fully functional. You'll find the stored procedures in the `Stored Procedures` folder of Database Explorer, as shown in Figure 11.20. Each stored procedure appears as a separate entry in the folder. Within each stored procedure, you can find external variables that you must supply as input to the stored procedure—the input variables appear with an at (@) sign in front of them.

Seeing how these stored procedures work is relatively easy. Right-click the stored procedure entry and select Execute from the context menu to start it. Try starting the CustOrderHist stored procedure. Because this stored procedure includes an input variable, you'll see the Run Stored Procedure dialog box shown in Figure 11.21. This dialog box contains a list of all of the variables the stored procedure supports. You must provide values for any of the input variables in the list. Some stored procedure variables have a default value, but that's not the case for the CustOrderHist stored procedure. Type **ALFKI** in the Value column and click OK. The stored procedure executes, but doesn't really show you much.

To work with a stored procedure in a way that produces a result, you manually create a page that includes a data source and a grid or other means of viewing the output. Interestingly enough, you can create a perfectly acceptable view without writing any code in many cases. You'll find this example in the `\Chapter 11\StoredProcedure` folder of the source code on the Sybex Web site.

FIGURE 11.20
Database Explorer contains a complete list of stored procedures for the selected database.

FIGURE 11.21
Whenever you execute a stored procedure, you must provide any required input values.

The first task is to create a data source using a `SqlDataSource` control. You could use other controls, but this one provides the best performance of the SQL Server-specific features. Click Configure Data Source on the `SqlDataSource` Smart Tag and you'll see the Configure Data Source wizard. Begin the process by selecting a data connection and clicking Next. This page also lets you create a new data connection, should you need one. The first page of interest appears in Figure 11.22. The default settings use a specific table for the input, but you can select stored procedures as an option, as shown in the figure.

Changing from the default setting takes you along a different path than configuring a standard data source. Click Next and you'll see the Define Custom Statements or Stored Procedures dialog box. Depending on your system, you might have to wait a minute or two to see the dialog box, but it will show up. The IDE has to query SQL Server about all of the stored procedures for the target database, so it may require a little time to complete the task. Choose the Stored Procedure option and select CustOrderHist from the list. Click Next and you'll see the Define Parameters dialog box shown in Figure 11.23. This figure shows the dialog box with the entries added.

When you click Show Advanced Properties, the IDE changes the display to show all of the information about input, which includes its data type and name. Notice that you could also provide a parameter source as input—the IDE configures the data source in a way that lets you pass the information at runtime, rather than design time.

Once you complete the parameter step, click Next and you'll see a Test Query dialog box. Click Test Query and you'll see a Parameter Values Editor where you can provide a specific input, or simply accept the test value you provided. Click OK and you'll see sample output. If the query completes as expected, click Finish—the data source is ready to use.

FIGURE 11.22
Choose a stored procedure as your data source, rather than a specific table.

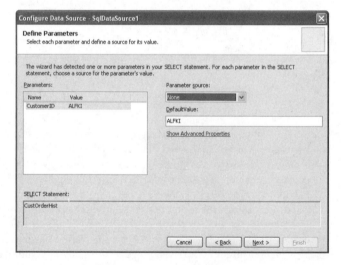

FIGURE 11.23
Provide any required data entries for the stored procedure you choose.

Now you have to decide on a means to display the data source. The GridView control provides the easiest and most reliable configuration. However, you can use any control that you want. All you really need to do is select the data source you created in the Choose Data Source field of the associated control's Smart Tag. When using a GridView control, it's usually a good idea to select the Enable Paging and Enable Sorting options so you can see the data in other ways. Figure 11.24 shows the no code results of using a stored procedure to display information from the database.

Not even the DataList control requires any coding on your part. Figure 11.24 shows this control as a comparison to the GridView control. Configuring the DataList control is a little more time consuming. You begin by defining the data source as normal. However, at this point, nothing displays on the control because you haven't told it what to display. To create the display, click Edit Templates. The Smart Tag actually changes to a different mode—one designed for editing the templates.

FIGURE 11.24
You don't have to write
code to create simple displays with stored proce-
dures in Visual Web
Developer.

·Begin the configuration process by selecting the ItemTemplate option in the Display field. This is a general item template, but you can configure the various template elements individually as well. For example, if you want alternating items to look different from a general item, select the AlternatingItemTemplate option. The area beneath the `DataList` control will change, at this point, and you can add both text and controls to the area.

Controls can have a connection to the database. You have to use the Smart Tags when creating a data binding because the data binding options don't appear in the Properties window. Select Edit DataBindings from the control's Smart Tag and you'll see a display similar to the one shown in Figure 11.25. (If you can't select the Field Binding option as shown, click Refresh Schema to re-create the connection with the database.) The display shows the three most common control properties to bind to a field in the database, but you can use any field that makes sense by checking Show All Properties. Once you associate a particular property with a data field, click OK and the IDE makes the appropriate changes automatically.

FIGURE 11.25
You don't have to write
code to create simple displays with stored proce-
dures in Visual Web
Developer.

Template editing doesn't end with the data you want to present. You can also control headers, footers, and separators. The DataList control is extremely flexible, so you can change it any way you want. After you configure the items, header, footer, and separators as needed, click End Template Editing on the DataList control Smart Tag. As soon as you end template editing, you'll notice that the appearance of the control changes to show the modifications you made.

Now comes the fun part. Select the Auto Format option on the DataList control Smart Tag. You'll see an Auto Format dialog box where you can choose a theme for the control. The left pane shows the theme options, while the right shows how the theme will appear with the template options you chose. That's why it's important to create the templates first—you want to see how the theme looks with your actual design. Once you select a theme, click OK and the DataList control will reflect the new formatting. Even though using the DataList control is a lot more work to configure, it's better than writing code to create the same display manually. The point is that you need to try the various viewing controls to discover which one saves you the most time and provides the best presentation of your data.

Modifying Stored Procedures

At some point, you'll want to modify the stored procedures that you create. You might need to change how they work, fix a bug in the routine, or simply see how you performed a task in the past. Whatever the reason, Visual Web Developer provides an editor for your stored procedures, so you don't need to leave the IDE to make changes. To begin the editing process, right-click the stored procedure that you want to modify and choose Open from the context menu. You'll see the editor shown in Figure 11.26 open with the stored procedure loaded.

The display might look a bit odd at first, but think about what you're doing for a second and it makes perfect sense. This display is actually a SQL statement that asks the DBMS to alter the stored procedure named CustOrderHist that includes a single input named @CustomerID, which is a variable of type nchar with a length of 5. The code for the stored procedure appears in the box below the ALTER PROCEDURE SQL statement.

After you edit the stored procedure, you save it just as you would any other file. In the background, the IDE sends the SQL request to the DBMS and asks it to make the change to the stored procedure. However, as far as you're concerned, you've simply saved a file.

FIGURE 11.26

Modify stored procedures using the local editor to avoid leaving the IDE.

Creating New Stored Procedures

The Visual Web Developer IDE lets you create new stored procedures. To create a new stored procedure, right-click the `Stored Procedures` folder for the target database and choose Add New Stored Procedure from the context menu. You'll see an editing window similar to the one shown in Figure 11.26. (You'll find this example in the `\Chapter 11\NewStoredProcedure` folder of the source code on the Sybex Web site.) The IDE does provide you with hints on creating your own stored procedure, so you don't start with a blank screen. However, you'll also notice differences between the window shown in Figure 11.26 and the one you use to create a new stored procedure—the most important of which is that the stored procedure begins with CREATE PROCEDURE, rather than ALTER PROCEDURE.

NOTE   SQL Server actually relies on a language called Transact-SQL (T-SQL) to perform tasks. This language is fully compatible with American National Standards Institute (ANSI) and International Standards Organization (ISO) SQL, but includes extensions that make the language more flexible. T-SQL can help you perform many programming tasks in addition to manipulating data using standard SQL statements.

The example is contrived, but I created it to demonstrate a few new features. Figure 11.27 shows the stored procedure for this example. Notice that the SQL statements appear in boxes. Because the stored procedure can execute more than one SQL statement depending on the input values, there's more than one box.

FIGURE 11.27

Creating a new stored procedure means processing the input and creating an appropriate SQL statement.

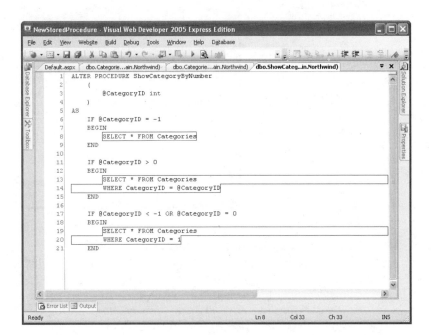

This stored procedure can take several routes depending on the input the user provides. For example, when the user provides a value of –1 (a value the CategoryID will never have), the stored procedure collects all of the records and passes them back to the caller. When the input value is greater than 0, the stored procedure returns a single record as long as that CategoryID exists, or no record at all if it doesn't. The stored procedure even includes an error handling mechanism. When the user supplied a value that can't exist in the table, the stored procedure sends the first record.

Now that you have a shiny new stored procedure, you'll want to test it. However, you can't simply assign a static value to this stored procedure and ensure that it works. The easiest way to handle this problem for testing is to add a textbox to the form and tell the user to enter a value. When you get to the Define Parameters page of the Configure Data Source wizard (see Figure 11.23, shown earlier), you choose QueryString as the data source. The change in the data source modifies the form, so you provide the control name (txtInput for this example) in the QueryStringField field. You can even define a default value when you want.

This example uses the FormView control, which displays a single record at a time as a form. To configure this control, you begin by setting the Choose Data Source field to the data source you created. Because the Categories table contains a Picture field, you have to edit the template. Click Edit Template. Remove the label and textbox associated with the picture. Because the FormView control could display more than one record, you should check the Enable Paging option. As an option, you can click Auto Format to choose a theme for the display. Figure 11.28 shows the output from this example.

FIGURE 11.28
The *FormView* control displays the output one record at a time as a form, rather than a grid.

Developing Stored Procedures with .NET

As described in the previous section, a stored procedure written with T-SQL can perform simple application tasks, such as comparisons, and manipulate data. Generally, a standard stored procedure provides all the functionality you need when you want to move the processing load from the client to the server in order to avoid the performance hit of moving large amounts of data over the network.

Most developers who work with T-SQL know that it's possible to perform many tasks, but also realize that T-SQL isn't a full-fledged language—it lacks basic support for programming constructions such as array and structures such as the for each loops. You won't find strong data typing in T-SQL and there isn't any way to create a class. In short, T-SQL is quite capable for many tasks, but it won't do everything as easily as a language such as Visual Basic or C#. That's where using the CLR support built into SQL Server Express comes into play.

Unfortunately, you pay a price for the flexibility that CLR provides. Creating a stored procedure that relies on CLR means creating a special kind of DLL—it requires the Class Library template. Because you can't create class libraries using Visual Web Developer, you need to rely on one of the other Express products, such as Visual C# Express. The coding technique itself can become relatively complex. You can see an example of the process in the DevX article at `http://www.devx.com/dot-net/Article/21286`. Another view of the same process appears as part of the Writing and Executing Your First Yukon CLR Procedure article at `http://www.c-sharpcorner.com/Longhorn/Yukon/First-CLR-Procedure.asp`. The bottom line is that this is a relatively complex process, so you need a good reason to use it.

Most small businesses will never need the functionality provided by the CLR support in SQL Server—it's simply overkill for the kinds of tasks that most small business perform. In fact, many developers find that T-SQL works fine for large projects as well. The only time that you really need the extra flexibility that CLR provides is when you need to perform complex manipulation of huge datasets.

Learning More about Stored Procedures

Stored procedures could easily require a book or perhaps two for a full explanation because you can do a lot with them. This section provides specifics on working with stored procedures with Visual Web Developer and a few hints about stored procedures as well, but you'll probably want to know a lot more about them at some point. One of the shorter (but useful) stored procedure tutorials online is the DevHood offering at `http://www.devhood.com/tutorials/tutorial_details.aspx?tutorial_id=49`. The author offers information at a relatively easy pace. If you want a longer basic tutorial, try SQL Server Stored Procedure Basics at `http://www.awprofessional.com/articles/article.asp?p=25288`. Another great tutorial appears as SQL Server Stored Procedures 101 at `http://www.devarticles.com/c/a/SQL-Server/SQL-Server-Stored-Procedures-101/`.

A number of sites offer short articles that tell how to handle specific issues. For example, the SQL Team.com site offers a number of stored procedure–specific articles including one on error handling at `http://www.sqlteam.com/item.asp?ItemID=2463`. You can find a list of undocumented stored procedures to use at SQL-Server-Performance.com (`http://www.sql-server-performance.com/ac_sql_server_2000_undocumented_sp.asp`). The MS SQL City at site also includes undocumented stored procedures at `http://www.mssqlcity.com/Articles/Undoc/SQL2000UndocSP.htm`, along with a wealth of other information.

Should you decide to use a stored procedure with an ASP file, rather than using ASP.NET for a particular solution, you can find everything you need in the Microsoft Knowledge Base article at `http://support.microsoft.com/support/kb/articles/Q164/4/85.asp`. Of course, half the fun of working with Visual Web Developer is that you have access to the resources that ASP.NET can provide. Consider this article an example of all the coding you'd need to do when using older technology.

Using Views

A view is a special kind of select query. It helps you create a particular perspective of the data in the database. Like a query, a view relies on a SQL statement to obtain the information. In fact, the editing window looks precisely the same as the one shown for queries in Figure 11.16. The big difference between a view and a query is how SQL Server Express works with them. Views provide a data perspective, a means of seeing the data in a certain way. On the other hand, a query requests something from the database—the concepts are the same, but the uses are different. The database also stores all of the views you create—a query appears as an external DTQ file. The following sections describe how to work with views.

Using the View Designer Toolbar

You'll see the View Designer toolbar every time you open an existing view for editing or create a new view. The View Designer toolbar looks a lot like the Query Designer toolbar described in the "Using the Query Designer Toolbar" section earlier in this chapter. Compare Figure 11.14 with Figure 11.29 and you'll find there are a few omissions from the Query Designer toolbar because you don't need to perform these tasks when working with views. The "Using the Query Designer Toolbar" section earlier in this chapter provides full descriptions of all the View Designer controls.

FIGURE 11.29
Use the View Designer toolbar to modify and verify the entries in a view that you create.

Creating a View

You can create as many views of your data as you need to understand it fully. To create a new view, right-click the Views folder and choose Add New View from the context menu. The IDE displays the Add Table dialog box shown earlier in Figure 11.6. Choose one or more tables, views (yes, a view can act as input to another view), or functions as needed. Once you select the input items, click Close. Now you configure the view just as you would a query. The example view contains just the Categories table—it includes all of the fields and is sorted by the CategoryName field. The example uses See-Categories as the view name. You'll find this example in the \Chapter 11\Views folder of the source code on the Sybex Web site.

After you create the view, you'll want to access it. Begin by placing a SqlDataSource control on the page. Select the Configure Data Source option on the Smart Tag menu to start the Configure Data Source wizard—follow the prompts to create the data source connection. One of the interesting parts about creating a view is that you can select it directly on the Configure Select Statement page of the Configure Data Source wizard. The Table or View Options field will contain the new view you created. Select the view and you can refine the selection, as shown in Figure 11.30.

Once you configure and test your view as a data source, you can create a means of viewing it. This example relies on a DetailsView control, which displays the data within a grid that you can configure in a number of ways. Begin by assigning the data source using the Choose Data Source field of the DataView control Smart Tag.

The control automatically configures itself to display any data that you defined for the data source. However, it doesn't always choose the correct presentation—as is the case for the Picture field. Click Edit Fields to display the Fields dialog box. The Selected Fields list shows all of the fields that the IDE provides automatically. You'll need to remove the Picture entry because the selection will display text—not a picture. In the Image Field folder of the Available Fields list, you'll see another entry for Picture. Highlight this entry and click Add to move it to the Selected Fields list.

FIGURE 11.30

It's easy to use and configure views as a data source.

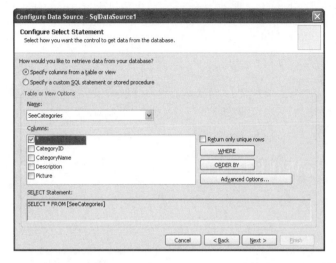

Interestingly enough, this control also supports templates. You can modify the header, footer, empty data entry, and the pager. Like many of the other controls, you can also use the Auto Format option on the `DataView` control Smart Tag to change the appearance of the output by adding a theme.

Using XML Support

One of the more useful additions to SQL Server Express is XML support. As you've seen in previous chapters, good XML support can be quite valuable for any Web site. Of course, you might wonder why someone would rely on XML files when they already have a perfectly good connection to SQL Server Express. There are a number of good reasons for using XML in place of a dynamic connection—perhaps you don't want the Web site user to see the live data or be able to access it through nefarious means. An XML file with regularly updated information provides much of the functionality of a live connection, but without the security risks.

The XML data might represent a particular view of the data that you don't want to maintain in the database. Creating the XML file from code as needed might be less expensive from a performance perspective than maintaining the live connection to a complex manipulation.

In some cases, the XML data might actually act as an input to the rest of your application. For example, you can safely gather user input in an XML file on your Web site, scan it for potential problems, such as scripts or viruses, and then add it to your database. Whatever reason you have for working with XML files, the following sections help you discover the connection between SQL Server Express and XML.

Creating an XML Index

SQL Server Express provides a special XML data type that you can use for a field. The XML data field can contain either a full XML page or an XML fragment. No matter what kind of XML the field contains, indexing it requires special techniques. The XML index makes working with XML fields easier. For the purposes of this demonstration, you'll want to temporarily add an XML data field to one of the existing databases such as Categories. Simply type the name of the field (this example uses `XML_Index`) when viewing the table definition and choose `xml` in the Data Type column.

Now that you have a new XML field, you can index it. Begin by highlighting the XML field. Click Manage XML Indexes and you'll see the XML Indexes dialog box shown in Figure 11.31. Click Add to add the new index, as shown in the figure. You don't have to do anything special to the index—it's ready for use.

FIGURE 11.31
XML data fields require special indexing through an XML index.

Using the XML Data Toolbar

The XML Data toolbar is accessible whenever you're working directly with XML data in the IDE. It includes features for moving between records with greater ease than if you have to scroll through the data manually. Figure 11.32 shows the controls for this toolbar. The following list describes each of the controls.

FIGURE 11.32
Use the XML Data toolbar to create, manage, and interact with XML data.

Go to Last Row

Create Schema

Go to New Row

Go to First Row

Create Schema Defines a schema based on the content and structure of the records within the XML file. A schema provides rules that maintain the integrity of the file and make it easier to important external data into a database table when both use the same schema. Generally, it's a good idea to use schemas to help enforce data input requirements when you plan to move data between XML and SQL files.

Go to New Row Places the cursor after the last row of data so that you can add a new row.

Go to Last Row Places the cursor at the last row of data in the file.

Go to First Row Places the cursor at the first row of data in the file.

Using the XML Schema Toolbar

The XML Schema toolbar appears whenever you work with an XSD file. The XML Schema toolbar contains features that make it easier to edit the schema. Figure 11.33 shows the controls for this toolbar. The following list describes each of the controls.

FIGURE 11.33
Use the XML Schema toolbar to create and managed XSD files.

Edit Key

Make Type Global

Zoom

Preview Dataset

Edit Relation

Zoom   Determines the magnification factor used to present the data. A higher zoom lets you see more of the data, while a lower zoom provides a better overview of all of the elements.

Preview Dataset   Displays the Dataset Properties dialog box shown in Figure 11.34. This dialog box contains a hierarchical view of the data elements within the schema. However, instead of presenting a graphical view of the schema, this dialog box displays the various element properties and makes it easier for you to decide how to work with the schema.

Make Type Global   Changes the entity from a simple to a complex entry so it can have a global presence.

Edit Relation   Displays the Edit Relation dialog box shown in Figure 11.35. This dialog box lets you modify the relations between various tables. The first table always contains the primary key, while the second contains the foreign key. The Key field contains the name of the relationship as it appears in the schema. You can also choose whether any constraints apply to just the foreign key or to both the primary and foreign keys.

Edit Key   Displays the Edit Key dialog box, which contains the name of the element and the key field. This dialog box also contains options for setting a primary key and defines whether the key is nullable.

FIGURE 11.34
Use the Dataset Properties dialog box to obtain a better view of the data properties of the schema.

FIGURE 11.35
Modify relations between tables as needed to show dependencies.

Defining an XML Schema

As your applications increase in complexity, you'll want to ensure that the XML data you collect remains secure. One way to improve security and maintain data integrity is to create a schema file. The best way to perform this task is to create the SQL Server Express database and associated tables first when you want to maintain a connection between the XML files and SQL Server Express. You can then drag and drop the tables onto the schema, as shown in Figure 11.36.

The IDE won't maintain any relationships normally found in the database—you must re-create them manually. Click Edit Relation and provide entries similar to the ones shown in Figure 11.35 to define the relationship between the two tables. The relation appears as a line between the two tables with a diamond in the middle, as shown in Figure 11.36. You'll find an example schema in the \Chapter 11\XMLSample folder of the source code on the Sybex Web site.

USING THE XML CONTROL

The XML control provides a convenient means of displaying XML data on-screen using XSLT without resorting to script. You'll find this example in the \Chapter 11\XMLSample folder of the source code on the Sybex Web site. The control is very simple. The DocumentSource property contains the name and location of the XML file, while the TransformSource property contains the name and location of the XSLT file. You don't have to do anything else to make this control work.

FIGURE 11.36

Create a schema by moving tables from the database to the design area.

Defining Your Development Goals

This chapter has demonstrated techniques you can use to work efficiently with SQL Server Express. The main idea is to think about where you want to process information to improve performance, reliability, and security. As your applications become more complex, you need to include the flexibility that these features provide. For example, a simple database application might not need a trigger, but you can bet that you'll want to use this feature as your database application grows. Of course, the big addition for SQL Server Express is the full XML support that it provides. Visual Web Developer users really need this support to create efficient Web applications.

Now it's time to play with the database. Try creating a new database, fill it with tables, add some views, and work with stored procedures. Database applications require that you fully understand how each of the individual features work toward a cohesive whole. Although you can build an application using nothing but stored procedures and a little glue code—the result is going to be inefficient because you aren't making best use of all the functionality that DBMS provides. Only by working with the various features can you discover how to use them with your particular application.

Chapter 12 explores the upper limit of what you can do with Visual Web Developer and SQL Server Express. No, you can't create the next multibillion dollar database for VISA with it, but you can create some impressive applications for a small to medium-sized business. The objective is to get close to the product limitations without actually bumping into them. For example, you can create an application that will serve the needs of multiple device types, and it's not even very hard. It's possible to create applications that incorporate middle-tier business logic. However, you probably can't create a very worthwhile application that spans multiple servers—at least not one that will work very well. Chapter 12 is all about exploring the limitations of Visual Web Express and understanding how they affect what you can do with the product.

Developing Multi-tier Applications

Many applications remain simple throughout their lifetime and don't cause their owners undo stress. Whenever possible, keep your applications simple—don't add gizmos that you really can't use. However, sometimes you do need some extra flexibility not only to make the application run better but also to keep the data safe and ensure that both the user and application follow all the rules. Complex applications that have multiple layers of support and business logic are multi-tier. Contrast this with single-tier applications (a simple Web page) or client/server applications (those where the Web page communicates directly with a backend application such as a database).

Developers create multi-tier applications for a number of reasons. Some applications are large enough that they require support from multiple servers—breaking the workload into smaller pieces helps create an environment where multiple servers can work well together. In some cases, multiple applications require the same component parts. For example, a database access routine might work well for more than one application, so there isn't a good reason to write the same code multiple times—breaking the code into tiers lets all applications access the common code. In some cases, breaking a complex application design into multiple pieces can reduce complexity—making it easier to code each piece rather than focus on the application as a whole. No matter what reason you have for creating a multi-tier application, the user interface, middle tier, and backend components must work well together to produce a cohesive whole.

Adding to the complexity of applications today is the need to support multiple device types. Most users now want to use the applications you develop on their desktop, laptop, Personal Digital Assistant (PDA), and cellular telephone. In addition, some companies use other device formats such as the digital notepad (see the Web site at `http://micro-wiz.com/warda/crosspadxp.html` for an example) and Tablet PC (see the Hewlett-Packard site at `http://www.hp.com/hpinfo/newsroom/feature_stories/2002/tablepc02.html` for an example). Some users expect computers to accept both keyed and handwritten input. Workers delivering goods might need a computer setup that looks and acts like a pad of paper. The point is that your need for a multi-tier application might revolve more around your need to support multiple devices than an actual application design requirement.

Binding with Middle-tier Objects

Most books on design divide the application environment for multi-tier applications into three areas. The user interface is the part of the application that the user sees. Actually, if you're used to the old client/server terminology—the user interface is the client—fat (normally a desktop application) or thin (normally a Web application), it doesn't matter. The middle tier contains all of the business logic, most of the security, all of the server interface, and even the server-side applications (such as data and event loggers). The backend normally includes the DBMS and any special software required to interact with it. You'll also find the backup systems here. Some large systems are now calling it a data store because they rely on exotic storage technologies to perform the task of managing data.

NOTE Visual Web Developer doesn't provide the capability of creating components. You'll need another language product such a Visual C# Express to create the .NET components used for the examples in this section. The only Microsoft language product currently capable of creating native (unmanaged) code COM and COM+ components is Visual C++ .NET. You can also create COM+ components using a language product such as Visual C# Express, using special attributes and construction techniques. This chapter describes how to create COM+ components using this technique. All of the components appear in compiled form on the source code CD (along with the source code should you wish to view it), so you don't need to worry about the actual component construction.

You already know that you can create a direct connection to the backend when necessary, but how about the middle-tier components that you might need to access? Fortunately, Visual Web Developer is also quite adept at creating these middle-tier connections. The following sections discuss the middle tier and demonstrate several middle-tier scenarios.

Understanding the Middle Tier

The middle tier is where you provide server-side resources that the client will use in connection with an application. The idea is to keep your data safe by hiding it behind the middle tier. When someone wants to access data on the server, they must run the gauntlet of server-side components guarding that data before obtaining access to it. However, it's important to think about the entire middle tier as a means of data hiding of various sorts. Most developers call the software used to create the middle tier, middleware. Generally, middleware is a series of components, rather than an actual application. Here are some of the tasks that the middle tier performs.

Security Ensures that the user has the required access. In addition, with .NET, you can determine whether the code has the required rights as well. Determining whether you have the right user accessing your site with the correct application is a significant way to improve security.

Calculations Provides feedback for calculated items. However, don't limit calculations to math—a calculation could be a date, time, or anything you want. The idea is that the middleware receives input from the client and uses that input to provide some kind of result. The reason that most companies perform this task in middleware, rather than at the back end, is to reduce the performance hit of returning the calculation. In addition, the middleware can restrict calculations to those who need them and accomplish the calculation based on the current application requirements.

Database access Creates secured and restricted access to the database. A direct connection to the database could mean that the user gains more access than a particular situation warrants. You might want to give the user full access to a table from a desktop application, but restrict that access from a Web application. You might go so far as to restrict access based on the user's current role. Middleware monitors that access to the database and frees up processing cycles on the database server so it can do what it does best—serving up data.

Data, error, security, performance, and other logging Monitors the system for unusual conditions, requests, or events. Many developers are afraid that users will see monitoring as a Big

Brother complex. However, monitoring has many legitimate and necessary uses. Checking data flow can help a developer create a better system setup—one more in tune with user requests. Logging errors tells a developer about problems with the application. Some forms of error logging can help the developer find and squash application bugs. Every Web application should include security monitoring—you never know when the bad guys will find a way in. It's also important to use performance logging as a means for checking system health—a good performance checking system can mean the difference between bringing an additional server online to save the day or watch the system crash due to an unexpectedly heavy load.

Redirection   Sends users to appropriate components to match specific needs or application loads. The browser that a user has installed on their system can make a big difference in the way they interact with your server—sometimes this means sending browser users to a component that can meet their specific needs. In some cases, you'll want to redirect user requests from a busy server to one that is less busy to improve application performance. Finally, you can use redirection for simple data hiding. The application loses track of the source of the information and doesn't really care as long as it continues to receive the data it needs.

Background processing   Creates a long-term processing session to let higher priority short-term tasks proceed. Sometimes a request requires many system resources to process and placing the request at the head of the list means that users with short requests have needless waits. Placing a request that requires a lot of system resources on the back burner means the short requests get processed in a timely manner, but that the long-term request is eventually fulfilled as well.

Creating Direct Connections

Many developers still consider the direct connection the best type to provide for the middle tier. Direct connection technologies such as Distributed Component Object Model (DCOM) and Component Object Model Plus (COM+) provide a stable communication medium with well-known features and functionality. Even though .NET component technology is newer, it offers the advantages of DCOM and COM+, with a few additional security features, such as code access checks added in for good measure. In addition, direct connections often provide enhanced security and use features such as an encrypted data stream to keep prying eyes at bay. Many developers also point out that direct connections usually provide higher performance than other connections, such as Web services, because they rely on various forms of data compression (Web services use XML, which is admittedly not very compact).

To create a direct connection to a local component, right-click the project entry in Solution Explorer and choose Add Reference from the context menu. You'll see the Add Reference dialog box shown in Figure 12.1. The .NET tab contains a list of components that appear in the Global Assembly Cache (GAC) on the local machine. Generally, you'll use this tab to access existing .NET Framework assemblies or assemblies used for multiple applications within your company. The COM tab contains native code components registered on the local machine. Remember that you must register COM+ components locally by exporting the COM+ application and installing the stub on the local machine. The Browse tab lets you locate components that exist on the local machine or even on a networked drive but that aren't registered. You'll normally use this technique to access custom assemblies that you design for use with one or two applications.

FIGURE 12.1
Use the Add Reference
dialog box to add
new references to
your project.

CREATING GLOBAL .NET CONNECTIONS

When you want to use a global assembly, highlight its entry on the .NET tab of the Add Reference dialog box. You can highlight multiple entries by Ctrl+clicking them. Click OK. For example, highlight the System.Data.SqlXml assembly and click OK. Visual Web Developer will automatically create a `Web.CONFIG` file for you, when your project doesn't have one already, and add the System.Data.SqlXml assembly reference shown here.

```
<assemblies>
    <add assembly="System.Data.SqlXml,
        Version=2.0.3600.0,
        Culture=neutral,
        PublicKeyToken=B77A5C561934E089"/>
</assemblies>
```

All of your referenced assemblies will appear within the `<assemblies>` element. The assembly reference includes the assembly name, version, culture (locale), and a public key token for security. The `PublicKeyToken` attribute is especially important because it identifies assemblies with a strong name—a prerequisite for inclusion in the GAC. (A strong name is a digital signature you add to the component—see the "Adding a Strong Name to the Component" section later in this chapter for details.)

CREATING COM, COM+, AND DCOM CONNECTIONS

Creating a reference using COM, COM+, or DCOM relies on the COM tab of the Add Reference dialog box. From a Visual Web Developer perspective, all three kinds of connections look the same. However, they're very different in reality. COM components exist on the local machine, while COM+ and DCOM components exist on a remote machine. COM+ relies on an installed stub for communication and actually relies on DCOM at a low level for direct communication, while DCOM relies on a configured setup.

To begin, you need to create the local registry entries for whatever communication technology you want to use. When working with COM+, the application you export provides all of the required information (see the "Creating the COM+ Application" section later in this chapter for details). When working with either COM or DCOM components, you'll use the RegSvr32 utility to register the component. Just type **RegSvr32 MyComponent.DLL** at the command prompt (where MyComponent.DLL is the name of your component and could have an EXE or OCX, OLE Custom eXtension, extension as well) and press Enter. You'll see a success message.

DCOM components require special configuration. Open the Component Manager console located in the Administrative Tools folder of the Control Panel and select the `Component Services\Computers\` `My Computer\DCOM Config` folder shown in Figure 12.2. This folder contains a list of all of the components registered on the local machine—not all of these component execute on a remote machine (in fact, the majority of the component execute locally).

NOTE   Older versions of Windows rely on the DCOMCnfg (Distributed COM Configuration) utility to configure DCOM for use. This utility works the same as the Component Manager console—just the appearance of the windows differs. To open this utility, select Start\Run, type **DCOMCnfg** in the Open field, and click OK. You'll see a list of components on the Applications tab that you can highlight. Click Properties to display a dialog box similar to the one shown in Figure 12.3.

Configure a component for use with DCOM by right-clicking the component entry and choosing Properties from the context menu. The example uses the Windows Media Player, but you can work with any component. You'll see the component Properties dialog box show in Figure 12.3. The Location tab is the most important for configuring the component because it determines where the component will execute. In this case, the Windows Media Player executes on a remote machine named WINSERVER. As far as .NET is concerned, the component is still executing locally—only this configuration change lets you use the remote component.

Make sure you check out the other tabs on the component Properties dialog box as well. The General tab contains the authentication level required to access the component. For example, if you're extremely paranoid about network communications, you can set the authentication level to Packet to ensure every packet provides authentication information. The Security tab lets you set access, launch, and configuration permissions for the component. The Endpoints tab lets you determine how the DCOM communication takes place—which protocols are used. Finally, use the option on the Identity tab to determine which credentials to use for authentication (interactive user, launching user, a particular user, or the system account).

FIGURE 12.2
DCOM components require special configuration using the Component Manager console.

FIGURE 12.3

Choose the location where you want a DCOM component to execute.

After you register and configure the component as needed, you can create a reference to it in .NET. Right-click the project entry in Solution Explorer and choose Add Reference from the context menu. This time, you'll select the COM tab. Highlight the component that you want to use and click OK. Visual Web Developer can't work with native code directly—it must use an interoperability layer to access the native code. Consequently, you won't see an entry for a COM, COM+, or DCOM component in Web.CONFIG—instead, the IDE creates a \Bin folder and places the interoperability module in there, as shown in Figure 12.4.

FIGURE 12.4

COM, COM+, and DCOM connections require use of an interoperability module.

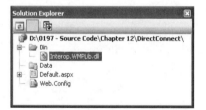

CREATING LOCAL CONNECTIONS

You can create local connections for either .NET or COM components. Local components aren't global—they might not be located on the local machine, but you haven't registered them for global use. To create this kind of connection, right-click the project entry in Solution Explorer and choose Add Reference. Select the Browse tab of the Add Reference dialog box shown in Figure 12.5. Notice that this dialog box accepts a variety of input types including DLL, EXE, and OCX files, as well as Type Libraries (TLB) and Object Libraries (OLB).

Unlike global assemblies, all local components appear in the \Bin folder—it doesn't matter whether the component relies on .NET or COM. The only difference is that the IDE copies the actual component into the \Bin folder for a .NET component, but relies on an interoperability assembly for COM components.

FIGURE 12.5
Use the Browse tab to locate local, unregistered components.

Developing Web Service Connections

Web service connections have a distinct advantage over direct connections. A direct connection requires that the client know about the server, know where the server physically resides, and knows enough about the server to make the connection. When you make a connection with a Web service, all you need is an URL. In both cases, you need to know about server security and you have to have an API to use, but Web services comes out ahead again here because using Web Services Description Language (WSDL), you can download the essentials of the API from the Web site. In short, Web services provide an enhanced environment for creating middle-tier connections.

WARNING The example in this section relies on advanced programming techniques that you can skip if you want. This technique is extremely useful, especially when you need to create components that work in a variety of environments. Using this technique, you can create one component that works with both local and remote applications. However, you don't have to master this technique immediately to use Visual Web Developer. In fact, you may find that you never have to use a technique quite this exotic to provide interoperability in your application.

You have many options for creating Web services using .NET alone, but you also have options for creating Web services using standard components. In fact, sometimes you don't have to create the Web service at all. The example in the "Using Google to Create a Site Search" section of Chapter 8 is really a kind of middle-tier Web service connection to a database—one that you didn't create but can access nonetheless. The "Managing the Application Using a Web Service" section of Chapter 15 will demonstrate another kind of Web service connection—one that you'll create to manage an application. In short, you have many opportunities to use Web services as a means of connecting to the middle tier.

NOTE This application works only on systems that have access to COM+ 1.5, which means that it won't work on Windows 2000 systems. It will work on newer versions of Windows such as Windows XP and Windows Server 2003. In addition, unlike other examples in this book, you must have Internet Information Server (IIS) installed to use this example because COM+ relies on IIS to create the Web service.

The example in this section provides a useful technique that works for more than one kind of connection. Your organization might have a number of older COM or COM+ components. In addition, you might want to gain the advantages of using .NET to create components that will work with both desktop applications and those that you create with Visual Web Developer. The technique shown here shows how to develop such a component, turn it into a Web service, and then access it from Visual Web Developer.

NOTE　You must have a copy of Visual C# or Visual Basic installed on your system to use this technique (Visual Studio 2003 or 2005 works fine). The technique relies on a special kind of class library project that you register and use from the local system as a COM+ component.

DESIGNING THE INTERFACE

Let's begin with the interface. You must create an interface for the class because COM and COM+ might not see the methods you expose otherwise. The interface must include two attributes: [Guid], which contains the Globally Unique Identifier (GUID) for the interface, and [ComVisible], which makes the interface visible to COM and COM+. You'll find that .NET automatically provides a GUID for you if you fail to include the [Guid] attribute, but you'll quickly find that this approach can leave your registry with tons of orphaned entries. Adding the [Guid] attribute is quick and easy, so it makes sense to use it to save time. Listing 12.1 shows the interface for this example. You'll find this example in the \Chapter 12\MyMathClass folder of the source code on the Sybex Web site.

LISTING 12.1:　Designing an Interface

```
[Guid("2D0B6B56-8572-4f25-8B13-E5CF81783E77")]
[ComVisible(true)]
public interface ISimpleMath
{
    Int32 DoAdd(Int32 Input1, Int32 Input2);
    Int32 DoSub(Int32 Input1, Int32 Input2);
    Int32 DoMul(Int32 Input1, Int32 Input2);
    Int32 DoDiv(Int32 Input1, Int32 Input2);
}
```

The interface just lists the methods that it supports. You implement this interface to build the component. The act of creating the interface provides a well-defined access method for the component that COM and .NET users understand equally well.

You might wonder where the mystery number for the [Guid] attribute comes from. Select the Tools ➢ Create GUID command and you'll see the Create GUID utility shown in Figure 12.6. (If you don't find this option on the Tools menu, you can also open the program at \Program Files\ Microsoft Visual Studio 8\Common7\Tools\GUIDGen.EXE.) Select option 4 as shown, and click Copy to place the new GUID on the clipboard. Paste the result into your code and remove the curly braces ({}), from either end of the GUID.

FIGURE 12.6

Define a GUID for your
component using the
Create GUID utility.

CREATING THE COMPONENT

The class comes next. You must implement the interface in your class to create the required linkage. Like the interface, the class uses the [Guid] attribute, but not the [ComVisible] attribute since the interface makes the methods public. The GUID that you use for the class must be different from the one you used for the interface. The [ClassInterface] attribute contains one of the ClassInterfaceType enumeration values. Always use AutoDual unless you have a good reason for using one of the other options (such as making the component available to only VB6 or only VC++ developers). Listing 12.2 shows the component code. You'll find this example in the \Chapter 12\MyMathClass folder of the source code on the Sybex Web site.

LISTING 12.2:   Define the Component Code Based on the Interface

```
[Guid("33933BDB-794D-4d3e-963A-D6FBCEE068E4")]
[ClassInterface(ClassInterfaceType.AutoDual)]
public class SimpleMath : ServicedComponent, ISimpleMath
{
    public SimpleMath()
    {
    }

    public Int32 DoAdd(Int32 Input1, Int32 Input2)
    {
        return Input1 + Input2;
    }

    public Int32 DoSub(Int32 Input1, Int32 Input2)
    {
        return Input1 - Input2;
    }
```

```
    public Int32 DoMul(Int32 Input1, Int32 Input2)
    {
        return Input1 * Input2;
    }

    public Int32 DoDiv(Int32 Input1, Int32 Input2)
    {
        return Input1 / Input2;
    }
}
```

Notice that this class inherits from the `ServicedComponent` class. This entry isn't too important when you want to use the component for COM or COM+ work, but Web services require it. What will happen if you don't include this entry is that COM+ will export the basic interface information, but won't create the required method declarations, so COM+ will appear to create the Web service and even IIS will seem to show that the Web service will work, but you won't be able to access the methods in the Web service. You'll find the `ServicedComponent` class in the `System.EnterpriseServices` namespace. Theoretically, you can also inherit from the Component class, which results in a less complex implementation, but can also introduce problems in using the Web service in some cases (the export isn't as precise as it could be).

The code for this example is purposely simple so that you can concentrate on the technique of creating the middleware connection, rather than the intricacies of the code itself. Any code that you normally use for a .NET class will work in most cases. However, there are special situations where you have to use the `InteropServices` namespace members such as the `Marshal` class to create a bridge between .NET and the Win32 environment. For example, when you want to pass a complex custom object, you need to marshal it because CLR won't know what to do with it.

ADDING A STRONG NAME TO THE COMPONENT

Creating the code is a good start, but you must perform one additional task—give the component a strong name. To do that, open a command prompt and use the `SN -k MyKey` command to create a key pair. This key pair signs the component to ensure that no one can tamper with it. You add the strong name to the top of the component (after the Using directives or Imports statements) file using code like this:

```
[assembly: AssemblyKeyFile(@"..\..\MyKey")]
```

Now you can compile the component. It's ready for use as either a COM or a COM+ application.

REGISTERING THE COMPONENT

Unlike .NET applications, you must register COM and COM+ components for use because the COM environment looks for component entries in the registry. However, you don't use the normal RegSvr32 utility to perform this task with .NET components; you use the RegAsm utility instead. The RegAsm utility has more than a few command-line switches, but you won't normally use most of them—they're for special purposes. The example component creates `MyMathClass.DLL`. To register this class in such a way that COM+ can use it, type **RegASM MyMathClass.DLL /tlb:MyMathClass.TLB** at the command prompt and press Enter. RegAsm will create all of the required registry entries to use `MyMathClass`. In addition, it creates a type library that you must have to add the component to COM+.

Before you make any changes to the code or recompile the component, make sure that you unregister the component from the registry. Again, you use the RegAsm utility to perform this task. In this case, type **RegASM MyMathClass.dll /unregister** at the command prompt and press Enter.

Using RegAsm is good enough when you want to use COM+ alone. However, in this example, you also want to access the component as a Web service. To make the component usable at this level, you must also register it in the Global Assembly Cache (GAC) using the GACUtil utility. Like RegAsm, GACUtil includes a number of interesting switches that you won't normally use. To register the example component, simply type **GACUtil -i MyMathClass.DLL** at the command prompt and press Enter. Figure 12.7 shows the results of using the RegASM and GACUtil commands to register the sample component.

FIGURE 12.7

Register the component that you want to use for a Web service and add it to the GAC.

Notice that the output from the RegAsm utility tells you that it registered the component types and that it exported these types to a type library file. If you don't see both entries, then the component registration won't work. Likewise, make sure that GACUtil tells you that it successfully added the assembly to the cache. The most common problem in adding an assembly to the cache is that the assembly lacks a strong name (see the previous section "Adding a Strong Name to the Component" for details).

Removing the assembly from the GAC is equally easy. Just type **GACUtil -u MyMathClass** at the command prompt and press Enter (notice that the DLL extension is omitted). Note that you must remove the component from the GAC before you unregister it, so the unregistration process follows the reverse order of registration.

CREATING THE COM+ APPLICATION

Now that you have a component to test with COM+, it's time to create the COM+ application. This is a two-step process. First, you create the COM+ application and then you add the component to it. However, when working with .NET components, you need to exercise a little extra care because sometimes the component will appear to register without problem, but you can't access the methods due to any of a number of errors.

To start the process, open the Component Services console found in the Administrative Tools folder of the Control Panel. Select the Component Services\Computers\My Computer\COM+ Applications folder. Right-click the folder and choose New ➢ Application from the context menu to create a COM+ application—you'll see the Welcome to the COM+ Application Install Wizard dialog box. Skip past the Welcome screen and you'll see the Install or Create a New Application dialog box. Click Create an Empty Application and you'll see the Create Empty Application dialog box shown in Figure 12.8.

FIGURE 12.8
Create a new COM+
application to hold the
.NET component.

Because we want to expose this application as a Web service, you have to make it a server application. Type an application name (the example uses COMPlusTest) and define an application type (it must be Server Application). Follow the rest of the prompts using the default options.

You're now the proud owner of a new COM+ application. However, this application doesn't have any components in it, so it won't do anything. Open the application and right-click the Components folder. Select the New ≻ Component option from the context menu. You'll see the COM+ Component Install Wizard.

The COM+ Component Install Wizard lets you add components to an existing application. Skip past the Welcome dialog box and you'll see the Import or Install a Component dialog box where you have several options for adding a component. Click Install New Component. You'll see a Select Files to Install dialog box. Highlight the TLB file created by RegAsm and click Open. (The example uses the TLB file located in the `\Chapter 12\MyMathClass\MyMathClass\bin\Release` folder on the Sybex Web site.) At this point, you'll see the Install New Components dialog box. Notice that it contains the name of the component and the component status, as shown in Figure 12.9.

FIGURE 12.9
Check the component
name and status to
ensure that it is installed
correctly.

It's important to check out this dialog box carefully because it can tell you whether the .NET component installed successfully. Make sure you check the component name to ensure that it's correct. Also, check whether COM+ found the interfaces. Errors in this dialog box usually indicate that RegAsm didn't work correctly (you had the wrong switches) or the component is missing one or more [ComVisible(true)] entries. Once you verify the entries, follow the rest of the prompts to add the component.

Now you can verify the COM+ application setup. Open the Interfaces, look for the ISimpleMath interface, and check out the methods. Your application should match the one shown in Figure 12.10. When any of the interfaces or methods is missing, it usually indicates some type of error in your code, such as missing [ComVisible(true)] entries or an invalid [ClassInterface(ClassInterfaceType.AutoDual)] entry.

FIGURE 12.10

Verify that the application setup is correct.

DEFINING THE WEB SERVICE

At this point, you could use the component using standard COM or COM+ techniques. That's great when you have a local connection, but what if you want to make this component available to someone who relies on an Internet connection? Microsoft has made it possible for users of COM+ 1.5 and above to expose a COM+ application as a Web service by making a few small changes to the application setup.

To begin the process, right-click the COM+ application entry in the Component Services console—COMPlusTest in this case—and choose Properties from the context menu. In the Properties dialog box, select the Activation tab and you'll see an entry for SOAP like the one shown in Figure 12.11 when you have COM+ 1.5 or above installed on your system.

To create a Web service, check the Uses SOAP option, as shown in Figure 12.11. Type a name for the Web service. Make sure that this name will make sense to anyone accessing the Web application because COM+ uses this name to create the required Internet Information Services (IIS) entry. The example uses MathTest because it's a simple descriptive name. Click OK.

At this point, you could run into a number of errors. The most common error is that you didn't register the component in the GAC. The second most common problem is that you don't have ASP.NET support installed on IIS. The \WINDOWS\Microsoft.NET\Framework\v2.0.40607 folder on your system contains the ASPNet_RegIIS.EXE utility that you can use to add ASP.NET support to IIS. This utility runs for several minutes, so don't become concerned about the registration time. Make sure that you restart IIS when you finish installing ASP.NET support. Another common problem is that IIS isn't running. It sounds odd, but IIS isn't always running on some development machines and you might not notice if you're not working on a Web project at the moment.

FIGURE 12.11

Only COM 1.5 and above users will have the SOAP entry available.

When the setup is successful, you can go to a special Web page for the application. For this example, it's `http://localhost/MathTest/Default.aspx`. This page displays a single link that takes you to the Web Services Description Language (WSDL) for the Web service. For this example, the WSDL appears at `http://localhost/MathTest/MyMathClass.SimpleMath.soap?WSDL`. Keep track of this WSDL URL because you need it to create a connection from outside applications to your COM+ application disguised as a Web service. This is also the time to check whether COM+ created a good WSDL file. Make sure you look for methods, as shown in Figure 12.12.

FIGURE 12.12

The WSDL that COM+ creates should show the methods you exported.

USING THE WEB SERVICE FROM VISUAL WEB DEVELOPER

The Web service created by COM+ is accessible from any outside source that has the proper permissions. Visual Web Developer is included in the list of sources. In fact, you can use this same Web service from the full version of Visual Studio .NET, or other language products such as Java or PHP. Web services provide great access to your code no matter what the other party is using.

To access the Web service, you need to create a Web reference. Right-click the project entry in Solution Explorer and select Add Web Reference from the context menu. You'll see an Add Web Reference dialog box. Type the WSDL URL for the Web service in the URL field and click Go. The Add Web Reference dialog box should access the Web service and display information about it similar to that shown in Figure 12.13.

FIGURE 12.13

The final confirmation that the COM+ application is accessible is the information that the Web service displays.

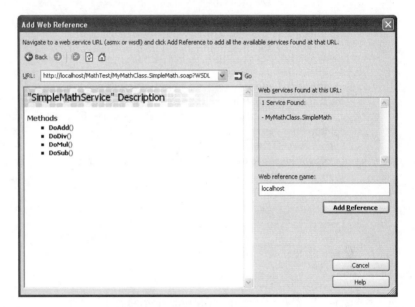

Click Add Reference to add the Web service to your application. Unlike local references, the IDE creates a `WebReferences` folder for a Web service, as shown in Figure 12.14.

FIGURE 12.14

Visual Web Developer creates special entries for each Web reference that relies on a folder structure.

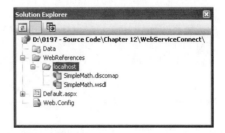

Notice that each server has a separate folder and included within that folder is the Web service entry, which includes a WSDL and a Discovery Map (DISCOMAP) file. The WSDL file looks precisely the same as the information shown in Figure 12.12. The DISCOMAP file contains a simple reference to the WSDL file so that Visual Web Developer can locate it again later, as shown here.

```xml
<?xml version="1.0" encoding="utf-8"?>
<DiscoveryClientResultsFile
    xmlns:xsi="http://www.w3.org/2001/XMLSchema-instance"
    xmlns:xsd="http://www.w3.org/2001/XMLSchema">
  <Results>
    <DiscoveryClientResult
        referenceType="System.Web.Services.Discovery.ContractReference"
        url="http://localhost/MathTest/MyMathClass.SimpleMath.soap?WSDL"
        filename="SimpleMath.wsdl" />
  </Results>
</DiscoveryClientResultsFile>
```

The DISCOMAP file is yet another form of XML used with Visual Web Developer. In this case, the `<DiscoveryClientResult>` tells the kind of reference that the DISCOMAP file contains and describes where to find it. The `url` attribute defines the remote location, while the `filename` attribute contains the local filename. Because Visual Web Developer creates the DISCOMAP file for you automatically, you should never edit it, but it's helpful to know that the file exists and how the IDE uses it.

Now you can create a Web form, add buttons and code to it, and test it. Before you can access the Web service, though, you need to add a reference for it. Here's the Visual Basic version.

```
Imports localhost
```

Listing 12.3 shows some code that you can use for testing purposes (the full example implements all four math functions). You'll find this example in the \Chapter 12\MyMathClass folder of the source code on the Sybex Web site.

LISTING 12.3:   Using the COM+ Application as a Web Service

```vb
Sub btnAdd_Click(ByVal sender As Object, ByVal e As System.EventArgs)
    ' Create the new Web service reference.
    Dim SMS As New SimpleMathService

    ' Obtain the output from the DoAdd() method call.
    txtOutput.Text = _
        SMS.DoAdd(Int32.Parse(txtInput1.Text), _
                  Int32.Parse(txtInput2.Text)).ToString()
End Sub
```

All you need to do is create an object based on the Web services class, SimpleMathService. This class includes all of the functionality required to interact with the Web service, including any custom methods such as DoAdd().

The next step is to use one of the methods to update the current application. In this case, the application retrieves two text values from the form, converts them to Int32 values, and passes them to the `DoAdd()` method. The `DoAdd()` method adds the values together and passes them back as an Int32 value, which the code converts to the string and displays on the form. Figure 12.15 shows typical output from this application.

FIGURE 12.15
The output of this application relies on middleware—a COM+ component on the server.

Understanding Limitations of the Express Product

Visual Web Developer and the other Express products offer limited support for multi-tier applications, especially those that have to service multiple device types. For example, to create a realistic test environment for a true multi-tier application, you really need to install IIS and that means changing the way that you work with Visual Web Developer. You lose many of the security features that Visual Web Developer provides with its built-in server, not to mention the extra overhead of working in this environment.

When you do want to create a multi-tier application, you must install more than one Express product on your system because Visual Web Developer doesn't allow you to create components. Consequently, you'll often find yourself switching between two IDEs while testing your application.

The use of two IDEs also limits your ability to debug the application. You can debug the component or you can debug the user interface, but you can't debug both. Because of the lack of linkage between tiers, you'll find that some debugging sessions don't net much more than frustration. Visual Web Developer works fine for simple applications, but you need the full Visual Studio Product to create complex multi-tier applications.

It's important to remember that Microsoft developed this product for use in small application development and for experimentation. Consequently, it's not surprising that Visual Web Developer lacks team development support and there isn't any way to add it to the product. When you find that you need more than one person to work on a project, it's time to move on to the full version of Visual Studio.

You'll even find a lack of some testing capabilities. For example, even though you can create XHTML applications with Visual Web Developer that include paging support, the product lacks an emulator (see the "Using the `ContentPager` Control" section later in this chapter for details). Unless you want to endure the complications of a real device, you need to install an emulator and hope that it works with the built-in Web server. In some cases, you'll find that the setup won't work. The "Working with Emulators" section later in this chapter discusses some capable emulators that you can use with Visual Web Developer.

Working with Multiple Device Types

Most developers have to face the prospect today of working with multiple device types. Users want to access their Web data using desktop, laptops, notebooks, PDAs, and cellular telephones. You can't even count on the kind of devices remaining constant—users frequently turn in their cellular telephones and PDAs to get the latest model. In short, you need a method of allowing access to the Web application that doesn't depend on a particular kind of device. The Web application should automatically accommodate whatever device the user attempts to use. The following sections describe this process in greater detail.

Understanding WAP/WML, XHTML Mobile, and cHTML

As a mobile device developer, you'll run into a wealth of new acronyms for specifications that you might not know about. This is especially true when working with cellular telephones because they represent one of the newest areas of application development. Sometimes it's tough to know which languages to pursue and where to find information about them.

One of the most popular languages today is eXtensible HyperText Markup Language (XHTML). The reason that this language is so popular is that it seeks to combine all of the previous mobile device presentation languages so that you have to consider only one, standards-based, language for your mobile device development. Unfortunately, the reality is that you must often support both older and newer technologies when working with mobile devices because some users will buy less expensive older models and attempt to access your application with them. You can learn more about this particular language at `http://www.w3.org/TR/xhtml1/` and `http://www.w3.org/TR/xhtml2/`.

Visual Web Developer provides support for XHTML 1.1. The use of this standard means that Visual Web Developer applications support most new devices and some older devices, but not all of the devices that could access your Web site. You can verify the use of the XHTML standard by creating a project with a `ContentPager` control and viewing the resulting `<DOCTYPE>` tag by right-clicking the Web page and choosing View Source from the context menu. Generally, you'll see a `<DOCTYPE>` tag such as this one:

```
<!DOCTYPE html PUBLIC "-//W3C//DTD XHTML 1.1//EN"
            "http://www.w3.org/TR/xhtml11/DTD/xhtml11.dtd">
```

You can create applications that support other standards using Visual Web Developer, but that means hand-coding the pages. Whether the additional coding is worth the effort depends on the project. When most of the people accessing your Web site use these older standards, you need to consider their needs. (Public Web sites should either check the client information of people accessing their Web site or rely on surveys to determine the kind and version of the browser that a visitor uses.) The rest of this section provides helpful tips you can use in gaining information about other mobile devices standards.

Two of the most important languages for developers are Wireless Markup Language (WML) (introduced by Nokia and Openwave) (`http://www.oasis-open.org/cover/wap-wml.html`) and Compact HyperText Markup Language (cHTML) (used as a source for i-Mode by NTT DoCoMo). These two languages describe the technique used to communicate with a mobile device such as a PDA or cellular telephone and therefore describe what you'll use to write applications for them. More importantly, these technologies present the starting point for mobile communications, and newer technologies tend to incorporate at least parts of these older specifications (not that the older specifications are out of use—new models come out that support them all the time). Fortunately, companies such as NTT DoCoMo, Nokia, Ericsson, and Openwave, part of the Open Mobile Alliance (OMA), do support XHTML, so these older specifications will become obsolete with time.

NOTE   The world of online development is in a constant state of flux. Most developers feel that XHTML will replace both WML and cHTML—articles such as the one entitled, "NTT DoCoMo Proposes XHTML as New WAP Standard" at `http://asia.internet.com/news/article.php/668041` tend to confirm that older technologies are on their way out. Other developers dispute this viewpoint, but you still need to consider your development options carefully. Make sure you consider eXtensible Hypertext Markup Language (XHTML) for complex applications with many elements. It helps you to display your application in segments with relative ease.

Many vendors use the Handheld Device Markup Language (HDML) (`http://www.w3.org/TR/NOTE-Submission-HDML-spec.html`) or WML because they're easy to understand. Both of these technologies use the concept of cards and decks to break up information into easily managed pieces. Of course, the mobile device that you use has to provide support for these standards (most older devices do) before you can use the tags within a document. Unfortunately, using any of these solutions normally prevents your Web application from appearing properly on a desktop machine.

You can obtain a wealth of specification information for WML (and other mobile technologies) at `http://www.wapforum.org/what/technical.htm`. It's surprising to see just how many WML specifications are already available online—make sure that you select the most current version of the specification when you do download it. The Wireless Developer Network has a tutorial on using WML at `http://www.wirelessdevnet.com/channels/wap/training/wml.html`.

One of the first places to look for cHTML information is the World Wide Web Consortium (W3C) site at `http://www.w3.org/TR/1998/NOTE-compactHTML-19980209/`. This discussion document helps explain some of the issues in using cHTML. A good introduction to i-Mode and cHTML appears at `http://www.devx.com/wireless/articles/i-Mode/i-ModeIntro.asp`. You can find an interesting article that explains how cHTML works, including example code, at `http://www.ddj.com/documents/nam1012432089/`.

Using the *ContentPager* Control

Creating an XHTML-compliant Web page will allow most devices to access it, but there's a problem to consider. Most mobile devices have small screens and limited display options. Trying to stuff a page that fits well on a desktop machine display onto a cellular telephone display isn't going to work. Consequently, you need some means for dividing the page into smaller pieces for mobile devices, while continuing to use the full capability of a desktop machine. Unfortunately, when working with Visual Web Developer, this means creating two sets of pages—one for the desktop and another for the mobile device. However, you can use a single Web page for all mobile devices, so the problem only involves a duplication of work at one level.

When working with a mobile device, the `ContentPager` control helps you create smaller pages with a minimum of effort. All you need to do is divide the page content into small segments and use the `ContentPager` control to move between them. Every mobile device will receive the same amount of text, so you need to balance the needs of very small devices with those that have larger displays.

To begin creating paged content, decide which elements will appear on every page and which elements you plan to display in sections. For example, a Web site header should appear on every page, but a section of content will appear on only one page. You also need to split content that appears in side areas from the main content and provide a link to it. Once you make these decisions, place the content that you plan to display in section in a container control, such as a `Panel`. Finally, place a `ContentPager` control at the bottom of the page. Figure 12.16 shows an example layout.

FIGURE 12.16
Section the output to
make it easier to display
on small devices.

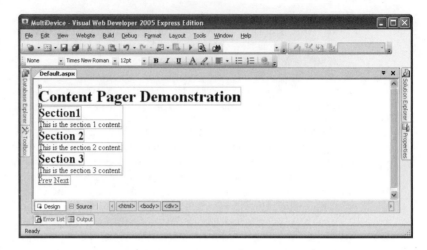

You also need to configure the `ContentPager` control. As a minimum, you must define the `ControlToPaginate` and the `ItemsPerPage` properties. The `ControlToPaginate` property contains the name of the control that contains the material to section—`pnlContent`, in this case. The `ItemsPerPage` property contains the number of items to display per page. The number of items is always one greater than the actual number of items because the `ContentPager` control adds a blank line at the bottom of the display. In this example, you need to include one line for the header and two lines for each of the sections, so the `ItemsPerPage` property contains a value of 4.

To see how this example works, you'll need an emulator. This section relies on the Openwave emulator (see the next section, "Working with Emulators," for details on downloading this emulator). Once you get Openwave installed and have restarted your machine, you'll want to test this product. If you installed the 6.2.2 version, all you get is the emulator. To start the emulator, select the Start ➢ Programs ➢ Openwave SDK 6.2.2 ➢ Openwave SDK 6.2.2 HTTP option. You'll see the emulator start. The emulator automatically goes to the Openwave test site on first use, but you can change that location by opening the SDK Configuration dialog box using the Tools ➢ Options menu. Select the Browse tab and change the Homepage field.

Unfortunately, Visual Web Developer doesn't know about the emulator. Start the application and you'll see the usual Internet Explorer display. Copy the address in the Address field to the clipboard and paste it into the Go field of the emulator. After a few seconds, you'll see how the page looks in the emulator. It should look like the display in Figure 12.17.

Working with Emulators

One of the problems that developers must solve when working with mobile devices is testing for multiple models. Because of this requirement, most developers turn to emulation software (a feature that Visual Web Developer doesn't have) to help test their applications. An emulator provides the equivalent environment of the mobile device that it's supposed to model. I stress the word *equivalent*, because most of these emulators don't provide a complete picture of the mobile device environment. You can rely on an emulator to tell you whether the application fits within the screen area that the mobile device provides, but you can't rely on it to tell you about memory issues or whether a particular device has a piece of support software you need. These other issues require testing on an actual device—something you should do for at least a subset of the mobile devices that you want to support.

FIGURE 12.17
Use an emulator to display the mobile device page so you can ensure it actually works.

Image courtesy of
Openwave Systems, Inc.

TIP   Keep apprised of the latest Microsoft mobility and embedded system developments at `http://msdn.microsoft.com/mobility/`. This Web site includes many of the links that you'll need to download the latest Microsoft products to make your Web Services mobile application development easier.

I chose the emulators used to test the application in the sections that follow because they provide a broad range of support, and you can download evaluation units. I also tested each of these emulators with Visual Web Developer—however, your experience might vary from mine, based on your system configuration. Here are the download locations so that you can get your copies of the products before you begin this section. The following sections assume that you've downloaded the software required for the installation.

- Microsoft eMbedded Visual Tools 3.0 (2002 edition): `http://www.microsoft.com/downloads/details.aspx?FamilyId=F663BF48-31EE-4CBE-AAC5-0AFFD5FB27DD` (full development package) or `http://www.microsoft.com/downloads/details.aspx?FamilyId=25F4DE97-AE80-477A-9DF1-496B85B3D3E3` (emulators only) or `http://www.microsoft.com/downloads/details.aspx?FamilyID=2dbee84a-bd94-4167-b817-2b2e548b2e92` (older full development version)

TIP   Because it's such a large download (205 MB), Microsoft provides eMbedded Visual Tools 3.0 (2002 edition) on a CD. You can order the CD to avoid the download time. In addition, even though Windows XP isn't listed as one of the supported platforms, developers find the product installs just fine on Windows XP. Make sure that you copy the CD key at the bottom of the download page when you do download your copy of eMbedded Visual Tools 3.0 from the Internet.

- Openwave SDK: `http://developer.Openwave.com/download/`

♦   Microsoft Smartphone 2003: `http://www.microsoft.com/downloads/details`
    `.aspx?familyid=8fe677fa-3a6a-4265-b8eb-61a628ecd462` (requires eMbedded
    Visual C++ 4.0) or Microsoft Pocket PC 2003 emulator for eMbedded Visual C++ 4.0
    at `http://www.microsoft.com/downloads/details.aspx?FamilyId=9996B314-0364-`
    `4623-9EDE-0B5FBB133652`.

Defining Your Development Goals

This chapter has provided you with some ideas for working with multi-tier applications, especially that all-important middle tier. Creating great applications often means dividing the applications into smaller parts to optimize the various code components. However, you must balance that requirement with the need to keep things simple—not to make the application any more complex than necessary. Increasing the complexity for most developers today is the requirement to not only create applications that work in a number of environments, but also on a number of devices. This chapter helps you balance all of that complexity while meeting the needs of everyone using the application.

Now it's time to put everything presented in the last three chapters to use. You now know that Visual Web developer can create relatively complex applications and support a number of devices. That it's possible to access any number of data sources and use the tools that Visual Web Developer provides to manage those data sources. Only you can determine how the various Visual Web Developer features can help you create robust applications that users can rely on. It's time to brainstorm some ideas, spend some time experimenting, and look at how Visual Web Developer can interact with the resources you have from other products to create a complete solution.

Once you have a complete application designed and partially developed, it's time to consider fit-and-finish issues. No one wants a drab application and Chapter 13 demonstrates some techniques for adding pizzazz to your next application. Yes, this chapter tells you how to use some of those processing cycles and other resources you saved by creating an efficient application to improve the user experience. An improved user experience usually equates to another kind of performance gain. Making the user more efficient usually nets better throughput than the best-tuned application can provide—of course, there's that matter of balance to maintain and Chapter 13 shows you how.

Part 5

Developing Full-blown Web Applications

In this section you will learn to:

- ◆ **Chapter 13: Designing Dynamic Pages with Pizzazz**
- ◆ **Chapter 14: Working with Client-Side Controls**
- ◆ **Chapter 15: Creating a Shopping Cart Application**

Chapter 13

Designing Dynamic Pages with Pizzazz

Most people like a Web site that has a little pizzazz—that something extra that dresses up the Web site and makes it fun to use. Pizzazz doesn't have to be an eye-popping array of snappy special effects that make the site unusable to anyone with any kind of special viewing need. Sometimes the subtle effects are better because they add a little surprise—one that the user can appreciate. For example, a mouse-over effect might not seem very exciting, but it's something small that the user will see and appreciate every time they use your Web site.

For many people, the concept of pizzazz goes hand in hand with what it does for them. Something glitzy that makes your Web site stand out attracts attention, but perhaps not the right kind of attention. However, a fully customizable site has a lot of pizzazz and it also does something for the user—it attracts the right kind of attention. Unfortunately, a one-size-fits-all approach won't work in this case. Some developers use hosted sites, others have setups that won't tolerate a lot of server-side processing, and still others need a level of customization that older technologies don't address. Consequently, this chapter provides several ideas on providing customization for your Web site, including both traditional client-side and server-side scripting, along with some additional Web Part techniques you can use. (All of these techniques require some kind of coding, unfortunately, but you still have quite a few choices.)

Depending on how you construct your Web site and the audience you're targeting, you might want to add various kinds of media to your Web site. Visual media presentations are the most common because they work even in a cubicle. Audio media is also popular, but it can cause problems in situations where quiet is the rule. In some cases, you'll want to combine both video and audio media to provide a movie-like experience for users. Of course, this technology also has some serious uses. For example, many tutorials benefit from the use of media, and you can use alternative media for other purposes as well. One of the least used forms of media is physical interaction. A good example of this form of media is a training site where the user provides input and the site reacts to that input. It's not quite the same as filling out a form because the reaction isn't the same every time.

Dynamic presentations are also important ways to add pizzazz to your Web site. Unfortunately, most dynamic presentations available today are cheesy advertisements for products of dubious quality. However, you could just as easily use these technologies to provide a tip of the day on your Web site or tidbits of interesting information. The idea is that dynamic presentations need not present just one kind of information—you can use the technology for many useful kinds of presentations.

Combining Themes, Scripts, and Other Techniques

Sometimes all the pizzazz you need for a Web site exists in technologies that you already know—combining these technologies in new ways can create the effects that you want. Chapter 4 describes how to use technologies such as master pages and themes. These two technologies can give your Web site a specific look. Chapter 5 tells you how to create a level of interactivity with the user. Sure, the interaction relies on form technology, but that might be all you need in many cases. Finally, Chapter 6 describes how to use scripts to accomplish a number of tasks. For example, using the `<Object>` tag might be all you need to display specialized content using a control that already exists on the user's machine. The sections that follow describe how you can combine these three essential techniques, along with other techniques described in previous chapters, to define a page with pizzazz.

Avoiding Pizzazz Overkill

One of the problems with learning a new technology is that you want to use it everywhere, even places where it doesn't make sense. A page with pizzazz often combines several technologies in subtle ways to produce a particular effect. For example, you might create a simple layout with an icon in the upper-left corner, a banner, a sidebar with a list of favorite URLs, and a main content area—it's a simple layout, yet it divides the information you want to present effectively. Add to the layout scripts that automatically change content based on user preferences and color based on a theme, and you have a page with pizzazz that the user will like.

Pizzazz overkill can occur in other ways. For example, you need to consider whether everyone can use the Web page that you design. A Web page that includes a lot of glitz or understated colors can cause more than a few problems. You need to ask whether a user that has scripting support turned off can see the page as you intended (even if some of the special features don't work). It's also important to determine whether the page is accessible (see Chapter 19 for details). Users with special sight, hearing, or cognitive needs will probably want to view your Web site as well, but a Web site with too much glitz could hinder their efforts.

Performance is another concern when you add pizzazz to a Web site. Every bit of pizzazz you add uses resources—consumes memory, hard drive space, processing cycles, and network bandwidth. The resources have a real world value, and you need to consider how much the pizzazz will cost. In addition, pizzazz has less tangible costs associated with it. For example, pizzazz increases the number of things that can break on the Web page, which reduces reliability. Pizzazz can also raise security concerns because it increases the number of potential holes that crackers can use to attack your site. In short, you have to moderate your desire to create a great looking page with the costs of creating it.

Using Layout, Themes, and Code Behind Effectively

Pages with a combination of layout, theme, and code behind support can provide a great visual presentation. You can create visual effects (see the "Creating Special Effects" section later in this chapter), add automatically updated materials (see the "Creating a Dynamic Presentation" section later in this chapter), or provide some type of media presentation (see the "Working with Media" section later in this chapter)—all with just these three technologies. The example in this section shows how you can incorporate some types of code behind in a manner that won't affect the presentation for users who don't have scripting enabled. Remember that many ASP.NET features automatically generate scripts behind the scene, so script support is a concern in some cases. You'll find this example in the `\Chapter 13\ThemeLayoutScript` folder of the source code on the Sybex Web site.

Begin by using the Layout ➤ Insert Table command to display the Insert Table dialog box shown in Figure 13.1. Notice that this dialog box already has the required information added. Make sure you set the number of Rows and Columns, along with the Width and Height fields. Add the Border and Padding attributes as well. The example provides a good basic layout that you can use for any task. The upper-right corner can contain a logo, the upper-left a header, a list of other destinations can appear in the lower-left corner, and the main content appears in the lower-right corner.

The IDE creates a layout that balances all four squares, which isn't going to work in most cases. What you really need is a layout that provides maximum space for the main content. The temptation is to precisely set the amount of space for each area, which means the layout is going to look perfect on your machine, but not for anyone else. A better choice is to set the space allotted for the upper-left corner as a total of the whole page, so the page sizes well, or to set the upper-left corner to a precise measurement, but not define the measurements for other areas.

To set the size of the upper-left corner, select the upper-left cell in Design view and choose the Style property in the Properties window. Click the ellipses in the Style property and you'll see the Style Builder dialog box. Select the Position tab and you'll see the positioning information shown in Figure 13.2. The two important settings are Height and Width. You can set them using a percentage of the entire page (as shown) or a precise measurement. Make sure you set just the Width setting for the lower-left cell as well. The width of the lower-left cell should match the width of the upper-left cell.

FIGURE 13.1

Design a layout scheme that will work well for your Web site.

FIGURE 13.2

Size the individual cells as needed to hold the information that you want to present.

One of the essentials of understanding this example is to know how various Web page features affect the event cycle. For example, the first addition to the Web page is an icon that the user can control. The icon is a representation of a feature—it can include anything that appears after the page initializes. To add a feature like this to your Web page, you need to add a DropDownList control to the Web page. Configure this control with the options the user can change. You also need to set the AutoPostBack property to True so that the user sees any changes instantly. The example has two icons that the user can choose for the upper-right corner. Changing the display is relatively easy, as shown here.

```
Sub ddlIcon_SelectedIndexChanged(ByVal sender As Object, _
                                 ByVal e As System.EventArgs)
    ' Set the icon according to user wishes.
    Select Case ddlIcon.SelectedValue
        Case "One"
            diIcon.ImageUrl = "~/Images/One.GIF"
        Case "Two"
            diIcon.ImageUrl = "~/Images/Two.GIF"
    End Select
End Sub
```

The code relies on a simple case statement to make the change. It simply changes the icon filename. Because the automatic post back also refreshes the display, the user sees the icon change immediately.

Not every feature is as easy to change as an icon or other physical feature. For example, you have to perform a lot more work to change the theme because the theme is set before the system initializes the Web page. The "Designing Your Own Themes" section of Chapter 4 describes how to construct a theme. You'll find two themes in the example folder that you can use for experimentation. This part of the example gives the user a choice—the ability to use either theme or no theme at all. You'll need to add a DropDownList control to the Web page and configure it with the themes the user can select. As before, you need to set the AutoPostBack property to True so that the user sees any changes instantly.

Here's a problem with some configuration changes. Because a theme change takes place before any control initialization, you can't read the controls—they don't exist at the time you need them. Cookies are likewise useless—they don't exist either. In fact, the only state mechanism that does exist (besides something like a database entry), is the query string. This kind of situation is where using the GET or POST method described in Chapter 5 comes in useful. Unfortunately, determining how to get the information to the Web page isn't the end of your worries. ASP.NET doesn't re-create the page every time it receives an automatic post back—it does that only when you create the page. Consequently, you have to create all of this functionality as part of a redirection back to the same page. With all of these requirements in mind, Listing 13.1 shows how to implement a page that has both a theme change and an icon modification.

LISTING 13.1:   Working with Theme Changes

```
Private Sub Page_Load(ByVal sender As Object, _
                      ByVal e As System.EventArgs) Handles Me.Load
    Dim ThemeName As String ' Holds the theme name.
    Dim IconName As String  ' Holds the icon name.

    ' Determine whether the query string contains setup values.
    If Request.QueryString.Count > 0 Then
```

```
        ThemeName = Request.QueryString.Item("ddlSelectTheme")
        IconName = Request.QueryString.Item("ddlIcon")

        ' If the query string doesn't contain a theme name, exit.
        If ThemeName.Length <= 0 Then
            Return
        End If

        ' If the query string doesn't contain an icon name,
        ' use the default setting.
        If IconName.Length <= 0 Then
            IconName = "One"
        End If
    Else
        ' Automatically return if there isn't a query string.
        Return
    End If

    ' Choose a theme setting based on the user request.
    Select Case ThemeName
        Case "Sunny"
            ddlSelectTheme.SelectedIndex = 0
        Case "Cloudy"
            ddlSelectTheme.SelectedIndex = 1
        Case "None"
            ddlSelectTheme.SelectedIndex = 2
    End Select

    ' Set the icon setting based on the user request.
    Select Case IconName
        Case "One"
            ddlIcon.SelectedIndex = 0
        Case "Two"
            ddlIcon.SelectedIndex = 1
    End Select

    ' Set the icon according to user wishes.
    Select Case ddlIcon.SelectedValue
        Case "One"
            diIcon.ImageUrl = "~/Images/One.GIF"
        Case "Two"
            diIcon.ImageUrl = "~/Images/Two.GIF"
    End Select
End Sub

Private Sub Page_PreInit(ByVal sender As Object, _
                    ByVal e As System.EventArgs) _
                    Handles Me.PreInit
```

```
        Dim ThemeName As String ' Holds the new theme name.

        ' Determine whether the query string contains a theme value.
        If Request.QueryString.Count > 0 Then
            ThemeName = Request.QueryString.Item("ddlSelectTheme")

            ' If the query string doesn't contain a theme name, exit.
            If ThemeName.Length <= 0 Then
                Return
            End If
        Else
            ' Automatically return if there isn't a query string.
            Return
        End If

        ' Choose a theme based on the user request.
        Select Case ThemeName
            Case "Sunny"
                Me.Theme = "Sunny"
            Case "Cloudy"
                Me.Theme = "Cloudy"
            Case "None"
                Me.Theme = ""
        End Select
    End Sub

    Private Sub ddlSelectTheme_SelectedIndexChanged( _
        ByVal sender As Object, ByVal e As System.EventArgs) _
        Handles ddlSelectTheme.SelectedIndexChanged

        ' Redirect the response so that it includes the
        ' required theme information.
        Response.Redirect("Default.aspx?ddlSelectTheme=" + _
                    ddlSelectTheme.SelectedValue + _
                    "&ddlIcon=" + ddlIcon.SelectedValue)
    End Sub
```

As you can see, changing a theme isn't nearly as simple as changing an icon, even though both of them require the same amount of effort during design time. The best place to begin this example is in the ddlSelectTheme_SelectedIndexChanged() method. The code calls this event handler when a user selects a different theme. Remember that the theme change can only occur in the Page_PreInit() method, but ASP.NET doesn't call this method except when the page loads. Consequently, the ddlSelectTheme_SelectedIndexChanged() method uses the Response.Redirect() method to create a new Web page that just happens to be the same as the one the user is currently viewing. Also, the Page_PreInit() method doesn't have access to any of the controls—they don't exist yet. The code overcomes this problem by creating a query string containing the current control status information.

When the redirection occurs, ASP.NET calls the `Page_PreInit()` method first to handle the pre-initialization event. Notice that the code first checks for query string using the `Request.QueryString.Count` property. It then extracts the current theme name from the `Request.QueryString.Item("ddlSelectTheme")` collection. When `ThemeName` is blank, the query string didn't contain a new theme name and the code exits. Setting the theme is the easy part; just supply a new theme name to the `Me.Theme` property.

The theme is set, but ASP.NET can't initialize the controls properly. The act of redirecting the page destroys this information. Consequently, when the page calls the `Page_Load()` method, it reconstructs the control settings from the query string using the `Request.QueryString.Item()` collection. However, you don't want to spend a lot of time performing an initialization if this isn't a new page, so the code first checks whether `ThemeName.Length` is greater than zero—if so, it completes the initialization. In this case, initializing the two controls is easy. All you need to do is change the `SelectedIndex` property value as needed.

This example also points out a potential problem. Notice that you also have to initialize the icon in the upper-left corner again. Remember that this is a new page, so even the icon information is gone. Depending on the number of controls you have on your Web page, the configuration issues can become quite complete, but you need to ensure that you reinitialize everything. Figure 13.3 shows typical output from this application.

FIGURE 13.3
Creating Web pages with configuration options, such as the ones shown here, adds pizzazz and also complexity.

Creating Special Effects

Many Web sites use special effects. They can add pizzazz to a Web site, while accommodating users that don't have scripting enabled in many cases. For example, if a user who doesn't have scripting enabled visits a Web site that has the mouseover special effect enabled, the only thing that will happen is that the user won't see the special effect. The information is still available, but with a little less pizzazz.

Mouseover with Internet Explorer and Older Browsers

The mouseover effect is one of the most common special effects that you'll find on Web sites. Whenever the user passes the mouse over a control or other page feature that has the appropriate code attached, the mouseover effect takes place. To create this effect, you actually need to track two events: `onmouseover` and `onmouseleave`, as shown in Listing 13.2. You'll find this example in the `\Chapter 13\SpecialEffect` folder of the source code on the Sybex Web site.

LISTING 13.2:   Creating a Mouseover Effect

```
<!DOCTYPE html PUBLIC "-//W3C//DTD XHTML 1.1//EN"
                     "http://www.w3.org/TR/xhtml11/DTD/xhtml11.dtd">
<html xmlns="http://www.w3.org/1999/xhtml" >
<head>
    <title>Special Effects Demonstration</title>
    <script type="text/javascript">
    <!--
        function HighlightControl(Control)
        {
            // Save the old settings.
            OldBackground.value = Control.style.backgroundColor;
            OldFontColor.value = Control.style.color;

            // Highlight the control so the user can see which
            // one is selected.
            Control.style.backgroundColor = "Blue";
            Control.style.color = "White";
        }

        function RemoveHighlight(Control)
        {
            // Return the control color to normal.
            Control.style.backgroundColor = OldBackground.value;
            Control.style.color = OldFontColor.value;
        }
    -->
    </script>
</head>
<body>
    <!-- These two hidden controls are used for the mouseover
         scripts. -->
    <input type="hidden" id="OldBackground" />
    <input type="hidden" id="OldFontColor" />

    <!-- These controls actually appear on screen. -->
    <h1>Special Effects Demonstration</h1>
    <p>
        <label id="lblInput" for="txtInput">Input: </label>
        <input type="text" id="txtInput" accesskey="I"
               onmouseleave="RemoveHighlight(this)"
               onmouseover="HighlightControl(this)" />
    </p>
    <p>
        <input type="submit" id="btnSubmit" value="Submit"
               accesskey="S"
```

```
                onmouseleave="RemoveHighlight(this)"
                onmouseover="HighlightControl(this)" />
    </p>

</body>
</html>
```

The code begins when a user passes the mouse over a control that has the `onmouseover` event defined such as `txtInput`. You generally won't use the mouseover effect for inactive controls such as `lblInput`—the effect shows the control that has mouse focus. In some respects, it actually helps make your page more accessible for those with low-vision needs, but generally, it's just a bit of pizzazz. The event fires and calls the `HighlightControl()` function. Notice that the code calls the function with the special `this` keyword, which refers to the current control. In effect, you're passing a reference from the current control to the function, which allows you to create generic functions that work for a number of controls.

The `HighlightControl()` function begins by saving the current control settings to hidden controls. You could also use a global variable to perform this task. The point is that you must save the data in some way because not every control has the same color scheme. For example, even if you use the standard colors, a pushbutton has a different background color than a text box. Notice that the control reference appears in `Control`. Unfortunately, using this technique means that you won't get any support from IntelliSense—you must know the various properties and methods that the control supports. The function ends by assigning a new color to the control background and text using the `backgroundColor` and `style.color` properties.

When the mouse leaves the current control, the control fires the `onmouseleave` event, which calls the `RemoveHighlight()` function. Like the `HighlightControl()` function, the `RemoveHighlight()` function receives a reference to the current control through the `this` keyword. The `RemoveHighlight()` function simply restores the original color settings to the control. Because the mouse can highlight only one control at a time and there isn't any chance that the mouse cursor can move from one control to another without firing the `onmouseleave` event, there's never a chance that you'll corrupt the control data by using a single pair of global variables to hold the old data. Figure 13.4 shows a typical example of a mouseover effect.

FIGURE 13.4
Mouseover effects can be subtle, but you can use any pizzazz technique desired.

The example uses a simple color change to demonstrate the effect of the mouseover. However, you aren't limited to color changes. You could use special icons, make sounds, or do just about anything else that makes sense for the browser environment. The basic principle is always the same. You handle the onmouseover and onmouseleave events so that the page can display the special feature and then remove it as soon as the user moves the mouse cursor.

Mouseover with Newer Browsers

The only problem with the code shown in Listing 13.2 is that it won't work with some newer browsers such as Firefox. Yes, it works fine with older browsers and Internet Explorer (all versions), but you won't see the mouseover effect in Firefox. Of course, this begs the question of why you can't simply use a script that works with Firefox. Unfortunately, older browsers don't understand the newer JavaScript coding techniques. Consequently, you're stuck building pages that pursue multiple standards, telling people with older browsers that the scripts won't work, targeting the older browsers, or focusing on one or two browsers and hoping for the best. It's not a very pretty picture and you shouldn't expect it to change in the near future.

To make a mouseover effect work with newer browsers, you need to enclose all of the HTML code within a <form> tag—controls don't exist without a form, even though you can see them in the various debugging screens. The newer browsers also don't understand the onmouseleave event used in Listing 13.2—you must use the onmouseout event instead (unfortunately, older browsers don't understand the onmouseout event, so you must include the onmouseleave event for them). Finally, you'll need to make some changes to the script—it's only a little more complex, as shown in Listing 13.3, but definitely more complicated than the simpler script shown in Listing 13.2. You'll find this example in the \Chapter 13\SpecialEffect folder of the source code on the Sybex Web site.

LISTING 13.3:   Using the Updated Mouseover Effect

```
function HighlightControl(Control)
{
    // Get the controls.
    var theOldBackground = document.getElementById("OldBackground");
    var theOldFont = document.getElementById("OldFontColor");

    // Save the old settings.
    theOldBackground.value = Control.style.backgroundColor;
    theOldFont.value = Control.style.color;

    // Highlight the control so the user can see which
    // one is selected.
    Control.style.backgroundColor = "Blue";
    Control.style.color = "White";
}

function RemoveHighlight(Control)
{
    // Get the controls.
    var theOldBackground = document.getElementById("OldBackground");
```

```
    var theOldFont = document.getElementById("OldFontColor");

    // Return the control color to normal.
    Control.style.backgroundColor = theOldBackground.value;
    Control.style.color = theOldFontColor.value;
}
```

Modern writers of JavaScript code can't get anywhere without going somewhere else first. Both of the scripts start by obtaining references to the controls that the script in Listing 13.2 accesses directly. You must use the `document.getElementById()` method or Firefox and other modern browsers will complain. The older technique of using the `document.all()` method should work, but the browser will complain about it nonetheless. Once you can access to the control, you can manipulate it much as you would any control—there isn't much difference between Listing 13.2 and Listing 13.3 in this area.

Presentation

Beauty is in the eye of the beholder, and nowhere is this truer than Web sites. In many cases, the artwork that a Web site provides can mean the difference between boring and exciting—the information is the same, but the presentation is different. However, unlike works of art that you see in a museum, beauty on a Web site is more of the architectural sort where form follows function. That's the point of the example in this section—a marquee provides important information to the viewer and a bit of pizzazz for the Web page. It's a functional architectural detail that you probably shouldn't skip.

TIP   You don't have to build all of the software required to provide a special effect on your Web site. Many third party vendors provide common special effects in easy-to-use packages. For example, you'll find a list of these products on the Advanced Presentation Tools Collection Web site at `http://www.jpowered.com/catalogue/specialeffects/`.

Many people are familiar with banner advertisements, which are essentially graphics with some intelligence added. The `<marquee>` tag is simpler to implement, yet you can dress it up in a number of ways. Fortunately, this tag seems to work with most browsers in use today. Here's a typical example of a `<marquee>` tag (the one used in the example).

```
<marquee id="ScrollTip"
         behavior="slide"
         direction="right"
         loop="infinite"
         scrollamount="5"
         scrolldelay="100"
         width="80%"
         bgcolor="yellow">
   This is the first message.
</marquee>
```

As you can see, the `<marquee>` tag provides a lot of room for customization. It actually has a number of other changes you can make. For example, you can attach style information to the `<marquee>`

tag to change the appearance of the information that it provides. The following list describes the special <marquee> tag features that you'll want to use to add pizzazz to your Web page.

behavior   Defines how the <marquee> tag presents the text. The slide option scrolls the text in one direction and stops when the text reaches the end. The alternate option scrolls the text between sides—when the text reaches one end, it reverses and moves toward the other side. The scroll option continuously scrolls the text in one direction—the text appears to scroll off one end of the display and reappears on the other end.

direction   Determines the direction of scroll, either right or left.

loop   Determines the number of times that the text scrolls. A value of infinite means the text continues to scroll forever.

scrollamount   Defines the number of pixels that the text moves per update.

scrolldelay   Defines the amount of time in milliseconds between updates.

bgcolor   Modifies the background color of the marquee. Using a contrasting or coordinating color can greatly add to the effect of the tag.

One of the complaints by some developers about the <marquee> tag is that it doesn't really change. Yes, the viewer sees the text that you want to provide, but it doesn't provide a resource for changing that text or any of the special effects. Fortunately, you can write a script that not only changes the text, but modifies the behavior of the display as well. To make matters even better, all of these modifications happen on the client machine automatically. Listing 13.4 shows a sample of what you can do. You'll find this example in the \Chapter 13\SpecialEffect folder of the source code on the Sybex Web site.

LISTING 13.4:   Designing a Marquee

```
function SetMarqueeFeatures()
{
    var SelType;     // Holds a random number

    // Choose a behavior.
    SelType = Math.round(Math.random() * 2);
    switch (SelType)
    {
        case 0:
            ScrollTip.behavior = "scroll";
            break;
        case 1:
            ScrollTip.behavior = "slide";
            break;
        case 2:
            ScrollTip.behavior = "alternate";
            break;
    }

    // Select a direction.
```

```
SelType = Math.round(Math.random());
if (SelType = 0)
    ScrollTip.direction = "right";
else
    ScrollTip.direction = "left";

// Set the scrolling.
ScrollTip.scrollAmount = Math.round(Math.random() * 10) + 5;
ScrollTip.scrollDelay = Math.round(Math.random() * 200) + 100;

// Set the message.
SelType = Math.round(Math.random() * 4);
switch (SelType)
{
    case 0:
        ScrollTip.innerText = "This is the first message.";
        break;
    case 1:
        ScrollTip.innerText = "Second message.";
        break;
    case 2:
        ScrollTip.innerText = "A third message.";
        break;
    case 3:
        ScrollTip.innerText = "The fourth message.";
        break;
    case 4:
        ScrollTip.innerText = "Showing the last message.";
        break;
}

// Set the timeout value for changes in appearance.
self.setTimeout("SetMarqueeFeatures()", 10000);
}
```

The page calls the `SetMarqueeFeatures()` function when the page loads using the `onload` event of the `<body>` tag. The code begins by creating a random number between 0 and 2 using `Math.round(Math.random() * 2)`. The first call to `Math.random()` produces a random number between 0 and 1. Multiplying this value by 2 creates a random number between 0 and 2, but it's a real number (one with a decimal) and not an integer (a whole number). The `Math.round()` function rounds the number as needed to produce an integer. The code uses the resulting random number to choose between one of the three `<marquee>` tag behaviors. The code uses this same technique to choose between a right and left scrolling direction.

The `scrollAmount` and `scrollDelay` property values are important because the user is going to see a change in the scrolling rate immediately. This particular change, more than most of the others you can make, will grab the user's attention every time the message changes, which ensures that user is at least aware of the messages that you want to provide.

The next task is to display a message, which relies on the same random number technique as before. The example hard codes several messages, which might not fulfill your needs if you have many pages with marquees and want to change the messages regularly. You could store the messages in an XML file or a database. The idea is to know how many messages there are and choose from them randomly as needed.

The final bit of code might look a little confusing at first, but it serves an important purpose. You use the `self.setTimeout()` function to time an event that occurs at a specific time interval. The event only happens once, so the example calls this function every time the marquee changes. The first argument is an expression—a call to the `SetMarqueeFeatures()` function in this case. The second argument contains the delay in milliseconds before the event occurs, so this example changes the marquee every 10 seconds. Figure 13.5 shows a typical example of a marquee that appears at the top of a page.

FIGURE 13.5

The *<marquee>* tag provides one of many presentation aids for Web developers.

Selection

One of the more interesting special effects that you can add to a Web page is also one of the more useful features. Any time you can provide the user with a suggestion about what to enter in a form, you'll find that you greatly reduce errors and improve the input you receive. Creating a form so that it automatically selects certain options based on previous user input represents one way to provide a suggestion. However, you don't want the form constantly changing its appearance either, so it's important to make the automatic selection timely. The best way to accomplish this task is to attach the selection code to the `onfocus` event, as shown here.

```
<label id="lblOption" for="selOption">Options: </label>
<select id="selOption" accesskey="O"
        onfocus="ShowPreference()"
        onmouseleave="RemoveHighlight(this)"
        onmouseover="HighlightControl(this)">
    <option>One</option>
    <option>Two</option>
    <option>Three</option>
</select>
```

The example in this section relies on input from the `txtInput` control. Type a number such as one, two, or three, into the text box and the contents of this drop-down list box changes automatically when the user selects `selOption`. The input and output of this example is simple, but you can create any level of complexity necessary. For example, you could even parse the input to locate specific bits of information that the code can use to make a decision on helping the user.

This special effect provides a lot of value, but it's not very hard to implement. Listing 13.5 provides an example of the code you'd need to include on your Web page to implement this special effect. You'll find this example in the `\Chapter 13\SpecialEffect` folder of the source code on the Sybex Web site.

LISTING 13.5:   Modifying an Input to Show the Preferred Response Based on Previous Input

```
function ShowPreference()
{
    // Convert the input to uppercase and then
    // choose an option.
    switch (txtInput.value.toUpperCase())
    {
        case 'ONE':
            selOption.selectedIndex = 0;
            break;
        case 'TWO':
            selOption.selectedIndex = 1;
            break;
        case 'THREE':
            selOption.selectedIndex = 2;
            break;

        // The default option occurs when the
        // user doesn't provide input.
        default:
            selOption.selectedIndex = 0;
            break;
    }
}
```

The code relies on a simple `switch` statement to choose between valid options. When working with a fixed number of choices, the `switch` statement is the best way to approach the problem. However, you'll need to choose a technique that best suits the result you want to achieve—in some cases, you might have to provide an equation or rely on data manipulation.

It's not possible to know how the user will type in the data you want to check. The best way to overcome this problem is to convert text to uppercase using the `toUpperCase()` function. Unfortunately, IntelliSense won't tell you that this particular function exists—it stops with the `value` property. In this case, you'd need to look at a JavaScript reference such as the one found at the W3Schools site at `http://www.w3schools.com/js/js_obj_string.asp`. This Web site provides a wealth of reference information that you can use when IntelliSense doesn't include everything you need.

A final bit of code shows how to implement the `default` case. Whenever you create a script like this, you should include a `default` case to ensure that the code chooses something. Otherwise, you could find that the code behaves strangely in some environments. Figure 13.6 shows how this particular feature works. Typing **Three** in txtInput and then pressing Tab to move to selOption automatically chooses Three as the value in selOption as well.

FIGURE 13.6
Automatic changes based on user input reduce the risk of user input errors.

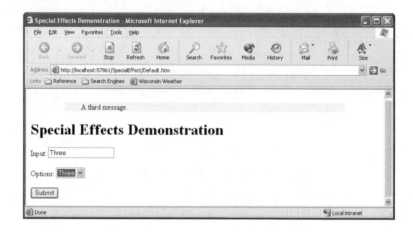

Progressive Input

Anything you can do to make the user's life easier normally reduces support costs and rework time for your code. Keeping forms simple and easy to understand is necessary when you don't know the experience level of the user. Consequently, creating a form that hides complex details unless the user actually needs them can garner a number of useful results. Not only will the user spend less time filling out the form, but also you'll spend less time answering questions.

This example relies on two techniques. First, you must hide the controls so that the user can't see them (or even select them). You can perform this task by using a simple set of style changes for the tags you want to hide. Second, you must provide a means for displaying the controls, but only when the user actually needs them. In most cases, you'll have to provide some kind of mechanism to perform this task. The following code shows how to structure the `style` attribute of tags to hide them completely.

```html
<p>
    <label id="lblSecondOpt" for="selSecondOpt"
            style="visibility: hidden; display: none;">
        Second Option:
    </label>
    <select id="selSecondOpt" accesskey="2"
            style="visibility: hidden; display: none;"
            onmouseleave="RemoveHighlight(this)"
            onmouseover="HighlightControl(this)">
        <option>A</option>
        <option>B</option>
        <option>C</option>
    </select>
</p>
```

Setting both the `visibility` and the `display` styles ensures that the user can't select the control or see it on screen. It's important to remember that the user can still see the tabs by viewing the source code for the page, but the tags won't appear on screen until the trigger event for displaying them occurs. You'll find these styles on the Layout tab of the Style Builder dialog box, as shown in Figure 13.7. You can access the Style Builder dialog box by clicking the ellipses in the `Style` property for any control in the Properties window.

FIGURE 13.7
Use the layout options to hide the less-needed controls on a page.

The second part of the task is to provide a trigger for displaying the optional input. Although this example only shows one level of progressive input, you can provide as many levels as needed to answer a particular need. Of course, too many levels aren't necessarily good either—at some level of complexity, the user becomes confused. Listing 13.6 shows the selection script for this example. You'll find this example in the `\Chapter 13\SpecialEffect` folder of the source code on the Sybex Web site.

LISTING 13.6:   Displaying Optional Controls Based on User Input

```
function ShowSecondOpt()
{
    // Determine whether the user has selected Two.
    if (selOption.selectedIndex == 1)
    {
        // Display the second option
        lblSecondOpt.style.display = "";
        lblSecondOpt.style.visibility = "visible";
        selSecondOpt.style.display = "";
        selSecondOpt.style.visibility = "visible";
    }
    else
```

```
        {
            // Otherwise, hide the second option.
            lblSecondOpt.style.display = "none";
            lblSecondOpt.style.visibility = "hidden";
            selSecondOpt.style.display = "none";
            selSecondOpt.style.visibility = "hidden";
        }
    }
```

The code begins by determining the value that the user selected from selOption. Always remember that JavaScript uses zero-based indexes, so the first option, One, actually has a selectedIndex value of 0. When the user selects Two, the code sets the style.display property for each of the controls to a blank string, which means the control uses the default value of displaying the control. The code actually has to set the style.visibility property of each control to visible to ensure the control displays as anticipated. When the user selects any other value in selOption, the code sets the two optional controls so they remain invisible.

Before this code activates, you need to add another event to selOption. The onchange event fires whenever the user changes the selection. This act calls the ShowSecondOpt() as shown here:

```
onchange="ShowSecondOpt()"
```

One of the elements you have to consider when working with code that modifies the presentation is interactions. Listing 13.5 shows a technique for modifying the selOption selection by changing the selectedIndex property value based on text that the user types into txtInput. That listing also has a potential for interaction. Changing the selectedIndex property value won't trigger the selOption onchange event. Consequently, you won't see the expected change. The easiest way to correct this problem is to add another call to the end of the ShowPreference() method, as shown here:

```
// Handle any change to the second option as well.
ShowSecondOpt();
```

Once you create the basic triggering mechanism and overcome any potential interactions, you can test the resulting progressive form. The big issue is to ensure that the progression is more help than hindrance, which means testing by users followed by a survey. Figure 13.8 shows how the optional selection looks when triggered by the selOption change.

Understanding the Ever Changing Browser Playing Field

Different browsers see pages differently, even when the page relies on ASP.NET. For example, start the Web Parts project in Chapter 6. Copy the address from the Address field in Internet Explorer and paste it to the Address field in Firefox (as an example). Figure 13.9 shows that the display is different, as are the requirements for using the page. For example, Internet Explorer displays a drop-down list box with a mouseover effect and automatic post back for changing the layout, while Firefox uses a drop-down list box and a separate command button.

FIGURE 13.8
Selective input is a helpful bit of pizzazz that reduces the complexity of forms.

FIGURE 13.9
Firefox and other browsers see ASP.NET pages differently than Internet Explorer.

The problem with this display is that it represents extra work. You couldn't write a single procedure for using even this simple page because elements like the catalog won't display the same way, or using the same steps in Firefox as when you use Internet Explorer. Because ASP.NET generates the code for you automatically, you also don't have any way of fixing the presentation. In short, you're stuck writing multiple operating procedures for the page—one for each browser that the users choose.

Pizzazz only works well when everyone has a level playing field—one in which the user can have certain expectations fulfilled for the browsers you have chosen to target for the application. When the only browser you support is Internet Explorer, it's relatively easy to create a user customization experience based exclusively on Web Parts. Unfortunately, not everyone is thrilled with Internet Explorer and the potential security risks it possesses. As an example, InfoWorld recently ran an opinion piece on the topic at `http://www.infoworld.com/article/04/12/03/49enterwin_1.html`.

Microsoft still owns the browser market, but their grip is loosening at little. According to a ComputerWorld article at `http://www.computerworld.com/developmenttopics/websitemgmt/story/0,10801,97754,00.html?source=NLT_AM&nid=97754`, 4.7 million people downloaded Firefox in its first month. Both the Mozilla Suite and Netscape increased their market share as well. In fact,

1 out of every 10 visitors to your Web site are probably using something other than Internet Explorer and there's good reason to expect that number to increase. However, this fact doesn't mean that developers will return to the unmanaged chaos of the browser wars era of computing. Browser developers are working harder to create standards-based products that work on the majority of Web sites.

The problem with using too much Microsoft gizmo technology on a public Web site is that you run into problems that you can't solve easily because you allow Microsoft to generate the underlying code for you. That's why you need to test your applications with several browsers and in multiple environments to ensure that they work well everywhere. You might be surprised to see how well the Microsoft code works as long as you don't test the boundaries of what it can do too much. In some cases, however, you'll still need to rely on direct coding techniques, such as using JavaScript, to ensure that the pages you create work for everyone.

Creating a Dynamic Presentation

Most Web pages contain a lot of static (unchanging) content. Even when the content changes from day to day, the content stays consistent during the entire viewing period. Dynamic content can keep users viewing the information on your site longer when used appropriately (and can just as easily drive them away when you make the Web site too dynamic). You create dynamic content by enforcing automatic changes to the appearance of the display. For example, the tip area could change periodically to show a new tip, even if the user hasn't changed Web pages. The following sections describe several types of low-cost dynamic content—the kind that doesn't require hours of programming and an investment in innovative technologies.

Using the Substitution Control

Imagine, for a moment, the cost of moving entire pages back and forth between the server to provide truly dynamic content. If you don't want to imagine that amount of wear and tear on your server, not to mention the resulting performance drop, then you'll want to discover the Substitution control. This control lets you designate a specific area of a Web page as non-cached (or dynamic). The rest of the Web page remains untouched during the session, but ASP.NET refreshes this one area to provide dynamic content that the user can see. The thing that sets this technique apart from other automatic refresh techniques presented in the chapter is that it doesn't rely on a client-side script—it relies on server-side processing, so you gain the advantages that server-side processing can provide, such as updates to database information.

The Substitution control provides only text output. Therefore, you can't use it to create an entire data form. However, you can use as many Substitution controls as needed to refresh just the text portions of a data form. You can also include tags as part of the output, so you could conceptually build whatever you want from standard HTML tags and create the output you want.

Before you begin working with the Substitution control, you need to set the Web page to use caching. The default setup assumes that you want to refresh all of the content every time the user requests a refresh. Generally, you want to refresh the content every time when working on the code for the project, but refreshing it every time on a production system wastes resources. Adding the OutputCache directive shown here solves the problem.

```
<%@ OutputCache Duration="120" VaryByParam="None" %>
```

The Duration attribute of the OutputCache directive defines how many seconds the system waits between refreshes of static data. In this case, the system will wait 2 minutes between refreshes. The

VaryByParam attribute tells which parameters to use to vary the output cache—the value of None is standard. You must provide both attributes.

Creating the function used to provide dynamic output to the Substitution control comes next. The example provides a static time output for comparison purposes as part of the Page_Load() event handler. This event handler outputs the time only for comparison purposes. Listing 13.7 shows both methods. You'll find this example in the \Chapter 13\Dynamic folder of the source code on the Sybex Web site.

LISTING 13.7:   Defining Substituted Output

```
Shared Function GetCurrentTime(ByVal Context As HttpContext) As String
    Dim Output As New StringBuilder()   'Output Data

    ' Get the User Name supplied as part of the context.
    Output.Append("User Name: " + _
                Context.User.Identity.Name + "<br />")

    ' Get the session time from the contentx.
    Output.Append("Session Time: " + _
                Context.Timestamp.ToLongTimeString() + "<br />")

    ' Get the current server time.
    Output.Append("Current Time: " + _
                DateTime.Now.ToLongTimeString() + "<br />")

    ' Return the entire string.
    Return Output.ToString()
End Function

Private Sub Page_Load(ByVal sender As Object, _
                        ByVal e As System.EventArgs) Handles Me.Load
    ' Display the static load time for the page.
    lblStartTime.Text = DateTime.Now.ToLongTimeString()
End Sub
```

The GetCurrentTime() method declaration is important. You must create this function as Shared as shown, and it must include the HttpContext input argument. The function must return a String value because that is the only kind of output that the Substitution control accepts. The IDE tends to produce unhelpful error messages at times when you forget any of these design requirements. For example, if you create the GetCurrentTime() method as Public, rather than Shared, the IDE will tell you there's an access error, but won't really help you fix the problem.

The Context object is extremely helpful—it includes a wealth of information you can use for creating the Substitution control output. For example, the Context object includes both Request and Response objects so that you can discover specifics about the client as needed. The code shows the User.Identity.Name property, which contains the username when the user logs into the Web page, and the Timestamp property, which contains the time at the user machine.

Notice the inclusion of the <br /> tag between lines of information. You can include any tags that you want in the output. If you want to create a table to display database information—there isn't any problem with you doing just that. However, you must create all output as HTML—don't use any ASP.NET tags because the system won't interpret them for you.

The code ends by obtaining the current server time and including it in the output. Figure 13.10 shows the output from this application. The static time—the time when the page is first opened, is a full minute behind the dynamic time. In addition, the `Substitution` control output appears on three lines because of the addition of the <br /> tags.

FIGURE 13.10

Use the Substitution control to output simple strings or formatted information.

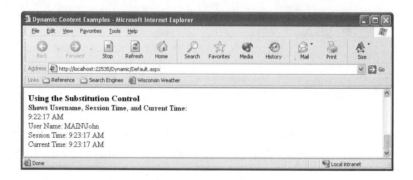

Using the *AdRotator* Control

Many developers view the `AdRotator` control as a means for creating click-through advertisements. It's true that you can use this control for that purpose. However, you could just as easily use it for other purposes. For example, you could use this control to display a tip of the day and point people to places to learn more information about the tip. An `AdRotator` control also provides an excellent method for making people aware of less-used content on your Web site or providing entertaining content (think joke of the day). Any rotating content works well with this control, so don't limit your choices.

You'll use a special tag to add an `AdRotator` control to your Web site. This control has only one essential attribute, `AdvertisementFile`, as shown here.

```
<asp:AdRotator ID="arAds"
               Runat="server"
               AdvertisementFile="Data/Ads.xml"
               BorderStyle="Groove"
               BorderWidth="10"
               BorderColor="#ffccff"
               Width="25%" />
```

The `AdvertisementFile` attribute tells the control where to find the content you want to display. This content must appear in a specially formatted XML file described later in this section. It usually pays to set off the `AdRotator` control in some way—the example uses a grooved border and some special coloration. Make sure you set at least the `Width` attribute as well so the controls take up the same amount of room across the display.

The special XML file is really just another kind of database. It includes one entry for every content item you want to display, as shown in Listing 13.8. You'll find this example in the \Chapter 13\ Dynamic folder of the source code on the Sybex Web site.

LISTING 13.8:   Creating a List of Display Entries

```xml
<?xml version="1.0" encoding="utf-8" ?>
<Advertisements>
    <Ad>
        <ImageUrl>../Images/One.GIF</ImageUrl>
        <NavigateUrl>~/Default.ASPX</NavigateUrl>
        <AlternateText>Back to this Site</AlternateText>
        <Impressions>80</Impressions>
        <Keyword>ImageOne</Keyword>
    </Ad>
    <Ad>
        <ImageUrl>../Images/Two.GIF</ImageUrl>
        <NavigateUrl>~/Default.ASPX</NavigateUrl>
        <AlternateText>Back to this Site</AlternateText>
        <Impressions>80</Impressions>
        <Keyword>ImageTwo</Keyword>
    </Ad>
</Advertisements>
```

As you can see, the example uses two entries that differ by the Graphics Interchange Format (GIF) file displayed. The root node for this file is `<Advertisements>`, which contains individual `<Ad>` elements. Each `<Ad>` element is an individual content entry, so you need to create one of them for each piece of content you want to display. An `<Ad>` element must contain the following entries.

<ImageUrl>   Defines the location of the image that the `AdRotator` control displays. You can use any common Internet display format including GIF, Joint Photographic Experts Group (JPEG), and Portable Network Graphic (PNG). The image can be any size, but you should strive for standard sizes to make the `AdRotator` output work better on the page. You don't have any limitations on the information the image contains.

<NavigateUrl>   Points to the redirection location. The user goes to this location after clicking the `AdRotator` control.

<AlternateText>   Contains the text to display when the image is unavailable. This text should describe the image so that people can understand the content you want to provide. Anyone using a screen reader also requires this content in order to hear a description of the image you provided.

<Impressions>   Determines the weighting of this image for display. The `AdRotator` uses a weighted random selection for images. Images with the same `<Impressions>` value have an equal chance of getting selected for display, while images with a lower value have less of a chance.

<Keyword>   Contains a keyword for this image so that you can track click-through events. The click information appears in the `aspnet_SiteCounters` table of the ASPNetDB database located in the \Data folder—setting `CountViews` to `True` tracks the number of times that the content appears on-screen, while setting `CountClicks` to `True` tracks the number of times that a user actually clicks on the content.

The default setup displays the AdRotator as a banner. However, you can change the AdType property to create a pop-up or pop-under window as well. Given the number of browsers that now include filters for both pop-up and pop-under windows, you'll probably want to use the default banner approach whenever possible. Figure 13.11 shows the banner content for this example.

FIGURE 13.11
The *AdRotator* has many uses that rely on rotating content.

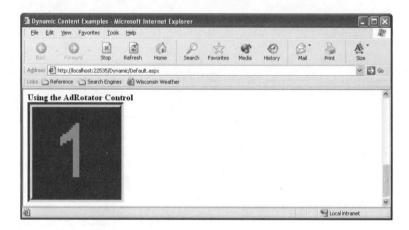

Working with Web Parts

Microsoft definitely designed some Web Parts for users. The "Using Web Parts to Automate User Customizations" section of Chapter 6 describes these Web Parts. You might not want to provide access to this powerful feature for novice users, but power users can definitely benefit from the functionality they provide. The Web Parts described in the sections that follow are more powerful—you wouldn't want to grant even power user access to them in some cases. Microsoft designed these controls to better meet the needs of administrators and developers.

Dressing Up the Web Parts

At some point, you'll want to dress up the appearance of the editors you create for the user. The style information appears as separate tags within the various zones, as shown in Listing 13.9. Each style entry affects a different part of the display. You'll find this example in the \Chapter 13\WebParts2 folder of the source code on the Sybex Web site.

LISTING 13.9: Developing Configurable Web Pages Using Web Parts

```
<asp:EditorZone ID="EditorZone1"
                Runat="server"
                HeaderText="My Editor Zone">
    <ErrorStyle BackColor="#FFFFCC"></ErrorStyle>
    <HeaderStyle BorderColor="#00008b"
                BackColor="#ffffcc"></HeaderStyle>
    <FooterStyle BorderColor="#00008b"
                BackColor="#ffffcc"></FooterStyle>
```

```
<PartTitleStyle ForeColor="#00008b"
                BackColor="#ffffcc"></PartTitleStyle>
<PartChromeStyle Font-Bold="True"
                 BorderColor="#00008b"
                 BackColor="#ffffcc"
                 ForeColor="#cc0066"></PartChromeStyle>
<PartStyle BorderWidth="5px"
           BorderStyle="Groove"
           BackColor="#ffffcc"
           BorderColor="#cc0066"></PartStyle>
<ZoneTemplate>
    <asp:AppearanceEditorPart Runat="server"
                              ID="AppearanceEditorPart1" />
    <asp:LayoutEditorPart Runat="server" ID="LayoutEditorPart1" />
    <asp:BehaviorEditorPart Runat="server"
                            ID="BehaviorEditorPart1" />
    <asp:PropertyGridEditorPart Runat="server"
                                ID="PropertyGridEditorPart1" />
</ZoneTemplate>
</asp:EditorZone>
```

You don't have to provide style information for every part of the zone, but it does help create a cohesive look when you do so. All of the part styles begin with the word *Part*, as shown. When you edit the <PartStyle> tag, you're changing the appearance of the part itself. The only odd entry in the list is the <PartChromeStyle> tag, which affects the outer area of the part entry. Think about the chrome on a car, it dresses up the outer boundaries of the car—that's what the chrome does for your application as well. Figure 13.12 shows an example of how chrome affects the editor display.

FIGURE 13.12
Dress up the editors you provide for the user once you finish configuring them.

TIP Many developers find it easier to work with the various zone settings from Source view once they create an initial design. Rather than opening each style entry separately in the Properties window, you can make all of the settings changes at once by copying the information from an existing zone and pasting it into a new zone.

Using the *BehaviorEditorPart* Control

The BehaviorEditorPart control helps you adjust a Web page for everyone's needs. This control lets you choose how a Web page acts in shared mode—the mode where everyone is affected. To use this control, you begin by adding it to an EditorZone, <ZoneTemplate> section as shown here:

```
<asp:BehaviorEditorPart Runat="server" ID="BehaviorEditorPart1" />
```

Listing 13.9 shows how the control looks in context with an EditorZone.

Of course, this is a powerful control, so you don't want to give just anyone access to it. You must adjust the security settings for Web Parts in the Web.CONFIG file for the application by adding the code shown in Listing 13.10 to the <system.web> section of the file. You'll find this example in the \Chapter 13\ WebParts2 folder of the source code on the Sybex Web site.

LISTING 13.10:   Authorizing Use of the *BehaviorEditPart* Control

```
<webParts>
    <personalization>
        <authorization>
            <allow users="MAIN\John"
                  roles="admin"
                  verbs="enterSharedScope"/>
        </authorization>
    </personalization>
</webParts>
```

Each user has a separate <allow> tag entry within the <authorization> section. To make this example work, you must change my information to match your information on your server. Once you make the change, you can run the example and you'll see a new BehaviorEditPart control as shown in Figure 13.13. To see this display, you must first select Shared in the Personalization Scope, choose Edit in Display Mode, and finally choose Edit from the drop-down list for a particular control.

As you can see, this control lets you change usage settings. All of these settings are Web Part properties. Here is a list of the properties that they change (the actual property name appears in parenthesis when it differs from the name the control uses on-screen).

Description   Provides a short description of the Web Part. The Web page automatically uses this information in tooltips, catalogs, and to meet other user needs.

Title Link (*TitleUrl*)   Provides a location for additional information about the Web Part. For example, you could explain the content of the Web Part and how to use it.

Title Icon Image Link (*TitleIconImageUrl*)   Contains an URL for an image used to represent the Web Part in the control's title bar.

FIGURE 13.13

Use the *BehaviorEditPart* control to modify the Web page properties for everyone.

Catalog Icon Image Link (*CatalogIconImageUrl*)   Contains an URL for an image used to represent the Web Part in the catalog of controls.

Help Link (*HelpUrl*)   Contains a link to the help file for the Web Part.

Help Mode (*HelpMode*)   Determines the mode used for navigating to the help file. The three common modes are modal, modeless, and navigate. When using the modal mode, the help opens in a separate window and the user must close the window before working any more with the application. When using the modeless mode, the help opens in a separate window, but the user doesn't have to close the window before working with the application again. When using the navigate mode, the help file opens in the current window and the user navigates back to the application window.

Import Error Message (*ImportErrorMessage*)   Contains the error message that the application displays when an error occurs during a Web Part import.

Export Mode (*ExportMode*)   Determines whether the user can export all, some, or none of the content of a Web Part. When you set a Web Part to allow export of non-sensitive data or all of the data, you must also change the <webParts> element in the Web.CONFIG file to allow export by adding the enableExport attribute like this: <webParts enableExport="True">. When you export the Web Part, the application creates a file with the WEBPART file extension. You can then import the Web Part into any other Web page that supports imports using the ImportCatalogPart control.

Authorization Filter (*AuthorizationFilter*)   Determines whether a user can add a Web Part to a page. Normally, this entry is blank so a user can add any Web Part as long as the user has proper permission and the Web page has the correct features enabled. However, you can set this value so the `WebPartManager` will check the Web Part for the specified string before it imports the Web Part. In short, this filter lets you control which Web Parts a user can add to a Web page without disabling the feature.

Allow Close (*AllowClose*)   Determines whether a user can close a Web Part.

Allow Connect (*AllowConnect*)   Determines whether the Web Part will allow other controls to form a connection with it for data exchange or other programmatic needs.

Allow Edit (*AllowEdit*)   Determines whether the user can edit the content of the Web Part.

Allow Hide (*AllowHide*)   Determines whether the user can hide the Web Part from view.

Allow Minimize (*AllowMinimize*)   Determines whether the user can minimize the Web Part.

Allow Zone Change (*AllowZoneChange*)   Determines whether the user can move a Web Part between zones.

Using the *DeclarativeCatalogPart* and *ImportCatalogPart* Controls

The `DeclarativeCatalogPart` and `ImportCatalogPart` controls represent two alternative methods of letting a user add content to a Web page. When working with the `DeclarativeCatalogPart` control, you create a list of useful, but optional controls to display on-screen. The `ImportCatalogPart` control lets the user import a new Web Part and place it on-screen. In both cases, the Web Part isn't part of the standard page and won't appear as part of a `PageCatalogPart` control as described in the "Adding New Items with the `CatalogZone`" section of Chapter 6.

Adding the `ImportCatalogPart` control is easiest. All you need to do is add the control to the page like this:

```
<asp:ImportCatalogPart ID="ImportCatalogPart1" runat="server" />
```

When the user opens the Web page and requests a catalog addition, they'll see an Imported Web Part Catalog section like the one shown in Figure 13.14. The user clicks Browse to display a Choose File dialog box and locate a file with a `.WEBPART` extension. Once the user selects the file, they'll see one or more Web Parts listed in the Imported Web Part list as shown in Figure 13.14. The user selects the Web Part and adds it to the display as normal.

The `DeclarativeCatalogPart` control requires a little more work. You must define the optional controls as part of the Web page. Listing 13.11 shows a typical example of the entries for a `DeclarativeCatalogPart` control. You'll find this example in the `\Chapter 13\WebParts2` folder of the source code on the Sybex Web site.

FIGURE 13.14
Importing Web Parts lets a user create a truly customized Web page.

LISTING 13.11:   Adding a *DeclarativeCatalogPart* Control to a Web Page

```
<asp:DeclarativeCatalogPart ID="DeclarativeCatalogPart1"
                            runat="server">
    <WebPartsTemplate>
        <asp:HyperLink ID="lnkSpecial"
                       Title="Special Hyperlink"
                       runat="server">
            The Special Link
        </asp:HyperLink><br />
        <asp:Label ID="lblSpecial"
                   Title="Special Label"
                   runat="server"
                   Text="The Special Label">
        </asp:Label>
    </WebPartsTemplate>
</asp:DeclarativeCatalogPart>
```

You can add any kind of control to this Web Part that you can add to a `PageCatalogPart` control. In addition, the user chooses the Web Part and adds it to the Web page as with the `PageCatalogPart` control. The main difference between the two controls is how the `WebPartManager` controls them. The `DeclarativeCatalogPart` control supplies what amounts to optional controls that you might not want every user to access.

Understanding How Much Customization to Provide

After working with the Web Parts examples in Chapter 6 and the additional examples in this chapter, you might think that users could spend all of their time rearranging page elements and not getting much work done. You could be correct. In fact, some users play around with the controls so much that their Web page become pretty much useless and you'll find that you spend too much time getting their Web page back into a usable state. In short, it's easy to provide too many customization features when using Web Parts, so you have to plan the page carefully.

The first concept to include in your plan is that you don't have to let the user customize everything—even if they ask for that right. Every Web page contains some material that the user will need no matter what they want to do with it. If the Web page is devoid of such content, you might want to ask whether you really need it. Consequently, make sure you identify any content that the user must have to use the page and exempt it from customization (or at least removal from the screen).

You also need to consider the experience level of the user. It's important to keep powerful controls out of the hands of novices who will have no idea of how to use them. In fact, you should consider whether some power users need all of the features that Web Parts could provide. To ensure that everyone gets the features they need, you need to either create separate pages (hard to maintain) or program the access based on the login user (difficult to write for bulletproof access). Generally, you should probably provide a user page and an administrator page to separate the two levels of controls at least.

Working with Media

Users once frowned on media because of the cheesy presentations assaulting them from their browser window—usually at the worst possible time. As developers become better at incorporating media in a workplace-sensitive manner and the need to present information, such as training sessions, that doesn't quite meet the text presentation that most Web sites use increases, so does the use of media. It's possible to create all kinds of different media—everything from static graphic animations to live presentations. This section discusses a few of the common media types that you can use to add pizzazz to your Web site.

NOTE   The available graphic formats for Web pages increases almost daily as developers discover new ways to present them. For example, Scalable Vector Graphics (SVG) rely on XML to store the data required to construction three-dimensional (3D) images on screen based on equations. The graphics have infinite resolution because they're based on vectors, rather than pixels. Of course, it also requires more time to process such an image because the browser has to re-create it for every request. Engineering and other graphics-intensive Web sites use SVG because standard graphics simply can't meet their needs. You can learn more about this technology at `http://www.w3.org/Graphics/SVG/`. Some companies, such as Adobe (`http://www.adobe.com/svg/main.html`) are also heavily involved in SVG research.

Media Uses

Media has many uses on the Internet. What was once a toy has become a tool as developers begin adding media for use in marketing products and as a means for making training more effective. In addition, major news stations now include video and sound on their Web sites to get the news across to a broader audience. Many corporations are also making use of media, as witnessed by the many media presentations that Microsoft is making available to developers. Good media can enhance content and make a boring Web site a joy to use. Generally, the best media enhances the user experience in some way. It helps the user understand a topic better than pure text can do. Here are some ways that you can use media to create a more effective Web site.

Training   Using video, sound, and static pictures can create a more effective training Web site. Users can see and hear the techniques they're supposed to learn, making the training better (people learn better when they experience a topic in more ways). In addition, the training takes on a human appearance. Instead of interacting with a computer, the person interacts with a trainer who just happens to appear on the computer.

Entertainment   Media can provide entertainment. For example, you could provide access to the video that you took of your vacation last year. Quite a few Web sites offer animated GIFs—those little graphics that provide a bit of a sparkle for any Web site. One of the more interesting places to find animated GIFs is the Webdeveloper.com Web site at `http://www.webdeveloper.com/animations/`. Another interesting place to look is Animation Factory at `http://www.animationfactory.com/animations/`. However, don't limit yourself because there are literally thousands of Web sites that offer free graphics.

Nonverbal information   Some topics don't lend themselves to easy description in text. For example, trying to explain precisely how a particular bird sounds is going to be hard when the user doesn't have the same frame of reference that you do. Both of you would have to have the same understanding of the sounds that birds make and even then, it would be hard. However, a simple audio file can say everything that the words can't.

Presentations   It doesn't matter what kind of presentation you want to make, most presentations work better when you include various kinds of media. Even a simple slideshow containing charts, graphs, and other information that backs up any claims you make can be very helpful. One place that can provide an interesting perspective on presentations used as advertisements is AdCritic at `http://www.adcritic.com`. If nothing else, you'll discover what other people have done incorrectly so you can avoid making the same mistakes.

Sometimes media can also cause problems. For example, imagine that you're sitting in a cubicle at work and everything is relatively quiet. Suddenly, you stumble on a Web site that plays marching music. The Web site has not only embarrassed you, but also disturbed everyone else in the office. The Web site developer could have avoided this problem by making the media optional—something that the user had to activate manually as a matter of choice. Generally, you want to make a Web site media optional unless you know that the user is expecting media of some type.

One rule of thumb to remember is that the more media you include on your Web site, the more platform-specific it becomes. Making a Web site platform-specific isn't a big problem when you know which browsers users will have installed on their system, but it's nearly impossible to determine this kind of information for a public Web site. Less platform-specific is better because more people can visit and enjoy your Web site. Most media makes Web sites platform-specific in one or more of the following ways.

Browser variances   Every browser has specific features that it supports, but not every browser supports every feature. Consequently, you might use a media tag that works well on one browser, but not on another. In addition, even when two browsers provide the same feature support, they'll likely support it in different ways, which means that the media might not look as expected on every system.

Plug-in problems   Some types of media require use of plug-ins—extra bits of code that you ask the user to add to a browser. For example, when you use RealAudio, you need a plug-in to hear the sounds that the data stream obtains for you. Not every add-in supports every browser. Consequently, you might lock some browser users out by simply choosing the wrong plug-in to implement the media you want to provide.

Client-side scripting   In some cases, you can implement media use through a client-side script. The script might support an add-in or object, or it might provide standalone functionality. In either case, the fact that many browsers don't provide full scripting support means that users of these browsers won't be able to enjoy the media you provide. This problem is especially worrisome when using Java applets because Internet Explorer 6 users have to download a Java runtime in order to use Java. Considering the Internet Explorer 6 share of the market, you could end up locking out many people.

Animated GIFs

The animated GIF file is the oldest form of animation on the Internet. You've probably seen the animated GIF on more than one Web site because it's very common. The little cartoon characters, twirling banners, and exploding stars that you see on various Web sites are probably animated GIFs.

TIP   It often helps to look at other people's animated GIFs as you create your own for ideas they might have used. To verify that an image on a Web page is an animated GIF from Internet Explorer, right-click the image and choose Properties from the context menu. You'll see the location and name of the image on the host system—any image that has a file extension of GIF and has an animated effect is an animated GIF. To save the image to your hard drive for better viewing, right-click the image and choose Save Picture As from the context menu. When you see the Save Picture dialog box, choose a location to save the image and click Save.

An animated GIF contains a series of still images that the browser plays back at the speed determined by the developer. You can add a number of special effects to GIFs and optimize them for size and playing speed. Most browsers do support this form of animation. The tools for creating an animated GIF are readily available and you can get some tools for little to no cost. Consequently, most developers experiment with this form of animation first.

Visual Web Developer supports animated GIF files, but it doesn't provide the tools required to create an animated GIF. To create an animated GIF, you need a drawing program to create the individual frames of the animation program and a program to put them together into a single file. One of the better products available on the market for creating animated GIF files is the GIF Construction Set from Alchemy Mindworks (`http://www.mindworkshop.com/alchemy/gifcon.html`). This product is shareware, so you can try it before you buy it. Figure 13.15 shows a typical editing session with this product. You'll find this example in the `\Chapter 13\Media\Images\Animated Graphic` folder of the source code on the Sybex Web site.

FIGURE 13.15

Create a series of frames and tell the browser how to display them.

On the left side of the display is a series of frames. The browser displays these frames one after the other. You add frames using the Edit ➤ Insert Block ➤ Image command. Double-click an image and you see the Edit Image dialog box on the right side of Figure 13.15. Notice that the Control Block field is checked and that the Delay field is set to 1. This is how you control the display time for each frame in your animation.

Placing an animated GIF on a Web page is relatively easy. All you need to do is find the image in Solution Explorer and drag it to the Design view. Visual Web Developer will create an `<img>` tag for you. It's important to configure the `<img>` tag for optimal display and to provide information for users who can't see the image on screen. Here's a typical `<img>` tag configuration for an animated GIF that you want to run continuously. (You'll find this example in the `\Chapter 13\Media\` folder of the source code on the Sybex Web site.)

```
<img border="1"
    src="Images/Animated%20Graphic/AnimatedTime.gif"
    width="90"
    height="90"
    alt="This is an animated GIF of a clock where the minute hand
        moves.  The clock has a red back with yellow hands and a
        yellow background.">
```

The use of an `<img>` tag points to the success of the animated GIF. Even when a browser doesn't provide the required support, which is rare, the use of this standard tag lets the user see the first frame of the animated GIF, so the Web page doesn't look bare. Consequently, always make the first frame of your animated GIF something that can stand alone so the user sees something useful even when the animation isn't available.

Sometimes you don't want the animated GIF to run continuously. You can add the `loop` attribute to the `<img>` tag to let the image animate for a set number of times and then stop. Figure 13.16 shows the output from this example.

FIGURE 13.16
The output application appears as an animated image that stops when finished.

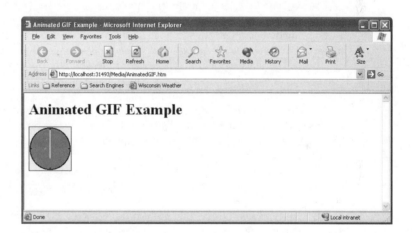

Audio

The next most popular media addition to Web sites (after animated GIFs) is audio. Some people actually play whole symphonies in the background, but that's the exception rather than the rule. In this case, you have two tags to choose from for adding audio to your Web page, and you could possibly add other techniques. Listing 13.12 shows the various techniques. You'll find this example in the `\Chapter 13\Media\` folder of the source code on the Sybex Web site.

LISTING 13.12:   Adding Audio to a Web Page

```
<!DOCTYPE html PUBLIC "-//W3C//DTD XHTML 1.1//EN"
                    "http://www.w3.org/TR/xhtml11/DTD/xhtml11.dtd">
<html xmlns="http://www.w3.org/1999/xhtml" >
```

```
<head>
    <title>Audio File Demonstration</title>
</head>
<body>
    <bgsound src="tada.wav" loop="1">
    <h1>Audio File Demonstration</h1>
    <p>
        <a href="tada.wav"
           title="This sound file makes the Tada sound, which is
                  often associated with the completion of a task." >
            Play a Sound
        </a>
    </p>
</body>
</html>
```

The `<bgsound>` tag is the first technique you can use. You define the audio file as part of the `src` attribute and can use the `loop` attribute to keep the sound file from playing continuously. It plays the audio immediately after the Web page loads. Most developers use this tag to provide background music for the Web site. It's popular on some product sites where the developer wants to extend the shopping experience to include the elevator music that the buyer would hear in the store. Generally, you should avoid using this approach unless you know that the user is expecting the sounds and won't open it up in an office environment.

The `<a>` tag is the second technique. Using this technique, you define the audio file you want to play as part of the `href` attribute. The sound plays only one time, so there isn't any need for the `loop` attribute. You should use the `title` attribute, in this case, to describe the sound to the user (avoiding any unpleasant surprises).

Another way to play sound files is to use the `<object>` tag. You can find a description of this technique in the "Developing with the `<Object>` Tag" section of Chapter 6. Using this technique, you can choose whether to play the sound immediately or wait for user input. In addition, the user gains access to the various controls that the Windows Media Player provides, so the user can play the file more than one time if desired or even pause the sound. This particular approach works great when you want to include sound within a training site so the user can pause the presentation as needed.

Video

Video is still somewhere rare on most Web sites. Yes, you'll find it in the expected locations such as news Web sites and online music stores, but most developers don't include video yet on the average Web site. As with audio, you have a number of options for playing video, as shown in Listing 13.13. You'll find this example in the `\Chapter 13\Media\` folder of the source code on the Sybex Web site.

LISTING 13.13:   Adding Video to a Web Page

```
<!DOCTYPE html PUBLIC "-//W3C//DTD XHTML 1.1//EN"
                      "http://www.w3.org/TR/xhtml11/DTD/xhtml11.dtd">
<html xmlns="http://www.w3.org/1999/xhtml" >
```

```
<head>
    <title>Movie Playback Demonstration</title>
</head>
<body>
    <h1>Movie Playback Demonstration</h1>

    <h2>Using the Inserted Picture Technique</h2>
    <p>
        <label id="lblMouseHover">Runs When Mouse Hovers: </label>
        <img id="imgMouseHover"
            border="1"
            dynsrc="Images/My%20Movie/TimeFlies.wmv"
            start="mouseover"
            loop="1">
    </p>
    <p>
        <label id="lblPageLoad">Runs When Page Loaded: </label>
        <img id="imgPageLoad"
            border="1"
            dynsrc="Images/My%20Movie/TimeFlies.wmv"
            start="fileopen"
            loop="1"></p>

    <h2>Using an Object Tag</h2>
    <p>
    <object width="200" height="225"
            classid="CLSID:05589FA1-C356-11CE-BF01-00AA0055595A"
            type="application/oleobject"
            id="WMP">
        <param name="filename" value="TimeFlies.avi">
        <param name="Appearance" value="0">
        <param name="AutoStart" value="0">
        <param name="AllowChangeDisplayMode" value="-1">
        <param name="AllowHideDisplay" value="0">
        <param name="AllowHideControls" value="-1">
        <param name="AutoRewind" value="-1">
        <param name="Balance" value="0">
        <param name="CurrentPosition" value="0">
        <param name="DisplayBackColor" value="0">
        <param name="DisplayForeColor" value="16777215">
        <param name="DisplayMode" value="0">
        <param name="Enabled" value="-1">
        <param name="EnableContextMenu" value="-1">
        <param name="EnablePositionControls" value="-1">
        <param name="EnableSelectionControls" value="0">
        <param name="EnableTracker" value="-1">
        <param name="FullScreenMode" value="0">
        <param name="MovieWindowSize" value="0">
```

```
            <param name="PlayCount" value="1">
            <param name="Rate" value="1">
            <param name="SelectionStart" value="-1">
            <param name="SelectionEnd" value="-1">
            <param name="ShowControls" value="-1">
            <param name="ShowDisplay" value="-1">
            <param name="ShowPositionControls" value="0">
            <param name="ShowTracker" value="-1">
            <param name="Volume" value="0">
        </object>
        </p>

        <h2>Using a Link</h2>
        <p>
            <a href="Images/My%20Movie/TimeFlies.wmv">
                Play Video
            </a>
        </p>

    </body>
    </html>
```

The first two techniques are similar—both rely on the <img> tag. However, you should notice a few differences in this case. First, you define the video source using the dynsrc (dynamic source) attribute. Using the dynsrc attribute lets the browser download the file and start playing it as pieces become available. (You can get an overview of the nonstandard attributes for the <img> tag at http://www.redbrick.dcu.ie/help/reference/html-tags/TAG_IMG.html.) Second, you must use the loop attribute in this case—video tends to replay itself in some browsers even though it shouldn't. Third, and most important, you need to define the start attribute because it defines when the video plays. In the first case, the user must pass the mouse over the video to play it and in the second, the video plays immediately when the page loads. Figure 13.17 shows how these two entries appear on the Web page.

A second approach is using the <object> tag. It's important to define a precise size for the video, in this case, using the width and height attributes (otherwise, the Windows Media Player tends to choose odd sizes that won't work with your video). You should also provide type information so that the <object> tag knows how to interact with the video. The code shows the most common type information.

TIP One other issue with this approach is that you have to use Audio Video Interleaved (AVI) files, not Windows Media Video (WMV) files. Unfortunately, current versions of Microsoft's products don't produce anything but WMV files, so you need a converter such as Fx Video Converter to create the AVI file. You can download this product at http://www.brothersoft.com/Multimedia_ Graphics_Video_Conversion_Fx_Video_Converter_20561.html. The vendor markets this product as shareware, which means you can try it before you buy it.

As with audio, you must define a number of <param> tags to go with the <object> tag. The code shows the common video settings, but you should experiment to see what works best with your video. You must provide a filename for the video, and experimentation shows that the filename works better when you don't need to include path information. In short, make sure the video appears in the same folder as the Web page used to display it. Figure 13.18 shows a typical Windows Media Player display for the example video using the settings shown.

The third technique is to use a simple <a> tag. All you need to do is assign a filename to the href attribute. Providing a description of the video as part of the title tag is also helpful, but might not be necessary given the way that most developers use video. You should make sure that your video includes captioning for people who can't turn up the audio (for example, due to workplace restrictions). The link method works differently for video, in most cases, than it does for audio (although the precise reaction depends on the browser). The user will normally see a copy of the Windows Media Player start, as shown in Figure 13.19, to play the video. The browser downloads a temporary copy of the video first and then plays the video, so this technique can take longer to start the video than other methods might.

FIGURE 13.17
Using the *<img>* tag lets the user see the presentation as part of the display.

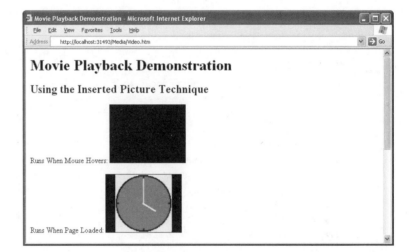

FIGURE 13.18
The *<object>* tag technique provides the user with access to controls.

FIGURE 13.19
A link downloads the image locally and then loads it into a local copy of Windows Media Player.

Interactive

Interactivity comes in a number of forms today—some of which you can use right now and other forms that are only in the testing phase. The most basic type of interactivity is the form. When a user fills out a form and your server receives it, a two-way communication takes place. The user is interactive, but in a static kind of way. Chapter 7 describes how to use forms.

The next level of interactivity is a form that mutates to meet specific needs. The "Selection" and "Progressive Input" sections earlier in this chapter describe this kind of interactivity. The form isn't static anymore, but it isn't dynamic. However, the improvements described in these two sections let companies create training programs where the user can learn something quickly. By combining video, audio, and special form effects, a user can feel as if the computer is interacting with them in a new way. Although the Web site is a continuous advertisement, the interactive tutorial on Web pages at http://www.davesite.com/webstation/html/ is a good place to see what you can accomplish with only a little work (some interactive tutorials are absolutely gorgeous, but you also have to pay to see them).

One of the better examples of interactive media is also free. If you've been following the latest in space technology, you know that the Mars rovers have made more than a little splash. They've lasted well over the time that NASA expected them to and have delivered some amazing pictures of Mars. Anyone who has ever wondered what it would be like to drive the Mars rover can do so at http://robotics.jpl.nasa.gov/tasks/scirover/operator/wits/homepage.htm. This Web site is an excellent example of an interactive media taken about as far as anyone can go today.

Many people are also discovering the wonders of interactive television. Given that some television stations are experimenting with online feeds to computer systems, it might not be long before you'll see an interactive video where you can become part of the show. Unfortunately, the technology isn't quite there yet and it's going to be quite a while before you can incorporate such technologies on your own Web site (perhaps as part of a video). To learn more about interactive television and discover how it might be coming to a computer near you, check out the Interactive Television Alliance at http://www.itvalliance.org/. Yahoo! provides a list of businesses that are currently involved with interactive television at http://dir.yahoo.com/Business_and_Economy/Business_to_Business/Entertainment_and_Media_Production/Television/Interactive/.

Defining Your Development Goals

This chapter has demonstrated many levels of pizzazz you can add to your Web site. Choosing the right level is a matter of planning the Web site, understanding what message you want to present to users, and discovering user needs that fit in with that message. Overall, the best strategy is the one that keeps the page simple, caters to user requirements, and still gives your Web site that something extra it needs to compete on the Internet.

Now it's time for you to consider the pizzazz factor for your Web site. It's important to think about these issues during the initial design phase, but to allow room for change as you create the critical components of your Web site as well. If you have an existing Web site, you might want to poll Web site users to determine what they would like to see changed on the current Web site. Make sure you consider functionality over glitz. Always ask what the user will get out of this feature, rather than simply assume that the user will love the eye candy you provide. Take time to create a plan that works and you'll find that the pizzazz you add is going to make a real difference in Web site statistics.

Chapter 14 discusses techniques for creating downloadable applications—the kind used for Web sites such as Windows Update. Many Web sites now use specialized applications to create an interactive environment. For example, you'll find specialized Web applications used for collaboration. The special application downloads over the Internet and creates a secure connection that two or more people use to discuss an important issue. Of course, someone with less than honorable intentions could misuse the environment the special application creates, so Chapter 14 also discusses techniques for easing user concerns and ensuring that the special application really is as secure as you tell the user it is.

Chapter 14

Working with Client-side Controls

Most Web applications get along just fine without the added complication of a custom control download. Creating a custom control can be time consuming, and users usually aren't willing to download them without good reason. However, you'll eventually run into an application requirement that needs a custom control. For example, a lot of conferencing software relies on custom controls to speed communication and to reduce the risks of someone's overhearing. Financial applications sometimes rely on custom controls for security reasons. You'll also find custom controls used for update applications. The most common example of a custom control used for this purpose is Windows Update.

Custom controls used over the Internet have to address a number of concerns, not the least of which is building the trust of the user. Besides quality control issues, you should sign a custom control used over the Internet. Signing ensures that no one has tampered with the control. The digital certificate that you use for signing the control comes from a reliable third party—one that everyone trusts. The digital certificate certifies that you really are who you say you are.

Once you overcome the basic issues of building, testing, and signing the control, you need to provide a means of downloading it from the Internet. Depending on the kind of control you build, the user usually needs to download the control to the local machine. In most cases, installation is automatic—the user doesn't do anything more than indicate that it's OK to install the control.

At this point, you have a control sitting on the user's machine. Now you have to build your Web pages to use the control. Of course, there's still plenty of room for problems. For example, a poorly designed control could cause memory problems on the user's machine. Controls also invite a number of security problems, so you need to ensure that the control works flawlessly (hopefully, but be prepared to fix bugs anyway).

NOTE This chapter represents a kind of upper limit of what you can do with Visual Web Developer Express and Visual C# Express. You can't fully test the functionality of the examples in this chapter using the built-in Web server because it doesn't provide enough configuration options. (It's possible to test the control itself and debug it before you deploy it to an IIS installation.) The examples won't work using just Visual Web Developer Express either—you need Visual C# Express to create the components and controls. In short, you can create these examples and use Visual Web Developer Express as a learning tool, but you're stretching it and the other Express products nearly to their breaking point. Developers who want to create full-fledged applications should probably rely on the full version of Visual Web Developer of Visual Studio 2005 to perform the task.

Understanding User Concerns about Custom Controls

Custom controls give the developer an immense amount of power and responsibility for the client system. Unlike scripts and other technologies, controls have direct access to the system resources and you don't even need to do anything of a cracking nature to gain that access. Greater trust brings with it greater responsibility. As a control developer, you have a greater responsibility to the user because of the trust that the user places in you.

A poorly constructed control can wreak havoc on a user system without even trying too hard. It's not just a matter of erasing data files or even causing the browser session to crash—controls are a lot more powerful than that. With a poorly constructed control, a developer can crash a system or cause so much damage that the user must format the hard drive and start over from scratch. No wonder many users are quite leery of working with controls. The point is that you must develop a rapport with the user and built trust. The controls you create must be free of bugs, reliable, secure, fast, and should not compromise the user's system. The second you lose the user's trust, you can be sure that you'll also lose any access that the control could provide.

Even after you gain the user's trust, you must consider other potential problems. For example, even a user who trusts you to provide a great control will have privacy concerns. A control can drain a computer system of every piece of private information and not leave much in the way of crumbs afterward. You can be sure that any breach of privacy is going to meet with a very negative response. Sometimes, a privacy breach is completely innocuous and your company might not even create the problem directly. If you can access your control, so can someone else. Consequently, you must have policies in place to ensure that any code you create meets strict privacy criteria and then perform testing to ensure that the code actually meets the criteria. This could mean hiring a hacker to test your control for breaches. Make sure you perform destructive outside testing on a test machine to ensure the integrity of your control.

Interception is another potential problem that users worry about when working with controls. You must consider interception at several levels. At the very least, a cracker could discover enough about the participants in a conversation over the Internet to engage in wrongful activity such as identity theft. Without proper safeguards, your conversation is completely open and the cracker won't have any problem listening to it. A more harmful type of interception occurs when a cracker actually begins to participate in the conversation. The man-in-the-middle attack is well known, but it still happens when a control relies on sloppy coding techniques. Make sure you use proper data encryption and rely on strong security measures to avoid tampering by outside parties. Again, make sure you have this part of your code tested by an outside party that specializes in this form of security. The extra time really gives you a better sense of security.

You might run into situations where the user isn't going to trust you no matter how diligently you test your control. Written policies and a great security record only go so far in building user trust. When the user is part of your company, you can force the issue of course, but other situations require more care. It always pays to have an alternative in mind when you work out a communication strategy. Some users will always trust the telephone over the computer, even though the telephone is theoretically more open to security breaches because it doesn't provide the encryption that your application can provide.

Creating a Custom Object

Objects—controls or components—can provide you with a great deal more flexibility in creating your Web application. You need to create a stand-alone object that the user can download. This limitation means that you have to create an object that can execute by itself using only the resources that the user machine is likely to possess, such as a copy of the .NET Framework. (You can create a software package to make up for gaps in the user's installation, but this approach is laden with pitfalls and quickly becomes messy because you can't assume anything about the user's machine.) Make sure you test the download technology to ensure that it works on a broad range of machines (one of the constant problems that many users complain about on some well-known Web sites, including Microsoft Windows Update).

NOTE   Even though you can create controls and components as part of a Visual Web Developer projects—they aren't stand-alone. You use them as part of the project. Chapter 18 describes these control templates (see the "Using the Built-in Control Template" section) and component templates (see the "Using the Built-in Class Template" section) in detail.

It's also important to give a strong name to any components or controls that you create—signing the name to ensure that no one can tamper with it. The "Adding a Strong Name to the Component" section of Chapter 12 describes how to perform this process. All of the components and controls in this chapter have a strong name, even though the chapter doesn't describe the process again as part of creating the component or control. The following sections show how to create a control to use as a Web application extension.

Understanding the Difference between Controls and Components

Many developers are unaware of the differences between controls and components. Both provide a modular method of adding functionality to an application and both rely on classes (essentially object blueprints). Instantiated classes create objects made up of code and data that expose functionality through properties, methods, and events. In short, both of them have many similarities that lead to confusion with some developers. The only problem is that controls and components serve distinctly different purposes.

The main difference between a control and a component is that a control provides an interface—something the user can see. The user interacts with controls directly and uses them to perform work. Consequently, controls are usually task oriented. Components hide in the background and the user is often unaware of their existence. Consequently, components are usually service or process oriented. Even though the underlying technology for controls and components is the same, the results (or output) are different.

NOTE   Visual Web Developer Express doesn't provide the capability of creating stand-alone controls or components. You'll need another language product such a Visual C# Express to create the .NET components used for the examples in this section. All of the controls and components appear in compiled form as part of the source code on the Sybex Web site (along with the source code should you wish to view it), so you don't need to worry about the actual control or component construction.

Designing a Control

The example in this section uses an augmented label to download content directly from a secret location on the Web server. A user clicks a link or button on the Web page and sees the content—the example uses a button. It's also possible to automate the download—you could use the page load event to perform the task, for example. You can use this technique for a number of tasks, such as displaying generalized help on-screen. Multiple applications can share the same help stored in a central location to reduce costs. This example isn't quite that complex—it downloads some special text and displays it on-screen. The use of a special label lets you either hard-code the target or provide it as properties. The whole purpose of this example is to demonstrate that you can create custom controls for direct communication and rely on a user event to activate the control.

TIP Don't assume that you're limited to .NET controls or that you even have to support the controls you want to use on your Web site. Microsoft provides a number of controls that you can access directly from a Web site at http://activex.microsoft.com. The Web site documentation tells you how to use the controls within a Web page as well.

Listing 14.1 shows the code you'll use to create the example in this section. Notice that the example actually inherits from a Windows form control, rather than a Web control. You'll find this example in the \Chapter 14\SampleControl folder of the source code on the Sybex Web site.

LISTING 14.1: Creating a Simple Control

```
[Guid("80299918-7D92-499e-B55B-5514649E759F")]
public class SpecialMessage : Label
{
    // Private global variables.
    Uri     _ResourceURL;   // Resource URL

    public SpecialMessage()
    {
    }

    public String ResourceURL
    {
        get
        {
            // Return the string that the user provided as input or
            // nothing when the URL is invalid.
            if (_ResourceURL == null)
                return "";
            else
                return _ResourceURL.AbsoluteUri;
        }
        set
        {
            // Use a try...catch block in case the user passes
            // something other than a valid URI.
            try
            {
                _ResourceURL = new Uri(value);
            }
            catch
            {
                // Display an error message.
                this.Text =
                    "Invalid URL: Use http://myserver/resource.htm";
            }
        }
    }
}
```

```csharp
public String ResourcePort
{
    get
    {
        // Return the current port string or a value or 0
        // when the URL is invalid.
        if (_ResourceURL == null)
            return "0";
        else
            return _ResourceURL.Port.ToString();
    }
}

public Boolean IsValidURL
{
    get
    {
        // Verify that the resource URL is valid. The _ResourceURL
        // variable is null when the URL is invalid.
        if (_ResourceURL == null)
            return false;
        else
            return true;
    }
}


public String GetResource()
{
    HttpWebRequest  Request;    // Web resource request.
    HttpWebResponse Response;   // Response from server.
    Stream          DataOut;    // Output data stream.
    StreamReader    ReadMe;     // Data from server.
    String          TheData;    // Contains the actual data.

    // If the URL isn't valid, then return.
    if (_ResourceURL == null)
        return "";

    // When the URL is valid, try to retrieve the data.
    this.Text = "Creating the Request";
    Request = (HttpWebRequest)WebRequest.Create(_ResourceURL);

    // Place the response code within a try...catch in case
    // the request is invalid.
    try
    {
        // Get the response.
```

```
            this.Text = "Getting the Response";
            Response = (HttpWebResponse)Request.GetResponse();

            // Obtain the data stream.
            this.Text = "Obtaining a Data Stream";
            DataOut = Response.GetResponseStream();

            // Build a link to the data.
            this.Text = "Creating the Data Link";
            ReadMe = new StreamReader(DataOut);

            // Retrieve the data.
            this.Text = "Retrieving the Data";
            TheData = ReadMe.ReadToEnd();

            // Clean up.
            this.Text = "Cleaning Up";
            ReadMe.Close();
            DataOut.Close();
            Response.Close();

            // Return the data.
            this.Text = TheData;
            return TheData;
        }
        catch (WebException WE)
        {
            // Return the exception information.
            return WE.Response + "\r\n" +
                    WE.Status + "\r\n" + WE.Message;
        }
    }
}
```

The example begins by declaring the `SpecialMessage` class. Notice that the class inherits from the `Label` class (the basis for the control of the same name). You should also define the `Guid` attribute with an appropriate GUID for the control. The "Designing the Interface" section of Chapter 12 describes how to perform this task. The class also contains one private global variable, `_ResourceURL`, of type `Uri` that contains the location of the secret resource. As with all well-designed controls, this control doesn't provide direct access to `_ResourceURL`; it relies on properties that provide error checking to do the job.

The `ResourceURL` property lets the developer using the control request a specific resource from the Web server. The example verifies only that the property receives a properly formatted Uniform Resource Identifier (URI)—it doesn't check to ensure that the resource is of the correct type, such as a text file. When the control receives an invalid URI, the code throws an exception and the `catch` statement displays an error message, rather than change the property value. The `get` part of the property returns either a null string (when the control hasn't received a URI) or the complete URI contained within `_ResourceURL`.

NOTE   The term *URI* defines any resource on the Internet, including various kinds of objects. A Uniform Resource Locator (URL) is a specific kind of URI. Microsoft chose to use the generic URI for the .NET Framework so that a single class could access any resource. You can use various properties and methods to ensure that the URI someone supplies is correct. For example, you can verify that the URI points to a file by checking the IsFile property.

The developer using the control will need methods for checking the control status. The example provides two methods. First, the developer can check the ResourcePort property, which contains the port number contained within _ResourceURL. In many cases, Web sites hide resources using a different port than the standard port 80. The second property, IsValidURL, is more direct. When the control receives an invalid URI, it ignores it, which means _ResourceURL remains null. A simple check of this variable provides an output value as to the validity of the URI.

The main part of the control is the GetResource() method. When the control has a valid URI, the code uses the URI to access the resource. Remember that this is a label control, so you can display status messages using the Text property. Generally, you don't need to perform this task when working with a label, but a user working with a slower connection to a large resource might want to see the status messages to ensure that the control is working as anticipated.

The first step is to create a connection between the client and the server using the WebRequest .Create() method. Unfortunately, you can't use the resulting WebRequest object directly—you must coerce it into a usable form, such as the HttpWebRequest object shown in the code.

Now that the code has a connection to the server, it can obtain the response to the request it made using the Request.GetResponse() method. Again, the resulting WebResponse object isn't very useful—you must coerce it into a usable object such as the HttpWebResponse object shown in the code. You might wonder why this call appears in a try...catch block when the original request doesn't. The request never fails because it's a request—the code doesn't receive the error information until it retrieves the response. Consequently, you must always place the response code in a try...catch block.

Once the code has access to the response, it creates a data stream to retrieve the response data using the Response.GetResponseStream() method. To read the response data, the code creates a new StreamReader, ReadMe. The code now relies on standard stream reading methods to obtain the data by using the ReadMe.ReadToEnd() method. The result ends up in TheData, which the code outputs to both the label and as a String to the caller. Notice that the code cleans up after itself by closing all of the open processing elements. The main error to watch for during the entire processing cycle is the WebException, which the code outputs to the caller as a String in the catch statement.

Designing a Component

Components generally provide a nonvisual service. The example in this section calculates the tax on a product. Although this isn't a complex component, it does demonstrate many useful component features. Listing 14.2 shows the code for this example. You'll find this example in the \Chapter 14\ SampleComponent folder of the source code on the Sybex Web site.

LISTING 14.2:   Creating a Simple Component

```
[Guid("CF8FE83E-5FFC-4bc0-82BE-8426F8BFE823")]
public class ComputeTax
{
    // Global variables used for calculation.
```

```
Single  _Rate;           // Contains the tax rate.
Decimal _TaxableSale;    // Contains the sale plus tax.
Decimal _TaxOnly;        // Contains just the tax.

public ComputeTax()
{

}

public ComputeTax(Single Rate)
{
    // Verify that the tax rate is within the acceptable range.
    if ((Rate > .01) && (Rate < 1.00))
        _Rate = Rate;
    else
        throw new ArgumentOutOfRangeException(
            "Rate", Rate, "Rate must be between .01 and 1.00.");
}

public Single TaxRate
{
    get
    {
        // Return the current tax rate.
        return _Rate;
    }
    set
    {
        // Verify that the tax rate is within the acceptable range.
        if ((value > .01) && (value < 1.00))
            _Rate = value;
        else
            throw new ArgumentOutOfRangeException(
                "Rate",
                value,
                "Rate must be between .01 and 1.00.");
    }
}

public Decimal TaxableSale
{
    get
    {
        return _TaxableSale;
    }
}

public Decimal TaxOnly
```

```
    {
        get
        {
            return _TaxOnly;
        }
    }

    public Decimal AddTax(Decimal SaleValue)
    {
        // Verify the user has provided a correct sales value.
        if (SaleValue < 0)
            throw new ArgumentOutOfRangeException(
                "SaleValue",
                SaleValue,
                "Sale value must be a positive number.");

        // Verify the user has defined a tax rate.
        if ((_Rate == 0) || (_Rate == null))
            throw new ArgumentNullException(
                "Rate",
                "You must define a tax rate before making this call.");

        // Calculate the sale amount with tax.
        _TaxableSale = SaleValue * (1 + Convert.ToDecimal(_Rate));
        _TaxOnly = SaleValue * Convert.ToDecimal(_Rate);

        // Return the computed tax amount.
        return _TaxableSale;
    }
}
```

The example begins with the class declaration. In this case, the class is stand-alone and doesn't inherit from any other classes. Always make sure that you include the Guid attribute with the class declaration in case the developer wants to use the GUID reference method described in the "Performing Tasks with Controls" section later in this chapter.

The class uses three private variables to store information about the tax computation. As with controls, you never provide direct access to internal component variables. Instead, always rely on properties to change the variable value. You can also use other techniques, such as allowing the developer to set the variable value with the constructor or as part of a method call.

This example shows how to use an overloaded constructor. Always provide a constructor that doesn't accept any input values when writing components for the Internet. You can't provide an input value to the constructor from the <Object> tag. However, including the overloaded constructors is a good idea when you expect the developer to use the component in more than one environment or in multiple ways. For example, you could access this component from the code behind and use the overloaded constructor that way.

It's essential to check your inputs no matter where they come from. In this case, the second constructor checks `Rate` to ensure that it falls within the proper value range. When the input fails to meet expectations, the code retains the current `Rate` value and throws an `ArgumentOutOfRangeException` exception. Make sure you use the correct exception or create a special exception. Don't throw a generic exception unless that's the most appropriate course of action—it seldom (if ever) is the correct selection. In addition, notice that the code provides complete information. The `ArgumentOutOfRangeException` exception supports several overloaded constructors that allow only partial information input, which isn't the best way to help the developer using your component to understand the situation.

You might wonder why the code uses exceptions, rather than handling the error within the component. Always use exceptions within components to allow the developer to handle the error within the application code. In this case, however, the component works within a scripted environment using the `<Object>` tag. There's little chance of catching any errors. Figure 14.1 shows the result of an error in this environment. In this case, the developer forgot to define the tax rate before requesting the taxable sales amount. The well-defined exception information tells the developer precisely what went wrong and which variable requires change. Consequently, this error is easy to repair.

The class includes several properties. The `TaxRate` property lets the developer set the tax rate in any environment, including a scripted environment. Notice that this property provides the same error handling as the overloaded constructor. The `TaxableSale` and `TaxOnly` properties provide outputs to the developer. It doesn't make sense to let the developer change them because the developer is requesting this information from the component. The `TaxableSale` property outputs the sales price of an item with tax included, while the `TaxOnly` property outputs just the sales tax for the item.

The `AddTax()` method determines the taxes for an item and returns the sales price with tax included. Notice that this method uses the `Decimal` data type. Always use the `Decimal` data type for financial calculations to avoid rounding errors. Converting numbers from human-readable base 10 numbers to computer-readable base 2 numbers normally results in some type of rounding error. When working with large numbers or even many iterations of small numbers, these rounding errors accumulate and present inaccurate results. The down side to the `Decimal` data type is that it requires more resources and incurs a performance penalty.

The `AddTax()` method begins by checking the inputs and throwing the correct exceptions when the input is incorrect. Notice that the code checks every input, which is a good component design feature. Never assume that someone else got their code right—always assume that the input data could have errors and you'll run into fewer reliability and security problems. The trade-off for these checks is a slight performance hit, but the performance hit is worthwhile in today's development environment.

After the code checks the inputs, it performs the required calculations and stores the information locally. The `AddTax()` method ends by returning the item price with tax included to the caller.

FIGURE 14.1
Providing well-defined exceptions means easier debugging in a scripted environment.

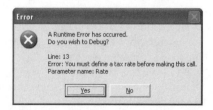

Deploying a Component or Control to the Client

Getting your control or component onto the client machine is an essential part of working with client-side controls. You can accomplish this task in a number of ways, not all of which are obvious from working with the Microsoft documentation and examples. The following sections describe one technique that you can use. A second technique appears in the "Performing Tasks with Controls" section later in this chapter.

Working with native code (non-.NET code) has one big advantage when using the <Object> tag—the tools that Microsoft created work perfectly with native code. When you create an <Object> tag for a native code COM DLL, you can provide a Codebase attribute that will show where to get the DLL when the user doesn't have it installed. The system automatically downloads, installs, and registers the control or component based on the entries you provide. This technique absolutely will not work with .NET controls and components for one very good reason—the .NET control or component requires a different set of utilities for registration. Consequently, Microsoft recommends an awkward reference method that doesn't provide you with the full functionality that the <Object> tag can provide. The sections that follow provide a unique solution that relies on generally unused <Object> tag behaviors and the Microsoft Installer.

Creating the *<Object>* Tag

You can't use the standard CAB when working with .NET components and controls because the technology is limited. The lack of support for .NET means that you can't use the Codebase attribute for the <Object> tag either. However, you do have an alternative—one that you don't see used very often. You can place a message between the opening and closing <Object> tag that contains the information required to download a control, as shown in Listing 14.3. You'll find this example in the \Chapter 14\FileDownload folder of the source code on the Sybex Web site.

LISTING 14.3:   Defining a Special *<Object>* Tag for .NET

```
<object classid="clsid:80299918-7D92-499e-B55B-5514649E759F"
        height="50"
        width="150"
        id="lblTest">
    <param name="Name" value="lblTest" />
    <param name="Text" value="Empty Space">
    <param name="ResourceURL"
        value="http://localhost:36868/FileDownload/SpecialMessage.TXT">
    The required control is missing.
    <a href="Downloads/InstallControl.msi">Install?</a><br />
    Press Refresh when the installation completes to see the control.
</object><br />
```

This <Object> tag contains all of the same elements as any other <Object> tag. However, notice the text between the opening and closing tags. The text includes a link for a Microsoft Installer (MSI) file. The text appears only when the object referenced by the GUID isn't present on the local machine. Consequently, the user will only see the message shown in Figure 14.2 when they need to install the component or control. Unfortunately, this particular feature is underused right now.

FIGURE 14.2
Adding text between the opening and closing *<Object>* tag lets you provide additional information.

When the user clicks the Install? link shown in Figure 14.2, the browser asks whether it should open or save the file. Make sure you instruct the user to click Open. At this point, the browser downloads the MSI file and starts the installation process. The installation looks like any other installation, and you can remove the component or control using the Add or Remove Programs applet in the Control Panel. Interestingly enough, this technique makes it easier to work with downloaded components and controls than using the standard method of creating a CAB file. Not only is it easier to remove the component or control when you're finished using it, but you can also determine the download location for the component or control.

Working with the Microsoft Installer

You have several choices for working with the Microsoft Installer (also called the Windows Installer). The two most practical choices are to use the Setup Project template in Visual Studio .NET or to rely on the Microsoft Installer SDK that's part of the Platform SDK, which you can download at `http://www.microsoft.com/msdownload/platformsdk/sdkupdate/`. However, if you want to save a lot of time and effort, use the batch file download found on the Desktop Engineer's Junk Drawer site at `http://desktopengineer.com/article.php?story=20041001112453379`.

This section relies on the easiest to use of the options, the Visual Studio .NET Setup Project template. To begin using this technique, you must create a new Setup Project. The Setup Project outputs an MSI file. All you need to do is provide a few configuration settings to create the MSI file. You'll find this example in the \Chapter 14\InstallControl folder of the source code on the Sybex Web site.

TIP   If you prefer working with XML, rather than creating a project in Visual Studio .NET or using the Microsoft Installer SDK, you can create the required MSI file using the XML2MSI utility found at `http://msi2xml.sourceforge.net`. In fact, this Web site also includes a utility for converting your MSI file to XML so that you can document its content. You can see an example of the output from this utility in the InstallControl.XML file found in the \Chapter 14\InstallControl\ Debug folder as part of the source code on the Sybex Web site.

The MSI file for this example has to perform two tasks and an optional third task. The two required tasks are to download and install the component or control. After the component or control is in its installed folder, the MSI file must provide some means of registering the component or control so that the Web page can use it. These two required tasks are the same tasks that the `Codebase` attribute of the `<Object>` tag normally performs. The MSI file can also perform the optional task of uninstalling the component or control when the user is finished using it.

TIP The Microsoft Installer is a relatively complex piece of software. It pays to know where you can find good documentation on it. Microsoft provides a complete list of the standard documentation at `http://msdn.microsoft.com/library/en-us/msi/setup/roadmap_to_windows_installer_documentation.asp`. You should also consider checking sites such as the Desktop Engineer's Junk Drawer at `http://desktopengineer.com/index.php?topic=0070MSI`.

Installing the component or control isn't much of a problem. You could perform that part of the task using the `Codebase` attribute. All you really need to do is tell the MSI file which applications files it should contain. The File System tab of the project opens automatically after you create it. To add a file, right-click the folder where you want the file to appear and choose Add ➤ File from the context menu. Figure 14.3 shows the files for this example—they all appear in the Application Folder, as shown. The `RegAssembly.EXE` file is a special application for registering the component or control. The `RegisterControl.BAT` file contains instructions for registering the component or control. The `SampleControl.DLL` file is the special control used for this example, but you can include any component or control you want. Finally, the `UnregisterControl.BAT` file contains the instructions for removing the component or control.

The MSI file won't know any more about registering the components or controls than the CAB file does, but it includes a special feature for performing custom actions. To see the custom actions, right-click the project entry in Solution Explorer and choose View ➤ Custom Actions from the context menu. Add Install and Uninstall actions to the project, as shown in Figure 14.4, by right-clicking the selected action and choosing Add Custom Action from the context menu. You'll see a Select Item in Project dialog box where you can choose the action to perform. This dialog box accepts only certain kinds of files—it specifically excludes the batch files that could perform the task, so you need to create a custom application to work with the batch files (see the "Registering the Component or Control" section later in this chapter for details).

FIGURE 14.3

Add the list of files that you want to install as part of the component or control.

FIGURE 14.4
Include any custom
actions required to
install the component
or control.

Each custom action is an executable and you can include all of the normal executable information in the Properties dialog box for each entry. The example requires only one change. You must include a /R argument for the Uninstall/RegAssembly.EXE entry to ensure that the special application removes the component or control registration. At this point, you can define any specific application information by clicking the project entry in Solution Explorer and changing the entries in the Properties window. Afterward, compile the installation program. Place all five resulting files (including the MSI file) in the download directory for your Web site. The example in the \Chapter 14\FileDownload folder of the source code on the Sybex Web site shows how to perform this task.

Signing the MSI File

After you set up the installation program, you'll need to decide whether to sign the MSI file. Signing the MSI file has a number of advantages, not the least of which is ensuring that no one can tamper with the file without raising flags. To begin this process, display the project Property Pages dialog box shown in Figure 14.5 using the Project ➤ Project Properties command. Check the Authenticode Signature option at the bottom of the dialog box.

FIGURE 14.5
Sign your MSI file to
prevent tampering and
to identify yourself to
the user.

InstallControl Property Pages	

Configuration: Active(Debug)   Platform: N/A   Configuration Manager...

Configuration Properties
    Build

Output file name: Debug\InstallControl.msi   Browse...

Package files: In setup file

Bootstrapper: Windows Installer Bootstrapper   Settings...

Compression: Optimized for speed

CAB size:
  ◉ Unlimited
  ○ Custom: Kb

☑ Authenticode signature

Certificate file: D:\0197 - Source Code\Chapter 14   Browse...

Private key file: D:\0197 - Source Code\Chapter 14   Browse...

Timestamp server URL: http://winserver/

OK   Cancel   Apply   Help

You must provide three inputs. First, you need a certificate. You can obtain certificates in a number of ways. The "Using the MakeCert Utility" section later in this chapter describes one technique; the "Using the Certification Authority Utility" section describes another. It's important to convert the certificate from the X.509 CER format to the Software Publisher Certificate (SPC) format using the Cert2SPC utility like this:

```
Cert2SPC JohnCert.CER JohnCert.SPC
```

You provide the name of the input and output files as arguments. The Certificate File field of the project Property Pages dialog box accepts only SPC entries.

Second, you must provide the Private Key (PVK) filename used to create the certificate. This file requires special command-line switches when you use the MakeCert utility. You should receive it automatically or at least have the option to export it when using other certificate techniques.

Third, you can provide an optional Timestamp Server URL entry. If you leave this field blank, the system will ignore the setting. Only use this setting when working with a certificate from a trusted Certificate Authority (CA). Don't use this field when working with a test certificate that you generate.

Adding the Authenticode information creates a few changes in the development environment. First, you must supply the private key password every time you build the project, so you won't want to add the signature until you have debugged your download application. Second, the user will see the Authenticode signature information when downloading the application. The Authenticode signature is required for many systems—the browser won't even offer to download the MSI file without it in some cases.

TIP Authenticode is an essential security technology for Web applications of all types. You can learn more about Authenticode technology at http://www.microsoft.com/technet/archive/security/topics/secaps/authcode.mspx. Unfortunately, not even Authenticode technology is completely bulletproof. Read about one issue that has occurred with VeriSign-issued certificates at http://www.verisign.com/developer/notice/authenticode/. Fortunately, such occurrences are incredibly rare, so Authenticode enjoys a good reputation in the user community.

StrongName VERSUS *Publisher* EVIDENCE

You have two major choices when signing a control or component using Visual Studio .NET. You use either the StrongName or Publisher evidence classes. The choice you make depends on how you want to use the control or component.

A strong name consists of a public/private key pair that a developer can generate on the local machine using the SN utility. The developer applies the certificate using the [assembly: AssemblyKeyFile("")] entry in the AssemblyInfo file. This kind of security relies on your ability to determine the public key in advance. A trusted source would need to send the public key to you or you could use a key pair generated for your own use. A strong name doesn't provide verification, nor can you determine who owns a key based on the information in the assembly alone. The StrongName evidence type is useful for personal or shared projects, but it isn't something you could trust for projects with someone you don't know.

On the other hand, Publisher evidence relies on an X.509 certificate (digital signature). A CA verifies the identity of an application independently of the development environment by identifying the developer directly. This technique ensures that you can trust the identity information because you trust the CA. You'd normally use this technique to validate code received from a third party whom you don't know.

Certificates come from a number of sources. Third-party certificates come from a Certificate Authority (CA) such as VeriSign (http://www.verisign.com), Entrust (http://www.entrust.com), or Thawte (http://www.thawte.com). These three companies create the certificates commonly used in public venues. You can also create a CA using the Certificate Services feature of Windows Server 2000 or 2003 (this feature doesn't come with workstation version of Windows, such as Windows XP). Microsoft also provides the MakeCert (Make X.509 Certificate) and Cert2SPC (X.509 Certificate to Software Publisher Certificate) utilities to create temporary, test certificates. The certificate generated by these utilities is good only for testing purposes because it doesn't contain the CA information. No matter what certificate source you use, you apply the certificate to an assembly using the SignCode utility.

You may read some texts that appear to say that one or the other form of evidence is better (usually with a strong emphasis on the Publisher evidence). Both forms of evidence have specific uses and you should use the form of evidence that best meets your needs. The important consideration is keeping the certificate or key file in a secure location to ensure that no one can sign code that you create. Neither form of evidence is worth anything once a third party has access to your key file.

Registering the Component or Control

As noted in the "Working with the Microsoft Installer" section earlier in this chapter, you can't provide direct access to a batch file within an MSI file, even if that's all you really need. The application presented in this section could fulfill any operating system (shell) access functionality required. However, in this case, the application specifically helps you create an environment for executing the one of the two registration batch files (the first registers the component or control, while the second unregisters it). Listing 14.4 shows the code you need for this portion of the example. You'll find this example in the \Chapter 14\RegAssembly folder of the source code on the Sybex Web site.

LISTING 14.4: Shell Access to Batch Files

```
// Track the progress of the registration or removal.
Process ControlProc;

private void frmMain_Load(object sender, EventArgs e)
{
    // Get the Windows directory.
    String WinPath = Environment.GetEnvironmentVariable("WinDir");

    // Get the current path.
    String PathInfo = Environment.GetEnvironmentVariable("Path");

    // Set the current directory to point to the installation
    // directory.
    String AppDir = Application.ExecutablePath.Substring(
        0, Application.ExecutablePath.IndexOf("RegAssembly") - 1);
    Directory.SetCurrentDirectory(AppDir);

    // Make sure the .NET Framework is installed.
```

```
    if (!File.Exists(
        WinPath + @"\Microsoft.NET\Framework\v1.1.4322\RegAsm.EXE"))
    {
        MessageBox.Show(".NET Framework not installed!");
        return;
    }

    // Verify the .NET path is in place.
    if (PathInfo.IndexOf(
        WinPath + @"\Microsoft.NET\Framework\v1.1.4322\") == -1)

        // Set the .NET path.
        Environment.SetEnvironmentVariable(
            "Path", PathInfo + ";" +
            WinPath + @"\Microsoft.NET\Framework\v1.1.4322\");

    // Determine the action to take.
    if ((Environment.CommandLine.IndexOf("/R") != -1) ||
        (Environment.CommandLine.IndexOf("/r") != -1))

        // Remove the assembly.
        ControlProc = Process.Start("UnregisterControl");

    else

        // Register the assembly.
        ControlProc = Process.Start("RegisterControl");

    // Wait until the process is complete.
    ControlProc.EnableRaisingEvents = true;
    ControlProc.Exited += new EventHandler(ControlProc_Exited);

    // Return the path to its original state.
    Environment.SetEnvironmentVariable("Path", PathInfo);
}

private void btnClose_Click(object sender, EventArgs e)
{
    // Close the form.
    Close();
}

void ControlProc_Exited(object sender, EventArgs e)
{
    // Enable the Close button so the program can end.
    btnClose.Enabled = true;
}
```

The code begins by declaring a very important variable, `ControlProc`. This variable tracks the activity of the shell process so that the application knows when the batch file is complete. Otherwise, the application could end prematurely with the registration or unregistration status of the component or control unsure.

The `frmMain_Load()` method executes immediately when the form loads, so the user doesn't have to do anything special and you can call this application from an MSI file without worrying about automation requirements. The code begins by obtaining the current Windows path and the path information provided by the user environment. The application requires this information to locate the .NET Framework, verify that it's installed, and provide access to the RegAsm and GACUtil utilities.

The next step is to point the application to the application directory using the `Directory` `.SetCurrentDirectory()` method. The current directory is the `\Windows\System32` folder because that's where the Microsoft Installer works. Of course, before the code can perform the redirection, it must determine the application folder using the `Application.ExecutablePath` property. An issue when using this property is that it includes the executable name, which the code must remove using string manipulation, as shown in the listing.

The code also needs to know the status of the .NET Framework. The example relies on a specific version, but you can check any version. All versions of the .NET Framework include the required RegAsm and GACUtil utilities—all work equally well in installing your control or component. Consequently, you might simply want to look for any version of the .NET Framework that will work with your control or component. In this case, the code looks for the `RegAsm.EXE` file using the `File.Exists()` method. If this file doesn't exist, then it's safe to assume the user doesn't have the .NET Framework installed either.

This example works by opening a command prompt and executing a batch file. The batch file contains the RegAsm and GACUtil commands discussed in the "Working with the Microsoft Installer" section earlier in this chapter. Consequently, the environment must contain a reference to the .NET Framework path or the commands will fail. The code looks for the .NET Framework reference in the path. If it doesn't exist, then the code adds it using the `Environment.SetEnvironmentVariable()` method. Note that you must separate the various paths with a semicolon, as shown in the code.

At this point, the code can perform one of two tasks. When the user provides the /R command line switch, the code will remove the control or component by unregistering it using the `UnregisterControl` `.BAT` file. Otherwise, the code calls on the `RegisterControl.BAT` file to register the component or control. Notice how the code keeps the control or component specifics external to the application. All you need to do to use this application with other controls or components is change the batch file—no code changes needed. In both cases, the `Process.Start()` method executes the batch file.

Once the code has created the process, it needs some way to track its progress and provide a report back to the application. To set up this state, the code relies on `ControlProc`, which contains a reference to the process. The code begins by enabling process events (they are disabled by default) using the `ControlProc.EnableRaisingEvents` property. It then points the `Exited` event to the `ControlProc_` `Exited()` event handler. When the batch file ends, the code calls `ControlProc_Exited()`, which enables the Close button. At this point, the user can click Close to close the application form. You could automate this process even further by having the `ControlProc_Exited()` event handler close the form.

Setting .NET Security

Even after you create a great download application, sign everything as needed, and add all of the code required to ensure a secure environment, you can run into problems getting the component to work on the client machine. In all cases, the problem will derive from changes made to the .NET environment to make it more secure. The default .NET environment (one without any changes) always runs controls and components created using the precautions mentioned so far in the chapter.

To create an environment where the control or component will run, you need to make one change to the code itself and the control or component user will need to make a configuration change to the .NET environment. The coding change is a simple attribute that you add to the beginning of the component or control namespace as follows:

```
[assembly: AllowPartiallyTrustedCallers]
```

The `AllowPartiallyTrustedCallers` attribute lets partially trusted code, such as that found in a Web browser, to call a strongly-named component or control. You can still control access to component or control functionality using other security attributes and tests within the code.

TIP A single chapter can't discuss all of the security features that .NET provides. You can find a complete treatment of the subject in my book, *.NET Development Security Solutions* (Sybex, 2003).

After you make the attribute change to the code, the user must also make a change to the .NET configuration using the Microsoft .NET Framework 2.0 Configuration console found in the Administrative Tools folder of the Control Panel. The user must create a special code group for your component or control and assign permissions to it (generally, you provide full trust, but you could possibly use limited trust levels as well). The following steps describe how to set up the required trust entry.

1. Open the `.NET Framework 2.0 Configuration\My Computer\Runtime Security Policy\ Machine\Code Groups\All_Code` entry shown in Figure 14.6. The code group entries define how a system reacts to code from various environments. A local control or component will have higher privileges than code you download from the Internet.

2. Right-click the `All_Code` folder and choose New from the context menu. You'll see a Create Code Group dialog box.

FIGURE 14.6
Create a new security policy for your component or control.

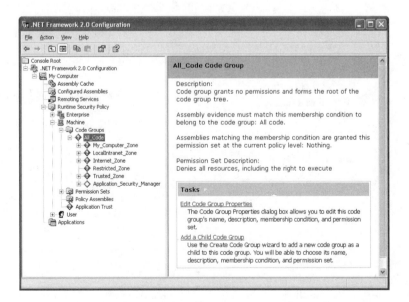

3. Type a name for the security settings in the Name field and a description in the Description field. Proper setting identification can reduce the number of errant and duplicate settings on your machine. In addition, proper identification makes it easy to remove settings you no longer need—making it easier to maintain a secure environment.

4. Click Next. You'll see the Choose a Condition Type dialog box. The condition type determines how the system identifies the code you want to work with. It's important to set this feature correctly because you don't want just anyone to have a given level of access to the system.

5. Select Strong Name from the Choose the Condition Type for this Code Group field. Using a Strong Name condition type ensures that only code signed with your digital signature receives the added permissions. Other code lacks the required Strong Name and therefore won't run with increased permissions.

6. Click Import. Locate the DLL containing the signature you want to use. Click Open. The Choose a Condition Type dialog box now has a signature in it, as shown in Figure 14.7. Notice that you can set additional limitations on the strong name by checking the Name and Version options (don't change the text in these fields). You can choose to allow any control or component signed with your digital signature to run by keeping the options cleared, choose a particular component or control by checking the Name option, and a specific component or control implementation by checking the Version option.

7. Click Next. You'll see the Assign a Permission Set to the Code Group dialog box. This is where you determine what rights the code has to execute. It's important to assign just the rights that the code needs, rather than take the easy way out and assign it rights to do anything. The goal is to let your code execute, not to give full trust to any code that might decide to piggyback onto your code. However, for testing purpose on a secure machine—one that isn't connected to the Internet, you can use the FullTrust setting.

8. Assign an existing set of rights to the code or create a new permission set, and then click Next. Click Finish. The Microsoft .NET Framework 2.0 Configuration console will add the new permission. Your code will execute with the rights you've assigned to it at this point.

FIGURE 14.7
Set the level of strong name support required to maintain a secure environment.

Interacting with the Client

Once you have a component to use, you can interact directly with the client over the Internet using techniques that are similar to those that you use for desktop communication. Even though you'll encounter differences, the basic concept is the same as you would use with any remote technology. What you need to do is establish communication with the remote system and then exchange data with it. The kind of data you exchange depends on whether the client has downloaded a component or control. The following sections help you discover the similarities and differences of interacting with a client using either a control or component.

Discovering the Visual Web Developer Port

Working with components and controls often means knowing which port Visual Web Developer will use for the Web server. This number is random. However, it remains the same for a particular project during each invocation. Consequently, you can perform testing against a specific port for a particular project.

The port number appears as part of the Solution (SLN) file that Visual Web Developer creates for you. After you create the project, build and start it one time (even if the project doesn't contain any information). The act of starting the Web server generates the random port number.

You'll find the SLN file in the `\Documents and Settings\`*User Name*`\My Documents\Visual Studio\Projects\`*Project Name* folder of your hard drive (where *User Name* is your name and *Project Name* is the name of the project you want to examine). Open the SLN file using a text editor such as Notepad and you'll find the `ProjectSection` entry shown here.

```
ProjectSection(WebsiteProperties) = preProject
    VWDPort = 5892
EndProjectSection
```

The `VWDPort` entry contains the port number for this project (but not any other project). When necessary, you can access the Web site directly by adding the port number to the URL like this:

```
http://localhost:5892/
```

Performing Tasks with Controls

Controls usually provide some type of visual interface, which means that you'll normally create scripts that affect the display in some way. Listing 14.5 shows two techniques for working with .NET controls using the `<Object>` tag. The first technique is the one that Microsoft recommends, but it has limitations that affect flexibility. The second technique is the one you should use when you require maximum flexibility, but it also has limitations that affect your ability to use the control on a public Web site. You'll find this example in the `\Chapter 14\TestControl` folder of the source code on the Sybex Web site.

LISTING 14.5:   Interacting with a .NET Control

```
<!DOCTYPE html PUBLIC "-//W3C//DTD XHTML 1.1//EN"
                      "http://www.w3.org/TR/xhtml11/DTD/xhtml11.dtd">
<html xmlns="http://www.w3.org/1999/xhtml" >
<head>
    <title>Control Test Example</title>
```

```
        <script type="text/javascript">
        <!--
            function ViewParams()
            {
                txtOutput.value = "";
                txtOutput.value = lblTest2.outerHTML;
            }
            function GetResource1()
            {
                txtOutput.value = lblTest1.GetResource();
            }
            function GetResource2()
            {
                txtOutput.value = lblTest2.GetResource();
            }
        -->
        </script>
    </head>
    <body>
        <h1>Control Test Example</h1>
        <object
            classid="http:SampleControl.DLL#SampleControl.SpecialMessage"
            height="50"
            width="100"
            id="lblTest1">
            <param name="Name" value="lblTest" />
            <param name="Text" value="Empty Space">
            <param name="ResourceURL"
              value="http://localhost:5892/TestControl/SpecialMessage.TXT">
        </object><br />

        <input id="bntGetResource1"
               type="button"
               onclick="GetResource1()"
               value="Get the Resource" /><br />

        <object classid="clsid:80299918-7D92-499e-B55B-5514649E759F"
               height="50"
               width="100"
               id="lblTest2">
            <param name="Name" value="lblTest" />
            <param name="Text" value="Empty Space">
            <param name="ResourceURL"
              value="http://localhost:5892/TestControl/SpecialMessage.TXT">
        </object><br />

        <input id="bntGetResource2"
               type="button"
```

```
            onclick="GetResource2()"
            value="Get the Resource" /><br />

    <input id="btnCheckHTML"
            type="button"
            onclick="ViewParams()"
            value="Check Control HTML" /><br />

    <textarea id="txtOutput" cols="50" rows="10" />
</body>
</html>
```

The page begins by creating an `<Object>` that relies on an HTTP reference, rather than a GUID to identify the control. The reference contains three parts. The first part uses `http` to identify the reference method. The second part (after the colon) identifies the resource on the Web site as `SampleControl.DLL`. The third part (after the pound sign) identifies the fully qualified name within the control as `SampleControl.SpecialMessage`.

The advantage of creating the object using the HTTP reference technique is that you don't have to register the component on the local machine. The browser doesn't even download the component to a permanent location on the system. The disadvantages of using this technique include a lack of flexibility and some potential security problems. The flexibility issue is best shown when you try to view standard `<Object>` tag properties such as `outerHTML`. The object reports that this property isn't available. In addition, this technique only works reliably when the user hasn't changed the .NET security configuration. Otherwise, you might have to provide the user with the instructions found in the "Setting .NET Security" section earlier in this chapter. Unfortunately, you can't automate the security setting process, so you have to rely on the user's ability to follow directions—definitely not the best assumption to make. Finally, because you have an open control connection to the server, there's a slight chance that a cracker could gain access to either the server or the client using .NET security holes. In short, even though this technique has definite advantages, such as the ability to use the control with clients on a public Web site, the disadvantages are equally devastating.

The second `<Object>` tag uses the GUID reference technique. You must provide a reliable GUID to use this technique, which is yet another reason to include the `Guid` attribute in your code (see Listing 14.1). The `clsid` portion of the reference identifies this methodology, while the GUID that follows identifies the control.

This method has all of the usual disadvantages of adding a COM control to a Web page, but these disadvantages are partially offset by the superior security that .NET provides. In other words, you can build a relatively secure control that resides completely on the client machine using this method. You have full access to all of the usual `<Object>` tag properties as well, as shown in Figure 14.8.

In fact, this would be the best method to pursue except for one problem. Normally, you'd see a `codebase` attribute as part of the `<Object>` tag. The `codebase` attribute doesn't appear, in this case, because there's no point in downloading the control from the Web site using this automated method. Microsoft designed the `<Object>` tag to interact with COM controls, not .NET controls. Consequently, when you attempt to download the control, the system will try to register it using RegSvr32, not the combination of RegAsm and GACUtil that a .NET control normally requires. Even if you build a CAB file that includes an INF file for installation purposes, you can't use this technique. The only way around this problem is to create an MSI file that includes the required setup and have the user download it to their system. The separate installation step is a nuisance, but definitely worth the effort.

FIGURE 14.8

Gain full access to your control using the GUID reference method.

No matter which method you use to reference the control, you still need to provide the same `<param>` tags to set up the control. In this case, you must assign a name to the control, as well as set its text value and the `ResourceURL` property that provides access to the special resource. Notice how this example relies on a port number to allow access to the resource using the built-in Web server. You can use this technique to access other resources as well, but will need to change the server and port information when moving the project to a production system.

TIP Microsoft supports a number of versions of the `<Object>` tag as part of ASP.NET. These server-side `<Object>` tag implementations let you work with .NET or COM controls from the server, rather than from the client. When you use this technique, you must create scripts that also run on the server. An advantage of using the server-side `<Object>` tag is that you don't need to consider client-side compatibility and security issues. Unfortunately, this technique also raises performance problems for the server and potential server-side security issues. The book doesn't discuss this technique because it does involve advanced coding techniques and could cause more problems than it solves. You can learn more about this technique at `http://msdn.microsoft.com/library/en-us/cpgenref/html/cpconserver-sideobjecttagsyntax.asp`.

The standard HTML controls on the form let you interact with the two objects. In both cases, you can access the `GetResource()` method. However, only the GUID reference method lets you also access the `outerHTML` property of the `<Object>` tag. Figure 14.8 shows the standard output from this example.

Performing Tasks with Components

Components generally work in the background. The example in this section uses a component to calculate the tax on the sale of a product. Any calculation or other background task works equally well with components. Listing 14.6 shows the code you'll need for this example. You'll find this example in the `\Chapter 14\TestComponent` folder of the source code on the Sybex Web site.

LISTING 14.6:   Interacting with a .NET Component

```
<!DOCTYPE html PUBLIC "-//W3C//DTD XHTML 1.1//EN"
                       "http://www.w3.org/TR/xhtml11/DTD/xhtml11.dtd">
<html xmlns="http://www.w3.org/1999/xhtml" >
<head>
    <title>Component Test Example</title>
    <script type="text/javascript">
    <!--
        function GetTaxData()
        {
            // Define the taxable rate.
            ComputeTax.TaxRate = .055;

            // Get the output values.
            txtOutput.value =
                "Sales Plus Tax: " +
                ComputeTax.AddTax(txtSalesPrice.value) + "\r\n" +
                "Tax Only: " +
                ComputeTax.TaxOnly + "\r\n" +
                "Stored Tax Rate: " +
                ComputeTax.TaxRate + "\r\n" +
                "Stored Sales Plus Tax: " +
                ComputeTax.TaxableSale;
        }
    -->
    </script>
    <object
        classid="http:SampleComponent.dll#SampleComponent.ComputeTax"
        id="ComputeTax">
    </object>
</head>
<body>
    <h1>Component Test Example</h1>
    <label id="lblSalesPrice" for="txtSalesPrice">Item Price: </label>
    <input id="txtSalesPrice" value="0" /><br />
    <input id="bntGetTax"
            type="button"
            onclick="GetTaxData()"
            value="Compute Tax" /><br />
    <textarea id="txtOutput" cols="50" rows="10" />
</body>
</html>
```

One of the first things you should notice is that the <Object> tag appears in the heading, not in the body. The placement of the <Object> tag is important. Keeping it in the heading means that the user won't see an annoying square block where the object is supposed to appear. Components don't have a visual interface, which means that you don't want to place them in the body.

The interface for this example is simple, as shown in Figure 14.9. The example relies on a single input, `txtSalesPrice`, and a single output, `txtOutput`. When the user clicks Compute Text, the page calls `GetTaxData()`.

The `GetTaxData()` function begins by setting the `ComputeTax.TaxRate` property value to 5.5 percent (0.055). You might wonder why the code didn't use the `<param>` tag to make this setting. This example uses the HTTP reference method, so the `<param>` tag has no effect—another limitation of using this method. Failure to set the `TaxRate` property in the code results in an error, even if you include the `<param>` tag.

Notice how the code creates a combined output string. The first call to `ComputeTax` invokes the `AddTax()` method. If you leave out this step, the property values that follow will be incorrect. The code then retrieves all of the property values so that you can see how they work. Figure 14.9 shows the output from these calls.

FIGURE 14.9
Use components to perform system or other nonvisual tasks.

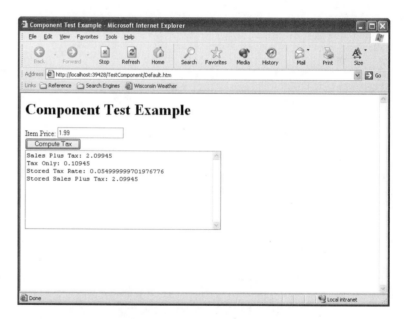

Considering the Security Issues of Using Controls

Security is an essential part of working with controls. You must maintain a secure environment to retain the user's trust. It's important to realize that security is problematic—that you can't rely on security to remain stable or even constant. Someone is going to find a way through your security measures, so you must couple good programming techniques with constant vigilance.

One way to improve your chances of creating a secure environment is to employ digital certificates on your Web site and in all your code. A digital certificate is a series of numbers forming an identity that acts as a key to lock and unlock files, identify a particular individual or company, and perform other cryptographic tasks. It's more secure than the public/private key combination generated by the Strong Name utility (`SN.EXE`). The "`StrongName` versus `Publisher` Evidence" sidebar earlier in this chapter provides an overview of digital certificate issues.

The following sections describe some significant security issues for control developers. Creating a secure environment for downloadable application elements means using Secure Sockets Layer (SSL) for communication, encrypting any data you send between machines, and verifying the user. Make sure you also read about the general security issues described in Chapter 17.

Using the MakeCert Utility

The MakeCert utility has a number of purposes, but the most important purpose for developers is creating test certificates. These certificates don't have a verifiable source, so you can't use them to sign a control, component, or installation program that you want to send to someone. However, they do allow you to set up and test your application realistically with all security measures in place. Here's the best command line to use when creating a certificate for testing.

```
MakeCert -sv JohnCert.PVK -n "CN=John Mueller" -m 24 -len 1024 -nscp JohnCert.CER
```

The -sv switch generates a private key file. You must have a private key file to sign anything with Visual Studio .NET. Always follow this switch with a filename that includes the PVK file extension.

The -n switch isn't mandatory, but you'll find that it's less confusing to use the certificate if you include it. Provide a name for your certificate using the CN (context name) entry as a minimum.

Always set a time limit for the certificate—even test certificates. The -m switch provides a convenient means to perform this task. Simply specify the number of months that you want to use the certificate for testing. Because this is a test certificate that could end up somewhere else, make the time interval short.

Use the -len switch to define the size of the key. Always use the same length for testing that you use for your actual certificate (the one used in the production environment) to ensure that you see accurate results.

You only need the -nscp (Netscape Client Authentication Extension) switch for the Web environment, and you might not even need it there if you can guarantee that everyone will use Internet Explorer. Even so, including this switch doesn't materially affect the certificate, so it's better to include it whenever possible.

Finally, you provide the name of the certificate you want to create. It's normally a good idea to use the same name for the certificate as you use for the private key file so that you can relate the two. In addition, the filename must end with the CER extension.

Using the Certification Authority Utility

A Certificate Authority (CA) is an organization that can verify who you are and provides a reputation that other people trust. Many organizations make use of third-party CAs to obtain digital certificates for signing their code. This is always the best approach if you intend to make your code available to third parties that don't know you or your organization. For example, this is the approach you should use when developing shrink-wrap software.

NOTE The CA setup for this section is a Windows 2000 server with all the latest patches and an enterprise CA installed. Your browser views will vary from the ones shown if you use a nonpatched version of Windows 2000 or a stand-alone CA. Some of the options mentioned in the following sections aren't available to systems that lack Active Directory support or if you perform the setup using a server that isn't a domain controller. However, even with these differences, the basic concepts are the same. You still need to obtain a code-signing certificate using the server options that you do have available.

Using a certificate generated by a third party isn't necessarily cost effective for an organization that plans to send its software to a few trusted partners who know the developer well. In this case, using the CA built into server operating systems such as Windows 2000 Server or the newer Windows 2003 Server is a less expensive alternative. Even a locally generated certificate store (a place for storing your certificate) identifies the issuing authority, making it a lot more difficult for someone to forge a key. The easiest way to obtain a certificate is to use your browser. The following steps show how.

1. Open your browser and access the certificate server using an URL similar to `http://YourServerName/CertSrv/Default.asp`. (The URL you type very likely points to your company's intranet site, rather than a location on the Internet.) Make sure your browser has scripting and cookies enabled (it probably will). You'll see the initial Microsoft Certificate Services Web site.

2. Select the Request a Certificate option, and click Next. You'll see a Choose Request Type screen. This is where knowledge of the various policies in the Policy Settings folder of the Certificate Authority console is helpful. Notice that the only entry is a User certificate. Double-click the User entry in the Policy Settings folder and you'll see a User Properties dialog box similar to the one shown in Figure 14.10. Notice that the User certificate doesn't include code signing. Consequently, this certificate would be useless for a developer.

3. Choose the Advanced Request option and click Next. You'll see an Advanced Certificate Requests screen. Because you probably don't have a smart card or an existing certificate, you'll need to choose the first (default) option of filling out a form.

4. Click Next. The Web server will tell you that it's downloading an ActiveX Control to your system. Be patient, the download can take a considerable amount of time even on a high-speed network. After some time, you'll see the form shown in Figure 14.11. This is where you fill in the requirements for your certificate.

FIGURE 14.10

Selecting the User certificate is useless for a developer.

FIGURE 14.11
FIGURE 14.11
Wait for the ActiveX
Control to download so
you can see this form.

5. Select the Code Signing option in the Certificate Template field.

6. Select a Cryptographic Service Provider (CSP) from the list in the CSP field. One of the best choices is the Microsoft Strong Cryptographic Provider, but even the Microsoft Base Cryptographic Provider 1.0 works well. The various CSPs feature different options such as key length. A longer key makes the key harder to break, but can also increase some factors such as code size.

7. Set the Key Usage option to Both so that you can use the Code Signing key for both needs.

8. Set the Key Size. A larger key is more secure, while a smaller key is more efficient. The minimum key size you should consider for code is 1,024, but some CSPs offer keys up to 16,384 bits in length. If your security needs are exceptional, you should also check the Enable Strong Private Key Protection option.

9. Check the Mark Keys as Exportable option. This check enables the Export Keys to File option. Check this option as well and type the name of a file in the File Name field. This step is essential because it gives you a physical key you can use as input to Visual Studio.

10. Select a Hash Algorithm option. Pay careful attention to this step. You must select one of the options that Visual Studio supports such as Secure Hashing Algorithm 1 (SHA-1) or Message Digest 5 (MD5). Don't select options such as MD2 or MD4 because you'll run into problems getting them to work right.

11. Click Submit. Internet Explorer will display a Generating Request message for a moment, and then you'll see a Create Private Key Password dialog box.

12. Type a password in the Password field, and again in the Confirm Password field. Click OK. Internet Explorer will display a success message.

Defining Your Development Goals

This chapter has demonstrated some of the techniques you can use to add downloadable code to your Web site. It's important to remember that downloadable code answers special needs—it's the option of last choice, rather than first choice. However, a well-designed control can make a significant difference in many applications. Not only do they affect the performance and security of the Web application you create, but you'll find that they make the user experience better and reduce support costs in some cases (in other cases, a custom control can become a real support nightmare). The bottom line is that custom controls really do answer special needs.

Now it's time to determine whether a custom control does have a part in your Web application. The first thing you should do is list any Web needs that a custom control could answer and determine whether you can do without them—that's right, it's better not to use a custom control unless you really need one. After you determine that you do need a better solution than the one that you have now, make sure you exhaust other alternatives first. For example, you might find that a combination of server-side and client-side scripting and fulfill the requirement. It's also important to look for third-party vendors that might meet the need. Once you exhaust all of the possibilities, begin designing your custom control. Make sure you think about all of the pitfalls before you put down one line of code because Web applications are a lot more demanding than the desktop in this area.

Chapter 15 moves beyond application components to a full application. This chapter helps you build a shopping-cart application from start to finish. When you finish, you'll understand how Visual Web Developer can help you build real-world applications—at least within reason. More importantly, this chapter puts all of the pieces together from previous chapters. It helps you make sense of the information you've received from previous chapters—including this one. After you finish this chapter, you should have a much better idea of what ASP.NET 2.0 brings to your development environment and how well Visual Web Developer uses those capabilities.

Chapter 15

Creating a Shopping Cart Application

As more and more people create an online presence, a place where they can buy and sell merchandise, the need for shopping cart applications—a means for tracking those purchases—becomes more important. You can build a modest shopping cart application using Visual Web Developer. It won't let you service a large number of customers, but should work well for many people. However, the importance of this chapter goes beyond the shopping cart application itself—this chapter shows how to combine many of the technologies discussed in the previous 14 chapters. Web pages are very simple in concept but can become quite complex in implementation. This chapter helps you understand how to combine the various features effectively.

Building a shopping cart application means a lot more than just settling on the products you want to sell and the price you expect to receive for them. Shopping cart applications require great database support, and you have to make them as bulletproof as possible. Privacy and security are big concerns as well. Anyone who's suffered a break-in of essential customer information will tell you that sales drop significantly once word gets out (and it generally will). You must also consider how the user will interact with the shopping cart and how to handle error conditions. For example, you must consider what to do when the user decides to abandon a shopping cart. As with real shopping carts, you can't simply leave all the abandoned shopping carts lying around—someone must restock the shelves with the products they contain and put the shopping carts away.

Before you can make your shopping cart accessible, you also have to perform stringent testing. Most developers know that they have to test the ability of the application to store orders correctly and perform the required math. It's even possible to include testing for credit card handling (you must determine whether the card number is even good). However, you also have to test the unusual. For example, many developers now test their code to see what happens when they place virus code in any of the input fields because some users will perform that act. Testing with multiple browsers is also necessary if you want to gain maximum benefit from your shopping cart application.

Understanding the Alternatives to a Custom Application

This section isn't about discouraging you from creating your own shopping cart application. Actually, creating a shopping cart application is a great idea even if you decide to use an off-the-shelf solution because you'll at least have a better idea of what you want after you go through a few iterations of the test cycle on your own application. Creating a shopping application also helps you understand how the various Visual Web Developer features work, so there are all kinds of good reasons to create a custom application. However, after you work with the application for a while, you might discover that it's too much work or that you simply can't get what you want from Visual Web Developer—at least, not everything you want. The reason to look for alternatives to a custom application has nothing to do with learning—it has everything to do with saving time and money. The following sections describe some of the alternatives to the custom application that you should consider before, during, and after you create your own shopping cart application.

Alternative Uses for Shopping Cart Applications

Don't get the idea that shopping cart applications only solve shopping needs. Yes, most shopping cart applications do appear as part of an online store, but that's not the only use for them. For example, you can create an information site where the user collects the information needed, and then downloads that information all at one time. Otherwise, the user has to download the information one piece at a time and that detracts from the information-gathering experience.

The Windows Update Catalog at `http://v4.windowsupdate.microsoft.com/catalog/en/ default.asp` provides an excellent example of an alternative strategy for working with shopping cart applications. This Web site uses the concept of a download basket, as shown in Figure 15.1. The benefit of this approach is that the user can collect everything in one place before downloading the required updates.

You could use the shopping cart scenario for any kind of object collection. A Web site might offer a collection of links for specific purposes. You could let the user gather these links into a shopping cart and add them to their browser all at one time. Even if you aren't making a permanent change, you could let the user download the various pages all at one time. In short, you need to think outside the traditional shopping cart uses to gain a full appreciation of just how beneficial this kind of software can be.

FIGURE 15.1
Use shopping cart applications any time you want to let the user collect objects of any kind.

Sidestepping the Pitfalls

No one will ever do things precisely the way that you do them, and this fact is the number one reason to consider creating a custom shopping cart application. You can search every corner of the Internet looking for the perfect application—the elusive one that has every feature that you ever envisioned—and you'll never find it. The perfect application is an illusion—even the application you build yourself won't perform every task as expected, but it'll be the closest match you can find. When you look for a complete solution or at least pieces you can incorporate into your own application, you need to look for something that you can live with—the application or component that does almost everything you want, but not quite. Remember that the goal of searching for an off-the-shelf solution is to save time and money, so you're exchanging a little functionality that you want for the time and money you need.

Another misconception is that an off-the-shelf solution won't require the extra work of testing. Whenever you install any software on your system, you have to test it fully—if for no other reason than to ensure that it really does work as advertised. However, because you expect a shopping cart application to handle sensitive data, such as the user's credit card information, you need to spend extra time ensuring that the off-the-shelf application you get is also safe. Users expect that your application will handle their data safely, no matter where you obtained it. You can avoid some problems by performing the proper research. Ask questions such as whether a third party organization tested the application for security problems. If possible, talk with other companies that have used the product. Always get a full demonstration of all product features whenever you can. Read online reviews about your shopping cart software of choice to get other viewpoints on potential problems.

A major part of the cost of implementing any software solution is training—a hidden cost that you might not initially think about. Even if you're a one-person business, you still need training on the software you use when you buy it off the shelf. One of the issues to consider is whether the vendor offers training. On-site training can be very effective, but expensive and not repeatable. Training tapes, followed by hands-on training, can offer a better solution when you have a motivated staff. The point is that when you build your own software, you must come up with a training solution yourself (which might not be any training at all if you both create and use the software). Third party software always requires some type of training, so custom software actually has a slight edge in this area at times.

Getting a Complete Solution

Sometimes the best solution is to get a premade shopping cart application that includes all of the required support such as training and access to the required online accounts. Try to get a product with a merchant account or built-in online payment support. Common online payment programs include Authorize Net, Worldpay, Nochex, and PayPal. Some of the companies that offer complete shopping cart solutions appear in the following list (note that I haven't listed a lot of the more interesting solutions, such as <cf_ezcart> ColdFusion Shopping Cart Application, `http://www.cf-ezcart.com`, because they don't support standard HTML, ASP, or ASP.NET).

Online Shopping Cart Software for Ecommerce `http://www.online-store.co.uk`

ShopJS `http://www.anweb.com/shopjs/`

3DCart `http://www.3dcart.com`

.netCart Shopping Cart `http://www.411asp.net/home/webapps/shopping`

Sometimes an ISP or Web hosting vendor can be a great source of information about shopping cart applications. For example, the Globalnet GNP Web Hosting site at `http://www.globalnet-promotions.com/free-commerce-shopping-cart-hosting-review.htm` contains a list of shopping cart applications of every description. You might also want to look at the list of solutions on Google at `http://directory.google.com/Top/Computers/Software/Business/E-Commerce/Shopping_Carts/`. Don't forget the Microsoft ASP.NET starter kits available at `http://asp.net/Default.aspx?tabindex=8&tabid=47`. One of these kits contains a shopping cart, and you'll find other components that you might want to add to the application. However, no matter where you obtain information about a complete solution, make sure you ask many questions and test the product features to ensure that you're getting what you need.

Obtaining Application Components

Getting a full-fledged shopping cart application might seem attractive until you look at the requirements for using it. At some point, you might decide that you'd prefer to build a solution of your own, but not the entire solution. Working with components that someone else has built provides some of the time and money savings that a full solution provides, but also lets you customize the application and ensure that it works almost as well for your specific needs as a custom application would.

TIP   Besides the one found in this chapter, you'll find a number of shopping cart development tutorials on the Internet. In many cases, these tutorials rely on other languages, but it's good to look through them anyway because you can pick up some good ideas or procedures. For example, Macromedia provides an in-depth article that focuses on technical issues such as Secure Sockets Layer (SSL) support at `http://www.macromedia.com/devnet/mx/dreamweaver/articles/build_shopping_cart.html`. In addition, this particular article includes a link to a hosted example of the shopping cart. You can learn more about SSL for Visual Web Developer in the "Using SSL to Communicate Credentials" section of Chapter 14.

Generally, you'll need to look through Web sites that cater to developers to find the components you need. For example, you'll find a full-fledged shopping cart application on the CodeToad site at `http://www.codetoad.com/asp/` and `http://www.codetoad.com/asp.net/`. You can download this code and customize it to meet specific needs. It's also possible to add component pieces from other examples on this site to your application.

Sometimes it's better to buy known good code from a third party vendor such as The ASP.NET Resource Index. This site contains a credit card charge program, .netCharge CC Processing, at `http://www.411asp.net/home/webapps/shopping/creditca`. By adding this component to your application, you can avoid many of the problems with creating the credit card charging software on your own. The idea is to reduce the time and money to create a shopping cart application, without losing the actual hands-on experience.

Developing a Merchandizing Plan

Before you begin designing your application, you need a merchandizing plan. This plan defines a number of shopping cart application elements including:

◆ Defining the layout of your store

◆ Determining how to present the products

♦ Creating a flow of product data from page to page

♦ Refining the user data you want to track

♦ Obtaining a merchant account for product payment

All of these elements define how you design your shopping cart application. For example, you need to consider whether the user has to log in to the Web site before or after shopping. The following sections discuss these issues.

Creating a Web Site Layout

Some people think that you can build a Web site with a good generic layout and that users will flock to it. The problem is that the generic Web site doesn't work. You must add a certain level of pizzazz to attract people's attention. In addition, you need to consider how everything will fit together. For example, you need to offer products at a good price, focus attention on the products you want to sell, and provide the user with enough information to make up for the lack of a physical buying experience. You have to do all of this work without the usual physical media that you might have relied on in the past.

Unfortunately, some online stores stop with the basics. However, have you ever noticed that real stores move their products around and change the path the shopper takes to encourage new sales? Every store does it—you walk in one day to find everyone hurriedly moving products around so that you have to memorize the new product locations—it seems like a cruel joke. However, there's a good reason for the changes—they force the shopper to see new products and perhaps spend a little more time in the store shopping. Likewise, you have to consider ways to move things around on your Web site without making the changes cumbersome for the user—remember that the next Web site is always a click away.

Presenting the Product

The way you present the product for sale can affect the shopping cart application and the results you get from it. For example, you need to consider whether you'll accept coupons that take a percentage off the sales price of the item. It's also important to consider how to handle sales and what to do about people who buy large quantities, rather than single items.

The display you create also affects ease of use. For example, you need to consider the checkout icon—the place the user clicks to purchase the items in their basket. Some Web sites include a Remove Item from Shopping Cart button directly on the product page; others place this functionality in the shopping cart application. You need to decide where this functionality will reside before you begin the design phase. An important issue to remember while making these decisions is consistency. Users are less confused when you offer consistent features, even when those features might not follow the latest trends in user design.

Product presentation also affects the page layout. For example, Figure 15.2 shows a typical view from Amazon.com. Notice that the layout includes a picture of the product and an offer to show a larger version of the image. The user can search inside the book and see other readers' reviews. Notice that the Add to Shopping Cart button appears in a different color in the upper-right corner—the buyer can't miss it. However, if you can't buy it today, Amazon offers to store it as a wish for someone else to buy. In short, the application accommodates future as well as present sales. To create a truly robust shopping cart application, you need to consider all of these features (and others that you brainstorm).

FIGURE 15.2

Page layout affects sales as well as the construction of your shopping cart application.

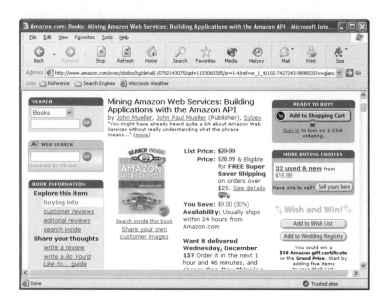

Developing the Product Data Flow

Once you decide the user interface issues, you need to consider how the data will flow within the application. For example, when you request that the user log in as part of the initial application screen, you need to track the user information in some way—usually through a database. A simple customer identification number might be all that you need to track the shopping cart as it moves through the sale and eventually to the checkout. The bottom line is that you need a user database of some sort to include shipping information and other important facts about the user.

No matter when the user logs in, you need to present the user with a list of products to buy. You could create an individual Web page for every product, but that probably wouldn't be very efficient. Most Web sites use a database to store the unique product information and then modify a single Web page with the required information. This feature works very much like the master pages described in the "Designing Master Pages" section of Chapter 4. All you do is fill in the blanks with product information that comes from the database.

A third piece of data flow is the shopping cart and the order it creates. You could simply store the shopping cart in memory and move it from page to page as the user shops. This technique depends on keeping every user separate and ensuring that there aren't any glitches on your system. Because you'll eventually need to generate an order within a database at some point, it's usually better to store the shopping cart on the server in a database during the entire process. Of course, you need some way to handle abandoned shopping carts when you use this technique. It's a choice of the complex database solution over the less reliable memory solution.

These three databases—user, product, and orders—are essential for any shopping cart application. You don't actually have to create three databases—you could store all three kinds of data in a single database using well-defined tables. The point is that the user data will likely include more than one table, as will the order information.

The product information could reside in a single table, but it's more likely that you'll need multiple tables to ensure that you can define the products fully. For example, you might want to include a list of items that other people buy as shown in Figure 15.3. You could generate this list in several ways—some Web sites simply use their search engine to locate suitable products. The application then displays those products that are selling best. You could also hand tune the list and include those that you either want to get rid of or that you want to sell along with the product as a special deal. The point is that you can create complex databases of information for your products, but the only thing you have to have is a list that includes a product name, description, and selling price.

FIGURE 15.3
Make the product listings robust to ensure that buyers can find what they want.

Tracking User Data

You have to track the user data at some point. The amount of user data you track depends on your system requirements. Requesting that the user log on before beginning the shopping experience is usually easier on the shopping cart developer because you can associate products with a specific user identifier. It's possible to track the user with this number during the entire transaction. Remember that Web servers have no concept of state, so you must have a method of tracking the user in place.

It's also a good idea to determine how to track the user data. Many shopping cart applications rely on cookies, which is a great technique to use until you want to interact with a user who has cookies turned off. Some shopping carts retain user information in a database on the server and use an identifier such as the Session ID to track the user. The advantage of this method is that the user doesn't require any special browser support to use it. Unfortunately, using this approach means that the header contains identifying information (such as the Session ID) that the server won't remember from session to session. A few shopping cart applications rely on a mix of both client-side and server-side tracking, which makes the code very complex, but also benefits from the advantages of both environments.

Getting Payment

You must open a merchant account with a local bank to handle the credit card transactions for your Web site. The bank exchanges the credit card information you provide for cash in an account, so you need to create this communication channel as part of creating your shopping cart application. It's best to find a bank that has a lot of experience working with the Internet and has a strong Internet presence. If possible, try to find a bank that uses a Web service to perform the transactions because a Web service is going to be a lot easier to use with Visual Web Developer. Avoid getting an account with a bank that uses a custom portal—such interfaces are difficult to write in Visual Web Developer, don't hide changes very well (so you'll spend lots of time rewriting the code), and don't lend themselves to use with third party products. It's also important to consider the rates that the bank charges for a merchant account—they vary a lot.

If you decide that none of your local banks can meet your needs, you can always rely on an online service such as PayPal. Even though most people associate PayPal with eBay, PayPal Web Services are completely separate from eBay Web Services. However, eBay developed both Web services.

PayPal is a system for taking care of all the financial details for purchases. For example, you can use PayPal on eBay to buy new products. However, eBay isn't the only place you can use PayPal. It's also possible to use PayPal to buy products on Amazon. PayPal isn't just a solution for big stores either; you'll also find PayPal on other Web sites such as Barefoot Productions shown in Figure 15.4. In short, PayPal is another form of payment service akin to a credit card, but without the potential security problems of credit cards because your information resides on a single secure site (at least you know where to go when your information is compromised).

You'd use PayPal Web Services if you wanted to add a simple payment mechanism to your own Web site. The purchases need not be for eBay or Amazon or any other particular online site—they can be for your own merchandise. Before you can use PayPal, you need to obtain new credentials from PayPal Developer Central at `https://developer.paypal.com`.

NOTE Some of you might already use eBay Web Services to market products online. You can't use the eBay Web Services credentials to access PayPal—you need PayPal specific credentials.

Once you obtain PayPal credentials, you'll notice that PayPal is willing to work with you to ensure that your application works flawlessly before you make it publicly available. This is a big advantage for anyone creating a custom application because you get a third-party check as part of the development process—something that's only available to larger companies in most cases.

FIGURE 15.4

PayPal is one solution for businesses that don't have a local bank that offers online credit card services.

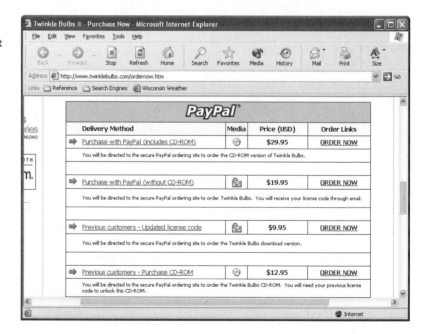

Amazingly, Visual Web Developer is set up to use PayPal with a minimum of coding on your part. PayPal uses a Simple Object Access Protocol (SOAP) interface to access the Web service. All you need to do is add a Web reference and then access PayPal as you would any local class from within Visual Web Developer. Both the "Using Google to Create a Site Search" section of Chapter 8 and the "Developing Web Service Connections" section of Chapter 12 discuss using Web services.

Creating the Required Databases

As previously mentioned, you must create three databases as a minimum for your shopping cart application. (The application actually places all of the related tables into one database file, but the tables do represent three types of individual data.) The first contains a product listing—the items that you want to sell. The second includes a list of customers registered to buy products from your Web site. The third contains a list of orders—items that you have sold to the customer. The following sections describe each of these databases in more detail. To make things easy, the application relies on a local SQL Server database that appears in the `\Chapter 15\ShoppingCart\Data` folder of the source code on the Sybex Web site. You can learn how to create a local database in the "Creating a Blank Database" section of Chapter 11.

Product Listing

The first piece of information that your shopping cart application requires is a list of products to sell. Someone can input this information using a management application that you create or you can simply use an existing database of items. The point is that you need to provide some information about the products you want to sell to the potential buyer. These listings can become extremely complex, especially when you begin including specialized information such as buyer comments. The example uses the simpler configuration shown in Figure 15.5 for demonstration purposes.

Notice that the database includes a `ProductID` field. You must include some unique method for identifying the product—one that's impossible to repeat. Otherwise, the shopping cart application is going to fail. The example relies on an `int` field type that it will need to manage using code. Theoretically, you could also use the `uniqueidentifier` field type because it automatically updates to the next value. However, you can run into problems using this field type when you need to create relationships between the various tables. A child necessarily has multiple copies of the unique value, making it impossible to create a relationship with a `uniqueidentifier` field.

FIGURE 15.5
The product listing database contains a single table, but you could include more.

TIP   Try to choose a numeric value, rather than a string, when creating the unique product identifier. You'll find that you get better performance when using a number, and data entry errors are less likely to cause unusable keys.

The other entries in the table describe the product. They include the product name, price, and description. You can't create a shopping cart information with any less information—more is better. The optional Picture field shows what the item looks like. This particular feature is so important that venues such as eBay often provide multiple pictures for each item—people want to know what they're buying.

The example application doesn't consider at least one feature that you'll probably want to include in a complete shopping cart application—the current inventory quantity. You don't want to attempt to sell something you no longer have. Some Web sites get around this issue by saying they'll put the item on back order or by offering used items (or sometimes both).

Customers

The customers database can become quite complex as well. A customer might have personal preferences, a wish list, shipping and billing addresses, multiple telephone numbers, and multiple credit cards. Each of these entries requires a separate table linked by the customer identifier. The example combines many of these features into a single table, as shown in Figure 15.6.

Notice that the CustomerID field uses the int field type, so the code needs to ensure that each entry is indeed unique; otherwise, the shopping cart application will fail. Generally, you'll want to make this a number that reflects any other sales sources, such as catalog sales so that every customer has just one identifier.

FIGURE 15.6

The customer database normally includes several tables linked with an identifer.

Orders

The orders database always requires at least two tables. The first contains the main order information, such as the customer identifier and the date. The second contains a list of items that the customer purchased for a particular order. Because these tables rely on other tables for input, you also have to create the required foreign keys. Figure 15.7 shows the structure for the orders table—the one that holds the order-specific information.

FIGURE 15.7
Use this table to track
individual orders.

This table contains the identifying information for the order as a whole. The example includes a unique order identifier and customer identifier, the order date, and a flag that shows whether the order is completed. Some applications include more status information. However, as you add more status information, users have a better chance of entering incorrect data. An order could end up with conflicting status indicators. Normally, it's best to keep the order database as simple as possible to enhance data integrity. Of course, you could always include a date that you shipped the product, rather than the simple status flag shown. Good application additions include tracking who filled the order and how you shipped it. Make sure you include a tracking number with the order if you track the shipping method. Nothing is more frustrating for the customer than to know that the order shipped, but not the details.

The Foreign Key Relationships dialog box includes two entries in this case. The orders table has a relationship with the customers table—you need the customer information to know where to send the product. The orders table must also supply its identifier to the order items table. Otherwise, you won't know which item entries belong to the order.

The order items table also requires input from other tables. Figure 15.8 shows the structure of this table and the associated relationships.

The order items table includes a pointer to the order identifier and the product that the customer ordered. The table defines the number of items ordered, but doesn't include a total price because an application can easily calculate this value as needed. You have to consider whether you'll reference the data later. The price of each product will fluctuate. If you think you'll need the total (based on today's prices) later, then you'll want to include a total field.

Defining the Table Relationships

You can easily get lost in all of the various tables, their contents, and relationships during the initial design process. For this reason, you'll want to create a physical representation of the various tables to ensure that you can see any problems. Unfortunately, both SQL Server Express and Visual Web Developer lack a graphic design tool, such as the Diagrams folder found in the full version of SQL Server, for seeing the database.

FIGURE 15.8
This table helps you track the individual items within an order.

The best way to overcome the problem of physical representation is to create a Data Component using the Add New Item dialog box (right-click the project entry in Solution Explorer and choose Add New Item from the context menu). Add data components for each of the tables and you can see the relationships between them, as shown in Figure 15.9. This technique provides an easy method for tracking your database design as you work with Visual Web Developer.

TIP Make sure you choose the * (All Columns) option in QueryBuilder when creating the Data Component. After you make changes, right-click the table with the changes and choose Configure from the context menu. When you see the Data Component Configuration Wizard dialog box, click Finish to update the table entries automatically.

FIGURE 15.9
Make sure you understand the table relationships before you begin coding.

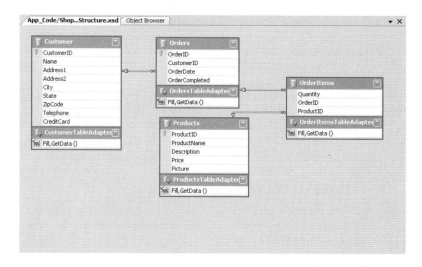

Designing Appropriate Management Applications

Once you design enough of your application, you'll also want to start building management applications for it. For example, you need a method for changing the product entries and a technique for seeing the orders. You'll also want to make it convenient for administrators to learn more about the application status and upload files when necessary. You'll need to decide how to provide the management features. A number of companies now have an all-Web application interface, even for the people working within the company, but using a desktop application is just as viable.

NOTE   You might wonder why I'm discussing management applications before the actual application. It helps to create at least some basic management applications before you begin writing code so that you can interact with the databases in comfort. After all, being a developer should mean creating the tools that you need to work efficiently. Consequently, you'll find that developing the tools you need before you write the application can help point out pitfalls in your design and make it easier to meet deadlines.

Many companies are turning to Web applications for management tasks because a Web page offers a level of mobility that a desktop application can't. You can access the Web page from anywhere needed to check the status of orders, make sure the Web site is functioning as anticipated, modify (add, remove, or update) customers, and make required database changes.

Choosing Management Tasks

One of the first things you'll want to create is a centralized access point for your tools, which means creating a method for accessing a particular tool. Although you can use any number of techniques for performing this task, this example shows a new control to try with ASP.NET 2.0. In this case, it uses the `RadioButtonList` to present a list of management options. These management options automatically change the appearance of the Web page based on code behind because the control provides automatic post back and calls the `rblMgntOption_SelectedIndexChanged()` method when a selection changes as shown here.

```
<asp:RadioButtonList
        ID="rblMgntOption" Runat="server"
        AutoPostBack="True" BorderStyle="Outset"
        BorderWidth="5px"
        OnSelectedIndexChanged="rblMgntOption_SelectedIndexChanged">
    <asp:ListItem Value="DoNothing" Selected="True">
        Do Nothing
    </asp:ListItem>
    <asp:ListItem Value="UpdateCustomers">
        Update Customers
    </asp:ListItem>
    <asp:ListItem Value="ChangeProducts">Change Products</asp:ListItem>
    <asp:ListItem Value="ReviewOrders">Review Orders</asp:ListItem>
    <asp:ListItem Value="GoHome">Return to the Main Page</asp:ListItem>
</asp:RadioButtonList>
```

Notice that the `RadioButtonList` control includes a series of `ListItem` entries, just as you would see for any list control. Each of these `ListItem` entries is a single option. The first option sets the

Selected attribute true so the page displays with one option selected. Using this control means you don't have to worry about groups or the placement of individual controls within a group. All you need to do is select Edit Items from the Common RadioButtonList Tasks SmartTag to display the List-Item Collection Editor dialog box shown in Figure 15.10. You can use this dialog box to change the option order, add new options, and remove options you no longer need, as well as configure the various options.

The RadioButtonList control requires some type of code behind support to function. Because the example application works with databases, the actual functionality resides in a central display method (explained in the next section of this chapter). However, you still need to define a task for the Return to the Main Page option, as shown here.

```
Sub rblMgntOption_SelectedIndexChanged(ByVal sender As Object, _
                                       ByVal e As System.EventArgs)
    ' Provide a means to go to the main page.
    If rblMgntOption.SelectedIndex = 4 Then
        Response.Redirect("Default.ASPX")
    End If

    ' Refresh the data.
    DataRefresh()
End Sub
```

This code checks the SelectedIndex property. Remember that this property is zero based, so the number is always one less than the actual selection. The Response.Redirect() method appears a lot in this chapter because it provides a very handy method for moving the customer from place to place in the store. The goal is to let the customer spend as much time as needed in the aisles, but to make the trip to the checkout stand as easy as possible.

FIGURE 15.10
Use the ListItem Collection Editor to add new options to a *Radio-ButtonList* control.

Displaying the Data

Writing one flexible method for displaying data is often easier than writing three methods to perform the task. This example shows one technique you can use to reduce the amount of code you need to write. A single method can display any of the databases that you will edit while working with the application. In fact, you'll find that the code for displaying each database isn't unique—only a few lines change depending on the database you want to work with, as shown in Listing 15.1. You'll find this example in the \Chapter 15\ShoppingCart folder of the source code on the Sybex Web site as part of the CartManage.ASPX.VB file.

LISTING 15.1:   Displaying the Data On-screen

```
Private Sub DataRefresh(Optional ByVal RecNum As Int32 = -1)
    ... Variable Declarations ...

    ' Determine whether the user has selected the Do Nothing option.
    If rblMgntOption.SelectedIndex = 0 Then
        ' Hide the data editing features.
        lblDataEdit.Visible = False
        dvDataEdit.Visible = False
        Return
    End If

    ' Make the data editing features visible.
    lblDataEdit.Visible = True
    dvDataEdit.Visible = True

    ' Create the database connection.
    Conn = New SqlConnection( _
        "Server=Main;" + _
        "Integrated Security=True;" + _
        "Database=ShoppingCartData;" + _
        "AttachDBFilename=" + _
      "D:\0197 - Source Code\Chapter 15\ShoppingCart\Data\Shopping.mdf")

    ' Create a data adapter based on the request. Set the unique
    ' details view features to ensure the user can only select the
    ' functional options.
    Select Case rblMgntOption.SelectedIndex
        Case 1
            Adapt = New SqlDataAdapter("SELECT * FROM Customer", Conn)
            dvDataEdit.AutoGenerateDeleteButton = True
            dvDataEdit.AutoGenerateInsertButton = True
        Case 2
            Adapt = New SqlDataAdapter("SELECT * FROM Products", Conn)
            dvDataEdit.AutoGenerateDeleteButton = True
            dvDataEdit.AutoGenerateInsertButton = True
```

```
        Case 3
            Adapt = New SqlDataAdapter( _
                "SELECT dbo.Orders.*, dbo.OrderItems.ProductID, " + _
                "dbo.OrderItems.Quantity FROM dbo.OrderItems " + _
                "INNER JOIN dbo.Orders ON " + _
                "dbo.OrderItems.OrderID = dbo.Orders.OrderID", Conn)
            dvDataEdit.AutoGenerateDeleteButton = False
            dvDataEdit.AutoGenerateInsertButton = False
    End Select

    ' Fill a dataset with the required information.
    DS = New DataSet("ShoppingData")
    Adapt.Fill(DS)

    ' Set up the details view.
    dvDataEdit.DataSource = DS
    dvDataEdit.AllowPaging = True
    dvDataEdit.AutoGenerateEditButton = True

    ' Select the record number.
    If RecNum > -1 Then
        dvDataEdit.PageIndex = RecNum
    End If

    ' Display the data.
    dvDataEdit.DataBind()
End Sub
```

The code begins by checking the rblMgntOption.SelectedIndex property. When the user chooses to do nothing, the code doesn't display the database. This is a nice option to add to your applications because it lets the user hide any sensitive information from other people during visits. When the user has selected one of the database options, the code makes a Label and a DetailsView control visible. The DetailsView control isn't configured—you use the same control for all of the databases.

The database connection requires three components in this case. However, the example also shows how to use other connection types. The code begins by opening a connection to the database using a SqlConnection object. It then defines the information the application will retrieve from the database using a SqlDataAdapter object. Finally, the code retrieves the data from the database and stores it in a DataSet. The DetailsView binds to the DataSet to display the information on screen.

Notice that the code uses the same connection, Conn, for all three displays because all the tables appear in the same database file. The connection uses a string to define the name of the server, determines whether you want to use integrated (Windows XP) security, defines the name of the database, and tells where the database is located. The Server argument is always the name of the machine that holds the database file, while the AttachDBFilename is the physical location of the database on the machine (which means you can put it anywhere).

The code creates a unique data adapter for each of the displays, so the code relies on the `rblMgntOption.SelectedIndex` value to determine which view to create. The `SqlDataAdapter` constructor accepts the T-SQL select statement as input, so the code can create `Adapt` in a single step. This section of code also determines the functionality of the `DetailsView` control, `dvDataEdit`. The user will have to create new records and delete old ones when working with the customers and products, but shouldn't perform these tasks with orders, so the code configures `dvDataEdit` differently in this case.

The next step is to create the `DataSet`, `DS`. The first step creates the object, while the second fills it with data using the `Adapt.Fill(DS)` method call. At this point, the code can display the data on-screen. To perform this task, the code begins by setting the `dvDataEdit.DataSource` property to point to the data source. It also sets display properties used by all three information presentations.

The next piece of code checks the content of an optional argument for this method. The optional declaration appears as part of the method declaration, `Optional ByVal RecNum As Int32 = -1`. All optional arguments must appear last. In addition, you must still define a type for the optional argument, along with a default value. Notice how the code tests this default value to determine whether it should set the record number for the example. Using this technique extends the functionality of `DataRefresh()` so it can display the initial data or the results of a change with equal ease.

The final step binds the dataset to the data view using the `dvDataEdit.DataBind()` method. You must perform this binding operation every time the dataset changes or the display won't change. Figure 15.11 shows a typical initial view (remember, there are three for this example). To change views, the user merely selects another database from the list.

FIGURE 15.11

A single method can display any of the data you need when you use flexible programming methods.

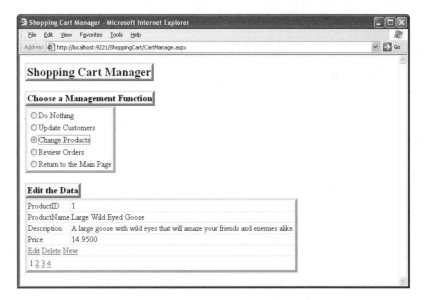

Changing Pages

It's unfortunate, but all of the automation you saw in Chapter 11 simply disappears whenever you want to do anything other than what Microsoft originally envisioned for you. For example, when working with the example in the "Creating a View" section of Chapter 11, you received paging support automatically. Figure 15.11 shows that this application also provides paging support—it must or the user would always see the first record. This example shows that adding any customization at all to the standard `DetailsView` control means that you have to provide the paging support. Fortunately, adding paging support isn't hard as shown here.

```
Private Sub dvDataEdit_PageIndexChanging( _
    ByVal sender As Object, _
    ByVal e As System.Web.UI.WebControls.DetailsViewPageEventArgs) _
    Handles dvDataEdit.PageIndexChanging

    ' Display the requested page.
    DataRefresh(e.NewPageIndex)
End Sub
```

This example shows the flexibility that adding the optional argument to `DataRefresh()` (see Listing 15.1) provides. The `DetailsViewPageEventArgs` object, e, provides a special `NewPageIndex` property with the page number that the user selected. All you need to do is refresh the data with the selected page number in mind.

Changing Modes

The `DetailsView` control shown earlier in Figure 15.11 also provides various modes of operation. Again, the automation you saw in Chapter 11 disappears when you perform any form of customization. This example provides edit, delete, and insert modes, besides the standard select mode shown in Figure 15.11.

You implement mode changes in two ways. First, you must create a generic mode-changing mechanism that handles all mode-changing events. Second, you must create specific mode-handling code for the event. This section discusses the generic mode-changing mechanism provided by the event handler shown in Listing 15.2. You'll find this example in the \Chapter 15\ShoppingCart folder of the source code on the Sybex Web site as part of the `CartManage.ASPX.VB` file.

LISTING 15.2:   Providing Generic Mode Changes for *DetailsView*

```
Private Sub dvDataEdit_ModeChanging( _
    ByVal sender As Object, _
    ByVal e As System.Web.UI.WebControls.DetailsViewModeEventArgs) _
    Handles dvDataEdit.ModeChanging

    If e.NewMode = DetailsViewMode.Edit Or e.NewMode = DetailsViewMode.Insert Then
        ' Hide the management options from view while editing.
        lblMgntOption.Visible = False
        rblMgntOption.Visible = False
```

```
        ' Disallow page changes again.
        dvDataEdit.AllowPaging = False
    Else
        ' Display the management options from view while editing.
        lblMgntOption.Visible = True
        rblMgntOption.Visible = True

        ' Allow page changes again.
        dvDataEdit.AllowPaging = True
    End If

    ' Change the display mode.
    dvDataEdit.ChangeMode(e.NewMode)

    ' Refresh the data.
    DataRefresh()
End Sub
```

Look again at Figure 15.11, and you'll notice that the program lets the user select other databases when working in select mode. This action would prove disastrous when in edit or insert mode. The user could accidentally change mode in the middle of an edit or new record creation and lose data. The code changes the appearance of the display for each mode based on the e.NewMode passed as part of the DetailsViewModeEventArgs argument. However, these visual changes don't change the appearance of the control.

The code uses the dvDataEdit.ChangeMode(e.NewMode) method to change the control's appearance. Of course, this change doesn't affect the on-screen appearance of the data. To make the on-screen change, the code also calls DataRefresh() without the optional argument. Interestingly enough, the code automatically retains the current record so the user sees a mode change, not a record change. Figure 15.12 shows a typical mode change to the edit mode.

FIGURE 15.12
The edit mode lets the user change the content of a database.

Creating New Records

Clicking the New link shown earlier in Figure 15.11 fires the `ItemInserting` event (pre-processing), followed by the `ItemInserted` event (post-processing). The application insists that you create an `ItemInserting` event handler, but the `ItemInserted` event handler is optional. In fact, unless you plan to provide some type of data massaging after the fact, it's better not to implement the `ItemInserted` event handler. Listing 15.3 shows the essential parts of the `ItemInserting` event handler. Note that the code in the listing isn't complete. You'll find the complete version of this example in the `\Chapter 15\ShoppingCart` folder of the source code on the Sybex Web site as part of the `CartManage.ASPX.VB` file.

LISTING 15.3:   Inserting Records

```vb
Private Sub dvDataEdit_ItemInserting( _
    ByVal sender As Object, _
    ByVal e As System.Web.UI.WebControls.DetailsViewInsertEventArgs) _
    Handles dvDataEdit.ItemInserting

    ... Variable Declarations ...

    ' Open the connection.
    Conn = New SqlConnection( _
        "Server=Main;" + _
        "Integrated Security=True;" + _
        "Database=ShoppingCartData;" + _
        "AttachDBFilename=" + _
      "D:\0197 - Source Code\Chapter 15\ShoppingCart\Data\Shopping.mdf")
    Conn.Open()

    ' Initialize DoInsert.
    DoInsert = New SqlCommand()

    Select Case rblMgntOption.SelectedIndex
        Case 1
            ' Create the SQL command.
            DoInsert = New SqlCommand( _
                "INSERT INTO [Customer] ([CustomerID], [Name], " + _
                "[Address1], [Address2], [City], [State], " + _
                "[ZipCode], [Telephone], [CreditCard]) VALUES " + _
                "(@CustomerID, @Name, @Address1, @Address2, " + _
                "@City, @State, @ZipCode, @Telephone, @CreditCard)", _
                Conn)

            ' Get the current CustomerID.
            CurrData = CType(dvDataEdit.Rows(0).Cells(1).Controls(0), _
                            TextBox)

            ' Create a parameter based on this value.
```

```
                Parm = DoInsert.CreateParameter()
                Parm.ParameterName = "CustomerID"
                Parm.DbType = DbType.Int32
                Parm.Value = Int32.Parse(CurrData.Text)
                DoInsert.Parameters.Add(Parm)

                ... Lots of Other Parameters ...

            Case 2
                ... Database specific SQL Command ...

                ... Lots of Parameters ...

        End Select

        ' Execute the query.
        Try
            DoInsert.ExecuteNonQuery()
            Conn.Close()
        Catch ex As Exception

        End Try

        ' Display the management options from view while editing.
        lblMgntOption.Visible = True
        rblMgntOption.Visible = True

        ' Allow page changes again.
        dvDataEdit.AllowPaging = True

        ' Change the display mode.
        dvDataEdit.ChangeMode(DetailsViewMode.ReadOnly)

        ' Refresh the data.
        DataRefresh()
    End Sub
```

The first task the code performs is creating a database connection. You always need to provide the same arguments for the connection including the server, security, database, and filename entries. This section shows how to use a command, rather than an adapter, to interact with the database. Consequently, you must open the connection because the command won't do it for you (the adapter does perform this task).

WARNING One error that some developers make when working with databases in Web applications is to assume the Web application has a state. They try to save resources by creating a global connection that will remain open for the entire session. The only problem is that Web applications have no state. Consequently, the connection always closes after the request even when you use a global variable. It's always better to use a local variable and to open and close the database connection for each request.

The next step is to create a command. The content of the command depends on the database you want to work with. All of the commands include the name of the database, the fields affected by the data insertion, and a series of values to insert into those fields. The information you provide is in standard T-SQL syntax. Of course, you must provide information to place in the data fields using the SqlParameter object, Parm. You can obtain this information from two sources. The first is the DetailsViewInsertEventArgs object, e, that the system passes to your event handler. The code retrieves the information from the Values property. Unfortunately, e isn't a reliable source of input data because of a bug in the .NET Framework.

A better source of information is dvDataEdit. Look again at Figure 15.12, and you'll notice that the data fields are actually TextBox controls. The code accesses these controls directly and retrieves the required information from them. Each DetailsView control consists of multiple rows of two columns—the name of the data field and the data within that field. Consequently, when you want to access the ProductID value in Figure 15.12, you would retrieve the value of the textbox (control 0) in row 0, cell 1 by placing dvDataEdit.Rows(0).Cells(1).Controls(0) in a local TextBox control, CurrData, and viewing the CurrData.Text property. The code can't access the textbox directly because the control could be anything (such as a check box) and the field could even contain multiple controls. Notice how the code uses CType() to convert the object to a specific control.

To create Parm, the code defines the parameter name, the data type, and a value. The parameter name must match the value name in the T-SQL statement without the @ (at) sign. The DbType value must come from the DbType enumeration as shown in the code. The parameter doesn't become permanent until the code assigns it to DoInsert using the Parameters.Add() method.

After the code creates the required command and its associated parameters, it performs the data insertion using the DoInsert.ExecuteNonQuery() method. After the insertion completes, the code closes the connection. Whenever you explicitly open the connection, you must also close it manually. Notice that the code executes the command within a Try...Catch structure. Even a perfectly formed command can fail for a number of reasons, so using a Try...Catch structure is essential. You can provide any level of error handling that you feel is appropriate. In many cases, you won't want to inform the user of the error, but you will want to create an event log entry for the network administrator.

NOTE The example doesn't provide any error handling to make the code easier to understand. A complete shopping cart application will provide full error handling. Chapters 16 and 17 provide information on various kinds of error handling and error trapping you can provide for applications.

The code ends by restoring the data editing view so the user can select another database if desired. Notice that the code also changes the mode using dvDataEdit.ChangeMode(DetailsViewMode .ReadOnly) to the selected or read-only mode. Figure 15.13 shows a typical view of the application in insert mode (using the customer database in this case).

Note that the display contains two options. When the user clicks New, the system calls the dvDataEdit_ItemInserting() event handler. Clicking Cancel doesn't call the inserting event handler, but it does call the dvDataEdit_ModeChanging() event handler, so you have to make sure the application works in both instances.

FIGURE 15.13

Use insert mode to add new records to a database.

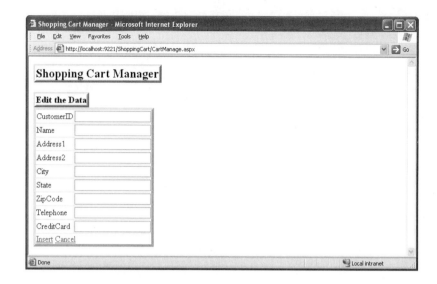

Updating Records

All of the databases require edit mode support. In many respects, this process differs only by the SQL command and the way you prepare the parameters. However, the orders database introduces special problems because you need to provide a means for updating both the `Orders` and the `OrderItems` tables. You could do this as part of a complex SQL command, but it's easier to handle the two tables separately. Listing 15.4 shows the essential code you need for this part of the example. Note that the code in the listing isn't complete. You'll find the complete version of this example in the `\Chapter 15\ShoppingCart` folder of the source code on the Sybex Web site as part of the `CartManage.ASPX.VB` file.

LISTING 15.4:   Editing Records

```
Private Sub dvDataEdit_ItemUpdating( _
    ByVal sender As Object, _
    ByVal e As System.Web.UI.WebControls.DetailsViewUpdateEventArgs)

    ... Variable Declarations ...

    ' Open the connection.
    Conn = New SqlConnection( _
        "Server=Main;" + _
        "Integrated Security=True;" + _
        "Database=ShoppingCartData;" + _
        "AttachDBFilename=" + _
      "D:\0197 - Source Code\Chapter 15\ShoppingCart\Data\Shopping.mdf")
    Conn.Open()
```

```vb
Select Case rblMgntOption.SelectedIndex
    Case 1
        ' Create the SQL command.
        DoUpdate = New SqlCommand( _
            "UPDATE [Customer] SET [Name] = @Name, " + _
            "[Address1] = @Address1, [Address2] = @Address2, " + _
            "[City] = @City, [State] = @State, " + _
            "[ZipCode] = @ZipCode, [Telephone] = @Telephone, " + _
            "[CreditCard] = @CreditCard " + _
            "WHERE [CustomerID] = @original_CustomerID", Conn)

        ' Get the current CustomerID.
        CurrData = CType(dvDataEdit.Rows(0).Cells(1).Controls(0), _
                        TextBox)

        ' Set the original CustomerID.
        Parm = DoUpdate.CreateParameter()
        Parm.ParameterName = "original_CustomerID"
        Parm.DbType = DbType.Int32
        Parm.Value = Int32.Parse(CurrData.Text)
        DoUpdate.Parameters.Add(Parm)

        ' Create a parameter based on this value.
        Parm = DoUpdate.CreateParameter()
        Parm.ParameterName = "CustomerID"
        Parm.DbType = DbType.Int32
        Parm.Value = Int32.Parse(CurrData.Text)
        DoUpdate.Parameters.Add(Parm)

        ... Lots of Other Parameters ...

    Case 2
        ... Database specific SQL Command ...

        ... Lots of Parameters ...

    Case 3
        Dim Completed As CheckBox    ' Special for order completed.

        ' Create the SQL command for the Orders table update first.
        DoUpdate = New SqlCommand( _
            "UPDATE [Orders] SET [OrderDate] = @OrderDate, " + _
            "[OrderCompleted] = @OrderCompleted " + _
            "WHERE [OrderID] = @original_OrderID", Conn)

        ... Lots of Parameters ...

        ' Get the current OrderCompleted.
```

```vbnet
                    Completed = CType(dvDataEdit.Rows(3).Cells(1).Controls(0), _
                                    CheckBox)

                    ' Create a parameter based on this value.
                    Parm = DoUpdate.CreateParameter()
                    Parm.ParameterName = "OrderCompleted"
                    Parm.DbType = DbType.Boolean
                    Parm.Value = Completed.Checked
                    DoUpdate.Parameters.Add(Parm)

                    ' Complete the Orders table update before moving on to
                    ' OrderItems
                    Try
                        DoUpdate.ExecuteNonQuery()
                    Catch ex As Exception

                    End Try

                    ... Database specific SQL Command ...

                    ... Lots of Parameters ...

            End Select

            ' Execute the query.
            Try
                DoUpdate.ExecuteNonQuery()
                Conn.Close()
            Catch ex As Exception

            End Try

            ' Display the management options from view while editing.
            lblMgntOption.Visible = True
            rblMgntOption.Visible = True

            ' Allow page changes again.
            dvDataEdit.AllowPaging = True

            ' Change the display mode.
            dvDataEdit.ChangeMode(DetailsViewMode.ReadOnly)

            ' Refresh the data.
            DataRefresh()
        End Sub
```

The code begins with the standard connection code. It then creates the `SqlCommand` object, `DoUpdate`. The T-SQL statement is a standard update command. It includes the name of the table and instructions on setting each of the fields. The T-SQL statement limits the update to a single statement using the `WHERE` clause. Notice that the current T-SQL statement doesn't include an entry for the `CustomerID` field. (The same holds true for the `ProductID` and `OrderID` fields.) The reason for this omission is that you never change the key field of a table. Consequently, with proper application design, the user should not be able to change the key field entries at all. In short, the current `CustomerID` field value will always match the `original_CustomerID` field value for the selected record.

Unfortunately, errors do happen and it would be nice to know that you have the correct values. The `DetailsViewUpdateEventArgs` object, e, includes both `OldValues` and `NewValues` properties. The `OldValues` property contains the original value of the field before the user changes it. Use this property, whenever possible, to obtain the `original_CustomerID` field value. The most reliable method of retrieving the `original_CustomerID` value is using the same method you use to obtain all of the other field values using the `CType(dvDataEdit.Rows(0).Cells(1).Controls(0), TextBox)` method. Once you have the required values, you create the `Parm` values. The products database works much like the customers database, so there's no need to explain it separately.

The orders database requires special handling, as previously mentioned. You need to work with the tables individually. Always update the parent table first and then the child table, or the database will complain about referential integrity issues. The code begins by creating a `SqlCommand` that works with the individual table, rather than both tables together, as the code does for the `DataRefresh()` method.

The `Orders` table also includes a special feature. Figure 15.14 shows that this table includes a Boolean value that the system creates as a `CheckBox`. Consequently, you need to change the code for retrieving the value as shown in the listing. The `Completed.Checked` property defines whether the order is complete.

FIGURE 15.14
Make sure you use the appropriate controls when working directly with the DetailsView.

Once the code creates the proper command and parameters for the `Orders` table, it uses the `DoUpdate.ExecuteNonQuery()` method to perform the change. The code then proceeds to create a command and parameters for the `OrderItems` table. The code doesn't execute this command immediately—it uses the standard code used by all of the other databases. This code performs the same tasks as inserting a new record. The code begins by executing the query. It then resets the display properties and sets the mode to `DetailsViewMode.ReadOnly`. The final step calls `DataRefresh()` to present the changes on screen.

Deleting Records

Removing records from the database turns out to be the easiest task of all (perhaps a reflection of the saying that it's easier to destroy than to create). Only the customers and products databases allow this action—you don't want to remove orders from the system by accident. Listing 15.5 shows the essential code you need to perform this task. Note that the code in the listing isn't complete. You'll find the complete version of this example in the `\Chapter 15\ShoppingCart` folder of the source code on the Sybex Web site as part of the `CartManage.ASPX.VB` file.

LISTING 15.5:   Deleting Records

```
Private Sub dvDataEdit_ItemDeleting( _
    ByVal sender As Object, _
    ByVal e As System.Web.UI.WebControls.DetailsViewDeleteEventArgs) _
    Handles dvDataEdit.ItemDeleting

    ... Variable Declarations ...

    ' Open the connection.
    Conn = New SqlConnection( _
        "Server=Main;" + _
        "Integrated Security=True;" + _
        "Database=ShoppingCartData;" + _
        "AttachDBFilename=" + _
      "D:\0197 - Source Code\Chapter 15\ShoppingCart\Data\Shopping.mdf")
    Conn.Open()

    Select Case rblMgntOption.SelectedIndex
        Case 1
            ' Create the SQL command.
            DoInsert = New SqlCommand( _
                "DELETE FROM [Customer] WHERE " + _
                "[CustomerID] = @original_CustomerID", Conn)

            ' Create a parameter based on the CustomerID.
            Parm = DoInsert.CreateParameter()
            Parm.ParameterName = "original_CustomerID"
            Parm.DbType = DbType.Int32
            Parm.Value = Int32.Parse(dvDataEdit.Rows(0).Cells(1).Text)
```

```
                DoInsert.Parameters.Add(Parm)

            Case 2
                ... Database specific SQL Command ...

                ... Lots of Parameters ...

        End Select

        ' Execute the query.
        Try
            DoInsert.ExecuteNonQuery()
            Conn.Close()
        Catch ex As Exception

        End Try

        ' Refresh the data.
        DataRefresh()
    End Sub
```

The code begins by creating the usual database connection. It then creates a SQL command that reflects the particular database in use. Notice that you need only the database name and the WHERE clause containing the specific record to delete.

As with other event handlers described in this section, you can use the e.Values property to obtain the value of the record to delete. However, you obtain better results by using the dvDataEdit .Rows(0).Cells(1).Text property. Notice that the code doesn't access any controls in the cell in this case—there aren't any. The controls exist only when you perform some type of edit. When the cell doesn't contain a control, the Text property contains the value of the cell.

Because the delete process never displays an editor, you also don't have to worry about returning the display to its pre-edit state or modifying the condition of dvDataEdit. The only tasks that this event handler must perform to complete the action is to call DoInsert.ExecuteNonQuery() to remove the record, close the database connection, and then call DataRefresh() to display the changes on-screen.

Creating the Front End Pages

The example shows two techniques for handling online applications. The first technique is modifying a single form to handle every need that the user might have. This technique appears in the "Designing Appropriate Management Applications" section of earlier in this chapter. The second technique combines several forms with blank areas to create specialized content. This section explores this second technique. The user moves from form to form and each of these forms modifies itself prior to presentation to display custom information for that user. The following sections lead you through the buying process for the shopping cart application.

Viewing a List of Products

Before someone visiting your Web site can buy anything, they need to see a list of potential purchases. Some Web sites have handled this problem by creating page after page of custom content in the past. Unfortunately, this approach is extremely time consuming and it isn't even very accurate. It's better to generate the display from the contents of the product database. That way, the information the user sees is accurate as of the moment that the browser makes the request—you can't get timelier than that. The example uses the PlaceHolder control to accomplish this task. The PlaceHolder control represents content that you plan to add later and it appears like this.

```
<asp:PlaceHolder ID="phProducts" Runat="server"></asp:PlaceHolder>
```

When you display this page without the appropriate code behind, all you see is a blank because the PlaceHolder control doesn't have any content. Listing 15.6 shows the code required to build content on the Web page using the PlaceHolder control. You'll find this example in the \Chapter 15\ShoppingCart folder of the source code on the Sybex Web site as part of the Default.ASPX.VB file.

LISTING 15.6:   Creating Content On-the-fly

```vb
Private Sub Page_Load(ByVal sender As Object, _
                      ByVal e As System.EventArgs) Handles Me.Load

    ... Variable Declarations ...

    ' Create the database connection.
    Conn = New SqlConnection( _
        "Server=Main;" + _
        "Integrated Security=True;" + _
        "Database=ShoppingCartData;" + _
        "AttachDBFilename=" + _
     "D:\0197 - Source Code\Chapter 15\ShoppingCart\Data\Shopping.mdf")

    ' Create the data adapter with the required select statement.
    Adapt = New SqlDataAdapter("SELECT * FROM Products", Conn)

    ' Fill a dataset with the required information.
    DS = New DataSet("ShoppingData")
    Adapt.Fill(DS)

    ' Define the Table.
    ProdTbl = New Table()

    ' Create content for the Web page.
    For Each DR In DS.Tables(0).Rows
        ' Create a new table row.
```

```
        ProdRow = New TableRow()

        ' Create a cell within the row.
        ProdCell = New TableCell()

        ' Define content for the cell.
        ThisLink = New HyperLink()
        ThisLink.NavigateUrl = "Products.aspx?ProdID=" + _
                            DR("ProductID").ToString()
        ThisLink.Text = DR("ProductName").ToString()
        ThisLink.ID = DR("ProductID").ToString()

        ' Add the content to the cell and the cell to the row. Place
        ' the row in the table.
        ProdCell.Controls.Add(ThisLink)
        ProdRow.Controls.Add(ProdCell)
        ProdTbl.Controls.Add(ProdRow)
    Next

    ' Add the table to the place holder.
    phProducts.Controls.Add(ProdTbl)
End Sub
```

The example code begins by creating a connection to the database. It then uses a data adapter to obtain the list of products from the Products table. Finally, it creates and fills a dataset. Now the code can display the data. However, it must display the data as links.

The code creates a Table object, ProdTbl, next. The ProdTbl output is a standard HTML table. The example uses this table to organize the product links.

At this point, the code begins a loop where it processes every product entry in DS.Tables(0). The code uses a DataRow, DR, to hold a single product entry. The loop begins by creating a row for the table and a single cell to place within that row. The cell will hold a single product link.

ThisLink is a HyperLink control that the code creates to hold a single product link. The product name appears in the Text property, the URL for the product appears in the NavigateUrl property, and the product identifier appears in the ID property. Notice the technique used to create the URL. The same page processes all products, even though the page will appear differently to the user depending on the product displayed. The query string holds the ProdID argument that contains a unique value, the product identifier from the database. Consequently, the Products.aspx page can identify which product to display based on its identifier.

Now that the code has all of the required objects, it builds a nested series of objects that result in a new table row. All of these controls create a standard HTML table, one tag at a time. The order in which you nest the various elements is important because the nesting affects the appearance of the table on-screen. When the table is complete, the code places the resulting table into the PlaceHolder control, phProducts. The user sees a series of product links similar to the ones shown in Figure 15.15.

FIGURE 15.15

Creating page content on-the-fly lets you provide up-to-date information.

Displaying Product Specifics

Once the user selects an interesting item, you'll want to display specifics about it and encourage the user to place the item in the shopping cart. Trying to create a separate Web page for each product isn't the most efficient way to perform the task unless the individual products are extremely different. Consequently, the next step is to display information about the product based on its entry in the products database using a single generic Web page. Listing 15.7 shows how to perform this task using just the product identifier as a source of information. You'll find this example in the \Chapter 15\ShoppingCart folder of the source code on the Sybex Web site as part of the Products.ASPX.VB file.

LISTING 15.7:   Showing Product Specifics

```
Private Sub Page_Load(ByVal sender As Object, _
                      ByVal e As System.EventArgs) Handles Me.Load

    ... Variable Declarations ...

    ' Create the database connection.
    Conn = New SqlConnection( _
        "Server=Main;" + _
        "Integrated Security=True;" + _
        "Database=ShoppingCartData;" + _
        "AttachDBFilename=" + _
     "D:\0197 - Source Code\Chapter 15\ShoppingCart\Data\Shopping.mdf")

    ' Create the data adapter with the required select statement.
    Adapt = New SqlDataAdapter( _
        "SELECT * FROM Products WHERE ProductID=" + _
        Request.QueryString.GetValues("ProdID").GetValue(0).ToString(), _
        Conn)
```

```
' Fill the dataset.
DS = New DataSet("ShoppingData")
Adapt.Fill(DS)

' Display the data on screen.
lblName.Text = DS.Tables(0).Rows(0).Item("ProductName").ToString()
lblDescription.Text = _
    DS.Tables(0).Rows(0).Item("Description").ToString()
lblPrice.Text = _
    "Your price today: " + _
    Format(Convert.ToDecimal( _
        DS.Tables(0).Rows(0).Item("Price")), "$#,##0.00")

' Store the product ID for later.
hidProductID.Value = _
    DS.Tables(0).Rows(0).Item("ProductID").ToString()
End Sub
```

The code begins by creating a database connection. It then creates a data adapter to access the product data. However, this request obtains just one product by including the WHERE clause. The query string, `Request.QueryString.GetValues("ProdID")`, contains the product identifier used to select the single record. Consequently, the code uses the `GetValue(0).ToString()` method to obtain this value in string form. Finally, the code creates a `DataSet`, DS, to hold the single record.

The display code shows how to implement a form view without using the FormView control. In this case, three Labels hold all of the information required for the buyer to make a decision. Notice that lblPrice requires special formatting. A raw Decimal value appears with four numbers after the decimal point and without a dollar (or other currency) sign. The Format() method accepts the Decimal value as input and outputs a formatted string, as shown in Figure 15.16.

FIGURE 15.16

Display as many specifics as needed to make the sale.

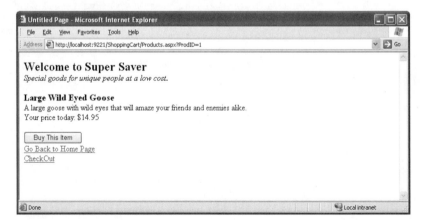

Figure 15.16 includes a Buy This Item push button. When the user clicks the Buy This Item button, the application must make a decision. The user must log into the system to make a purchase. If the user isn't logged in, the `btnBuy_Click()` event handler calls a login page to accept the buyer's login information. Otherwise, it calls a Web page that places the item in the buyer's shopping cart as shown in Listing 15.8. You'll find this example in the `\Chapter 15\ShoppingCart` folder of the source code on the Sybex Web site as part of the `Products.ASPX.VB` file.

LISTING 15.8:   Adding Products to the Cart

```
Sub btnBuy_Click(ByVal sender As Object, ByVal e As System.EventArgs)
    ' Determine whether the user is logged in.
    If (Request.Cookies.Count = 0) Or _
       (Request.Cookies("UserID") Is Nothing) Then

        ' Get the user logged in.
        Response.Redirect( _
            "Login.ASPX?ProdID=" + _
        Request.QueryString.GetValues("ProdID").GetValue(0).ToString())

    Else
        ' Go directly to the shopping cart.
        Response.Redirect( _
            "ShoppingCart.ASPX?ProdID=" + _
        Request.QueryString.GetValues("ProdID").GetValue(0).ToString())

    End If
End Sub
```

Notice that the code uses the query string again to transfer information to the next page. In many cases, the query string represents the best method to use to transfer information because you can track what the user is doing with greater ease. Using a query string can reduce support costs.

The user identifier is another matter. You don't want this information displayed publicly. In fact, you don't even want this information transferred directly from page to page, so the application relies on a cookie to perform the job. However, the user might not have logged in yet, so the `Request.Cookies.Count` is 0, or the user might have stray cookies (odd, but it happens), so you also need to check for the user identifier using `Request.Cookies("UserID")`. When either of these conditions are true, the code redirects the buyer to the login page using the `Response.Redirect()` method. Otherwise, the code redirects the buyer to the shopping cart page. In both cases, the code passes the product identifier as part of the query string.

Logging the User into the System

It's important to create a secure environment for logging into the system. In fact, you might want to use SSL for everything in this chapter. For the sake of clarity, the example avoids some of the security you would normally use, including the user password. The example simply asks for a username. Type the wrong username—one that doesn't appear in the customer database—and you'll see an error Web page. Otherwise, the system redirects the buyer shopping cart page. The system creates a cookie to store the user identifier after a successful login. Listing 15.9 shows how all of these events take place in the example. You'll find this example in the \Chapter 15\ShoppingCart folder of the source code on the Sybex Web site as part of the Login.ASPX.VB file.

LISTING 15.9:   Defining a User Login

```vb
Sub btnSubmit_Click(ByVal sender As Object, _
                    ByVal e As System.EventArgs)

    ... Variable Declarations ...

    ' Create the database connection.
    Conn = New SqlConnection( _
        "Server=Main;" + _
        "Integrated Security=True;" + _
        "Database=ShoppingCartData;" + _
        "AttachDBFilename=" + _
      "D:\0197 - Source Code\Chapter 15\ShoppingCart\Data\Shopping.mdf")

    ' Create a request using the user name.
    Adapt = New SqlDataAdapter( _
        "SELECT * FROM Customer WHERE Name='" + txtUserName.Text + "'", _
        Conn)

    ' Attempt to get the customer record.
    DS = New DataSet("CustomerData")
    Adapt.Fill(DS)

    ' Check for the CustomerID
    If DS.Tables(0).Rows.Count = 0 Then

        ' Tell the user the account doesn't exist.
        Response.Redirect("LoginError.ASPX")

    Else

        ' Otherwise, place the CustomerID in a cookie and redirect the
        ' user to the shopping cart page.
        Response.Cookies.Add(New HttpCookie("UserID", _
                DS.Tables(0).Rows(0).Item("CustomerID").ToString()))
        Response.Redirect( _
            "ShoppingCart.ASPX?ProdID=" + _
        Request.QueryString.GetValues("ProdID").GetValue(0).ToString())
    End If

End Sub
```

The code begins by creating a connection to the database. It then creates a data adapter that queries the customer database for the username entered on the Web page in txtUserName.Text. The code creates a DataSet, DS, and fills it with the customer record. DS always contains a record when the customer exists, so checking DS.Tables(0).Rows.Count tells the code whether the customer is valid or not.

When the customer name is valid, the code creates a cookie to hold the user identifier using the Response.Cookies.Add() method. Because this cookie lacks an expiration date, the browser deletes it immediately after the session ends. After the code creates the cookie, it uses the Response.Redirect() method to send the buyer to the shopping cart. Notice that the code passes the same product identifier that the user chose on the products Web page shown in Figure 15.16.

Displaying the Shopping Basket

Eventually, the user will want to see a list of items in the shopping basket. Some Web sites force the user to go to a special location to perform this task. The example simply displays the shopping cart after the user selects each item—much as you would look into a shopping cart at the store after selecting an item from the shelf. The example doesn't use a very complex shopping cart display because other parts of the example have already shown how to display product information (see the "Displaying the Data" section earlier in this chapter). Listing 15.10 shows how to create a simple shopping cart display Web page. You'll find this example in the \Chapter 15\ShoppingCart folder of the source code on the Sybex Web site as part of the ShoppingCart.ASPX.VB file.

LISTING 15.10:   Showing the Products

```
Private Sub Page_Load(ByVal sender As Object, _
                        ByVal e As System.EventArgs) Handles Me.Load

    ... Variable Declarations ...

    ' Don't perform any extra processing for a postback.
    If Page.IsPostBack Then
        Return
    End If

    If Not Request.QueryString.Item("ProdID") Is Nothing Then
        If Request.Cookies.Get("Products") Is Nothing Then
            ' Create an item list for just the current item.
            ItemList = Request.QueryString.Item("ProdID") + "=1"

            ' Create a cookie to include the new item.
            Response.Cookies.Add(New HttpCookie("Products", ItemList))
        Else
            ' Get the current items and combine with the new item.
            ItemList = Request.Cookies.Get("Products").Value + "&" + _
                        Request.QueryString.Item("ProdID") + "=1"

            ' Update the cookie to include the new item.
            Response.Cookies.Set(New HttpCookie("Products", ItemList))
```

```
            End If
    End If

    ' If there isn't anything to do, exit.
    If ItemList Is Nothing Then
        Return
    End If

    ' Create the dataset.
    DS = New DataSet("OrderedItems")
    DS.Tables.Add(New DataTable("Orders"))
    DS.Tables("Orders").Columns.Add("ProductID", GetType(Int32))
    DS.Tables("Orders").Columns.Add("Quantity", GetType(Int32))

    ' Split the string into a list of items.
    Items = ItemList.Split(Convert.ToChar("&"))
    lblItemNoteB.Text = Items.Length.ToString()

    ' Process each of the items.
    For Each Item In Items

        ' Split the ProductID from the Quantity.
        ItemSplit = Item.Split(Convert.ToChar("="))

        ' Create a new table entry.
        DR = DS.Tables("Orders").NewRow()

        ' Add the data.
        DR("ProductID") = Int32.Parse(ItemSplit(0))
        DR("Quantity") = Int32.Parse(ItemSplit(1))

        ' Place the data in the table.
        DS.Tables("Orders").Rows.Add(DR)
    Next

    ' Display the items on screen.
    gvItems.DataSource = DS
    gvItems.DataBind()
End Sub
```

It's important to remember that Web pages have no state information. Consequently, if you provide a shopping cart update function as part of the Page_Load() event handler, you must provide some means of detecting when a page load is part of a post back versus a product addition. The Page.IsPostBack property provides this information. When this value is true, the page loads as the result of a user click on a post back control on the Web page, rather than as a redirection from another Web page for a product addition. The code simply returns when this happens so that the buyer doesn't end up with extra items in their shopping cart.

When another Web page calls the shopping cart page, the shopping cart page expects a product identifier as part of the query string. However, a user might decide to call the page directly without the product identifier, so you must include code to detect this condition. If someone calls the page without a product identifier, then the `ItemList` is going to contain nothing and the code returns. You should probably add error-handling code at this point, but the choice is up to you. The important factor is that the code doesn't add an item to the shopping cart.

The shopping cart list appears in a single cookie. The cookie uses a special encoding technique to hold the list of items in an amazingly small space. All you really need is the product identifier and the number of items the user wants (the example is hard wired for one item, but you can easily add code to allow other quantities). Therefore, a single item appears as a product number, followed by an equals sign, followed by the quantity, such as 2=1 for one of product number 2. The buyer hopefully purchases more than one item, so the code separates each item pair by an ampersand (&). Two items might appear as 2=1&3=1 for one of product number 2 and one of product number 3. Using this technique, an entire shopping cart can appear in just a few bytes on the user's hard drive.

You must also differentiate between the first product that the buyer selects and those that follow. When the buyer adds the first item, `Request.Cookies.Get("Products")` won't have a value. The code creates a new string value with the single item. It then uses the `Response.Cookies.Add()` method to add the single item to the list of cookies. However, after the first product, the code must obtain the other items first, and then add the new item to `ItemList`. The code then uses the `Response.Cookies.Set()` method (notice the difference in method names) to change the existing cookie.

The Web page now has access to a list of shopping cart items in a string, which isn't very useful. The code creates a `DataSet`, DS, next to hold the shopping list for display purposes. Because there isn't a database to construct the table within DS, the code creates the table manually. Notice that the code creates the table first, and then adds the columns to the table.

Now it's time to break the data into pieces and store the information in DS. The `ItemList.Split()` method splits the string into an array of product strings (product identifier and quantity pair). It places the number of items into `lblItemNoteB.Text` so the buyer can see how many items appear in the shopping cart.

A `For Each...Next` loop processes the array items and splits them into value pairs using the `Item.Split()` method. Now that the code has the values split into individual pieces, it can create a new `DataRow`, DR, to hold the single row of data. The code places the individual data elements into DR, and then adds DR to DS using the `DS.Tables("Orders").Rows.Add()` method. The loop continues until it processes all of the shopping cart items.

Eventually, the code creates a dataset that contains all of the shopping cart items. It sets the `gvItems.DataSource` property to DS and displays the result using the `gvItems.DataBind()` method. Figure 15.17 shows a typical shopping cart display.

Making the Sale

The buyer eventually adds all of the required items to the shopping cart and wants to check out. The Buy Items push button shown in Figure 15.17 lets the buyer place an order. Obviously, this act can lead to a wealth of additional pages where the buyer selects a credit card and performs other tasks. The example takes a shortcut and stores the credit card locally. Eventually, the application must store the order, which is the important part of making a purchase for the seller. Listing 15.11 shows the required code to store an order. You'll find this example in the `\Chapter 15\ShoppingCart` folder of the source code on the Sybex Web site as part of the `ShoppingCart.ASPX.VB` file.

FIGURE 15.17
Display the content of the
user's shopping basket
before making the sale.

LISTING 15.11: Entering the Order

```
Sub btnBuy_Click(ByVal sender As Object, ByVal e As System.EventArgs)

    ... Variable Declarations ...

    ' Open the connection.
    Conn = New SqlConnection( _
        "Server=Main;" + _
        "Integrated Security=True;" + _
        "Database=ShoppingCartData;" + _
        "AttachDBFilename=" + _
     "D:\0197 - Source Code\Chapter 15\ShoppingCart\Data\Shopping.mdf")
    Conn.Open()

    ' Get the current records to determine the next available OrderID.
    Adapt = New SqlDataAdapter("SELECT * FROM Orders", Conn)

    ' Fill a dataset with the required information.
    DS = New DataSet("OrderData")
    Adapt.Fill(DS)

    LastOrder = _
        Convert.ToInt32( _
            DS.Tables(0).Rows(DS.Tables(0).Rows.Count - 1).Item(0))

    ' Create the order entry first.
    DoInsert = New SqlCommand( _
        "INSERT INTO [Orders] ([OrderID], [CustomerID], " + _
        "[OrderDate], [OrderCompleted]) VALUES (@OrderID, " + _
        "@CustomerID, @OrderDate, @OrderCompleted)", Conn)

    ' Create the OrderID parameter.
```

```vbnet
        Parm = DoInsert.CreateParameter()
        Parm.ParameterName = "OrderID"
        Parm.DbType = DbType.Int32
        Parm.Value = LastOrder + 1
        DoInsert.Parameters.Add(Parm)

        ... Lots of Parameters ...

        ' Perform the query
        Try
            DoInsert.ExecuteNonQuery()
        Catch ex As Exception

        End Try

        ' Get the list of items to process.
        ItemList = Request.Cookies.Get("Products").Value

        ' Split the string into a list of items.
        Items = ItemList.Split(Convert.ToChar("&"))

        ' Create one OrderItem entry for each product.
        For Each Item In Items

            ' Split the ProductID from the Quantity.
            ItemSplit = Item.Split(Convert.ToChar("="))

            ... Database specific SQL Command ...

            ... Lots of Parameters ...

            ' Perform the query
            Try
                DoInsert.ExecuteNonQuery()
            Catch ex As Exception

            End Try

        Next

        ' Close the connection when complete.
        Conn.Close()

        ' Clear the Products cookie.
        Response.Cookies.Remove("Products")

        ' Thank the buyer for the order.
        Response.Redirect("Thanks.ASPX")
    End Sub
```

You can use a number of techniques for obtaining an order number or even set the database to provide it for you automatically. The example begins by creating a connection to the database, setting up an adapter to retrieve the current orders, and then looking at the last order in the list to determine the next order number in line. This technique works fine for simple Web sites, but you'll want to set up something better for a Web site with high volume. The last order number ends up in LastOrder.

Now that the code knows which order number to use, it creates an entry in the Orders table. All the code needs is the order number in LastOrder, the client identifier that appears in the UserID cookie, the current date, and a value of False for the OrderCompleted field.

After the code adds the new record to Orders (which tends to prevent another buyer from using the order number), it requests the list of products from Request.Cookies.Get("Products").Value. The code splits the values using the same method described in the "Displaying the Shopping Basket" section earlier in this chapter. Although this might seem like unnecessary extra work, always remember that Web pages have no state. Consequently, the page doesn't know about the dataset created earlier in the Page_Load() event handler.

Instead of creating a dataset to hold the data, the btnBuy_Click() method begins creating records in the OrderItems table—one for each shopping cart item in the list. The loop eventually ends and the code closes the connection to the database.

The next step is essential. The code removes the product list from the cookies so that the shopping cart is empty again using the Response.Cookies.Remove() method. If you fail to perform this task, the shopping cart will remain full until the buyer closes the browser and the browser deletes the cookie for you. Consequently, if the buyer visits your Web site again to get a missed item, the shopping cart will remain intact and you'll lose a sale (or experience the woes of an irate buyer who received two of everything). The code ends by redirecting the buyer to a thank-you Web page.

Defining Your Development Goals

The shopping cart application in this chapter is basic, but it provides a good basis on which to build the online shopping experience of your dreams. You've discovered the benefits of creating the application as simply as possible—adding all of the constraints required to make sure the application works as you envisioned. No one wants a virus lurking around on their system after a cracker crashes the application, steals all the credit card information, and loses any sales visitors requested during the day. Online applications can become a nightmare, but you can manage it with careful planning. You really can make this shopping cart application work.

Of course, the first task you must perform is to determine whether someone has already done all of the required work. Yes, there's a nice feeling when you create something on your own, but most businesses don't have time to reinvent the wheel. If you can't find an application that does everything you need, you can look for third party add-on products to make your programming journey a little easier. The bottom line is that you should have fun with this application and make it as useful as you like, but make sure you spare yourself a little pain whenever possible too. At the very least, you should try this application out so you can put everything discussed in Chapters 1 through 14 together into a cohesive picture.

Chapter 16 starts a new topic—putting the finishing touches on your application. The least loved, but most needed, changes include debugging your application completely. Chapter 16 helps you discover that debugging isn't just a painful way to experience your application—you really do gain something by debugging the application fully. In many cases, the best gain is the knowledge you acquire about your application. Most applications are so complex that developers don't realize how hard they are to understand until they try to debug them. The resulting experience builds knowledge and helps the developer understand coding in a way that a well-working application could never demonstrate.

Part 6

The Finishing Touches: Debug, Secure, and Distribute Your Application

In this section you will learn to:

Chapter 16

Debugging Your Application

Many developers view debugging as a task that "real programmers" don't need to perform. Unfortunately, debugging (the act of looking for errors in code) is something that everyone has to perform because no one writes perfect code. The programmers who do write nearly perfect code are the same programmers who rely on debugging, just as an author relies on good editors to help proof a manuscript.

Somewhere, hidden in a remote location you didn't think to check, is a bug (a coding error) that someone is going to encounter. The moment that the user encounters the bug, an error will occur and your application could crash and, in a worst-case scenario, take the rest of the system with it. Of course, bugs figure into other potential problems—just as bugs in Microsoft applications receive constant attention as crackers use them to gain access to the user's system. In short, debugging is an essential task to perform even if you do write the mythical perfect code.

Fortunately, Visual Web Developer provides a wealth of debugging aids for you. In many cases, you don't have to do anything special to make these aids work. The IDE simply provides them for you. Interpreting the various windows and debugging features can take a little time, so this chapter not only tells you that they exist but how to interpret them as well.

Visual Web Developer also provides two ranges of debugging. Localized debugging helps you find bugs on your system as you create the application. Remote debugging helps you locate bugs that show up only when someone accesses the application from another location. It's important to perform both ranges of checking to ensure that your application runs as intended in all situations.

Understanding Why Debugging Is Important

Debugging is the only effective means you have for fully testing your application and preventing outside entities from using your application for nefarious reasons. Good testing methodologies rely on both expected and unanticipated input to expose bugs that you explore using debugging techniques. Users look at bugs as non-entities devoid of any characteristics. All a user knows is that a bug causes the program to crash and lose data. You can't afford to have that perspective. Bugs have personalities, in that they vary by

- Type
- Cause
- Effect
- Severity
- Other factors that you include in your personal classification system

Smart developers rely on the bug personalities to define the presence and the cure for the bug. Debugging is the act of defining, detecting, categorizing, and fixing the bug. All newly developed applications have bugs—some of them are quite difficult to locate because they exist within the coding logic, some are simply a matter of not adding a required feature, and some exist as part of the development environment. For example, your application could experience an error because there's a bug in the .NET Framework—an error you must report if you have any hope of ever getting it fixed by Microsoft.

Bug classification determines when and where you'll detect the bug. It also defines how difficult the bug is to locate and the amount of help you can anticipate receiving from the IDE. You can classify bugs into the following four types:

◆ Syntax

◆ Compile

◆ Runtime

◆ Semantic

The following sections describe the four bug classifications and help you understand how each of them affects your debugging efforts. More importantly, these classifications provide you with a better idea of just why debugging is so important.

TIP   The best way to find bugs is to know your coding style. Keeping notes helps you understand patterns in your programming so that you can correct techniques that lead to bugs. More importantly, understanding your personal style helps you develop techniques for finding bugs based on past mistakes. Knowing what you did in the past can help you locate and squash bugs today.

Considering Syntax Errors

Syntax errors are the easiest errors to avoid but are also some of the hardest errors to find. A syntax error can include a spelling mistake, misuse of punctuation, or a misuse of a language element. When you forget to include an `End If` for an `If...Then` statement in Visual Basic, it's a syntax error. Likewise, C# developers encounter syntax errors if they fail to provide a closing curly brace. Syntax errors even occur in HTML. Forgetting a closing tag can cause a syntax error in many cases. The idea is that syntax errors occur when the code is misspelled, ill formed (lacking a required element), or used incorrectly in other ways.

Typos are a common syntax error. They're especially hard to find when you make them in variable names. For example, all programming languages view `MySpecialVariable` and `MySpecialVariable` as two different variables, but you might miss the typing error. You can rely on Visual Web Developer to find most variable typos for you as you write your code.

NOTE   Visual Basic developers will remember the `Option Explicit` declaration from previous versions. This declaration still exists, but the IDE now adds it by default. You would have to tell the IDE not to add this declaration to the code. One reason the IDE adds this feature automatically is to reduce the probability of a typo existing within the code.

You can easily miss some of the subtle aids to locating syntax errors if you don't view tasks that the IDE performs carefully enough. The balloon help shown in Figure 16.1 for the `Request.MapPath()` function provides a cue that you could miss. The IDE displays the balloon help shown in the figure only when it recognizes the function name that you type. When you don't see the balloon help, it's a cue that the IDE doesn't recognize the function name, and you need to look at your code. You might find that you haven't included a reference or a required statement, but you can also use this method to detect typos and other syntax errors.

FIGURE 16.1

Balloon help assists you in locating syntax errors in your code.

```
Request.MapPath (
  ▲ 1 of 2 ▼   string HttpRequest.MapPath (string virtualPath)
  virtualPath: The virtual path (absolute or relative) for the current request.
```

TIP   No matter what you do, a few syntax errors can slip by and cause bugs in your program. You can look at the errors for hours and not actually see them because you've worked with the code for so long. Asking someone else to look at your code often helps because that person isn't familiar with the code. Make sure that you ask someone with the same or better programming skills that you have to ensure that they understand your code. It's also essential that you comment your code heavily to help the other person understand what it's supposed to do.

Syntax errors also include errors in logic (the construction of expressions in your program). You can create a loop that processes the loop structure statements once too often or not often enough. An If statement can use an expression that works most of the time but isn't quite right, so it doesn't produce the correct result all of the time. Code with logic errors runs because the IDE and compiler don't know that the expression is incorrect. The only way to find this kind of syntax error is to debug the program. See the "Using the Visual Web Developer 2005 Express Debugging Features" section later in this chapter for details.

Considering Compile Errors

The .NET language compiler contains a syntax checker, among other features. The IDE uses the compiler to look for errors that prevent the program from running properly. For example, when working with Visual Basic, you might create an If...Then statement and not include the corresponding End If statement. The syntax-checking portion of the compiler runs constantly, so the IDE finds some mistakes almost immediately after you make them.

The IDE uses the compiler to find many of the syntax errors that you make and displays an error indication similar to the one shown in Figure 16.2. When you create a syntax error, the IDE displays the location with a squiggly underline, normally in red. Hover the mouse over the error to see what it is, as shown in Figure 16.2.

NOTE   The Visual Web Developer IDE uses different colors to display various error conditions. For example, the default compiler error uses a blue squiggly underline. The color of the underline provides another clue as to the kind of error that you made and helps you fix it more quickly. It's also important to know that you can modify the colors that the IDE uses to highlight errors. Choose the Tools ➤ Options command to display the Options dialog box. The Environment\Fonts and Colors folder contains the color options for errors. Select the error type that you want to change in the Display Items list and modify the presentation as needed.

FIGURE 16.2

The IDE displays some syntax errors.

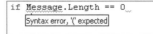

```
if Message.Length == 0
   Syntax error, '(' expected
```

Missing elements are another syntax error that the IDE finds with relative ease. For example, when working with Visual Basic, if you fail to include an End If for an If...Then statement, the IDE always finds it and displays an error presentation similar to the one shown in Figure 16.2. However, in some cases, the IDE won't find syntax errors until you try to run the program. In addition, the IDE might not always find the precise error location—sometimes it highlights another area of the block where a syntax error occurs. Fortunately, these situations are rare, so you'll generally get great help from the IDE when it comes to syntax errors.

The compiler also finds many of the punctuation errors that you can make in your code. When a line of Visual Basic code becomes too long, and you try to move to the next line without adding a continuation character, the compiler notices the error and tells you about it. On the other hand, since C# doesn't require the use of continuation characters, you won't see this kind of error when working with the C# language. The assistance you get is language specific based on the errors that the syntax-checking feature of the compiler is designed to recognize. The complier also notes missing periods between elements of a statement or missing parentheses from function calls.

Considering Runtime Errors

Some errors aren't the result of poor coding practices. Runtime errors happen when something outside your application is incorrect. A disk access request can fail, or the user can type the wrong information. In both cases, the application environment causes the problem. Your application code is correct, but the program still fails because of this external error.

Runtime errors are the reason why many large companies such as Microsoft run beta programs. (A beta program is a vendor-sponsored method of getting a program before the developers have finished it for the purpose of testing and evaluation.) A large base of users can help you find runtime errors that depend on a particular machine configuration or a specific kind of user-entry technique.

NOTE Don't confuse runtime errors with errors that occur at runtime. You can observe a syntax error at runtime. The fact that the syntax error occurs when the application is running doesn't mean that the error suddenly changes into a runtime error. Most errors can occur while the application is running (at runtime), but runtime errors (as a category) always occur when the application is running.

Unlike other kinds of errors, the IDE never provides help with runtime errors and it's not even very easy to anticipate them. Code that you know will work well can still fail in the runtime environment because this environment is so uncertain. You can trap runtime errors or change the program flow to ensure that they don't happen, but the fact remains that you won't see a runtime error until you run your application on enough machines to expose it. Unfortunately, you'll find that while runtime errors are hard for you to find, crackers are drawn to them as bugs are to light. Coding defensively—anticipating whatever can go wrong will—is the only way to overcome this particular kind of error. For example, consider this code.

```
void btnTest_Click(object sender, EventArgs e)
{
    TextReader OpenFile;   // References the Open File

    // Open the file for reading.
    OpenFile = new StreamReader("DoesNotExist");

    // Display the contents on screen.
    txtOutput.Text = OpenFile.ReadToEnd();
```

```
        // Close the file after reading it.
        OpenFile.Close();
    }
```

You won't find anything wrong with this code. It should work as presented as long as the requested file exists. However, because the file doesn't exist, the application displays the error shown in Figure 16.3 when the user clicks btnTest.

FIGURE 16.3
Runtime errors occur because the environment is incorrect.

The error isn't in the code—it's in the environment. Because the file DoesNotExist is missing, the application experiences an error. You can trap such an error using the technique shown here.

```
    void btnTest_Click(object sender, EventArgs e)
    {
        TextReader  OpenFile;    // References the Open File

        try
        {
            // Open the file for reading.
            OpenFile = new StreamReader("DoesNotExist");

            // Display the contents on screen.
            txtOutput.Text = OpenFile.ReadToEnd();

            // Close the file after reading it.
            OpenFile.Close();
        }
```

```
        catch (FileNotFoundException FNFE)
        {
            txtOutput.Text = "The file wasn't found.";
        }
        catch (Exception ex)
        {
            txtOutput.Text = "Unexpected Exception: " +
                ex.Message;
        }
    }
```

The difference, in this case, is that the code traps the error. The try...catch statement tells the compiler that you expect one or more errors to occur. Each error is an exception that the catch portion of the statement handles. The FileNotFoundException exception handles the specific case where a file is missing. However, you don't know that this is the only exception that will occur. You could rely on the .NET Framework documentation to tell you about every error, test every possible error condition, pass the error on to the next level, or simply provide a generic exception handler for the Exception class, as shown in the listing. The point is that when you run the code this time, the user will see a nice error message, rather than the output shown in Figure 16.3. More importantly, the application won't crash—it recovers from the runtime error.

Considering Semantic Errors

A particularly difficult error to find and understand is the semantic error, which is an error that happens when the application code and logic are correct, but the meaning behind the code isn't what you intended. For example, you could use a Do...Until loop in place of a Do...While loop when writing Visual Basic code. Even if the code is correct and you use the correct logic, the code won't produce the result that you expected because the meaning of a Do...Until loop is different from a Do...While loop.

The meaning that you assign to your code has to match the words that you use to write the code. Just as a good book uses precise terms, a good program relies on precise statements to ensure that compiler understands what you want to do.

Introducing semantic errors in subtle ways is easy. Writing an equation the wrong way can result in output errors. When you use the wrong equation to determine the next step in a loop, the problem becomes worse because the error looks like a syntax or runtime error. The steps between loops or the expression used to make a decision are very important. The most common error is leaving the parentheses out of an equation. The application interprets $1 + 2 * 3$ as 7, but $(1 + 2) * 3$ as 9. The missing parentheses are easy to miss when you are frantically searching for an error.

In many cases, you won't even receive a notification such as the one shown in Figure 16.3 when a semantic error occurs. The application appears to work fine, but the output is incorrect. Unless you specifically test for incorrect output, the application could enter the production environment flawed. One method of testing for semantic errors is to include Debug.Assert() method calls within your code, as shown here.

```
    void btnTest2_Click(object sender, EventArgs e)
    {
        Int32 Test = 1 + 2 * 3;
        Debug.Assert(Test == 9, "Test Should Equal 9!");
    }
```

This method appears in the `System.Diagnostics` namespace, so you'll need to add the additional reference to your code. When the runtime environment encounters the `Assert()`, it determines whether the test condition is true. When the condition is false, you'll see an error dialog box similar to the one shown in Figure 16.4. The dialog box tells you about the error and asks whether you want to proceed. The point is that the error is no longer hidden—you can find it based on your expectations for the code.

FIGURE 16.4

Use the `Assert()` method to locate semantic errors in your code.

Using the Visual Web Developer 2005 Express Debugging Features

You don't have to rely on code alone to find the bugs in your code. Once you know that a bug exists, you can use various resources that the IDE provides to locate the bug. However, locating the bug doesn't always mean a lot. After all, you might see the bug without really knowing how to fix it. The IDE also provides the resources you need to test alternative code or change values. The following sections describe the resources that the IDE provides for testing your code in the form of visual aids.

Using the Debug Toolbar

The Debug toolbar automatically appears every time you start an application for debugging. However, many developers display it all the time so they can start the application for debugging without using the menu. This toolbar (see Figure 16.5) contains all of the features needed to step through code one statement at a time. The following list describes the toolbar features.

Windows Displays a list of debugging windows. This isn't a complete list of windows—only the currently available debugging windows. For example, when you're not in debugging mode, you'll see only the Immediate window—the Locals, Watch, and Call Stack window entries appear only while in debug mode.

Hexadecimal display Changes the numbers in the various debugging windows from decimal to hexadecimal. The change in base lets you switch between numbers that most humans understand very well to those that the computer understands. Sometimes you can't easily see an error in one base, but it becomes quite clear in another.

FIGURE 16.5

The Debug toolbar contains a number of features to make runtime debugging easier.

Step out   Moves the statement pointer from the current method to the next statement in the method that called it. The application executes all of the statements between the current position and the end of the current method without forcing you to step through the individual steps.

Step over   Moves the statement pointer over a called method. The application executes all of the statements within the called method, but you don't have to step through them one statement at a time.

Step into   Moves the statement pointer into the called method and places the pointer on the first statement within that method. This feature lets you see the details of a called method.

Show next statement   Places the statement pointer on the next statement that the application will execute or on the current statement if it contains executable code. Use this feature to see where the statement pointer will go next when you see a series of structure or variable declarations statements.

Restart   Restarts the current application. The debugger resets all variables to their pre-execution state. Use this option when you want to start the application over without executing the remaining statements.

Stop debugging   Stops the debugger. Use this option to return the IDE to editing mode.

Break all   Places the IDE in debug mode for all of the currently attached applications. In most cases, you use this feature when debugging multithreaded applications.

Start or continue   Starts the application. The IDE is still in debug mode and it will stop application execution when you next click Break All or the IDE encounters a breakpoint (a special stop indicator) in the code.

Using the Immediate Window

The Immediate window is one of the most useful debugging features that Visual Web Developer has to offer. You can use this feature to test the validity of statements or check the value of variables. It also lets you change the value of variables or the properties of objects while debugging. Consequently, you can use this feature to perform "what if" analysis of your code while looking for an answer to coding problems. Figure 16.6 shows a typical view of the Immediate window with a query in place.

FIGURE 16.6

Use the Immediate window to test alternative values and code.

```
Immediate Window                                                      ☒
? txtOutput
{System.Web.UI.WebControls.TextBox}
    base {System.Web.UI.WebControls.WebControl}: {System.Web.UI.WebControls.TextBox}
    AutoCompleteType: System.Web.UI.WebControls.AutoCompleteType.None
    AutoPostBack: false
    CausesValidation: false
    Columns: 0
    Controls: {System.Web.UI.EmptyControlCollection}
    MaxLength: 0
    ReadOnly: false
    Rows: 0
    Text: ""
    TextMode: System.Web.UI.WebControls.TextBoxMode.SingleLine
    ValidationGroup: ""
    Wrap: true
```

> **TIP** You can execute single commands to the IDE using the Immediate window. Simply type the > (greater than) symbol and start typing the command you want to issue. For example, if you want to open a file, you could type **>File.OpenFile** and press Enter. When you type `File` without the > symbol, IntelliSense displays the members of the File class, not the File menu. However, if you want to issue a number of commands, you should use the Command window instead.

The Immediate window provides full IntelliSense support. Whenever you type a . (period), IntelliSense shows the members of the object that you're working with. This means that you can continue to work with objects even while debugging the application and perform additional tests to see what works best.

Changing the values of variables is one of the tasks you'll perform most often. To change a variable or property value, simply type the variable or property name and set it equal to a value. For example, if you wanted to change the `txtOutput.Text` property value to Hello, you'd type **txtOutput.Text = "Hello"** and press Enter. The Intermediate window displays the new property value on the line after the entry you make.

It's also possible to evaluate any expression within the Immediate window. For example, you could type **? txtOutput.Text == "Hello"** and press Enter to determine whether the `txtOutput.Text` property contains the value Hello. Notice the addition of the ? to the entry. The ? tells the IDE that you want to perform a query, rather than work directly with the variable. The expression must appear in the correct form, as well, for the language you're using. For example, C# requires a == (double equals sign) for Boolean expressions.

The ? is actually shorthand for the `Debug.Print()` method. You can use any of the `Debug` class methods within the Immediate window without adding the > symbol. However, if you want to issue a debug command, then you must add the > symbol.

The Immediate window also supports the use of Mark mode. You use this mode to work with any previously issued command. For example, if you didn't type quite what you want to type for a previous command, simply highlight the incorrect part of the command and start typing the correction. The Immediate window automatically copies the old command as you type the changes—reducing the amount of typing you must perform to issue any command.

Eventually, you'll end up with many entries in the Immediate window. To remove old entries, right-click the window and choose Clear All from the context menu. You'll also notice that this menu contains options for cutting, copying, and pasting entries in the Immediate window.

Using the Command Window

The Command window has a lot in common with the Immediate window. For example, you can evaluate variables and display their values (see the previous section, "Using the Immediate Window," for details). However, the main purpose for using the Command window is to issue commands. For example, type the word File and you'll see a list of associated File menu commands, as shown in Figure 16.7. Notice that the Command window always provides a > symbol on every line that you use to type commands.

FIGURE 16.7

Output commands to the IDE using the Command window.

Sometimes it's inconvenient to move your hands from the keyboard to display another window. You can switch windows by using a command. For example, if you want to move from the Command window to the Immediate window, type **immed** and press Enter. Here's a list of shortcuts for moving between windows.

- ◆ callstack (Call Stack window)
- ◆ cmd (Command window)
- ◆ immed (Immediate window)
- ◆ locals (Locals window)
- ◆ View.Output (Output window)
- ◆ watch (Watch window)

NOTE Unlike the full version of Visual Studio .NET, Visual Web Developer doesn't include any macro capability. Normally, you could request macro execution from the Command window, but this feature isn't available.

Using the Output Window

The Output window performs a number of important tasks. You'll actually see two versions of this window. The first is the Build output shown in Figure 16.8. The second, Debug, contains the output from various startup and debugging tasks. Use the Show Output From drop-down list box to change the views.

Figure 16.8 shows a successful build. You'll also find any errors that the application encounters during the build process in this view. Double-clicking on any error in the list takes you to the location of the errant code. Consequently, you can build the application and then visit each error that the compiler finds in turn.

FIGURE 16.8
Verify the results of a
build operation using the
Output window.

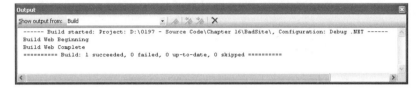

The Debug view of the Output window always contains startup messages when you start the application. Figure 16.9 shows a typical example of the messages that Visual Web Developer generates for a simple application. Looking through the list of loaded entries can help you determine the source of startup failures or other problems later during application execution. By following the list of startup entries, you can determine errors such as loading the wrong version of a referenced DLL.

FIGURE 16.9
See debugging state-
ments as your code exe-
cutes to determine how
events take place.

The Output window also displays debugging messages that you produce using a number of **Debug** class methods. You place these entries in your code and they execute only when you debug your application. Figure 16.10 displays some entries produced using the essential **Debug** class methods.

FIGURE 16.10
Add debugging state-
ments to your code to see
events and code flow.

To produce these entries, you need to include special code in your application. Here are the entries used to produce the output in Figure 16.10.

```
// Display the value of the variable.
Debug.Print("Printed: " + Test.ToString());
Debug.WriteLine("Written: " + Test.ToString());

// Display an indented line.
Debug.Indent();
Debug.Print("This line is indented.");
Debug.Unindent();

// Display a line only when a specific condition exists.
Debug.WriteLineIf(Test <= 9, Test, "Test Error");
```

The Debug.Print() and Debug.WriteLine() methods work about the same from an Output window perspective. The difference comes in the flexibility that each method offers. When using Debug.Print(), you can provide a list of values as an array in the second argument. On the other hand, the Debug.WriteLine() method lets you specify an error category as the second argument. Neither of the second arguments shows up in the Output window but do affect any listeners that you create for your application (writing debug listeners is a complex topic that won't appear in this book). Note that there's also a Debug.Write() method you can use to write several entries on the same line, rather than placing them on separate lines.

The Output window doesn't allow much in the way of formatting, but you can indent text to make the various levels easier to see. For example, you might want to indent each layer of calls in your application. Use the Debug.Indent() and Debug.Unindent() methods to add and remove levels from the output. You can use the Debug.IndentLevel property to determine the current indent level of your code. The Debug.IndentSize property lets you set the number of spaces between each indent level.

Sometimes you don't want to display a debug statement every time in the Output window. You can control debug statement output using the Debug.WriteLineIf() method. The first argument is an expression that controls the display of the debug statement. Whenever the statement is true, the debug statement appears in the Output window. Note that you also have access to the Debug.WriteIf() method when you want to display the output on the same line.

The "Considering Semantic Errors" section earlier in this chapter discusses the use of the Debug.Assert() method. You can also create a condition where the assertion always occurs using the Debug.Fail() method, as shown here.

```
// Display a failure.
Debug.Fail("It Failed", "This is a failure message.")
```

It's important to realize that the Debug.Fail() method always displays an assertion, so you can't use it in the regular code flow. However, you can use it as part of a Catch statement or as part of an optional code flow. Figure 16.11 shows typical output from both the Debug.Assert() and Debug.Fail() methods. Notice that this content looks very much like the information in the dialog box shown in Figure 16.4, so the Output window provides the means for you to preserve the assertion information.

FIGURE 16.11
Assertions and failures also appear in the Output window.

Using the Error List Window

Visual Web Developer provides a number of methods for managing application errors. The Error List window presents a list of the problems in your code. The window separates the entries into errors, warnings, and messages, as shown in Figure 16.12. Notice that the window shows the number of each entry type at the top of the window. In addition, you can set the window to display any combination of errors, warnings, and messages by clicking the appropriate entry at the top.

FIGURE 16.12

Determine which errors the IDE has detected using the Error List window.

The Error List window is always active when you're writing your code. Whenever you make a mistake that the system catches as you type, it appears in the Error List window. In addition, the IDE adds any errors that it finds when it compiles your code to the list. Consequently, you can simply go down the list to locate the current problems in your code. Double-click any entry and the IDE takes you to that error in the code.

It's easy to reconfigure the Error List window to meet your specific needs. All of the configuration options appear on the context menu that appears when you right-click the window. Besides the options that you expect to see on the list such as Copy and Delete, you'll also find the Sort By and Show Columns submenus. These submenus define how the window orders any error entries and what information it displays about them. You can sort the entries by priority, category, default order, description, file, line, column, and project. The displayable columns include category, default order, description, file, line, column, and project (the IDE always displays the error priority).

Using the Locals Window

The Locals window helps you see the active state of local application variables. This window contains a list of all the variables associated with the current method or property. It doesn't show variables outside the current scope. For example, if you have a global variable, it won't appear in this window even if the current method or property performs some task with the variable. You'll see the values of any arguments used to call the method. The Locals window shows the variable name, value, and type, as shown in Figure 16.13.

The entries show the local variables for the btnTest2_Click() method shown in Listing 16.1. The sender and e variables are part of the arguments for the method, while Test appears within the method. Click the plus sign next to any variable and you'll see the properties and objects it contains (if any). You'll find this example in the \Chapter 16\BadSite folder of the source code on the Sybex Web site.

FIGURE 16.13

All of the local variables appear in the Locals window.

LISTING 16.1: Exploring the Locals Window

```
void btnTest2_Click(object sender, EventArgs e)
{
    // Create a variable based on a math expression.
    Int32 Test = 1 + 2 * 3;

    // Display the value of the variable.
    Debug.Print("Printed: " + Test.ToString());
    Debug.WriteLine("Written: " + Test.ToString());

    // Display an indented line.
    Debug.Indent();
    Debug.Print("This line is indented.");
    Debug.Unindent();

    // Display a line only when a specific condition exists.
    Debug.WriteLineIf(Test <= 9, Test, "Test Error");

    // Display a failure.
    Debug.Fail("It Failed", "This is a failure message.");

    // Ensure the value is correct.
    Debug.Assert(Test == 9, "Test Should Equal 9!");
}
```

Notice that some of the variables listed in Figure 16.13 contain magnifying glass icons in the Value column. When you click this icon, you'll see a list of Visualizers, including the text, XML, and HTML Visualizers shown in the figure. Select any of the Visualizers from the list and you'll see the value displayed in that format. Using Visualizers helps you see the data in a specific format. This technology is especially helpful when working with Visual Web Developer because you often run into XML data embedded within an object.

Depending on how you set up a method, you might see some interesting calling arguments. In this case, `sender` is a `Button` control—the one handled by this event handler. This means you have access to a global variable, `btnTest2`, at a local level.

Figure 16.13 shows one local variable that isn't declared anywhere—`this`. Every method and property has access to the `this` object, which refers to the local application. The `this` object contains a reference to the application as a whole and everything that the application contains, as shown in Figure 16.14. Consequently, even though the Locals window legitimately accesses only local variables, the `this` object provides a view of the application as a whole.

FIGURE 16.14

Every local method has access to the *this* object, which contains access to some global elements.

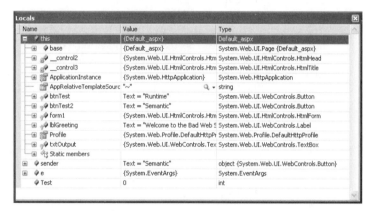

The best way to use the Locals window is to view just local variables and occasionally glimpse the application. When you need to view specific variables, especially those at the global level, then you really need to use the Watch window described in the next section of this chapter. The Watch window not only lets you reduce the number of items you have to track but also lets you organize the variables so that you can perform debugging with greater ease.

Using the Watch Window

The Watch window provides a custom view of variables, expressions, and objects within your application. You'll place variables, expressions, and objects that you want to watch in this window. The easiest way to do this is to highlight the code in question and drag it to the window. The Watch window also allows you to type variables and functions by hand. You can create multiple Watch windows for a given debugging session. The Watch window shows the variable name, value, and type, just like the Locals window, so the two windows operate similarly. Figure 16.15 shows a typical view of the Watch window.

FIGURE 16.15

Watching the values and objects in your application can help track tricky bugs.

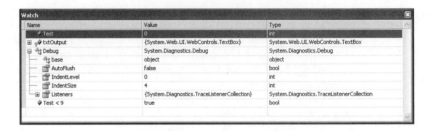

In this case, you see a local variable, an object on a form, a class with static properties, and an expression. The local variable is also available in the Locals window, but these other entries help you understand why the Watch window is so useful. For example, when working with objects, you don't need to drill down to find it in the `this` object. In fact, you can go further than shown in Figure 16.15. When you want to view just one property in the object, you can use dot syntax within the Watch window to see it directly—you could see the `txtOutput.Text` property directly, rather than have to find it in a list of properties.

The ability to create expressions in the Watch window is also important. You can look for important changes as you step through the application. For example, you could use this method to determine precisely when one variable becomes greater than another variable in the code. The changes signify the point where an error occurs in the execution of your application.

One of the biggest problems with using the Watch window is that you can develop tunnel vision. You can become so focused on the variables that you choose to watch that you miss clues to resolving an application error. That's why the Locals window is so important. This window shows you all of the variables for the current method or property. When you begin feeling that you're missing something—it's usually time to move from the Watch window to the Locals window long enough to see if anything is happening within the application that you need to know about.

Using the Call Stack Window

The Call Stack window answers the question of how the application got to the current point of execution. Every time the application makes a call, CLR adds the call to the call stack. When the call returns, CLR removes it from the call stack. In short, the Call Stack window shows you a list of pending calls, which tells you how the application accessed the current function, as shown in Figure 16.16.

FIGURE 16.16

Determine the path used to reach a method using the Call Stack window.

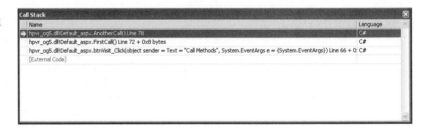

The call at the top of the stack is the current call. As you progress down the list, you get closer to the original calling point. In this case, the original caller is the btnVisit_Click() event handler. However, that entry contains a lot more useful information, as shown here (the entry normally appears on one line, but is split due to space requirements).

```
hpvr_og5.dll!Default_aspx.btnVisit_Click(object sender = Text = "Call Methods",
    ~CASystem.EventArgs e = {System.EventArgs}) Line 66 + 0x8 bytes
```

The entry begins by telling you the name of the DLL, hpvr_og5.dll. You won't recognize the name of this DLL because Visual Web Developer generates it for you when you compile the application. The Default_aspx Web page appears within the DLL, which contains the btnVisit_Click() method. This method requires two input arguments. Notice that the call stack tells you the input argument type, name, and default value. For example, sender is an object type that has a default Text property value of Call Methods. The entry ends with the location of the btnVisit_Click() method within the source file and the number of bytes that this method requires.

Sometimes it's not enough to look at the Call Stack window. Fortunately, double-clicking an entry takes you to that method within the source code. Viewing the code doesn't alter the call stack, nor does it change the order of execution, but it does help you understand the program flow better.

Managing Breakpoints

Knowing how to use the windows isn't helpful until you know how to stop the application at precise points of execution. One way to stop application execution is to click Break All on the Debug toolbar shown in Figure 16.5. However, this method isn't very precise. Breakpoints address the need for precision. Whenever your application is running in debug mode and it encounters a breakpoint, the debugger stops the application so you can examine the values and single step through the order of execution. Only when the application stops precisely do the various debugging windows become helpful.

Working with breakpoints is very easy. To add a breakpoint to a line of code, right-click the line of code and choose Breakpoint ➤ Insert Breakpoint from the context menu. The IDE highlights the line of code in red (as a default) and places a circle in the left margin of the IDE, as shown in Figure 16.17.

In this case, the code stops at the line that assigns a value to Test, Int32 Test = 1 + 2 * 3;. You can't place breakpoints on lines of code that simply declare a variable—the code doesn't allow you to see an action, so there really isn't a good reason to stop there. The breakpoint indicates the start of a command. In other words, the application won't actually assign a value to Test until you step past this line of code using any of the step commands on the Debug toolbar such as Step Over (you can also use the options on the Debug menu if you wish).

FIGURE 16.17

Add breakpoints to your code to stop execution in selected places.

Removing a breakpoint is just as easy as adding one. To remove the breakpoint, right-click the line of code containing the breakpoint and choose Breakpoint ➢ Remove Breakpoint from the context menu. Sometimes, however, you don't actually want to remove the breakpoint—you simply want to disable it for a while. In this case, choose the Breakpoint ➢ Disable Breakpoint command instead. The line remains highlighted as before, but the IDE displays a hollow circle, as shown in Figure 16.18. The breakpoint remains in place, but the IDE won't stop at it during the debugging process.

FIGURE 16.18
Disabled breakpoints let you maintain the breakpoint position without stopping.

At some point, you'll want to use the disabled breakpoint again. Use the Breakpoint ➢ Enable Breakpoint command to enable the breakpoint again.

Visual Web Developer also provides a number of global breakpoint commands that you'll find on the Debug menu. For example, you can enable all of the breakpoints in an application using the Debug ➢ Enable All Breakpoints command. Note that many of these global commands appear only when you need them. For example, you won't see the Enable All Breakpoints entry on the Debug menu when none of the breakpoints are disabled.

When you run your application in debug mode, the breakpoints become active. As soon as the application encounters a breakpoint, execution stops in that thread and you can begin stepping through the code. The IDE highlights the breakpoint line in yellow and you'll see an arrow in the breakpoint circle, as shown in Figure 16.19.

FIGURE 16.19
Encountering a breakpoint when the application is running stops the current thread.

Defining Your Development Goals

This chapter has helped you understand the levels and ranges of debugging that Visual Web Developer provides. You've seen the debugging tools that Visual Web Developer provides in action. Debugging is an essential task—one that every developer must understand completely or the current situation with faulty applications will never resolve itself. From some perspectives, this is the most important chapter in the book because many developers don't really understand debugging well. It doesn't matter whether you write a "Hello World" application or the next must-have tool for users, every application requires debugging.

Now it's time to develop your debugging skills. One way to do this is to create code with errors purposely to see how the system reacts. Interestingly enough, you won't find much help in this area, even though working with broken code is a very good way to develop debugging skills. Try exchanging a broken application with a friend so that you don't know what to expect. It's only by seeing simple cases of errors that you can begin to see patterns in complex applications. Simple studies help you understand the problems that certain classes of bugs can create so that you can spot them faster in real applications.

Chapter 17 describes another important area of application development—security. Most developers know that users expect secure applications and every developer wants to avoid becoming the next one mentioned in a trade press magazine as leaving a huge gaping hole in an application that crackers exploited. Security is an important issue because crackers have become quite adept at finding and using security holes in applications for their own purposes. Chapter 17 helps you understand the risks and overcome them without devoting your life to tracking down every potential problem, real or not.

Chapter 17

Designing Secure Applications

Previous chapters have already discussed security issues. For example, the "Considering the Security Issues of Using Controls" section of Chapter 14 describes how to generate certificates and shows how to use them in Secure Sockets Layer (SSL) communications. All of these security topics are important. Explore any newspaper or magazine today, and you'll find that security is a topic of discussion in many venues, even those outside the developer community. This chapter discusses security in earnest. It won't discuss the topics that appeared in other chapters, but will provide a general discussion of security for your applications. For example, you'll find sections that discuss general security issues and that consider the need to create a security plan for both your organization and the applications you create.

This chapter also discusses specialized controls you can use to verify data that a user provides. The techniques extend to gaining information about the data methods received from other parts of the application and helping you understand how to build a cohesive security picture for your application. Only when your application provides the required level of security at all failure points can you feel reasonably sure that application security is as good as you can make it.

WARNING   Security isn't an issue that you visit once or twice during the life of your application—you visit this issue constantly. In fact, it's better to assume that a cracker is going to break through your security and maintain vigilance based on that assumption. Yes, good barriers will keep honest people honest and even deter some less-skilled individuals, but a determined cracker will always find a way to break down your security precautions.

Understanding the Common Security Issues

It's important to understand the general security issues of the .NET environment. More importantly, it's important to understand how .NET interacts with the online environment supported by Visual Web Developer. One of the most secure computer environments is one in which the computer has no outside access at all. In fact, locking the computer by itself in a closet somewhere with the on/off switch locked off is possibly the most secure environment of all, but it's hardly usable. Using a computer means exposing it to some level of risk from security intrusions. The more public and connected the computer, the less secure it becomes. In fact, think for a moment about software such as a firewall, virus protection, or spyware detectors. All of this software has one thing in common—it reduces the connectivity that the computer provides in some way, making the computer less accessible. Accessibility—the ability of the computer to communicate—represents a security risk. The following sections describe how .NET helps and how it doesn't help your security efforts.

Considering the Security Issues that .NET Resolves

When Microsoft started designing .NET, the world of computing was moving from the local area network (LAN) and wide area network (WAN) to the Internet. The individual user and group approach Windows used didn't necessarily reflect the best way to pursue security in a distributed environment. In addition, the current environment was too open to potential attacks from outside.

To overcome the security problems inherent in Windows, Microsoft enhanced the role-based security approach originally found in COM+ to work as a general programming methodology. In addition, the managed environment maintains better control over resources that tend to create problems in the unmanaged Windows environment. These two security changes, along with the object-oriented programming strategy of the .NET Framework, summarize what you'll find as security enhancements in the .NET Framework. Here's a list of the critical security enhancements for the .NET Framework.

Evidence-based security   This feature determines what rights to grant to code based on information gathered about it. The Common Language Runtime (CLR) (pronounced "clear") examines the information it knows about an assembly and determines what rights to grant that code based on the evidence. CLR matches the evidence against a security policy, which is a series of settings that define how the administrator wants to secure a system. Web applications generally have fewer rights than desktop applications, but as demonstrated in the "Setting .NET Security" section of Chapter 14, you can change the security policy to meet specific needs.

Code access security   CLR uses this feature to determine whether all of the assemblies in a calling chain (stack) have rights to use a particular resource or perform a particular task. All of the code in the calling chain must have the required rights. Otherwise, CLR generates a security error that you can use to detect security breaches. The purpose of this check is to ensure that a cracker's code can't intercept rights that it doesn't deserve. Only .NET provides the unique ability to validate code security, as well as user security (the older Windows system concentrated all efforts on the user). A piece of code that can execute locally might not execute over the Internet because of this feature.

Defined verification process   Before the Just-in-Time (JIT) compiler accepts the Microsoft Intermediate Language (MSIL) assembly, it checks the code that the assembly contains for type safety and other errors. This verification process ensures that the code doesn't include any fatal flaws that would keep it from running. The checks also determine whether an external force has modified strongly named code. After JIT performs these checks, it compiles the MSIL into native code. CLR can run a verified assembly in isolation so that it doesn't affect any other assembly (and more important, other assemblies can't affect it).

Role-based security   If you know how role-based security works in COM+, you have a good idea of how it works in .NET. Instead of assigning security to individuals or groups, you assign it based on the task that an individual or group will perform. The Windows security identifier (SID) security is limited in that you can control entire files, but not parts of those files. Role-based security still relies on identifying the user through a logon or other means. The main advantage is that you can ask the security system about the user's role and allow access to program features based on that role. An administrator will likely have access to all of the features of a program, but individual users may have access only to a subset of the features.

Cryptography   The advantages of cryptography are many. The concept is simple—you make data unreadable by using an algorithm, coupled with a key, to mix up the information. When the originator supplies the correct key to another algorithm, the system returns the original data. Over the years, the power of computers has increased, making old cryptography techniques suspect. The .NET Framework supports the latest cryptographic techniques, which ensures that your data remains safe.

Separate application domains   You can write .NET code in such a way that some of the pieces run in a separate domain. It's a COM-type concept where the code is isolated from the other code in your program. Many developers use this feature to load special code, run it, and then unload that code without stopping the program. For example, a browser could use this technique to load and unload plug-ins. This feature also works well for security. It helps you run code at different security levels in separate domains to ensure true isolation.

Determining Where .NET Can't Help

Security is a problem precisely because it's a system designed by one person to thwart access to resources by another person. What one person can create, another can just as easily destroy. In fact, it's always easier to destroy than to create—so crackers have a significant advantage over those of us trying to create a secure environment. Consequently, security is an ongoing process. You need to know the threats your system faces so that you can monitor and protect against them.

Most developers focus on writing bulletproof code and adding as many security precautions to the code as possible without slowing application performance to a crawl. Although the .NET Framework provides a good basis for building applications with robust security, it can't protect you from other sources of security problems. The sections that follow detail these security problems. They provide suggestions on how you can use .NET along with other strategies to reduce problems to a minimum.

BALANCED CODING REQUIREMENTS

One of the biggest security problems you'll face is the balanced coding requirement. Everyone wants a secure application, but they aren't willing to pay the price to get it. Secure code necessarily uses more resources and runs more slowly (all other things being equal) than nonsecure code. Secure code also introduces reliability problems (the code would rather fail than provide access to an intruder) and is less flexible (it's less tolerant of hostile environments). It doesn't matter whether the code fails gracefully when a security problem occurs—all the user sees is that the code has failed. When enough users complain that the secure code you wrote doesn't allow them to be completely lazy, management will likely request that you relax the rules. Management will also ask you to rewrite the code when it works too slowly on antiquated equipment or requires too many resources. At some point, all of the competing requirements balance and you have an application that everyone can live with. The result is likely less secure than it should be.

The .NET Framework helps you create code that's amazingly secure, but generally, that code won't meet the balance that you need. The question becomes, how secure do you actually need the code to be? For example, you could put your collection of milk bottle caps in Fort Knox and be assured that the collection is perfectly safe. However, does a milk bottle cap collection really need that much security? You must answer the level of security question. It's important to make this decision as part of the design process before you begin writing code. Security works well only when you design the application to use it, rather than bolt it on later.

However, the decision you make can have unanticipated and unwelcome consequences. Consider the scenario where a hole in your security—one that you decided not to fill because filling it caused too much of a performance hit—acts as a conduit for cracker activity on your system. The cracker manages to gain access to the system through the application you built. It's not a big deal for the current application because it doesn't store any critical data, but the cracker has also inadvertently gained access to the database containing customer credit card information. The design decision probably seemed acceptable for this one application, but not when viewed from a whole system perspective. In short, you must make your design decisions—discover the point of balance—based on the needs of the entire system and not just one application or group of people.

STUPID USER TRICKS

You've likely seen all of the jokes, heard all of the stories, and seen some of user-related problems yourself. The most horrid story I've read appears in an InfoWorld article titled "Stupid User Tricks." One is about a traveler who had taped both the dial-in phone number for his server and his password to the outside of his laptop carrying case. (See `http://www.infoworld.com/article/ 03/01/24/030127Security_1.html` for details.) Finding plenty of horror stories is never a problem—solving the security issues that users create is another story.

After 18 years of consulting, one of the first security scans I perform at a client site is to check the area surrounding desks for pieces of paper with passwords on them. Invariably, I usually find at least one piece of paper with not just one, but several passwords on it. The passwords aren't even hard to figure out. It almost seems that the user is determined to make it easy for the janitor to make off with all of the company passwords.

TIP   One of the reasons that users write down passwords is that network administrators insist on using interesting passwords such as jk$LL12Z# to make life harder for crackers. Unfortunately, these passwords are nearly impossible for users to remember and with the continuing advances in computer technology, even these difficult passwords will remain viable for only so long. A better approach is to use a pass-phrase. A pass-phrase relies on an easily remembered phrase that's difficult to guess because of its length. For example, you could use a phrase such as "I love listening to Pink Floyd at 8:00." This phrase is 39 characters long, includes both uppercase and lowercase letters, and has numbers and special characters, including spaces, which most cracking tools don't consider today. You can read more about this technique at `http://www.pcmag.com/article2/ 0,1759,1736152,00.asp`.

To an extent, the .NET security features can help overcome problems users create. No, it won't automatically detect Post-it notes placed on the monitor, but it does ensure that the user doesn't gain rights to resources by using code incorrectly. Code access security helps in this regard. For example, when a user requests access to a file, the user's rights are checked and the rights of the code are checked. If either check fails, then access to the file fails.

Training, well-written *policies* (instructions for handling various security situations), and *rules* (requirements that everyone must meet) with some teeth in them can also help with user security problems. However, this is one area where you'll continually have problems because people will normally find a way around rules that are inconvenient. The .NET Framework can help here as well. You can write code such that the network administrator controls security policies, not the user. This technique makes it possible for the network administrator to monitor problems and ensure the program has a reasonable chance of maintaining a secure environment.

SOME EXTERNAL FORCES

Most people associate external forces that threaten security with crackers. This group does receive a lot of attention from the media, which is why they're the group that many programmers consider first (and perhaps last). While crackers do cause a great many problems, they aren't the only external force to consider.

Employees on the road or recently let go from the company can cause a great deal of harm to your applications. The problem is twofold:

◆ Using the old Windows security system, an application might execute at the same privilege level whether the employee accesses it from a desktop or from a remote location. The .NET Framework considers this issue by adjusting the rights of an application based on the zone in which it executes.

◆ An employee is much more familiar with the security setup and organization of your system than any cracker. Unfortunately, this is a problem that .NET can't help you solve. Someone determined to break into your system is almost certainly going to do it. The only way to overcome this problem is to monitor the system constantly.

Other programs can also affect your application—at least if it's a Web-based application. In a day when distributed applications can rely on services that your program can provide, it's possible that some other programmer you've never met will cause a security problem on your system and not even realize it. The .NET Framework helps you solve this problem by adhering to standards-based security. New standards such as WS-Security and WS-Inspection make it easier to write programs that work across platforms and provide a secure environment. You can learn more about these standards at Web Services Specifications site (`http://msdn.microsoft.com/library/en-us/dnglobspec/html/wsspecsover.asp`).

Inept network management can also cause serious problems. A network administrator could restore old policies to a server or overwrite the recently patched files for your application. Newer versions of Windows have some protection for both of these issues. For example, Windows File Protection can help ensure that only the latest version of your files remain on disk. The .NET Framework also helps by making version checks before it loads files and executes them. An overwritten file would have the wrong version number and .NET would display an error indicating this fact. This fix may not make the user very happy, but at least you'll know the cause of the problem.

Another source of external problems is the connections you create with other businesses. Distributed applications are becoming more common as companies invest more in Web services. The problems with distributed applications are many, and you can't expect the .NET Framework to solve them all. Many of the strategies for overcoming this problem hinge on standards-based application development such as using the WS-Security standard for your application.

Wireless devices present one of the most prevalent and least understood security problems for developers today. Some wireless networks aren't secure. Anyone with the proper equipment can come along and access the network from outside the company. Some people are using this technique to spread illicit email using company Internet connections without anyone knowing. The .NET Framework can't do anything about this kind of security problem—you must overcome it by securing the wireless network.

Something's always attacking your data, even nature. Fortunately, keeping your data safe, or at least knowing when someone has tampered with it, is relatively easy because this is an area where security professionals have spent a lot of time. First the bad news—if you have any kind of data transfer at all (even on a LAN), be prepared for situations when that data is compromised. The good news is that the .NET Framework uses the latest technologies, such a cryptography to secure your information.

POORLY PATCHED SYSTEMS

Patches are problematic no matter how you look at them. First, there's the problem that the existence of a patch tells many users that the vendor didn't test the program well. Second, there's the issue of compatibility. Some patches actually cause more problems than they fix by creating compatibility problems or introducing new problems onto a system.

Although these issues are probably not going away any time soon, you still need to patch your system to ensure that it has the latest security features and that any security holes are fixed. You need to think about the results of not patching your system and consider how the lack of patches affect any programs you produce on the system. With this in mind, you'll want to use three tools to check your system for problems before you begin developing a new program.

Windows Update   Always check Windows Update to verify the status of any patches for your system. Windows Update works automatically. All you need to do is select the updates you want to download. The one mistake that some developers make is not reading the information about a patch (or any other update for that matter) before they install it. This may lead to problems on a development machine. You can find Windows Update at `http://www.windowsupdate.com/`. It also pays to check the Windows Update Catalog at `http://v4.windowsupdate.microsoft.com/catalog/en/default.asp`.

Microsoft System Update Services (SUS)   Microsoft SUS can reduce the burden of updating multiple machines for a business. This system helps you download and distribute updates in a safe environment. Learn more about this product at `http://www.microsoft.com/windows2000/windowsupdate/sus`. (Microsoft is changing the name of SUS to Windows Update Services or WUS.)

Microsoft Baseline Security Analyzer (BSA)   Windows setups can become quite complex. It's easy to miss an update when you have multiple pieces of software to consider. Add to this problem the issue of individual driver updates, and security can become a considerable problem. The Microsoft BSA won't solve all of your problems, but it can help by providing a comprehensive list of problems within a system. Learn more about this product at `http://www.microsoft.com/technet/security/tools/mbsahome.mspx`.

NOTE   Some people report problems downloading and using the updated drivers that Microsoft provides as part of Windows Update and other update services it supports. Generally, it's a better idea to obtain driver updates directly from the vendor to ensure that it will work with your system. In addition, never update a driver unless you experience the issue that the driver addresses or the driver contains a security update that you must install to maintain your system.

INEPT ENTERPRISE POLICIES

I actually knew of a moderately sized business that lacked a real network administrator and had a policy in place that made every network user an administrator. The person who was supposed to administrate the network was simply too lazy to set up the required features and didn't want to hear user complaints about not being able to access a particular file or feature. Imagine what would happen if a cracker decided to attack the company's Web application. The network would transmit administrator commands from every infected machine and eventually crash under the weight of infection.

Setting enterprise policies is one case when the .NET Framework might actually increase the number of security problems your application will have to face. Microsoft assumes that every network administrator is faithful, loyal, hardworking, conscientious, and knowledgeable. The .NET Framework is set up to ensure that the network administrator has maximum access to security features. Unfortunately, some network administrators just aren't up to the task and you'll have to find ways to overcome this problem.

Training is one way to help network administrators fulfill their new role with the applications you create. Many will find it quite surprising that they can control who uses a particular function within their components and specific features in an application. However, the best strategy is to use imperative and declarative security effectively in your applications to ensure that they maintain some level of security even if the network administrator doesn't do anything at all.

Distributed applications are notorious for opening security holes because these applications make hidden resources visible to users through an Internet connection. It's amazing that some companies don't have security policies in place to protect from these problems. What's even more amazing is that a few companies actually end up opening new holes in their firewall and other security features to enable an application to work. For example, some companies still rely on Distributed Component

Object Model (DCOM) applications to create distributed applications. The .NET Framework isn't the only solution at your disposal, but by using modern Web services techniques, you can greatly reduce the risks distributed applications impose. Fortunately, Visual Web Developer can help you create robust Web applications that keep security holes to a minimum through the use of Web services.

One of the most interesting security problems is one in which a company follows all other best practices, but then fails to lock up the computer so that no one can access it physically. If someone can gain physical access to a server, they can control the server in a relatively short time. A worst-case scenario occurs when the company not only leaves the computer in the open, but also thoughtfully provides a monitor and keyboard so that anyone entering the room can modify the server setup. Although the best policy is to lock up the computer, there are alternatives if you must keep the computer in plain view. For example, you can add physical locking to the system. SecurityWare (`http://www.securityware.com`) provides a number of specialized computer-locking mechanisms that make physical access a lot more difficult.

WINDOWS FILE PROTECTION VULNERABILITIES

Windows File Protection is thought to be a safe way to install executable files on a system because those files are supposedly signed. Unfortunately, there's a well-known method to create files that Windows File Protection will trust even if they aren't signed by an appropriate digital certificate. You can read the detailed version of the problem on the Bugtraq site at `http://archives.neohapsis.com/archives/ntbugtraq/2002-q4/0122.html`. A Microsoft security bulletin on the topic appears at `http://www.microsoft.com/technet/security/bulletin/MS00-072.asp`.

The interesting thing about the .NET Framework is that it doesn't rely on this security mechanism. When you sign a control, component, or application, CLR verifies the signature. The signature uses a hash mechanism that exists outside the Windows File Protection environment, so CLR ensures the security of the file. You can always check the token used to secure a file with a strong name that's contained within the Global Assembly Cache by viewing the content of the `\WINDOWS\assembly` folder. Figure 17.1 shows a typical example of the content of this folder.

FIGURE 17.1

Managed files use a unique signature system that ensures their integrity.

Creating a Security Plan

Crackers depend on a certain level of disorganization within a company in order to employ their trade. The social engineering attacks that most crackers use rely on the user not knowing whom to contact regarding company policy or even knowing that the company doesn't have a security policy. That's why it's important to create a security strategy for you or your organization before you even begin coding the application. The strategy should spell out how you plan to approach certain issues, such as a password inadvertently lost or a breach of the database. Even if your application affects only you because you run a one-person shop or you're experimenting, it's important to consider security issues before you begin coding so that security is part of your application design from the outset. In short, you need some type of strategy that eventually becomes a written security plan.

Security plans are great, but you need to translate that plan into code. New programming features in Visual Studio .NET rely on your ability to define the application user. For example, you can't develop a role-based security strategy for an application until you know which roles the users could fulfill as they use the application. Some developers brainstorm roles they think an organization will need, but this leaves holes from unused roles in the application implementation and makes the application more complicated to configure.

The developer also needs to decide how to implement security. You can configure security at the client, the server, or both. Security can appear as an internal programmed function, something the administrator can configure using an MMC snap-in or other tool, a user-controlled application feature, or an add-on implemented as needed for distributed requirements. In many cases, an application requires several levels of security and uses more than one method for implementing it. The application design should specify what type of security to implement and qualify how to implement it. Never hardwire the security into a Web application—always implement the main security features at the server.

Another consideration is the type of security you want to implement. You have a choice of traditional Windows security, newer role-based security, or third-party implementations. Third-party implementations are important because Windows doesn't fill every gap in the modern application. For example, if you choose to use the SOAP or some other XML-derivative to transfer data, you'll need a third-party product to secure the information in most cases (using a secure server connection does help).

Most developers find that role-based security works best at the server. It enables the developer or network administrator to create a security policy based on the tasks the user must perform, rather than focusing on the user's job title or other personal information. Role-based security is extremely flexible because you can employ it programmatically or rely on the network administrator to configure it. A developer also has the option of enforcing a minimum-security level and allowing the network administrator to enforce more stringent security measures as needed.

Configuring ASP.NET

Visual Web Developer works with ASP.NET to provide a specific level of security for your applications. Generally, you add special attributes to your code, in addition to actual security checks, to implement application security. Control and component security generally relies on a combination of attributes and coded security checks too, but always requires some level of configuration, as demonstrated in the "Setting .NET Security" section of Chapter 14. Applications can also require configuration, but this configuration information appears as part of the Web.CONFIG file. ASP.NET itself also requires some level of configuration in the form of local and server policies. The following sections describe the generic issues you need to consider—look for specific issues in application, control, or component sections of the book.

Working with the Configuration Web Site

The `System.Web.Security` namespace is the one that you'll use for the majority of your Web security needs—no matter what type of application you want to create. For example, this namespace contains the `PassportIdentity` class. The following sections describe essential security that you can provide using a combination of the `Web.CONFIG` file and classes such as the `FileAuthorizationModule` class.

TIP   Microsoft has scaled back their goals for Passport according to a ComputerWorld article at `http://www.computerworld.com/managementtopics/outsourcing/itservices/story/0,10801,96838,00.html`. Passport is still a solid technology, and you'll find it useful for some types of security needs, such as when you host a number of satellite companies or groups from partner companies. This chapter won't include a Passport example due to space concerns. However, you can find such an example in my book, *.NET Development Security Solutions* (Sybex, 2003).

DEFINING FILE SECURITY USING THE *FILEAUTHORIZATIONMODULE* CLASS

The `FileAuthorizationModule` class doesn't look like very much from the description in the help files. However, this class is exceptionally important because it's one of the few distinct links between Windows security and the security employed by the .NET Framework. Whenever a caller requests a resource such as a file, the `FileAuthorizationModule` class authenticates the caller against the Windows Access Control List (ACL). This isn't the role-based or code access security that a .NET application normally relies on to authenticate a caller.

TIP   Web security takes a number of forms. While the classes in the `System.Web.Security` namespace can help you keep your data safe to a certain extent, most applications still require additional security measures such as the WS-Security standard (`http://www-106.ibm.com/developerworks/webservices/library/ws-secure/`). You can read about a number of products on the market today to help developers make the most of the potential of WS-Security in the InfoWorld article at `http://www.infoworld.com/article/03/04/15/15appnews_1.html`.

The tie-in with older Windows technology is important. For example, without this link, ASP.NET impersonation (the use of a default account in place of the standard user account to access a resource) wouldn't work. This class also provides a way for you to restrict access to certain resources such as a file to specific callers using standard security measures. This means that someone who accesses the site using a PDA will have the same rights to that file as if they were accessing it from their desktop—a good feature when used to deny or grant access to a resource based on credentials, rather than other factors.

An alternative to using the `FileAuthorizationModule` class is to rely on the `UrlAuthorizationModule` class. Although this option might seem more in line with the .NET way of working with security, you must manually enter the information used for authorizations purposes in the `Web.CONFIG` file. Here's an example of an authorization entry:

```
<authorization>
    <allow users="John"/>
    <allow roles="Administrators"/>
    <deny users="Guest"/>
    <deny roles="Guests"/>
</authorization>
```

In this case, the user named John and anyone in the Administrators role would gain access to the resource, but CLR would deny the user named Guest and anyone in the Guests role access. The problem with this technique is that it doesn't necessarily work well with all callers (including wireless devices where the user name or role is ambiguous at times) and it keeps the authorization information in plain text form on the Web server. In short, using the FileAuthorizationModule class method is the more secure choice in this case. CLR uses the FileAuthorizationModule class automatically when you fail to include an <authorization> section in the Web.CONFIG file.

You can learn more about the various roles of these two classes in security in Microsoft Knowledge Base article 306590 at http://support.microsoft.com/default.aspx?scid=kb;[LN];306590. Note that using the FileAuthorizationModule class can result in errors due to a bug in the .NET Framework implementation. See Knowledge Base article 317955 at http://support.microsoft.com/default.aspx?scid=kb;[LN];317955 for details.

DEFINING FORM SECURITY USING THE *FORMSAUTHENTICATION* CLASS

The FormsAuthentication class can help you overcome some of the issues with authenticating clients who can't use the more secure Windows login. For one thing, it helps you create an environment in which ASP.NET authenticates the caller, but it doesn't matter quite as much who the caller is, where the caller is located, or what device the caller is using. This form of authentication relies on special server configuration, application configuration, and a few programming tricks. Listing 17.1 shows the first part of this application. You'll find this example in the \Chapter 17\ FormAuthorize folder of the source code found on the Sybex Web site.

LISTING 17.1:   Defining the Login Page

```
private void btnLogin_Click(object sender, System.EventArgs e)
{
    HttpCookie  AuthCookie; // Authorization cookie.

    // Verify the user has proper access.
    if (!FormsAuthentication.Authenticate(txtName.Text,
                                    txtPassword.Text))
        throw new SecurityException(txtName.Text +
                                " is not authorized!");

    // If the user is authenticated, generate a cookie.
    AuthCookie = FormsAuthentication.GetAuthCookie(txtName.Text, true);

    // Place the cookie in the response.
    Response.Cookies.Add(AuthCookie);

    // Redirect to the default page.
    Response.Redirect(Request.QueryString.Item("ReturnUrl"));
}
```

This example begins by calling one of the secure pages on the Web site. Because `Default.ASPX` is the only available Web page, the example calls it. However, the user never sees the Web page because the server automatically redirects the user to the `Login.ASPX` page shown in Figure 17.2. Notice the `ReturnUrl` argument in the query string—the server automatically adds it for you so that you can create code that knows where the user started. All of these tasks happen without any code on your part, but you need to know that they occur.

FIGURE 17.2

The login page appears automatically when the user requests a secure page.

At this point, the login page waits for the user to type a user name and password, and then click Login. When the user provides the required information, the code calls on the `FormsAuthentication.Authenticate()` method to authenticate the user against the data stored in the `Web.CONFIG` file. This method of authentication doesn't rely on the standard Windows names and passwords—a caller must appear in a separate credential database to access the page.

NOTE The application is currently set to accept `John` as the user name and `hello` as the user password. You can create a hash for any password you wish by modifying the `FormsAuthentication.HashPasswordForStoringInConfigFile("hello", "SHA1")` line of code shown in Listing 17.3.

At this point, ASP.NET has authenticated the user or the application has generated a `SecurityException` and the caller hasn't gained access to anything. The code stores the authentication information in a cookie and redirects the caller to the target page.

You can't ask for forms authentication and not provide any data to support it. The `Web.CONFIG` file requires additional entries to make this type of authentication work. Listing 17.2 shows the changes you need to make.

LISTING 17.2:   Modifying the *Web.CONFIG* File

```
<!-- Use the Login.ASPX form for authentication. -->
<!-- <authentication mode="Forms">
  <forms loginUrl="Login.ASPX" requireSSL="true"> -->

<!-- Use this line for testing with Visual Web Developer. -->
 <authentication mode="Forms">
```

```
<forms loginUrl="Login.ASPX">

    <!-- Create a list of credentials. -->
    <credentials passwordFormat="SHA1">
        <user name="John"
              password="AAF4C61DDCC5E8A2DABEDE0F3B482CD9AEA9434D" />
    </credentials>

  </forms>
</authentication>

<!-- Deny access to users who aren't authenticated. -->
<authorization>
    <deny users="?" />
</authorization>
```

You need to pay careful attention to several features of this configuration file. First, notice the `requireSSL="true"` attribute. It's extremely dangerous not to include this entry because the user's name and password appear in plain text otherwise. You should also set the server to use SSL by changing the Secure Communications entry on the Directory Security tab of the application Properties dialog in the Internet Information Services console. (You could also change just the entry the particular file, but securing the entire application is better.)

WARNING   Visual Web Developer doesn't support SSL. To test this example with Visual Web Developer, you must use the second <forms> element—the one that doesn't require SSL. Use the first <forms> element when you move the application from your local machine to a production server.

Second, notice the `passwordFormat="SHA1"` attribute. All of the passwords in the credentials list are hashed using the SHA1 encryption standard. Listing 17.3 shows one technique you can use to obtain the required information. Because the cracker could access the configuration file, you want to keep all sensitive data encrypted.

Third, notice that the `<authorization>` element now contains a `<deny>` child. This entry specifically denies access to any unauthenticated callers.

Once ASP.NET authenticates the user, the application redirects them to the `Default.ASPX` page. In this case, the page shows several of the other `FormsAuthentication` object features. Listing 17.3 shows the code for this portion of the example.

LISTING 17.3:   Generating Forms Authentication Statistics

```
private void Page_Load(object sender, System.EventArgs e)
{
    // Get the information for the current user and display it.
    lblOutput.Text = "Forms Cookie Name: " +
        FormsAuthentication.FormsCookieName +
        "<BR/>Forms Cookie Path: " +
        FormsAuthentication.FormsCookiePath +
```

```
    "<BR/>Is SSL Required? " +
    FormsAuthentication.RequireSSL;

// Hash a password for storage in the configuration file.
lblHashPwd.Text = "Hashed Password for hello:<BR/>" +
    FormsAuthentication.HashPasswordForStoringInConfigFile(
        "hello", "SHA1");

// Sign out.
FormsAuthentication.SignOut();
}
```

The code begins by listing a few statistics for the page. Notice that you can determine the SSL status of the page before you do anything. Always check the FormsAuthentication.RequireSSL property to ensure that the application uses SSL. The code uses the FormsAuthentication.HashPasswordForStoringInConfigFile() method to generate a hash for the password for user John using the SHA1 standard. Finally, the application logs off using the FormsAuthentication.SignOut() method. Figure 17.3 shows typical output from this application.

FIGURE 17.3
The default page shows the hash value for "hello" along with status information.

Using the Login Controls

Many Web sites today provide a login system that anyone can use. For example, you might sign up to use a list server or gain access to the latest information on a news server. You might also want to make this system part of a shopping cart application (see Chapter 15). The point is that you want to know who these people are, but you don't necessarily want to limit their access to the Web site. Generally, the user signs up for access and you send them an email granting access to the Web site after checking their credentials. The following sections describe a list of controls that make setting up this kind of login system a lot easier. In fact, you'll find that you don't have to do much work at all to make it operational. You'll find this example in the \Chapter 17\Login folder of the source code on the Sybex Web site.

USING THE ASP.NET WEB SITE ADMINISTRATION TOOL FOR SECURITY

Many of the login controls, such as the actual Login control, contain a special Administrate Website option on the associated Smart Tag. You won't see this particular link anywhere else. Choose this option and you'll see the ASP.NET Web Site Administration Tool shown in Figure 17.4.

FIGURE 17.4
Use the ASP.NET Web Site Administration Tool to create users and roles, and set Web site security.

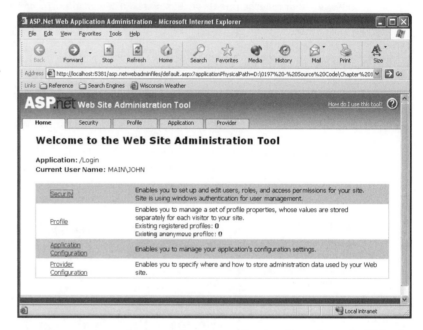

This utility helps you create a secure environment for your application. It works at the Web site level, not at the global server level. The settings that it creates appear in the AspNetDB.MDB file in various tables. For example, when you create roles, they appear in the aspnet_Roles table. The user data appears in two locations. You'll find the user entries in the aspnet_Membership table and the roles that these users occupy in the aspnet_UsersInRoles table. The general per user security profile information appears in the aspnet_Profile table. Because you can protect the database, creating a security setup using this technique is safer than using the Web.CONFIG file discussed earlier in this chapter. However, you can't make changes as quickly and this method isn't as compatible as the Web.CONFIG file—it works only with ASP.NET 2.0. In short, you must choose the kind of security you want to create based partly on the needs of the system.

NOTE Some security settings still reside within the Web.CONFIG file—the ASP.NET Web Site Administration Tool simply makes managing the settings easier. For example, allowing or denying access still requires use of the <authorization> element with <allow> and <deny> child elements. View the Web.CONFIG files in the \Chapter 17\Login folder of the source code on the Sybex Web site for details.

When you initially set up a Web site, the first link you'll want to click is Security. The Security page, shown in Figure 17.5, lets you set the kind of authentication the Web site uses and defines, whether the application relies on role-based security. Always use role-based security for pure ASP.NET applications because it provides the highest level of security and requires the least amount of programming.

FIGURE 17.5

Modify the security settings before you perform any other tasks.

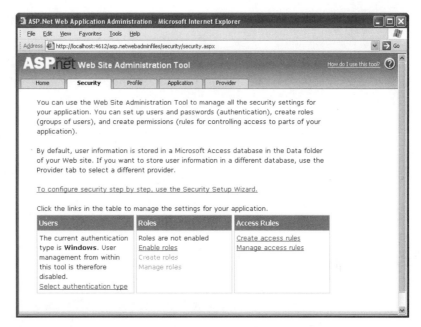

The tool lists two choices when you choose the Select Authentication Type option. You can choose local security, where the application relies on integrated Windows authentication based on the server entries and Internet security, where the user must log in using a form. The settings are a little misleading. You should use local security whenever you create a private Web site—one where you know the users in advance. Use the Internet setting when you plan to allow unknown users to create an account and receive access after you approve them. To gain maximum benefit from the examples in this chapter, you should select the Internet option. Otherwise, the various security forms have less effect on the actual functioning of the Web site. When you select the Internet option, the form shown in Figure 17.5 changes to let you add new users to the Web site. (See the "Creating New Users" section of the chapter for additional information.)

After you add the initial users to the Web site, you'll need to determine whether you want to enable roles for them. It's important to create roles that the users will actually fill, not roles that you think you might need at some point. Excess roles create security gaps that you won't want in your application. When you click the Enable Roles option shown in Figure 17.5, the system enables the Create Roles and Manage Roles options. You use these links to work with roles for this application—the roles don't affect the Web server as a whole. Click Create Roles and the ASP.NET Web Site Administration Tool will display a text box where you add a role name. Enter all of the roles you want to create first, and then click the Manage link for each role. Add users to each role based on that user's needs.

The directory structure you create makes a big difference when you begin setting up the access rules using this tool. You can't choose individual files, so you must arrange the individual Web pages in folders where you can apply the same access rule to the entire folder. For example, you'll want to make the login folder accessible to everyone, including anonymous users, but the data folders available only to logged-in users. An administrative folder might provide access only to the administrators group and you might have statistical folders available to power users. Figure 17.6 shows settings for the Administrative folder for this example. In this case, the settings would deny access to anonymous users.

FIGURE 17.6

Make user settings changes as needed to provide a secure application environment.

TIP   Don't assume that you can't fine-tune your security setup. The settings you create with the ASP.NET Web Site Administration Tool provide only a starting point. You can also make changes by adding code to your application. For example, you can display content based on whether the user is in a specific role. Consequently, you have very fine control over the security of your application, but you must mix settings and coding techniques to obtain this control.

USING THE ASP.NET WEB SITE ADMINISTRATION TOOL FOR PROFILES

Even though profiles aren't necessarily security specific, you can use them to help manage security. You access the profiles by selecting the Profile link on the main ASP.NET Web Site Administration Tool page shown in Figure 17.4. A profile is essentially a variable that you add to the application and assign to a group, as shown in Figure 17.7. When the group names match role names, you can use these variables to make decisions about the application based not only on the security role, but also on the properties assigned to that role.

You can create only one property with a specific name for a particular group, but you can create the same property for multiple groups. For example, you can't create multiple instances of the SeeStatistics property for the Visitors group, but you can create this same property in both the Administrators and the Visitors group. The profile properties actually appear in the Web.CONFIG file, as shown here.

```
<profile>
    <properties>
        <group name="Visitors">
            <add name="SeeStatistics"
                defaultValue="False"
                type="System.Boolean" />
```

```
            </group>
            <group name="Administrators">
                <add name="SeeStatistics"
                    defaultValue="True"
                    type="System.Boolean" />
            </group>
        </properties>
    </profile>
```

Consequently, you can manage these settings without using the ASP.NET Web Site Administration Tool, but using the tool makes working with the settings a lot easier. The point is that you can make these settings, change them, and use them in your code to make decisions without making any coding changes. You add flexibility to the application environment without having to rewrite or recompile your code.

FIGURE 17.7
Use profile variables to change the behavior of your application without compiling it again.

LOGGING EXISTING USERS IN

The Login control is the most essential for creating a secure Web site using the techniques described in this section. It's the only control that you must include somewhere in the Web site. Otherwise, no one can log in and therefore, no one can see the data you want to provide.

NOTE   The example is set to use George Smith as the username for the Visitors group and John Mueller as the username for the Administrators group. In both cases, use "hello" as the password. Obviously, these entries are only samples and you can change the setup to meet specific needs.

Configuring this control is a little odd. You can simply dump the control on the page and not do anything with it, or you can set it to perform certain tasks automatically. In general, the only feature you really need to define is where to go after the user logs into the Web site using the `DestinationPageUrl` attribute. Here's a typical Login control setup.

```
<asp:Login ID="liMain" Runat="server" AccessKey="L"
           CreateUserUrl="~/NewUser.aspx"
           CreateUserText="Create New User Account"
           DestinationPageUrl="~/MyData/DataPage.aspx"
           InstructionText="Type your name and password."
           BorderPadding="5" BorderStyle="Ridge"
           PasswordRecoveryText="I Forgot My Password"
           PasswordRecoveryUrl="~/RecoverPassword.aspx"
           HelpPageText="Get Password Help"
           HelpPageUrl="~/HelpOnPasswords.aspx">
    <InstructionTextStyle BorderStyle="Ridge" BorderWidth="4px"
                          BackColor="Black" ForeColor="White">
    </InstructionTextStyle>
    <FailureTextStyle Font-Bold="True" ForeColor="Red"
                      Font-Size="Large" >
    </FailureTextStyle>
</asp:Login>
```

The entries you choose to use depends on what login features you want to provide. For example, you need to provide only the `CreateUserUrl` and `CreateUserText` attributes when you want to allow outsiders to create a new user. Of course, the user changes don't actually take effect until the administrator approves them (unless you allow unfettered user creation on your Web site).

WARNING   The login page won't work correctly if you don't name it `Login.ASPX`. The system automatically redirects all user requests to `Login.ASPX` when the user isn't logged in. Fortunately, you don't have to implement any special logic to return the user to the page they requested. The `Login` control automatically handles the `ReturnUrl` query string variable for you. All the user has to do is login and the redirection occurs automatically.

The `InstructionText` is optional, but it provides the user with helpful information, especially when you are working with less experienced users. Make sure you include a distinctive `<InstructionTextStyle>` element to focus the user's attention on this additional information. You might also want to define the `HelpPageText` and `HelpPageUrl` when you're working with many novice users. The help page should provide clear instructions on how to use each of the options. In addition, you might want to provide the email address of the support center for your company.

Users are going to forget their passwords. It doesn't matter what kind of user you work with, there's a very good chance that even advanced users will forget their password from time to time. Consequently, you should always define the optional `PasswordRecoveryText` and `PasswordRecoveryUrl` entries to help the user regain access to the Web site. As part of this addition, you'll also want to define a `<FailureTextStyle>` element to ensure that the user actually notices when an error has occurred. Notice that this control performs all these tasks without any code—all you need to provide is the proper settings changes.

As part of the login page, you should also show the user their current login status. You provide this information as part of the LoginView control. As a minimum, you'll want to provide both a logged-in message and a logged-out message. However, you can also provide messages based on the user's role. For example, you might want to include special information for administrators. Here's a typical example of the LoginView control at work.

```
<asp:LoginView ID="LoginView1" Runat="server">
    <RoleGroups>
        <asp:RoleGroup Roles="Administrator">
        <ContentTemplate>
            Welcome Administrator<br />
            <asp:HyperLink ID="hlSeeData1" Runat="server"
                           NavigateUrl="MyData/DataPage.aspx">
                See the Data
            </asp:HyperLink><br />
            <asp:HyperLink ID="hlAdminister" Runat="server"
                           NavigateUrl="Administrative/AdminPage.aspx">
                Manage the Web Site
            </asp:HyperLink>
        </ContentTemplate>
        </asp:RoleGroup>
    </RoleGroups>
    <LoggedInTemplate>
        You are currently logged in.<br />
        <asp:HyperLink ID="hlSeeData2" Runat="server"
                       NavigateUrl="MyData/DataPage.aspx">
            See the Data
        </asp:HyperLink>
    </LoggedInTemplate>
    <AnonymousTemplate>
        You are currently not logged in.
    </AnonymousTemplate>
</asp:LoginView>
```

The <LoggedInTemplate> element provides the information for logged-in users. The system doesn't limit you to using text—you can include any required controls as well. The example includes a link for the logged-in user to return to the main data page. The <AnonymousTemplate> element provides a simple message for anyone visiting the Web site. This is the message that anyone visiting the Web site sees when they first visit because everyone is anonymous at the outset.

The <RoleGroups> element begins a series of entries that defines specific messages for users in specific roles. The example provides a special message for the Administrator group. You create a RoleGroup control by selecting the Edit RoleGroups option on the LoginView control Smart Tag. Provide the names of the roles that you want to support and then define the special messages for each group. You can perform this task using Design view, but sometimes this task is easier using Code view because you can copy message elements from other templates. Figure 17.8 shows typical output from this application. This figure shows a logged-in administrator.

FIGURE 17.8

Design whatever style of login you need with a few simple settings changes.

LOGGING USERS OUT

It's important to offer the user an opportunity to log out of the system on every protected Web page. Otherwise, some users will simply remain logged in, even after they leave your Web site to visit other locations. Although the system will eventually time out and force a logoff, your Web site will remain more secure and perform better when you let the user log out of the system. The LoginStatus control lets you add login and logout functionality to your Web pages. All you need to define is the logout URL, as shown here.

```
<asp:LoginStatus ID="lsLogout" Runat="server"
                  LogoutPageUrl="../Login.aspx" AccessKey="L" />
```

CREATING NEW USERS

Whether you allow anyone to create new users on your Web site depends on the kind of Web site you own. A Web site that provides access to news stories or other reading material might simply want to track which users are reading what material, which means that security isn't the focus of logging in and you can provide free access to the feature. On the other hand, you might want to provide a means for letting administrators quickly add users to a Web site. You use the same CreateUserWizard control, but the control appears on an administrator page instead of on an easily accessible part of the Web site. The CreateUserWizard control also offers an incredible amount of customization potential. You can define your own processing steps and even include specialized functionality.

The actions that the CreateUserWizard control performs when someone creates a new user depends on the level of customization you incorporate. A basic setup creates a new user who doesn't belong to any role. Consequently, a user could request access to the Web site, but not actually gain any access to it until you assign the user to a group when you set the Web site security up correctly. The example uses this approach. You can create a new user, but the user gains access to the Web site only after the administrator adds the user to a role. Here's a basic CreateUserWizard control setup.

```
<asp:CreateUserWizard ID="CreateUserWizard1" Runat="server"
                      CancelDestinationPageUrl="~/Login.aspx"
```

```
                    ContinueDestinationPageUrl="~/Login.aspx"
                    CompleteSuccessText="Successfully created"
                    DisableCreatedUser="True"
                    DisplayCancelButton="True">
    <WizardSteps>
        <asp:CreateUserWizardStep Runat="server"
                                  Title="Sign Up for Your New Account">
        </asp:CreateUserWizardStep>
        <asp:CompleteWizardStep Runat="server" Title="Complete">
        </asp:CompleteWizardStep>
    </WizardSteps>
 </asp:CreateUserWizard>
```

To make even the basic control functional, you must provide a `ContinueDestinationPageUrl` argument property. Because this control doesn't provide a means of escape (getting back to previous page) by default, you should set the `DisplayCancelButton` argument to True and provide a `CancelDestinationPageUrl` argument value. The `CompleteSuccessText` argument shows what the user will see for a successful addition.

This control works by creating a series of steps for the user to follow to sign up for your Web site. A default control includes just two steps. The first displays the sign-up page shown in Figure 17.9. You can change this page as needed. The second displays a completion page.

FIGURE 17.9

The default page requests a minimum of user information to create an account.

The `<WizardSteps>` element contains a list of steps that the user must complete to create a new account. You can add any number of intermediate steps or change the default steps as needed. This flexibility lets you create a new account creation process of any complexity. You add additional steps using the `WizardSteps` property in Design view. Click the ellipsis and you'll see the Wizard Steps Collection Editor dialog box where you can add and remove steps as needed.

CHANGING PASSWORDS

Many Web sites make it easy to create an initial account, but nearly impossible to change your password later. Given the security breaches that Web sites suffer today, allowing the user to change their password whenever necessary is important. The ChangePassword control makes adding this feature extremely easy. Here's a typical example of this control.

```
<asp:ChangePassword ID="cpPassword" Runat="server"
                    CancelDestinationPageUrl="~/MyData/DataPage.aspx"
                    ContinueDestinationPageUrl="~/MyData/DataPage.aspx">
</asp:ChangePassword>
```

The control needs only two essential arguments. The CancelDestinationPageUrl argument tells the control where to send the user after clicking Cancel. Likewise, the ContinueDestinationPageUrl argument defines where to redirect the user for a successful change. Generally, you'll set both destinations the same. Figure 17.10 shows a typical view of the ChangePassword control in action.

FIGURE 17.10

Use the ChangePassword control to reduce the complexity of user password changes.

RECOVERING A PASSWORD

Nothing saps customer support resources like sending users lost passwords. The PasswordRecovery control automates the process. This is an extremely simple control to use, as shown here.

```
<asp:PasswordRecovery ID="PasswordRecovery1" Runat="server"
                      SuccessPageUrl="~/Login.aspx">
</asp:PasswordRecovery>
```

All you need to provide is the SuccessPageUrl attribute so the control knows where to send the user after a successful recovery. The actual recovery is a three-step process. The user begins by proving a name and clicking Submit. The next step, shown in Figure 17.11, requests the user's special question. In this case, it's the name of the user's cat. When the user answers the question successfully, the system sends their password to the email account that the user supplied. The combination of the special question and the email destination makes this process reasonably safe.

NOTE   You must configure an email server on the Application tab of the ASP.NET Web Application Administration Tool to use the PasswordRecovery control. Simply click the Configure SMTP E-mail Settings link, and you'll see settings that you can use to update the email information for your server.

FIGURE 17.11
Reduce user support
costs by automating
password recovery.

Checking All Incoming Data

One of the most common exploits for any Web application that relies on forms is to trick the form into doing something the originator didn't envision. Unfortunately, Web applications often prove difficult to monitor for these kinds of errors. The reasons include the use of text for all entries, the lack of strong data typing, and the problems of forcing scripts to perform tasks normally associated with full-fledged programming languages. Fortunately, ASP.NET provides validators to make it easier to maintain security by ensuring that the user can input only values that you want to use.

An Overview of Validators

Validating Web applications can become quite complex, so Microsoft provides validators. A validator is a special control that ensures the user enters the right type of data and in the proper range. Each kind of validator performs a specific check, so you might use several validators together to provide full data entry coverage for your application.

Although validators vary in functionality, all validators require an error message found in the Text property that the user sees and uses to correct the error on the Web page. For example, when a user types a value that's outside the correct range, the RangeValidator displays the error message in the Text property. In addition, all validators provide a ControlToValidate property that you use to associate the control with the validator. (Some validators might require two controls as input.) Visual Web Developer supports several validator types, but here are the types you'll commonly use for applications.

CompareValidator The CompareValidator accepts two controls as input and then compares the value of each control. If the two controls don't match the condition you specify, the CompareValidator displays an error message. The name of the second control appears in the ControlToCompare property. The Operator property defines the comparison between the two controls. For example, if you choose the GreaterThan option, the value of the control listed in the ControlToValidate property must be greater than the value of the control listed in the ControlToCompare property. A Type property ensures that the second control contains data of the correct type, but this is almost superfluous because the two controls won't compare if their types don't match.

RangeValidator The RangeValidator ensures the input in a control falls within a range of values. The MinimumValue and MaximumValue properties contain the limit of values the user can input. You'll use the Type property to determine what type of data the control will accept. The RangeValidator accepts common types including string, integer, double, date, and currency. If the input doesn't fall within the selected range of values or is of the wrong type, the control will display an error message.

RegularExpressionValidator The RegularExpressionValidator uses an expression consisting of a specially formatted string that defines the kind of input required to validate the content or format of the input. For example, you could use an expression that evaluates input for all numeric entries or all character entries. You'll find that the Microsoft help topics tend to focus on the format of the expression, as do the built-in expressions. However, the example in this section will show you how to build an expression that defines the content of the expression. The expression used for comparison with the input of the target control appears in the ValidationExpression property. Click the ellipsis in this property to display the Regular Expression Editor dialog box shown in Figure 17.12.

FIGURE 17.12

The Regular Expression Editor helps you choose a predefined expression or create one of your own.

RequiredFieldValidator This is the easiest of validators to understand. If the target control is blank, the validator displays an error message. Some developers use an asterisk in place of the error message and simply display one error message for all required fields. However, the use of a custom error message for each controls means that you can provide example input for each field.

ValidationSummary Most of the validation controls display errors immediately after the control loses focus. Some users can find this behavior distracting or frustrating. Use the ValidationSummary to display a list of page error at one time and in one place. Set the Display property of the validator control to None in order to suppress the standard display and make it appear in the summary instead. Figure 17.13 shows a typical Web page with a ValidationSummary control.

Notice that I haven't mentioned any need for application code. All of the validators perform their job without any coding on your part. The only work you need to perform is configuring the validator as described in the list. The validator performs the rest of the work for you at that point.

All of the validators provide client-side support. This feature forces the client to fix any errors in the form before the browser will send it to the server. Using a validator means that your server will have to react to fewer poorly formatted messages and will work more efficiently. Of course, validators can only check for specific problems.

You can use multiple validators on one field to ensure that the application detects as many problems as possible. In addition, the CustomValidator enables you to create special validators that can react to some unique conditions. Unfortunately, the CustomValidator requires you create code to make it functional, which makes a CustomValidator the custom programming solution for special situations.

FIGURE 17.13

Use a *ValidationSummary* control to consolidate form error messages.

WARNING   Visual Web Developer still includes and supports the `CustomValidator` control, but you should avoid using it. Microsoft has marked this control as obsolete. You might not see this control in the next update of ASP.NET. Even so, the `CustomValidator` control can be quite useful in special situations.

Using Validators in an Application

Validators only require that you provide any required settings for use. The example in this section shows all of the essential validators so you can see how they work with a form. Listing 17.4 shows the test code for this example. You'll find this example in the `\Chapter 17\Validators` folder of the source code on the Sybex Web site.

LISTING 17.4:   Using Validators to Check Data Input

```
<form id="frmValidatorTest" runat="server">
<div id="Heading">
    <asp:Label ID="lblGreeting" Runat="server"
               Text="Validator Test Example"
               Font-Bold="True" Font-Size="X-Large"></asp:Label>
</div>
<div id="TestArea">
    <p>
        <asp:Label ID="lblTestEntry" Runat="server"
                   Text="Type Some Test Text: "
                   AssociatedControlID="txtTestEntry"></asp:Label>
        <asp:TextBox ID="txtTestEntry" Runat="server"></asp:TextBox>
```

```
        <asp:RequiredFieldValidator
            ID="rfvTestEntry" Runat="server"
            ErrorMessage="You must provide a text entry!"
            ControlToValidate="txtTestEntry" Display="None" >
        </asp:RequiredFieldValidator>
        <asp:RegularExpressionValidator
            ID="revTestEntry" Runat="server"
            ErrorMessage="Type 2 to 15 Characters Only!"
            ControlToValidate="txtTestEntry" Display="None"
            ValidationExpression=
    "[ABCDEFGHIJKLMNOPQRSTUVWXYZabcdefghijklmnopqrstuvwxyz]{2,15}">
        </asp:RegularExpressionValidator>
        <asp:CompareValidator
            ID="cvTestEntry" Runat="server"
            ErrorMessage=
                "txtTestEntry Doesn't Compare with txtCompare!"
            ControlToValidate="txtTestEntry"
            ControlToCompare="txtCompare" Display="None">
        </asp:CompareValidator>
    </p>
    <p>
        <asp:Label ID="lblCompare" Runat="server"
                Text="This Entry Used for Comparison Only: "
                AssociatedControlID="txtCompare"></asp:Label>
        <asp:TextBox ID="txtCompare" Runat="server">
            CompareMe
        </asp:TextBox>
    </p>
    <p>
        <asp:Label ID="lblNumeric" Runat="server"
                Text="Type a Number Between 1 and 10: "
                AssociatedControlID="txtNumeric"></asp:Label>
        <asp:TextBox ID="txtNumeric" Runat="server"></asp:TextBox>
        <asp:RequiredFieldValidator
            ID="rfNumeric" Runat="server"
            ErrorMessage="You must provide a numeric entry!"
            ControlToValidate="txtNumeric" Display="None">
        </asp:RequiredFieldValidator>
        <asp:RangeValidator
            ID="rvNumeric" Runat="server"
            ErrorMessage="Type a value between 1 and 10!"
            ControlToValidate="txtNumeric" Display="None"
            MinimumValue="0" MaximumValue="10" >
        </asp:RangeValidator>
    </p>
    <p>
```

```
        <asp:Button ID="btnSubmit" Runat="server"
                    Text="Submit"
                    AccessKey="S" PostBackUrl="Default.aspx" />
    </p>
</div>
<div id="SummaryArea">
    <p>
        <asp:ValidationSummary ID="Summary" Runat="server"
                               HeaderText="Error Summary" />
    </p>
</div>
</form>
```

The kinds of validators you use will depend on the kind of input you expect from a control. The example uses three controls, as shown earlier in Figure 17.13. The first contains text input and relies on the `RequiredFieldValidator`, `RegularExpressionValidator`, and `CompareValidator` controls to ensure validity. The `RequiredFieldValidator` control doesn't require any special configuration.

The `RegularExpressionValidator` control requires some means of determining correct output. Although you can rely on the Microsoft supplied templates, in some cases, they won't fulfill most needs. Generally, you'll have to provide a template. The template for this example looks like this:

```
[ABCDEFGHIJKLMNOPQRSTUVWXYZabcdefghijklmnopqrstuvwxyz]{2,15}
```

The information within brackets tells the `RegularExpressionValidator` control which characters are acceptable. A cracker can't send a virus script to your server using the characters shown. The numbers within curly brackets define the acceptable character limits. A user can provide any input that relies on characters between 2 and 15 characters long. This comparison could introduce problems in some cases. Notice that the list of acceptable characters doesn't include a period or spaces. You could conceivably set up a situation where the user can't provide the required input.

The `CompareValidator` control also requires special input. In this case, `txtTestEntry` must compare with `txtCompare`. This control can provide you with help when the user provides a value that doesn't match a value you expected. Generally, you won't need to use it, but it's nice to know the control is available when you do. Because of the three controls provided in this example, the only text that the user could type that would pass the tests is "CompareMe".

Numeric input requires different handling from text input. When working with numbers, you're normally looking for a value between two ranges. Consequently, the numeric input relies on the `RequiredFieldValidator` and `RangeValidator` controls. Like the text input, the `RequiredFieldValidator` control ensures only that the user provides some kind of input—it doesn't require specific input.

The `RangeValidator` control requires that you provide the `MinimumValue` and `MaximumValue` attributes. These two attribute ensure that the input is a number that falls between the required minimum and maximum value. The user can't provide a script and have it pass the test. For that matter, typing three, in place of 3, won't pass the text either. The user must provide numeric input for this validator to accept the input. Figure 17.14 shows output from the various checks performed by this example.

FIGURE 17.14

Validation reduces the chances of someone sending you data that you don't want.

Hardening Your Applications against Outside Intrusion

As important as security and validation are, you still need to do more to protect your application from hostile influences. Of course, your first line of defense is constant vigilance—make sure you check your application for damage, look for unwanted (or unexpected) files on your system, and verify that your database is intact whenever possible. A check here or there can make a significant difference in your system's security. The following sections describe some other tactics you can use to keep crackers at bay.

Preventing Data Leaks

Your Web site has a data leak. It doesn't matter how well you secure the site or whether the people using it are trustworthy, the data leak is there. Many developers discount the problem of data leaks because they think they have followed every security procedure. However, data leaks occur not because of a programming problem, but because of an implementation problem. Displaying any information at all on a Web site causes an information leak for your organization. Of course, since the purpose of a Web site is to provide information to viewers, your application wouldn't be worth very much without at least a small information leak. In addition, some kinds of information leaks are actually good for your organization, such as when you announce a new product.

Part of your responsibility as a developer is ensuring that your design doesn't leak data that is better left private. For example, make sure your templates, databases, and Web pages contain only the information that they need to contain. Of course, these data sources still have to provide functionality, so you can't leave them blank. Make sure that you don't confuse protected company information with essential user information. You still have to make the Web page accessible and it still requires good help to avoid confusing the user.

Data leak protection can take other forms. For example, your organization might rely on a database to supply information for Web pages. At some point, your program will need to access the required database record, extract the data, apply it to a page, and output the result. This setup provides a perfect opportunity to scan for forbidden words, such as the name of a new secret project, during the extraction phase using regular expression parsing. Obviously, this form of data leak protection won't fulfill every need—a smart user who is determined to leak information will find some other words to do it. This limitation is the same reason that spam filters are only partially successful.

Many people complain that digital rights management is a bad thing and it can be a bad thing when used for the wrong purposes. This book doesn't discuss matters that are legal, philosophical, or ethical, except when it comes to working with code. Information leaks occur when someone passes data from your Web site to a second person that shouldn't view it. The data transfer can occur as part of covert information sharing or as an accidental data release as part of an email. If you want to maintain the secrecy of proprietary company information that you must make available on the Internet, make sure you use digital rights management. Even if someone obtains a copy of the file, it's useless without the password required to open it for viewing. After you decide to protect the file using some type of encryption (such as password protection for Adobe Acrobat files), you should also use data encryption to transfer the data. Ensuring that no one can access your data without permission and then guarding the data through encryption doesn't accomplish much if you don't protect the means for obtaining it. Make sure that your security measures really do keep unwanted people out of the system.

Encrypting Your Data

Data encryption is an essential data protection technique today and you really can employ it on Web sites. You have a number of choices to make, such as the use of symmetric or asymmetric encryption. Remember that the asymmetric technique found in the `System.Security.Cryptography.AsymmetricAlgorithm` class relies on a public/private key pair, making it the logical choice for Web communications because you can trust others with the public key, while keeping the private key safe on your system. The use of two keys makes it possible to work with others in a secure manner without exposing yourself to needless risk.

Encryption also relies on an encryption technique and a specific hash algorithm. When working with Web-based algorithms, you need to consider the likes, dislikes, and requirements of the other participants in a data exchange. The most common encryption technique in use today is Rivest, Shamir, and Adleman (RSA). You can find this algorithm in the RSA class and the implementation in the `RSACryptoServiceProvider` class.

Some developers see data encryption as an all-or-nothing undertaking. The facts are less clear. You actually have multiple encryption choices and strategies to choose from when working with Web applications. However, you can group these approaches into whole message or individual element categories. When you use SSL to create an application, the system encrypts the entire message. Encryption and decryption time is one reason why SSL communication takes so much time. Likewise, you can implement channel sinks to perform the task if you don't want to rely on a pure SSL approach. A channel sink lets you maintain control over the communication.

Encryption always increases the size of the message, consumes additional processing time, and generally slows everything down. Consequently, the smart developer uses enough encryption to ensure that sensitive data remains safe, but not so much encryption that the system slows to an unacceptable speed. Desktop applications have faster communication channels, so full message encryption isn't quite as much a burden as with Web applications. Partial message encryption is much faster and resource efficient when working with Web applications.

Defining Your Development Goals

This chapter has explored general security issues—those that affect your application and even your entire computer system as a whole. You can't ignore security issues in today's environment. Too many crackers are waiting to probe your application, locate the hole they want to use, and compromise your system for you to ignore security in even the smallest application. This chapter provides tools you need to combine with the security topics in other chapters in this book to create a good security setup for your application.

It's time to begin setting up your security strategy. In fact, you should have security polices in place before you write even one line for code. Make security part of the foundation of your application and include it at every level of the design and implementation process. Make sure you schedule security testing and revise your security strategy as needed. Planning is an essential part of creating a robust security environment for both your application and your organization.

Chapter 18 helps you discover downloadable applications. Generally, you use downloadable applications when a control or component won't perform the task fully. In some cases, the user will have to install the application to make it functional. A downloadable application provides functionality needed between business partners or as part of a solution for a work-at-home scenario. Downloadable applications are well-defined methods of providing interaction between trusted entities. In short, this chapter visits an area that is equally in the future as it is available today.

Chapter 18

Creating Downloadable Applications

Downloadable applications are a special kind of software where the user can work with the application from a Web page, rather than having it stored on the local desktop. A downloadable application differs from controls and components that the user can download because they're self-contained and perform a specific task. One way to view downloadable applications is as a variant of the helper application that browsers have always relied on to display some types of data. For example, when you click a PDF link online, the browser will more than likely open a copy of Adobe Acrobat Reader to view the information.

The Internet, trade press, and just about every other source you can imagine have discussed downloadable applications for years. For example, Microsoft has considered creating downloadable forms of its Office products. However, you'll notice that they haven't done it and part of the reason is that creating large downloadable applications isn't practical without the required resources such as network bandwidth. It's possible to create small- or even medium-sized downloadable applications. For example, you could probably create a calculator program and offer it as a downloadable application on your Web site.

Needless to say, any time you create an application that the user downloads and executes from the Internet, there's going to be security concerns. You need to address user fears about downloading and using the application. Obviously, a downloadable application requires a higher level of trust than components or controls discussed in previous chapters (see Chapter 14 for details about controls and components in general). As part of allaying fears about your downloadable application, you also need to address setup and configuration issues.

This chapter addresses downloadable applications in several forms (both component and control) and considers how you can access them as you would any helper application. The Visual Web Developer environment comes with several examples of downloadable applications that you can use as examples and as a basis for ideas for your own applications.

The final section of the chapter considers the alternatives to downloadable applications. Leaping onto an interesting technology is only natural for a developer, but it might not be the best solution for the user. Sometimes you can achieve just as much using standard technologies as you can a downloadable application. This section discusses the various possibilities. Once you've looked at the other alternatives, you can determine whether downloadable applications are the best solution for your needs.

Considering Potential Security Problems

Most users view the Internet as a comfortably anonymous place where they don't have to volunteer any information or expose their identities in any way unless they really want to. Consequently, you have people running around pretending to be all kinds of things they aren't. Scripts expose some of the privacy of individuals, controls and components expose a little more, and there's little chance of hiding much with a downloadable application. Consequently, downloadable applications make people feel uncomfortable—people view them as a personal assault on privacy and, as a result, on security as well (the two go hand in hand for most people, even though they really are separate issues). The "Developing a Privacy Policy" section of Chapter 5 discusses privacy policies—make sure your privacy policy addresses any use of personal information that a downloadable application might require.

Any time you download content to the client machine without really knowing what effect that content will have, you risk damaging the user's system. The End User Licensing Agreement (EULA) found with most software packages is evidence that software companies understand this issue far too well. However, well-informed users understand there's still a commitment from shrink-wrap companies to resolve any difficulties an installation might create that they might not get as part of an application download. A downloadable application has the highest probability of creating problems of any content the user might get, so naturally the user is leery of accepting such content.

It's also unlikely that you'll post a precise analysis along with accompanying source code of your downloadable application. Users tend to suspect the hidden nature of the downloadable application you create. Because a downloadable application will likely execute at the same privilege level as the user, you could gain access to financial records and the like without the user's knowledge. In short, the user has to have considerable trust that your company won't steal sensitive information.

An issue that you might not consider is the security risks for your company when you create a downloadable application. Crackers often depend on obtaining code that they can analyze and check for holes. Your company could open a gaping hole in its security defenses by creating a downloadable application. A downloadable application could have a buffer overflow or other problem that a cracker exploits to gain access to the server. Because of the nature of these errors, a security breach might go unnoticed for days or even weeks. Every moment that the cracker has access to your system is another moment that the cracker can challenge your system integrity and you might lose data (or even control of the system). Generally, by creating a downloadable application, you have more to lose from a security perspective than the user—even though the user will fail to notice this problem.

Security breaches need not occur at either the client or server end of the conversation. The fact that the conversation occurs over the open Internet also creates potential problems. A cracker could listen to the conversations and hope to break the encryption you use to secure it. For example, anyone relying on the Data Encryption Standard (DES) might as well forgo encrypting their data because this encryption technology has become relatively easy to crack as computers have become more powerful. Fortunately, .NET developers have access to the Advanced Encryption Standard (AES), which is the only form of encryption that you can rely on to remain secure—for the moment at least.

NOTE Breaking the DES encryption was big news at one time (1998, in fact), but now it's old information. Unfortunately, many downloadable applications still use it. Even the U.S. government has moved away from DES and is moving away from Triple-DES because it's unlikely to remain secure for very long (see the NetworkWorldFusion article at `http://www.nwfusion.com/research/2001/0730feat2.html` for details). You can find archived stories about the DES security problem in places such as Hasten Down the Wire (`http://www.michaelfraase.com/index.php/hasten/des_cracked_again/`) and the Cryptography Mailing List (`http://www.privacy.nb.ca/cryptography/archives/cryptography/html/1999-01/0120.html`). Look at the dates and you'll see that DES has been unusable since 1998. Now, consider the fact that many online stores still rely on DES for transactions and you'll begin to understand why well-informed users balk at using many types of online communication. Any system that relies on DES or even Triple-DES is suspect—make sure you give users a good reason to trust you by using AES.

Considering Client-side Setup and Configuration Issues

Many developers are under the assumption that application installations must follow a prescribed regimen of setting up the Windows Installer and creating complex application destinations. Microsoft was the originator of this philosophy, and it worked well during the days when the desktop was the only source of applications that Windows users had. However, many applications, such as the downloadable applications described in this chapter, now arrive from other sources. A complex installation scenario no longer works because the user can't even be sure that the application elements reside on the local hard drive (rather than on your Web server). Consequently, Microsoft changed course, as it so often does, and went back to the installation technique from the days of DOS XCopy.

NOTE For those of you who don't know what the Disk Operating System (DOS) is, it's the original operating system for the PC. The character mode DOS allowed a user to work with one application at a time. The user didn't see fancy graphics and wasn't able to multitask. The system was quite simple and many people still think DOS is worth keeping around for specific tasks. XCopy is a utility that originated with DOS. It lets someone copy an entire application, including data, from one location to another without any fancy installation or other requirements. Everything the application needs resides in a single main folder (sometimes with subfolders). XCopy can copy everything, including the subfolders, using a single command.

Of course, you might think I've gone quite mad in introducing an old technology as a means for getting your downloadable application onto the user's machine, but the technique really does work. Microsoft has fought an uphill battle on the subject, so you'll find articles such as "Determining When to Use Windows Installer Versus XCopy" (`http://msdn.microsoft.com/library/en-us/dndotnet/html/xcopywininst.asp`) on the Microsoft Developer Network (MSDN) Web site.

The problem is that XCopy isn't the right solution for every application. For example, it can actually cause problems when working with Internet Information Server (IIS) as described in the "Troubleshooting Deployment" article at `http://msdn.microsoft.com/library/en-us/vsintro7/html/vxtbstroubleshootingdeployment.asp` (see the "Web applications deployed using the Xcopy command cannot be debugged" heading for details). Note that this article prescribes using the Copy Project utility and provides a link to another article that describes how to use it. However, Microsoft is heading toward more use of XCopy by incorporating product features that make using it easier. For example, check out the new emphasis on XCopy support for SQL Server Express at `http://msdn.microsoft.com/library/en-us/dnsse/html/sseoverview.asp`.

To use the XCopy command, you type **XCopy** *SourceFile* at the command prompt (where *SourceFile* is the name of the file you want to copy) and press Enter. The source file argument can rely on DOS wildcard characters where * is any number of characters and ? is a single character. For example, *.DOC would copy files with any filename and the .doc file extension. The following list contains optional arguments you can use with the XCopy command.

Destination Specifies the location of the new files—replace Destination with the new file location. You may optionally use Destination to change the name of the copied file as well, but this feature works well only when you copy a single file.

/A Copies only files with the archive attribute set, doesn't change the attribute.

/C Continues copying even when errors occur.

/D:Month-Day-Year Copies files changed on or after the specified date. If no date is given, copies only those files whose source time is newer than the destination time.

/E   Copies directories and subdirectories, including empty ones. Same as /S /E. May be used to modify /T.

/EXCLUDE:File1[+File2]...   Specifies a list of files containing strings. Each string should be in a separate line in the files. When any of the strings match any part of the absolute path of the file to be copied, that file will be excluded from being copied. For example, specifying a string like \obj\ or .obj will exclude all files underneath the directory obj or all files with the .obj extension, respectively.

/F   Displays full source and destination filenames while copying.

/G   Allows the copying of encrypted files to a destination that doesn't support encryption.

/H   Copies hidden and system files also.

/I   If the destination doesn't exist and copying more than one file, assumes that the destination must be a directory.

/K   Copies attributes. Normal XCopy will reset read-only attributes.

/L   Displays files that would be copied.

/M   Copies only files with the archive attribute set; turns off the archive attribute.

/N   Copies using the generated short names.

/O   Copies file ownership and ACL information.

/P   Prompts you before creating each destination file.

/Q   Doesn't display filenames while copying.

/R   Overwrites read-only files.

/S   Copies directories and subdirectories except empty ones.

/T   Creates directory structure, but doesn't copy files. Doesn't include empty directories or subdirectories. /T /E includes empty directories and subdirectories.

/U   Copies only files that already exist in destination.

/V   Verifies each new file.

/W   Prompts you to press a key before copying.

/X   Copies file audit settings (implies /0).

/Y   Suppresses prompting to confirm that you want to overwrite an existing destination file.

/-Y   Prompting to confirm you want to overwrite an existing destination file.

/Z   Copies networked files in restartable mode.

NOTE   You can substitute a folder (directory) for the file when using XCopy. Supplying a folder name lets you copy the entire folder to another location. Add the /S switch and you can copy the folder and any subfolders it contains.

Creating Standard Components

This section of the chapter shows how to use the built-in class template to create a component for your downloadable application. The component isn't stand-alone—you use it with other applications.

However, the build process directly incorporates the component into your application—you don't have to worry about providing a means for the user to download the component. For a comparison with external components, see the component-specific sections of Chapter 14. The following sections describe how to work with a built-in component.

Designing the Component

The first step in this example is to add a component to the project. To add a built-in component to your application, select the Class template in the Add New Item dialog box (right-click the project entry in Solution Explorer and choose Add New Item from the context menu). Type a name for the class and click Add. If this is the first class you've added, the IDE will ask whether you want to create the class in the Code folder so you can use it anywhere within the Web site. Click Yes. The IDE creates the Code folder and places the class within it.

A component normally provides some type of background processing. In this case, the component makes a comparison and returns a color value based on an input. You might use such a component to provide a visual indicator based on numeric input. Listing 18.1 shows the code you'll need for this example. You'll find this example in the \Chapter 18\BuiltInComponent folder of the source code on the Sybex Web site.

LISTING 18.1: Creating a Built-in Component

```
' Create an enumerated range of results.
Public Enum Colors
    Red = -65536
    Yellow = -256
    Green = -16744448
End Enum


' Define the private variables used to hold propery values.
Dim _CompareValue As Int32

Public Sub New()
    ' Initialize the properties.
    _CompareValue = 0
End Sub

Public Sub New(ByVal InitValue As Int32)
    ' Initialize the properties.
    If (InitValue >= 0) And (InitValue <= 100) Then
        _CompareValue = InitValue
    Else
        Throw New ArgumentOutOfRangeException( _
            "InitValue", InitValue, _
            "InitValue must be between 0 and 100")
    End If
End Sub
```

```
Public Property CompareValue() As Int32
    Get
        Return _CompareValue
    End Get
    Set(ByVal value As Int32)
        ' Make sure the comparison value is in the correct
        ' range.
        If (value >= 0) And (value <= 100) Then
            _CompareValue = value
        Else
            ' Throw an error for an incorrect value.
            Throw New ArgumentOutOfRangeException( _
                "CompareValue", value, _
                "CompareValue must be between 0 and 100")
        End If
    End Set
End Property

Public Function CalcColor() As Colors
    ' Return a color based on the current value of _CompareValue.
    If (_CompareValue >= 0) And ( CompareValue <= 33) Then
        Return Colors.Red
    ElseIf (_CompareValue > 33) And (_CompareValue < 67) Then
        Return Colors.Yellow
    Else
        Return Colors.Green
    End If
End Function
```

The example begins with an enumeration. Using enumerations makes your code easier to understand and reduces the complexity of working with your component. In this case, the enumerated values translate to an Alpha Red Green Blue (ARGB) color value (where alpha is the measure of the transparency of the color). The combination of the four values produces a specific color indication on-screen. In this case, the three numbers equate to the ARGB for red, yellow, and green. The enumeration shows that you can create enumerations with specific values—an important consideration, in this case, because the code uses the value to reproduce the color on-screen.

The class has two constructors. Always create a constructor that doesn't require any input values to ensure someone can use the component on a Web page. The second constructor accepts the value you want to use for comparison purposes. Notice that the second constructor ensures that the input value is within the correct range. When the value is outside the correct range, the code throws an `ArgumentOutOfRangeException` exception, rather than handle the error within the component code.

The class includes the `CompareValue` property so that the developer using the control has access to the comparison value as needed. The `Get` portion of the property returns the `_CompareValue` value. The `Set` portion of the property uses the same technique as the second constructor to change the `_CompareValue` value. Always check every input to reduce the risk of getting a bad input value.

The CalcColor() method doesn't accept any input value. You could certainly create an override that would accept the comparison value as input. The method performs a numeric comparison and returns an enumerated color value based on the input. Using the technique shown reduces the risk of misinterpreting the method output.

Adding the Component to a Web Page

Now that you have a new component to use, it's time to add it to a Web page. The example Web page relies on a text box for input of the comparison value, a pushbutton to provide a means of performing the comparison, and a label for output. Because this is an ASP.NET application, all of the processing occurs as part of the code behind. Listing 18.2 shows the code you'll need for this example. You'll find this example in the \Chapter 18\BuiltInComponent folder of the source code on the Sybex Web site.

LISTING 18.2:   Using the Built-in Component

```
Sub btnCheck_Click(ByVal sender As Object, ByVal e As System.EventArgs)
    Try
        ' Create the value checking component.
        Dim CheckValue As New Calculate(Int32.Parse(txtInput.Text))

        ' Change the output background color.
        lblOutput.BackColor = _
            Drawing.Color.FromArgb(CheckValue.CalcColor())

        ' Change the foreground color so the user can see the text.
        If (CheckValue.CalcColor() = Calculate.Colors.Yellow) Then
            lblOutput.ForeColor = Drawing.Color.Black
        Else
            lblOutput.ForeColor = Drawing.Color.White
        End If

        ' Create an output string.
        lblOutput.Text = _
            txtInput.Text + " is a " + _
            CheckValue.CalcColor().ToString() + " number."

    Catch AOR As ArgumentOutOfRangeException
        ' Display the problem on screen.
        lblOutput.Text = "Input Error: " + AOR.Message

    Catch ex As Exception
        ' Display a generic message.
        lblOutput.Text = "Unknown Error: " + ex.Message

    End Try
End Sub
```

The first thing you'll notice when using a built-in component is that you don't have to provide a reference to it—the IDE provides access to the component without the addition of a reference. Consequently, the code begins by instantiating an object based on the class. The code uses the second constructor to supply an input value directly, rather than as a second step.

You can use the `CalcColor()` method to provide output in several ways. The first method uses the color value to change the `lblOutput.BackColor` property using the `Drawing.Color.FromArgb()` method. Assigning an ARGB color to the enumeration, rather than allowing the compiler to assign a value, lets you assign the color directly.

The second use of the `CalcColor()` method compares the output color to one of the enumerated values. The example outputs black text when working with a yellow background and white text when working with either a red or green background. The idea is to improve the readability of the display.

The third use of the `CalcColor()` method displays the color name as part of the application text output. When you use the output in this way, the code automatically translates the output to a color name, rather than a numeric value, as shown in Figure 18.1.

FIGURE 18.1

This example shows three kinds of output from a single method call.

The example provides two levels of error trapping. The first level is the `ArgumentOutOfRangeException` specific exception output by the component. It's better to check for specific errors when you can to ensure that you can provide the best help possible to the user. The second level is a generic exception. Even though this second level keeps the application from failing completely, the output message is less helpful because the application isn't trapping a specific error.

Creating Standard Controls

Sometimes you need a special control for an application. You won't use the control in other projects—just this project. That's where a built-in control can come in handy. You add the control directly to the current project. For a comparison with external controls, see the control-specific sections of Chapter 14. The following sections describe how to work with a built-in control.

Designing the Control

The first step in this example is to add a control to the project. To add a built-in control to your application, select the Web User Control template in the Add New Item dialog box (right-click the project entry in Solution Explorer and choose Add New Item from the context menu). Type a name for the control and click Add.

Creating a built-in control isn't precisely the same as working with stand-alone controls because they rely on Web technology. You create what amounts to a specialized kind of Web page fragment and use it within the application. Consequently, this example on a `RadioButtonList` (`rblColorSelect`) and a `Label` (`lblOutput`) as a starting point. Listing 18.3 shows the code you'll need for this example. You'll find this example in the `\Chapter 18\BuiltInControl` folder of the source code on the Sybex Web site.

LISTING 18.3:   Creating a Built-in Control

```
' A structure to hold a color name and associated
' ARGB value.
Public Structure ColorType
    Dim ColorName As String
    Dim ColorValue As Int32
End Structure

' Contains the current list of colors.
Dim _ColorValues As ColorType()

<Browsable(False)> _
Public Property ColorValues() As ColorType()
    Get
        Return _ColorValues
    End Get
    Set(ByVal value As ColorType())
        ' Verify that there is an input value.
        If (value Is Nothing) Or (value.Length = 0) Then
            Throw New ArgumentNullException( _
                "InitColors", "You must provide a list of colors.")
            Return
        End If

        ' Assign the values to _ColorValues
        ReDim _ColorValues(value.Length)
        _ColorValues = value

        ' Fill the color list with names.
        rblColorSelect.Items.Clear()
        For Each Entry As ColorType In _ColorValues
            rblColorSelect.Items.Add(Entry.ColorName)
        Next

        ' Set the default option.
        rblColorSelect.SelectedIndex = 0

        ' Set the label up for use.
        lblOutput.Text = _
            _ColorValues(0).ColorName
```

```vbnet
            lblOutput.BackColor = _
                Drawing.Color.FromArgb(_ColorValues(0).ColorValue)

            ' Save the data as a cookie.
            Response.Cookies.Add( _
                New HttpCookie("SavedColorValues", _
                                CreateColorString(_ColorValues)))
        End Set
    End Property

    Public ReadOnly Property CurrentColorName() As String
        Get
            ' Return just the color name.
            Return _ColorValues(rblColorSelect.SelectedIndex).ColorName
        End Get
    End Property

    Public ReadOnly Property CurrentColorValue() As Int32
        Get
            ' Return just the color value.
            Return  ColorValues(rblColorSelect.SelectedIndex).ColorValue
        End Get
    End Property

    Private Function CreateColorString(ByVal Input As ColorType()) _
        As String

        Dim Counter As Int32    ' Loop counter variable.

        ' Define the output string.
        Dim Output As New StringBuilder()

        ' Process each of the input elements.
        For Counter = 0 To Input.Length - 1

            ' Create a string from the individual color values.
            Output.Append(Input(Counter).ColorName + "=" + _
                        Input(Counter).ColorValue.ToString())

            ' Add a semicolon separator only when this isn't the
            ' last entry.
            If Counter < Input.Length - 1 Then
                Output.Append("&")
            End If
        Next
```

```vbnet
    ' Return the completed string.
    Return Output.ToString()
End Function

Private Function CreateColorArray(ByVal Input As String) As ColorType()
    Dim Elements As String()    ' Holds name/value strings array.
    Dim Output As ColorType()   ' Contains the output data.
    Dim Counter As Int32        ' Loop counter variable.
    Dim NameValue As String()   ' A name/value pair.

    ' Divide the string into name/value pairs.
    Elements = Input.Split(Convert.ToChar("&"))

    ' Now that we know how many name/value pairs there are, define the
    ' array size.
    ReDim Output(Elements.Length)

    ' Place one name value pair in each Output element.
    For Counter = 0 To Elements.Length - 1

        ' Split the name/value pair.
        NameValue = Elements(Counter).Split(Convert.ToChar("="))

        ' Place the values in the output.
        Output(Counter).ColorName = NameValue(0)
        Output(Counter).ColorValue = Int32.Parse(NameValue(1))
    Next

    ' Return the result.
    Return Output
End Function

Sub rblColorSelect_SelectedIndexChanged(ByVal sender As Object, _
                                        ByVal e As System.EventArgs)
    ' Set the output to display the newly selected color.
    lblOutput.Text = _
        _ColorValues(rblColorSelect.SelectedIndex).ColorName
    lblOutput.BackColor = _
        Drawing.Color.FromArgb( _
            _ColorValues(rblColorSelect.SelectedIndex).ColorValue)
End Sub

Private Sub Page_Init(ByVal sender As Object, _
                      ByVal e As System.EventArgs) Handles Me.Init
    If (Request.Cookies("SavedColorValues") Is Nothing) Then

        ' Set the colors to their default values.
        ReDim _ColorValues(2)
        _ColorValues(0).ColorName = Drawing.Color.Red.Name
```

```
            _ColorValues(0).ColorValue = Drawing.Color.Red.ToArgb()
            ... Two Other Default Color Entries ...

        Else
            ' Retrieve the stored colors and use them to create the array.
            _ColorValues = _
                CreateColorArray(Request.Cookies("SavedColorValues").Value)
        End If

        ' Fill the color list with names.
        rblColorSelect.Items.Clear()
        For Each Entry As ColorType In _ColorValues
            rblColorSelect.Items.Add(Entry.ColorName)
        Next

        ' Set the default option.
        rblColorSelect.SelectedIndex = 0

        ' Set the label up for use.
        lblOutput.Text = _
            _ColorValues(0).ColorName
        lblOutput.BackColor = _
            Drawing.Color.FromArgb(_ColorValues(0).ColorValue)
    End Sub

    Public Sub ChangeColorSelection(ByVal NewColor As Int32)
        ' Verify the value is in range.
        If (Not NewColor < _ColorValues.Length - 1) Then
            Throw New ArgumentOutOfRangeException( _
                "NewColor", NewColor, _
                "Value is not within the range of colors listed.")
        End If

        ' Change the selection.
        rblColorSelect.SelectedIndex = NewColor

        ' Set the label up for use.
        lblOutput.Text = _
            _ColorValues(rblColorSelect.SelectedIndex).ColorName
        lblOutput.BackColor = _
            Drawing.Color.FromArgb( _
                _ColorValues(rblColorSelect.SelectedIndex).ColorValue)
    End Sub

    Public Function GetColorSelection() As Int32
        ' Return the selected index value.
        Return rblColorSelect.SelectedIndex
    End Function
```

```
Public Sub UseDefaultColors()
    Dim Values(2) As ColorType  ' Contains the default values.

    If (Not Request.Cookies("SavedColorValues") Is Nothing) Then

        ' Set the colors to their default values.
        Values(0).ColorName = Drawing.Color.Red.Name
        Values(0).ColorValue = Drawing.Color.Red.ToArgb()
        ... Two Other Default Color Entries ...

        ' Change the color values.
        Me.ColorValues = Values
    End If
End Sub
```

This example begins by defining a data structure to store color values. In this case, the structure includes the color name as well as the ARGB for that color. Each color requires a single entry, so the private variable, _ColorValues is an array of ColorType. The ColorValues property exposes this value to the developer using the control. Notice that the example sets the <Browsable> attribute to False to ensure that the developer doesn't attempt to modify this property from the Properties window in design view. You could expose the property by creating a custom property page for it, but that task is beyond the capability of Visual Web Developer Express—you really need the full version of Visual Studio .NET to perform this task.

Setting _ColorValues requires more than the usual amount of work because this is a user control, rather than a stand-alone control. The code begins by verifying the developer has provided a valid array as input. When the developer fails to provide a valid array, the code throws an ArgumentNullException exception. The next step is to assign the new array to _ColorValues. Notice that the code must redimension _ColorValues to ensure it has just enough entries to contain the new array. The next three steps set up the visual components to display the new color values—the control doesn't perform this task for you automatically. Finally, there's an odd step where the code creates a cookie containing the new values using the Response.Cookies.Add() method. The reason you must perform this step is that Web pages have no state. The only way to preserve the new color choices is to create a cookie (or other storage medium) to hold them. The code uses the CreateColorString() method to convert the _ColorValues array to a string.

Sometimes an outside process might need to know the current color or color value. The CurrentColorName and CurrentColorValue perform this task. Both properties work the same— they simply return different structural elements.

The example includes two methods for converting a ColorType array to a string and back again: CreateColorString() and CreateColorArray(). Cookies work only for string values, so you must convert everything else to a string. In many cases, the task is simple, but complex data types, such as a ColorType array, require special handling.

The CreateColorString() method begins by creating a StringBuilder, Output, to hold the results of the conversion. The actual conversion process begins by combining the two ColorType fields, ColorName and ColorValue, into a name/value pair that's separated by an equal sign. The separator you choose is important—it can't appear in the data that you're trying to separate. Many developers use the equal sign because it's uncommon in actual data, but be prepared to use other characters such as the circumflex (^). The code then checks whether this is the last element in the array. If it isn't, the code adds an ampersand to the end of the string. The ampersand separates name/value pairs—making it easier to convert the data back later. Again, make sure you choose a unique character.

WARNING   Choose separator characters carefully. Remember that you're working with HTML, which means that you must escape some characters, such as the semicolon (;) and space. Using unescaped characters can produce odd results. For example, using the semicolon truncates the string after the first name/value pair. The code creates the complete string, but the cookie accepts information only up to the first semicolon. Generally, it's best to use the equal sign and ampersand when you can—these characters are always safe to use within a cookie.

The CreateColorArray() method begins by using the Split() method to create an array of name/value pairs. The next step is to process each name/value pair within the array and place the appropriate information into a ColorType array. Notice that the code again uses the Split() method to perform this task. The double use of the Split() method is the reason why you should use different separator characters for the name and value, and for the name/value pairs.

The rblColorSelect_SelectedIndexChanged() event handler is private to the control. It only changes the text and background color of lblOutput to match the current user selection. The reason you want to keep this event handler private is to circumvent outside efforts to corrupt the internal functionality of the control. The ChangeColorSelection() method makes this functionality public. However, notice that this method checks the input values before it allows a change and ensures the system updates the display properly. The GetColorSelection() method retrieves the currently selected color. You could easily use a property to perform the same task—it's a matter of personal preference in this case.

The Page_Init() method is probably the most important part of the control because it sets up the visual elements for each post back. The method begins by viewing two possible kinds of display. The first occurs when the user provides a cookie containing the name/value pairs created by the CreateColorString() method. The second occurs when the page relies on the default colors. In both cases, the code creates a _ColorValues array. The next step is to create the list of colors in rblColorSelect, so the user sees the correct color names. The code also selects the first color. The final step is to set lblOutput to display the correct color name and highlighting.

The final method, UseDefaultColors(), lets the developer set the control back to its default setting. Theoretically, you could simply delete the cookie that holds the current user colors. After experimenting for a while, however, it becomes obvious that retaining the cookie can have performance benefits if you expect the user to change the colors again. Consequently, the UseDefaultColors() method sets the cookie to the default colors, rather than deleting the cookie. Notice how the code uses the control's ColorValues property to perform this task. Using the property saves a little coding, but you could also place the code within the UseDefaultColors() method.

Adding the Control to a Web Page

Adding the built-in control to the Web page is a bit different from using a stand-alone control. Instead of selecting the control in the Toolbox, you drag and drop it where you want from Solution Explorer. This action produces a different result from using a stand-alone control as well. The IDE begins by registering the ASCX files with the Web page using a special tag, as shown here.

```
<%@ Register TagPrefix="uc1"
         TagName="SpecialSelect"
         Src="SpecialSelect.ascx" %>
```

The registration contains three attributes. The `TagPrefix` defines the prefix that the IDE will use for the control within the Web page. The `TagName` contains the class name for the control. The `Src` points to the location of the file on disk. After the IDE registers the control, it places a tag for it on the Web page, as shown here.

```
<uc1:SpecialSelect id="selTest" runat="server">
</uc1:SpecialSelect>
```

Notice that the tag includes the prefix, uc1, and the name of the control, SpecialSelect. The Web page uses the control as it would any other control and you can access any properties you define for the control on the Web page. Listing 18.4 shows the code you'll need for this example. You'll find this example in the \Chapter 18\BuiltInControl folder of the source code on the Sybex Web site.

LISTING 18.4:   Using the Built-in Control

```
Sub btnCheck_Click(ByVal sender As Object, ByVal e As System.EventArgs)
    ' Display statistics about the current control settings.
    txtOutput.Text = "Color Name and Value: " + _
                     selTest.CurrentColorName + " (" + _
                     selTest.CurrentColorValue.ToString() + ")" + _
                     vbCrLf + "Currently Selected Item: " + _
                     selTest.GetColorSelection().ToString()
End Sub

Sub btnChange_Click(ByVal sender As Object, _
                    ByVal e As System.EventArgs)
    Dim Colors(4) As SpecialSelect_ascx.ColorType

    ' Define the colors.
    Colors(0).ColorName = Drawing.Color.Blue.Name
    Colors(0).ColorValue = Drawing.Color.Blue.ToArgb()
    ... Four Other Colors ...

    ' Change the colors.
    selTest.ColorValues = Colors
End Sub

Sub btnDefaultColors_Click(ByVal sender As Object, _
                           ByVal e As System.EventArgs)
    ' Use the default color scheme.
    selTest.UseDefaultColors()
End Sub

Sub btnSelect_Click(ByVal sender As Object, _
                    ByVal e As System.EventArgs)
    Try
        ' Choose a new item from the list.
        selTest.ChangeColorSelection(Int32.Parse(txtItem.Text))
```

```
        Catch AOR As ArgumentOutOfRangeException
            ' Display an error if the input is incorrect.
            lblError.Text = AOR.Message
            lblError.Visible = True
        End Try
    End Sub

    Private Sub Page_Load(ByVal sender As Object, _
                          ByVal e As System.EventArgs) Handles Me.Load
        ' Turn off error messages.
        lblError.Visible = False
    End Sub
```

All of the code in this part of the example is event handler related—it all helps you understand how the control works. The btnCheck_Click() method displays statistical information about the control. It displays the current color name and color value, along with the current selection number. Figure 18.2 shows a typical example of the output from this event handler.

The btnChange_Click() method creates a ColorType array. It fills the array with a list of colors. The final step is to assign the new colors to the control using the ColorValues property. Figure 18.2 shows the alternative color list.

The btnDefaultColors_Click() method returns the colors to their default setting. It relies on the control's UseDefaultColors() method to perform this task. You should always provide a means of returning the control to a default state when the setup could require more than a few lines of code.

FIGURE 18.2
Built-in controls can combine functionality and make creating pages faster.

The btnSelect_Click() method lets the user change the selection programmatically using the ChangeColorSelection() method. The ChangeColorSelection() method throws an exception for incorrect input, so you should provide some type of error display when using this technique in your own controls. The example uses a hidden label to display the information by making it visible and filling the label with the error information. Figure 18.3 shows typical error output. The Page_Load() event handler resets the error message as needed by making the label invisible.

FIGURE 18.3

Provide error output as needed to make the control user friendlier.

Using the *FileUpload* Control

You can do a lot with forms on a Web site. Adding user controls and interacting with the client in other ways extends your ability to gather information. However, at some point, you might need more information than these sources can provide. For example, you might need access to an application log that the user has compiled. The FileUpload control can help with these additional information needs. It displays a text box and browse button on-screen that lets the user specify a file for upload. You must provide a separate upload button whose event handler contains code to upload the file.

The amount of checking you perform on the file depends on the application requirements. You can use the PostedFile property to check the information that the user plans to upload. In all cases, you should quarantine the file in a special folder so that you can virus scan it and check for other problems. Listing 18.5 shows the code you'll need for this example. You'll find this example in the \Chapter 18\FileUpload folder of the source code on the Sybex Web site.

LISTING 18.5:   Uploading Files from the Client

```
Sub btnUpload_Click(ByVal sender As Object, _
                    ByVal e As System.EventArgs)
    Dim UploadPath As String    ' Server side upload path.
    Dim UniqueStr As String     ' Date/Time stamp.
    Dim Contents As TextReader  ' File content.

    ' Create a unique DateTime string.
    UniqueStr = Request.LogonUserIdentity.Name + "_" + _
                DateTime.Now.ToShortDateString + "_" + _
                DateTime.Now.ToLongTimeString()
    UniqueStr = UniqueStr.Replace("/", ".")
    UniqueStr = UniqueStr.Replace("\", ".")
    UniqueStr = UniqueStr.Replace(":", ".")

    ' Determine the file status.
    If fuUpload.HasFile Then

        ' Create the upload path.
        UploadPath = _
            "C:\Uploads\" + UniqueStr + "_" + fuUpload.FileName

        ' Upload the file.
        fuUpload.SaveAs(UploadPath)

        ' Display the status message.
        lblStatus.Text = _
            "File saved as " + UniqueStr + "_" + fuUpload.FileName
        lblStatus.ForeColor = Drawing.Color.Black
        lblStatus.Visible = True

        ' Get all of the information from the PostedFile property.
        With fuUpload.PostedFile

            ' Display file statistics.
            lblStats.Text = _
                "Content Length: " + .ContentLength.ToString() + _
                "<br />Content Type: " + .ContentType + _
                "<br />Filename: " + .FileName

            ' When the file contains text, display the text as well.
            If .ContentType.ToUpper = "TEXT/PLAIN" Then
                Contents = New StreamReader(.InputStream)
                lblStats.Text = lblStats.Text + _
                    "<br />Contents: " + Contents.ReadToEnd()
            End If
```

```
        End With

    Else
            ' Display an error message.
            lblStatus.Text = "You must provide a filename!"
            lblStatus.ForeColor = Drawing.Color.Red
            lblStatus.Visible = True
    End If
End Sub
```

The code begins by creating a unique file string. You must create a unique file string because multiple users could attempt to upload files with the same name at the same time. In addition, a user might determine an initial upload is incorrect and attempt to upload a new version of the same file later. The newest file always overwrites older files of the same name. The example uses a combination of the user name, the date, and the time. Unfortunately, all three values contain characters that you can't use in a filename. The example solves this problem by using the Replace() method to change the character to an acceptable value.

Determining the status of the FileUpload control, fuUpload, comes next. The HasFile tells whether the user has supplied a filename. If not, the code displays an error message. Otherwise, the code begins processing the file by obtaining the value in the FileName property. The code uses the SaveAs() method to upload the data from the client machine. Afterward, the code displays a successful upload message for the user that includes the augmented filename.

The example also displays statistics that you can obtain from the PostedFile property. All files allow you to display the content length, the Multipurpose Internet Mail Extensions (MIME) content type, and the filename supplied by the user. When the example detects a MIME type of TEXT/PLAIN, it processes the file and displays the content as well. Figure 18.4 shows typical output from this example. Notice that the FileUpload control automatically clears the filename after the user uploads it.

FIGURE 18.4
Let users upload files as needed to your Web site to augment other kinds of information.

TIP Most vendors have begun using MIME types for more than browsers—you'll find them in many applications today. The biggest reason is that you'll find standard MIME types across platforms. You can see a list of MIME standards at `http://www.mhonarc.org/~ehood/MIME/MIME.html`. Another good source of information about MIME is at `http://www.hunnysoft.com/mime/`.

Designing Custom Smart Tags

You may have seen Smart Tags used as part of many Office products. The developer or environment attaches Smart Tags to various controls so that the user can perform tasks faster. It's also possible to attach Smart Tags to Web pages. These mini-applications detect specific content and let the user interact with it in new ways.

The Smart Tags are already on the user's system in many cases. Some of them come with Microsoft Office and other applications, for example, or you can provide a download for custom Smart Tags on your Web site. In addition, many third party vendors provide Smart Tags. All of these applications run within a host environment—similar to the way that the Microsoft Management Console (MMC) hosts various snap-in applications, such as Component Services. The host for the examples in this section is a browser, but you'll see other hosts in use.

The following sections describe two Smart Tag scenarios. The first is using the Smart Tags that come with Microsoft Office. Because Microsoft Office appears on so many desktops, you can count on having access to these Smart Tags when the majority of your Web site visitors work within the enterprise environments using Windows desktops. Of course, you should be ready to accommodate other users on a public Web site or explain this requirement to users on a private Web site. The second is using third party Smart Tags that you can either download from the Internet or purchase for special needs within your company. For example, you can find special Smart Tags for use within legal firms that make Web content easier to work with.

Adding Standard Smart Tags to a Web Page

You already have at your disposal a wealth of Smart Tags that perform common tasks such as creating an address or properly formatting a date. The problem is that working with these Smart Tags isn't necessarily common knowledge—you don't find them used a lot online because many developers don't realize just how common they really are. Microsoft Office installs all of the Smart Tags in the following sections—at least all of the versions of Microsoft Office that support Smart Tags (they won't work with users who are still clinging to Office 97 and older). When you think about how many people have Microsoft Office installed, you begin to realize just how easy it would be to add these Smart Tags to a Web page and be reasonably sure that anyone visiting the Web site will benefit. Of course, public Web sites should provide alternatives for users who don't have the proper Smart Tags installed. You'll find this example in the `\Chapter 18\SmartTag` folder of the source code on the Sybex Web site.

NOTE The following examples won't work if you didn't install Smart Tag support with Microsoft Office in most cases. One exception is the Address and Places Smart Tag, which you get as part of most Windows installations. Discover more about this Smart Tag in the "Using the Address and Places Smart Tag Plug-in" section later in this chapter.

CREATING THE WEB PAGE ENTRIES

Using any type of Smart Tag requires special entries on your Web page. Most of the entries appear within the <head> tag, rather than the <body> tag, which is why you can't really see them in Design view. The first set of attributes actually appears in the <head> tag like this (other <head> tag attributes removed for the sake of clarity).

```
<html xmlns:o="urn:schemas-microsoft-com:office:office"
      xmlns:st1="urn:schemas-microsoft-com:office:smarttags"
      xmlns:st2="urn:schemas:contacts">
```

These entries define three namespaces. Namespaces are identifiers for a resource you want to use. The first is the Microsoft Office namespace. The second is a general namespace for Smart Tags. The third namespace is a special entry for contact information. The Uniform Resource Name (URN) (pronounced "earn") portion of the namespace tells the browser that this is identification information. The remainder of the namespace is a declaration of the identifier, which are schemas, or organized listings of data in this case. A schema defines the data construction.

NOTE   An URN is not an URL. The URNs used with Smart Tags exist on the client machine—not at a location on the Internet. Consequently, when the user doesn't have the required support installed on the local machine, the browser ignores the URN. The page still displays, but not with the intended functionality that the Smart Tag will add.

The next step is to describe the Smart Tags that you want to use. Every Smart Tag requires at least one entry. These descriptions tell the browser how to react to the Smart Tag entry. Listing 18.6 shows all of the descriptions for the Smart Tags that Microsoft Office supports natively.

LISTING 18.6:   Adding Smart Tag Descriptions to a Web Page

```
<o:SmartTagType
    namespaceuri="urn:schemas-microsoft-com:office:smarttags"
    name="stockticker"/>
<o:SmartTagType
    namespaceuri="urn:schemas-microsoft-com:office:smarttags"
    name="PersonName"/>
<o:SmartTagType
    namespaceuri="urn:schemas:contacts" name="Sn"/>
<o:SmartTagType
    namespaceuri="urn:schemas:contacts" name="GivenName"/>
<o:SmartTagType
    namespaceuri="urn:schemas-microsoft-com:office:smarttags"
    name="Street"/>
<o:SmartTagType
    namespaceuri="urn:schemas-microsoft-com:office:smarttags"
    name="address"/>
<o:SmartTagType
    namespaceuri="urn:schemas-microsoft-com:office:smarttags"
    name="place"/>
```

```
<o:SmartTagType
   namespaceuri="urn:schemas-microsoft-com:office:smarttags"
   name="City"/>
<o:SmartTagType
   namespaceuri="urn:schemas-microsoft-com:office:smarttags"
   name="State"/>
<o:SmartTagType
   namespaceuri="urn:schemas-microsoft-com:office:smarttags"
   name="PostalCode"/>
<o:SmartTagType
   namespaceuri="urn:schemas-microsoft-com:office:smarttags"
   name="time"/>
<o:SmartTagType
   namespaceuri="urn:schemas-microsoft-com:office:smarttags"
   name="date"/>
<o:SmartTagType
   namespaceuri="urn:schemas-microsoft-com:office:smarttags"
   name="phone"/>
```

Each entry in the list includes three items. The first item tells the browser that this is an entry for a Smart Tag, which appears as part of the Microsoft Office namespace. The o: preceding each entry ties it to the Microsoft Office declaration in the <head> tag. The second item is the location of the definition for this Smart Tag. This entry uses an URN, just as the entries in the <head> tag do. The third item is the human-readable name for the Smart Tag.

The vendor provides the information you use as a basis for the <SmartTagType> tags as part of an XML file where the Smart Tag file is stored, or on a registry entry. All the Microsoft Office Smart Tag files appear in the \Program Files\Common Files\Microsoft Shared\SmartTag folder of your machine. The registry entries appear in the HKEY_CURRENT_USER\Software\Microsoft\Office\ Common\SmartTag\Recognizers key.

A special object processes all this information for Internet Explorer. You must add the following <Object> tag to activate Smart Tag processing on a Web Page. (See the "Using the <Object> Tag" section of Chapter 6 for additional information about the <Object> tag.)

```
<Object classid="clsid:38481807-CA0E-42D2-BF39-B33AF135CC4D"
        id=IETag></object>
```

Notice the <Object> tag doesn't include any parameters or arguments. You can't interact with this object in any way. The id value you assign is important because you use it to identify the object to the browser.

The final generic step is to add styles to identify the actual content for the Smart Tags to the browser. This is one situation where embedded styles are essential. In addition, unlike most styles, this style doesn't affect the appearance of the content—the style affects the behavior of the content. Here are the two styles you need to work with Smart Tags.

```
<style>
   st1\:*{behavior:url(#IETag) }
   st2\:*{behavior:url(#IETag) }
</style>
```

Notice the two styles point to a behavior URL that has the same identifier as the object. The style behavior URL and the object identifier must match or the Web page won't work.

Don't expect a Smart Tag you use on a Web page to have the full functionality that it has in a Microsoft Office document. The Smart Tag knows that you're using it in a Web environment and limits the context menu choices to those that are appropriate for a Web venue. Even so, Smart Tags can reduce the work that a user needs to perform to accomplish tasks, so they serve an important purpose.

USING THE STOCKS AND FUNDS SMART TAG PLUG-IN

The Stocks and Funds Smart Tag detects a stock symbol and provides the user with access about that symbol. Beside all the generic entries needed to support Smart Tags, you supply the special tag shown here.

```
<st1:stockticker w:st="on">MSFT</st1:stockticker>
```

The stock symbol, MSFT, placed in the `<stockticker>` tag acts as input for the Smart Tag. When you hover the mouse over the purple line that appears under the stock symbol, you see an i within a circle and a square, as shown in Figure 18.5. Click on the i and you see a context menu.

This example shows some of the power of Smart Tags on your Web page. The entry appears as text and yet the user can do three things with it: get a stock quote, obtain a company report, or get the latest news about the company in question.

FIGURE 18.5

Use Smart Tags to provide the user with data manipulation options.

USING THE NAME SMART TAG PLUG-IN

The Microsoft Office options you have installed affect the functionality of the Name Smart Tag, so you'll want to test this Smart Tag with the same Office features that you expect your users to have installed. The Name Smart Tag can do everything from help you set up an appointment with the person to creating email or addressing an envelope. Here's the code you need to add to create a Name Smart Tag entry.

```
<st1:PersonName w:st="on">
    <st2:GivenName w:st="on">George</st2:GivenName>
    <st2:Sn w:st="on">Smith</st2:Sn>
</st1:PersonName>
```

After you install the proper support, the Name Smart Tag becomes exceptionally useful. Figure 18.6 shows the common options you'll see for a standard Office installation. Because each Office product adds features to this particular Smart Tag, the options you see will vary depending on what you have installed on your system.

FIGURE 18.6

Decide in advance how much Smart Tag functionality the user receives.

TIP Sometimes less is better when it comes to Smart Tags. You could easily replace the Name Smart Tag with a simple link that sends an email to the person you want to contact. Just how easily you can replace this Smart Tag depends on which features you need to use.

USING THE ADDRESS AND PLACES SMART TAG PLUG-IN

The Address and Places Smart Tag provides driving instructions and a map as the user needs them, as shown in Figure 18.7. The interesting part about this Smart Tag is that you get at least this minimal support without having any major Microsoft Office features installed (you generally need at least one product installed to use this Smart Tag).

FIGURE 18.7

Some Smart Tags are useful even without Microsoft Office support.

The code for creating an Address and Places Smart Tag is a little more complex. Here's the code you normally need.

```
<h3>An Address</h3>
<p>
   <st1:Street w:st="on">
      <st1:address w:st="on">
         1313 Mockingbird Lane
      </st1:address>
   </st1:Street>
</p>
<h3>A Place</h3>
```

```
<p>
   <st1:place w:st="on">
       <st1:City w:st="on">Indianapolis</st1:City>,
       <st1:State w:st="on">IN</st1:State>
       <st1:PostalCode w:st="on">46290</st1:PostalCode>
   </st1:place>
</p>
```

Notice that you need both a `<Street>` and an `<address>` tag to create an address. Likewise, to describe a place, you need a number of tags including the `<place>` tag. The remaining elements describe a particular city, state, and postal zone. The reason for these dual tags is that you can create lists. A `<Street>` tag can contain multiple `<address>` tags so you could describe a list of related entries.

USING THE TIME AND DATE SMART TAG PLUG-IN

The Time and Date Smart Tags won't work unless you have the correct Microsoft Office features installed, most notably, Schedule Plus. The tags let you set up meetings or perform other tasks based on the time or date you enter. Here's the code you need to create a Time Smart Tag.

```
<st1:time Hour="12" Minute="22" w:st="on">12:22 pm</st1:time>
```

Notice that this tag includes special attributes: `Hour` and `Minute`. Because time display formats can vary from place to place, you need to provide an easily recognizable time value for the Smart Tag. The Date Smart Tag works about the same as the Time Smart Tag, as shown here.

```
<st1:date Month="4" Day="29" Year="2004" w:st="on">
   29 April 2004
</st1:date>
```

As with the Time Smart Tag, you must provide an absolute date using the `Month`, `Day`, and `Year` attributes. The actual order of the attributes is unimportant as long as you provide all three entries.

DISABLING SMART TAGS ON YOUR SITE

Some people don't like Smart Tags because they see them as a means of gaining more information than is required. They don't want their site content to appear as part of a Smart Tag and have no desire to share their information using Smart Tag technology. It's true that Smart Tags have a lot to offer, but developers can also abuse them and the Web sites from which they receive data. Fortunately, it's relatively easy to prevent someone from using the content on your site as part of a Smart Tag solution. All you need to do is include the following `<meta>` tag at the beginning of every Web page.

```
<meta name="MSSmartTagsPreventParsing" content="TRUE">
```

The name attribute defines the kind of information this `<meta>` tag contains—a request that Smart Tags not parse the page. The content attribute defines all content as off limits. Adding this `<meta>` tag doesn't have any effect on any Smart Tags that you add to your Web page.

The purpose of this tag is to disable any Smart Tag support added to a browser. A browser with Smart Tag support could visit your site and automatically add Smart Tags to keywords. The addition wouldn't affect your site, but it would affect how the user sees the site and that's what concerns many people.

USING THE TELEPHONE SMART TAG PLUG-IN

The Telephone Smart Tag is another Smart Tag that won't work unless you have certain Microsoft Office features installed. Generally, installing Schedule Plus is enough to activate this tag. There aren't any special requirements for this tag, as shown here.

```
<st1:phone w:st="on">(317)572-3201</st1:phone>
```

Getting Prebuilt Smart Tags

A number of third party vendors provide additional Smart Tags. You can view and sometimes download these Smart Tags at `http://office.microsoft.com/en-us/marketplace/EY010504821033.aspx`. Microsoft also produces some special Smart Tags such as the Euro conversion Smart Tag that you find at `http://www.microsoft.com/downloads/details.aspx?FamilyID=5879FD92-6119-4B59-9A62-A7164AC67F40&displaylang=EN`. Here are some additional Smart Tag sources you should consider exploring.

ActiveDocs (*http://www.activedocs.com/?from=msomp***)** Helps you create your own custom Smart Tags for classes of information you need to track. This means you could create additional Smart Tags that you can add to a Web page as needed to provide support to the end user.

DataPortal (*http://www.nereosoft.com/dataportal20.htm***)** Helps you create Smart Tags for managing your database applications. For example, you could create a Smart Tag where all the user needs to do to interact with a database is to type the database name. The keyword triggers a response that helps the user create database connectivity without really knowing anything about the connection itself. The emphasis is on the data.

LexisNexis (*http://support.lexisnexis.com/lndownload/***)** Provides a Smart Tag for developers who work with the legal community. For example, the Case Name Smart Tag can search for a case name, legal reviews, and verdict information based on a case keyword typed by the user.

ProWrite (*http://www.nereosoft.com/prowrite.htm***)** Lets you print Avery labels from contact information. You could use this feature to let someone print a label for your company from a Web page when mail contact is required for a transaction. For that matter, you could use the same technique to create labels for items you want to deliver to a customer based on Web site form data.

WestCiteLink (*http://www.westlaw.com/citelink***)** Provides a Smart Tag for developers who work with the legal community. This Smart Tag specializes in finding and working with citations.

WorldLingo (*http://www.worldlingo.com/microsoft/smart_tag.html***)** Provides Smart Tags that translate text. You can also obtain quotes for translating large documents, uncovering business practices in other countries, and getting country-specific data.

These are just a few of the Smart Tags you can obtain. News sites such as MSNBC and travel sites such as Expedia also provide Smart Tags that help you perform tasks with their service. The idea is to provide the Smart Tags that users of your Web site can use best.

Developing Downloadable Application Alternatives

You might think at this point in the chapter that downloadable applications are the greatest technology to come along. However, you also know that they come with a list of potential problems that you might not overcome—at least not easily. The problem with any powerful technology is that it comes with equally powerful issues that you have to overcome. Sometimes, the best technology is the one that provides just what you need in the smallest package and with the least amount of work. In short, downloadable applications aren't the answer to every problem. You should look for alternatives before you begin creating the downloadable application.

One of the best methods of replacing a downloadable application is to use a series of self-altering Web pages. You can see an example of this kind of technology in the shopping cart example described in detail in Chapter 15. The various pages in this application appear to perform tasks that are similar to those in desktop applications, yet the application relies on a combination of client-side and server-side processing to perform the task in a standard way. In other words, even though the user has to trust you enough to enable scripting, the application doesn't require anything exotic—certainly not as exotic as a downloadable application.

In some cases, the best solution is to create a desktop application with an Internet interface. Network administrators find it easier to test desktop applications on their systems and verify their functionality, rather than depend on a Web application they can't control. The Web application could change and cause problems that the network administrator hadn't considered at the outset. The result is often the same, only the method you use differs. The user sees a desktop application, but underneath the desktop application is a Web application that interacts with online data sources.

You could rely on a combination of scripting and standard components or controls to accomplish tasks. Chapter 6 shows how to use this technique in a number of ways, most importantly, the `<Object>` tag. Any object that you can create with a desktop application, you can also create using a script on the client machine. The only prerequisite is that the user trusts you enough to let you work with these objects. Since many of these objects already appear on the user's machine and the user understands them, you'll likely run into fewer objections than trying to get the user to accept a downloadable application. Of course, you must fit your application requirements within the confines of what the typical user has installed.

Sometimes an acceptable third party product is the best approach. For example, most people accept Adobe Acrobat Reader as a reasonably safe product. You can embed PDF files in your Web site along with a `FileUpload` control (see the "Using the `FileUpload` Control" section earlier in this chapter for details). A user could download the PDF, fill out any required forms, and upload it to your site. The PDF could include any forms of interaction that the file format supports. For example, you'll find a list of Adobe Acrobat Reader add-ins at the FreeDownloads Center (`http://www.freedownloadscenter.com/Search/adobe_acrobat_reader.html`).

Defining Your Development Goals

This chapter has demonstrated how to create, implement, and use downloadable applications in a number of ways. One favorite technique on private Web sites is to use a specialized Smart Tag. In fact, this might be the best way to introduce users to the idea that Web pages can do more than present static displays or even dynamic information. A well-designed Web page can do many of the same tasks that desktop applications can perform—the only difference is the Web connection. Of course, that Internet connection makes a lot of difference, so this chapter has also helped you understand user concerns that you have to address.

The problem that you must consider is whether a downloadable application is the best way to provide the functionality that a user requires. In some cases, you might want to use other approaches or even rely on a desktop application that provides a Web interface. Applications that users won't touch don't accomplish anything, so you must consider your company culture as much as you consider the usefulness of this technology.

Chapter 19 addresses an important issue, no matter what kind of Web project you create. Creating accessible Web sites is an important part of the work you perform as a developer. Accessibility means making the Web page friendly for those who have special needs of any kind. For example, a Web page that uses certain color combinations can be invisible to someone with color blindness. Likewise, adding multimedia to a Web site is great for pizzazz, but not such a great means of providing a single source of information—someone who can't hear or see won't be able to use the content on such as Web site. Even small things can affect the accessibility of a Web site. For example, you might see well enough to make out 6-point type on the screen, but most people can't read text that small. Consequently, using small type might cost you visitors. Chapter 19 addresses the full range of accessibility issues so you can create great Web sites that everyone can use.

Creating Accessible Pages

One of the most important user elements of any Web page you design is the accessibility it provides. Accessibility, in this case, is a measure of how well the user can interact with the page. It doesn't matter how well you design a Web page if someone can't see it. Not seeing a page comes in many forms—everything from not being able to decipher page elements due to color blindness to not being able to distinguish the minute text used to provide content. Accessibility covers a broad spectrum of other interface issues that appear in this chapter as well.

Fortunately, making a Web page accessible is easier now than ever before. You simply need to add a few items that you might not have added in the past. In many cases, all you need to do is define properties that make it easier for accessibility aids to understand the content of your page and relay it to the user. Of course, you may also need to verify that the resources you want to use will actually work and provide a little additional content to help those who can interact with the Web page in a certain way. For example, you can provide a description of a picture or other informational graphics for those who can't see or have limited vision.

You don't even have to perform this task completely on your own. Visual Web Developer provides a number of tools to make the task easier for you. In addition, you'll find a wealth of tools on the Internet for checking the accessibility of your Web page. Making a Web page accessible doesn't necessarily mean spending hours slaving away at code that you don't think anyone will actually use. Sometimes, accessibility is a matter of presenting the page in a way that you hadn't considered in the past.

Reasons to Design with Accessibility in Mind

Many developers are under the misconception that accessibility refers to code that they add to an application in order to make it usable by people with special needs, such as blindness. By adding special attributes to HTML tags, a person using a screen reader can visualize the page content and interact with it. While this is certainly one definition of accessibility, it's also the least productive and most narrow-minded interpretation. Unfortunately, it's the most prevalent view of accessibility used by government and industry today because it's the viewpoint that enjoys legal status. A broader definition helps everyone because most people have some type of special need—it might simply be the need to enlarge text when their eyes are tired, but the need is still real and Web sites that cater to this need have a distinct advantage.

NOTE Most countries in the world today have some type of legal requirement for accessibility in place. In general, these legal requirements define how you must set up both hardware and software for someone who has a special need. Businesses are often exempt from these requirements unless they have a relationship with the government—any participation in the accessibility program is purely optional for individuals. To learn more about the accessibility requirements for the United States, see the Section 508 requirements at `http://www.section508.gov`. Many countries rely on a standard based on the Web Content Accessibility Guidelines, which are stricter than the U.S. standards. Learn more about these guidelines at `http://www.w3.org/TR/WAI-WEBCONTENT`.

The best way to view accessibility is as a means of making people comfortable, not as an extra expense that the business or individual must bear. A business that pursues accessibility as a means for attracting and keeping new clients is certainly going to see a profit from their efforts. In addition, the company's employees benefit from better health, which in turn pays dividends in reduced sick time for the company. An application, whether desktop or Web-based, that's accessible is easier to use than one that lacks accessibility features. You might even find that adding accessibility features pays for itself by reducing application support costs.

The whole concept of accessibility is an important one that the developer needs to make a part of the design process. Unfortunately, most developers ignore it until the last second and only pay attention to it as part of a legal requirement. Yet something as simple as making an application or Web site screen reader accessible can net large gains for anyone who chooses to use a screen reader. Some developers would say that this statement proves their point because only those with vision deficiencies would rely on a screen reader.

Although I have good vision, I use the screen reader provided with Windows on any Web site with a lot of content (if the Web site will allow such use). The reason is simple. Using a screen reader helps me to concentrate on the content offered by the Web site. I get more out of the information I hear because I'm not constantly distracted by other Web site features, ads, or other embellishments. In addition, if the content is easy enough to understand, I can perform other tasks while my computer reads to me. Many people choose to multitask today in order to get their work completed—using a screen reader allows multitasking. The user can listen to the Web site content while performing some other task. This little tip is a real time saver when you read (listen to) as many trade journals as I do.

Including Alt attribute and bubble help (tool tips) in an application may seem like something that no one would use—especially with graphics—because the developer assumes that the user can see the image on screen. The fact is that some applications and Web sites alike present many images in such a way that deciphering them is difficult. The Alt attribute and bubble help provide clues for those with good vision, as well as those who might require a little additional help. The pop-up explanation becomes a source of additional information that everyone can use.

TIP Lest you get the idea that accessibility affects only application use and that developers are solely engaged in creating applications, there are many other areas of involvement, such as training. You can find an excellent piece written by David M. Peter, "Usability and Accessibility—Everyone Learning" on the effects of accessibility on training at `http://www.cdlr.tamu.edu/dec_2002/Proceedings/david_peter.pdf`. This white paper helps you understand how accessibility can affect training goals and requirements. It also shines a light on the issue of accessibility as a methodology that affects everyone.

Carpal tunnel syndrome is the scourge of our society. One of the main causes of carpal tunnel syndrome for office workers is the keyboard and mouse. The accessibility requirements designed to ease access for those who lack good coordination also helps those who have normal use of their arms by reducing the effort required to input information. A business could easily write off the cost of improving the accessibility of their software by reducing the number of cases of carpal tunnel syndrome. In fact, because of the high cost of medical assistance, even one case of carpal tunnel syndrome prevented could pay for the required upgrades and anything after that would be money saved.

TIP Carpal tunnel syndrome is a lot more serious and widespread than most people think. You can obtain a good overview of the topic at the National Institute of Neurological Disorders and Stroke (NINDS) Carpal Tunnel Syndrome Information Page (`http://www.ninds.nih.gov/disorders/carpal_tunnel/carpal_tunnel.htm`). There's a lot of good information for computer users at the MSU—Computer Science and Engineering Web site (`http://web.cps.msu.edu/facility/avoid-ct.php`).

Even the colors used to present information on screen can affect the productivity of those who use the application. For example, many of the same color combinations that cause problems for those with color blindness also cause eyestrain for those with normal vision. Meeting accessibility requirements for color composition can also net surprising results in reduced headaches and time off spent recovering from symptoms such as dry eyes.

TIP If you want to obtain a quick overview of color blindness, check out the article entitled, "Can Color-Blind Users See Your Site?" at `http://msdn.microsoft.com/library/en-us/dnhess/html/hess10092000.asp`. You might also want to visit the Color Perception Issues Web site at `http://www.firelily.com/opinions/color.html`.

The benefits from programming with accessibility in mind are more numerous than I've already listed in this section, and we'll explore them as the chapter progresses. The bottom line is that programming with accessibility in mind helps everyone. It benefits all users by making the computer easier to use. Businesses benefit with better sales, increased employee productivity, reduced costs, and improved customer relations. In short, you should embrace this technology with open arms because it has something for everyone.

Making Controls Accessible

Depending on the accessibility goals you set for your Web site, you can perform various levels of changes to its design. As a minimum, you should make the standard controls that you use accessible. In some cases, you can add additional information to improve the accessibility of existing controls. Visual Web Developer natively supports many of these attributes—you'll have to add other attributes by hand in Source view, but the effort is well worth the results. The following sections describe how you can make controls more accessible.

Adding Accessibility Attributes to Standard Controls

You don't need to sweat a lot to greatly improve the accessibility of your Web site. In fact, all you really need is a few simple attributes that you can add using the Properties window. In short, you don't even have to remember the names of these properties—all you need to do is remember to provide content for them. The following list of attributes can help you create accessible Web pages. The

ASPX name of the property appears first, the HTML name second (that's right, the same properties work for both page types).

AccessKey/AccessKey   This attribute enables a user to access a screen element, such as a text box or a pushbutton, quickly. You can use this attribute with most of the ASP.NET controls. In addition, you can use it with the <A>, <AREA>, <BUTTON>, <INPUT>, <LABEL>, <LEGEND>, and <TEXTAREA> HTML tags.

AssociatedControlID/For   This attribute associates one element with another element. For example, you could use it to associate a label specifically with its associated text box. The value of this attribute must match the ID attribute value of the target element.

TabIndex/TabIndex   This attribute defines the element's position in the tabbing order for a form. It helps the developer control the flow of the page. Defining a tabbing order makes the page easier to understand and use.

ToolTip/Title   This attribute provides ancillary information about the associated element. The ancillary information describes the purpose and content of the element in most cases. In some cases, a developer can also use this attribute to provide basic help information for the element.

Using these attributes is relatively easy. All you need to do is think about how the user will employ the control when making accessibility choices. For example, you need to associate a label with another control only when the label actually references that control. On the other hand, all controls should have a tab index to ensure that the user sees the correct page flow when pressing Tab. Listing 19.1 shows the code you'll need for this example. You'll find this example in the \Chapter 19\AccessibleControl folder of the source code found on the Sybex Web site.

LISTING 19.1:   Using Basic Accessibility Attributes

```
<p>
    <label id="lblGreeting">Accessible Control Demonstration</label>
</p>
<p>
    <label id="lblOutput"
           for="txtOutput"
           tabindex="1">
        Check the Application:
    </label><br />
    <input id="txtOutput"
           type="text"
           accesskey="C"
           title="Holds the application output."
           tabindex="2" />
</p>
<p>
    <input id="btnTest"
           type="button"
           value="Test"
           accesskey="T"
           title="Creates application output that appears in the textbox."
           tabindex="3" />
```

```
</p>
<p>
    <a id="hlASXP"
        title="Displays a page that shows the same attributes in HTML form."
        accesskey="A"
        tabindex="4"
        href="ASPXVersion.ASPX">
        See the ASXP Version
    </a>
</p>
```

All of this content appears within the <body> tag of the example. I chose the HTML version because it's easier to understand. In addition, when you run the ASPX version and view the source it produces, you'll notice that it's amazingly close to the code shown here—the server simply converts the ASPX page into this HTML equivalent.

The first thing you should notice is that `lblGreeting` doesn't appear to have any of the accessibility tags mentioned in the list. Sometimes your Web pages will have one or two controls that lack attributes too, so don't worry about it when you can't come up with attributes you should use to make the page accessible. In this case, `lblGreeting` isn't associated with any other control, it doesn't require a tooltip or speed key because the user won't actually interact with it, and the tab index is 0, which is the default. However, this control is the exception, rather than the rule.

The `lblOutput` control includes attributes that are common for labels. It uses the `for` attribute to create a connection between it and `txtOutput`. Although the naming convention makes the connection apparent to developers, the `for` attribute makes the connection apparent to many accessibility aids such as screen readers, which makes it easier for the user to interpret the display. The `tabindex` attribute is important because the user can actually tab to the label, unlike desktop applications where tabbing tends to skip nonfunctional display elements such as labels.

The `txtOutput` control is one that the user will interact with, so it requires different attributes. The `AccessKey` attribute makes it easier for users who can't use the mouse to select the control quickly. All the user needs do is press Alt+C to access the control. Unfortunately, the accessibility aid won't tell the user about this key combination in most cases. The best solution is to use the first character of the associated label as a quick selection key. However, you can also format the label text to include underlines so the user knows which key to use. The `title` attribute provides balloon help. In addition, most accessibility aids will make use of this text. For example, a screen reader will read the text to the user to help in visualizing the display.

TIP It's easy to get stuck in a rut when typing the `title` attribute information in an application. Some developers will start every title attribute entry with the word *click*, even when the user obviously knows that a click is required. Imagine waiting several minutes for a page to finish because of long `title` entries and hearing the word *click* repeatedly. Using short and descriptive `title` entries works much better and increases the user's ability to understand the Web page content.

The example code also includes typical entries for buttons and hyperlinks. In all cases where a user will interact with the control directly, rather than using it as a visual aid (such as when working with a label), you should include the `title` attribute and provide an `AccessKey` attribute as well. Some controls do have other special entries you can make—many of which appear in the remainder of the chapter.

Using Alternative Attributes to Improve Accessibility

The common attributes described in the "Adding Accessibility Attributes to Standard Controls" section of the chapter always work, even with some of the older browsers on the market. However, sometimes you want to provide more information than these common attributes can provide. This section describes alternative attributes that you can use on your Web page.

Many alternative attributes also work with every modern browser on the market, but you can't count on them to work quite as often with older browsers. The issue isn't one of standardization. The problem with many attributes today is that developers don't know they exist, don't understand how to use them, or don't know which attributes are actually standardized. As with accessibility tags, you can find a list of accessibility attributes in the "Index of HTML elements and attributes" section of the HTML Techniques for Web Content Accessibility Guidelines 1.0 specification (http://www.w3.org/TR/WCAG10-HTML-TECHS). The following list provides a quick overview of these attributes and tells how they're used.

Abbr   This attribute contains an abbreviated form of the data found in a table cell. A screen reader could use this information to output a short form of a long, repetitive table entry.

Axis   This attribute places the cell of a table within a conceptual category. The Axis acts as a single dimension within an *n*-dimensional space. The user can request the browser organize the data using a particular category as a basis.

Class   This attribute assigns a class name to the element. Browsers often use this feature to select characteristics for the element from a Cascading Style Sheet (CSS) file. More than one element on a Web page can share the same Class attribute value.

Dir   This attribute defines the direction of the text on screen when Unicode doesn't define the direction. The acceptable values include ltr (left-to-right) and rtl (right-to-left).

HREFLang   This attribute defines the language used by a resource pointed at by an HREF attribute. Developers commonly use this attribute with the <LINK> and <A> tags.

ID   This attribute assigns an identifier to the element. Browsers can use this feature to select characteristics for the element from a CSS file. However, the most common use of this attribute is as a means to identify a particular element within a script or other means of page processing.

Label   This attribute assigns a value to the element. The current specification uses this attribute only with the <OPTION> and <OPTGROUP> tags.

Lang   This attribute defines the language used by or associated with a particular element. Developers can use this attribute to help speech and search engines to interact more successfully with Web page elements. In addition, this attribute can help the browser provide correct language-specific interaction, such as the use of punctuation.

Rel   This attribute describes the relationship between the current document and the target URL. For example, you can use this attribute with the <LINK> and <A> tags to describe where the link goes. Acceptable values include alternate, designates, stylesheet, start, next, prev, contents, index, glossary, copyright, chapter, section, subsection, appendix, help, and bookmark. This attribute is important in telling the viewer what to expect from the link. For example, when a link points to a help page, you'd use the rel attribute with the help value.

Rev   This attribute describes the relationship between the target URL and the current document. In other words, it tells the viewer what to expect when clicking the Back button on the browser. The acceptable values and uses for this attribute are the same as for the rel attribute.

Style   This attribute assigns the inline style for an element. For example, the developer could use it to assign font characteristics to a `<Label>` tag. In general, you'll want to avoid using this attribute and assign a style to tags using an external CSS file. Using an external file enables users to substitute the styles they want to use to view a particular page.

UseMap   This attribute associates an image map with the element. The `UseMap` value must match the value of the Name attribute of the `<MAP>` tag used to define the image map. Developers can use this attribute with the `<IMG>`, `<INPUT>`, and `<OBJECT>` tags.

Many of the attributes provided as part of the specification perform special tasks. For example, the `Abbr`, `Axis`, `Headers`, and `Scope` attributes appear only with the `<TD>` and `<TH>` tags used with tables. If you're using a product such as Visual Web Developer to create your Web applications, the IDE will generally provide you with a list of acceptable attributes for a particular tag. The problem with relying too heavily on the input provided by an IDE is that the IDE will often supply vendor-specific, as well as standardized, attributes. In sum, you need to exercise care to ensure that your Web page uses only standardized attributes to ensure maximum flexibility.

Using Alternative Tags to Improve Accessibility

You also have access to a number of specialized tags that aid in accessibility. In most cases, these tags also serve other purposes, so using them provides a double benefit. Here are a few of the tags you should try.

Abbr   This tag lets you define the meaning behind abbreviations on a Web page. An abbreviation is a shortened form of a word that may not form a word in and of itself as an acronym will. For example, people often use WI, Wis, and Wisc as abbreviations for Wisconsin.

Acronym   This tag lets you define acronyms on first use in a Web page. Defining the acronym helps those who don't know what it means, yet lets you to use the acronym for those who expect to see it. An acronym is a word formed from the initial letters of the words of a compound term. For example, Rapid Application Development (RAD) qualifies as an acronym because it's composed of the initial letters of several words and produces a pronounceable result.

Code   This tag defines an area of the Web page containing example computer code. You always use this tag for complete listings. Use the `<samp>` tag for code snippets and other code samples, and the `<var>` tag for code variables. The reason you want to add these tags to computer code is to avoid confusing the screen reader when it comes to the odd combinations of letters used for computer code. Don't use this tag for actual computer code, such as scripts, within the Web page.

Dfn   This tag lets you define terms that the viewer might not understand the first time they appear on the Web page. Not everyone understands the technical jargon used for every trade, so defining the terms on first use makes the Web page easier to use, yet lets experienced viewers skip the material.

Kbd   This tag defines keyboard text on the Web page. Use this tag whenever you want the viewer to perform a task using the keyboard. The tag provides both visual and aural cues that let the viewer know that you want them to perform an action. You might use this tag within a procedure for setting up an application that the viewer has downloaded.

Samp   This tag defines an area of sample computer code—not a full listing, but a code snippet used for explanation purposes. As with the `<code>` tag, don't use this tag for actual computer code, such as scripts, within the Web page.

Var   This tag defines a variable used as part of a code explanation within a Web page. As with the `<code>` tag, don't use this tag for actual computer code, such as scripts, within the Web page.

Organizing the Web Page

You can organize Web pages using a number of techniques. In fact, there's a wealth of such techniques throughout the book. However, from an accessibility perspective, you can see the vast majority of the organizational techniques you need to use with forms and tables. The following sections discuss both accessible forms and tables.

Working with Forms

Web forms present a few accessibility challenges. For example, it's very easy to add speed keys to a desktop application by adding an ampersand (&) in front of the letter you want to use as a speed key. Not only does this addition add the speed key, but it also underlines the letter so the user knows which key to press along with the Alt key. Web pages have no such resource—you need to perform extra coding to make the speed keys work correctly.

WARNING   Avoid assuming too much about the capabilities of the browser and other software that the user will employ to access your Web site. For example, some screen readers aren't compatible with the `AccessKey` attribute associated with the on screen elements. Normally, the user can press Alt, followed by the `AccessKey` value to access a specific screen element. Read more about this problem in the Q306448 Knowledge Base article titled, "INFO: Some Screen Readers Are Not Fully Compatible with Access Keys" at `http://support.microsoft.com/default.aspx?scid=kb;en-us;306448`.

Figure 19.1 shows a data entry form. This form isn't functional—its only function is to show some accessibility features. You'll find this example in the `\Chapter 19\AccessibleForm` folder of the source code found on the Sybex Web site.

You should notice a few features about this page. First, each of the labels preceding a field has an underlined letter. This letter doesn't add any functionality as it would for a Windows application. All that the underlining does is provide a visual cue for the viewer. To add the keyboard shortcut, you must include the `AccessKey` attribute as part of the `<input>` tag for the text box. Consequently, the keyboard shortcut is associated with the actual text box, rather than the label preceding it. (You can also follow the Microsoft conventions where the label is the focus of the shortcut—read about it at `http://msdn.microsoft.com/workshop/author/dhtml/reference/properties/accesskey.asp`.)

Unfortunately, you have to use the underlined characters carefully. The `AccessKey` attribute accepts a single letter as input. Every shortcut is an Alt key combination. In short, if you have more than 36 fields (letters A through Z and numbers 0 through 9) on a form, then you'll run out of `AccessKey` attribute combinations. (Theoretically, you can use a single key more than once, but this often confuses the viewer more than helps them.)

This page also provides balloon help for every field. Like the table example discussed earlier, you'll use the title attribute to create the balloon help. It becomes obvious, in this case, that the balloon help appears only when hovering the mouse over the field. Selecting the field with the keyboard doesn't display the balloon help. Fortunately, all the screen readers I tested say the title attribute text even if it doesn't appear on screen.

Interestingly enough, the special effects demonstrated on this page are more the result of careful programming than special effects. Listing 19.2 shows the code for this example. Notice that the Web page in Figure 19.1 looks formatted, even though there's little or no formatting for the controls in this example.

FIGURE 19.1
Using this simple
data entry form will
demonstrate the use
of both tooltips and
keyboard shortcuts.

LISTING 19.2: Adding Accessibility Features to a Form

```
<!DOCTYPE html PUBLIC "-//W3C//DTD XHTML 1.1//EN"
                    "http://www.w3.org/TR/xhtml11/DTD/xhtml11.dtd">
<html xmlns="http://www.w3.org/1999/xhtml" >
<head>
    <title>Simple Data Enty Form</title>
    <link rel="stylesheet" type="text/css" href="SampleStyle.CSS">
</head>
<body>
    <form id="frmDataEntry"
          title="This form demonstrates data entry principles."
          name="frmDataEntry">

        <h1>Data Entry Form</h1>
        <div>
            <label id="lblName" for="txtName">
                <span class="underline">N</span>ame:
            </label>
            <input id="txtName"
                   class="data_entry"
                   title="Full name of the person."
                   accessKey="N"
                   type="text"
                   name="txtName">
        </div>
```

```
        ... Other Form Entries ...

    <div> </div>
    <div>
        Press <kbd>Alt+H</kbd> or click the
        <A id="lnkHelp"
            title="Obtain help on this page."
            accessKey="H"
            href="Help.htm"
            rev="Start"
            rel="Help"
            name="lnkHelp">
            Help link
        </A>
        to view help information for this page.
    </div>
    <div> </div>
    <div>
        <input id="btnSend"
                title="Send the data."
                accessKey="S"
                type="submit"
                value="Submit"
                name="btnSend">
    </div>
</form>
</body>
</html>
```

Many of the coding elements, such as the use of the for, title, and AccessKey attributes, appear in the "Adding Accessibility Attributes to Standard Controls" section of the chapter. However, notice the use of the <span> tag to underline the speed key in lblName. The <span> tag doesn't add any actual formatting and you could override its effect by using a different CSS page for the Web site. However, the effect, in this case, is to underline the first character in the label.

The help link at the bottom of the page also uses some special formatting. For example, the <kbd> tag surrounds the Alt+H text because you want the user to perform this act. The actual link, lnkHelp, contains the usual accessibility attributes, along with the rev and rel attributes. The rel attribute tells the user about the information on the linked page—a help page in this case. The rev attribute tells the user what kind of page will appear when clicking the Back button after viewing the linked page. The combination of these two links helps the user to navigate your Web site with greater ease by providing positional cues.

The CSS for this Web page adds quite a bit to the output you see. For example, many Web sites would use tables to align the text entry fields on the page. However, this example uses a simple CSS file entry, as shown here.

```
.data_entry
{
    left: 11%;
    width: 250px;
    position: absolute;
}
```

Notice that the bottom of the page in Figure 19.1 shows a help link. All of your data entry forms should include some type of help. Figure 19.2 shows the sample help for this example. It also includes a link at the bottom of the page to return to the data entry form. Like the data entry fields, both of these links include a keyboard shortcut that makes them easy to access. The text associated with the link tells the reader what key combination to press in order to access the link quickly.

Working with Tables

Look anywhere on the Internet and you'll find a wealth of tables. Unfortunately, most of those tables will prove confusing to viewers with special needs because the page uses them as an organizational aid, rather than for their intended purpose. Accessibility friendly tables store information, rather than layouts. However, accessible tables contain a few other elements than just information. This section of the chapter provides an overview of the two table types commonly used on Web sites that are easiest to read using a screen reader.

FIGURE 19.2
Your data entry forms should include some type of help dialog.

Before you begin working with tables, however, it's important to know about some special attributes you can use with them. The following list describes some table-specific attributes that you can use with tables to make them easier for the viewer to understand.

Headers This attribute contains a space-delimited list of cells that form the header for a table. Using this attribute helps users of screen readers because the screen reader will announce that the cells are part of a header. Developers also use this attribute with style sheets.

Scope This attribute often appears in place of the Headers attribute for simple tables. It defines the set of data cells that are associated with a header cell. Acceptable values include row, col, rowgroup, and colgroup. The rowgroup and colgroup values associate the header cell with a group of data cells.

Summary This attribute defines the purpose and content of a table. Providing a summary means that someone using an accessibility aid can determine whether they want to listen through the entire table. The summary attribute also helps focus the viewer's attention on the table as a whole before hearing about the specific elements.

Tables come in a variety of sizes, content, arrangements, and formatting, so it's not possible to discuss every possible table type in a section of one chapter. The examples shown in Listing 19.3 consider two typical table types and their accessibility features. You'll find this example in the \Chapter 19\AccessibleTables folder of the source code found on the Sybex Web site.

LISTING 19.3: Adding Accessibility Features to Tables

```
<!DOCTYPE html PUBLIC "-//W3C//DTD XHTML 1.1//EN"
                      "http://www.w3.org/TR/xhtml11/DTD/xhtml11.dtd">
<html xmlns="http://www.w3.org/1999/xhtml" >
<head>
    <title>Accessible table Demonstration</title>
    <link rel="stylesheet" type="text/css" href="SampleStyle.CSS">
</head>
<body>
    <h1 id="lblTitle">Table Demonstration</h1>
    <h2 id="lblTableType1">Table Type 1</h2>
    <p>
        <table id="tblType1"
               title="Shows some features every table should have."
               summary="This is a demonstration table.">
        <tr>
            <th title="This column stores the first column of data."
                id="Column1">
                Column 1 Heading</th>
            <th title="This column stores the second column of data."
                id="Column2">
                Colunn 2 Heading</th>
            <th title="This column stores the third column of data."
                id="Column3">
                Column 3 Heading</th>
        </tr>
        <tr>
```

```
            <td headers="Column1">Column 1 Row 1</td>
            <td headers="Column2">Column 2 Row 1</td>
            <td headers="Column3">Column 3 Row 1</td>
        </tr>

        ... Other Rows ...

        <tr>
            <td colspan="3"
                headers="Column1 Column2 Column3">
                Columns 1 through 3 Row 3
            </td>
        </tr>
        </table>
    </p>
    <h2 id="lblTableType2">Table Type 2</h2>
    <p>
        <table id="tblType2"
                title="Shows some features every table should have."
                summary="This is another demonstration table.">
        <tr>
            <th title="This square purposely left blank.">
            </th>
            <th title="This column stores the first column of data."
                scope="col">
                Column 1 Heading</th>
            <th title="This column stores the second column of data."
                scope="col">
                Colunn 2 Heading</th>
            <th title="This column stores the third column of data."
                scope="col">
                Column 3 Heading</th>
        </tr>
        <tr>
            <th title="This is the first row of data."
                scope="row">
                Row Heading 1</th>
            <td>Column 1 Row 1</td>
            <td>Column 2 Row 1</td>
            <td>Column 3 Row 1</td>
        </tr>

        ... Other Rows ...

        </table>
    </p>
</body>
</html>
```

You should notice a few construction details about these tables. First, notice that each table has a `title` attribute. The `title` attribute describes what the table contains (demonstration information). In addition to the `title` attribute, the tables also include the `summary` attribute. Many accessibility aids treat the two attributes differently, so you should include both in your tables.

Second, the column headings rely on the <TH> tag pair, not the <TD> tag pair. If you use the <TD> tag pair for the column headings, the accessibility aid won't know it's a heading and will read it as data. The same holds true for row headings. If you include a row heading, such as the one shown in Table Type 2, then make sure you use the <TH> tag pair for just the heading (not the data). Data should always appear within the <TD> tag pair.

Third, each of the headings also produce balloon help containing additional information using the `title` attribute—the `summary` attribute is unnecessary (and unsupported) for headings. The screen real estate for Web applications is often limited, which means that developers use short headings whenever possible. The addition of balloon help makes it possible for the user to receive additional information. To use this feature, add a title attribute to each of the headings. When users hover the mouse over the heading, they'll receive additional information about that heading.

The two table types demonstrate different accessibility support features. Table Type 1 demonstrates use of the `headers` attribute, while Table Type 2 demonstrates use of the `scope` attribute. In both cases, the purpose is to provide header information to text-only browsers and certain types of accessibility aids. Both attributes work equally well.

The choice of which one to use depends on the kind of table you want to create. In the first case, the deciding factor is that the last row of the table uses the `colspan` attribute, so it spans three columns. Using the `headers` attribute lets you associate each cell with the specific headers that support it. Notice that the last row has three headings associated with it. Make sure you separate the header identifiers with spaces, not with commas or other separator characters. Table Type 2 has both column and row headers, so using the `scope` attribute is easier. Otherwise, you'd have to type complex entries for each cell. Figure 19.3 shows the output from this example.

Figure 19.3 shows that a table can contain a lot of formatting information that doesn't necessarily appear in the Web page. This is another demonstration of the power of CSS. All of the formatting you see appears in the sample CSS file, as shown here.

```
Table
{
    padding-right: 1px;
    padding-left: 1px;
    padding-bottom: 1px;
    padding-top: 1px;
    width: 80%;
    border-right: silver thick ridge;
    border-top: silver thick ridge;
    border-left: silver thick ridge;
    border-bottom: silver thick ridge;
    margin: 1px;
}

TH
{
    border-right: blue outset;
    border-top: blue outset;
```

```
        border-left: blue outset;
        border-bottom: blue outset;
    }

    TD
    {
        border-right: green thin solid;
        border-top: green thin solid;
        border-left: green thin solid;
        border-bottom: green thin solid;
    }
```

Because this code affects all of the table entries, you have to make only one change to adjust the appearance of the table. Make sure you include entries for the table, the headers, and the data, or the table won't contain all of the formatting that it could. Especially important are the border settings because they provide separation between table cells. You can also use CSS to adjust the colors, fonts, and other table features.

FIGURE 19.3
An example of the two types of tables commonly used on Web sites

Working with Graphics

Graphics by their very nature are visual. Depending on the graphic and the equipment that the viewer uses, it might require perfect vision to see a graphic. You might find yourself asking whether that's a picture of a van or a sports utility vehicle (SUV) depending on the skill of the photographer. In short, graphics can be a very confusing means of communication despite the fact that they dress up a Web site and give it real pizzazz. That's why this section is so important. You can use graphics to good effect on a Web site and offer help to people who can't make quite make them out at the same time by using the attributes in the following list.

Alt   This attribute provides a short description of a graphic element on screen. In many cases, you'll combine it with the `LongDesc` attribute to ensure that the user receives a complete description of the graphic element.

LongDesc   This attribute provides a reference to a Web page or other resource that contains a long description of a complex graphic element. For example, the developer would use this attribute with a chart or a graph. The referenced page would provide a text description of the content of the chart or graph so users who rely on screen readers can understand the information conveyed by the graphic image. This attribute often appears with the `Alt` attribute.

Of these two attributes, the `Alt` attribute sees the most common use because more developers know about it. An `Alt` attribute provides a short description of a Web site element. When the user hovers the mouse over the element or selects the element in some other way (such as using a screen reader), a browser that supports the `Alt` attribute will provide descriptive information about the screen element. In many cases, the help is in the form of an audio description or the appearance of balloon help. However, the rendering of the `Alt` attribute depends on the browser you use.

TIP   It's often helpful to have a number of tools to test your Web site. Of course, buying these tools can become quite expensive, so getting free or low cost solutions is always helpful. The Sayz Me text-to-speech reader (`http://sayzme.sourceforge.net`) is one such solution. It provides basic text reading capability that helps you hear what your page will sound like to someone who can't see it.

Some pictures literally are worth a thousand words. The problem with placing all the thousand words in an `Alt` attribute is that they'd be hard to read and not every user will want to hear them. Imagine waiting for a screen reader to finish saying all this information before moving on to the next element on the Web page. The `longdesc` attribute provides a link to another page with a complete text description of complex graphics. In general, the description should talk about every element of the graphic. You want to create a word picture that matches the graphic element. Listing 9.4 shows how to use these two attributes. You'll find this example in the `\Chapter 19\AccessibleGraphics` folder of the source code found on the Sybex Web site.

LISTING 19.4:   Using the *Alt* and *LongDesk* Attributes on a Web Page

```
<!DOCTYPE html PUBLIC "-//W3C//DTD XHTML 1.1//EN"
                      "http://www.w3.org/TR/xhtml11/DTD/xhtml11.dtd">
<html xmlns="http://www.w3.org/1999/xhtml" >
<head>
    <title>Sample of ALT and LONGDESC Attributes</title>
</head>
<body>
    <h1 align=center>Using the ALT and LONGDESC Attributes</h1>

    <p>Simple graphics only require use of the ALT attribute.</p>
    <img align=middle
```

```
            alt="A green diamond shape that contains the word New in red."
            src="new.GIF">

    <p>Complex graphics require both the ALT and the LONGDESC
        attributes</p>
    <img align=middle
            alt="A picture of John"
            src="JohnPic.JPG"
            height=200
            width=150
            longdesc="JohnDesc.HTM">
    <a href="JohnDesc.HTM"
        title="A text description of John's picture.">[D]</a>
    </body>
    </html>
```

Figure 19.4 shows the output from this example. As you can see, the first image is simple, so it doesn't require the use of the `longdesc` attribute. However, as you can see from Listing 19.4, the example still uses the `Alt` attribute. Although this first image is simple, notice that describing it still presents problems. Drawing a word picture of any graphic element is going to take time, but it's an essential task.

The second image is more complex than the first. In this case, I used my picture, but any complex graphic qualifies as something that you'll want to describe in more detail than an `Alt` attribute will allow. As you can see from Listing 19.4, the second image uses the `longdesc` attribute in addition to the `Alt` attribute.

FIGURE 19.4
Make sure you use the right set of tags to describe graphic elements based on their complexity.

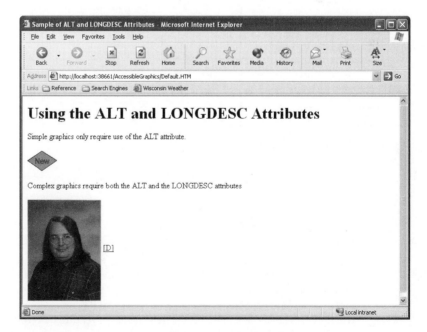

Unfortunately, if you click the second picture shown in Figure 19.4 when using Internet Explorer, nothing will happen. Even the 6.0 version of Internet Explorer lacks support for the LongDesc attribute. This means that you wasted your effort unless you can come up with another solution to the problem. You'll notice that Listing 19.4 contains a strange looking [D] link in it that takes you to the same URL as the LongDesc attribute. The [D] link is the W3C solution to the problem, and you should always include it with your Web page so that everyone can access the long description for a graphic element.

The JohnDesc.HTM file that contains the long description for my picture is relatively simple text. You can see the text shown in Figure 19.5 by clicking the [D] link shown in Figure 19.4.

You should know about a special feature in this file. To format the text, I included the following tag.

```
<p align=justify style="LEFT: 15%; WIDTH: 70%; POSITION: relative">
```

Normally, you won't format your text using this technique because the viewer may have a style sheet that works better for their particular needs. However, in this case, I chose to include the formatting information. Notice that the tag doesn't include any mention of font size and that all layouts rely on percentages. This tag will work for most users, even those who need to use large text displays, because the formatting is flexible. It's still better to use an external CSS file, whenever possible, but you can use this approach for simple formatting on simple pages.

FIGURE 19.5
Create word pictures that describe complex graphics you use on your Web site.

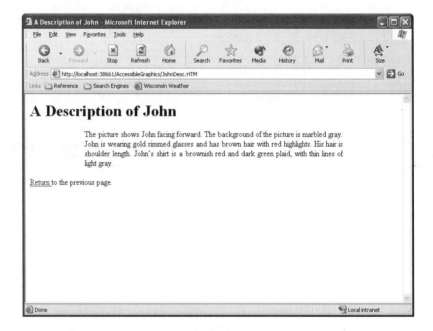

Using the *<NoScript>* Tag

Not everyone allows scripts when they browse the Internet, so you should prepare for a non-scripting scenario. To overcome this problem, you can add the <NoScript> tag to any Web page that includes a client-side script. The purpose of the <NoScript> tag is to provide output for users who don't have a browser that supports scripting or who have turned scripting off. Even though this information appears in the accessibility chapter of the book because you'll run into more people with scripting turned on when addressing accessibility needs, this particular feature helps everyone who visits your Web site.

If the client-side script on your Web site performs a simple task that you can easily explain in text, you can provide a description of the task within the <NoScript> tag. For example, if the client-side script creates a cookie on the user's system that holds user settings between sessions, you can explain this fact in the <NoScript> tag. The loss of the cookie won't affect the content presented by the Web site—it's a convenience for the user. Listing 19.5 shows how to use the <NoScript> tag to convey information about scripting on your Web site. You'll find this example in the \Chapter 19\NoScript folder of the source code found on the Sybex Web site.

LISTING 19.5:   Using the <NoScript> Tag to Convey Information

```
<!DOCTYPE html PUBLIC "-//W3C//DTD XHTML 1.1//EN"
                      "http://www.w3.org/TR/xhtml11/DTD/xhtml11.dtd">
<html xmlns="http://www.w3.org/1999/xhtml" >
<head>
    <title>&lt;NoScript&gt; Test Web Page</title>
    <link href="MyStyle.css" type="text/css" rel="StyleSheet">
    <script type="text/JavaScript">
    <!--
        function btnTest_OnClick()
        {
            txtOutput.value = "Hello World";
        }
    -->
    </script>
</head>
<body>
    <h1>Welcome to the &lt;NoScript&gt; Test Web Page</h1>
    <noscript>
        Your browser doesn't support scripts. The only task the scripts
        on this page perform is to display Hello World in the output
        textbox when the user clicks Click Me or remove the text when
        the user clicks Reset.
    </noscript>
    <p>
        <label><span class="underline">O</span>utput Textbox</label>
        <input id="txtOutput"
               tabindex="1"
               title="This is the output textbox."
               accesskey="O"
               type="text"
               value="Page Output" /><br />
        <input onkeypress="btnTest_OnClick()"
               id="btnTest"
               title="See a change in the text box."
               accesskey="C"
               onclick="btnTest_OnClick()"
               tabindex="2"
```

```
                    type="button"
                    value="Click Me" />

            ... Reset Button ...

        </p>
    </body>
</html>
```

The example uses standard HTML in this case. The script appears within the header area. When the user clicks Click Me, the button calls `btnTest_OnClick()`. This script sets the value of `txtOutput` to a new value. Of course, the code only works when the user has scripting enabled. When scripting isn't available, the content of the `<NoScript>` tag appears, as shown in Figure 19.6. Browsers that do have scripting enabled won't display this information.

WARNING   The `<NoScript>` tag can't fix many problems that people have seen on Web sites. For example, it can't fix the malfunctioning banner ad that wants to store user information locally so that it can detect a hit rate for that user. In addition, the `<NoScript>` tag won't fix gadgets such as using objects. Using the `<NoScript>` tag won't make animations and special sound effects work because there isn't any text equivalent for these features. In general, if you can represent a non-scripting fix for a client-side scripting problem as a combination of standard HTML tags and text, then the `<NoScript>` tag will probably work.

One innovative use of the `<NoScript>` tag involves adding a special link to the text within the `<NoScript>` tag. Selecting this link will post the page back to the server. The server can then perform any data calculations using a server-side script. This approach allows you to use a single page for everyone. The example shown in Listing 19.6 performs the simple task of adding two numbers together, but does so in such a way that the users with scripting support use client-side scripting and those that don't use server-side scripting. You'll find this example in the `\Chapter 19\NoScript` folder of the source code found on the Sybex Web site.

FIGURE 19.6
The *<NoScript>* information appears only when the browser lacks scripting.

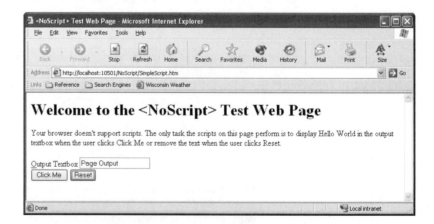

LISTING 19.6:   Accessible Friendly Scripting Code

```
<%@ Page Language="VB" %>

<!DOCTYPE html PUBLIC "-//W3C//DTD XHTML 1.1//EN"
    "http://www.w3.org/TR/xhtml11/DTD/xhtml11.dtd">

<html xmlns="http://www.w3.org/1999/xhtml" >
<head id="Head1" runat="server">
    <title>Accessible Friendly Script Demonstration</title>
    <script language=javascript>
    <!--
        function DoAdd()
        {
            var Value1 = parseInt(TheForm.InValue1.value);
            var Value2 = parseInt(TheForm.InValue2.value);
            TheForm.Output.value = Value1 + Value2;

        }
    -->
    </script>
    <script runat="server">
        Sub GetValue(ByVal Name As String)
            If (Request.QueryString(Name) Is Nothing) Then
                Response.Write("0")
            Else
                Response.Write(Request.QueryString(Name))
            End If
        End Sub
        Sub DoAdd()
            Dim Value1 As Int32 ' Holds the first value.
            Dim Value2 As Int32 ' Holds the second value.

            ' Verify there is data to process.
            If ((Request.QueryString("Input1") Is Nothing) Or _
                (Request.QueryString("Input2") Is Nothing)) Then
                Response.Write("0")
            Else
                ' Try to convert the data to numbers.
                Try
                    Value1 = Int32.Parse(Request.QueryString("Input1"))
                    Value2 = Int32.Parse(Request.QueryString("Input2"))
                Catch FE As FormatException
                    ' Output 0 when the user doesn't supply valid
                    ' information.
                    Response.Write("0")
                    Return
                End Try
```

```
                        ' Output the calculation result.
                        Response.Write(Convert.ToString(Value1 + Value2))
                End If
            End Sub
        </script>
    </head>
    <body>
        <form id="TheForm" runat="server" method=get>
            <h1 align="center">Math Demonstration</h1>
            <div>
                <input type=text
                       id="InValue1"
                       accesskey=1
                       title="This is the first input value."
                       tabindex=1
                       name=Input1
                       value=<%GetValue("Input1")%> />
                <label> Input Value 1</label>
            </div>

            ... Another Input and Output Textbox ...
            <div>
                <button onclick=DoAdd()
                        title="Click this button to add the numbers."
                        tabindex=4
                        id=AddNumbers
                        accesskey=A>
                    Add
                </button>
            </div>
            <div>
                <noscript>
                    <div>
                        Your browser doesn't support scripts.
                        Use this button instead.
                    </div>
                    <button type=submit
                            title="Click this button to add the numbers."
                            id=NoScriptAdd
                            accesskey=N
                            tabindex=5>
                        No Script Add
                    </button>
                </noscript>
            </div>
        </form>
    </body>
</html>
```

This example doesn't use code behind—it includes the ASP.NET code directly in the header of the Web page to make the explanation clearer. You can perform the same task using code behind. Notice that the example has two script sections. The first script section runs on the client, so it doesn't include the `runat` attribute. The second script section runs on the server. You'll notice that both sections contain a `DoAdd()` function and that this function adds two numbers together. The two functions don't conflict because one function runs only on the client and the other runs only on the server.

The `GetValue()` function is important when working with server-side scripting because the two inputs will lose their values otherwise. This function simply accepts the value from the `QueryString` and outputs it again using `Response.Write()`. If there isn't a value to output, then the function outputs a 0.

These functions work in various ways, depending on whether the client has scripting enabled. The server-side scripting begins with the `<input>` tags used for the two input and one output text boxes. Notice the `value` attribute is set equal to `<%GetValue("Input1")%>` for the two input text boxes. The output text box `value` attribute equals `<%DoAdd()%>`. In all three cases, the server-side script executes when the user posts data to the server.

The example includes two `<button>` tags. The first `<button>` tag always appears on screen. Users with scripting enabled will see only this first button. Clicking the button calls the client-side `DoAdd()` function. The output of this function overrides any value provided by the server-side `DoAdd()` function when the page loaded, but only when scripting is active. Users who don't have scripting enabled see both buttons, as shown in Figure 19.7. Clicking the first button won't do anything, but clicking the second button posts the page back to the server. The server processes the two inputs, refreshes their content, and provides an output to the output text box.

FIGURE 19.7
This figure shows what the page will look like if the client doesn't provide scripting support.

Testing Your Page for Accessibility Errors

At some point, you need to test your Web page for conformance to both the HTML standards and accessibility requirements. Most of the available HTML check utilities that you purchase test an entire Web site. You'll receive a report on the compliance level of all your pages at one time. It's sort of the same as using a compiler to check for errors in your code. Shareware and freeware checkers will often let you check one page at a time. Don't discount these options because they work very well for smaller

Web sites. The following list describes some of the accessibility and HTML testers that you should consider for testing your Web pages.

Bobby   This utility provides a quick check that you can use for any existing Web site. Simply feed the online version of Bobby an URL and you'll receive a report about it. Using the online version is free. The vendor also provides a full version of Bobby that will check an entire Web site without entering the individual pages for a price. Although Bobby does a great job of accessibility checking, the vendor doesn't guarantee that the product will locate every problem. You can learn more about this product at `http://bobby.watchfire.com/bobby/html/en/index.jsp`. See the "Using Bobby to Test Accessibility" section for a demonstration of this product.

Lynx   This is a text-only browser that comes in versions for the Macintosh and Windows. It helps you check your Web site by displaying it in text only. This check helps you see your Web site as a screen reader will see it—making it possible to detect and correct problems with greater ease. Learn more about this product at `http://lynx.browser.org`. You can also use the online version found at `http://www.delorie.com/web/lynxview.html`.

NIST Webmetrics Tool Suite   This group of tools from the National Institute of Standards and Technology (NIST) helps you test the usability and accessibility of a Web site. For example, Web Static Analyzer Tool (WebSAT) ensures your Web page meets specific usability goals. The Web Variable Instrumenter Program (WebVIP) helps track user interaction so you know how well users are finding Web site features. There are more tools on this Web site and NIST updates them regularly. You can learn more at `http://zing.ncsl.nist.gov/webmet`.

Opera   Like Lynx, this browser enables you to see your Web site as a screen reader will see it. However, unlike Lynx, this product also helps you turn certain features on and off as needed for comparison. For example, you can toggle images off so you can see how Alt attribute will look. Opera is available for a number of platforms including Windows, Macintosh, and Linux. You can learn more about it at `http://www.opera.com`.

W3C HTML Validation Service   This Web site checks the HTML on your Web page for conformance to World Wide Web Consortium (W3C) recommendations and standards. An error on this Web site means that the coding for your Web page is incorrect, even if most browsers will read it, so this tester goes beyond usability and accessibility requirements. Don't get the idea that passing the test on this Web site automatically makes your Web site accessible. Passing the test on this Web site means that your code is correct. However, making sure you code is correct is a good first step to ensuring that you can add accessibility features. Learn more about this utility at `http://validator.w3.org`.

Web Design Group HTML Validator   This Web site checks the HTML on your Web page or, as an alternative, on your computer. It also provides an option to validate a single page or the entire site. I also found that this site is a little less picky than the W3C HTML Validation Service about which pages it will check. This Web site seems to output about the same information as the W3C Web site, but it may not provide complete validation of your Web site. You can learn more about this tool at `http://www.htmlhelp.com/tools/validator`.

The following sections walk you through the process of using two of the freeware utilities to verify your Web site's code and accessibility. The reason I chose these particular utilities is that they're thorough, free for the asking, and not dependent on a particular platform.

W3C HTML Validation

The first level of Web site checks will ensure that your code is correct. Syntactically correct code doesn't necessarily work, but it does follow all of the rules provided by the World Wide Web Consortium (W3C). The reason I emphasize syntactically correct code is that some developers don't check their code for accuracy, while others don't check their code for bugs. You must make sure that your code works and that it's syntactically correct before you perform accessibility check. To make a syntax check, go to the W3C HTML Validation Service at `http://validator.w3.org`. As you can see from Figure 19.8, you begin by entering the Web site URL, selecting any display options, and then clicking Validate this Page.

Sometimes the Web page won't validate correctly because it lacks a `<!DOCTYPE>` tag or character set entry. You can override these problems by selecting a value from the Character Encoding or Document Type fields. However, these selections will skew the results you obtain and you should add the proper tags to your Web page as soon as possible. After you override the selections, try to validate the page again. If it still won't validate, your Web page has serious problems that you should fix immediately.

Validating a page doesn't mean that it's error free—it simply means that you've fixed enough problems for the tool to tell you about the remaining errors. Figure 19.9 shows typical output from the W3C HTML Validation Service. This figure concentrates on the errors—you can also view an outline of your Web page, numbered source listing, and a parse tree of the data.

Notice that the output shown in Figure 19.9 shows the precise location of the error as the parser sees it. The output page also includes a brief message on the error and optionally provides some information on how to fix it. Generally, you'll find that this setup works well for simple errors, but doesn't provide enough information to fix complex errors.

FIGURE 19.8

Use the W3C HTML Validation Service to ensure that the code on your Web page is correct.

FIGURE 19.9

The W3C HTML
Validation Service
provides complete
information on the
errors on your
Web page.

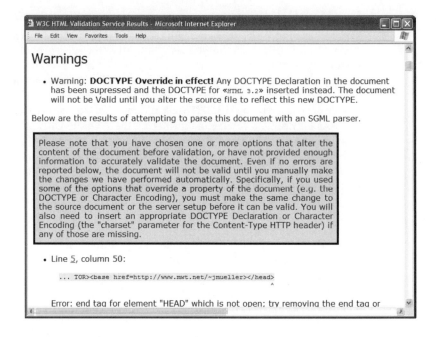

Using Bobby to Test Accessibility

One of the oldest and most relied on methods for checking Web sites for accessibility is Bobby. The fact that Bobby is free only makes it more popular. Bobby will check a single page of a Web site for free and provide a seal of approval should the Web site pass. The Bobby check relies mainly on the honor system, so you should make sure that your Web site actually passes the tests before you request use of the seal.

You can check out this valuable resource (shown in Figure 19.10) at `http://bobby.watchfire.com/ bobby/html/en/index.jsp`. As you can see from Figure 19.10, the Web site performs both Web Content Accessibility Guideline 1.0 and Section 508 (U.S. government approved) checks on a Web site of your choosing. You'll notice almost immediately that the Web Content Accessibility Guideline check is more intense than the Section 508 check, but performing both checks can point out errors on your Web site.

All you need to do is enter a Web site URL, select the test you want to run, and then click Submit. Bobby retrieves the Web site, checks it for errors, and prints a report for you. I thought that my pure text Web site would pass on the first try, but, as shown in Figure 19.11, my Web site at `http://www.mwt.net/ ~jmueller/` still had five glitches to fix. I've since corrected the problems with my Web site and posted an updated version.

Notice that all of these errors are "user checks." A user check error is one that you have to check manually and determine if your site is in compliance. In many cases, Bobby will raise a question that you can answer by saying that your site is in compliance. You can determine the error locations by looking for question marks on the Web page displayed above the report. Every question mark represents an issue that you need to consider, and some locations will contain more than one question mark because they break more than one rule.

Every user check in the report also contains a link you can use to obtain additional information. Generally, the additional information tells you what you need to do in order to correct the error and the rationale behind the rule. In some cases, the help also shows short code snippets with generic implementation information. The point is that you can find out the specifics of the problem using your own Web page as a source of the information.

FIGURE 19.10
Bobby ensures that
your Web site meets
the required accessibility
requirements.

FIGURE 19.11
Even pure text Web
sites can experience
accessibility problems.

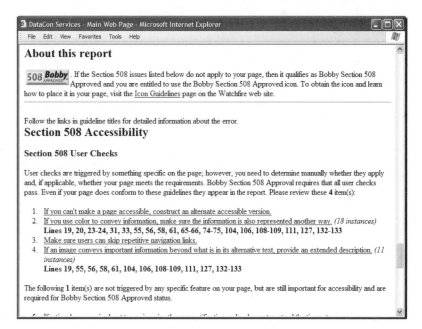

Defining Your Development Goals

This chapter presented an overview of accessibility issues that you need to consider for your Web site. Accessibility is extremely important because many people need the functionality to interact with your Web site. The few additional minutes you spend defining properties on a Web page can mean the difference between someone who uses the content you provide and someone who clicks the next link. In the end, that's what accessibility is all about—making sure that everyone can interact with your Web site. A lack of interaction means a lack of interest in what you have to provide.

Now it's time for you to get involved. If you haven't already built your Web site, make sure you include accessibility as one of the design items. Including accessibility as part of your design saves time later and makes the addition almost invisible. Anyone who's already built a Web site should consider testing it thoroughly for accessibility needs. You might be losing visitors at this very moment because they can't use the content you have to provide. Businesses should be especially aware of accessibility issues because a lack of accessibility can cost you sales.

Chapter 20 helps you move your Visual Studio .NET 2003 applications to the Visual Web Developer environment. Of course, this chapter applies only to Web applications since Visual Web Developer doesn't support desktop applications. However, many of the techniques you learn in this chapter apply equally well to desktop applications. In short, this is a good chapter to read for anyone who's performing an upgrade.

Chapter 20

Converting Visual Studio 2003 Applications

At some point, you'll decide that you no longer want to maintain two versions of your Web applications on your machine—you'll want to move your old projects to Visual Web Developer Express. Unfortunately, like most moves, this one isn't painless. Microsoft has made progress in reducing the complexity of moving an application over the years, but you still have to do some of the work yourself. Sure, the IDE performs some tasks, such as converting the project file automatically, but you still have other issues to consider, such as replacing older code with new.

This chapter helps you perform application upgrades with a lot less pain. You can automate some tasks and eliminate others through careful planning. In some cases, you can get the IDE to help you perform the upgrade, even if the IDE won't perform the task automatically for you. These techniques help you get most applications converted or at least far enough along the way that you shouldn't run into problems. However, you might still run into a few applications that cause problems simply because of the unique environment in which they run. For example, this chapter won't help much if your application runs in a mixed .NET and Java environment.

After you convert an application, you also need to consider how to test it. A standard set of tests will check the application for user-related problems. For example, a standard test suite will ensure that the user actually ends up saving a file when using the File ➤ Save command. These test suites are also valuable when testing your updated code, but they won't test everything. This chapter also points out a few special tests you should run on your code to ensure that it isn't hiding any odd version-related problems—issues that tend to sneak up on your when you least expect it.

Understanding the Process Is One Way

When you decide to move an application from Visual Studio .NET 2003, it's important to understand that the process is one way—at least to an extent. You can take the first step toward moving the application—converting the project file from its current version to the new Visual Studio 2005 version without any problem. The IDE saves the old project file and you can still use it to work with the application using Visual Studio .NET 2003. However, once you move beyond this first step, moving back becomes difficult because you would have to reverse any changes you make to the code. (Consequently, make sure you save a backup of your original Visual Studio .NET 2003 project.) The following sections describe the conversion process and examine some of the changes that you can expect to see as a result.

Performing the Conversion

The conversion process begins when you open the Visual Studio .NET 2003 project file using Visual Web Developer Express. To perform this task, use the File ➤ Open ➤ Project/Solution command instead of opening a Web site as usual. Locate the SLN file for the project that you want to convert and click Open. The Visual Web Developer Express IDE automatically recognizes that the product is a Visual Studio .NET 2003 project and starts the Visual Studio Conversion Wizard. The following steps take you through the process of performing the conversion. You'll find this example in the \Chapter 20\Convert folder of the source code on the Sybex Web site.

1. Click Next to get past the Welcome dialog box. You'll see the Choose Whether to Create a Backup dialog box shown in Figure 20.1. It's always better to be safe than sorry, so creating a backup of your old project file is always a good idea.

FIGURE 20.1

Choose a backup option from this dialog box.

2. Choose a backup option. I strongly recommend creating a backup. In most cases, you want to place the backup in a separate folder to make it easier to find later. The example uses the same project folder, but creates a Backup subfolder for the backup information.

3. Click Next. You'll see a Ready to Convert dialog box that contains a summary of the actions that the Visual Studio Conversion Wizard will take. This is your last chance to change your mind.

4. Click Finish. It's at this point that you could see any of a number of error messages. The most common error is going to be the one shown in Figure 20.2. The IDE can't tell whether the server has the proper support installed. Remember that Visual Studio .NET 2003 relies on a separate IIS server to work with Web projects and that you've been using the built-in Web server for most of the projects in this book. Generally, you can still continue with the conversion process, but you'll have to address any errors that the conversion program detects later.

FIGURE 20.2

Make sure you address any error messages that the conversion program displays.

5. Click OK after you record any error messages. Once the conversion process is complete, you'll see a Conversion Complete dialog box. This dialog box contains an option for displaying the conversion log when the wizard is closed.

6. Check the Show the Conversion Log When the Wizard is Closed option and click Close to close the Conversion Complete dialog box. Visual Web Developer Express displays a conversion report similar to the one shown in Figure 20.3.

FIGURE 20.3

Review the conversion log for errors before you try using the converted application.

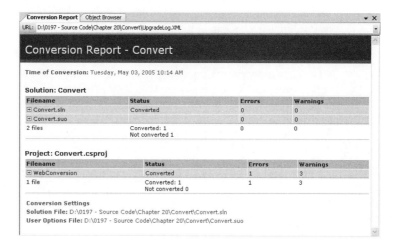

You'll notice from Figure 20.3 that the conversion program experienced three warnings and one error when converting the simple example. It's important to review these problems and correct any outstanding issues before you begin working with the project itself. Click the plus sign (+) next to the `Project: Convert.csproj` entry shown in Figure 20.3 and you'll see a list of actions that the conversion program performed as shown in Figure 20.4.

FIGURE 20.4

The Visual Studio Conversion Wizard performs a series of complex steps to update your application.

In this case, none of the issues are major. The warnings deal with changes in the visibility of various methods within the application—these changes are normal for a conversion so you don't need to worry about them. The error is a problem that could arise when you review the project before you convert it. The Visual Studio .NET 2003 IDE locks certain files and directories as it performs its job. In this case, the IDE kept one of the folders locked. You can easily address this problem later.

Understanding the Conversion Process

Converting your code produces a wealth of changes. The biggest change is the solution file. If you don't make a backup of this file, you have little chance of using the project from Visual Studio .NET 2003 if you change your mind later. This is the one change that's completely one way and you don't have any way to reverse it unless you make a backup of the requisite files.

The changes are sometimes subtle. In fact, sometimes it's simply a different way of accomplishing the same task. Often, it pays to try various techniques using both IDEs so that you can see the differences and come up with a plan to work through them. In some cases, you might even consider continuing to perform some design work using Visual Studio 2003 just to ensure that the code is compatible across the multiple development environments that you use. Consider the simple Web page described in Listing 20.1.

LISTING 20.1:   A Simple Web Page in Visual Studio 2003

```
<form id="Form1" method="post" runat="server">
  <p>
     <asp:Label id="lblGreeting" runat="server"
             Font-Bold="True" Font-Size="Large">
        Project Conversion Example
     </asp:Label>
  </p>
  <p>
     <asp:Label id="lblInput" runat="server"
             AssociatedControlID="txtInput">
        Type Some Text:
     </asp:Label>
     <asp:TextBox id="txtInput" runat="server" accessKey="I"
               ToolTip="Type some text to display on screen.">
     </asp:TextBox><br>
     <asp:Button id="btnTest" runat="server" Text="Test"
               ToolTip="Display the text you typed on screen.">
     </asp:Button>
  </p>
  <p>
     <asp:Label id="lblOutput" runat="server" Visible="False">
     </asp:Label>
  </p>
</form>
```

This page shows the Visual Studio .NET 2003 method of accomplishing the task. When you create the same page using Visual Web Developer Express, you'll notice some differences. (You'll find the Visual Web Developer Express version of the example in the \Chapter 20\VWDExample folder of the source code on the Sybex Web site.) A few of the differences are easy to overcome and won't cause any problems for Visual Studio .NET 2003. For example, Visual Web Developer Express encases the page elements in a <Div> tag that Visual Studio .NET also supports, but doesn't use. The addition of this tag won't cause any problems.

However, some of the changes do present compatibility issues. For example, consider this code snippet for the <asp:Label> tag.

```
<asp:Label ID="lblGreeting" runat="server"
          Font-Bold="true" Font-Size="Large"
          Text="Project Conversion Example">
</asp:Label>
```

Notice that the code relies on a Text property that Visual Studio 2003 doesn't support. If you decide to move code from Visual Web Developer Express back to Visual Studio 2003, you would potentially need to change every label in the project—not a very appealing modification, but quite doable.

The <asp:Button> tag also changes somewhat. In this case, Visual Web Developer Express adds an attribute, OnClick, as shown here.

```
<asp:Button ID="btnTest" runat="server" Text="Test"
           ToolTip="Display the text you typed on screen."
           OnClick="btnTest_Click" />
```

The change won't work within Visual Studio 2003 properly, so you'd need to remove it in that environment. In short, you not only have to look for changes to existing programming code, but new code as well.

Another change is the <% @Page> directive. Here's the Visual Studio 2003 version.

```
<%@ Page language="c#" Codebehind="Default.aspx.cs"
    AutoEventWireup="false" Inherits="Convert.WebForm1" %>
```

The Visual Web Developer Express version is similar, but different. Here's the version for this project.

```
<%@ Page Language="C#" AutoEventWireup="true"
    CodeFile="Default.aspx.cs" Inherits="_Default" %>
```

The visual Web Developer Express version uses a new CodeFile attribute in place of the Codebehind attribute used by Visual Studio 2003. The AutoEventWireup attribute is automatically set to true, rather than false. Finally, even the standard class definition is different, so you'd possibly need to change that as well.

Understanding Visual Web Developer 2005 Express Limitations

Visual Web Developer Express supports the .NET Framework and ASP.NET 2.0, so it might be tempting to think that an application will convert without errors. The problem is that many developers don't separate the underlying technology from the features that IDE provides. Figure 20.4 shows a report for a conversion—you can see there are many changes, even for a simple application. The previous section,

"Understanding the Conversion Process," describes these changes in greater depth. These errors show that Visual Web Developer Express won't convert even a simple application without problems.

Once you begin working with more complex applications, you'll find that the number of changes increases greatly. At some point, you'll find the added complexity results in a lot more errors and eventually you'll find that you spend a great deal of time converting an application that shouldn't have presented any problems because it doesn't rely on any third party products. The biggest limitation of converting an application so it works within Visual Web Developer Express is that Microsoft has made enough changes to the product that the conversion process can't complete without error.

As the version of Visual Studio .NET gets older and the number of applications features increase, the number of errors increase substantially as well. Even though Microsoft tries to provide backward compatibility through the update process, Visual Web Developer Express can't overcome an accumulation of errors—just as any other language product would have a difficult time overcoming the same problems. Generally, you should have a strategy for performing upgrades that either relies on using an older version of the language product or performs incremental upgrades so you can control the magnitude of any updates you have to perform.

WARNING   Sometimes the conversion utility doesn't do a very good job about alerting you to conversion errors. In fact, it won't alert you to some issues at all. The next section, "Overcoming Potential Conversion Problems," provides some insights into where you should look for problems when you find a converted application doesn't work as anticipated.

Adding third party products to the picture only complicates things. To convert a project that relies on a third party product, you need a version of the product that works in both environments. Most products don't transition well from Visual Studio .NET 2003 to Visual Web Developer Express. In fact, you can probably count on needing an updated version of the product before you can perform any conversion. Once the conversion is complete, you'll need to perform any product updates manually unless the vendor provides an appropriate conversion utility (most don't). Consequently, the third party product that saved you so much time last year will cost considerable time during the update to Visual Web Developer Express this year. In fact, you might want to continue using an older version of Visual Studio .NET when you rely on a number of third party solutions and you aren't sure how fast these solutions will receive updates.

Visual Web Developer Express can't convert anything other than Visual Studio .NET projects. The old Visual Basic 6 application on your system won't convert with any of the Express languages. However, you can use the various utilities that Microsoft provides to convert the application. In fact, you can see Microsoft's conversion strategy for Visual Basic 6 at `http://msdn.microsoft.com/VBRun/default.aspx?pull=/library/en-us/dv_vstechart/html/appmigrationstrat.asp`.

Overcoming Potential Conversion Problems

You're going to run into a few problems with your converted code. The problems aren't insurmountable, but you must consider them nonetheless. The following sections help you understand a few of the more difficult conversion issues. Most of them don't have a right or wrong solution—simply a solution that works best for you. For example, when you upgrade, you might find that you have to upgrade custom components and controls as well. Maintaining two versions of these components and controls can be difficult, so you need to think about the conversion technique that will work in your particular environment. Sometimes the best solution is not making the upgrade at all when the work involved surpasses the benefits you gain.

Considering Deprecated Features

Even if you use just the .NET Framework and ASP.NET 1.1 for your Visual Studio 2003 application, Microsoft has made changes to the latest update and you'll find that not everything converts properly. For one thing, Microsoft has deprecated (gotten rid of) some of the features found in the older version of the .NET Framework. The techniques are different, so you have to make changes to your code.

Most of the changes are for the better. Microsoft has found ways of helping you accomplish a given task using fewer resources. Listing 20.2 shows an example of using a custom event source using Visual Studio 2003.

LISTING 20.2:   Using a Custom Event in Visual Studio 2003

```
Private Sub btnTest_Click(ByVal sender As System.Object, _
                          ByVal e As System.EventArgs) _
                          Handles btnTest.Click

    Dim eLog As EventLog                ' Holds the event log reference.
    Dim eLogEntry As EventLogEntry    ' A single entry.

    ' If you want to create a special log, then you need
    ' to register an event source first (as you already did in your
    ' example code).
    If (Not eLog.SourceExists("MyEventSource")) Then

        ' Create the new event source.
        eLog.CreateEventSource("MyEventSource", "MySpecialLog", ".")

    End If

    ' Register the new event source.
    eLog = New EventLog("MySpecialLog")
    eLog.Source = "MyEventSource"

    ' Create an entry.
    eLog.WriteEntry("MyEventSource", _
                    "Special Message", _
                    EventLogEntryType.Information, _
                    12, _
                    22)
End Sub
```

Notice that in this example, you must create an EventLog object to work with a custom event source. In addition, you provide standard strings as input to the CreateEventSource() method. Notice that there's an event registration process in this code as well. Listing 20.3 shows the same example using Visual Web Developer Express.

LISTING 20.3:   Using a Custom Event in Visual Web Developer Express

```
Protected Sub btnTest_Click( _
    ByVal sender As Object, ByVal e As System.EventArgs)

    ' If you want to create a special log, then you need
    ' to register an event source first (as you already did in your
    ' example code).
    If (Not EventLog.SourceExists("MyEventSource")) Then

        ' Create the new event source.
        EventLog.CreateEventSource( _
            New EventSourceCreationData( _
                "MyEventSource", "MySpecialLog"))

    End If

    ' Create an entry.
    EventLog.WriteEntry("MyEventSource", _
                        "Special Message", _
                        EventLogEntryType.Information, _
                        12, _
                        22)

End Sub
```

In this case, you don't have to create an `EventLog` object because Microsoft marked the `EventLog` class methods as shared. Consequently, the application saves resources that it would otherwise need to create the custom event log. You do need to create an object to register the custom event source. Instead of using strings, the `CreateEventSource()` method now requires you to define an `EventSourceCreationData()` object to hold the data. It's a small change, but one that you'd need to consider as part of the conversion process. This is one of the extreme examples of code rewriting, but it's an important example as well. You'll spend time working with the code once you perform a conversion because the conversion process doesn't accomplish everything for you.

Of course, the example code further points to the process of conversion being one way. Once you make these changes, you can't easily move the code back to Visual Studio 2003.

Considering Difficult Conversion Issues

Generally, custom components and controls that you create yourself don't pose the problems that third party solutions do because you have the source code. The same holds true for any libraries you create. In both cases, you can choose to upgrade the code as needed to meet certain expectations for the converted application. However, now you have to consider what to do about the component, control, or source code library. You have a number of choices.

◆ Maintain the current code and live without the upgrade

◆ Upgrade the current code and all applications that rely on the external code (component, control, or library)

◆ Create two code bases—one for each version of the component, control, or library that you need to use

◆ Attempt to use the component or control as is from the latest version of the .NET application

There isn't a right answer in this list. All of these solutions work, but they work in specific conditions. When you have a huge code base consisting of applications that work well today and you don't see a pressing need to upgrade, then maintaining the current code might be the best solution. On the other hand, someone who has just a few applications and needs the features provided by Visual Web Developer Express might decide to upgrade all of their applications as well as the components and controls. The point is that you need to consider the problems that the conversion will present before you begin the conversion.

Something that many developers don't consider is how an upgrade will affect their code libraries. Code libraries aren't as isolated as components and controls, so often you can't attempt to use the current version of the code from the new application. Your ability to use the existing code is determined by how you created the code library. For example, you might have a better chance of using it when the code library hides the details of the code within classes.

Testing the Converted Application

At some point, you'll have a shiny new converted application. Of course, you don't even know whether the application will work. In many cases, you'll have to search through the code by hand looking for deprecated features and clean up any mysterious errors that suddenly appeared during the conversion process before you can do anything else.

During the examination process, when you're searching for errors and odd conversion problems, you should also make notes within the code. The Task List can become your best friend during this process. Make comments using the special keywords that appear in the task list. The default keywords include HACK, TODO, UNDONE, and UnresolvedMergeConflict. It's actually best to add new keywords to the list for the conversion process. To perform this task, select the Tools ➤ Options command to display the Options dialog box. Check Show All Settings in the Options dialog box. Select the Environment\Task List folder shown in Figure 20.5.

FIGURE 20.5

Add task list keywords for the conversion process and use them to add items to your task list.

Beginning all of the keywords with the word, `Convert`, as shown in Figure 20.5 makes their purpose clear. You can create as many keywords as needed to clearly define the tasks you need to perform or to designate areas of the code that can cause problems so that you can find them with greater ease during testing.

The test phase should begin with unit testing—just as you do when putting the application together initially. Performing unit testing helps you locate obvious problems quickly. Breaking the code up into pieces also helps you ascertain the effects of the conversion with greater accuracy. Because the point of conversion is to gain a benefit in flexibility, functionality, or performance, you want to be sure you can point out these differences and quantify them.

Perform integration testing next. Again, you're looking to put the application back together as you originally did. This is the point where good notes come into play. Notes can help you figure out the best way to put the application together and point out any problems that you had in the past. It's a good idea to know about these problems because you don't want to blame an existing condition on the conversion. Make sure you make a record of issues that you can definitely track now as a conversion issue. It's also important to continue looking for application differences and track any changes you notice. Track both positive and negative changes—both are important.

Some developers would stop when they had the application put together and call the application finished. However, you need to perform at least one additional step in the testing process—user testing. Users who have used the application every day are bound to notice differences that you don't see. It's not that they're any more adept than you are, but they work with the application continuously, so even small changes become obvious. Users also help you quantify the quality of the change—how it affected performance, reliability, usability, and other user-related issues.

Stress testing is a good addition to your repertoire if you don't already perform this task. It's not only important to determine what it takes to make the application fail but also to determine how it fails. The way in which the application fails can tell you a lot about the changes that the conversion has created. You can determine whether Microsoft really did fix the bugs that you had expected them to fix. It's also possible to see whether the application runs twice as fast, as you thought it would, or it has become a memory hog, which is an effect that you wanted to avoid. Using stress testing makes it possible to see how the application will fail so you know what to expect when the stress condition actually occurs.

Exporting Templates

Templates represent a type of conversion. You're converting a project or project item into a form that someone else can use. Fortunately, this process is a lot less error prone than converting an old .NET project into another form. The output works very reliably, and you'll find that it's a great way to share both projects and code.

To start the export process, you select the File ➤ Export Template command. You'll see the Export Template Wizard dialog box shown in Figure 20.6. This dialog box lets you choose the project you want to export (you must have the project loaded into the IDE) and the kind of export you want to perform. You must select the correct language from the list—this wizard won't translate a C# program into a Visual Basic program.

The following sections describe how to perform a project or an item template export. Both of these sections assume that you're starting at the Export Template Wizard dialog box shown in Figure 20.6.

FIGURE 20.6

Choose the kind of
export that you want
to perform from Visual
Web Developer.

Creating a Project Template

A project template lets you share a project setup with someone else. The project template contains everything that your project contains. Consequently, if you built personal Web sites for a living and have a set of features that you always provide, you create the initial project and save it as a template. Using this technique saves time because you'll always start the project at the point where you're customizing it, rather than building the entire project from scratch every time.

The goal then is to build only part of an application—the common part that you'll use more than one time. If the application is already complete, then it's probably too late to build a good template from it because someone else would end up removing more material than they would use from the project. Of course, it isn't always easy to guess the point at which the template becomes the most usable, so you might have to try a few times before you get just the right setup. Use the following steps to export a project template. You'll find the export example in the \Chapter 20\SimpleSite folder of the source code on the Sybex Web site.

1. Select Project Template in the Export Template Wizard dialog box.

2. Choose the project from the project list and the language that the project uses from the list of available language choices.

3. Click Next. You'll see the Select Template Options dialog box shown in Figure 20.7. The figure shows the various entries filled out so you can see examples of what to enter.

4. Choose a template icon. Type a name for your project—make sure the name is descriptive because the user will have to select the project based on the name you provide. Type a description that tells the user of your template what to expect as output.

5. Choose the options you want to use for the template. Check the Automatically Import the Template into Visual Studio option when you want to make this template part of your personal setup. Check the Display an Explorer Window on the Output Files Folder if you want to see the output folder when the template is complete.

FIGURE 20.7
Determine the icon, template name, and description you want to use for the template.

6. Note the location of the template output shown in the Output Location field. Highlight the content of the field and press Ctrl+C to save this information to the clipboard.

7. Click Finish. The Export Template Wizard creates a ZIP file containing all of the elements of your project. Depending on the options you selected, you might also see an Explorer window like the one shown in Figure 20.8 containing your project.

FIGURE 20.8
The Explorer window displays the ZIP file containing your project template.

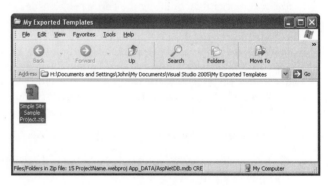

If you chose the Automatically Import the Template into Visual Studio option, you'll want to perform one additional check. Choose the File ➤ New ➤ Web Site command to display the New Web Site dialog box. Your template will appear in the My Templates section as shown in Figure 20.9. Notice that the project uses the icon you selected, has the name you chose, and provides the description you typed into the wizard. Try creating a project using the template to verify that it works as anticipated.

FIGURE 20.9
Verify that your template actually appears where you thought it would.

Of course, this entire process begs the question of what you should do with project templates that don't quite work as anticipated. Simply erase the ZIP file from your exported template folder (see Figure 20.8). In addition to the exported template folder, you'll need to remove the two entries for this project from the language folder for your Visual Web Developer installation. For example, when you create a Visual Basic project, you'll need to find the entries in the \Documents and Settings\Your Name\My Documents\Visual Studio\ProjectTemplates\Visual Web Developer\VisualBasic and \Documents and Settings\Your Name\Application Data\Microsoft\VWDExpress\8.0\ProjectTemplatesCache\Visual Web Developer\VisualBasic folders. Consequently, this change isn't permanent—it's merely convenient.

Creating an Item Template

Sometimes you don't need to save an entire project—all you need is an item from that project. For example, you might create a Cascading Style Sheet (CSS) file that you want to use with every project. You can save just this item as a template. The following steps show you how to create a new item template. You'll find the export example in the \Chapter 20\SimpleSite folder of the source code on the Sybex Web site.

1. Select Item Template in the Export Template Wizard dialog box.

2. Choose the project from the project list and the language that the project uses from the list of available language choices.

3. Click Next. You'll see the Select Item To Export dialog box shown in Figure 20.10. While it's possible to select more than one item to export, you'll generally get better results when you export one item at a time.

4. Click Next. You'll see the Select Item References dialog box shown in Figure 20.11. It's important to export all of the references that this item uses (which might not be any at all for an item such as a graphic). However, don't include any references that the item doesn't need. For example, even if your project uses the System.XML.DLL, don't export it unless the item actually uses it.

FIGURE 20.10
Choose the items that
you want to export from
the selected project.

FIGURE 20.11
Select only the references
that the item you want to
export actually uses.

5. Click Next. You'll see the Item to Export dialog box shown in Figure 20.7. The wizard offers you the same choices for an item that it does for a project.

6. Choose a template icon. Type a descriptive name for the item. Type a description that tells the user of your template what to expect as output.

7. Choose the options you want to use for the template. Check the Automatically Import the Template into Visual Studio option when you want to make this template part of your personal setup. Check the Display an Explorer Window on the Output Files Folder if you want to see the output folder when the template is complete.

8. Note the location of the template output shown in the Output Location field. Highlight the content of the field and press Ctrl+C to save this information to the clipboard.

9. Click Finish. The Export Template Wizard creates a ZIP file containing all of the elements of your project. Depending on the options you selected, you might also see an Explorer window like the one shown in Figure 20.8 containing the item you exported.

As with the project template, you'll want to verify that the item template actually appears in the list of items that you can use. In this case, right-click the project in Solution Explorer and choose Add New Item from the context menu. You'll see the Add New Item dialog box shown in Figure 20.12. Notice that the template appears in the My Templates section.

FIGURE 20.12

Verify that the template you created is accessible from the Add New Item dialog box.

You can remove an item template you no longer need using the same technique as for a project template. Begin by removing the template from your exported templates folder shown in Figure 20.8. In this case, you would remove the template entries from the `\Documents and Settings\Your Name\Application Data\Microsoft\VWDExpress\8.0\ItemTemplatesCache\Visual Web Developer\VisualBasic` and `\Documents and Settings\Your Name\My Documents\Visual Studio\ItemTemplates\Visual Web Developer\VisualBasic` folders.

Defining Your Development Goals

This chapter has provided some guidelines for moving an application from Visual Studio .NET 2003 to Visual Web Developer Express. You've discovered the pros and cons of such a move and learned about the pitfalls you'll encounter. Of course, planning helps reduce any potential problems that you might encounter. The biggest concept this chapter promotes is detailed testing after the application conversion to ensure that you don't miss any hidden version-related problems with the converted application.

Now it's time for you to plan your first application update. Start with a small project. In fact, you might want to start with a simple project you create in Visual Studio .NET 2003 for the sole purpose of testing. Don't make the test application too simple or you won't run into any significant problems that you need to consider as part of a real project upgrade, but don't spend a lot of time with this first application either. The point is to go through all of the steps defined in this chapter on a trial run to ensure that you have a good process in place before you begin the real conversion process.

You won't always want to use Visual Web Developer Express for your projects, which is the reason that Chapter 21 appears in this book. At some point, you'll want to move larger projects to the robust environment that the full version of Visual Web Developer can provide. Chapter 21 provides you with tips and hints on performing such an upgrade. More importantly, you'll discover where to look for potential upgrades to the application as a whole so it works more efficiently and reliably.

Moving to Visual Studio 2005

You may never need this chapter. Visual Web Developer Express is a great product and you might find that it provides everything you need. In fact, if you're happy with Visual Web Developer Express, it's a great idea to stick with what works. However, you may eventually run up against some of the limitations expressed in various chapters of this book. When you find that you're creating a few too many workarounds to make Visual Web Developer Express work, it's time to move up to Visual Studio 2005 and the full version of Visual Web Developer. Moving to Visual Studio 2005 means you'll gain access to a lot of functionality that Visual Web Developer Express doesn't provide, such as access to Server Explorer.

This chapter addresses the code movement process from a little project to big project perspective. The little projects you created using Visual Web Developer Express have grown in size and complexity until you can no longer maintain them using that product—you need something designed to manage larger applications. Of course, it's not just physical size that determines the kind of programming environment you need—in many cases, you'll also need better functionality, access to additional tools, and an increased number of project templates. Moving your code can also buy all of these added features.

After you make the move from Visual Web Developer Express, you need to test your code in its new environment. You'll want to look for all of the normal usage problems, but it's also helpful to ensure your code is actually using all of those new features you needed. Consequently, you need to perform tests that check for code use within the application to ensure you're seeing the kinds of changes that you had expected.

Working with your code in the full version of Visual Web Developer also means it's far more likely that you'll also use a full version of IIS, rather than the built-in Web server. Consequently, you'll want to know how to compile the code before you check it to see how it really performs. This chapter also discusses how to use the new ASPNet_Compiler utility.

Finally, removing Visual Web Developer Express and replacing it with Visual Web Developer can produce some unwanted problems. The most critical of these problems is that your system might suddenly decide to ignore the ASP.NET file extensions. The code is correct, but it doesn't execute correctly. The final section of this chapter describes how to fix the problem.

Preserving Your Code

You've spent a lot of time putting the code together for your application, so it's important to preserve that investment as you move the application from Visual Web Developer Express to Visual Web Developer (the full version of the product available is part of Visual Studio .NET 2005). Fortunately, this process is a lot easier than converting a project from previous versions of Visual Studio .NET. All you really need to do is get the code onto Internet Information Server (IIS), define it as an application, and create a solution (SLN) file for it. The following sections describe this process and help you make the big move without losing any code.

WARNING   Never assume that anything is going to work right the first time. If you haven't made a backup of your code already, make sure you do it before you move it to Visual Web Developer and IIS. Even though this process is relatively safe, you don't want to take any chances with the code you worked so hard to create.

Moving the Code to IIS

Moving the code to IIS isn't as simple as creating a folder for your application and hoping for the best. You need to create an application environment on IIS for the application. Of course, you'll begin by creating a folder within the `\Inetpub\wwwroot` folder and copying the code to it. Copy everything but the SLN and SUO files.

At this point, you need to change the folder into an application. The following steps show how to accomplish this task.

1. Open the Internet Information Services console found in the Administrative Tools folder of the Control Panel. You'll see a display similar to the one shown in Figure 21.1. The precise arrangement of folders and even Web sites on your system will differ from the one shown here, but the point of interest is the folder holding your code. The example uses the SimpleSite example from Chapter 4.

FIGURE 21.1
Locate the folder containing your application code in the Internet Information Services console.

2. Right-click the folder containing the source code and choose Properties from the context menu. Select the Directory tab. You'll see a Properties dialog box like the one shown in Figure 21.2.

3. Click Create. IIS creates a new application with a name based on the folder name for the source code.

4. Select the Scripts and Executables option in the Execute Permissions field. Changing this option lets the ASP.NET executable code perform its task. Check the Write option. If you don't choose this option, the IDE won't be able to save code changes to the folder.

FIGURE 21.2

Select the Directory tab to change your source folder into an application.

5. Choose the Documents tab. Remove the existing documents and add `Default.ASPX` to the list, as shown in Figure 21.3. Making this modification ensures that the user automatically sees the default page for your application when they open the Web site.

FIGURE 21.3

Set the default page so the user automatically sees the first page of your Web application.

6. Select the ASP.NET tab. You'll see ASP.NET specific information, as shown in Figure 21.4. Make sure you have the correct version selected for this application (IIS defaults to the latest version installed on your machine) and perform any required configuration editing.

At this point, your application is ready to use. You'll want to perform any required security and other standard setups that you would with any Web application. For example, you might want to create custom Web pages for the various error messages that your Web site can display.

FIGURE 21.4
Verify the ASP.NET information for your system and perform any required configuration.

The ASP.NET configuration can become important depending on what you expect from the application. Figure 21.5 shows the ASP.NET Configuration Settings dialog box that appears when you click Edit Configuration on the ASP.NET tab of the Properties dialog box. This dialog box contains a wealth of settings that are available only to ASP.NET users. The settings affect only the current application, so you can easily set each application as needed.

All of the tabs provide valuable settings. However, for the developer just moving the application to a server, the Application tab shown in Figure 21.5 is the most important. Notice that this tab lets you set a default master page and default theme for the application. When a page doesn't specify a master page or theme value, ASP.NET automatically applies these values. Check the Enable Debugging option when you want to debug your new application. Make sure you adjust the timeout setting as needed, too. Otherwise, you'll experience timeouts whenever the server needs to use resources with a longer load time, such as a database.

FIGURE 21.5
Change the ASP.NET configuration as needed once you move the application to IIS.

Creating a Solution File

Moving the code to IIS and configuring IIS to use it correctly is actually the hardest part of the process. However, you still want to set up your IDE to work with the application you've moved to IIS. The first step is to make sure that you don't have an SLN file in that folder. Otherwise, Visual Studio .NET will attempt to use the old SLN, and you'll see some very odd results on-screen. The following steps get you started.

1. Select the File ➢ Open ➢ Web Site command to display the Open Web Site dialog box. Start with Step 5 if you're using a remote connection.

WARNING   The Web server must have FrontPage Server Extensions installed when you use a remote connection. Otherwise, the Visual Studio .NET IDE displays an error message when it attempts to open the Web site. See the next section, "Fixing FrontPage Server Extension Problems," for details on fixing this problem. You don't have to have FrontPage Extensions installed to use a Local IIS connection.

2. Choose the Local IIS option when using a local connection and you'll see the Local Internet Information Server display shown in Figure 21.6.

FIGURE 21.6

The Local Internet Information Server display lets you choose local projects.

3. Highlight the project you want to use and click Open. The IDE opens the Web site for you.

4. Select the File ➢ Save All command. The IDE displays a Save File As dialog box where you can enter the name of the solution file. You can now access the solution as you would any other solution on your system.

5. Chose the Remote Sites option when using a remote connection, and you'll see the Remote Sites display shown in Figure 21.7.

6. Type the location of the Web site you want to open. As an alternative, you can click Browse and use the Select a Folder URL to Open dialog box to find the Web site.

FIGURE 21.7
Use a remote site connection for Web applications on other machines.

7. Click Open. The IDE loads the project from the remote Web site. This process can require a few minutes when the project is large.

8. Select the File ➤ Save All command. The IDE displays a Save File As dialog box where you can enter the name of the solution file. You can now access the solution as you would any other solution on your system.

Fixing FrontPage Server Extension Problems

Remote Web sites can run into problems when you move an application from Visual Web Developer Express to IIS because a remote connection requires FrontPage Server Extensions. Some developers won't even have this feature installed because they don't need it in many cases. Begin by verifying you have the FrontPage Server Extensions installed by opening the Add or Remove Programs applet found in the Control Panel. Click Add/Remove Windows Components. Locate Internet Information Services (IIS) and click Details. The exact FrontPage version number can vary by Windows version, but you should have this option checked in the Internet Information Services (IIS) dialog box shown in Figure 21.8.

When you don't have this feature installed, check the option to install it as you would any other Windows feature. Once the new feature is installed, restart IIS by right-clicking the computer entry in the Internet Information Services console shown earlier in Figure 21.1 and choosing All Tasks ➤ Restart IIS from the context menu. Adding FrontPage Server Extensions to IIS won't add them to your application, so you need to configure the application next.

Open the Server Extensions Administrator console found in the Administrative Tools folder of the Control Panel. You'll see a misnamed fpmmc (short for Server Extensions Administrator) window like the one shown in Figure 21.9. The following steps show you how to configure your application to use FrontPage Server Extensions.

FIGURE 21.8
Verify that you have
FrontPage Server Extensions installed.

FIGURE 21.9
Use the Server Extensions
Administrator to configure your application.

1. Locate your application in the left pane.

2. Right-click the application entry and choose All Tasks ➤ Configure Server Extensions from the context menu. You'll see the New Subweb Wizard dialog box.

3. Click Next. You'll see the Subweb Name dialog box.

4. Type a name for your application in the Title field. Generally, using your application name works fine.

5. Click Next. You'll see the Access Control dialog box. This dialog box contains two entries. The default entry uses the same administrator as the parent Web for this subweb. This is the only option you should choose unless you have a custom administrator that you want to use—most people don't because the default administrator works fine.

6. Click Next. You'll see a completion dialog box.

7. Click Finish. The Server Extensions Administrator configures your application to use FrontPage Extensions. It's easy to verify that the process worked as expected. Simply open the application in the Internet Information Services console and view its Properties page. You'll see a Server Extensions tab like the one shown in Figure 21.10.

FIGURE 21.10
Verify that your
application now has
FrontPage Server
Extensions support.

Testing Code in the New Environment

Moving an application to IIS, configuring, and creating an SLN file for it isn't the end of the road. Actually, it's the beginning of the real work for you as a developer. Before you do anything else, make sure you rebuild the entire solution. Keeping old files around is a sure way to cause yourself untold grief. Make sure you use the Built ➤ Rebuild Solution command, rather than just click the Build Solution button on the Build toolbar.

After you compile the solution completely, try accessing it from a browser. In many cases, the Web site will run just fine. However, even though things look fine, it doesn't mean they are fine. Make sure you test each page to ensure that it loads and works as anticipated in the new environment.

Unfortunately, a move doesn't always go as anticipated. Finding even one page that doesn't work right is your signal that you might need to perform more extensive testing. The tips and techniques in the "Testing the Converted Application" section of Chapter 20 work just as well for applications that you have moved to a new location. Use these techniques to locate the sources of problems in your application and remedy them prior to making the application available to end users.

Compiling Your Code Using *ASPNet_Compiler.EXE*

One of the tasks you'll want to perform after changing versions of Visual Web Developer is to compile your code. The compilation process helps you assess your code in a number of ways. First, you can use this technique to develop a list of possible problems with your code. The compiler will output errors that you won't normally see, and you can simply send those errors to a text file for later analysis. Second, using the compiler helps you check your code more quickly. The pages will load at the same speed as they do for the user. Consequently, you can see how the Web pages perform in the new environment. You'll find the ASPNet_Compiler utility in the \WINDOWS\Microsoft.NET\Framework\v2.0.40607 folder of your drive. It uses the command-line syntax shown here.

```
ASPNet_Compiler [-?] [-m MetabasePath | -v VirtualPath [-p PhysicalDir]]
[TargetDir]
```

The compiler doesn't need very much information to get started. You must supply some information or the utility will display an error. For example, you must supply a path to the Web server folder. The following list tells you about the various command-line options.

-?   Displays a list of options that you can use with this utility.

-m *MetabasePath*   Provides the full Internet Information Server (IIS) metabase path to the application. You can't use this switch with either the −v or −p switches.

NOTE   The metabase is essentially a database of information about IIS. Think of it as a kind of IIS registry. Microsoft moved the IIS settings out of the registry and into the metabase to allow developers to make changes to IIS without rebooting the system. Because the metabase is separate from the registry, you can also move the IIS settings to another machine with few problems. You can learn more about the metabase at `http://www.microsoft.com/technet/prodtechnol/windows2000serv/technologies/iis/tips/metabase.mspx`. Another good article to read is the one on the WindowsNetworking.com site at `http://www.windowsnetworking.com/kbase/WindowsTips/WindowsNT/AdminTips/IIS/IISMetabaseRegistry.html`.

-v *VirtualPath*   Provides the virtual path to the application you want to compile. The virtual path is the location of the application, as the user would see it. For example, if the user accesses the application using `http://myapp`, you would provide /myapp as the virtual path. You can't use this switch with the −m switch.

NOTE   If you omit both the −m and −v switches, the ASPNet_Compiler utility assumes that you want to compile the default application as listed in the IIS metabase.

-p *PhysicalDir*   Provides the physical location of the application on the hard drive. If you omit this switch, the ASPNet_Compiler utility uses the IIS metabase to locate the application. You must use this switch with the −v switch.

-nologo   Runs the ASPNet_Compiler utility without displaying a logo. You can use this switch with automated processing techniques.

The final optional argument is `TargetDir`. You use this argument to define the physical path of the compiled application. If you don't provide this argument, the ASPNet_Compiler utility will compile the application in place (within the same physical location as the application source code).

Fixing File Association Problems

You're going to run into problems with IIS file associations on your system. No matter what you do, IIS is going to suddenly forget that it can process ASP.NET pages at some point unless you keep your machine going 24 hours a day and never change anything—an impractical setup for many people. Fortunately, Microsoft realized early on that you would need some method for repairing IIS and provided some utilities to do the job. The following sections describe the two utilities you need to keep your copy of IIS worry free.

Using the ASPNet_RegIIS Utility

One of the most common problems that you'll experience with IIS is that it forgets how to process the ASP.NET and associated pages. Your first cue that something is wrong is that IIS suddenly starts displaying error messages whenever someone requests an ASP.NET page. Of course, a good many other problems can occur to cause this problem, but don't rule out IIS as a source of the problem. You can verify IIS as a source of problems by looking in two areas.

The first source of problems occurs when the ASP.NET services don't start up correctly. You can verify this source of problems by opening the Services console found in the Administrative Tools folder of the Control Panel. Check the ASP.NET Admin Service and ASP.NET State Service entries shown in Figure 21.11. If these entries show Stopped status, even though the service is set for automatic startup, the problem is usually one where a registration problem has occurred and the service can't locate the resources it needs.

FIGURE 21.11
Determine whether the ASP.NET services can access the resources they need.

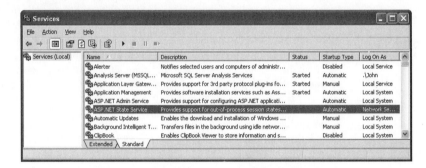

Another problem that occurs is that IIS actually loses the file extension support it requires. If IIS doesn't know what to do with a particular file extension, it usually displays an error message or does something unexpected (such as displaying your source code on-screen when available).

You can verify a file extension problem by opening the Internet Information Services console located in the Administrative Tools folder of the Control Panel. Open the Web site that hosts your application. Right-click the application and choose Properties from the context menu. Select the Directory tab. You'll see the Properties dialog box shown in Figure 21.12. Click Configuration and you'll see the Application Configuration dialog box shown in Figure 21.12.

FIGURE 21.12
Set the default page so the user automatically sees the first page of your Web application.

Notice that the Application Configuration dialog box contains entries for every file extension that this copy of IIS supports. The extensions appear in the first column of the Application Mappings table and in this case, ASPX isn't one of them. The second column contains the path and name of the DLL that supports the file extension, while the third column shows which verbs (actions) the DLL can handle. An error in any of the three columns usually indicates a problem with the IIS setup.

NOTE   Always locate the ASPNet_RegIIS utility for the version of ASP.NET that you want to use with your Web application. Each version of the .NET Framework will have a separate folder in the \WINDOWS\Microsoft.NET\Framework folder. Select the folder that contains the version you want to use.

It's possible to fix some of these problems using manual techniques and you can certainly try a manual registration or fixing the file extensions if you think the error is minor. However, in most cases, you'll need to register ASP.NET again to ensure proper IIS operation. You use the ASPNet_RegIIS utility found in the \WINDOWS\Microsoft.NET\Framework\v2.0.40903 folder of your system to perform this task. Here are the most commonly used command-line options for this tool.

-i   Install this version of ASP.NET on IIS. Using this option updates all of the script maps, updates the file extensions, registers any DLLs, and generally makes the same changes and a new installation as part of the Visual Studio .NET Setup application would make. This option also updates any existing features to the version of ASP.NET that you're installing. Use this option when you want to ensure that the ASP.NET installation completely refreshes and fixes any major errors in the system.

NOTE   Script mapping is the process of matching an application to a particular version of the .NET Framework for execution. ASP.NET supports the concept of maintaining multiple versions of the .NET Framework on a machine so that you can use the version that application relies on, rather than the latest version installed. This approach makes it less likely that your application will break because of an upgrade to ASP.NET. During an update, you must decide whether to maintain the current mapping—support for the current version of the .NET Framework—or update to the latest version of the .NET Framework. All of the options that discuss the script map (some sources use scriptmap) are referring to this process of maintaining the correct version of ASP.NET for each application. The ASP.NET Web site at http://www.asp.net/faq/SideBySide.aspx has an article that details the process for using more than one version of ASP.NET on a system.

-ir   Perform all of the tasks required to register ASP.NET on IIS. This option doesn't perform any updates. Consequently, this option completes much faster than the −i option, but isn't as complete.

-iru   Install this version of ASP.NET on IIS. This switch is the same as the −i option, but it verifies that no existing applications are using ASP.NET first. When the utility detects existing applications, it performs the installation and registration, but maintains any existing script maps so the existing applications don't break.

-enable   Enables ASP.NET in the IIS security console (IIS 6.0 or later) when used with the −i, −ir, or −r command-line switches. You don't need to use this switch with older versions of IIS (including Windows XP, which is version 5.1 in most cases).

-disable   Disables ASP.NET in the IIS security console (IIS 6.0 or later) when used with the −i, −ir, or −r command-line switches. You don't need to use this switch with older versions of IIS (including Windows XP, which is version 5.1 in most cases).

-s *Path* Install the script maps for this version of ASP.NET at the specified path, rather than use the default path. This instruction follows the script map path recursively to install all subdirectories as well. Generally, you don't want to use this option unless you have a custom IIS setup.

-sn *Path* Install the script maps for this version of ASP.NET at the specified path, rather than use the default path. This instruction doesn't use recursive installation, so you only obtain the script map at the top level. Generally, you don't want to use this option unless you have a custom IIS setup.

-r Install this version of ASP.NET and update all of the script maps starting at the IIS metabase root for all of the script maps below the root. (See the note about the IIS metabase in the "Compiling Your Code Using ASPNet_Compiler.EXE" section earlier in this chapter.) This switch updates all of the script maps regardless of the original version.

-u Uninstall this version of ASP.NET. This switch automatically updates existing script maps to the highest version of ASP.NET still installed on the machine. If this is the last version of ASP.NET on the machine, then the application removes the existing script maps and your ASP.NET applications will no longer run.

-ua Uninstall all versions of ASP.NET on the machine. This switch also removes all script maps— your ASP.NET applications will no longer run.

-k *Path* Remove all script maps to any version of ASP.NET from the specified path. This switch removes the script maps recursively, so it removes all of the script maps for an entire application. Any subapplications will also stop working.

-kn *Path* Remove all script maps to any version of ASP.NET from the specified path. This switch doesn't remove the script maps recursively, so other applications in a path are unaffected. Only the application specified by the path variable is affected by the change.

-lv List all versions of ASP.NET installed on the machine. The output information includes the version status and installation path.

-lk List the paths of the IIS metabase keys where the ASP.NET script map is defined, along with the ASP.NET version. Keys that inherit the ASP.NET script map from a parent don't appear in the listing.

-c Install the client side scripts for this version of ASP.NET to the \aspnet_client subdirectory of each IIS site directory.

-e Remove the client-side scripts for this version of ASP.NET from the \aspnet_client subdirectory of each IIS site directory.

-ea Remove the client-side scripts for all versions of ASP.NET from the \aspnet_client subdirectory of each IIS site directory.

-w Install the Web administrator tool.

-wu Remove the Web administrator tool.

-wct *ConnectionType* Change the connection type for the Web administrator tool. The ConnectionType value can include HF (hosted and forms authentication), HW (hosted and windows authentication), and L (local authentication).

-config+ Enable remote access to configuration information. This is a good option for team development on a private network, but an open invitation to cracker activity on a public system.

-config- Disable remote system access to configuration information. Always use this option for public Web sites.

? Display the complete list of help switches.

The −i command-line switch is usually the only option you need when you want to fix errors in the ASP.NET setup. Start the utility at a command prompt so you can see the progress it makes. Figure 21.13 shows a typical installation sequence.

FIGURE 21.13
Verify that the installation takes place without error on your system.

NOTE   Performing a fresh installation of ASP.NET can require several minutes to complete. Don't disturb the system during this process—go get a cup of coffee instead. Be patient—the process won't complete for several minutes even on a fast system.

Figure 21.13 has two important pieces of information in it. First, the utility completes by providing a success message. Second, it tells you there are errors. Check the error log in the folder specified. In most cases, you'll see an error message telling you that the W3SVC service didn't start in a timely manner. If this is the only error that you see (it will appear at least twice) and the Web service is currently operating as anticipated, you don't have to worry about the errors. In some cases, you will have to start the Web service manually, but in many cases you won't. Make sure you also check your ASP.NET services and manually start them if needed. Finally, check the Application Configuration dialog box again. Figure 21.14 shows that the dialog box on the test system now shows the correct entries for ASP.NET. Compare this dialog box to Figure 21.12 and you'll see that ASP.NET adds a lot of file extensions.

FIGURE 21.14
ASP.NET adds a lot of file extensions to your Application Configuration dialog box.

Using the ASPNet_RegSQL Utility

As with ASP.NET, sometimes you'll lose the SQL Server connection for your Web applications. The ASPNet_RegSQL utility helps you fix any connectivity problems without reinstalling SQL Server and ASP.NET. This utility operates separately from the ASPNet_RegIIS utility, so you might have to use both to restore application functionality completely when you rely on a database to implement certain features.

Unlike the ASPNet_RegIIS utility, the ASPNet_RegSQL utility comes with two interfaces. The first operates at the command line, while the second uses a wizard to accomplish its work. Because the ASPNet_RegSQL utility is more complex than the ASPNet_RegIIS utility, you'll want to use the wizard version of the utility whenever possible. The following sections describe both interfaces.

USING THE COMMAND LINE

You'll use the command line-interface for the ASPNet_RegSQL utility when you work with scripts or when you don't feel the wizard provides sufficient access to a particular feature. Generally, the command-line version is harder to use and error prone. That said, here are the connection-oriented command-line switches for this utility.

WARNING   The command-line switches are case sensitive. If you use the wrong case, the utility will fail in most cases, and might perform unanticipated and unwanted actions in other cases. You must use the dash (-) rather than a slash (/) when typing a command-line switch. Failure to use the dash always results in an error.

-?   Displays a complete list of switches for this utility.

-W   Places the utility in wizard mode. This is the best mode to use for reconfiguring the SQL Server connection. See the "Working with the ASPNet_RegSQL Utility Wizard" section later in this chapter for details.

-S *Server*   Specifies the name of the server when creating a connection.

-U *Username*   Defines the name of the user when creating a connection.

-P *Password*   Defines the user password when creating a connection.

-E   Sets the utility to authenticate the user with Windows credentials, rather than a username and password when creating a connection.

-C *ConnectionString*   Contains the arguments required to create the connection. The connection string takes the place of the username, password, and server name command-line switches. Don't include a database name as part of the connection string.

-sqlexportonly *Filename*   Sets the utility to generate a SQL script file for adding and removing the desired SQL Server features. The utility doesn't actually perform any changes when you specify this switch. You can use this switch with the -A, -R, -ssadd, and -ssremove switches.

Once you create a connection to SQL Server, you can perform various application service tasks. Here's a list of application service command-line switches.

-A [all | m | r | p | s | c | w]   Use this switch with any of the optional keywords to add a feature to the SQL Server connection. You can use multiple switches together by specifying them as separate switches (-A m -A r) or by combining them into one switch (-A mr). The features include:

    all   All features

    m   Membership

r   Role manager

p   Profiles

s   Site counters

c   Personalization

w   SQL Web event provider

-R [all | m | r | p | s | c | w]   Use this switch with any of the optional keywords to remove a feature from the SQL Server connection. You can use multiple switches together by specifying them as separate switches (-A m -A r) or by combining them into one switch (-A mr). The features include:

all   All features, including all common tables and stored procedures

m   Membership

r   Role manager

p   Profiles

s   Site counters

c   Personalization

w   SQL Web event provider

-d *Database*   Contains the name of the database to use with application services. ASP.NET uses a default name of `aspnetdb` when you don't supply this value.

-Q   Sets the utility to perform all tasks quietly. You don't see confirmation or error messages. This is the mode to use with scripts and other forms of automation.

Besides application services tasks, you can also use the ASPNet_RegSQL utility to modify the cache dependency options. Here's a list of the command-line switches you use to perform this task.

-d *Database*   Contains the name of the database to use for the cache dependency options. ASP.NET uses a default name of `aspnetdb` when you don't supply this value.

-ed   Enables the database for SQL cache dependency.

-dd   Disables the database for SQL cache dependency.

-et   Enables a particular table for SQL cache dependency. You must specify the -t command-line switch to use this switch.

-et   Disables a particular table for SQL cache dependency. You must specify the -t command-line switch to use this switch.

-t *Table*   Contains the name of the table to enable or disable for SQL cache dependency. You must also supply -et or -dt command-line switch.

-lt   Lists all of the tables enabled for SQL cache dependency.

The final set of command-line switches let you use the ASPNet_RegSQL utility to modify the session state options. Here's a list of the command-line switches you use to perform this task.

-d *Database*   Contains the name of the database to use for the session state when the -sstype command-line switch type is set to c (custom).

-ssadd   Adds support for the SQL Server mode session state.

-ssremove   Removes support for the SQL Server mode session state.

-sstype [t | p | c] Defines the type of session state that SQL Server supports. These options include:

t Defines a temporary session state. ASP.NET uses the `tempdb` database to store information. Stored procedures for managing the session appear in the ASPState database. ASP.NET doesn't persist any information when you start SQL Server. This is the default setting.

p Defines a persisted session state. ASP.NET uses the ASPState database to store both state information and the stored procedures for managing the session. The information stays in place even after you restart SQL Server.

c Defines a custom session state. ASP.NET stores both the state data and the stored procedures used to manage the session state in the custom database that you supply. You must combine this option with the –d command-line switch.

WORKING WITH THE ASPNET_REGSQL UTILITY WIZARD

The command-line version of the ASPNet_RegSQL utility works great for scripts, but you have a better option when making manual changes. Use the –W command-line switch to place the ASPNet_RegSQL utility into wizard mode. When you use this switch, you'll see the ASP.NET SQL Server Setup Wizard appear. The following steps take you through the process of using this wizard.

1. Click Next to get past the Welcome dialog box. You'll see a Select a Setup Option dialog box. When you select the Remote Application Services Information from an Existing Database, the wizard takes you through a three-step process that removes SQL Server support from the system and then exits. The steps that follow assume that you're using the Configure SQL Server for Application Services option.

2. Select Configure SQL Server for Application Services and click Next. You'll see the Select the Server and Database dialog box shown in Figure 21.15. This dialog box lets you choose the server and database that you want to work with, along with supplying your credentials for access to the server.

FIGURE 21.15
Choose the server and database that you want to configure.

3. Choose the server and database that you want to work with. Choose an authentication option. Click Next and you'll see a confirmation dialog box.

4. Click Next. The application will work for a few minutes as it configures the database. Eventually you'll see a completion dialog box.

5. Confirm that the configuration succeeded without error. Click Finish.

Defining Your Development Goals

Moving from Visual Web Developer Express to Visual Web Developer (the full version in Visual Studio 2005) isn't something that everyone should do. Although Microsoft would have you believe that everyone should make the move, the reality is that many people find working with Visual Web Developer Express a great experience that provides everything they need. However, if you do find you want to make the move, then this chapter provides an outline of everything you need to do. Using the techniques described in this chapter helps you avoid many of the pitfalls that turn some upgrade projects into fiascos.

Now it's your turn to do some planning. You need to figure out when to make your move—changing development applications in the middle of a project is something you should avoid unless it's necessary. Make sure you have some goals set for the upgrade. For example, consider what you expect to gain for every application and make those expectations part of a checklist you create. Ensure the testing regimen you create also verifies that the application actually makes use of the new functionality. In some cases, you might have to write new procedures and policies for working on code that considers these new features. For example, if you didn't have access to a testing utility before, such as the ActiveX Control Test Container, you'll want to add procedures for using it into your development process.

Congratulations! You've reached the last chapter of the book. However, your journey should also include the appendixes for this book. Appendix A helps you locate useful third-party utilities. All of these utilities are quite helpful, but most of them didn't appear anywhere in the book, so you won't have the complete story until you visit the appendix. Appendix B tells you how to avoid common development errors. None of these techniques appear in the book—I based them on a number of sources, so they do reflect real-world problems. Appendix C describes how to work with character codes on Web pages. You might be surprised at the number of techniques you can use to get a special character to appear on-screen. Appendix D provides 52 helpful tips you can use to optimize Windows better and faster. Try reading one at the start of every week and you'll find that you have a wealth of new ideas by the end of the year. Make sure you contact me at `JMueller@mwt.net` if you have any questions about this book. I'd also love to hear about your experiences working with Visual Web Developer Express. Also, look on my Web site at `http://www.mwt.net/~jmueller/` for updates and additional information.

Appendix A

Helpful Third-Party Tools

Throughout this book, you discovered a number of resources that would help you perform some tasks faster or with less effort. In some cases, a product added the special functionality required to make working with Visual Web Developer possible. I usually placed the special products in a separate section or used them to demonstrate a particular development process. The book also references a number of Web sites that feature special information—these helpful Web sites normally appear as part of notes or tips. This appendix is an extension of all those special sections, notes, and tips—it contains a number of helpful third-party tools that will make your Visual Web Developer experience better.

Of course, this appendix begs the question of why these third-party products and sites don't appear somewhere in the main part of the book. In many cases, these products fulfill a special need that I didn't demonstrate or they duplicate a functionality that you'll already find. This appendix contains additional information that I thought you'd find helpful, but didn't find a place in the main part of the book for whatever reason.

I'm always on the lookout for great third-party products, and I like to know about Web sites with helpful information. These sites often appear in my newsletter (sign up at `http://www.freeenewsletters.com`). I also provide them as updates to the book on my Web site at `http://www.mwt.net/~jmueller/`. If you know of a special third-party product or Web site that has information that would help users of this book, please let me know by writing to me at `JMueller@mwt.net`.

Working with XML

Visual Web Developer does provide usable XML editing capabilities. You can discover more about these capabilities in Chapters 2, 5, 7, 8, 9, 11, and 13 as part of various examples. However, if you work with XML a lot, you might need a little better functionality than Visual Web Developer provides. You have many choices for XML editors on the market. Perhaps the most powerful of the XML editors available now is XMLSpy. However, you can also choose from a number of freeware or less expensive shareware versions as well. The following sections describe three XML editor choices that you might want to try.

Using Netpadd

Netpadd (`http://www.netpadd.com`) is a freeware product that has some interesting features, but is also very simple to use. To write XML using this product, you need to type all of the information manually. There's little automation in this product, so when you create an opening tag, you must create the closing tag to go with it. The feature that makes this product better than the native Visual Web Developer support is that it's very configurable and shows the various XML elements in more colors that the Visual Web Developer environment does (making it easy to locate just what you want).

The display, shown in Figure A.1, is very much like the display you'd see in Notepad, rather than the heavily formatted display provided by products such as XMLSpy that some newer developers find confusing. Netpadd does provide keyword highlighting for your XML file, which makes viewing the information a lot easier. Use the Options ➤ Hilite ➤ XML menu options to define which file types receive highlighting.

FIGURE A.1

Netpadd provides an easy-to-understand display of the XML file.

One of the more interesting features that Netpadd provides for XML developers is multiple data views. For example, you can use the View ➤ XML Tree command to display a tree view like the one shown in Figure A.2. Other commands let you view the XML in other ways. Use the View ➤ XSL Transformation command to display the information as transformed by an XSL file. This particular view is very helpful when working with Web services because you can fine-tune your XSL file without making numerous requests to the Web service.

You'll also like the special dialog boxes that Netpadd provides. For example, the View ➤ Special Characters command displays the Special Characters dialog box. Select the character you want to use and click either Paste or Paste as HTML to place the symbol in your document. If you've ever wasted time looking up language codes online, you'll really like the Language Codes dialog box (displayed using the View ➤ Language Codes command). Simply select the language you want to use and click Paste.

Using XMLwriter 2.5

XMLwriter 2.5 (`http://www.xmlwriter.net`) is a try-before-you-buy product. I won't say that this product is shareware in the strictest sense because the trial period limits use to 30 days. That said, the trial period means you can download the product and try it before making a buying decision, which makes the buying decision easier.

FIGURE A.2

View your XML files in various ways using Netpadd's View commands.

Unlike many other XML editors on the market, XMLwriter 2.5 also uses a Notepad-style document display for editing, as shown in Figure A.3. This product automatically assumes you want to use color coding for keywords. You'll also find the use of automation nice. For example, when you type an opening tag, XMLwriter 2.5 automatically creates a closing tag for you. Load a schema for your XML file and you'll be able to choose tags directly from the TagBar displayed on the left side of the screen. The IDE also features an XML checker. Simply right-click the document and select Validate XML File from the context menu. Any errors appear in a TODO list at the bottom of the IDE.

This product includes a number of features that the serious XML developer will need. For example, you can build projects using XMLwriter 2.5. Creating a project organizes the files and makes it easier to build the links you need. XMLwriter 2 comes with built-in support for all of the standard files—including XML, XSL, XSLT, HTML, XHTML, CSS, DTD, XSD, and text. In addition, you can open some types of image files, such as the GIF, JPG, and PNG files used by many Web sites. However, the files you can open aren't actually limited to these types. You can add new types to the list, as long as XMLwriter 2.5 can read them (which means that you can add any text-based file extension).

The IDE itself is fully configurable using any of the Options dialog box entries. Fortunately, the default setup is quite usable. For example, the tabbed presentation means you can see multiple versions of your XML file with ease. If you want to see a tree view of your document, simply right-click the document and select View As Tree from the context menu. Figure A.4 shows a typical example of the tree view. You can also choose a browser view for your document.

Using XMLSpy 2005

Altova's XMLSpy comes in a number of different packages—everything from a simple product designed for the less professional user to an enterprise package designed for large project use. This section describes the professional edition that you can download at `http://www.xmlspy.com/download_xmlsuite_professional.html`. You can find a list of the other versions at `http://www.xmlspy.com/download.html`. No matter which version of XMLSpy you download, it's not a free ride—you'll have to pay for this product, at some point, unless you decide not to use it at all.

FIGURE A.3
XMLwriter 2.5 uses a document style editor, but provides many features found in high-end products.

FIGURE A.4
Select a tree view to see
the overall layout of your
XML document.

The XMLSpy difference first appears when you install the product. The installation program offers to make all kinds of changes to your system. You'll expect some of the changes, such as modifying file associations so they open with XMLSpy—others are unique, such as adding a content menu to Internet Explorer for editing XML files in place. You can even set XMLSpy up to perform certain types of validation on HTML files by modifying the normal product behavior to view HTML files as XML. The actual product consists of three components: XMLSpy (edits XML files), MapForce (helps you create XSLT files for data mapping), and StyleVision (lets you graphically create style sheets). In short, you're getting a lot more than a simple XML editor. The features that surprised me most, though, appear as part of the main product. For example, XMLSpy includes a complete spelling checker so you can locate misspellings in your data.

NOTE   Altova is quite fanatical about protecting their product. Before you can even open the product, you must request an evaluation key and provide them with your name, company name, and email address. The product enforces the 30-day rule by hiding entries in the registry—uninstalling the product and reinstalling doesn't reset the usage timer.

Opening XML the first time can be a confusing experience. The product provides more windows for manipulating XML than the average developer will ever use, as shown in Figure A.5. Shown in the Project window is a series of examples—more examples than you might imagine for a product of this type. You can find an example for every kind of XML-related file and for just about every situation. Simply double-click the file you want to open it and work with it in the editor. XMLSpy also provides tools for adding data, changing the schema, verifying the document is well formed, and too many other tasks to mention.

Unlike many other XML products, XMLSpy doesn't provide a tree view. It provides the grid view shown in Figure A.6 instead. Many developers prefer the grid view when working with complex data because it better illustrates the relationships and it can prove easier to work with. You can't get this particular view with Visual Web Developer.

FIGURE A.5

XMLSpy is definitely a professional level product designed for serious work.

FIGURE A.6

Obtain a detailed view of the data in context using the grid view.

XMLSpy provides a range of other views too. For example, click the Browser tab and you'll see how the page will appear to the user in a browser. You can also view the schema associated with the XML page and view the style sheet, when there is one. The one drawback with the Automatic view (the one that shows the Style Sheet view) is that you must create a special SPS file with StyleVision before you can use it. Some developers might find the additional work cumbersome when they have a lot of data to work with that was created without the Altova product line.

Editing Graphics

For most developers, one of the more important additions to Web sites is graphics. In most cases, Web sites will include everything from animated GIFs to pictures from your last vacation. The "Working with Media" section of Chapter 13 tells you about various kinds of media you can use with a Web page and you can learn specifically about animated GIFs in the "Animated GIFs" section of that chapter. However, you'll have other graphics needs and will likely need other products to answer those needs. The following sections provide a few product suggestions. All of these products provide professional results and you can download them to try before you buy.

Using Paint Shop Pro

Jasc Software (recently purchased by Corel) actually produces a number of graphics products that you might want to try. For example, you can use Photo Album to organize the pictures for your Web site, Animation Shop to create various kinds of animations (including animated GIFs), and WebDraw to create Scalable Vector Graphics (SVG). You can see a list of these products at `http://www.jasc.com/products`. (If you buy Paint Shop Pro, you might also want to check online for add-on filters and other features produced by third parties. Use these add-ons with care, however, since the add-on authors don't document their products very well in some cases.) However, one of the better products for Web site developers is Paint Shop Pro. Using this product, you can scan images, grab screenshots, create new images, touch up images and drawings, translate existing images to other file formats, organize images, and perform a wealth of other tasks.

TIP   You can find a wealth of interesting software packages on the Internet with a little time and perseverance. For example, many Web sites offer mapping as part of their output. One source of good mapping software is MapInfo (`http://www.mapinfo.com`). You might also want to check out a free product called the GIMP (`http://www.gimp.org`), which the author updates regularly with new features.

NOTE   Paint Shop Pro is not strictly a shareware product. You can download and use it for 60 days. After the 60 days, you must purchase the product or remove it from your machine.

The Paint Shop Pro installation sets up the product to work with a number of file types and you can choose others from the list. You have access to all of the common Web formats (GIF, JPEG, PNG) and a myriad of others (TIF, BMP, PCX, CGM, and too many others to list here). Jasc designed Paint Shop Pro to work with bitmap files, rather than vector files such as those produced by CorelDraw or AutoCAD. Even so, you can import vector graphic files into Paint Shop Pro and at least view them. Figure A.7 shows a view of Paint Shop Pro with a number of files loaded.

The product almost provides too many controls, but all of these controls help you perform tasks very precisely. For example, you'll find that the Overview window helps you keep watch on the big picture as you make small changes to the image. This window also provides information about the image. You can discover the image size, it's color depth, and other information that will help decide issues such as whether to resize the image or use fewer colors on a Web site.

Paint Shop Pro supports the concept of layers. By adding layers, you can make changes to just the parts of a picture that you want without worrying about making accidental changes to other areas. In addition, you can remove a layer when no longer needed. For example, you could create a layer with construction lines and then delete that layer when you don't need it any longer.

Of course, all of these features could prove confusing. Paint Shop Pro provides an excellent help system. In fact, you can use the Help ➢ Learning Center command to display a Learning Center window like the one shown in Figure A.8. The Learning Center contains tutorials arranged by topic. When you want to discover how to use a new Paint Shop Pro feature, simply choose the applicable tutorial.

Paint Shop Pro comes with a number of other features not discussed in this appendix. For example, you can perform a number of photographic edits, such as red eye removal. In addition, Paint Shop Pro comes with full script support so that you can record tasks that you perform regularly—making graphics editing less time consuming. Overall, Paint Shop Pro is a full-featured graphics application that lets you perform most editing tasks at a fraction of the cost of higher-end products.

Using Antechinus Draw Magic

C Point produces a number of graphics products, including Antechinus Animator for creating animated images (including animated GIFs) and Antechinus Audio Editor for working with audio files of all sorts. However, one of the most interesting products is Antechinus Draw Magic (`http://www.c-point.com/download2.htm`). This product is a different kind of drawing program. You don't work with graphics in the same way as you do any other image editor.

FIGURE A.7
Paint Shop Pro can open more file types than most graphics applications.

FIGURE A.8
Tutorials help reduce the learning curve of a comprehensive application.

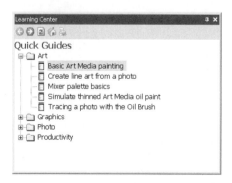

Every element on a page is an individual unit. You drag and drop controls onto the form and edit them in a manner that's very familiar to developers. In fact, you even have access to a Property Sheet window for controlling the various controls as shown in Figure A.9.

The product comes with libraries of images that you add to a form and manipulate as you would controls in Visual Web Developer. You can construct complex images using pieces from various sources. In fact, you can even click the OLE button to add actual controls to the form. Drawing bitmaps is also a little different. First, you add a bitmap control, and then you edit it using the editor shown in Figure A.10.

FIGURE A.9
Draw Magic provides an interface that developers will understand well.

FIGURE A.10
Add and modify bitmaps using this editor that you access from a bit-map control.

At this point, you might well wonder where the drawing part of this product comes into play. Antechinus Draw Magic includes several options on the File menu for exporting your drawing as a bitmap (raster image) or a metafile (vector image). The resulting file looks and acts just like any other image. Only you know that you used a control-like interface to create it. The technique provided by this product lets you create everything from standard graphics to flowcharts with equal ease—making it an excellent tool for someone creating a business or professional Web site.

Using VCW VicMan's Photo Editor

The VCW VicMan's Photo Editor (`http://www.vicman.net/vcwphoto/index.htm`) is one of many useful freeware products available on the Internet. In fact, this company makes several freeware products that you can try and professional versions of products that you can buy at `http://www.vicman.net/index.htm`. However, don't get the idea that this product works with just photographs, although that's its main purpose. You can associate this editor with a number of file extensions including JPEG and GIF.

The help file for this application is good, but it can take a while to find important topics at times. The VCW VicMan's Photo Editor also comes with an animated tutorial that you'll find quite helpful, and you'll probably want to view it the first time you start the application.

You'll find that the VCW VicMan's Photo Editor has a very flexible and colorful interface, as shown in Figure A.11. It's easy to move the editing elements around as needed to accommodate your editing needs. Resizing the elements is equally easy, even though the various boxes don't display the usual sizing arrows when you move the cursor to the edge.

The VCW VicMan's Photo Editor comes with all of the tools you might expect. However, one of the tools is exceptionally welcome—the Magic Wand. Unlike a conventional editor, selecting this tool and then pointing to an area of the image selects all of the elements of a particular color. Given photographs are often patches of mixed colors, this tool makes it incredibly easy to select a specific area, even if it's irregular. The Tolerance setting adjusts how much the color must vary from the one you selected to choose an area.

Using the Gradient tool lets you add special effects to your photograph. It's most useful for creating interesting background effects, but you can use it for other tasks too. For example, it's a perfect way to add a bit of shine to a car or that special glint to someone's eye.

The Gamma correction tool helps when an image is too light or dark. You can get rid of shadows and make an image look brighter. It's possible to change individual areas of the color spectrum or all of the color channels at once.

The bottom line is that most Web site developers run into situations when they can really use help with photographs. The VCW VicMan's Photo Editor lets you make sensible changes very quickly. No, you can't use it to create believable fake photographs, but you can use it to make your photographs look better.

Using Map This

Map This (`http://home.swipnet.se/~w-48421/mapthis.html`) is a freeware image map creator. An image map associates URLs with specific locations on an image that you provide on an HTML page. The image can include anything you want—a picture of a summer home, the topics you provide on your Web page, anything that you can dream up. When a viewer clicks a specific image map area, known as a hot spot, the image map takes them to that location on your Web site. Most Web sites use image maps to provide a little pizzazz and functionality combined.

NOTE Image maps do present problems for viewers with accessibility needs, however, so you should use them carefully and make them accessible when you do. You can find an excellent tutorial for creating accessible image maps at http://www.jimthatcher.com/webcourse5.htm.

You can use Map This to create hotspots of any shape or complexity. The Area List shown on the left side of Figure A.12 displays a list of hotspots for the current image and tells you about the hotspot type using the shape icon. You can also right-click an image area and choose Edit Area Info from the context menu to display the Area dialog box shown in the figure. Both options let you modify the area information. Adding information to the Internal Comment About This Area field automatically adds the Alt attribute required to make the image map marginally accessible.

FIGURE A.11
Working with photographs is easy with VCW VicMan's Photo Editor.

FIGURE A.12
Create image maps for your Visual Web Developer projects with relative ease.

Map This can save you considerable time and effort when working with image maps because Visual Web Developer doesn't provide the required resources to create a .MAP file. Normally, you need to create the code by hand. Using Map This lets you create the complex image map code using a graphical interface (and not writing any image map code at all). Here's a typical example of an image map code for an HTML page.

```
<MAP NAME="CountryLake">
    <!-- #$-:Image Map file created by Map THIS! -->
    <!-- #$-:Map THIS! free image map editor by Todd C. Wilson -->
    <!-- #$-:Please do not edit lines starting with "#$" -->
    <!-- #$VERSION:1.30 -->
    <!-- #$DESCRIPTION:Just a test map to show what can be done without
                      resorting -->
    <!-- #$DESCRIPTION:to lots of writing down points and wasting time.
     -->
    <!-- #$AUTHOR:Todd Wilson -->
    <!-- #$DATE:Mon Jul 08 18:51:43 1996 -->
    <!-- #$PATH:D:\src\MapThis\4release\files\examples\ -->
    <!-- #$GIF:lake.gif -->
    <AREA SHAPE=RECT COORDS="213,296,289,336" HREF="door.html">
    <AREA SHAPE=CIRCLE COORDS="499,355,14" HREF="liferaft.html">
    <AREA SHAPE=POLY
        COORDS="637,362,551,366,550,373,545,375,448,366,371,367,347,
                367,336,367,293,356,256,352,0,356,0,477,640,478,637,
                365,637,362,637,362"
        HREF="lake.html">

    ... Lots of Other <AREA> Tags ...

    <AREA SHAPE=default HREF="tryagain.html">
</MAP>
```

The comments are Map This specific. They tell the application how to set up the environment and provide project information. However, all of those <AREA> tags define hotspots on the Web page. Imagine trying to create the correct coordinates for all of the hotspots you want to add to a Web page by hand—especially when you need to use the POLY shape.

To use the resulting image map in your Visual Web Developer projects, save the image map using a MAP extension in Map This. In Visual Web Developer, select the image that you want to use. Add the image map filename to the UseMap property of the image (the Microsoft-supplied help would have you believe that you need to create this information by hand). Figure A.13 shows a typical example of a Web page with an image map on it. Notice that the hotspot includes an Alt attribute, in this case, so the browser displays balloon help.

Using the Antechinus C# Editor

This book contains more than a few pieces of C# code and VB code that you need to create with something other than Visual Web Developer Express. You can download one of the other Express product options, get the full version of Visual Studio .NET, or rely on a third-party alternative. The Antechinus C# editor is an excellent alternative third-party product.

FIGURE A.13
Add image maps to your
Visual Web Developer
projects using the
UseMap property.

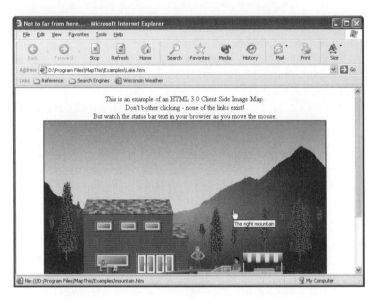

The Antechinus C# editor got its start when some developers expressed dissatisfaction with the editor provided with Visual Studio .NET for C# development. The fact that some developers complained about the Visual Studio .NET editor isn't a surprise for anyone who's developed applications for long. The editor, along with other tools such as third-party libraries, represents the developer's custom tool for creating code. Because each one of us is different, it's not surprising that a one-size-fits-all approach to the editor doesn't work.

More than a few developers are also looking for alternatives to the rather steep purchase price of Visual Studio .NET. Not every developer is convinced that .NET programming is in their future and the Visual Studio .NET package could represent an expensive experiment. Because the .NET Framework and the .NET Framework SDK are free, all that a developer really needs is a good editor to get started coding C#.

NOTE   The Antechinus C# Editor relies on the .NET Framework, so you'll need to install the released version of the .NET Framework to use it. The installation program provided on the CD won't install the .NET Framework for you. However, if you install Visual Web Developer Express (http://lab.msdn.microsoft.com/express) or the .NET Framework SDK (http://www.microsoft.com/downloads/details.aspx?FamilyID=9B3A2CA6-3647-4070-9F41-A333C6B9181D&displaylang=en) before you install the Antechinus C# Editor, you'll have the required support.

Of course, using a general editor deprives the developer of the features that a C#-specific editor can provide, such as context-sensitive help and keyword highlighting, so any alternative a developer chooses must provide some basic level of functionality. The Antechinus C# Editor (http://www.c-point.com/download2.htm) from CPoint Pty Ltd. does provide all of the required functionality for a C# editor, yet has a different interface from the one provided by Visual Studio .NET. This section will briefly explore the Antechinus C# Editor. Figure A.14 shows an example of the Antechinus C# Editor with a project file loaded.

The first difference you'll notice when using the Antechinus C# Editor is that it deals with source code files and doesn't rely on a Solution file as the center of the application universe. This is actually a big plus because many of the examples you'll see online lack any kind of Solution file, so the Visual Studio .NET IDE has to build one as part of "importing" the application. You do have complete control over the project settings using the Project Options dialog box shown in Figure A.15. Many developers find this method of setting project options easier than the relatively complex set of dialogs and folders provided with Visual Studio .NET.

FIGURE A.14

The Antechinus C# Editor provides simpler interface than the one provided by Visual Studio .NET.

FIGURE A.15

The Project Options dialog box gives you complete control over the project options.

NOTE Some of the options demonstrated in this section are available only to registered users. For example, the trial version lacks support for using projects. However, even with the trial version, you can create individual files and compile them into an executable. (You can't create multiple file examples without project support.) The trial version will also show features such as key word highlighting. In short, the editor itself is fully functional, but you'll find some of the functionality required to create complete applications is missing.

The Antechinus C# Editor is missing what some developers would consider an exceptionally important feature—there's no designer support. However, newer versions of the Antechinus C# Editor include a Visual Forms view as shown in Figure A.16. The editor is similar to Visual Studio in that you have an Object Bar from which to choose controls and a Property Sheet window for changing properties, but the effect is very reminiscent of older C++ editors, rather than the designers provided with Microsoft products. In addition, this editor doesn't provide separate tabs for the designer and code views—you switch between them using the View menu options.

The designer limitation means you may have to perform some hand coding for forms. Some developers actually find this easier, but you'll need to consider this omission from a productivity standpoint. Moving objects around in a graphical environment is easier than moving them around by modifying coordinates in source code. Still, not every project involves a visual interface. You can create a multitude of components and controls without worrying too much about graphics.

Something to note about the Antechinus C# Editor is all of the helpful menu options it provides. For example, this editor actually works better than the Microsoft product for adding documentation to your C# code. The Doc menu contains the entire list of C# documentation options—all you need to do is select the documentation option you need from the list. You'll also find menu options for working with HTML, so this product will let you make quick changes to Web pages when necessary. Finally, the Antechinus C# Editor is very much oriented toward using scripts and code templates to reduce coding time. You can save the snippets of code that you use regularly and save typing time.

FIGURE A.16

The Antechinus C# Editor has a few limitations when designing forms.

In sum, the Antechinus C# Editor is a good alternative to the Visual Studio .NET IDE if you don't plan to work on large applications that require many graphics. This is the perfect editor for anyone writing a lot of component and control code or working on Web site code (which is why the product appears in this appendix). It's also a good way to get to know C# without extra widgets to get in the way. Using this editor forces you to learn about the code that the Visual Studio .NET editor creates (and sometimes botches) in the background.

Appendix B

A Guide to Common Development Errors

All developers make mistakes. Part of the coding learning process is making mistakes and then learning from those mistakes. The difference between a good code writer and a great developer is often the willingness to make mistakes and learn from them. However, you don't always have to have a brick wall of bad code fall on you to learn a new technique or discover how to avoid errors. Sometimes, all you need to do is look at what someone else has done and obtain the lessons learned without making the same mistake. This appendix falls into the "learn from someone else's error" category—it contains a list of common errors that Web developers make and discusses how to avoid them.

Plan Before You Write Code

It doesn't matter how small your project is, a failure to plan before you begin writing code is always an error. The problem is that these small projects tend to get bigger before you finish writing the application. Even personal projects can become labyrinthine in short order. Think about it this way—just as a builder needs a plan to construct a house, you need a plan to construct your application.

You could easily tell whether a builder decided to build a house without using a plan, and it's just as easy to determine when someone writes an application without one, as well. Application users can see that the application has design flaws because it doesn't work as anticipated. The plan that you use doesn't have to be very complicated, but you do need to think about these questions:

- What will the application do?

- How will the application accomplish its task?

- When will the application run?

- Who will use the application?

- Why is the application important?

Professional developers use a number of complex methods, such as the Unified Modeling Language (UML) (http://www.omg.org/gettingstarted/what_is_uml.htm), and applications, such as Microsoft Visio (http://office.microsoft.com/en-us/FX010857981033.aspx), to answer these questions. Because most Visual Web Developer applications are much smaller than these huge undertakings, you can normally answer the questions quite easily. Don't make this more complicated than you need to. You might answer the first question by saying that the application will display the pictures on your Web site.

The reason you want to go through this process is to ensure that you've thought about the application that you want to create. It's easier to answer the questions before you write any code instead of fixing the code later. Writing your answers down also helps you avoid making the application into something that you didn't intend. This is a common problem for everyone; even developers with a lot of experience write applications that quickly grow beyond the original intent.

Avoid Performance Bottlenecks

Web pages present all kinds of ways to waste resources and perform tasks more often than necessary. As the technology you use to create a Web page becomes more complex, the number of ways to create a performance bottleneck also increases. For this reason, you want to consider how to perform a specific task. Some developers feel obligated to use ASP.NET just because they're using Visual Web Developer to create their application. However, the smart way to develop the Web site is to rely on the least complex solution. Whenever possible, use standard HTML for static information to conserve resources. A help file doesn't change very often, so using HTML will conserve resources. The following sections describe other ways to avoid performance bottlenecks.

Use *Page.IsPostBack* to Control Resource Use

When you need to use ASP.NET to create a Web page, you can avoid some common performance bottleneck issues through careful programming. For example, it's very likely that your Web page will contain one or more areas of initialization code. Letting this initialization code run every time the user calls the Web page can use resources inefficiently. Check whether the controls are already initialized using the `Page.IsPostback` property like this:

```
If (Not Page.IsPostback) Then
    ' Initialize the controls.
    MyControl.Text = "Hello"
    ... Other Controls ...
End If
```

Of course, this technique works only for static control initialization. A control that changes with every call will probably need initialization. In addition, remember that Web pages don't include the concept of state. ASP.NET pages keep track of the control state using various background techniques. Consequently, you might find that you do need to initialize some controls on each call. The point is to try the control using a static initialization whenever possible.

It's important to note that using `Page.IsPostback` can also help you avoid some difficult-to-find bugs in your Web page. For example, you might change the property value of a control programmatically in response to a user request. However, the change doesn't appear to stick—the control shows the old data on every call. The code to change the control looks fine, so you spend hours looking for the problem with a debugger. After a long search, you discover the problem occurs because the code re-initializes the control's property on every call.

Perform Client-side Validation

Whenever possible, use client-side scripts to validate form entries for accuracy. Using server-side validation can result in a lot of extra network bandwidth usage, especially for large forms. When using server-side validation, the client sends the form to the server for approval every time the user moves to the next field on the form. Although you might not notice a large performance penalty when using a high-speed connection, the content back-and-forth validation traffic can cause significant performance problems when working on a low-speed connection such as dial-up.

Of course, you don't want to open a security breach in your setup and you must accommodate users who keep their scripting turned off. Consequently, you can't always use client-side validation, even if the performance hit of server-side validation is more than you'd like. When this situation occurs, try to divide the form into those elements that you must validate on the server and those that you can validate on the client. Using aggressive post-processing can help a lot in this regard. Sometimes you can wait to catch the error when it first reaches the code behind for your application, rather than at the client or as part of a server-side validation control. However, make sure you do validate every entry the user makes.

Save the View State Only When Needed

All of the server-side controls that you use with Visual Web Developer set the `EnableViewState` property to `True` by default. What this means is that every control saves its state as part of the hidden __VIEWSTATE variable. The client and server send this information back and forth. Saving the view state information for a small control such as a text box isn't very resource intensive. However, when you start working with data grids, the price for saving that information increases dramatically. It's nothing for the variable to consume 10 KB or more of space, which means that you're transferring a lot of information for every call. Figure B.1 shows an example of a page that contains just a small data grid with eight entries on it.

FIGURE B.1

Saving the view state makes sense when the control actually needs the information.

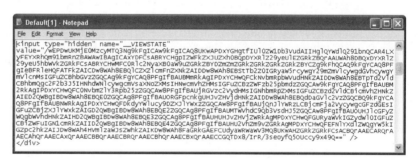

Even this example is relatively resource intensive. The version of the page that saves the view state for the data grid consumes 5.6 KB, while a second version that doesn't use view state requires only 3.9 KB. (You'll find this example in the \Appendix B\ViewState folder of the source code on the Sybex Web site. The HTML sent to the browser with view state enabled appears in Test1.HTM, while the disabled version appears in Test2.HTM.) It's the same information, but in a smaller package. Add server-side validation to this example and you have a performance disaster in the making. Here's the best part. You can disable the view state and not lose any functionality. Because the data grid is rebuilt every time the client makes a request, saving the view state doesn't provide anything of value.

Don't get the idea that it's always a bad idea to enable the view state. Some controls, especially those with static data that the server won't re-create for every call, do need the view state enabled. However, using this feature only when you need it can make your application run a lot faster.

TIP You can always disable the view state of a control you can't see when the page is active. For example, the IDE will enable the view state for the SqlDataSource control, even though you can't see this control on-screen. Controls that you can't see don't have a view state that you should save.

Set the Session State

The session state, like the view state, stores information about the application. However, the session state affects the application as a whole, rather than the status of a single control. Consequently, the session state has a larger effect on the functioning of your application. Unfortunately, as with the view state, the IDE always enables the session state. You can set the session state to one of three values: `True`, `False`, or `ReadOnly` using a page directive like this.

```
<%@ Page EnableSessionState="True" %>
<%@ Page EnableSessionState="ReadOnly" %>
<%@ Page EnableSessionState="False" %>
```

Setting the session state to `True` lets the application both read and write session state variables. Consequently, you can save session state information from one invocation of the page to another. However, this setting also consumes the most resources. Setting the session state to `ReadOnly` will let the application read the session state, but not change it. This setting is good when you need to work with the session state information because it uses fewer resources. Finally, set the session state to `False` to ensure that the application doesn't store the session state. Interestingly enough, this setting works more often than you might think.

Setting the session state to `ReadOnly` or `False` won't reduce the Web page size any (as demonstrated by `Test3.HTM`). However, you'll notice that the page loads significantly faster. In fact, the example page found in the `\Appendix B\ViewState` folder of the source code on the Sybex Web site is quite fast when you set the session state to `False` and noticeably faster when you set the session state to `ReadOnly`. The time savings come from the reduced preparation that the server must perform to display the page. Even with the session state set to `False`, the example page, which displays the Categories table from the Northwind database, performs all standard tasks without a problem.

You also have several options for storing session state information in the `Web.CONFIG` file. In this case, you can use the `<sessionState>` element to set the session state `Off` (no session state at all), `InProc` (the application stores the settings locally), `StateServer` (the settings appear on a remote server specifically designated for that task), `SQLServer` (the settings appear within a SQL Server database), or `Custom` (a custom configuration scenario that you create). A complete explanation of these options is outside the scope of this appendix, but generally, you'll want to use the `Off` option to get the best performance as shown here.

```
<configuration
 xmlns="http://schemas.microsoft.com/.NetConfiguration/v2.0">
    <system.web>
        <sessionState mode="Off" />
    </system.web>
</configuration>
```

Use Pure HTML Whenever Possible

Every time you drop an ASP.NET server control on the page, you're using processing cycles. The ASP.NET control requires server-side processing in all cases and additional client-side processing in some cases. Using pure HTML for the same task is far more efficient. Consequently, when you have a choice between an HTML tag and an ASP.NET control to implement a label, choose the HTML tag whenever possible.

Keep Your Data Safe

Security is the most talked-about development issue today. It's true that better security will keep your data safer. In addition, well-designed security can reduce user confusion and frustration. However, security isn't the only consideration for data security. You also need to consider the reliability of adding, accessing, modifying, and deleting data as part of your application design. Underlying both of these issues is the code that you write. Using the development techniques in the following sections not only makes your data more secure but more reliable as well.

PUTTING THE TIME BACK INTO ACCESS

One of the biggest problems that developers face is time. Often, accountants, managers, and others who don't develop code for a living only understand the ticking of the clock and see how the expenditure of time affects the bottom line. The outside world has tried to quantify developer productivity for years. In a race to deliver code within the time expectations of management, developers often cut corners and leave out the code that we all know should appear in the application.

Would it surprise you to know that most of the errors and security issues in code are there because of time issues? Even the best developers get flustered and fail to provide adequate checks in their code because it's easier to deliver the code now, rather than hear marketing whine one more time. Time is the enemy of security. Bowing to the demands of time, rather than exercising prudent programming practices, is the biggest mistake that any developer can make.

Fortunately, the .NET Framework automatically adds code to perform many required security checks. The Common Language Runtime (CLR) uses these automatic code additions to perform security checks during runtime. Unless you trap the error, however, the user sees an ambiguous security error message, rather than a precise message stating how to fix the problem. The .NET Framework does improve the situation, but can't fix it completely.

Explaining the dichotomy of time versus quality to your boss isn't an easy undertaking and will be impossible if you can't quantify the argument in some way. It's important to put the science back into the art of programming by creating an underpinning of quality within your organization. For example, how many developers actually use a checklist to ensure they've met every programming need (such as the need to include security exception checking within the code)? A checklist requires validation, but once validated, it can provide the best means of quantifying your progress to those who need to know.

Checking Every Input

Relying on strong data typing, using all of the proper data transfer techniques, and keeping global variables to a minimum all help keep your data safe. However, it's far better to check the data every time you use it. Checking every input might seem like a waste of time, but it's the only way to ensure that you have good data to work with. It's far better to find bad data before you use it than to catch it as an exception or not catch it at all. With this in mind, the following list provides some items you need to check when working with incoming data.

Check the data range.   A data range defines the acceptable values for data input. For example, when you define a value in your code as Int32, it means that the user can enter any value from –2,147,483,648 through +2,147,483,647. However, your application might not find this range acceptable. When this happens, you must include special code in your application to check for potential error conditions. You might want to accept numbers from 0 to 40,000 in your code, which is outside the `Int16` value range, but well within the `Int32` value range. In short, a data range is specific to the need at hand. Generally, you'll find that value data types are the easiest to range check because they have predefined ranges. The .NET Framework supports more value types than you might think. For example, the .NET Framework considers a color used for drawing (`System.Drawing.Color`) a value type. You can see the full list of .NET Framework value types at `http://msdn.microsoft.com/library/en-us/cpref/html/frlrfsystemvaluetypeclasshierarchy.asp`.

Check the data length.   Many of the exploits that crackers use depend on the application not checking the length of the incoming data. For example, the buffer overrun technique has become so popular because few developers check the length of incoming data. Fortunately, for the .NET developer, CLR does much of the length checking automatically and raises an exception immediately after it detects data of the wrong length. Even so, CLR only checks for extreme cases—you still have to perform checks for your particular application. Data that's too short can be just as much a problem as data that's too long. For example, if your program needs a string that it will then parse for appropriate data, it could fail if it suddenly runs out of data before the parsing is complete. Ensuring the data is as long as you need before you begin any processing is the best way to avoid certain kinds of problems. Make sure you tell the user about these requirements (length limits) and present clear messages about the error when it does occur.

Control unnecessary characters.   Unnecessary characters are any characters that your application doesn't require as input. For example, if your application doesn't require any slashes, then you shouldn't accept them as input. Likewise, you should avoid any numeric or control character input unless you actually need them to make the application work properly. Crackers have devised a number of interesting exploits over the years to make use of extra characters. The problem is especially severe for Web applications where an application could actually end up combining several fields together if the cracker provides specific input. (It's easier to create combined fields in a Web application because form data isn't strongly typed and there's less direct separation of the data through use of individual variables.)

TIP   You may think that checking individual characters in a string isn't worth the effort. Until you actually see some of the exploits that crackers use, it might seem that character checking is a solution in search of a problem. The Security Focus site article titled "Abusing Poor Programming Techniques in Webserver Scripts V 1.0" at `http://www.der-keiler.de/Mailing-Lists/securityfocus/secprog/2001-07/0001.html` shows that this is a significant problem.

Verifying Every Output

Just as you check every input, you also need to check every application output to provide maximum security. Although this application feature isn't quite as important as checking inputs, you should still consider adding it to your application. You don't know when a compromised system will modify the data between the time that your code receives the data as input and the time it sends it as output. A system is only as good as the security that the entire system provides and most systems have a number of security holes that you need to watch.

Use the same checks for data output as you do for data input. In other words, ensure that the data is of the correct type, the right size, contains only the characters you expect, and is within the correct range. Whenever these checks fail, you know that something is wrong. Security is going to be one of the main culprits, but also be willing to look for errors in your code. Output checks often help you locate bugs in your application by locating the source of the error more precisely.

PROVIDING PRECISE HELP

It always pays to provide good help with your application. A good help file can prevent many kinds of user input errors by showing the user precisely what your application expects to receive. Reducing input errors makes it possible to perform thorough analysis of the errors that remain, which reduces security risks from incorrect input in the end.

Some data types present special challenges that your application must handle to ensure data integrity, as well as address security concerns. For example, a date is a common data entry item that could present problems. First, you need to consider the format of the date. A user could type 1 June 2003, 06/01/2003, June 1, 2003, 2003/06/01, or any other acceptable variant. Desktop applications usually don't have many problems with dates, but they can become a problem with Web applications because the application must parse the date into an acceptable format. Allowing just one type of entry and telling the user about the precise data format will reduce the security problems—it's easier to determine when the data is correct.

Note that providing precise help won't eliminate all data entry errors. Some users will insist on attempting to enter data using whatever means they think best. In addition, there are biases to consider. A particular locale may use a specific date form, and the user will use that form out of habit. Even so, most users will get the point after a few tries, making good help beneficial. When you begin noticing patterns of constant abuse despite the help, your security screens should go up and you should consider the kind of user making the error.

Work Smarter, Not Harder

Computer languages generally provide more than one way to accomplish a task. In addition, the .NET Framework sometimes provides more than one class you can use for a given task. Add to this complexity the options that you have with a given technology, such as configuring your Web site, and you might think it impossible to use the best strategy all of the time. In fact, you probably won't use the best technique every time, but that's where the learning process comes into play. Maintaining an electronic notebook of what works and when is probably the best thing you can do for yourself. At some point, you'll have a whole book of pointers that will help you work smarter, rather than harder, to write great code. The following sections describe a few techniques you can try.

Try the *HttpServerUtility.Transfer* Method

Depending on what you're trying to accomplish, you don't always need to use the `HttpResponse .Redirect()` method to send the user to a new URL. Using this method incurs an extra round-trip between the client and the server, which produces a performance hit. In addition, the extra round-trip always invites unwanted introduced errors. When you don't plan to do anything but change the user's Web page, you can rely on the `HttpServerUtility.Transfer()` method instead. This method performs the transition at the server—the client sees the new Web page on the first trip.

Of course, using the `HttpServerUtility.Transfer()` method also means that you won't have an opportunity to perform client-side tasks before the new page appears. For example, when you rely on cookies to transfer certain kinds of data, you might find that the page doesn't work as expected. You want to test this method in various situations before you assume that the performance benefit is worth a coding change.

Use Exceptions Carefully

Exceptions are an essential part of good application design, so you need to use them as required. However, you should remember a simple rule about exceptions—they occur only under exceptional circumstances. Always use exceptions in controls or components to signal an error—don't display the error information from within the control or component. In addition, you might have to use exceptions to pass information to the next method in a call stack when a lower method can't handle the error. What you need to avoid is using an exception as a means of changing application flow or sending messages between application layers. The reason is simple: exceptions are very costly from a resource perspective. In addition, exceptions always produce a noticeable delay in execution.

Whenever possible, use standard coding techniques to change the execution path or pass data. For example, the server spends a lot less time processing an `If...Then` statement than it does unwinding the stack to process an exception. Likewise, passing a structure between methods is a lot faster than using an exception to create a complex message store.

The unfortunate part about exceptions is that they don't affect only one person or only your code. Every time the server processes an exception, it robs processing cycles from other applications. The exception generally runs at a higher priority than normal code does. Consequently, an application that uses enough exceptions in the wrong way can greatly reduce the work that a server can perform.

Use All Available Resources

You might be surprised to learn that most developers use only a small percentage of the resources available to them when writing code. In many cases, it's a problem of not knowing about a particular environment feature—it really is tough to keep all of those namespaces, classes, methods, events, and properties in your head. Because most projects today are on very short schedules, the developer has little reason to look for alternatives. Therefore, many developers continue to use inefficient programming techniques that result in less than optimal code because the technique is familiar—the developer doesn't have to do anything special to use a known technique. The following sections provide a few ideas of where to look for interesting new techniques that you can use to create better applications without a lot of work.

Rely on SQL Server Stored Procedures

SQL Server stored procedures can make your code run more efficiently in many cases. Whenever you can define a static query—one in which only the arguments change—use a stored procedure rather than a local command. Using a stored procedure lets SQL Server store the command locally—reducing network traffic. In addition, SQL Server compiles stored procedures, which means the request executes faster. The combination of all of these elements makes well-defined stored procedures execute faster and with fewer resources.

However, don't be afraid to use local commands as needed. Any ad hoc query requires a local command. When you can't define a query very well in advance, creating odd-looking stored procedures with convoluted logic can actually make the application run slower. When you need to choose between a stored procedure and a local command, decide whether you can state the query as a change in variables. If you can't, use a local command.

Using stored procedures can help you avoid some security issues. For example, stored procedures often resist script attacks when a local command won't. A script attack is one in which a cracker adds special coding to one, two, or more fields on a form to gain unauthorized access to an application. Of course, making sure that you check every input reduces the problems of script attacks for local commands as well.

Precompile the Application

Precompiling your application makes the page load faster. This process occurs automatically the first time a user requests the page after you make a change. Unfortunately, if you change many pages, the load on the server can increase dramatically at precisely the wrong time—during peak server usage.

In the past, developers had two options for combating the performance and resource problems of compilation. They could use a third-party utility to walk the Web site structure and request each Web page in turn, or they could perform the task manually. ASP.NET 2.0 comes with the AspNet_Compiler.EXE utility. You'll find it in the `\WINDOWS\Microsoft.NET\Framework\v2.0.40607` folder of your hard drive. The advantage of using this utility is that you can perform a compilation of all Web pages in your application during nonpeak hours. Simply make all of the changes you want to make, upload them at one time, and run the compiler.

However, this utility has another significant advantage. You can compile the application on a development server and then upload just the compiled code to your production server. Using this technique means that the source code is no longer accessible on the Web site—only the compiled page is. Crackers have a lot harder time creating havoc on your Web site when they only have compiled versions of your Web pages to work with.

Appendix C

Working with Common Character Codes

Character codes are an important part of Web development because they help developers overcome various Web page display problems. For example, a greater than or less than sign normally signifies part of an HTML tag. To display these characters on screen, you must use a character code.

Developers commonly use two forms of character codes. First, you can replace the character directly using an entry from a chart. Second, you can replace the character programmatically using code. The technique you choose depends on how the Web page uses the character code. The direct replacement technique works best when you know the character at the time you develop the Web page. The programmatic approach works best for user entry or other runtime needs. This appendix describes both techniques.

Direct Replacement Using a Chart

Direct character replacement means providing an escaped (substituted) form of the character as part of the HTML so it appears on the page. In some cases, you can make the character more readable by using a special keyword. Here are five common examples to consider.

◆ > (greater than)

◆ < (less than)

◆ & (ampersand)

◆ " (double quote)

◆   (non-breaking space)

If you decide to use this approach, make sure you use the International Organization for Standardization (ISO) ISO-8559 standard. You can find a list of ISO-8559 characters at `http://www.ramsch.org/martin/uni/fmi-hp/iso8859-1.html`. Notice that all of these characters begin with an ampersand and end with a semicolon.

Another, perhaps more practical, method of replacing characters with an escaped character is to use the character's Unicode number. In this case, you create the escaped character by adding a number sign and the Unicode number to the escape sequence. For example,   is a space. Although this form is less readable than using the keywords, you can use it to create any character. You can find a list of Unicode characters and their associated numbers at `http://www.unicode.org/charts`. Make sure you have the appropriate language support loaded when you use foreign language characters.

Because the number technique is so useful, you might want to create an application to display the numbers and their associated characters as a table. Listing C.1 shows one application you might try. You'll find this example in the \Appendix C\CharReplace folder of the source code on the Sybex Web site.

LISTING C.1:   Displaying Character Escape Sequences

```html
<form id="ShowChars" name="ShowChars" method="get">

   <h1>Direct Character Replacement</h1>

   <p>
       <label id="lblStart" for="txtStart">
           Starting Character Number:
       </label>
       <input id="txtStart"
               name="txtStart"
               type="text"
               title="Contains the beginning character number."
               value="32" /><br />
       <button id="btnSubmit"
               type="submit"
               title="Sends the request for processing.">
           Submit
       </button>
   </p>

   <table id="CommonChars"
           summary="Contains a list of common character replacements."
           title="Common Character List"
           border="2">
       <thead title="Table Heading">
           <tr>
               <th>Code</th>
               <th>Char</th>

               ... Additional Header Entries ...

           </tr>
       </thead>
       <tbody title="Table Data">
           <script language="javascript">
           //<!--
               var RowCount = 0;   // Counts the rows.
               var ColCount = 0;   // Counts the columns.
               var CharCount = 32; // Tracks the character number.
```

```
            // Process the input number, if any.
            var HREFValue = location.href.split("?");
            var StartValue;       // Holds the starting number.

            // When there is a query string to process.
            if (HREFValue.length > 1)
            {
                // Divide the first input into a name/value pair.
                StartValue = HREFValue[1].split("=");

                // Display the value and use it for the table.
                ShowChars.txtStart.value = StartValue[1];
                CharCount = StartValue[1];
            }

            // Display 9 rows.
            for (RowCount=0;RowCount<=8;RowCount++)
            {
                // Create a new row.
                document.writeln("<tr>");

                // Display 8 columns.
                for (ColCount=0;ColCount<=7;ColCount++)
                {
                    // Write the character code.
                    document.writeln(
                        '<td title="Code &amp;#"' + CharCount +
                        ';">&amp;#' + CharCount + ';</td>');

                    // Write the character.
                    document.writeln(
                        '<td title="Chararacter &#' + CharCount +
                        ';">&#' + CharCount + ';</td>');

                    // Update the character count.
                    CharCount++;
                }

                // End the current row.
                document.writeln("</tr>");
            }
        //-->
        </script>
    </tbody>
</table>

</form>
```

The code begins by displaying the text box you'll use to enter the starting character value and a button for submitting the new value. The page also includes a header for a table containing the escape character values. Figure C.1 shows a typical display. In this case, the output begins with the space character. However, you can begin with any legal Unicode value.

The table body relies on a script. The code begins by checking for a query string. The HREFValue array contains two entries when the HTML reference includes a query string. For the sake of clarity, the example leaves out some error trapping that you should include—it assumes that no one has tampered with the query string. When using this example in a production environment, you would add checks for the input values and possibly use the POST method in place of the GET method.

When the HTML reference contains a query string, the code splits it into a name value pair. Again, the code assumes that the query string contains just one name value pair. The code assigns the result to txtStart.value so it displays the correct starting number on screen and CharCount so the character count starts at the correct number.

The example uses a hard-coded 9-row by 8-column table for display because this size fits well on most displays. However, you could easily change these values to suit any need. The table code begins by creating a new row with the opening <tr> tag. It then begins writing column values to the display. The columns include two kinds of values—the code used to create the character and the resulting character. The example is basically accessible because it includes the title attribute for both entries. The table entries end by adding the closing </tr> tag.

You might not want to go online to find the starting character number. Fortunately, you can also use the Character Map utility to locate this number. Figure C.2 shows what this utility looks like.

FIGURE C.1

Displaying a list of escape character values can help you create difficult characters quickly.

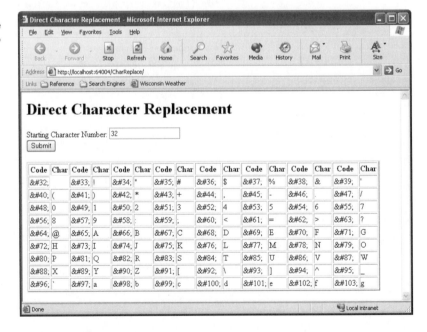

Code	Char	Code	Char	Code	Char	Code	Char	Code	Char	Code	Char	Code	Char	Code	Char
 		!	!	"	"	#	#	$	$	%	%	&	&	'	'
(	(	)	)	*	*	+	+	,	,	-	-	.	.	/	/
0	0	1	1	2	2	3	3	4	4	5	5	6	6	7	7
8	8	9	9	:	:	;	;	<	<	=	=	>	>	?	?
@	@	A	A	B	B	C	C	D	D	E	E	F	F	G	G
H	H	I	I	J	J	K	K	L	L	M	M	N	N	O	O
P	P	Q	Q	R	R	S	S	T	T	U	U	V	V	W	W
X	X	Y	Y	Z	Z	[	[	\	\	]	]	^	^	_	_
`	`	a	a	b	b	c	c	d	d	e	e	f	f	g	g

FIGURE C.2

Character Map makes it easy to learn the numbers associated with special characters.

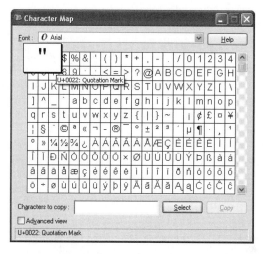

Simply select the character you want and look at the number that appears at the bottom of the dialog box. Unfortunately, this is a hexadecimal number. You can easily convert the hexadecimal number to a decimal number using the Calculator that comes with Windows.

Using Direct JavaScript Code

JavaScript provides a means of creating escaped output that is extremely simple. All you need to do is use the `escape()` function like this:

```
ResultVal.value = escape(InputVal.value);
```

In this case, the raw input appears in `InputVal.value`, while the output appears in `ResultVal.value`. The only requirement is that `InputVal.value` contain a string, which means you don't have to do anything special with the input except from a security standpoint (you still don't want someone to send a virus to your Web server). You'll find this example in the `\Appendix C\Direct` folder of the source code on the Sybex Web site.

The only problem with this technique is that it's standard—you have no control over the character replacement. In many cases, you won't care. You really do want to use the standard escaping technique for user input. The `unescape()` function removes the escaping from the string, so the entire process is very easy from beginning to end. However, sometimes you need better control over the output, which is where the technique shown in the next section comes into play.

Using Indirect JavaScript Code

For most people, working with Web sites is a unique experience because they encounter unexpected oddities that they haven't had to consider in the past. When you type a space into a word-processed document, nothing odd happens—the computer simply accepts the character. However, look at the word processor again. Notice how the word processor automatically looks at the space and uses it to determine where to split lines of text. The word processor does treat the space differently—it treats it as a delimiter (a fancy term that programmers use to mean a character that has a special meaning).

Likewise, when you add a hyphen to a word, the computer could choose to split the sentence in the middle of the word. The hyphen acts as a delimiter.

The Internet also uses delimiters for a number of purposes, including URLs. When a Web server sees a space, it could assume that it has reached the end of the URL or the beginning of a new input parameter (or a number of other things). Consequently, you must replace spaces, question marks, and other characters with other characters that don't work as delimiters. You might have noticed this practice at work when you fill out a form on the Internet. The browser commonly replaces a space between two words with %20 or a plus sign (+). The Web server interprets these special character sequences as a space.

At first, you might think that the character replacement is random, but there's some method to the madness. In fact, it's relatively easy to write a JavaScript function that performs the character replacement so you don't need to worry about it. Listing C.2 shows this function. You'll find this example in the \Appendix C\Indirect folder of the source code on the Sybex Web site.

LISTING C.2:   Replacing Characters in a String

```
function ReplaceCharacter(InputStr, Replace, UseInstead)
{
   // Define the length of the inputs.
   var InputLength = InputStr.length;
   var ReplaceLength = Replace.length;

   // Determine whether either input has a 0 length. If so,
   // the function can't succeed. However, because this is
   // a recursive function, the function does need to return
   // the original string.
   if ((InputLength == 0) || (ReplaceLength == 0))
      return InputStr;

   // Locate the first replacement value.
   var ReplaceIndex = InputStr.indexOf(Replace);

   // If the replacement value doesn't appear within the string,
   // then return. Again, keep the recursive nature of the
   // function in mind.
   if (ReplaceIndex == -1)
      return InputStr;

   // Create a string that includes the first part of the original
   // string and the replacement character, but not the rest of the
   // string.
   var Output = InputStr.substring(0, ReplaceIndex) + UseInstead;

   // Use recursion to process the string again if there is more data
   // to process.
   if (ReplaceIndex + ReplaceLength < InputLength)
```

```
        // Keep adding to the output string after each recursion.
        Output += ReplaceCharacter(
            InputStr.substring(ReplaceIndex + ReplaceLength, InputLength),
            Replace,
            UseInstead);

        // Return the output during each recursion.
        return Output;
    }
```

This might look like a lot of very complicated code, but it's actually an easy program. It uses a special technique called recursion to perform its work. In recursion, the programmer writes a program that solves the simplest form of a problem, and then has that program keep calling itself until it achieves that simple form. No matter how complex the input is, the program can solve it (given enough memory and time) because eventually the input will reach this simple solution.

In this instance, the program keeps calling itself until one of several conditions occurs. First, the program could run out of text to process. Second, the program might have some text left, but it might not contain the special character you want to replace (such as a space). If that's the case, then the program has already performed all of the required work, so it can stop.

Once the program determines there's data to process, it uses the substring() function to look for that character in the string. The substring() function returns just the first part of the string—the part that doesn't contain the special character. To this string, the code adds the replacement characters, such as %20 for a space.

It's at this point that the recursion process occurs. The code still has the other part of the string to consider—the last half. The first half of the string is free of the special character, but not the second half. When the code detects that there's still string to process, it calls itself again with the last half of the string. This process continues until the code has processed all of the input string. Figure C.3 shows typical output from this program.

The important consideration for this example is that you have complete control over the escaping process. You can escape any character, even those that JavaScript doesn't process using the escape() function. In addition, you can use any replacement that works. For example, you can choose to use something other than %20 to replace a space.

FIGURE C.3
The example program shows how you can perform URL encoding.

Appendix D

52 Indispensable Visual Web Developer Tricks and Techniques

This appendix contains 52 helpful hints that you can use to create better ASP.NET 2.0 applications. There's one tip for each week of the year. As you build applications using Visual Web Developer, you'll find new ways to get work done faster. Now that I've shared my tips with you, I'd love to hear about any tips you might have. Write me at JMueller@mwt.net to share them with me.

1. Always use HTML tags whenever possible to make your code run faster and with fewer compatibility problems. However, make sure you take advantage of the powerful features that ASP.NET provides. Whenever you can display complex data using one or two ASP.NET tags instead of a multitude of HTML tags, the ASP.NET tags are a better choice from a productivity perspective.

2. Don't be afraid to use the Class View window when working with Web services, controls, and components. This window displays important information that you can use to create classes faster and find the classes, methods, properties, and events you need in large projects. The Class View window doesn't appear by default, so many developers miss it. Use the View ➢ Other Windows ➢ Class View command to display the window.

3. Specifically release resource-intensive objects, such as SQL Server connections and commands, using the Dispose() method. In some cases, the garbage collector won't release the resources fast enough for your application. The resulting resource error can hide in many forms. For example, in some situations, .NET will complain that a timeout occurred when the problem is really resource usage related. Yes, the code timed out, but it timed out because it was waiting for resources from the resource pool.

4. Whenever you create client-side scripts, try to create a server-side alternative that caters to users who don't have scripting enabled. Place the server-side code within a <NoScript> tag so only clients who lack the client-side functionality will see the server-side alternative.

5. The <Object> tag can introduce compatibility issues on your Web page—Internet Explorer is the only product that supports it completely. However, using this tag can also help you create flexible Web pages that have a robust interface.

6. Always remember that you can create database applications programmatically or using Database Explorer with Visual Web Developer Express. Using Database Explorer is generally faster and easier. However, the programmatic approach can provide better flexibility and is more tolerant of certain types of input errors.

7. Visual Web Developer Express sets the random port address for a project the first time you start it. The port number controls the address that the browser uses to access the built-in Web

server. You can find the port number in the project's solution (SLN) file. The information appears in the `ProjectSection` section as the `VWDPort` entry.

8. Make your Web page easier to reconfigure and more accessible as well, by using Cascading Style Sheets (CSS) to define all page formatting. All you need to do to format a new Web page after creating the CSS file is to add a reference to the CSS file. In some cases, you might also need to define a class for a particular page element to apply alternative formatting.

9. Use the Add New Online Template feature found in the various New dialog boxes to add functionality to Visual Web Developer. This feature lets you access both Microsoft and third-party templates that add functionality to your working environment—potentially reducing the time required to complete tasks.

10. You can find Visual Web Developer Frequently Asked Questions (FAQs) at `http://lab.msdn.microsoft.com/express/faq/default.aspx`. This Web site provides helpful answers to common questions that you might have as you begin using Visual Web Developer to create increasingly complex projects.

11. Use the Object Browser as a means to explore the various namespaces, classes, method, properties, and events in the .NET Framework. It's also easy to use this tool to work with COM components and any other code you can access. You can display this window using the View ➤ Object Browser command.

12. The standard Options dialog box displayed using the Tools ➤ Options command displays only a subset of the options at your disposal. Check the Show All Settings option to display a complete list of settings at your disposal.

13. The ASP.NET 2.0 page that you write isn't the HTML the client browser sees. In some cases, it helps to understand precisely how ASP.NET creates Web pages so you can create code that's more efficient. Use the View ➤ Source command in Internet Explorer to view the actual output of an ASP.NET page.

14. Get the latest Visual Web Developer tips and tricks on the Visual Web Developer 2005 Express Edition forum at `http://www.asp.net/Forums/ShowForum.aspx?tabindex=1&ForumID=175`.

15. Make sure you investigate the Smart Tags provided with the Visual Web Developer controls. These Smart Tags can greatly reduce development time by making configuration a lot easier. In most cases, the Smart Tags let you configure common items—you'll still need to use the Properties window to perform complex setups using less common properties.

16. Select the WebParts controls that you use in an application with care. Although you must include a `WebPartManager` and `WebPartMenu` control, the other controls are optional and you should use only those controls that you actually need. Giving the user too much control over the appearance of a Web page can actually become more disruptive than helpful. Some users will tend to play with the display, rather than get useful work accomplished.

17. Visual Web Developer Express, along with ASP.NET 2.0, store many application settings, including some user data, in the `ASPNetDB.MDB` file found in the `\Data` folder of any application you create. Studying the effects of application changes you make on this database can help you understand how ASP.NET works better. For example, you can demonstrate that ASP.NET 2.0 really does encrypt all user data.

18. If you have trouble seeing some of the highlighting that the Visual Web Developer IDE provides, you can change it using the options in the `Environment\Fonts and Colors` folder of the Options dialog box that you access using the Tools ➤ Options command. This folder also lets you change the font used to display code, information within windows, and other IDE features. Using a larger font often reduces eye fatigue and helps you see errors with greater ease.

19. Explore the list of top 10 interesting things you can do with Visual Web Developer at `http://lab.msdn.microsoft.com/express/vwd/top10/default.aspx` to find ideas to use in your own projects. This list will likely change as Microsoft receives input from developers.

20. Use the site counters that ASP.NET 2.0 provides to your advantage. Site counters are useful anytime you want to monitor the performance of a page or page elements. Always use the `SiteCounters.Write()` method to track the data when working with an entire page. Otherwise, set the `CountClicks` property of the control you want to monitor to `True` and add values to the `CounterGroup` and `CounterName` properties.

21. The ASP.NET 2.0 `SiteMapPath` control provides the best method for presenting a path from the current page to the home page. This control appears in the Navigation tab of the Toolbox.

22. Don't assume that every component or control is a good candidate for use with the `<Object>` tag. Consider how the component or control will react to a Web environment and whether the control will display correctly. Components generally provide better overall functionality because they lack a visible interface.

23. Make sure you add validation controls to sensitive Web pages to ensure that the user fills in all required information. The most common validation control, `RequiredFieldValidator`, ensures that the user provides the requested information. Using this control reduces the risk of a user's leaving out important information that you need for contact or problem resolution. The most powerful validation control, `RegularExpressValidator`, ensures the data is in the correct format. Use this control to reduce the risk of users' providing unexpected information for highly formatted fields, such as telephone numbers.

24. Place application settings in the correct files. Use the `WEB.CONFIG` file to store application-specific settings. The `MACHINE.CONFIG` file is the place to store settings that affect your Web site as a whole. Using the correct configuration file reduces the amount of work you have to perform when your Web site requires configuration changes.

25. Create task entries in your code as needed by adding the appropriate keywords in comments. The common keywords include HACK, TODO, and UNDONE. You can add other keywords using the options in the `Environment\Task List` folder of the Options dialog box accessed using the Tools ➤ Options command.

26. Visit the Visual Web Developer Express Guided Tour Web site at `http://beta.asp.net/GuidedTour/default.aspx` for additional ideas on how to use this product. Microsoft will very likely add to the beginning tutorial and provide updates as necessary. Consequently, you could find new material over time.

27. Always test your ASP.NET applications using more than one browser if you plan to offer the Web page on a public Web site. For example, you might want to test the Web page using Internet Explorer and Firefox to ensure maximum compatibility. Despite Microsoft's claims, ASP.NET pages don't always display as anticipated in other browsers, so multiple browser testing helps reduce unpleasant surprises.

28. Database Explorer can help you create displays automatically in some cases—just drag and drop the table you want to view to the form. However, this technique performs formatting for you that you might not want. You can control this formatting using the options in the `Database Tools\Table Designer` folder of the Options dialog box that you can access using the Tools ➤ Options command.

29. Use the ASP.NET command-line utilities found in the `\WINDOWS\Microsoft.NET\Framework\v2.0.40607` folder of your hard drive to your advantage. For example, the ASPNET_RegBrowsers utility lets you register the capabilities of the browsers that you expect Web site users to use. The browser definitions appear in the `\WINDOWS\Microsoft.NET\Framework\v2.0.40607\CONFIG\Browsers` folder. Use the ASPNET_RegIIS utility to register or unregister a particular version of ASP.NET on a system. Likewise, you use the ASPNET_RegSQL utility to register a particular version of ASP.NET with SQL Server.

30. Never use the Data Encryption Standard (DES) to encrypt data on your Web site because this encryption technique is exceptionally easy to break with modern computers. Use Triple DES with care on Web pages and only for compatibility with older systems. Use the Advanced Encryption Standard (AES) whenever possible for maximum security.

31. The animated GIF is the most common and most compatible form of pizzazz that you can add to a Web site. Most browsers support the animated GIF and you can find a wealth of tools to work with them. In fact, some Web sites offer predefined animated GIFs that you can use on your Web site without becoming an artist (make sure you use a trustworthy Web site so you don't download an animated GIF with a virus in it).

32. Database connections that you create using Database Explorer appear in the `Web.CONFIG` file associated with the project. You can find these settings as part of the `<connectionStrings>` element. In some cases, you can modify the settings manually to correct errors in the database entry.

33. It pays to visit the Channel 9 Web site at `http://channel9.msdn.com` to learn more about various Microsoft projects. The Web site contains the latest information about various Microsoft projects including video. In addition, you can often find useful projects for Visual Web Developer that you won't find in other places.

34. Many developers like to see a grid when designing forms. Other developers like to use a tighter (or looser) grid than the default settings allow. You can control the design of your forms better using the options found in the `Display\Display` folder of the Options dialog box that you can access using the Tools ➤ Options command.

35. ASP.NET 2.0 includes a number of new login controls that make working with users a lot easier. These controls appear under the Login tab of the Toolbox. Make sure you include the new `PasswordRecovery` control in your list of necessary tools to reduce support costs for your application.

36. Never assume that a Web site is secure simply because you implement Secure Sockets Layer (SSL) and verify the user's identity. Make sure you also check code privileges to ensure that your security policy allows the code to perform the requested task under a given set of conditions. Many security breaches occur because a user executes code outside a safe environment.

37. Learn from the daily coding experiences of Brian Goldfarb, one of the Visual Web Developer Express developers, through his blog at `http://blogs.msdn.com/bgold/category/6057.aspx`.

38. Use the ASP.NET 2.0 `Menu` control to provide a path from the current page to other pages on your Web site. You can use this control to provide a means of accessing child pages, or simply as a means of finding other locations. The `Menu` control lets you define both dynamic (indexed) and static locations. This control appears on the Navigation tab of the Toolbox.

39. Visual Web Developer comes with a number of file extension mappings by default. For example, when you double-click an SLN (solution) file in Windows Explorer, the Visual Web Developer IDE loads the project for you. You can add new file extensions to the list by adding new file extensions using the features in the `Text Editor\File Extension` folder of the Options dialog box that you can access using the Tools ➢ Options command.

40. Find the latest tips and tricks for using ASP.NET 2.0 efficiently on the ASP.NET Tips and Tricks forum at `http://www.asp.net/Forums/ShowForum.aspx?tabindex=1&ForumID=134`.

41. Smart Tags provide a wonderful way to add value to your Web pages. You can use the standard Smart Tags, third-party Smart Tags, and even custom Smart Tags to provide context-based functionality. However, because Smart Tags rely on the `<Object>` tag, you'll find that some browsers won't support them. Consequently, while Smart Tags offer a way to provide value-added content, you won't want to use them for essential content on a Web page.

42. Always provide a method to return a Web page to its default settings when using WebParts. Some users will change things so much that the page becomes a mess and it's easier to start the configuration from scratch. Make sure you tell the user the results of setting the Web page to its default state (that they will lose all of their settings).

43. Microsoft has increased the XML capabilities of ASP.NET 2.0. Make sure you use this new functionality to create robust applications that are easy to move to other locations. Generally, if you can use XML, rather than a database, to store information, the XML is easier to work with for simple data.

44. Always provide a written security policy. Even if you're a one-person shop, writing a policy down and using the written policy when writing code ensures that you apply the policy evenly and completely. As the size of a business grows, the need for a complete and comprehensive security policy increases. In addition, make sure you review the security policy annually, as a minimum, to ensure that it covers new threats and business conditions.

45. If you program in more than one language, it's annoying to have the IDE behave one way when working with one language and another way when working with a second language. You can modify this behavior by setting generic settings for all languages. Make changes using the options in the `Text Editor\All Languages` folder of the Options dialog box that you can access using the Tools ➢ Options command.

46. Discover the Media Tracker sample application for Visual Web Developer at `http://channel9.msdn.com/ShowPost.aspx?PostID=23091`. This sample application performs the useful task of helping you track your media. However, it's also a very good way to learn more about Visual Web Developer coding techniques. You can download the application at `http://channel9.msdn.com/Photos/ZippedFiles/826da073-19ec-41a2-b20f-e9d81190ae1f.zip`.

47. Don't expect validation controls to perform all of the security work for your Web pages. Make sure you add code to your Web page to check for issues that the validation controls can't check. In addition, never assume that your method receives the data it needs from another method—always verify the data to reduce the risk of problems such as buffer overruns.

48. Using an XML file to hold the menu entries for a `Menu` control lets you update the entries without visiting each Web page manually. To keep the menus on your Web site updated, all you need to change is a single XML file. The Menu controls will update automatically during the next user visit.

49. Whenever you include the ability to remove (delete) content from a Web page using WebParts, include a `CatalogZone` control so the user can add the content back. Otherwise, the user won't be able to add the content back onto the Web page. Because ASP.NET encrypts the user settings automatically, the administrator can't change the settings either. In short, the only way to change the settings back if you don't include the `CatalogZone` control is to remove the user settings from the database and instruct the user to start the configuration process from scratch.

50. Getting help is important. Sometimes the built-in help doesn't provide what you need, but using online help is extremely slow and cumbersome. You can strike a balance using the settings found in the `Help\Online` folder of the Options dialog box that you can access using the Tools ➢ Options command.

51. Although this book explores a lot of the new ASP.NET 2.0 functionality, you can learn more about ASP.NET 2.0 at `http://msdn.microsoft.com/asp.net/whidbey`.

52. Reduce your workload, whenever possible, by using Visual Web Developer automation. For example, you can create Web pages more quickly by defining master pages and themes. These two complementary technologies let you add all of the common formatting in one or two steps, and then concentrate solely on the content for that Web page.

Glossary

This book includes a glossary so that you can find terms and acronyms easily. It has several important features you need to know about. First, every acronym in the entire book appears here—even if there's a better than even chance that you already know what the acronym stands for. (The book does exclude common acronyms such as units of measure and most file extensions because these terms are easy to find in other sources and most people know what they mean.) This way, there isn't any doubt that you'll always find everything you need to use the book properly.

Second, these definitions are specific to the book. In other words, when you look through this glossary, you're seeing the words defined in the context in which they're used in this book. This might or might not always coincide with current industry usage because the computer industry changes the meaning of words so often.

Finally, I've used a conversational tone for the definitions in most cases. This means that the definitions might sacrifice a bit of puritanical accuracy for the sake of better understanding. The purpose of this glossary is to define the terms in such a way that there's less room for misunderstanding the intent of the book as a whole.

WHAT TO DO IF YOU DON'T FIND IT HERE

While this glossary is a complete review of the words and acronyms in the book, you'll run into situations when you need to know more. No matter how closely I look at terms throughout the book, there's always a chance I'll miss the one acronym or term that you really need to know. In addition to the technical information found in the book, I've directed your attention to numerous online sources of information throughout the book. Few of the terms that Web site owners use will appear here unless I chose to use them in the book. Fortunately, many sites on the Internet provide partial or complete glossaries to fill in the gaps:

Acronym Finder `http://www.acronymfinder.com/`

Free Online Dictionary Of Computing (FOLDOC) `http://nightflight.com/foldoc/`

Microsoft Business Users Glossary `http://www.microsoft.com/atwork/glossary.mspx`

Microsoft Encarta `http://encarta.msn.com/`

Microsoft Management Console (MMC) Glossary `http://msdn.microsoft.com/library/en-us/mmc/mmc/mmc_glossary_gly.asp`

Microsoft .NET Glossary `http://www.microsoft.com/NET/basics_glossary.aspx`

Microsoft Security Glossary `http://msdn.microsoft.com/library/en-us/dnanchor/html/securityanchor.asp`

TechEncyclopedia `http://www.techweb.com/encyclopedia/defineterm.jhtml?term=COM`

Webopedia `http://webopedia.internet.com/`

yourDictionary.com `http://www.yourdictionary.com/`

Some entries in this list are quite specialized. For example, the Microsoft Management Console (MMC) Glossary provides definitions for terms that you'll encounter when using one of the Consoles found in the Administrative Tools folder of the Control Panel. You can find other Microsoft Glossaries listed at `http://www.microsoft.com/resources/glossary/default.mspx`. If you still don't find what you need, try the Microsoft Search page at `http://search.microsoft.com/`, type the word *glossary*, add a specific area such as network, and click Go.

A

access control entry (ACE)

Defines the object rights for a single user or group. Every ACE has a header that defines the type, size and flags for the ACE. Next comes an access mask that defines the rights a user or group has to the object. Finally, there's an entry for the user's or group's *security identifier (SID)*.

access control list (ACL)

Part of the Windows NT–based operating system security *application programming interface (API)* used to determine both access and monitoring properties for an object. Each ACL contains one or more *access control entries (ACEs)* that define the security properties for an individual or group. There are two major ACL groups: security access control list (SACL) and discretionary access control list (DACL). The SACL controls Windows auditing feature. The DACL controls access to the object.

accessibility

A measure of a user's ability to interact with an application. For example, applications should provide both mouse and keyboard access to every control to ensure that the user can reach the control for use. An application should support all devices without providing specialized support for a particular device unless necessary. A Braille input device should receive no special treatment beyond that required for a keyboard.

ACE

See *access control entry*.

ACL

See *access control list*.

Active Server Pages (ASP)

A special type of scripting language environment used by Windows servers equipped with *Internet Information Server (IIS)*. This specialized scripting language environment helps the developer create flexible Web applications that include server scripts written in a number of languages such as VBScript, JavaScript, JScript, and PerlScript. The use of variables and other features, such as access to server variables, helps the developer create scripts that can compensate for user and environmental needs as well as security concerns. ASP uses HTML to display content to the user. Recent extensions to ASP in the form of *Active Server Pages eXtended (ASPX)* provide a broader range of application support functionality, improved debugging, new features such as *code behind*, and improved performance. Note that you need to install the .NET Framework to use ASPX pages.

Active Server Pages eXtended (ASPX)

An extension of *Active Server Pages (ASP)* that includes a number of new features such as the ability to use separate Web page and coding files. ASPX is normally associated with Microsoft's .NET Framework, a new tokenized application platform. Consequently, the technology relies on the objects that the .NET Framework provides, which includes additional functionality, ease of coding, and improved security.

Active Template Library (ATL)

A special set of header, source, object, and executable files created by Microsoft. The main purpose of ATL is to reduce the size and dependence of COM objects created for use in environments where memory and network bandwidth are a potential problem. For example, an ATL object won't normally rely on the *Microsoft Foundation Classes (MFC)*. In many cases, the ATL executable is self-contained and doesn't rely on anything other than standard Windows core files. While ATL executable files are smaller than their MFC counterparts, they're also more complex to develop and often require the developer to write more code in order to obtain a similar result.

advanced encryption standard (AES)

The mathematical basis for performing symmetric encryption and decryption of data. The algorithm originally appeared as the Rijndael algorithm, after its inventors (Joan Daemen and Vincent Rijmen). This is a block cipher that can accept a number of data block sizes and key lengths. Many companies now use this algorithm as a replacement for the *DES* and Triple DES algorithms.

AES

See *advanced encryption standard*.

alpha red green blue (ARGB)

The creation of a color based on the combination of red, green, and blue that defines it. Generally, each color can have a value between 0 and 255 on modern displays. The alpha component defines the transparency of the color where a color with a value of 255 is opaque and a color with a value of 0 is transparent.

American National Standards Institute (ANSI)

An organization dedicated to creating standard implementations of common technologies. For example, this group created the *American Standard Code for Information Interchange (ASCII)* character standard commonly used for application development.

American Standard Code for Information Interchange (ASCII)

A standard method of equating the numeric representations available in a computer to human-readable form. For example, the number 32 represents a space. The

standard ASCII code contains 128 characters (7 bits). The extended ASCII code uses 8 bits for 256 characters. Display adapters from the same machine type usually use the same upper 128 characters. Printers, however, might reserve these upper 128 characters for non-standard characters. For example, many older Epson printers use them for the italic representations of the lower 128 characters. This is the standard character set used by all Windows 9*x* implementations.

ANSI

See *American National Standards Institute*.

API

See *application programming interface*.

applet

A helper or utility application that normally performs a task within a specialized environment such as a browser or as part of an operating system. Java is one of the most commonly used languages for creating applets for browser applications. Another example is the Control Panel applications used to configure Windows. In both cases, the applications perform a limited task within a specialized environment.

application

One or more executable files that include machine-readable code and specialized data. The complete program or group of programs. An application is a complete environment for performing one or more related tasks. Applications perform tasks for the user or system based on a specific need.

application programming interface (API)

A method of defining a standard set of function or method calls and other interface elements. It usually defines the interface between a high-level language and the lower level elements used by a device driver or operating system. The ultimate goal is to provide some type of service to an application that requires access to the operating system or device feature set.

ARGB

See *alpha red green blue*.

ASCII

See *American Standard Code for Information Interchange.*

ASP

See *Active Server Pages.*

ASPX

See *Active Server Pages eXtended.*

ATL

See *Active Template Library.*

attribute

An attribute expresses some feature peculiar to an object. When referring to a database, each field has an attribute that expresses what type of information it contains, the length of the field, the field name, and the number of decimals. When referring to a display, the attribute expresses pixel color, intensity, and position. In programming, an attribute can also specify some type of object functionality, such as the method used to implement security.

Audio Video Interleaved File Format (AVI)

A special file format that contains both audio and visual in digital format. AVI is one of the most popular method for transmitting multimedia files across the Internet.

AVI

See *Audio Video Interleaved File Format.*

AWT

Abstract Windowing Toolkit.

B

bandwidth

A measure of the amount of data that a device can transfer in a given time. For example, the amount of data that a processor can send to memory every second. In many cases, bandwidth also considers software limitations, such as the estimated bandwidth of an Internet connection.

binary

(1) A numbering system that uses only two digits: 0 and 1. (2) A method used to store worksheets, graphic files, and other nontext information. The data store can appear in memory, but most often appears in a file on disk. While you can use the DOS TYPE command to send these files to the display, the contents of the file remain unreadable. Other binary files include programs with extensions of *EXE, DLL,* or *COM.*

Boolean

A method of determining whether a statement is true or false using rules of logic. Boolean values are often used to help a computer determine whether it needs to take a certain course of action based on current system or application conditions.

browser

A special application, such as Internet Explorer, Opera, FireFox, or Netscape, normally used to display data downloaded from the Internet. The most common form of Internet data is the *HTML (HyperText Markup Language)* page. However, modern browsers can also display various types of graphics and even standard desktop application files such as Word for Windows documents directly. The actual capabilities provided by a browser vary widely depending on the software vendor and platform.

buffer overrun

A memory condition normally associated with a variable in which the application assigned more data to the variable than the variable is capable of holding. The excess data runs into other memory locations, which corrupts the information in those memory locations. In many cases, the buffer overrun affects other variables. However, when used maliciously, a buffer overrun can also overwrite other areas of memory such as code blocks or the application stack, causing the application to fail or perform tasks that the originator didn't intend.

C

CA

See *certificate authority.*

CAB

See *cabinet file.*

cabinet file (CAB)

(1) A compressed-format file similar to the ZIP files used to transfer code and data from one location to another. Only developers who work with Microsoft language products normally use the CAB format, but anyone working in the Windows environment could use them by creating the file with the Compress utility. You can also decompress the file using the Expand utility. (2) A single file created to hold a number of compressed files. A related set of cabinet files can be contained in a folder. During installation of a program, the compressed files in a cabinet are decompressed and copied to an appropriate directory for the user.

cache

A storage area for data, code, or other resources normally associated with memory or a special file on a hard drive. Both hardware and applications rely on the cache to improve performance.

cascading style sheets (CSS)

A method for defining a standard Web page appearance using formatting information. The formatting may include headings, standard icons, backgrounds, and other features that would tend to give each page at a particular Web site the same appearance. The reason for using CSS includes speed of creating a Web site (it takes less time if the developer doesn't have to create an overall design for each page) and consistency. Changing the overall appearance of a Web site also becomes as easy as changing the style sheet instead of each page alone. CSS is also a standards-supported technology, so it represents an easy method for developers to create Web pages that will work in standards-compliant browsers.

CD

Compact disc.

certificate authority (CA)

The originator of a digital credential. An organization or group that independently verifies the identity of a requestor and issues credentials that reflect that identity. The credentials are in the form of a certificate that the requestor can use for a number of purposes, such as identification of an email source or signing a component. To provide any value, both parties in an information exchange must trust the CA. In some cases, this means using a public CA such as VeriSign. However, in other cases, it means that third parties must trust the private company issuing the certificate. For example, some Windows server versions provide the means to issue private certificates.

cHTML

See *Compact HyperText Markup Language.*

class identifier (CLSID)

A method of assigning a unique number to each object used by Windows. These numbers normally appear in the registry and Windows uses them for reference purposes. The number normally appears in the form {00000000-0000-0000-0000-000000000000}, but can take on other forms as well. This term also refers to various high-level language constructs used by programming languages.

client

The requestor and recipient of data, services, or other resources from a file or other server type. This term can refer to a workstation or an application. Often used in conjunction with the term *server*, this is usually another PC or an application.

CLR

See *Common Language Runtime.*

CLSID

See *class identifier.*

CN

Context name.

code behind

A Web page coding technique where the display (user interface) code resides in a file separate from the file containing the code to make the Web page functional. This type of Web page scripting technology is most closely associated with *Active Server Pages eXtended (ASPX)*. The advantage of this approach is that the developer spends less time looking for application code—reducing some task times such as debugging. Code behind helps promote code reuse by keeping the code and the user interface separate. The use of a separate code file also means that the same code file could serve multiple Web pages through the use of generic routines. The code behind portion contains all of the functions and methods that the Web page uses to control various display elements and to perform programming tasks in the background such as opening a database connection. The code behind file normally has the same name as the ASPX page, with the programming language suffix appended. For example, if the user interface portion of the application is Default.ASPX, the code behind portion might appear in the `Default.ASPX.CS` file when using C# as the coding language.

COM

See *Component Object Model*.

COM+

See *Component Object Model Plus*.

Common Language Runtime (CLR)

The engine used to interpret managed applications within the .NET Framework. All Visual Studio .NET languages that produce managed applications can use the same runtime engine. The major advantages of this approach include extensibility (you can add other languages) and reduced code size (you don't need a separate runtime for each language).

Compact HyperText Markup Language (cHTML)

A specialized form of the *HyperText Markup Language (HTML)* specially designed for mobile device use. Pages creating with cHTML have the same appearance as HTML. However, cHTML doesn't support *Joint Photographic Experts Group (JPEG)* images, tables, image maps, multiple fonts or font styles, background colors or images, frames, *cascading style sheets (CSS)*, or more than two colors. All user tasks in cHTML rely on the use of four buttons, rather than on a full keyboard, including cursor forward, cursor backward, select, and back/stop. The Japan-based Access Company originated cHTML for use with i-mode devices. The protocol is used less now that most companies are developing around the *eXtensible HyperText Markup Language (XHTML)*.

compiler

A program that converts English-like statements into machine instructions in an executable or intermediate form. In some cases, the executable code can run without assistance on the host machine (called a native executable). In other cases, the intermediate code requires compilation into an executable form. This secondary form can rely on an interpreter, such as Beginner's All-Purpose Symbolic Instruction Code (BASIC), or runtime engine, such as Java, or it can use a secondary compiler or linker to change an object format into a standard native executable (C).

Component Object Model (COM)

A Microsoft specification for a binary-based, object-oriented code and data encapsulation method and transference technique. It's the basis for technologies such as *OLE (Object Linking and Embedding)* and ActiveX (compontents and controls). COM is limited to local connections.

Component Object Model Plus (COM+)

An updated version of both the *Component Object Model (COM)* and *Distributed Component Object Model (DCOM)* that includes features for modern remote and disconnected applications. COM+ applications are registered on the server and client machines using standard installation programs and specialized administrative tools. The technology can use both standard connected and queued communication. Later versions of COM+ can even act as Web services with the proper configuration.

connectivity

A measure of the interactions between clients and servers. In many cases, connectivity begins with the local machine and the interactions between applications and components. *Local area networks (LANs)* introduce another level of connectivity with machine-to-machine communications. Finally, *wide area networks (WANs)*, metro area networks (MANs), intranets, and the Internet all introduce further levels of connectivity concerns.

console

(1) A type of character-mode application that normally runs at the DOS (command) prompt. A console application normally performs a simple or utilitarian task that doesn't require the *graphical user interface (GUI)* associated with most application development today. (2) The generic term for a workstation used to monitor server status information. In most cases, the workstation and server are the same device. Most people associate consoles with a character mode interface, but this isn't a requirement. (3) A short version of the longer term *Microsoft Management Console (MMC)*.

constructor

An Object Oriented Programming (OOP) term that describes the special method the application operating environment calls during object instantiation. The constructor contains code that ensures the object is functional. Developers often use the constructor to initialize global variables, set operating environment conditions, and perform other object creation tasks.

cookie

A value stored in one or more special files managed by a Web browser. The cookie can hold site-specific settings or other information specific to Web pages. In addition, the cookie can last just for the current session or the browser can hold it until some future expiration date. A developer always saves and restores the cookie as part of a Web page programming task using a programming language such as ASP, ASP.NET, JavaScript, Java, VBScript, or CGI. In most cases, this is the only file that a developer can access on the client site's hard drive. The cookie could appear in one or more files anywhere on the hard drive, depending on the browser currently in use. Microsoft Internet Explorer uses one file for each site storing a cookie. Netscape Navigator uses a single file named COOKIE.TXT to store all of the cookies from all sites.

counter

(1) An application designed to measure performance on a Windows system. The counter is part of a performance object. It's normally stored with other counters associated with the same performance object within a *dynamic link library (DLL)* on the host machine. A counter may allow monitoring of one or more instances of the same type of device or other object as individual performance statistics. (2) A specialized programming structure used to track application data. In some cases, the counter is a specialized object the developer adds to the application for the purpose for statistical data collection.

cracker

A hacker (computer expert) who uses their skills for misdeeds on computer systems where they have little or no authorized access. A cracker normally possesses specialty software that allows easier access to the target network. In most cases, crackers require extensive amounts of time to break the security for a system before they can enter it. Some sources call a cracker a black hat hacker.

cryptographic service provider (CSP)

A specialty company that deals in certifying the identity of companies, developers or individuals on the Internet. This identification check allows the company to issue an electronic certificate, which can then be used to conduct transactions securely. Several levels of certification are normally provided within a specific group. For example, there are three levels of individual certification. The lowest merely verifies the individual's identity through an Internet mail address; the highest requires the individual to provide written proof along with a notarized statement. When you access a certified site or try to download a certified document such as a component, the browser will display the electronic certificate on-screen, allowing you to make a security determination based on fact.

CSP

See *cryptographic service provider*.

CSS

See *cascading style sheets*.

D

DAC

Dedicated administrative connection.

data encryption standard (DES)

An unsafe method of data encryption that relies on symmetric key encryption. This methodology was originally introduced in 1975 and standardized by ANSI in 1981. As computer technology has improved, the encryption technique has become easier to crack, making it an unreliable means of protecting data.

data source name (DSN)

A name assigned to a database connectivity description, such as an *Open Database Connectivity (ODBC)* connection. Applications use the DSN to make the connection to the database and gain access to specific database resources such as tables. The DSN always contains the name of the database server, the database, and (optionally) a resource such as a query or table. Many database technologies such as *Object Linking and Embedding - Database (OLE-DB)* rely on the use of DSN connection information.

database

A data collection that consists of one or more storage elements and any associated objects. The organization of the database depends on the features and functionality of the *Database Management System (DBMS)* used to maintain it. A database normally uses a hierarchical or tabular format. A hierarchical database relies on nodes connected in any of a number of ways, such as record pointers. The tabular format relies on rows (records) made up of columns (fields). A database can appear as a single file, as part of a collection with the DBMS, as part of a worksheet for a spreadsheet, or any other organized disk format.

Database Management System (DBMS)

A method for storing and retrieving data based on tables, forms, queries, reports, fields, and other data elements. Each field represents a specific piece of data, such as an employee's last name. Records are made up of one or more fields. Each record is one complete entry in a table. A table contains one type of data, such as the names and addresses of all the employees in a company. It's composed of records (rows) and fields (columns), just like the tables you see in books. A database may contain one or more related tables. It may include a list of employees in one table, for example, and the pay records for each of those employees in a second table. Sometimes also referred to as a Relational Database Management System (RDBMS) that includes products such as SQL Server and Oracle.

DBMS

See *Database Management System*.

DCOM

See *Distributed Component Object Model*.

DCOMCnfg

Distributed Component Object Model Configuration utility.

delimiter

(1) A special symbol or symbols used to separate text. For example, many programming languages use the single (') or double (") quote to separate text elements. (2) A boundary between two different objects. The boundary normally consists of a special symbol or group of symbols. A delimited file contains variable length records. Each field normally uses a comma as a delimiter. Each record normally uses a carriage return as a delimiter.

DES

See *data encryption standard*.

digital subscriber line (DSL)

A term used to refer to any of a number of technologies that allow higher communication rates over standard telephone lines than normally allowed using standard modems. DSL is normally used between a remote location such as a home or office and the switching station or ISP. It isn't used between switching stations. Types of DSL include asynchronous DSL (ADSL), symmetric DSL (SDSL), and high bit-rate DSL (HDSL). The technologies vary by their ability to pack data onto the copper line, distance from the switching station, and other characteristics. ADSL allows communication from 1.5 Mbps to 9 Mbps downstream (to the remote connection) and 16 Kbps to 640 Kbps upstream (from the remote connection). SDSL allows communication up to 3 Mbps in both directions. HDSL allows communication up to 1.544 Mbps in both directions.

digital video disc (DVD)

A high-capacity optical storage media with capacities of 4.7 GB to 17 GB and data transfer rates of 600 KBps to 1.3 GBps. A single DVD can hold the contents of an entire movie or approximate 7.4 CD-ROMs. DVDs come in several formats including DVD-R, DVD-RW, DVD+R, DVD+RW and DVD-RAM that allow read-only or read-write access. Newer dual-layer DVDs promise even greater storage capacities. All DVD drives include a second laser assembly used to read existing CD-ROMs. Some magazines will also use the term *digital versatile disk* for this storage media.

directory

A storage unit description used with DOS, many character mode applications, and the Windows command prompt. Directories provide a means of separating files into different locations based on type or use. Using directories makes it easier to locate data and use applications.

DISCO

See *Discovery of Web Services*.

DISCOMAP

Discovery of Web Services Map File.

Discovery of Web Services (DISCO)

A service that is designed to make it easier to locate and use Web services. This particular service is *SOAP* specific, originally defined and supported by Microsoft. Other vendors, such as IBM, now use the technology as well. The DISCO service relies on a special protocol named SOAP Contract Language (SCL) to allow the discovery of services by remote computers.

disk operating system (DOS)

The underlying management software used by older PCs to provide basic system services and to allow the user to run application software. The operating system performs many low-level tasks through the basic input/output system (BIOS). The revision number determines the specifics of the services that DOS offers; check your user manual for details.

distributed application

An application that resides on more than one machine; normally a client and server, but not necessarily limited to this configuration. The application could include multiple levels of clients and servers, commonly referred to as tiers. The application is composed of multiple interchangeable elements. For example, a server component could service more than one application type. The application elements are loosely coupled (both systems require access only to self-describing messages) and the developer can replace each element with updates as needed as long as the new element provides the same interface to the client.

Distributed Component Object Model (DCOM)

A binary data transport protocol that interacts with the *Component Object Model (COM)*, and is used for distributed application development. This protocol enables data transfers across the Internet or other non-local sources, but is usually limited to a *local area network (LAN)* or *wide area network (WAN)* environment. DCOM adds the capability to perform asynchronous, as well as synchronous, data transfers between machines. The use of asynchronous transfers prevents the client application from becoming blocked as it waits for the server to respond.

DLL

See *dynamic link library*.

DOS

See *disk operating system*.

DSL

See *digital subscriber line*.

DSN

See *data source name*.

DVD

See *digital video disc*.

dynamic link library (DLL)

A specific form of application code loaded into memory by request. It's not executable by itself like an EXE is. A DLL does contain one or more discrete routines that an application may use to provide specific features. For example, a DLL could provide a common set of file dialogs used to access information on the hard drive. More than one application can use the functions provided by a DLL, reducing overall memory requirements when more than one application is running. DLLs have a number of purposes. For example, they can contain device-specific code in the form of a device driver. Some types of COM objects also rely on DLLs.

E

ECMA

See *European Computer Manufacturer's Association*.

element

(1) A single data value within an array. (2) One node of an *eXtensible Markup Language (XML)* data structure. An element can contain values, other elements, or appear empty. Elements can also contain attributes that appear as name/value pairs. Properly formed elements appear as HTML tags with stricter usage rules. For example, the element must include a closing tag.

ELUA

See *end user licensing agreement*.

emulator

A specialized application that provides the same features and functionality as the target device. The device on which the emulator runs is normally more capable than the emulated device. For example, emulators commonly enable a developer to test

applications designed for use on personal digital assistants (PDAs) using the standard PC.

encryption

The act of making data unreadable using a mathematical conversion. The data remains unreadable unless the reader provides a password or other key value. Encryption makes data safe for transport in unsecured environments like the Internet.

end user licensing agreement (ELUA)

The contract between the buyer and seller of products, especially computer software. The contract defines a license that allows the user to install and interact with the software application.

error trapping

The additional code required to detect, analyze, repair, report, and overcome errors in an application. An error-trapping routine normally locates the precise origin of the error, determines the error type, and defines a course of action for repairing the error whenever possible. If the application can't recover, the error-trapping routine helps the application fail gracefully after reporting the source and cause of the error to the application user.

European Computer Manufacturer's Association (ECMA)

A standards committee originally founded in 1961. ECMA is dedicated to standardizing information and communication systems. For example, it created the ECMAScript standard used for many Web page designs today. You can also find ECMA standards for product safety, security, networks, and storage media.

event handler

A special method or function that reacts to specific system or user events such as clicking a button on a form or the loss of focus for a textbox.

event log file (EVT)

(1) A file used to hold the event log entries for a particular aspect of system performance. For example, there are separate files for application, security,

and system entries. Each log file can hold several different event types including audit, informational, warning, and error events. (2) An application event destination. The application never interacts with the EVT file itself since more than one application requires access to the EVT file at one time. A well-designed application will always use the Windows API to perform this task.

EVT

See *event log file*.

EXE

See *executable file*.

executable file (EXE)

(1) A binary file that contains machine code (procedural steps the machine can understand), instructions, and data that an operating system can read to perform tasks. An executable file normally contains an application, but it can contain any form of code and resources. (2) A file containing tokenized data where a token relates to a specific instruction. A special runtime application reads the tokens, interprets them, and sends the results binary machine code to the operating system for execution. The use of tokens lets a single executable work on more that one operating system or machine type, but slows application execution.

eXtensible Hypertext Markup Language (XHTML)

A cross between *eXtensible Markup Language (XML)* and *HyperText Markup Language (HTML)* specifically designed for Internet devices such as *personal digital assistants (PDAs)* and cellular telephones, but also usable with desktop machine browsers. Because this language relies on XML, most developers classify it as an XML application builder. The language relies on several standardized namespaces to provide common data type and interface definitions. XHTML creates modules that are interpreted based on a specific platform's requirements. This means that a single document can serve the needs of many display devices.

eXtensible Markup Language (XML)

(1) A method used to store information in an organized manner. The storage technique relies on hierarchical organization and uses special statements called tags to separate each storage element. Each tag defines a data attribute and can contain properties that further define each data element. (2) A standardized Web page design language used to incorporate data structuring within standard HTML documents. For example, you could use XML to display database information using something other than forms or tables. It's actually a lightweight version of Standard Generalized Markup Language (SGML) and is supported by the SGML community. XML also supports tag extensions that allow various parts of a Web-based application to exchange information. For example, once a user makes a choice within a catalog, that information could be added to an order entry form with a minimum of effort on the part of the developer. Because XML is easy to extend, some developers look at it as more of a base specification for other languages, rather than a complete language.

eXtensible Style Language Transformation (XSLT)

The language used within the eXtensible Style Language (XSL) to transform the content provided in an *eXtensible Markup Language (XML)* file into a form for display on screen or printing. An XSL processor combines XML content with the formatting instructions provided by XSLT and outputs a new document or document fragment. XSLT is a *World Wide Web Consortium (W3C)* standard.

F

FAQ

See *frequently asked question*.

File Transfer Protocol (FTP)

One of several common data transfer protocols for the Internet. This particular protocol specializes in data transfer in the form of a file download or upload. The site presents the user with a list of available files in a directory list format. An FTP site may choose DOS or UNIX formatting for the file listing, although the DOS format is extremely rare. Unlike HTTP sites, an FTP site provides a definite information hierarchy using directories and subdirectories, much like the file directory structure used on most workstation hard drives. Generally, FTP transfers require a special application, but some browsers now include this capability. FTP transfers occur without encryption, so security is an issue unless the owner of the FTP site encrypts the individual files.

filter

An application, piece of hardware, or driver that accepts raw data as input, processes it in some way, and then outputs it as a finished product. Filters perform a variety of tasks including data translation, enhancement, and reduction. For example, a sound filter that changes Pulse-Code Modulation (PCM) data into Adaptive Differential Pulse-Code Modulation (ADPCM) data performs data translation. Another sound filter could perform data enhancement by adding a reverberation effect. A third sound filter could control the intensity of the sound by performing data reduction. Filters also affect data. For example, you can request that an application remove entries from a data stream provided by a *Database Management System (DBMS)*.

firewall

Hardware or software (or a combination of both) used to prevent unauthorized access to a private network. The firewall can use any of a number of techniques to detect unauthorized packets and deny access to them. Some firewalls not only check incoming packets but outgoing packets as well. There are many types of firewalls including packet filter, application gateway, proxy server, and circuit-level gateway. For maximum protection, the proxy server normally works best in a hardware configuration.

folder

A specialized area for storing files on the hard drive. Folders help you manage both data and applications by breaking them up into smaller and easier to recognize groups. The folder acts as a storage receptacle. The DOS and command prompt equivalent term for folders is *directories*, the same term used by many other operating systems.

frequently asked question (FAQ)

A document that contains answers to questions that many people ask. FAQs generally reduce support costs by providing answers to commonly asked questions that people can find in one place. Vendors use FAQs for many purposes including both hardware and software support.

FTP

See *File Transfer Protocol*.

G

GAC

See *global assembly cache*.

GACUtil

Global assembly cache utility.

GIF

See *Graphics Interchange Format*.

global assembly cache (GAC)

A central repository used by the .NET Framework for storing public managed components. The GAC contains only components with strong names, ensuring the integrity of the cache. In addition, the GAC can hold multiple versions of the same component, which ensures that applications can access the version of a component that they need, rather than the single version accessible to all applications.

globally unique identifier (GUID)

A 128-bit number used to identify a *Component Object Model (COM)* object within the Windows registry. The GUID is used to find the object definition and allow applications to create instances of that object. GUIDs can include any kind of object, even nonvisual elements. In addition, some types of complex objects are actually aggregates of simple objects. For example, an object that implements a property page will normally have a minimum of two GUIDs: one for the property page and another for the object itself.

graphical user interface (GUI)

(1) A method of displaying information that depends on both hardware capabilities and software instructions. A GUI uses the graphics capability of a display adapter to improve communication between the computer and its user. Using a GUI involves a large investment in both programming and hardware resources. (2) A system of icons and graphic images that replaces the character-mode menu system used by many older machines including "green screen" terminals that are connected to mainframes and sometimes to cash registers. The GUI can ride on top of another operating system (such as DOS, Linux, and Unix) or reside as part of the operating system itself (such as the Macintosh and Windows). Advantages of a GUI are ease of use and high-resolution graphics. Disadvantages include cost, higher workstation hardware requirements, and lower performance over a similar system using a character mode interface.

Graphics Interchange Format (GIF)

One of several standard file formats used to transfer graphics over the Internet. There are several different standards for this file format—the latest of which is the GIF89a standard used on most Internet sites. CompuServe originally introduced the GIF standard as a method for reducing the time required to download a graphic and the impact of any single-bit errors that might occur. A secondary form of the GIF is the animated GIF. It allows the developer to store several images within one file. Between each image within the file are one or more control blocks that determine block boundaries, the display location of the next image in relation to the display area and other display features. A browser or other specially designed application will display the graphic images one at a time in the order in which they appear within the file to create animation effects.

GUI

See *graphical user interface.*

GUID

See *globally unique identifier.*

H

hacker

An individual who works with computers at a low level (hardware or software), especially in the area of security. A hacker normally possesses specialty software or other tools that allows easier access to the target hardware or software application or network. The media defines two types of hackers that include those that break into systems for ethical purposes and those that do it to damage the system in some way. The proper term for the second group is *crackers.* Some people have started to call the first group "ethical hackers" or "white hat hackers" to prevent confusion. Ethical hackers normally work for security firms that specialize in finding holes in a company's security. However, hackers work in a wide range of computer arenas. For example, a person who writes low-level code (like that found in a device driver) after reverse engineering an existing driver is technically a hacker. The main emphasis of a hacker is to work for the benefit of others in the computer industry.

Handheld Device Markup Language (HDML)

A technology that predates most standardized efforts, such as the *Wireless Access Protocol (WAP),* for transmitting Internet content to cellular telephones. It's a proprietary language that users can only view using OpenWave browsers. The associated transport protocol is the Handheld Device Transport Protocol (HDTP). A user types a request into the phone, which is transferred to a gateway server using HDTP. The gateway server translates the request to *HyperText Transport Protocol (HTTP),* which it sends to the Web server. The Web server provides specialized HDML content, which the gateway server transfers to the cellular telephone using HDTP. To use this protocol, the Web server must understand the text/x-hdml *Multipurpose Internet Mail Extensions (MIME)* type.

HDML

See *Handheld Device Markup Language.*

HTML

See *HyperText Markup Language.*

HTTP

See *HyperText Transfer Protocol*.

HTTPS

See *HyperText Transfer Protocol Secure sockets*.

HyperText Markup Language (HTML)

(1) A data presentation and description (markup) language for the Internet that depends on the use of tags (keywords within angle brackets <>) to display formatted information on-screen in a non-platform-specific manner. The non-platform-specific nature of this markup language makes it difficult to perform some basic tasks such as placement of a screen element at a specific location. However, the language does provide for the use of fonts, color, and various other enhancements on-screen. There are also tags for displaying graphic images. Scripting tags for using scripting languages such as VBScript and JavaScript are available, although not all browsers support this addition. The <OBJECT> tag addition allows the use of ActiveX controls. (2) One method of displaying text, graphics, and sound on the Internet. HTML provides an ASCII-formatted page of information read by a special application called a browser. Depending on the browser's capabilities, some key words are translated into graphics elements, sounds, or text with special characteristics, such as color, font, or other attributes. Most browsers discard any keywords they don't understand, allowing browsers of various capabilities to explore the same page without problem. Obviously, there's a loss of capability if a browser doesn't support a specific keyword.

HyperText Transfer Protocol (HTTP)

One of several common data transfer protocols for the Internet. HTTP normally transfers textual data of some type. For example, the *HyperText Markup Language (HTML)* relies on HTTP to transfer the Web pages it defines from the server to the client. The *eXtensible Markup Language (XML)* and *Simple Object Access Protocol (SOAP)* also commonly rely on HTTP to transfer data between client and server. It's important to note that HTTP is separate from the data it transfers. For example, it's possible for SOAP to use the Simple Mail Transfer Protocol (SMTP) to perform data transfers between client and server.

HyperText Transfer Protocol Secure sockets (HTTPS)

A secure form of HTTP that relies on the secure sockets encryption technology to transfer data.

I

IDE

See *Integrated Development Environment*.

identifier (ID)

The name used to reference a function, procedure, object, or variable. An identifier generally begins with a character, followed by any number of characters and numbers. Some older systems place limits on identifier length, but most newer systems don't. In addition, some identifiers must appear in a specific format, such as the *globally unique identifier (GUID)* Windows relies on to identify components and controls.

IIS

See *Internet Information Server*.

IL

See *Intermediate Language*.

infrastructure

The underlying base of an organization or system. One way to view infrastructure is a foundation on which all other elements of a system or organization are attached. Many vendors use this term to indicate the compatibility of their product with existing installations.

Integrated Development Environment (IDE)

The development environment used to write application code. An IDE provides all of the tools needed to write an application using one or more specialized editors. The IDE normally includes support for development language help, access to any tools required to support the language, a compiler, and a debugger. Some IDEs include support for advanced features such as automatic completion of language statements and balloon help showing the syntax for functions and other language elements. Many IDEs also use color or highlighting to emphasize specific language elements or constructs.

Intermediate Language (IL)

The common language that all .NET compilers output. The *Common Language Runtime (CLR)* interprets the tokens that reside in the IL. The use of a tokenized output ensures that all languages can share the functionality provided by the .NET Framework. Because CLR understands this one common language, any compiler that produces it is compatible with .NET.

Internet Information Server (IIS)

Microsoft's Web server that runs under the Windows Server operating system. IIS includes all of the standard Web server features including *File Transfer Protocol (FTP)* and *HyperText Transfer Protocol (HTTP)*, along with both mail and news services.

Internet Protocol (IP)

The information exchange portion of the TCP/IP protocol used by the Internet. IP is an actual data transfer protocol that defines how the sender places information into packets and transmits from one place to another. TCP (Transmission Control Protocol) is the protocol that defines how the actual data transfer takes place.

Internet server application programming interface (ISAPI)

A set of function calls and interface elements designed to help developers create applications for Microsoft's *Internet Information Server (IIS)*. Essentially, this set of API calls provides the programmer with access to the server itself. This technology makes it easier to provide full application access to the Internet server so the developer can perform tasks such as Web page redirection, security checks, and incoming data parsing. There are two forms of ISAPI: filters and extensions. An extension replaces script-based technologies like CGI. Its main purpose

is to provide dynamic content to the user. A filter can extend the server itself by monitoring various events like user requests for access in the background. You can use a filter to create various types of new services such as extended logging or specialized security schemes. Most developers use technologies such as *Active Server Pages (ASP)* in place of ISAPI because these technologies are easier to use. For example, ASP makes it easy to modify a file without the need to recompile it. However, ISAPI is still used for speed critical applications such as the *Simple Object Access Protocol (SOAP)* listener used by some SOAP implementations.

Internet service provider (ISP)

A vendor that provides one or more Internet-related services through a dial-up, *digital subscriber line (DSL)*, Integrated Services Digital Network (ISDN), cable television, or other outside connection. Normal services include email, newsgroup access, full Internet Web site access, and personal Web page hosting.

IP

See *Internet Protocol*.

ISAPI

See *Internet server application programming interface*.

ISO

International Organization for Standardization.

ISP

See *Internet service provider*.

J

Java Development Kit (JDK)

A special set of application development tools, resources, example code, help files, and other resources designed to help a programmer create Java applications. The JDK normally contains a full set of development tools and a copy of the *Java Runtime Enviroment (JRE)*. However, most developers will require one or more third-party solutions to create a complex Java application. For example, unlike many languages today, Java doesn't provide *Simple Object*

Access Protocol (SOAP) support, so the developer would require a third-party library to create an application that relies on SOAP.

Java Runtime Environment (JRE)

Another name for the *Java Virtual Machine (JVM)*. This set of files provides Java support on the host machine allowing it to run Java applications.

Java Virtual Machine (JVM)

The application used to interpret the Java language originally developed by Sun Microsystems. This includes both text and byte code .CLASS files containing common routines. Java is similar to C++, but eliminates many of the complex programming constructs and uses a more restrictive security scheme. Many operating systems have a Java Virtual Machine including most versions of Windows, Mac OS, and Unix. The use of text files means that Java applets can run on any number of operating system platforms without modifications, but the use of an interpreter implies slower execution speed.

JavaScript (JS)

A file containing a program written in JavaScript; a language with a C-like syntax. Don't confuse Java and JavaScript; the two languages aren't the same. Most browsers support JavaScript and developers like to use it for local and remote applications alike. There are many versions of JavaScript, including Microsoft JScript and the *European Computer Manufacturer's Association (ECMA)* ECMAScript.

JDK

See *Java Development Kit.*

JIT activation

See *Just-in-Time activation.*

JIT compiler

See *Just-in-Time compiler.*

Joint Photographic Experts Group (JPEG)

A standard graphics file format used on the Internet. This is a vector file format normally used to render high-resolution images or pictures. (The current

version of the file standard supports 16.7 million colors.) JPEG provides lossy graphic compression that makes the image file considerably smaller. However, the image loses detail as the amount of compression increases. The file extension also appears as JPG. Other standard Internet graphics formats include Graphics Interchange Format (GIF) and Portable Network Graphics (PNG).

JPEG

See *Joint Photographic Experts Group.*

JRE

See *Java Runtime Environment.*

JS

See *JavaScript.*

Just-in-Time activation (JIT activation)

An application, component, control, or service execution method that starts executing the code only as needed, rather than allowing it to remain in memory. Server resources are always scarce, so good resource management techniques are essential. The latest component resource management techniques normally include gaining access to resources only when needed, then releasing them immediately. However, older components were designed to gain access to all of the resources required to perform a task early, then hold onto those resources until no longer needed. Using JIT activation means that even if a client holds onto a component reference, Windows can still use physical resources required by that component until they're needed again by the application. Windows monitors all of the components that are marked as JIT enabled. When a certain time period has elapsed without any method calls, the component deactivates, and the resources that it's using are returned to the resource pool. As far as the application is concerned, the component is still active and the reference to it is still valid. The next time the application makes a method call to the deactivated component, Windows reactivates it and allocates the resources that it requires. This entire process occurs in the background without any programmer input. Newer technologies, such as .NET, have extended JIT to include every aspect of the application.

Just-in-Time compiler (JIT compiler)

A specialized applications that tranforms code into executable form with Just-in-Time activation in mind.

JVM

See *Java Virtual Machine*.

L

LAN

See *local area network*.

local area network (LAN)

Two or more devices located in a relatively small physical area connected together using a combination of hardware and software. The devices, normally computers and peripheral equipment such as printers, are called nodes. An NIC (network interface card) provides the hardware communication between nodes through an appropriate medium (cable or microwave transmission). The actual connection is provided through cables, in many cases, but can also rely on radio waves, infrared, and other technologies. There are two common types of LANs (also called networks). Peer-to-peer networks allow each node to connect to any other node on the network with shareable resources. This is a distributed method of files and peripheral devices. A client-server network uses one or more servers to share resources. This is a centralized method of sharing files and peripheral devices. A server provides resources to clients (usually workstations).

M

master page

A document that acts as a template for other documents. The master page does include common content such as pictures and text that will appear on all pages created using it. However, it doesn't contain any unique data. Instead, the page created with the master page contains unique data for that page.

MD5

See *Message Digest 5*.

Message Digest 5 (MD5)

The mathematical basis for creating a message digest (a value) based on the content of the message. The basis of this technology is that no two messages will produce the same message digest. Consequently, the recipient can validate the content of a message by performing the calculation and comparing it to the message digest value. MD5 is a one-way hash, which means that it isn't used for encrypting and decrypting the data. Professor Ronal Rivest created MD5 in 1991 to verify the authenticity of digital signatures.

MFC

See *Microsoft Foundation Classes*.

Microsoft Database Engine (MSDE)

This term also appears as Microsoft Desktop Engine and Microsoft Data Engine in various publications. MSDE is a miniature form of SQL Server that enables developers to create test database applications. Microsoft designed this engine for use by one person, usually the developer, although you can potentially use it for up to five people. The developer accesses MSDE through a programming language *Integrated Development Environment (IDE)* or using command-line utilities. In some cases, MSDE is also used to provide access to a remote copy of SQL Server. Some third-party products, such as MSDE Query, provide a *graphical user interface (GUI)* for MSDE.

Microsoft Foundation Classes (MFC)

The set of code libraries required to make many Microsoft applications work. These files contain the shared classes used as a basis for creating the application. For example, a push-button is a separate class within these files. Normally, you'll find the MFC files in the Windows SYSTEM folder; they use MFC as the starting letters of the filename.

Microsoft Installer (MSI)

(1) A technique for installing applications within Windows that allows later removal even if the system configuration has changed. This technique also provides support for additional vendor information, partial installations, multiple configurations, and installation recovery. (2) A file format containing instructions for

installing Windows applications. The file is actually a database that contains specialized instructions and data in a specific format that's read by the Microsoft installer application.

Microsoft Management Console (MMC)

A special application that displays special programs called snap-ins that help the user manage Windows, a device, or an application. MMC acts as an object container for Windows management objects such as Component Services and Computer Management. The management objects are actually special components that provide interfaces that allow the user to access them within MMC to maintain and control the operation of Windows. A developer can create special versions of these objects for application management or other tasks. Using a single application like MMC helps maintain the same user interface across all management applications.

MIME

See *Multipurpose Internet Mail Extensions*.

MMC

See *Microsoft Management Console*.

MSDE

See *Microsoft Database Engine*.

MSDN

Microsoft Developer Network.

MSI

See *Microsoft Installer*.

Multipurpose Internet Mail Extensions (MIME)

The standard method for defining the content of Internet messages. This standard allows computers to exchange objects, character sets, and multimedia using email without regard to the computer's underlying operating system. MIME is defined in the Internet Engineering Task Force (IETF) Request for Comment (RFC) 1521 standard.

N

National Institute of Standards and Technology (NIST)

A government agency that helps business develop and apply technology, measurements, and standards. In some cases, NIST also performs independent research and shares the finding with business.

NIST

See *National Institute of Standards and Technology*.

O

Object Library (OLB) file

This file contains interface information for an object of any type (usually with the same filename). The OLB file lets the developer see the various interfaces provided by a component. In addition to interfaces, the developer will also see the methods, properties, and list of acceptable property values (when available) associated with the object.

Object Linking and Embedding - Database (OLE-DB)

A low-level database access technology that relies on COM and a vendor-supplied OLE-DB provider rather than the SQL used by *Open Database Connectivity (ODBC)*. OLE-DB is designed to work with both remote and local databases. In addition, it can access database managers that don't rely on SQL such as those found on mainframe computers. OLE-DB and ODBC are cooperative, rather than competing data access technologies. OLE-DB, when coupled with ActiveX Data Objects (ADO), is designed to replace older database technologies such as Remote Data Objects (RDO) and Data Access Objects (DAO).

ODBC

See *Open Database Connectivity*.

OLB

See *Object Library file*.

OLE-DB

See *Object Linking and Embedding - Database*.

OMA

Open Mobile Alliance.

Open Database Connectivity (ODBC)

One of several methods for exchanging data between DBMSs. In most cases, this involves three steps: installing an appropriate driver, adding a source to the Data Sources (ODBC) applet in the Control Panel, and using specialized statements, such as Structured Query Language (SQL), to access the database.

P

P3P

See *Platform for Privacy Preferences*.

parameter

A value received by a function or procedure from another function or procedure, the command line, or some other source.

PDA

See *personal digital assistant*.

PDF

See *Portable Document Format*.

personal digital assistant (PDA)

A small handheld computing device such as a Palm Pilot or Pocket PC. People normally rely on these devices to accomplish personal tasks such as taking notes and maintaining an itinerary during business trips. Some PDAs rely on special operating systems and lack any standard application support. However, newer PDAs include some level of standard application support because vendors are supplying specialized compilers for them. In addition, you'll find common applications included, such as browsers and application office suites that include word processing and spreadsheet support.

platform

A description of the combination of software and hardware used to create a computing system. For example, many users use a combination of the Windows operating system and an Intel processor. The combination often appears as the Wintel platform. In some cases, a discussion will only use the operating system as the basis for a platform. A developer might create applications only for the Windows platform. The use of the term *platform* is often ambiguous and requires the actual platform type to make the meaning clear.

Platform for Privacy Preferences (P3P)

A Worldwide Web Consortium (W3C)–sponsored technique for ensuring privacy through specialized programming techniques. The specification defines methods of communicating information requests, use, storage technique, and requirements to the requestor. The requestor then decides whether the requirements are acceptable and optionally transfers the necessary information.

plug-in

A descriptive term for helper applications, components, or controls that a container (host) application uses to provide optional functionality. Plug-ins appear in a number of forms such as a sound processing system for playing streaming audio normally downloaded as a separate item for container applications such as browsers. The container application provides an environment in which the plug-in can operate. The container application calls on the plug-in to perform specialized tasks that the developer of the container application chose not to include.

PNG

See *Portable Network Graphic*.

Portable Document Format (PDF)

A formatted, book-like, document format originally created by Adobe. This document format initially captured the output of desktop publishing applications. Many other applications, especially graphics applications, now output to the PDF format. Users can view PDF files using the free Acrobat Reader utility.

Portable Network Graphic (PNG)

A graphics file format (pronounced *ping*) similar to the *Graphics Interchange Format (GIF)* used for Internet graphics. This graphics format is newer than the GIF and many developers consider it superior because it uses a newer compression mechanism. Many developers use the PNG file format because it doesn't rely on patented technology as the GIF format does.

Private Key (PVK) file

A file containing the private key used to encrypt data or other content sent from one location to another.

protocol

A set of rules used to define a specific behavior. For example, protocols define how networks and the Internet transfer data. Other protocols define how data is formatted within files. Most protocols rely on some type of standardization process to achieve development community support.

PVK

See *Private Key file*.

Q

query

A request or question made by a user of an application program using an interface. The query can appear as part of a form or other type of input, or the user can make the query as part of a script when using automation. Common queries include search requests for documents or a request to perform a task such as checking the status of the computer hardware. The data returned by the query can appear in a number of locations, including databases and flat file storage.

R

RAM

See *random access memory*.

random access memory (RAM)

The basic term used to describe volatile data storage within a computer system. RAM comes in a variety of types such as Direct Rambus Dynamic Random Access Memory (DRDRAM), Double Data Rate Synchronous Dynamic Random Access Memory (DDR SDRAM), Dual-Ported Video RAM (VRAM), Extended Data Out Dynamic Random Access Memory (EDO DRAM), and Static Random Access Memory (SRAM). Each of these RAM types has specialized features. These special features make some kinds of RAM more acceptable for some storage tasks than others.

registry

A specialized hierarchical database used to hold settings, configuration, file associations, and other information for Windows. The registry is a hierarchy or tree consisting of keys and associated values. The operating system searches the registry tree for keys that it requires, then requests values for those keys in order to perform tasks such as configure an application. The registry is organized into hives. Each hive contains settings for a particular operating system element such as user information and hardware configuration. Users share common hives such as those used for hardware, but have separate hives for their information as long as Windows is configured to provide separate desktops for each user.

registry key

A registry entry; a method of organizing registry data. It provides the structure required to hold configuration values and other information required by both Windows and the applications it runs. Each registry key resides within a hive and can contain zero or more values. Children of registry keys are called subkeys.

registry setting

The combination of a registry key and one or more registry values that describe an option such as an application configuration value. A registry setting could describe where to find additional values for an executable file. The setting provides a complete description of a single data element.

registry value

An individual piece of data within the Windows registry database. Each value provides some type of information associated with a registry key, such as configuration information, a *globally unique identifier (GUID)*, human readable value, numeric value, binary sequence, or other appropriate data. The common registry data types include: string, DWORD, binary, multi-string, and expandable string. Of these values, the string data types are the easiest to read and understand.

Remote Procedure Call (RPC)

One of several methods for accessing data within another application. RPC is designed to look for the application first on the local workstation, and then across the network at the applications stored on other workstations.

Rivest Shamir Adleman (RSA) algorithm

An authentication technology named after its creators that relies on a private-public key pair to create a set of credentials. The credentials are then used as a means of identification for logging into various network resources. Using this methodology allows for secure data transmission as well as user-oriented features such as one password login to the network.

RPC

See *Remote Procedure Call*.

RSA

See *Rivest Shamir Adleman algorithm*.

runtime error

A fault that occurs while an application executes, which usually generates a message describing the problem and can cause the application to terminate prematurely.

S

Scalable Vector Graphics (SVG)

A vector-based method of describing a graphic using XML. Vector graphics are infinitely scalable because they rely on math definitions, rather than bitmaps. They also require less storage space than bitmap graphics. Unfortunately, SVG requires more display time, processing power, and resources. It also requires a special XML parser and display application.

script

Usually associated with an interpreted macro language used to create simple applications, productivity enhancers, or automated data manipulators. Most operating systems support at least one scripting language. You'll also find scripting capability in many higher-end applications such as Web browsers and word processors. Scripts are normally used to write small utility-type applications rather than large-scale applications that require the use of a compiled language. In addition, many scripting languages are limited in their access of the full set of operating system features.

SDK

See *Software Development Kit*.

Secure Hashing Algorithm 1 (SHA-1)

The mathematical basis for encrypting and decrypting data used with the Digital Signature Standard (DSS) introduced by the *National Institute of Standards and Technology (NIST)*. DSS also relies on Digital Signature Algorithm (DSA) to provide the digital signature functionality.

Secure Sockets Layer (SSL)

A digital signature technology used for exchanging information between a client and a server. Essentially an SSL-compliant server will request a digital certificate from the client machine. The client can likewise request a digital certificate from the server. Companies or individuals obtain these digital certificates from a third-party vendor such as VeriSign or another trusted source that can vouch for the identity of both parties.

security identifier (SID)

The part of an access token that identifies the object throughout the network; it's like having an account number. The access token that the SID identifies tells what groups the object belongs to and what privileges the object has.

server

(1) A specialized computer designed to answer client requests for services such as printing and centralized file storage. (2) An application or workstation that provides services, resources, or data to a client application or workstation. The client usually makes requests in the form of Object Linking and Embedding (OLE), Dynamic Data Exchange (DDE), *Distributed Component Object Model (DCOM)*, *Component Object Model Plus (COM+)*, *HyperText Markup Language (HTML)*, or other command formats. The server response to a request is service, resource, data, error message, or an access denied message.

SHA-1

See *Secure Hashing Algorithm 1*.

SID

See *security identifier*.

Simple Object Access Protocol (SOAP)

A protocol that provides the means for exchanging data between a requestor and a server. Originally, SOAP provided the means for binary technologies such as *Component Object Model (COM)* to exchange data with other binary technologies such as Common Object Request Broker Architecture (CORBA) using *eXtensible Markup Language (XML)* as an intermediary. However, SOAP is often used as the basis for Web services communication today. A developer could also use SOAP on a *local area network (LAN)* or in any other environment that requires machine-to-machine communication and the two target machines provide the required infrastructure.

SLN

See *Solution file*.

SOAP

See *Simple Object Access Protocol*.

Software Development Kit (SDK)

A special add-on for developers to an operating system or an application that describes how to access its internal features. For example, an SDK for Windows would show how to create a File Open dialog box. Programmers use an SDK to learn how to access special Windows components such as the *Component Object Model (COM)* or the Media Player.

Solution (SLN) file

The file used by Visual Studio and other development environments to store application settings such as special file views and a list of the files contained within the application. The solution file is the central storage location for application-specific information that doesn't affect the actual application code.

SPC

Software Publisher Certificate.

SQL

See *Structured Query Language*.

SSL

See *Secure Sockets Layer*.

string

Two or more characters connected to form a word or other character-based information. Strings normally provide human readable data, but you can find non-human (machine) readable forms. For example, even though a path and filename normally appear in a string, you have to know how to read the string to interpret it correctly.

Structured Query Language (SQL)

Most *Database Management Systems (DBMSs)* use this language to exchange information; many also use it as their native language. SQL provides a method for manipulating data controlled by the DBMS. It defines which table or tables to use, determines what information to get from the table, and resolves how to sort the information. A typical request will include the name of the database, table, and columns needed for display or editing purposes. SQL can filter a request and limit the number of rows using special features.

Developers also use SQL to manipulate database information by adding, deleting, modifying, or searching records. The IBM Almaden Research Center designed SQL between 1974 and 1975. Oracle introduced the first product to use SQL in 1979. SQL originally appeared on mainframe and minicomputers. Today it's a favorite language for most PC DBMS as well. There are many versions of SQL.

SVG

See *Scalable Vector Graphics*.

T

T-SQL

See *Transact-Structured Query Language*.

Tagged Image File Format (TIFF)

A bit-mapped (raster) graphics file format used on the PC and Macintosh. The TIFF file format offers a broad range of color formats including black and white, gray scale, and color. One of the advantages of using TIFF is that it provides a variety of compression methods and offers smaller storage form factor. Files on the PC often use a TIF extension.

TCP/IP

See *Transmission Control Protocol/Internet Protocol*.

TIFF

See *Tagged Image File Format*.

TLB

See Type Library file.

Transact-Structured Query Language (T-SQL)

A Microsoft variant of the *Structured Query Language (SQL)* designed for use with SQL Server.

Transmission Control Protocol/Internet Protocol (TCP/IP)

A standard communication line protocol (set of rules) developed by the U.S. Department of Defense. The protocol defines how two devices talk to each other. TCP defines a communication methodology where it

guarantees packet delivery and also ensures that the packets appear at the recipient in the same order they were sent. IP defines the packet characteristics.

Type Library (TLB) file

This file contains interface information for a specific component (usually with the same filename). The TLB file lets the developer see the various interfaces provided by a component. In addition to interfaces, the developer will also see the methods, properties, and list of acceptable property values (when available) associated with the component.

U

UI

See *user interface*.

UML

See *Unified Modeling Language*.

Unicode character

A double byte (16-bit) character used to represent more than the character set used by the English language. Unicode character sets are standardized by international convention. Advanced operating systems normally rely on Unicode for enhanced language support and consistent data handling. This is the standard character set used by newer versions of Windows, although all versions of Windows can still use ASCII characters when needed for compatibility purposes.

Unified Modeling Language (UML)

A specialized form of presentation used to express the design of an application.

Uniform Resource Identifier (URI)

A generic term for all names and addresses that reference objects on the Internet. A URL is a specific type of URI. See also *Uniform Resource Locator (URL)*.

Uniform Resource Locator (URL)

A text representation of a specific location on the Internet. URLs normally include the protocol (`http://`, for example), the target location (World Wide Web or www), the domain or server name (mycompany), and a domain type (for example, com for commercial). (Many URLs don't include the www portion of the address anymore.) It can also include a hierarchical location within that Web site. The URL usually specifies a particular file on the Web server, although there are some situations when a Web server will use a default filename. For example, asking the browser to find http://www.mycompany.com would probably display the DEFAULT.HTM or INDEX.HTM file at that location. The actual default filename depends on the Web server used. In some cases, the default filename is configurable and could be any of a number of files. For example, *Internet Information Server (IIS)* offers this feature, so the developer can use anything from an HTM, to an ASP, to an XML file as the default.

Uniform Resource Name (URN)

A managed resource identifier. Being a managed resource means that a URN is guaranteed to be unique. Companies that want to use a URN must apply for a Namespace Identifier (NID) from an authority such as the Internet Assigned Numbers Authority (IANA). The NID appears as part of every resource reference that the company creates.

unmanaged code

A .NET programming term for natively compiled code that runs directly under DOS or Windows. Native code executes without the benefit of the *Common Language Runtime (CLR)*.

URI

See *Uniform Resource Identifier*.

URL

See *Uniform Resource Locator*.

URN

See *Uniform Resource Name*.

US-CERT

United States Computer Emergency Response Team.

user interface (UI)

The portion of an application that contains user accessible controls and data manipulation elements. The user interface for a Windows application is commonly comprised of buttons, text boxes, static text, graphics, and other design elements.

UTC

Universal Time Code.

V

VBE

See *Visual Basic Editor*.

VBS

See *Visual Basic Script*.

Visual Basic Editor (VBE)

A development environment normally used to create and edit *Visual Basic Script (VBS)* or Visual Basic for Applications (VBA) code. VBE is also the extension used for many modern script files. The VBE extension replaces the Visual Basic Script (VBS) extension used in the past.

Visual Basic Script (VBS)

A file containing a program that relies on a subset of the full Visual Basic language. Users normally rely on VBS to create small applications and macros. Visual Basic Script or VBScript works well as a stand-alone language. Many developers also use it within Web pages and as part of *Internet Information Server (IIS) Active Server Pages (ASP)*.

W

W3C

See *World Wide Web Consortium*.

WAN

See *wide area network*.

WAP

See *Wireless Access Protocol*.

Web Services Description Language (WSDL)

A method of describing a Web-based application (Web service) that's accessible through an Internet or intranet connection. The file associated with this description contains the service description, port type, interface description, individual method names, and parameter types. A WSDL file relies on namespace support to provide descriptions of common elements such as data types. Most WSDL files include references to two or more resources maintained by standards organizations to ensure compatibility across implementations.

WebSAT

Web Static Analyzer Tool.

WebVIP

Web Variable Instrumenter Program.

wide area network (WAN)

An extension of the *local area network (LAN)*, a WAN connects two or more LANs together using a variety of methods. A WAN usually encompasses more than one physical site, such as a building. Most WANs rely on microwave communications, fiber optic connections, or leased telephone lines to provide the inter-network connections to keep all nodes in the network talking with each other.

Windows Scripting Host (WSH)

The Windows capability to write and execute scripts at the system level. This service allows the user to reduce the number of repetitive tasks required to get applications to work together. A user can use a script, for example, that scans their hard drive for errors, backs it up, then optimizes it—all without any work on the user's part except for the initial script execution. The user may have to perform additional work if the script encounters an error, but nothing more than the user would normally do. Scripts can employ one of two default languages, JavaScript or VBScript. The user can also create scripts via languages such as REXX and Perl when working with a third party add-in product.

Wireless Access Protocol (WAP)

A method of providing secure access for mobile devices of all types to Web-based application content through a gateway. The underlying technology works much like *Handheld Device Markup Language (HDML)*, but using standardized and secure access techniques. This technology supports most mobile networks including Cellular Digital Packet Data (CDPD), Code-Division Multiple Access (CDMA), Global System for Mobile Communications (GSM), and Time Division Multiple Access (TDMA). Supported mobile device operating systems include PalmOS, EPOC, Windows CE, FLEXOS, OS/9, and JavaOS. The technology can support pages in either *Wireless Markup Language (WML)* or *HyperText Markup Language (HTML)* format although WML is preferred because it better supports mobile device requirements.

Wireless Markup Language (WML)

An XML-based language used to communicate with *Wireless Access Protocol (WAP)* devices such as cellular telephones or *personal digital assistants (PDAs)*. Most cellular telephones provide support for WML. The pages are served in a manner similar to the used by the *Handheld Device Markup Language (HDML)*.

wizard

A specialized application or application module that reduces the complexity of using or configuring an operating system, application, or other component. A wizard normally relies on procedural steps and simple questions to obtain the information needed to perform a complex task.

WML

See *Wireless Markup Language.*

World Wide Web Consortium (W3C)

A standards organization devoted to Internet standards, especially security issues. This organization is also involved in other issues such as defining the special <OBJECT> tag used to implement ActiveX technology. The W3C also defines a wealth of other HTML and XML standards. The W3C first appeared in December 1994, when it endorsed the *SSL (Secure Sockets Layer)* standard. In February 1995, it also endorsed application-level security for the Internet.

WSDL

See *Web Services Description Language.*

WSH

See *Windows Scripting Host.*

X

XHTML

See *eXtensible Hypertext Markup Language.*

XML

See *eXtensible Markup Language.*

XSLT

See *eXtensible Style Language Transformation.*

Z

ZIP

A file that acts as a container for other files. The ZIP normally provides some level of data compression to make the resulting package smaller than the individual files. Some operating systems such as Windows XP provide built-in support for the ZIP file. However, in many cases, you need to buy or download an application that provides the ZIP file functionality.

Index

Note to the reader: Throughout this index **boldfaced** page numbers indicate primary discussions of a topic. *Italicized* page numbers indicate illustrations.

This program was reproduced by Wiley Publishing, Inc. under a special arrangement with Microsoft Corporation. For this reason, Wiley Publishing, Inc. is responsible for the product warranty. If your diskette is defective, please return it to Wiley Publishing, Inc., who will arrange for its replacement. PLEASE DO NOT RETURN IT TO OR CONTACT MICROSOFT CORPORATION FOR SOFTWARE SUPPORT. This product is provided for free, and no support is provided for by Wiley Publishing, Inc. or Microsoft Corporation. To the extent of any inconsistencies between this statement and the end user license agreement which accompanies the program, this statement shall govern.